Close Encounters

Second Edition

To our daughters—Gabrielle, Kristiana, Kirsten, Leila, and Rania.
They possess many of the qualities that people
value in relationships. Our relationships with them bring joy to our lives.

Close
Encounters

Second Edition

Communication in Relationships

Laura K. Guerrero
Arizona State University

Peter A. Andersen
San Diego State University

Walid A. Afifi
University of California, Santa Barbara

SAGE Publications
Los Angeles • London • New Delhi • Singapore

For information:

Sage Publications, Inc.
2455 Teller Road
Thousand Oaks, California 91320
E-mail: order@sagepub.com

Sage Publications Ltd.
6 Bonhill Street
London EC2A 4PU
United Kingdom

Sage Publications India Pvt. Ltd.
B 1/I 1 Mohan Cooperative Industrial Area
Mathura Road, New Delhi 110 044
India

Sage Publications Asia-Pacific Pte. Ltd.
33 Pekin Street #02-01
Far East Square
Singapore 048763

Printed in the United States of America

Library of Congress Cataloging-in-Publication Data

Guerrero, Laura K.
Close encounters: Communication in relationships/Laura K. Guerrero, Peter A. Andersen, Walid A. Afifi. — 2nd ed.
    p. cm.
Includes bibliographical references and indexes.
ISBN 978-1-4129-4953-8 (pbk. : alk. paper)
    1. Interpersonal communication. I. Andersen, Peter A. II. Afifi, Walid A. III. Title.

BF637.C45.G83 2007
153.6—dc22

2006101371

Printed on acid-free paper

07   08   09   10   11   10   9   8   7   6   5   4   3   2

Acquiring Editor:	Todd R. Armstrong
Editorial Assistant:	Katie Grim
Production Editor:	Sarah K. Quesenberry
Copy Editor:	QuADS
Typesetter:	C&M Digitals (P) Ltd.
Proofreader:	Caryne Brown
Cover Designer:	Candice Harman
Marketing Associate:	Amberlyn M. Erzinger

Brief Contents

DETAILED CONTENTS

PREFACE

We are pleased and privileged to release the second edition of *Close Encounters.* We wrote the first edition of this book in response to the increasing number of upper-division courses on relational communication and advanced interpersonal communication being taught at colleges and universities across the country. Since writing the first edition, an increasing number of courses in relational communication are being offered, and research on close relationships has continued to flourish. Indeed, it was challenging to incorporate all the new research on relational communication into this edition, and because of space limitations, we could not include everything we wanted to include. Nonetheless, we believe that this edition contains a nice mix of current and classic research related to communication in relationships. Our goal in writing *Close Encounters* continues to be to produce an informative yet readable textbook that will help students to understand their relationships better and be more critical consumers of information about relationships. This book is research based. We strive to present concepts and theories in more depth than the average textbook on interpersonal communication while writing in an accessible style. For us, writing this textbook is a rewarding experience; it lets us reach beyond the pages of scholarly journals to share information with students who are eager to learn more about relationships.

APPROACH

The book takes a relational approach to the study of interpersonal communication by focusing on issues that are central to describing and understanding close relationships, particularly between romantic partners, friends, and family members. One of the most exciting trends in the field of personal relationships is the interdisciplinary nature of research and theory. Scholars from fields such as communication, family studies, psychology, and sociology, among other disciplines, have all made important contributions to scholarly knowledge about relationships. This book reflects the interdisciplinary nature of the field of personal relationships while focusing strongly on interpersonal communication.

ORGANIZATION

In line with our relational approach, this book is organized loosely around relationship trajectories. We use the term *trajectory* loosely because all relationships are different, with no two following exactly the same path. Nonetheless, from a communication process perspective, it is helpful to think of how relationships progress from initial meetings toward farewells. Of course, interesting and important communication occurs throughout the course of a relationship. For example, conflict can be studied in terms of a couple's first big fight, the mundane disagreements that people have on a fairly regular basis, the conflicts that enhance relational functioning, or the argument that ultimately marks the destruction of a relationship. Thus even though this book is organized somewhat chronologically, we believe that relationships do not always unfold in a linear fashion and that many types of events, such as having conflict, communicating love, and managing uncertainty, occur at various stages during the course of a relationship.

CHANGES IN THIS EDITION

There are many significant changes in this edition of *Close Encounters*. All the chapters now start with a scenario that features fictional characters dealing with communication issues. Each chapter ends with a section called "Summary and Application." These new chapter endings tie back to the scenarios at the beginning of each chapter so that students can see how the information they learned can be applied to a specific situation. Throughout each chapter, we refer to the opening scenarios at various times to provide examples of how the concepts we discuss relate to real-life situations. With the exception of Chapter 1, all the chapters now include at least one "Put Yourself to the Test" box. Our students have told us that they find these boxes very helpful in identifying their communication style as well as some of the characteristics of their relationships.

New research has been added to each chapter. Interestingly, when we wrote the first edition of this book, some people commented that we probably did not need whole chapters focusing on uncertainty and expectancies (Chapter 4), privacy and secrets (Chapter 12), and relational transgressions (Chapter 13). Yet these three areas of research have blossomed over the past few years, and we found ourselves adding numerous studies to each of these chapters. New areas of research have been added to other chapters as well, including sections on date initiation, cohabitation,

friends with benefits, affectionate communication, the chilling effect, and parent-child communication following divorce. In addition, the conflict chapter is centered on a new six-strategy system for measuring conflict communication that emerged in our thinking after sorting through the latest literature. These are just a few of many new concepts and theories that have been added to this edition.

FEATURES

In addition to the features already discussed, *Close Encounters* is designed to appeal to students and professors alike based on the following features:

Current, Interdisciplinary Research: The research in *Close Encounters* reflects the interdisciplinary nature of the study of personal relationships and draws from across the social science disciplines while maintaining a focus on communication. This edition has been carefully updated to include recent cutting-edge research on interpersonal communication.

High-Interest Topics: Intriguing subjects, such as long-distance relationships, cross-sex friendships, flirting, sexual interaction, cohabitation, and the "dark side" of relational communication, are explored in depth.

Put Yourself to the Test Boxes: These exercises, found throughout the book, assess various aspects of students' own relationships and communication styles.

Highlights: These boxes take a closer look at issues in relational research and challenge students to think critically about research and popular concepts.

Discussion Questions: These questions, which are found at the end of each chapter, can help students prepare for class, or they can be used as springboards for classroom discussion. Some instructors also have students write position papers in response to some of the discussion questions.

Instructor's Resource CD: The new instructor's resource CD includes class activities, suggestions for film and television clips that can be used during class, test bank questions, and PowerPoint slides.

ACKNOWLEDGMENTS

Writing a textbook is an exciting challenge as well as a daunting task. As we worked on this edition of *Close Encounters*, our dens were cluttered with articles, and our families (and in some cases our young children and babies) had to listen to the click-click-click of our computer keyboards even more than usual. The support of our families and colleagues was critical in helping us complete this project, and we owe them our sincere gratitude. We are especially indebted to our partners—Vico, Janis, and Tammy, who provided not only social support but also examples and feedback. Laura also wishes to extend thanks to her sister, Cindy Hill, who helped with some of the photos; and her nephews, Garrett and Brent, and niece, Julie, who along with her own daughters posed in some of the pictures, as did Cindy's nephew, Cody. In line with acknowledging the children in our lives, Walid would like to mention his nieces, Leah, Loulwa, Tala, Hannah, and Kayli, as well as his nephew, Derek.

We would also like to thank the many people who helped during the writing and editing process. We are especially grateful to our editor, Todd Armstrong, whose excitement about the second edition was contagious, and to Sage for stepping in to publish a second edition. Thanks also to our editorial assistants, Katie Grim and Sarah Quesenberry, and to our excellent team of copyeditors at QuADS. Holly Allen, our editor for the first edition, also deserves a word of thanks. A conversation between Laura and Holly back in 1998 started the *Close Encounters* ball rolling.

We have also received formal and informal feedback from many valued colleagues and reviewers, including (but not limited to) Katherine Adams, Jess Alberts, Guy Bachman, Brant Burleson, Daniel Canary, Victoria DeFrancisco, Kathryn Dindia, Renee Edwards, Kory Floyd, Michael Hecht, Susanne Jones, Leanne Knobloch, Pamela J. Lannutti, Sandra Metts, Claude Miller, Paul Mongeau, Larry Nadler, Sylvia Niehuis, Donna Pawlowski, Sue Pendall, Sandra Petronio, Denise Solomon, Brian H. Spitzberg, Glen Stamp, Claire Sullivan, Paul D. Turman, Richard West, Christina Yoshimura, and Stephen Yoshimura. A special thanks goes to Judee Burgoon (Laura and Walid's Ph.D. adviser and an exceptional role model) who suggested that we use the term *Close Encounters* as part of the title.

Finally, we would like to thank all the students we have had in our classes over the years. We use some of their examples in this book, and we have incorporated their feedback into this second edition. Just as important, lively dialogue with students has helped sustain our enthusiasm for teaching courses on interpersonal communication and relationships. We hope this book contributes to spirited discussions about relationships in your classrooms as well.

—L. K. G
—P. A. A.
—W. A. A

1

CONCEPTUALIZING RELATIONAL COMMUNICATION

Definitions, Principles, and Relational Messages

People accomplish a lot by communicating with others. For example, Jake is having trouble with his statistics homework, which is due tomorrow. His friend and roommate, Dave, is a whiz at math, so Jake tries to persuade Dave to stay home (rather than go to a party) and help him. Su-Lin recently arrived in the United States as an international student and feels a lot of uncertainty about the university and student life. However, after joining a couple of student clubs and getting to know some of her classmates, she is starting to feel more comfortable in her new surroundings. Kristi's husband moves out of the house and tells her he wants a divorce. Rather than sitting at home alone moping around and feeling sorry for herself, Kristi drives over to her parents' house, where she receives comfort and support from her mother.

Personal relationships are central to being human. McAdams (1988) suggested that, "through personal relationships, we may find our most profound experiences of security and anxiety, power and impotence, unity and separateness" (p. 7). People are born into relationships and live their lives in webs of friendships, family networks, romances, marriages, and work relationships. In fact, research has shown that when people talk, the most common topics are relationship problems, sex, family, and romantic (or potentially romantic) partners (Haas & Sherman, 1982). The capacity to form relationships is innate and biological, a part of the genetic inheritance that has enabled the human race to survive over time. Humans have less potential for survival, creativity, and innovation as individuals than in relationships. Experts in personal relationships attempt to unlock the mysteries of these universal human experiences, assist people with problematic relationships, and help people achieve greater satisfaction in their close encounters.

As the examples of Jake, Su-Lin, and Kristi illustrate, communication plays a central role in our relationships. Whether we need help, comfort, or reassurance, communication is the tool to help us accomplish our goals. Relationships cannot exist unless two people communicate with each other. "Bad" communication is often blamed for problems in relationships, whereas "good" communication is often credited with preserving or saving relationships. In this introductory chapter, we take a closer look at what constitutes both communication and relationships. First, however, we provide a brief history of the field of personal relationships. Then, we define and discuss three important terms that are central to this book: *relationships, interpersonal communication,* and *relational communication.* We also discuss issues related to each of these concepts and end the chapter with a discussion of various types of relational messages.

THE FIELD OF PERSONAL RELATIONSHIPS: A BRIEF HISTORY

People have been curious about their relationships for thousands of years, but the formal study of personal relationships is a fairly recent phenomenon. Today, we take the study of personal relationships for granted; but a few decades ago, the scholarly investigation of relationships was considered unscientific and a waste of resources. In 1975, two of the finest and earliest relationship researchers, Ellen Berscheid and Elaine Hatfield (formerly Elaine Walster), were publicly criticized by Senator William Proxmire of Wisconsin for their research on love. Proxmire gave the "Golden Fleece Award" for wasteful government spending to the National Science Foundation for supporting Berscheid and Walster's research on love with an $84,000 grant. The Senator's objections to "squandering" money on love research were twofold: (1) Scientists could never find an answer to the mystery of love; and (2) even if they did, he didn't want to hear it and was confident that no one else did either (E. Hatfield, personal communication, August 20, 1999). Of course, like many Americans, Proxmire had problematic relationships of his own and had just been divorced at the time he gave his "award." Months of harassing phone calls and even death threats to Berscheid and Walster followed (E. Hatfield, personal communication, August 20, 1999). Even Elaine Hatfield's mother's bishop, whose name is changed in the letter below, got into the act.

Dear faithful in Christ:

This week, the *Chicago Tribune* announced that the National Science Foundation will unravel the most sacred mysteries of love and life. Soon they will be in a position to dictate to the whole world. If "Science" were not such a sacred cow, we would all laugh at such ponderous nonsense. Who has granted these "scientists" the ability to see into men's minds and hearts? Are their "findings" going to eliminate pride, selfishness, jealousy, suffering, and war? Sex research. Birth control. "Swinging." This is not the face of America.

Rev. Richard S. Moody
Bishop, Diocese of Chicago (Hatfield & Rapson, 2000, pp.77–78)

Within decades, however, most people, including priests and politicians, would come to realize that understanding the many facets of close relationships is as important as research on earthquakes or nutrition. Most people now find social scientific knowledge compatible with personal, political, and religious beliefs. In fact, some churches conduct premarital workshops and marriage encounters based on relationship research. Bookstores and newsstands are crammed with books and magazines that focus on every aspect of relationships, providing advice (of variable quality) on topics such as "How to Deal With His Ex" (Nanus, 2005), "Who Not to Marry" (McKinnell, 2006), and how to "Catch Her Eye" (Beland, 2005), as well as offering "Five Sex Tips for . . . What can lesbians and gay men teach each other about great sex?" (Westernhoefer & Mapa, 2006) and "6 Secret Ways to Turn Her On" (Miller, 2004), just to name a few pieces of advice found in the popular press. One important function of scientific research on relationships is to provide a check-and-balance system for the popular advice given in the media. Critical consumers can compare the scientific literature with the popular, but sometimes inaccurate, advice they receive in magazines, best-selling books, and television shows. Box 1.1 presents one such comparison.

Several major tributaries have contributed to the now steady stream of scholarly research on personal relationships. The early pioneers in the field could not have envisioned the vast amount of research on relationships that exists in several disciplines today. The young field of personal relationships has always been interdisciplinary, although it sometimes took years for scholars from different disciplines to discover one another's work. Duck

BOX 1.1   Highlights

The Importance of Being a Critical Consumer: Comparing John Gottman With John Gray

People are bombarded with advice about relationships from best-selling books, magazine articles, and talk shows. How accurate is this advice? The answer is, it depends. Sometimes, the advice given in the media is consistent with social science research; at other times it is not. In a *Psychology Today* article, Marano (1997) put John Gray to the test by comparing his credentials and conclusions to those of John Gottman. John Gray is the author of the number one best seller in nonfiction *Men Are from Mars, Women Are from Venus*. John Gottman is one of the premier social psychologists in the study of personal relationships. So how did Gray stack up to Gottman? Here is what *Psychology Today* reported after researching and interviewing both men.

	John Gray	John Gottman
Education	Ph.D. through correspondence school	Ph.D. from the University of Illinois
Licensing	Driver's license	Licensed psychologist
Number of journal articles	None	109
Number of couples formally studied	None	760
The cardinal rule of relationships	Men and women are different	What people think they do in relationships and what they actually do are very different.
Defining statement	"Before 1950, men were men and women were women."	"It's the everyday mindless moments that are the basis of romance in marriage."
What makes a marriage work?	Heeding gender stereotypes	Making mental maps of each other's world
What makes a marriage fail?	Gender differences in communication style	Gender stereotypes; reactions to stress
What they say about each other	"John who?"	"I envy his financial success."

SOURCE: From Marano, H. E., Gottman and Gray: A Tale of Two Relationship Gurus, in *Psychology Today*, November/ December 1997. Reproduced with permission from *Psychology Today*, copyright © 1997 www.psychologytoday.com

(1988) commented that the field of personal relationships is unusual because it is truly interdisciplinary and has the power to affect people's everyday lives. Groups of scholars from disciplines such as communication, social psychology, child development, family studies, sociology, and anthropology are all in the business of studying human relationships.

In subsequent sections, we take a closer look at how research in interpersonal communication, social psychology, and other disciplines has contributed to the establishment and evolution of the field of personal relationships.

Contributions of Interpersonal Communication Research

Although the earliest research in this area dates back to the 1950s, the study of interpersonal communication began in earnest in the 1960s and 1970s (Andersen, 1982). Previously, communication scholars had been mainly preoccupied with public speeches, political rhetoric, and mass communication. In the 1960s, scholars realized that most communication takes place in small groups and dyads consisting of close friends, family members, and romantic partners (Miller, 1976). The study of interpersonal communication thus began to focus on how people communicate in dyads and small groups. The first books on interpersonal communication emerged soon thereafter (see McCroskey, Larson, & Knapp, 1971).

Scholars also began to realize that interpersonal communication differs depending on the type of relationship people share. Miller and Steinberg (1975) proposed that the defining characteristics of interpersonal relationships are that they are unique, in most respects irreplaceable, and require an understanding of the psychological makeup of the partner. In contrast, noninterpersonal or "role" relationships, such as those with store clerks or phone operators, possess few unique qualities, are entirely replaceable, and involve only stereotypic perceptions of roles.

These shifts in communication scholarship reflected broader social changes. In part, the youth movement of the 1960s represented a rebellion against a society perceived to be impersonal and manipulative. Sensitivity training, encounter groups, and other personal-growth movements of the 1960s and 1970s turned people's attention inward to the dyad and to close relationships.

The evolution of interpersonal communication as one of the primary emphases in the communication discipline was a natural outcome of the realization that relationships are the primary locus for communication. In addition, scholars recognized that relationships are inherently communicative phenomena. It is difficult to imagine how human relationships might exist in the absence of communication. This realization was well stated by Miller (1976): "Understanding the interpersonal communication process demands an understanding of the symbiotic relationship between communication and relational development: communication influences relational development, and in turn (or simultaneously) relational development influences the nature of the communication between parties to the relationship" (p. 15). Since the 1970s, the sophistication of interpersonal and relational communication research has increased, and the work has become more theoretically driven (Andersen, 1982).

Contributions of Social Psychology

Early research in social psychology also laid the groundwork for the scientific investigation of interpersonal relationships, with much of this work focused on social development and personality differences. From the late 1950s through the mid-1970s, however, social psychologists increasingly began studying interaction patterns related to group and dyadic processes (for some of the major early works, see Altman & Taylor, 1973; Berscheid & Walster, 1969; Heider, 1958; Thibaut & Kelley, 1959). This movement was not limited to social psychologists in the United States; in Great Britain, Argyle and his associates also spent several decades studying aspects of relationships (see Argyle & Dean, 1965; Argyle & Henderson, 1985).

During this time, several highly influential books were published. For example, Thibaut and Kelley's (1959) *The Social Psychology of Groups* eventually led to an explosion of research on social exchange processes in groups and dyads, bringing issues such as rewards (the positive outcomes people get from relationships) and reciprocity (the way one person's behavior leads to similar behavior in another) to the forefront. Berscheid and Walster's (1969) *Interpersonal Attraction* also had a major impact on both interpersonal communication research and the study of dyadic behavior in social psychology. This book focused on emerging relationships between strangers, as much of the early research in social psychology did (see Altman & Taylor, 1973). A short time later, however, relational research began to focus on love, and the study of close relationships began to bloom (see Berscheid & Walster, 1974; Rubin, 1970, 1973). Finally, Altman and Taylor's (1973) *Social Penetration: The Development of Interpersonal Relationships*, which examined the role of self-disclosure in relationships, helped generate research in communication, relationship development, and relationship disengagement.

The prestigious *Journal of Personality and Social Psychology* also includes a section on "Interpersonal Processes"; indeed, this journal publishes some of the best research on relationships. However, until the mid-1980s, there were no journals devoted entirely to the study of relationships. In fact, the first professional conference devoted entirely to interpersonal relationships was held in the 1980s, again indicating the youthfulness of the field of personal relationships compared with other academic disciplines (see Kelley, 1986). This conference, which was organized primarily by social psychologists, laid the roots for the creation of two organizations that focused exclusively on personal relationships: the International Network on Personal Relationships (INPR), which was established by Steve Duck, and the International Society for the Study of Personal Relationships (ISSPR), which was founded by Robin Gilmour and Steve Duck. In 1984, the INPR established the first journal dedicated solely to the study of personal relationships, the prestigious *Journal of Social and Personal Relationships*. A decade later the ISSPR launched a second journal called *Personal Relationships*. Now, these two scholarly societies have merged into one professional association, the International Association for Relationship Research (IARR).

Roots in Other Disciplines

Although the most identifiable bodies of research on personal relationships come from scholars in communication and social psychology, disciplines such as family studies, sociology, developmental and child psychology, clinical psychology, humanistic psychology, and anthropology have made important contributions as well. One study reported that approximately 37% of the research on personal relationships comes from social psychologists and

another 37% comes from communication experts. In addition, sociologists and family studies scholars contribute substantially to the field of personal relationships (Hoobler, 1999).

This interdisciplinary element gives the field of personal relationships a richness and diversity of ideas that is often absent in other fields. It is precisely because scholars in the various disciplines— communication, social psychology, sociology, family studies, and so on—think in different ways and have different theoretical and methodological approaches that the field of personal relationships has been so vital and is evolving so quickly (Duck, 1988).

Although this book draws on knowledge from various fields, the primary focus is on communication in close relationships. Next, we define and discuss three terms that are central to this book: relationships (role, interpersonal, and close), interpersonal communication, and relational communication. Box 1.2 gives definitions for each of these key terms.

RELATIONSHIPS

Think about all the different people with whom you interact in a given day. Do you have relationships with all of them or only some of them? With how many of these people do you have close or intimate relationships? Defining the term *relationship* can be tricky. When do we cross the line from interacting with someone to having a relationship? And when do we move from having a casual or functional relationship to having a close or intimate relationship?

Features of Relationships

According to many relationship scholars, the basic ingredient for having a relationship is that two individuals share some degree of behavioral interdependence (Berscheid & Peplau, 1983). This means that one person's behavior somehow affects the other person's behavior, and vice versa. Based on this definition, we have relationships with a variety of people, including the salesclerk who helps us make a purchase, the waiter who takes our orders and serves us dinner, and the boss whom we rarely see but on whom we depend for leadership and a paycheck.

BOX 1.2   Highlights

Definitions of Key Terms

Role relationship: Two people who share some degree of behavioral interdependence, although people in such relationships are usually interchangeable, they are not psychologically or behaviorally unique. One person in a role relationship can easily replace another.

Interpersonal relationship: Two people who share repeated interactions over time can influence one another, and have unique interaction patterns.

Close relationship: Two people in an interpersonal relationship that is characterized by enduring bonds, emotional attachment, personal need fulfillment, and irreplaceability.

Interpersonal communication: The exchange of nonverbal and/or verbal messages between people, regardless of the relationship they share.

Relational communication: A subset of interpersonal communication that focuses on the expression and interpretation of messages within close relationships. Relational communication includes the gamut of interactions from vital relational messages to mundane everyday interactions.

These basic "relationships," known as **role relationships**, are not true interpersonal relationships. Rather, role relationships are functional and/or casual, and are often temporary; also, people in such relationships are usually interchangeable and are not unique. A close or intimate relationship with someone requires more than simple behavioral interdependence.

In addition to basic behavioral interdependence, **interpersonal relationships** require that two individuals influence each other in meaningful ways, that they have unique interaction patterns, and that they have repeated interactions over time. Our **close relationships** have all the features of interpersonal relationships plus three more. Specifically, close relationships are characterized by emotional attachment, need fulfillment, and irreplaceability. When we have a close relationship with someone, we feel connected to that person emotionally; he or she can make us feel happy or sad, proud or disappointed. Similarly, close relational partners fulfill critical interpersonal needs, such as the need to belong to a social group, to feel loved and appreciated, or to care for and nurture someone. Our closest relationships are also characterized by **irreplaceability**.

This means that the other person has a special place in our thoughts and emotions as well as in our social network. For example, you may only have one "first love" and one "best friend," and there may be one person in particular to whom you reach out in times of crisis.

It is important to recognize, however, that the distinctions between these three types of relationships are sometimes blurred. This is because our close relationships contain some of the same features as interpersonal and role relationships. For instance, Kristi's close relationship with her mother is partially defined by her role as a daughter. Behavioral interdependence also characterizes all relationships, but as people move from role to interpersonal to close relationships, this interdependence becomes more enduring (Berscheid & Peplau, 1983). In role relationships, such as those we have with salesclerks or waiters, behavioral interdependence is fleeting. Need fulfillment is also part of all three types of relationships, but the needs that our closest relationships fulfill are more central and personal than the needs that other relationships fulfill.

Types of Relationships

Another way to think about relationships is to categorize them based on type. In fact, we do this every day in our ordinary language. For example, we refer to some relationships as "friendships" and to others as "romances" or "marriages." We introduce someone as our "best friend," "brother-in-law," "wife," and so forth. These categorizations, although simple, help us understand the type of relationship we share with someone.

Relationships come in all shapes and sizes. When college students think about what constitutes a close relationship, they mainly think about dating or romantic relationships. However, as the different categories or types just listed suggest, we live in a web of relationships that includes family members, lovers, acquaintances, coworkers, employers, and so forth. We also have "blended" relationships, such as those with a teacher who also becomes a friend or with a coworker who becomes a lover.

Moreover, most of us are apt to think only of typical "mainstream" relationships. Traditionally, the media, as well as most research, has focused on young, white, middle-class heterosexuals (Wood & Duck, 1995). But relational researchers have begun to examine many other types of relationships as well, including gay, lesbian, and bisexual relationships (Huston & Schwartz, 1995; Kurdek, 1991); polygamy (Altman & Ginat, 1996); cohabitation between unmarried individuals (Cunningham & Antil, 1995); single-parent families, orphans, and interracial couples (Gaines, 1995; Williams & Andersen, 1998); cross-generational and Internet relationships (Lea & Spears, 1995); and long-distance relationships (Rohlfing, 1995). Unfortunately, research in these areas still lags far behind the research on heterosexual romantic relationships. For example, Peplau and Spalding (2000) reported that of the 312 articles published in the *Journal of Social and Personal Relationships* from 1980 to 1993, only 3 focused on some aspect of sexual orientation.

Because this book is based on the existing research, the majority of the discussion necessarily revolves around romantic relationships between heterosexuals. We also discuss research related to friendships and family relationships, albeit less

often. We make an effort, however, to include relevant work on understudied relationships whenever possible. Thus, as you read this book, keep in mind that the traditional models of relationships do not apply to all relationships. Nonetheless, many types of relationships have elements in common: connection and conflict, joy and grief, meetings and departures. Indeed, the more scholars study less common relationships, the more they conclude that all relationships are part of the same patchwork quilt. Of course, there are important differences sprinkled in with the similarities. Relationships are as unique as the different combinations of patchwork that create a quilt, and individuals in certain types of relationships do encounter particular difficulties that can affect communication processes. For example, Huston and Schwartz (1995), in their research on gay men and lesbians, stated, "The relationships formed by lesbians and gay men are in many ways very similar to heterosexual ones; in other ways distinct factors influence relationship formation and survival" (p. 120). Gay and lesbian couples, as well as interracial couples, often have to deal with societal prejudices and pressures with which opposite-sex and same-culture couples do not have to cope.

Characteristics Distinguishing Different Relationship Types

All types of intimate relationships vary on a number of different characteristics or dimensions. First, relationships can be either **voluntary** or **involuntary.** That is, people make a conscious choice to be involved in some of their close relationships, but they enter other close relationships without choosing to do so. For instance, children cannot choose their family; rather, they are born or adopted into relationships with parents, siblings, aunts and uncles, grandparents, and other relatives. In contrast, people typically choose their friends. In most Western cultures, people also choose their romantic partners, whereas in many other cultures spouses are selected through arranged marriages, thus becoming less voluntary.

Second, relationships are characterized by their **romantic** versus **platonic** nature. Typically, friendships and relationships with family members are platonic, which means they do not include sexual attraction or sexual involvement. Dating and marital relationships, in contrast, are often marked by romantic feelings and sexual activity. Of course, some relationships fall in the middle. Sometimes an individual has romantic or sexual feelings for someone who is only supposed to be a good friend, or someone feels little sexual attraction for a well-liked dating partner. "Friends with benefits" also blur the line between relationship types because partners have sex within the context of a friendship but don't consider themselves to be a romantic couple (Hughes, Morrison, & Asada, 2005). In cases such as these, the line between romance and friendship may not be clear. In addition, both platonic and romantic relationships can be characterized as **intimate**. In everyday use, some people use the terms *intimate* and *sexual* synonymously. But intimate relationships are defined by the characteristics mentioned previously: enduring behavioral interdependence, repeated interactions, emotional attachment, and need fulfillment. Thus people can have intimate relationships with friends, family members, and romantic partners.

Third, relationships can be either **satisfying** or **dissatisfying**. Satisfying relationships make people feel good about themselves. The relational partners feel close and connected, and emotions usually are more positive than negative (Kelly, Fincham, & Beach, 2003). Dissatisfying relationships, in contrast, often make people feel badly about themselves. Partners frequently feel disconnected from one another, and emotions generally are more negative than positive. All relationships go through rough stretches, and some dissatisfaction is not only inevitable but also can lead partners to work through and solve problems, which can improve the relationship. Any relationship can be characterized by some degree of satisfaction or dissatisfaction. Think of the different close relationships that you have. You are likely to feel more satisfied in some of these relationships than others. For example, you might share a close relationship with both your siblings, but you tend to be happier when you are with your brother than when you are with your sister, perhaps because you have more in common with your brother and get into more conflicts with your sister.

Fourth, relationships can be either **long term** or **short term**. For many people, their sibling relationships are the longest lasting relationships they will experience—from childhood through old age. The history that siblings share with one another is unique. Other relationships are short term, sometimes by choice and other times due to circumstances. Think about old friends you have lost touch with but wish you could contact. Commitment levels also help determine if our relationships are long or short term. If you are highly committed to your romantic partner, you are more likely to be in a long-term relationship than to want to "play the field" and see other people. Some romantic relationships fall in the middle. For instance, if you are in a romantic relationship that is on a "commitment roller coaster," you and your partner may frequently break up and make up. In any case, both commitment levels and relational length define the nature of a given relationship.

Other dimensions characterize types of relationships. For example, Fitzpatrick (1988) suggested that marriages can be viewed in terms of how **traditional** or **nontraditional** the relationship is. In traditional marriages, husbands and wives adhere to established gender roles, with the man expected to earn more money and the woman expected to take primary responsibility for the home. In nontraditional marriages, these gender roles are blurred, and partners must negotiate how tasks will be handled. Fitzpatrick also suggested that marriages differ based on how **connected** or **separate** partners are. Partners who value connection are highly interdependent and readily share their experiences with each other. These couples are also likely to engage in activities together with common friends. In contrast, partners who value separation are likely to be less self-disclosive and to engage in more activities without their spouses, such as spending time with friends. Finally, Fitzpatrick distinguished marriages based on whether spouses tend to avoid or engage in conflict. Conflict avoiders dislike conflict, often because they believe that disagreement is unpleasant and can harm the relationship; **conflict engagers** believe that it is important to air grievances and to discuss problems.

Finally, some scholars have labeled **sex** or **gender** as a component defining different types of relationships (Wood, 1996). Sex refers to an individual's biological makeup as male or female, whereas gender refers to how masculine, feminine, or androgynous the person is, with androgynous individuals possessing some feminine and some masculine traits (Bem, 1974). Sex is biologically determined, whereas gender is socially and culturally constructed. Sex can help define family relationships into categories such as father-son or father-daughter, or romantic relationships into categories such as lesbian, gay, or heterosexual. Much of the research on friendship makes these distinctions by comparing male friendships to female friendships, or same-sex friendships to cross-sex friendships. Other research focuses on gender by looking at how masculine, feminine, or androgynous individuals are within a relationship. For example, a romantic couple consisting of a feminine person and a masculine person is likely to function much differently than a romantic couple consisting of two androgynous individuals. In this book, we use the term *sex* to refer to biological sex (male vs. female) and the term *gender* to refer to culturally constructed images of men and women as masculine versus feminine.

Need Fulfillment in Close Relationships

Researchers suggest that a plethora of human needs are satisfied in close personal relationships: the three most central interpersonal needs being affection, inclusion, and control (Schutz, 1958). In the scenario at the beginning of this chapter, each person used communication to try to fulfill one of these needs. Kristi went to her mother for affection and social support. Su-Lin joined student clubs and talked with classmates to satisfy her needs for inclusion. Finally, Jake tried to exert behavioral control by persuading Dave to stay home and help him with his statistics homework.

Affection. Our need for **affection** is satisfied through our ability to love other people and through having other people love us (Schutz, 1958). Throughout life, our need for love and affection is satisfied through close relationships. Neglected infants who are never touched suffer from "failure-to-thrive syndrome"

and even risk death (Andersen, 1999; Montagu, 1971/1978). Adults who regularly give and receive affection report more psychological and physical health, as well as better relationships (Floyd, 2006). Affection, according to Schutz (1958), occurs only in dyads. Inclusion and control, in contrast, can occur either "between pairs of people or between one person and a group of persons" (p. 23). Affection forms the basis for our most powerful relationships.

Social Inclusion. Feeling part of a group is another crucial need (Schutz, 1958). It is through primary group relationships that basic needs such as safety and survival are satisfied. As Ruesch (1951) observed, being part of a family or group enhances feelings of security and increases one's "chance for survival in a troubled world" (p. 36).

Humans evolved as members of hunting and gathering bands of 100 to 200 people (Donald, 1991). This may explain why belonging to groups—from youth groups to corporations, from sports teams to service clubs, from street gangs to fraternities and sororities—is so important to most people. In any case, Schutz (1958) suggested that feeling included is a crucial part of social development that enables us to have successful interactions and associations with other people. A lack of social interaction and inclusion can contribute to loneliness and low self-esteem (Segrin, 1998).

Behavioral Control. The third basic interpersonal need revolves around the need people have to feel in control of their lives (Schutz, 1958). People in successful interpersonal relationships share control over their lives (Scott & Powers, 1978), including important decisions involving work, money, sex, children, and household chores. Indeed, a whole body of research suggests that partners who share tasks and resources in a fair manner are more satisfied with their relationships (see Chapters 9 and 10). In contrast, partners who believe they lack control or who are denied free choice may deliberately sabotage their relationships, defy rules, and engage in other destructive behavior. For example, if you have a friend who always shows up late, you might retaliate by leaving before he or she arrives. Prohibition of a relationship by parents sometimes increases the attractiveness of the relationship. According to Cialdini (1988), this effect is based on the idea that objects or people observed to be scarce or hard to obtain are most attractive. This explains why advertisers offer "limited time offers" and sales "while the supply lasts" and why people who are "hard to get" are more attractive than people who are "easy to get"—except, of course, if they are easy for us to get but hard for others to get.

Goals in Relationships

Of course, humans are driven by more than needs; they also have aspirations and goals. College students' goals might include graduating, making friends, acquiring skills, partying, meeting their future spouse, getting into graduate or professional school, living up to parental expectations, and preparing for a career. Spouses' goals might include maintaining a happy marriage, raising their children to be "good" people, buying their dream home, and saving for retirement. Within the context of interpersonal interaction, Canary and Cody (1994) suggested that people strive for three overriding and sometimes related sets of goals: self-presentational goals, relational goals, and instrumental goals.

Self-Presentational Goals. These goals have to do with the image we convey to others. Andersen (1999) claimed that "selling ourselves is the most common objective of persuasion" (p. 265). Other scholars have contended that people often resemble actors on a stage, trying to present themselves in the most favorable light possible (see Chapter 2). Indeed, a central set of communication principles suggests that we are as attractive, credible, competent, or honest as others think we are. Objective personal qualities sometimes have little to do with our image, especially when we first meet people. From an interpersonal standpoint, we are what people think we are. As Andersen (1999) put it, "Impressions we form of others are not just part of the communication game, they are the whole game" (p. 265). Not surprisingly, people spend a lot of time trying to look and act just right for that big date or that important interview. For example, before attending her first student club meeting, Su-Lin might purposely dress like a student from the United States so that she will fit in.

Relational Goals. These goals have to do with how we communicate our feelings about others, including the type of relationships we desire. Canary and Cody (1994) maintained that "nothing brings us more joy than our personal relationships. We spend significant amounts of time, energy and emotion in the pursuit of quality relationships" (p. 6). At every stage in a relationship, we have goals and plans for the future of that relationship. For example, you might want to meet that attractive student in your class, impress your date, avoid the person who won't let you alone, or spend time with your sister whom you haven't seen all year. Canary and Cody (1994) described three primary groups of relational goals. The first is activity based and involves sharing an activity with someone, such as attending a party or going skiing. The second is relationship based and involves wanting to initiate, escalate, maintain, or deescalate a relationship. The third is advice based and involves giving advice to peers and parents.

Instrumental Goals. These goals have to do with accomplishing specific tasks, including obtaining goods and services that promote self-advancement. For example, making money, getting good grades, buying a car, getting a ride to school, and completing a homework assignment are all instrumental goals. Usually, although not always, instrumental goals involve other people. Often, people facilitate attainment of instrumental goals by asking for advice or assistance from a friend, getting permission from a parent or boss, eliciting support from a friend, or influencing someone's attitudes or behaviors (Canary & Cody, 1994). Whereas achieving relational goals involves *giving* advice to help others, achieving instrumental goals involves *seeking* advice and assistance to meet one's own task-related goals. Thus, in the scenario involving Kristi and her mother, Kristi may reach instrumental goals related to coping with a divorce by asking her mom for advice. It is through networks of relationships that many of our instrumental goals are facilitated. For example, suppose you want to get a pay raise at work. To do this you have to communicate your wishes to your boss, and you also have to make a convincing argument that your performance merits a raise. People in close relationships also commonly try to achieve instrumental goals. For instance, Jake wanted his roommate to stay home and help him with his homework. Think about the times you asked a friend for a favor, tried to persuade others to see the movie that you wanted to see, or perhaps asked a family member to lend you some money. All these situations involve instrumental goals.

PRINCIPLES OF INTERPERSONAL COMMUNICATION

Whether you are trying to fulfill self-presentational, relational, or instrumental goals, communication is the vehicle through which you attain these goals. This is not to say that all communication is strategic and goal oriented. Much of our communication is relatively mindless and routine (Burgoon & Langer, 1995; Langer, 1989). Nonetheless, communication is the mechanism by which relationships are developed, the glue that holds them together, and often the means by which they are dissolved.

The terms *interpersonal communication* and *relational communication* describe the process whereby people exchange messages within the context of different types of relationships. The goal of message exchange is to co-create meaning, although as we shall see shortly, not all message exchanges are effective and miscommunication occurs frequently. A broader concept than relational communication, **interpersonal communication** refers to the exchange of messages, verbal and nonverbal, between people, regardless of the relationship they share. These people could be strangers, acquaintances, coworkers, political candidate and voter, teacher and student, superior and subordinate, friends, or lovers, to name just a few relationship types. Thus interpersonal communication includes the exchange of messages in all sorts of relationships, ranging from functional to casual to intimate. **Relational communication**, in contrast, is narrower in that it typically focuses on messages exchanged in intimate, or potentially intimate, relationships. In this section, we focus on specific principles related to interpersonal communication.

Verbal and Nonverbal Messages

The first principle is that *interpersonal communication consists of nonverbal and verbal messages*. Although much of our communication consists of verbal messages, nonverbal communication is at least as important as verbal communication (Andersen, 1999). In fact, some studies suggest that 60% to 65% of the meaning in most interactions is derived from nonverbal behavior. When emotional messages are exchanged, even more of the meaning may be gleaned from nonverbal behaviors (see Burgoon, Buller, & Woodall, 1996). Words are not always to be trusted. For example, someone can say "I love you" and not really mean it. But the person who spends time with you, gazes into your eyes, touches you lovingly, tunes into your moods, interprets your body language, synchronizes with your behavior, and uses a loving tone of voice sends a much stronger message. Nonverbal actions often do speak louder than words. As Eliza Dolittle sings in *My Fair Lady*,

> Don't talk to me, show me. When we sit together in the middle of the night, don't talk at all just hold me tight. Anyone who's ever been in love can tell you that this is not time for a chat.

Nonverbal communication encompasses a wide variety of behaviors, including **kinesics** (facial expressions, body movement, and eye behavior), **vocalics** (silence and the way we say words, including vocal pitch, loudness, tone, and speed), **proxemics** (the way we use space), **haptics** (the use of touch), **appearance** (physical attributes such as height, weight, and general attractiveness, as well as clothing), **environmental cues** (such as using candles and soft music to set a romantic mood), and **chronemic cues** (the use of time, such as showing up for a date early or late). Clearly, these types of behaviors can send powerful messages. Of course, interpersonal communication also consists of many forms of verbal behavior, including self-disclosure, small talk, and verbal content. Self-disclosure, through which people reveal information about themselves to others, is a particularly important form of interpersonal communication (see Chapter 5). The use of formal or informal language, nicknames, and present or future tense are other examples of verbal behavior that affect interpersonal interactions. For example, when dating partners first start talking about sharing a future, such communication is likely to reflect a shift toward a more committed relationship.

Communication as Inevitable

The second principle is that *one cannot not communicate in interpersonal settings.* In one of the important early works on communication, Watzlawick, Beavin, and Jackson (1967) stated, "Activity or inactivity, words or silence, all have message value: they influence others and these others, in turn, cannot not respond to these communications and thus are themselves communicating" (p. 49). Thus, unless two people simply do not notice each other, some degree of communication is inevitable when they are in contact. Even if someone does not mean to send a message, something that person says or does is likely to be interpreted as meaningful by the other person. This does not mean, however, that everything people do is communication. For communication to occur, a person has to send a message intentionally, or a receiver has to perceive and assign meaning to a behavior. So, for example, if you are blinking in a normal fashion while interacting with a friend, your friend is unlikely to attach any meaning to such an ordinary, involuntary, and biologically based behavior. Similarly, not every body movement counts as communication since many of these movements go unnoticed. But some of the movements you make and most of the words you say will be received and interpreted by others, making it impossible not to communicate at some level (Andersen, 1991).

To illustrate, recall the last time you sat down next to a stranger—perhaps at the mall, in a movie theater, or on a bus. What did you notice about the person? Did you check to see if he or she looked friendly before sitting down? Did you notice his or her appearance? Did he or she look older or younger than you? If you can answer any of these questions, Andersen (1991) argued, communication took place because you perceived and interpreted the stranger's behavior. In our relationships, much of what we do is interpreted as meaningful by our partners. For example, a smile might be perceived as heartfelt or condescending, while a neutral facial expression might be perceived as reflecting boredom. Even silence can communicate a message. For instance, if a close friend stops calling you and does not return your messages, you will likely suspect that something is wrong. Perhaps your friend is mad at you, or perhaps he or she is ill or depressed. In either case, your interpretation of your friend's silence will probably lead you to communicate with her or him in particular ways that will, in turn, further influence the exchange of messages between you.

Content Versus Relational Information

The third principle is that *every message contains both content and relational information.* Bateson (1951a) observed that messages, whether verbal or nonverbal, send more than literal information; they also tell people something about their relationship: "Every courtesy term between persons, every inflection of the voice denoting respect or contempt, condescension or dependency, is a statement about the relationship between two persons" (p. 213). Bateson (1951b) labeled these two functions of communication the report and command features of messages. The **report** function refers to the literal content of the message; the **command** function refers to the part of the message that signals status and other aspects of the interpersonal relationship.

Building on Bateson's work, Watzlawick et al. (1967) labeled these two functions the **content** and **relationship** levels of communication:

> The report of a message conveys information and is therefore synonymous in human communication with the content of the message. . . . The command aspect, on the other hand, refers to what sort of message it is taken as, and ultimately to the relationship between the communicators. (p. 51)

Thus, a statement as simple as "Hand me your book" contains both content (namely, the request to hand over the book) and information about the relationship. This relational information depends on whether the request is delivered in a harsh, polite, sarcastic, bored, or warm vocal tone. It also depends on the communicator's facial expressions, posture, gestures, use of touch, attire, eye contact, and a host of other nonverbal behaviors. Finally, the context or situation can affect how the relational information in a message is interpreted.

Another example may be helpful. Suppose that late on Friday afternoon your romantic partner calls and asks, "So what are we doing tonight?" At the content level, this seems to be a simple question. But at the relationship level, this question could be interpreted in a variety of ways. You might think, "It sure is nice to know that we always do something together on Friday nights, even if we don't plan it in advance." Alternatively, you might think that your partner takes you for granted and assumes that you have nothing better to do than wait around for her or him to call before you make plans. Or, if you had argued with your partner the day before, you might think that this is his or her way of making up. Yet another possibility is that you might think your partner always leaves it up to you to decide what to do. Based on which relational information you get from the message, you are likely to react in very different ways.

Effectiveness and Shared Meaning

The fourth principle is that *interpersonal communication varies in effectiveness*, with the most effective messages leading to shared meaning between a sender and a receiver. When one person sends an intentional message, understanding occurs when the receiver attaches approximately the same meaning to the message as did the sender. Of course, such perfectly effective communication may never occur, since people typically attach somewhat different meanings to the same messages. It is impossible to get inside people's heads and to think their thoughts and feel their emotions. Thus, it is difficult to truly

and completely understand "where someone is coming from." Nonetheless, communication is most effective when the sender and receiver attach very similar meanings to a behavior. Less effective (or less accurate) communication occurs when sender and receiver attach different meanings to a behavior.

Guerrero and Floyd (2006) provided a way of thinking about how different types of message exchanges are more or less effective. In their model (see Figure 1.1), communication necessitates that a sender encodes a message or a receiver decodes a message. Therefore, behaviors falling in the box labeled **unattended behavior** do not qualify as communication. The types of exchanges in the other boxes are all relevant to interpersonal communication, but the most effective form of communication, **successful communication**, occurs when a sender's message is interpreted correctly by a receiver. For example, Jake may ask Dave to stay home and help him, and Dave may understand what Jake wants him to do.

Other exchanges are less effective. **Miscommunication** occurs when someone sends an intentional message that is misinterpreted by the receiver. For example, you might teasingly say, "I hate you" to someone who takes your message literally. **Attempted communication** occurs when someone sends an intentional message that the receiver fails to receive or interpret; in other words, he or she misses the message. For example, you might hint that you want to leave a party you think is boring, but your partner might not get the message and keep on socializing. **Misinterpretation** occurs when someone unintentionally sends a message that is misconstrued by the receiver. For example, you might be scowling simply because you are in a bad

	Behavior Not Interpreted	Behavior Interpreted Inaccurately	Behavior Interpreted Accurately
Behavior Sent With Intention	Attempted communication	Miscommunication	Successful communication
Behavior Sent Without Intention	Unattended behavior	Misinterpretation	Accidental communication

Figure 1.1 Types of Communication and Behavior

mood after a long, trying day at work, but your roommate misinterprets your facial expression as reflecting anger toward her or him. Finally, **accidental communication** occurs when someone does not mean to send a message, but the receiver observes the behavior and interprets it correctly. For example, you might try to hide your joy at acing an exam from a classmate who studied harder than you and did poorly, but your classmate sees your nonverbal reaction and correctly assumes that you did well. Although such communication is an authentic representation of your feelings, your emotional expression would be ineffective because it communicated a message you did not intend (or want) to send. As you can see, all these forms of communication can affect the communication process and people's relationships. Certainly, effectiveness is important to high-quality communication; but it is not an attribute of all interpersonal communication.

Symmetry in Communication

Finally, *interpersonal communication can be symmetrical or asymmetrical.* This fifth principle of communication, which is taken from Watzlawick et al. (1967), emphasizes the dyadic nature of the communication process. That is, communication unfolds through a series of messages and countermessages that contribute to the meaning people attach to a given interaction. **Symmetrical communication** occurs when people exchange similar relational information or messages that are similar in meaning. For instance, a dominant message may be met with another dominant message (Jake says, "Help me with my homework," and Dave responds, "Do it yourself!"), or an affectionate message may be met with another affectionate message (Kristi's mother says, "I love you," and Kristi says, "I love you too"). Nonverbal messages can also be symmetrical, as when someone smiles at you and you smile back or when your date gazes at you lovingly and you touch her or him gently on the arm.

Asymmetrical communication occurs when people exchange different kinds of information. One type of asymmetry arises when people exchange messages that are opposite in meaning. For example,

a dominant message such as "I need you to help me with my homework now!" might be met with a submissive message such as "Okay, I'll cancel my plans and help you." Or Kristi's declaration of love to her soon-to-be ex-husband might be met with a guilt-ridden silence and shuffling of feet, after which he says something like, "I'm sorry that I don't love you anymore." Another type of asymmetry occurs when one person uses more of a certain behavior than another. For instance, imagine that Su-Lin is from an Asian culture where people generally touch each other less than people from the United States do. During a social gathering, a new friend of Su-Lin's might casually touch her arm five times, whereas Su-Lin might only initiate touch once. Although there is some symmetry because both Su-Lin and her new friend engage in some touch, the difference in the amount of touch each person initiates constitutes a source of asymmetry. As these examples suggest, the verbal and nonverbal messages that two people send and receive work together to create a unique pattern of communication that reflects their relationship.

PRINCIPLES OF RELATIONAL COMMUNICATION

As mentioned previously, relational communication is a subset of interpersonal communication that focuses specifically on messages exchanged within relationships. Most often, research on relational communication examines messages in relationships that are, were, or have the potential to become intimate. Thus, all the principles of interpersonal communication discussed previously are applicable to communication in relationships. Relational communication includes the entire range of communication behaviors, from vital relational messages to mundane everyday interaction. Thus, relational communication reflects the nature of a given relationship at a particular time. Communication both constitutes and defines relationships. In other words, communication is the substance of close relationships. Wilmot (1995) provided several principles of relational communication that are consistent with these ideas. These principles are paraphrased on page 15.

Relationships Emerge Across Ongoing Interactions

Relationships form not out of thin air but across repeated interactions. Cappella (1988) argued that "experience and common sense tell us that relationships are formed, maintained and dissolved in interactions with partners. At the same time interactions reflect the kind of relationship that exists between the partners" (p. 325). According to Wilmot (1995), "Relational definitions emerge from recurring episodic enactments" (p. 25). In part, relationships represent collections of all the communication episodes in which two partners have engaged over time, and each episode adds new information about the relationship. In new relationships, each episode may add considerably to the definition of the relationship. Even in well-developed relationships, critical turning points such as a declaration of love, a heated argument, or an anniversary can alter the course of the relationship.

Relationships Contextualize Messages

In various relationships, messages have different meanings. For example, a frown from your relational partner does not have the same meaning as a frown from a stranger; a touch from your mother does not mean the same thing as a touch from your date or spouse; disclosure from an acquaintance at work communicates differently than disclosure from a good friend. In Wilmot's (1995) words, "Relationship definitions 'frame' or contextualize communication behavior" (p. 27). Thus, the context is critical to understanding the message. According to Andersen (1989), "It has become axiomatic that no human action can be successfully interpreted outside of its context. The term 'out of context' has become synonymous with meaningless or misleading" (p. 27).

Relational Types Overlap One Another

While some relationships fit into neat categories, such as boyfriend, coworker, wife, or student, many relationships fit more than one category. For example, a colleague might also be a basketball teammate, a close friend, and a fellow member of a service organization. As Wilmot (1995) put it, "Relational types are not necessarily mutually exclusive—their boundaries are often fuzzy" (p. 28). Moreover, relationships often move from one category to another, as when a coworker becomes a friend, a friend becomes a dating partner, or a fraternity brother becomes an employee. In these "fuzzy" relationships, people can be uncertain about how to behave appropriately, especially when they are using different relational definitions.

Relational Definitions and Communication Episodes Frame Each Other

This paraphrase of Wilmot's (1995) fourth principle suggests that relational communication is a dynamic, interrelated process. As definitions of a relationship change, so does communication within that relationship, and vice versa. For instance, if you start dating a coworker, your communication with that person will reflect this change in relationship status. You are likely to discuss more intimate topics and to engage in more frequent interaction. Of course, your conversations at work might remain somewhat formal if you both want to project a professional demeanor. Similarly, two rivals at work who are stuck together in a stalled elevator might pass the time by talking and joking. As a result, they might reassess their relationship and see each other in a friendlier, less competitive light.

RELATIONAL MESSAGES

People can send a variety of messages to one another about their relationships. After reviewing the literature from a range of disciplines, Burgoon and Hale (1984, 1987) outlined seven types of relational messages that people commonly communicate to one another: (1) dominance/submission, (2) level of intimacy, (3) degree of similarity, (4) task-social orientation, (5) formality/informality, (6) degree of social composure, and (7) level of emotional arousal and activation. These messages, which have been referred to as the *fundamental relational themes*, all reflect the nature of a relationship. Of these seven

SOURCE: Copyright: Robert Trawick/iStockphoto.com   SOURCE: iStockphoto.com

Photo 1.1   Note how the two types of touches depicted in these photos send different relational messages related to intimacy, dominance, formality, and task-social orientation.

themes, dominance/submission and intimacy are the two primary dimensions that characterize relationships (Burgoon et al., 1996).

These seven message themes are important within all types of interpersonal interactions, but especially in close relationships. In role relationships, relational messages stay fairly constant, with people generally following prescribed rules and scripts. For instance, in manager-employee relationships, a certain level of formality, friendliness, dominance, and task orientation usually prevails across most interactions. In contrast, in intimate relationships, the range and impact of relational messages are typically much greater. For example, a romantic couple might be hostile during an argument and then become intimate when making up; a parent might act with an unusual level of formality and dominance during a serious talk with a child; or, friends might have a hard time switching gears and moving from a conversation to a task. Such messages can have a powerful impact on how relational partners view each other and their relationship.

Dominance/Submission

Dominance is often defined as the actual degree to which a person influences others and **submission** as the actual degree to which a person gives up influence and/or yields to the wishes of others. As such, dominance is a "social and relational phenomenon. Dominance is determined by the subservient or submissive responses of others. It is not dominance unless it works" (Burgoon et al., 1996, p. 306). Dominance is closely related to power and status, with **power** defined as a person's ability to control valuable resources and **status** defined by a person's place in a social hierarchy (Patterson, 1983). For example, your boss is likely to have power because she controls your work schedule and has the power to promote you or give you a raise. She also has status because of her position within the company. And, because she has power and status, she may be able to influence you more easily. Similarly, your friends are likely to be able to influence you to some extent because you like them and want to maintain positive relationships with them.

Dominance is communicated in a variety of ways. Verbal statements that take the form of commands are a key form of dominant behavior, as are many verbal messages delivered using assertive or aggressive language. Nonverbal behaviors can also reflect dominance. For example, dominant individuals tend to look at people more when they are speaking and less when they are listening (Exline,

Ellyson, & Long, 1975), which suggests that they believe what they are saying is more important. Dominant individuals also tend to take up more space and to speak in a moderately loud, fast, and authoritative tone of voice. Interestingly, dominant individuals also have the prerogative to violate norms by keeping others waiting, dressing casually when others are expected to dress formally, talking for longer periods of time than others, and initiating touch (Burgoon et al., 1996). (More information on dominance is provided in Chapter 11.)

Level of Intimacy

According to Burgoon and Hale (1984), intimacy is a multidimensional construct that has five subthemes: (1) affection/hostility, (2) inclusion/exclusion, (3) trust, (4) depth/superficiality, and (5) intensity of involvement. Intimate communication conveys affection, inclusion, and trust. It is also high in depth. In other words, intimate communication deals with personal rather than superficial topics. In addition, intimate communication is typically characterized by high levels of nonverbal involvement and positive affect, which means that the two people are actively engaged in conversation and attentive to each other.

Intimacy is conveyed in a variety of ways. Verbal statements of affection, such as "I love you," are highly valued within relationships (Marston, Hecht, & Robers, 1987). Personal nicknames, such as "honey bunny" for a romantic partner or "pumpkin" for a child, also convey intimacy. Self-disclosure is important in communicating intimacy as well. As you will learn in Chapter 5, self-disclosure occurs when individuals reveal personal information about themselves to others. The more in-depth this self-disclosure is, the more intimate the communication. Nonverbal behaviors are extremely powerful in conveying intimacy. A special set of behaviors called **nonverbal immediacy cues** send messages of physical and psychological closeness as well as interpersonal warmth (Andersen, 1985). Primary immediacy cues include touch, close proxemic distancing, direct body orientation, forward lean, and attention gaze. Andersen also included positive affect cues, such as smiling and vocal warmth as part of nonverbal immediacy. (More information on intimacy is provided in Chapter 8.)

Degree of Similarity

Shows of similarity are an important way for people to identify with one another and to show inclusion. Similarity is achieved through a wide array of verbal cues, such as expressing similar opinions and values, agreeing with each other, reciprocating self-disclosure, and communicating empathy and understanding. Nonverbal cues conveying similarity are very common. For example, people may sit in similar positions or mirror one another's facial expressions. Indeed, research has shown that people's emotions are often "contagious," with one person's emotional state influencing the other's, leading to similar displays of affect (Hatfield, Cacioppo, & Rapson, 1994). Other research has shown that people often adapt their vocal intonations and speech to match that of their friends or other people they like (Street & Giles, 1982). For example, you might pick up some of the slang that a friend uses, and you might talk with a slightly different accent when at home with your family on the East Coast than when with friends from the Midwest. Street and Giles (1982) referred to this process as **communication accommodation**, whereby people's verbal and nonverbal behaviors become more similar to those around them. Generally, when we like people and identify with them, our behavior becomes more similar to theirs. In contrast, when we dislike people and want to dissociate ourselves from them, our behavior becomes more dissimilar to theirs. People who are trying to fit in with a new group or culture tend to accommodate; so it would not be surprising for Su-Lin to accommodate to the communication style of her new friends in the United States.

People also alter their physical appearance to show similarity and dissimilarity. For example, group members might get tattoos, as many players on college basketball teams do. In addition, body piercings can reveal that people belong to a particular group or generation. More temporary signs of similarity, such as getting similar haircuts or wearing similar clothing, are common as well. Clothing, jewelry, and tattoos can also identify people as members of a group. Thus, people communicate similarity and dissimilarity in a variety of verbal and nonverbal ways. Such messages help form a foundation for inclusion in or exclusion from groups and can also signal individuals' connection to one another.

Task-Social Orientations

As noted previously, some people are connected only through task-oriented or role relationships. Examples of task-oriented relationships include teachers and students, superiors and subordinates, doctors and patients, and lawyers and clients. Unless a friendship develops, communication between these people generally focuses almost exclusively on the task at hand—for example, getting a good grade, doing a job properly, seeking medical treatment, or trying to win a settlement. In contrast, our close relationships, as well as many of our casual acquaintanceships, tend to be characterized by more social orientations. Here, communication involves conversing and having fun, rather than trying to accomplish a particular task. Importantly, our closest relationships often include both task and social orientations. For example, a married couple may have a task orientation when doing chores together or discussing important issues, such as how to discipline a rebellious child. But this same couple may shift to a social orientation when they are out having fun with some friends or spending a quiet, romantic evening together away from their rebellious child.

Burgoon and Hale (1987) found certain types of communication to reflect a task orientation. Specifically, when people seemed sincere, work oriented, reasonable, and more interested in the task at hand than the conversation, they were rated as being highly task oriented. This makes sense. Think about a time when you tried to have a serious conversation with a romantic partner. Perhaps you were concerned about a problem that had emerged in your relationship, and you were intent on working it out. How would you feel if your partner seemed uninterested in solving the problem? What if she or he wanted to watch TV instead of talking or kept changing the subject to something less serious? These actions probably would be distressing to you because your task orientation would be in direct contrast to your partner's more social orientation.

Formality/Informality

When an interaction is formal, people maintain their distance, and the overall tone of the interaction is serious. In contrast, informal interactions are characterized by less distance and a more casual approach. One of the key verbal behaviors associated with formality is forms of address. For example, calling your professor Dr. Brown is more formal than calling her Dr. B, which is more formal than calling her Lisa. Similarly, the way you address your romantic partner's parents sends a strong message regarding formality. Should Rosa call her boyfriend's father Mr. Garcia or José? If Rosa married her boyfriend, should she still call her father-in-law Mr. Garcia or José, or should she call him Dad? These seemingly trivial differences in forms of address can affect the intimacy level of the relationship. In some cases, too much formality sends a strong negative message. For instance, someone who considers you a close friend might be offended by your use of formal address. When parents are angry with a child, they sometimes use the child's full name ("Jonathan Martin Hall, stop that this minute!"), and romantic partners sometimes use formal names sarcastically during an argument ("Whatever you say, MISS Green!"). Of course, using too little formality can also send a strong negative message. For example, calling your date Gabby when he prefers Gabriel (or she prefers Gabrielle!) would not be a wise move on a first date, nor would it be wise to call your spouse by a nickname such as "sweet-ums" when at a formal company party.

Nonverbal cues are also important in conveying formality. Burgoon and Newton (1991) found that interactions characterized by anxiety cues (such as speaking too fast, using nonfluencies like "um," and twisting one's hands in one's lap), inexpressiveness (such as neutral facial expressions and a lack of gestures and vocal animation), and low levels of eye contact combined to convey formality. This is probably because people are less comfortable in formal than informal situations. Environmental cues are important in conveying formality as well. To illustrate, think about the different ways that lunch might be served at a birthday party. If there are assigned seats and someone serves you lunch, the atmosphere is probably more formal than if everyone helps themselves to a buffet and finds a place to sit or stand while eating. Similarly, the way people use time differs based on the level of formality. If the birthday party is a formal affair, people are expected to be there on time, or at least before the meal is served. Time of arrival is more lax if the party is a casual affair.

Degree of Social Composure

Social composure is related to the level of anxiety and communication competence people show in a given interaction. When people are socially composed, they appear confident and sure of themselves, and other people are likely to regard them as competent communicators. Social composure is conveyed through verbal cues such as making strong, convincing arguments and saying the appropriate words at the right time. For example, if you are arguing with your roommate about the household chores, you will appear composed and competent if you present a logical argument about why you think the chores are not being distributed fairly. If you are asking someone out on a date, you will appear more composed if you make your request in a charming and appropriate fashion ("I feel so comfortable with you; I'd enjoy spending more time with you. Would you like to go to a party with me next Saturday night?"), rather than if you stammer or become tongue-tied.

Nonverbal behavior also sends powerful messages about social composure. Canary and Cody (1994) listed several types of nonverbal messages that are related to competence and composure. These include (1) maintaining a high level of, but not continuous, eye contact; (2) speaking in a confident, moderately fast, and fairly loud voice, and including purposeful pauses; and (3) wearing clothing that is appropriate for the situation. In contrast, low levels of social composure and competence are conveyed by anxiety cues such as nonfluent speech, moistening one's lips, and fidgeting. Other behaviors such as looking down before responding to a question, displaying smiles that look fake or insincere, and taking too long to resume one's speaking turn are also associated with a low level of social composure (Burgoon et al., 1996; Canary & Cody, 1994). So if your heart starts pounding when you are arguing with

your roommate or asking someone out, you might appear anxious and sound nervous, which could undermine perceptions of your composure.

Level of Emotional Arousal and Activation

Relational messages also influence the emotional tone of an interaction. Interactions can be characterized by two emotional dimensions: (1) **pleasantness**, which refers to how positive or negative the emotions experienced are, and (2) **activity**, which refers to how active or bored a person feels (see Burgoon et al., 1996). For example, if you are in an argument with your romantic partner, the interaction is likely to be characterized by low pleasantness and high activity. But if you are having a serious, loving conversation with your romantic partner about your future together, the interaction is likely to be high in both pleasantness and activity. Other times, interactions are characterized by low activity. For example, two strangers sitting next to each other at the department of motor vehicles might chat to pass the time, but they are unlikely to be very involved in the conversation. Instead, such interactions are typically socially polite (pleasant) but low in activity. In other situations, such as having to talk to someone you would rather avoid, the interaction is likely to be low in both pleasantness and activity.

Research has shown that people usually perceive moderate to moderately high levels of arousal as most appropriate when interacting with relational partners, particularly when arousal is positive (see Burgoon et al., 1996). Negative forms of arousal include experiencing distress or nervousness; positive forms of arousal include experiencing excitement, interest, and elation. We do not expect our friends and loved ones to be nervous around us, except maybe at the beginning of a relationship, but we do expect them to be interested and involved in the conversations we have with them. Perhaps surprisingly, research also suggests that individuals sometimes are less relaxed with people they like than with people they dislike (Burgoon et al., 1996). This is because people care more about making a good impression on those they like and because they are often more affected by what close relational partners say about them than by what strangers say.

In any given interaction, these relational messages work synergistically to create a pattern of themes that reflects the nature of a relationship at a particular point in time. Over time, different patterns of themes emerge to characterize the type of communication and the type of relationship that people share. Think about your closest relationships. How would they compare in terms of these message themes? Chances are that each relationship is characterized by a somewhat unique profile of relational messages.

SUMMARY AND APPLICATION

This chapter introduced you to the field of personal relationships and provided information on key concepts that will be discussed throughout this book. After reading this chapter, you should have a better appreciation for the complexity of your relationships and the communication that occurs within them. Communication does not occur in a vacuum. Rather, communication is shaped by contextual and relational factors, and communication both reflects and influences the nature of a given relationship. In the scenarios that opened this chapter, Jake's communication with Dave reflects his expectation that a good friend should help him at a time of need. Su-Lin's communication is shaped by the context of being in a new cultural environment, and Kristi's communication is embedded within a social network that includes her husband and her family.

Communication is essential for accomplishing personal and relational goals, as well as for fulfilling the basic human needs of affection, inclusion, and control. Only through communication can Jake persuade Dave to help him, and only through communication can Dave give Jake the knowledge that he needs to do well in his statistics assignment. It is through communication that Su-Lin will learn about and adapt to the U.S. culture, and it is through communication that her new friends will learn more about her and her

culture. The scenario involving Kristi also highlights how communication reflects people's goals and needs: Kristi's husband used communication to inform her that he wanted a divorce; in turn, Kristi searched for comfort by communicating with her mother. While the importance of communication in these scenarios and in everyday life may be obvious to you, it is amazing to think about how much we rely on communication every day in so many ways.

This book is designed to help you better understand how communication functions within your close relationships. We do not provide a blueprint or list of "rules" for how to communicate effectively in relationships. Instead, we summarize research related to significant relational communication topics in the hope that you will be able to apply the concepts and theories we discuss to your own life. As this chapter has shown, being able to communicate effectively is a key to good relationships, and having good relationships is a key to a happy life.

DISCUSSION QUESTIONS

1. What qualities distinguish your close relationships from your casual relationships?

2. In this chapter, we defined interpersonal communication as the exchange of nonverbal and verbal messages between people, regardless of their relationship. Do you agree or disagree with this definition of interpersonal communication? What types of behavior should not count as communication?

3. As illustrated by the comparison of John Gottman and John Gray, there is a lot of popular press material on relationships that does not necessarily correspond with what researchers have found. Why do you think the public is so fascinated with popular books, talk shows, and magazine articles on relationships? What type of role, if any, do you think relationship researchers should play in this process?

2

COMMUNICATING IDENTITY

The Social Self

Cindy has a page on Facebook with over 200 people on her friend list. Several of her favorite quotes are on her page, with her personal motto "carpe diem" in a prominent position under her name. She posted some quotes in Italian because she is proud of her ethnic background and feels a connection to her relatives who live in Rome. Her page indicates her current relationship status, which is updated as warranted. Cindy has posted over 300 pictures; most are of her partying with her friends and sorority sisters or performing in a local dance company. A few are from her trips to Italy. She also has tons of messages on her message board/"wall," with some friends wishing her happy birthday, others making inside jokes, and yet others reminiscing about the previous night or just saying hi.

What does Cindy's Facebook page say about her? It lets others know whether she is dating or not (even though the information she posts may or may not be true), gives others a sense of how popular she is (from the number of "friends" on her list), gives strangers a glimpse into who she is, and generally provides a peek into her personal and social life. Whether her presentation of herself is effective or not probably depends on who views her page. Cindy's page certainly speaks to her friends in important ways; through her pictures and wall she is able to identify herself as a good friend to certain people. Her page also communicates to her classmates and potential friends; her Facebook can help shape their impression of her before they really get to know her. But what if potential employers, professors, or her parents look at her page? These are the questions that people are increasingly asking as the popularity of Facebook and other similar Web sites grows. It is striking that, like everyday face-to-face interaction, such Web sites portray different identities depending on the audience they are targeted at.

Of course, the Internet is but one venue that people use to present and manage their identities. Identity management occurs in face-to-face interaction, over the telephone, and even in letters. Research on identity management, which has focused most often on face-to-face contexts, offers a glimpse into how people develop and maintain their perceptions of self. Identity management is particularly important at the beginning of relationships when people try to make a good initial impression, but it is also important in well-developed relationships.

In this chapter, we examine how people use communication to manage their identities during social interaction. First, we briefly discuss the development of personal identities and the role that relationships play in their development. Second, we discuss some general issues related to identity management, such as whether trying to make a good impression is deceptive and manipulative or is simply a natural, often unconscious, process. Finally, we review the literature on three perspectives of identity management: Goffman's (1959) dramaturgical perspective, Brown and Levinson's (1987) politeness theory, and research on facework.

THE DEVELOPMENT AND EXPANSION OF IDENTITIES

Sociologists, anthropologists, psychologists, family researchers, and communication scholars, among others, have studied how our identities affect us throughout our life. Although several definitions have been offered, we define identity as "a theory of self that is formed and maintained through actual or imagined interpersonal agreement about what self is like" (Schlenker, 1985, p. 67). The key theme underlying this definition is that "a person's identity is forged, expressed, maintained, and modified in the crucible of social life, as its contents undergo the continual process of actual or imagined observation, judgment, and reaction by audiences (oneself and other)" (Schlenker, 1985, p. 68). In other words, the way we see ourselves is shaped by our interactions with other people, our anticipated interactions, and the way they respond to and judge us.

Identity, Perceptions, and Social Interaction

Our identities help us understand ourselves in relation to the world around us. Self-esteem and identity are part of a person's **theory,** or **vision,** of self. Self-esteem refers to how positively or negatively we view ourselves. People with high self-esteem generally view their traits and behaviors in a positive light, whereas people with low self-esteem mostly see their traits as negative. Identity defines who we are and what we are like (see Schlenker, 1985) by

specifying the characteristics that define us (African American, student, smart, attractive, introvert) and placing us on a comparative continuum with others (smarter than John, not as smart as Haley). Unlike self-esteem, however, our identity is not necessarily based on whether we consider these aspects of ourselves to be positive or negative qualities. Identity simply specifies what these qualities are.

Self-esteem and identity, although sometimes related, are distinct. For example, both Cindy and her friend Lindsay may see themselves as partiers who like to have fun. However, Cindy may think that partying is a cool aspect of her personality, while Lindsay may be depressed because she realizes that partying is interfering with her success in school, yet she can't seem to stop. Thus, while part of each of their identities, partying could contribute to high self-esteem for Cindy and to low self-esteem for Lindsay. In this chapter, we focus on identity and identity management rather than self-esteem, despite their influences on one another.

Social identity theory provides an explanation of how our identities are developed and maintained as well as how our identity or self-view is intricately linked to our membership in social groups. These social groups can be either as broad as religious or ethnic groups or as narrow as small cliques—for example, Italian American, bisexual, Catholic, alumnus of West High School, a resident of the Bronx, a member of "the big four" (a self-labeled group of friends with whom a person grew up). Based on Cindy's Facebook, you would probably associate her with at least two key groups—her sorority and her dance company. A key principle of social identity theory is that membership is characterized by in-group behaviors that signal membership and define someone as being a part of a group or as an outsider (see Hogg & Abrams, 1988) and accordingly promote differential behavior toward that person. Group members may dress a certain way, get similar tattoos, talk with an accent, use particular gestures, play the same sports, or have conversational routines that identify themselves as belonging to the group. To maintain positive views of ourselves, we may also be motivated to think of "our" groups as better than other groups. It is not uncommon to think that our way of doing things is the best, what we wear looks the best, what we say is the smartest, our view of the world is the most reasonable, our perspective on a conflict is a sensible one, our values are the ones most connected to God, our beliefs are correct, and so forth.

The impact a group has on your identity is influenced by several factors, including how central the group is to your self-view (see Oakes, 1987). So, for example, an ethnic group association may be important for someone like Cindy, who has visited relatives in Rome, but unimportant to people who have little connection to their ethnic roots. Several studies have also shown that minority groups are especially likely to identify with their ethnic backgrounds. African Americans or Latinos, for example, see their ethnicity as a more central part of themselves than do Caucasians (see Jackson, 1999). In fact, people in minority groups are typically more aware of their membership in that group than are majority members. Why is that? Events on a day-to-day basis remind them of their minority status. Think about this: How many black mannequins have you seen in clothing stores? Unless you are visiting a store in a neighborhood that is primarily African American, the answer is likely to be "none." Because clothes look a bit different on black skin than on white skin, African Americans have to imagine how that piece of clothing would look on them.

Think about the examples in your exams and textbooks: How many of them describe the lives of individuals with a homosexual orientation? Probably very few. The research on gay relationships is not abundant. Thus, despite our efforts to accommodate all sexual orientations in this book, gay, lesbian, or transgendered students have to think about whether the examples fit in their lives. In all these cases, group identity is more salient to minority-group members because their lives are surrounded by reminders that they don't "fit" into the majority group's way of thinking or doing.

To clarify the way in which group identities and personal identities are merged, Hecht (1993) introduced the **communication theory of identity**. He argued that identity construction can be viewed through four "frames of identity" or "lenses" (see also Hecht, Collier, & Ribeau, 1993; Hecht, Warren, Jung, & Krieger, 2004). First, identity is viewed through a **personal** frame. In this sense, identity is an image we construct within ourselves: We perceive ourselves to possess certain characteristics and not others. Second, identity can be viewed through an **enactment** frame. In other words, identities develop through communication with others; the way we respond to others and the way they respond to us reflect and shape our theories of self. Third, identity can be viewed through a **relationship** frame whereby we define ourselves in terms of relationships with other people. For example, your identity might be shaped by the kind of friend, romantic partner, and son or daughter you are. Moreover, you might portray yourself differently depending on whether you are with your best friend, a first date, your spouse, or your parents. Finally, identity can be viewed through a **communal** frame. As such, our identities are integrally tied to the groups to which we belong, and the development of our identities often is constrained by our cultural or group identities. For example, in childhood we are taught rules of cultural appropriateness, such as norms of politeness. These rules become so ingrained that they necessarily affect our identities.

These four frames work together to affect identity development (Hecht, 1993). All couples routinely deal with identity issues, but interracial or intercultural couples often face special challenges (Williams & Andersen, 1998). They must each deal with who they are as individuals—for example, as a white man and an African American woman (personal frame). They must also deal with how they present themselves to others (enactment frame), what it means to be an interracial couple (relationship frame), and how to best blend their different cultural backgrounds (communal frame). Scholars are increasingly aware of these identity-related challenges in interracial or interethnic relationships. Although research on these couples is somewhat rare, available studies have shown that the difficulties they face may include differences in language, conflict styles, communication preferences, and sexual scripts, as well as pressure from family and friends to dissolve the relationship (see Gaines & Liu, 2000; Williams & Andersen, 1998). In the past, most U.S. states banned interracial marriages, with Alabama most recently removing that law in 2000 (Hartill, 2001). As a result of ethnic norms and societal pressures confronting them, census data show that interethnic couples in the United States are more likely than same-ethnicity couples to get divorced (Bramlett & Mosher, 2002). On the other hand, most other studies show that there are very few differences in the quality of inter- and intraracial couples and emphasize that the differences within an interracial couple, if managed, may help the bond grow between the partners in such relationships (Troy, Lewis-Smith, & Laurenceau, 2006).

In fact, one theory in particular seems especially well suited to explaining the possible benefits to interracial relationships. Specifically, A. Aron and E. N. Aron's (1986, 1996) **self-expansion theory** helps explain how identity influences the development of close relationships after first impressions are made. Self-expansion theory is framed around three primary predictions. First, people seek to expand the self, to be more than they are. Studies have shown that a fundamental human desire is to broaden our experiences and extend our identity (E. N. Aron & A. Aron, 1996). We do not seem satisfied with a static sense of self. Instead, we seek to develop our sense of self as part of our physical, cognitive, and emotional development. For example, if you are good at oil painting, you might try other kinds of art, such as ceramics or watercolors. If you like reading or watching television, you may search for new types of books or shows you have not seen previously.

Second, one reason people enter into relationships is the opportunities they provide to expand their identities. One of the best ways to expand the self is by becoming close to someone who can contribute to our identity development by exposing us to new experiences. Obviously, interracial or interethnic relationships are filled with such possibilities. Aron, Aron, and Smollan (1992) found that the more partners defined their relationship as a meshing of both identities, the closer they were likely to be. Figure 2.1 shows the inclusion-of-others-in-self scale that these authors have used in their studies. They have consistently found that close relationships are characterized by an expansion of self through inclusion of others. Rather than having two separate identities, people in close relationships merge identities, thereby allowing each partner's identity to expand through new experiences. In a novel test of this prediction, Aron, Paris, and Aron (1995) asked students to list as many self-descriptive words or phrases that came to mind in response to the question, Who are you today? The students did this four times in a 10-week period and answered questions about whether they had fallen in love during the task. Consistent with the theory's prediction, those who reported falling in love during the task showed a marked increase in the number of self-definitions they could list, an indication that their identity had expanded. This does not mean, however, that in strong relationships partners are completely intertwined. It is important to keep in mind that the theory emphasizes the importance of self in relationships. As such, losing one's sense of self or one's

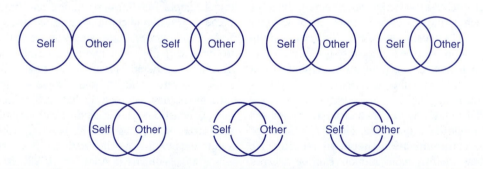

Figure 2.1   The Inclusion-of-Others-in-Self Scale: Which Drawing Best Describes Your Relationship?

SOURCE: Copyright © American Psychological Association.

individual identity in favor of a relational identity is not what the theory would predict as a "healthy" relationship outcome. Instead, the theory predicts that close relationships are those in which both individuals have strong self-identities that can grow from the new experiences that each partner's identity brings.

Third, a relationship's success depends on the ability of the relationship to expand the partners' experiences and sense of self. A common phenomenon in many relationships is stagnation; that is, over time the relationship gets bogged down by routine, which decreases satisfaction for both partners. Self-expansion theory offers an interesting explanation and remedy for this common problem. Specifically, A. Aron and E. N. Aron (1986, 1996) argued that relationships stagnate when they stop serving a self-expansion function, when personal and relational growths stop. While the theory, to our knowledge, has not been applied to interracial relationships, its premises seem especially well suited to the identity-expansion opportunities found there.

Of course, ethnicity is not the only aspect of identity that challenges relational partners. Sexual identities often occupy an important position in individuals' sense of self in relationships. As a starting point, we can think of the ways in which we manage public expressions of our sexuality and/or sexual orientation. These expressions, which include how we initiate relationships with prospective partners, whether we hold hands in public, or whether we are comfortable with intimate displays of public affection, send messages about ourselves to other people. Such decisions are somewhat benign for heterosexual couples because that sexual orientation is normative. The decision to initiate a relationship, hold hands, or engage in intimate behaviors in public becomes much more significant identity issues for gay or lesbian couples.

The double trouble of identity in interracial gay couples were studied by Steinbugler (2005), who interviewed eight black/white couples, four of whom were heterosexual, two were gay, and two were lesbian. Her results provide a fascinating glimpse into the ways in which people manage these important identities. One of her participants (a 28-year-old black gay male dating a white male) reflected on the couple's behavior this way:

> We have a lot of PDA [public displays of affection] but not overt, not, not loud PDA. It's very quiet. For example . . . we'll walk and one of us will rub the other on the back. Or if we hold hands it's sort of brief, very brief. (p. 435)

He continued by noting that he felt more comfortable with these expressions "when I know for a fact that there are other gay people around." His words emphasize the public nature of our identities and suggest that his sexual orientation occupies a more central position in his construction of self than his ethnicity, at least in the context of his public interactions with his boyfriend.

PRINCIPLES OF IDENTITY MANAGEMENT

This couple's experience serves as an entry to discussing the ways in which identity affects how we perceive ourselves, how others perceive us, how we behave, and how we evaluate our behavior and our relationships with others. Seven principles provide a good summary of this research.

Identity and Hierarchical Structure

The first principle is that *our identities provide us with a hierarchical structure of who we are.* Although we define ourselves in myriad ways, our identity helps organize these many characteristics into a hierarchical structure that fluctuates according to context (Schenkler, 1985). The content of our identity includes our relationships (boyfriend, friend, son), roles (student, basketball player, law clerk), goals (live in Europe, get a job helping others), personal qualities (friendly, honest), accomplishments (3.5 GPA, president of an organization), group/cultural membership (sorority member, Asian), and appearance (am moderately attractive, like Abercrombie clothes), among others. These contents vary in the degree to which they centrally define who we are. The more central they are to our definition of self, the more likely they are to be stable across our lifetime and to be prominent as we present ourselves to others during interactions. Think back to Cindy and her Facebook page.

Although its content gives visitors to that page a good sense of Cindy's identity structure, Cindy is probably only displaying part of that structure when she edits that page. Thus people who frequent her page might have biased impressions about Cindy. For example, they might think that Cindy cares for her friends more than her family, when actually the reverse is true.

Identity and the Looking-Glass Self

The second principle is that *the feedback we receive from others helps shape our identities.* Charles Horton Cooley (1922) first developed the notion of the looking-glass self, a metaphor that described his belief that identity is shaped by feedback from others. He argued that social audiences provide us with an image of ourselves like the one we see when we look into a mirror. The way people treat us is reflected in the way we see ourselves. For example, think of how you came to believe that you were smart enough to pursue a college degree. Your identity as an intelligent person was most likely cultivated through interactions with parents, teachers, and/or peers. Perhaps a specific teacher in high school said you were smart enough to go to college, or your parents or spouse gave you positive feedback and encouragement, or a friend kept complimenting you on your ability to learn quickly. Regardless of the source, one or more of these people likely helped develop that aspect of your identity. Many parts of our identities are similarly formed through our interactions with significant others.

Identity and the Interpretation of Feedback

The third principle is that *our identities help us interpret feedback from others.* Just as people's feedback affects our identities, so too, our identities affect how we perceive feedback from others (Schlenker, 1980). For example, people like Cindy who see themselves as extroverts will likely react very differently than those who define themselves as introverts when someone says to them, "You're awfully quiet today." The emotions they experience

and the perceptions of what the statement means, as well as what it means about the sender of the message, and their intent—all are influenced by their identity as an introvert or extrovert, to say nothing of other aspects of their theory of self.

Research also suggests that we are likely to interpret feedback from others as consistent with our identity (Swann, 1983; Swann & Read, 1981). For example, people who consider themselves attractive may interpret someone's negative comment about their appearance as an expression of envy rather than a true reflection of their attractiveness. An unattractive person may interpret that statement as consistent with their negative self-image. Moreover, we are generally more likely to remember information that is consistent with our identity and to discount information that is inconsistent (Kahneman, Slovic, & Tvesky, 1982). However, some research suggests that this tendency applies only to those aspects of our identity that are central to our definition of self and for which we have strongly held beliefs (Stangor & Ruble, 1989). For less central aspects of self, inconsistent information is more easily assimilated. For example, a 21-year-old who is just beginning to adopt an identity as someone who enjoys drinking on weekends may struggle mightily when a friend tells him that she thinks people who drink are irresponsible. This feedback may influence his identity development and his relationship with her. However, if the negative feedback comes after drinking has become a more stable aspect of the person's identity, it is less likely to affect his identity, though more likely to affect his relationship with her.

Identity, Expectations, and Behavior

The fourth principle specifies that *identity incorporates expectations and guides behavior.* The central characteristics that we see ourselves possessing create social expectations for our behavior (Schenkler, 1985), as well as self-fulfilling prophecies (Merton, 1948). These expectations strongly influence how we act (Bandura, 1986). As such, our identity carries with it expectations of how people with that identity typically behave. To live up to that identity means to behave in a certain manner. For example, if a

SOURCE: Copyright: iStockphoto.com/Karen Struthers

Photo 2.1 The concept of the looking-glass self specifies that our identities are shaped by how others see us. Do you think the image you have of yourself matches what others see?

person's identity includes being a good student, he or she must behave in ways that reflect such a characteristic or the identity will not be maintained. Such individuals are likely to study harder and to attend classes more regularly than those who see themselves as average or poor students. If they perceive themselves to be an excellent athlete, their daily workouts become central to their identity. Note that these behaviors set up a **self-fulfilling prophecy** because people who study and attend class more are likely to get better grades, and people who work out more are likely to be better athletes. A self-fulfilling prophecy occurs when an expectation exists that something will happen, and a person behaves in a way (often unconsciously) that actually makes it more likely that the anticipated event will occur. In any case, the maintenance of our identity requires us to behave in an identity-consistent manner.

Identity and Self-Evaluation

The fifth principle is that *identity influences our evaluations of self.* The expectations and behavioral guidelines connected to identity provide people with comparison points against which to judge their performance (Schenkler, 1985). As a result, our identity influences our evaluation of how well or poorly we performed. For example, good students are likely to get upset if they receive a C on an exam or a paper, whereas those who see themselves as poor students might be delighted to receive a C. Interestingly, self-esteem and identity may be most closely connected through this expectation-evaluation link. Unrealistically flattering self-definitions lead to expectations of self that are unlikely to be met, which leads to a string of perceived failures. As a result, self-esteem can suffer.

Identity and Goal Achievement

The sixth principle is that *identity influences the likelihood of goal achievement.* The achievement of goals is facilitated by the presence of qualities that are consistent with that particular goal. Thus people who see themselves as good students are likely to get better grades because they see studying and attending class as important behaviors that help them maintain their identities. The same type of process influences goal achievement in our relationships. For example, the likelihood that Bill will achieve his goal of dating Jeff depends on the extent to which Bill believes he possesses the characteristics desired by or appealing to Jeff. If an important aspect of Bill's identity is his sensitivity and Jeff prefers a dating partner who is relatively tough, Bill might feel he has little hope of attracting Jeff. Self-fulfilling prophecies are also related to goal achievement. For instance, if Cindy believes that she can make it as a dancer on Broadway, she is likely to have confidence, be more motivated, and perhaps work harder, all of which will make it easier to achieve her goal.

Identity and Relationships

The final principle is that *our identities influence what social relationships we choose to pursue and maintain.* Robinson and Smith-Lovin (1992) found that people prefer interactions with individuals who provide identity-consistent feedback, even if such feedback produces emotional hurt. In other words, those who define themselves in negative terms, such as not intelligent, unconsciously seek partners who confirm that negative identity. Why would this be the case? Apparently people distrust feedback that is not consistent with what they believe, so they perceive those who offer such feedback as dishonest and less likable (Swann, Griffin, Predmore, & Gaines, 1987). The consequences of this tendency can be serious, especially for abused women, who often unconsciously find themselves attracted to individuals with the same characteristics as those who abused them in the past.

Identity-consistent behavior may be particularly important in established relationships. Swann, De La Ronde, and Hixon (1994) examined this issue by investigating whether our preference for "authentic" feedback (feedback consistent with our identity) or "positive" feedback (feedback that is more favorable than our view of self) changes according to the stages of our relationships. They asked partners in dating relationships and marriages about their self-identity, their partner's assessment of their identity, and the level of relationship intimacy. Their results showed that a shift occurs between dating relationships and marriages. Although intimacy was highest in dating relationships when a partner's feedback to the individual was more positive than the individual's view of her or his self, the most intimate marriages were those in which "authenticity" prevailed—that is, in which the partner's view of the individual matched the individual's view of her or his self. It seems that we want others to view us through rose-colored glasses while dating but that successful marriages are those in which the partners view each other in a more authentic way.

In sum, how we view ourselves plays a critical role in what interactions we select, what relationships we pursue, and how these interactions and relationship develop. Thus far, however, we have not addressed how we communicate our identity to others, how we manage to maintain our identity despite threats to its validity, and what social rules are in place to help us navigate the pitfalls of identity management. In the next section, we focus on communication and discuss how identity management influences our behavior across a variety of situations.

COMMUNICATING OUR IDENTITIES TO OTHERS

Antonio: I hold the world but as the world, Gratiano; A stage where every man must play a part, And mine a sad one.

Gratiano: Let me play the fool.

—William Shakespeare, *The Merchant of Venice,* Act I, Scene I

Shakespeare's writing popularized the notion that "all the world's a stage" upon which we are merely actors. Scholars have also widely embraced this concept when describing the process of identity management (see Tracy, 1990). To better understand how people use communication to present themselves in a positive light, research and theory will be discussed related to three general perspectives: (1) self-presentation, (2) Goffman's (1959, 1967, 1971) dramaturgical approach (the approach most closely aligned with Shakespeare's famous reference to people as actors on a stage), and (3) Brown and Levinson's (1987) politeness theory, including preventive and corrective facework. In general, our efforts at **self-presentation** reflect the things we do to portray a particular image of self to others (e.g., I'm a rebel, I'm smart, I'm helpless, I'm creative), while the latter two approaches involve activities that are more generally ingrained as part of everyday interaction (e.g., politeness, image maintenance, image repair). Obviously, these perspectives share more similarities than differences because they all deal with ways in which our behavior manages identity needs.

General Issues in Self-Presentation

On any given day, chances are that you are presenting an image of yourself to others; trying to portray a certain impression of yourself to your boss, your parents, your teacher, or your boyfriend/girlfriend. Doing so requires managing your behavior to hide or minimize potential faults while maximizing strengths. Here is where Cindy's Facebook page is especially relevant. The image she presents to her friends (e.g., partier) is likely to be quite different from the image she wants to display to prospective employers when she interviews for jobs. In fact, Cindy might be worried or even embarrassed to learn that someone who was considering hiring her looked her up on the Web. Some people question whether impression management is hypocritical, manipulative, and deceptive; reflects communication competence; or simply represents the way people unconsciously present themselves to others. We summarize what research has to say about these questions next.

Is self-presentation hypocritical, manipulative, or deceptive? When discussing self-presentation in class, we typically find that a majority of students think, at first, that self-presentation is the height of

hypocrisy, is evidence of insecurity, is tantamount to being phony, or is downright deceptive. Moreover, many students are uncomfortable with the notion that we are chameleon-like in our behavior, changing according to the audience and situation. Are we not trying to deceive the audience into thinking we are something or someone we are not? The answer is no, not typically. Most instances of self-presentation are merely a matter of highlighting certain *aspects* of ourselves for different audiences. We may possess elements of intelligence, sociability, respect, crassness, career orientation, and laziness in our identity, but we segregate these elements when communicating to various audiences. This segregation is not deception because those characteristics are all real aspects of ourselves. For example, Cindy may display her social side to her friends and her serious side to teachers and employers. Her family might see both these sides of Cindy's personality.

Of course, people do fabricate identities. Indeed, the news is full of people leading double lives, faking their résumé or individuals in an Internet chat room posing as someone or something they are not. These instances, and others like them, are examples of deceptive self-presentations. Most of us, however, have neither the ability nor the desire to completely fabricate our identity.

Other, less extreme examples may relate to your life experiences more directly. Have you ever hidden your anger or sorrow from others and "put on a happy face," feigned interest in a boring conversation, or acted as if you liked someone you actually disliked? People manage their emotions for a variety of reasons (Guerrero & Floyd, 2006), but all involve a belief in the importance of self-presentation. We may not want people to know that we are angry or sad because we want to look composed, we may not show boredom because that would be disrespectful, and we may not express our dislike because that would disrupt group dynamics.

Attempts to manage impressions in the hope of advancing a desirable image of ourselves sometimes backfire. A key element of a successful performance is that it is perceived as sincere (Goffman, 1959) and as a true reflection of one's personality. Cases in which individuals are caught lying in their efforts to manage their identity produce the opposite results from those sought. Research has shown that when deception is detected, it produces detrimental personal and relational consequences (Buller & Burgoon, 1994; O'Hair & Cody, 1994; see also Chapter 13). Indeed, honesty is an important impression that we want to foster in others because it goes to the core of our identity. Being perceived as untrustworthy or fake will likely put in doubt the sincerity of all other positive qualities that we have successfully portrayed and that accurately reflect who we are.

Exaggerating the truth or putting too much effort into self-presentation sometimes produces negative outcomes as well. For example, research on narcissism (self-focusing behavior) has shown that boastful individuals are generally rated as less socially attractive and are liked less than those who enact less self-promotion (Vangelisti, Knapp, & Daly, 1990). These findings show that behaviors meant to bolster one's image in the eye of an audience can fail if the person is perceived as selfish or insincere. Schlenker (1980, 1984, 1985) discussed a dilemma that people often face of having to choose between presenting the best possible image of self and presenting a plausible or realistic image. Jones and Wortman (1973) used an example of a first date to show how this dilemma may affect our behavioral choices. When people on a first date describe their positive qualities and accomplishments, they can come across as conceited and unattractive. But if they neglect to mention these qualities and accomplishments, they may be perceived as closed or uninvolved. Thus, the ideal self-presentation strikes a balance between positivity and plausibility.

How is self-presentation related to communication competence? According to researchers who study communication competence, people who are socially skilled have a knack for engaging in behavior that is both polite and situationally appropriate (Spitzberg & Cupach, 1988). People who possess these skills are also generally more successful at developing relationships. This makes sense when you think about the many ways you manage impressions based on the audience and the situation. For example, you would probably not have many friends if you acted as formally with them as you would during a job interview. Similarly, you would probably not be hired if you acted the way you do at a party,

when meeting a prospective employer. Among friends we act relaxed, discuss social activities, get a little crazy, and often trade stories about humorous events. We want to promote ourselves as a good friend, a good person, and someone who can contribute to the group's fun. During the job interview, we want to emphasize very different aspects of ourselves—as a reliable colleague, a smart person, and someone who can contribute to the company's development. If we switch gears this way, does this mean that we are phonies? No. It means we understand that we must fulfill different roles for different audiences, just as they do for us. Being flexible in terms of the roles that we play can help us be more effective communicators, as long as we are not manipulating others for nefarious purposes.

Studies confirm that people change their behavior based on the audience and/or the situation. As mentioned previously, to be socially competent, people must strike a balance between showing their most positive characteristics and still appearing modest. Interestingly, this balance is affected by whether we are interacting with friends or strangers. Research suggests that we are more likely to present an overly favorable impression of ourselves to strangers than to friends. We assume that strangers do not know much about us, so the importance of disclosing favorable information about ourselves is relatively high. In contrast, our friends probably already know of our accomplishments, so pointing them out again would likely be perceived as conceited, thus backfiring. Moreover, our friends probably know us well enough to recognize realistic from unrealistic stories, while strangers may be unable to make such a distinction. Tice, Butler, Muraven, and Stillwell (1995) conducted five studies that compared the differences in people's self-presentations to friends and to strangers. They concluded that "people habitually use different self-presentation strategies with different audiences, relying on favorable self-enhancement with strangers but shifting toward modesty when among friends" (p. 1120).

Several studies also show that we vary the impression that we project of ourselves based on the audience or situation. For example, Daly, Hoggs, Sacks, Smith, and Zimring (1983) observed restroom behavior of men and women in restaurants and bars. They recorded the amount of time that people spent preening (adjusting their clothes, straightening their hair, looking at themselves in the mirror) and then asked them about their relationship with the person with whom they attended the establishment. Not surprisingly, they found that those who spent the most time managing their appearance were in the newest relationships. In fact, research on affinity-seeking behavior (behavior done to attract others) discovered a variety of impression management activities that we do early in relationships to increase our partner's attraction to us (Daly & Kreiser, 1994). These include attending carefully to how we look, appearing interested in what the person has to say, emphasizing similarities, and portraying an image as a "fun" person. In sum, the way people present themselves to others is flexible and dynamic, with people managing their behavior differently depending on the situation and the audience so as to maximize positive impressions and social competence.

To what extent is self-presentation a deliberate, conscious activity? Self-presentation is so commonplace that it often becomes routine, habitual behavior that is encoded unconsciously. DePaulo (1992) offered several examples of habitual impression management behavior, including the postural etiquette that girls learn as they are growing up and the ritualistic smiles given by the first runner-up at beauty pageants. Other examples include the ritualistic exchange of "thank you" and "you're welcome," table manners, classroom etiquette, and the myriad taken-for-granted politeness strategies (which we will address in more detail later in this chapter). These behaviors were probably enacted deliberately and consciously at some time but have since become automatic aspects of interaction.

However, at times even behaviors that are typically habitual become more deliberate. Specifically, when we especially want to make a good impression or when we expect difficulty in achieving our desired impression, our self-presentational activity will likely be more deliberate and controlled (Leary & Kowalski, 1990; Schlenker, 1985). For example, when you first meet the parents of your girlfriend or boyfriend, you will probably be more aware than usual of your posture, politeness rituals, and other normally habitual impression management behaviors. Your deliberateness in enacting these behaviors may be further

heightened if your partner's parents do not approve of the relationship and/or you expect resistance from them. In sum, in certain circumstances we are very deliberate and conscious in our use of impression management tactics—for example, on first dates, at the dean's office, or in an interview—but most of our self-presentational strategies are relatively habitual and performed unconsciously.

Even people who claim not to care about what others think of them tend to manage their identities in ways that make them more socially competent, providing further evidence that self-presentation is often an unconscious, habitual process. Schlenker and Weigold (1990) compared "autonomous" individuals, who claim to be individualistic and not to care about audience opinions, with individuals who claim to place significant weight on others' attitudes. If self-presentational concerns are irrelevant to autonomous individuals, then we would expect their attitudes to be unaffected by audiences. Instead, Schlenker and Weigold found that autonomous individuals changed their attitudes "if expressing their actual beliefs would have jeopardized their appearance of independence" while more socially driven individuals did so "in order to conform to the expectations of their partner" (p. 826). In other words, both autonomous and more socially driven people are motivated to maintain a certain image of themselves; it is just the kind of image that differs. Thus, even those who claim not to care about societal attitudes seem to be motivated by self-presentational concerns. Indeed, research shows that those who are not sensitive to audience characteristics and self-presentation needs are less successful relationally and professionally than those who are (Schlenker, 1980). This suggests that there is considerable social incentive for people to adapt their behavior based on the audience.

The Dramaturgical Perspective

In his classic book *The Presentation of Self in Everyday Life,* Goffman (1959) advanced a revolutionary way of thinking about identity management— the **dramaturgical perspective**. Borrowing from Shakespeare, Goffman used the metaphor of theater to describe our everyday interactions. Specifically, he argued that we constantly enact performances that are geared for particular audiences, with the purpose of advancing an image that is beneficial to us. In other words, we are always concerned about appearances and work to ensure that others view us the way we would like them to.

Goffman, like others, argued that we are highly motivated to present a positive image of ourselves to others. Indeed, the evidence for such a claim is strong. For example, several studies have shown that some sexually active individuals refrain from using condoms because they are afraid that such an action may imply that they (or their partners) are "uncommitted" or "diseased" (Lear, 1997). Holtgraves (1988) argued that gambling enthusiasts pursue their wagering habits partly because they wish to portray themselves as spontaneous, adventurous, and unconcerned about losing money. Snow and Anderson's (1987) yearlong observational study revealed how homeless people present themselves to their communities in ways that help restore their dignity. For instance, a 24-year-old male who had been homeless for 2 weeks told them,

> I'm not like the other guys who hang out at the "Sally" [Salvation Army]. If you want to know about street people, I can tell you about them; but you can't really learn about street people from studying me, because I'm different. (p. 1349)

This man clearly made an effort to distance himself verbally from what he considered to be an undesirable identity: being homeless. In fact, distancing was the most common form of self-presentation that these authors found among the homeless.

Since Goffman's early work, scholars have outlined certain conditions under which impression management becomes especially important to us (Schlenker, Britt, & Pennington, 1996). Although researchers still consider impression management to be something that is always salient to us, the following three conditions seem to make it especially important.

Condition 1: The behavior reflects highly valued and central aspects of the self. We are especially concerned about the success of our impression management when we try to portray an image that is at the core of our identity than when our efforts involve less central aspects of ourselves. For example, if Cindy sees herself as particularly outgoing but only moderately career oriented, she is likely to portray herself as more social than professional. Situations such as planning a party or college reunion are therefore likely to call forth a particularly strong need for Cindy to present a social rather than a professional image.

Condition 2: Successful performance is tied to vital positive or negative consequences. If the success of a cherished relationship depends on your ability to convince your partner of your commitment, the importance of your impression management efforts is heightened. You might start sending your partner flowers, giving her or him gifts, and saying "I love you" more often as ways of showing you are a devoted, committed partner. In a similar vein, if you are told that your raise at work is contingent on being a team player, you may devote considerable attention to that aspect of your identity. Consistent with this notion, studies have shown that we are especially motivated to be perceived in a positive light when interacting with attractive or highly valued others (see Jellison & Oliver, 1983; Schlenker, 1984). In one study, participants were less likely to ask for help on a task from attractive opposite-sex strangers than from unattractive opposite-sex strangers, presumably because of their desire to come across as competent to attractive others (Alain, 1985).

Condition 3: The behavior reflects directly on highly valued rules of conduct. We all consider certain rules of conduct to be especially important. For example, some people strongly believe that engaging in conflict in a public setting is inappropriate (Jones & Gallois, 1989). These people will be especially careful not to engage in public conflict because violating that norm would be especially threatening to the public identity they wish to portray. Similarly, some people believe that public displays of affection are inappropriate. If a friend shows too much public affection to such people, they might become embarrassed and unaffectionate to try to maintain a comfort level. When important relational rules such as these are violated frequently, it not only is very face threatening but often leads to relationship deterioration (Argyle & Henderson, 1984; Metts, 1994).

It is worth noting that these three factors are quite prominent in close relationships, especially in the early stages, when partners are busy trying to make positive first impressions (Swann et al., 1994). In early relational stages, people typically display central aspects of themselves to their partners (Condition 1); success in these displays can make the difference between attracting or repelling a potential friend or romantic partner (Condition 2); and ground rules are often set as to what rules of conduct will be most highly valued (Condition 3). For these reasons (and others discussed throughout the chapter), studying identity and identity management is critical to understanding the success and failure of relationships.

To the extent that the three conditions outlined here are salient, people will engage in impression management. Consistent with his dramaturgical perspective, Goffman (1959) referred to social behavior designed to manage impressions and influence others as a performance. An actor gives a performance in front of a set of observers, or an audience, and in a particular location, which Goffman referred to as the stage.

Front Versus Back Stage. As in any theatrical venue, there are two stage locations: front and back. The front stage is where our performances are enacted, our behaviors are observed by an audience, and where impression management is particularly important. Conversely, the back stage is where we can let our guard down and do not have to think about staying in character. According to Goffman (1959), the back stage is "where the performer can reliably expect that no member of the audience will intrude" (p. 113). In the backstage and surrounding area, which Goffman referred to as **wings**, we can often find materials and individuals who assist us in giving a successful performance. For example, cologne/perfume, a hairbrush, and a mirror are backstage materials that we use to improve our appearance, thereby increasing the potential success of our self-presentational performance on a first date. We might also ask friends to assist us in improving our appearance or to give us information about the person whom we are about to date. In fact, one of the primary ways that we gain information about someone is by consulting other people (see Baxter & Wilmot, 1984; Berger, 1987). This information is used to improve our impression-management strategies. Answers to questions such as "Is he dating anyone right now?" and "Does she like sports?" can help reduce uncertainty and give people an idea of how to manage their impressions (see Chapter 4). For example, if you learn that someone you want to date is interested in sports, you might portray yourself as a sports enthusiast and invite that person to a college sporting event. If you learn that the person dislikes sports, you will probably take a different approach.

Tedeschi (1986) made a distinction similar to front and back stages by comparing public versus private behavior, with public behavior being subject to observation and private behavior being free from such scrutiny. Indeed, several studies have shown that we often behave differently in public than in private (see Baumeister, 1986). Can you think of something that you typically do only in the back stage? Singing is a common example of a backstage behavior. Many people are too embarrassed to sing in front of others (in the front stage), but when pressed, they admit to singing in the shower or in their cars (which are both backstage regions). In a similar vein, hygienic activity, despite its universality, is reserved for backstage regions. Relationships also determine if we are in the front or back stage. For example, unless you have a good singing voice, you would probably not sing in front of strangers, but you might sing with your best friend or a romantic partner. When people are with their closest friends and intimate partners, behaviors that typically are reserved for the back stage are often moved to the front stage. You might not swear in public but may do so with your closest friends. Our close friends and family members are backstage, so they get a more authentic and unrehearsed version of us. Again, we are reminded of Cindy's Facebook. The pictures that are posted (some by her, and others of her but posted without her consent) are often things that were done in backstage settings (with friends, at home, and so forth), but are presented on the front stage and viewed by whoever visits the page. This mixing of back and front stages on these Web pages is dangerous for identity management but hasn't been adequately studied.

Role, Audience, and Context. Whether behaviors occur in the front or back stage depends on the role enacted, the audience being targeted, and the context in which the activities are performed. For example, you might feel free to sing in front of strangers at a karaoke bar in another city but not in a bar that you hang out in regularly. Similarly, some teenagers manage their use of swearing with parents or other adults to advance an identity of being proper and respectful. With their friends, in contrast, they might want to convey a care-free, rebellious, and "cool" identity that is bolstered by swearing. The only viable criterion on which performance success is judged is whether it successfully advances the image that the performer desires to advance for a particular audience (Baumeister, 1982; Leary, 1995; Schlenker, 1980). When a performance threatens the image that one wants to convey to a certain audience, it is reserved for the back stage. Thus, in the swearing example, the teenagers would consider swearing a backstage activity when they are interacting with their parents but a front-stage activity when they are interacting with peers. Thinking back to Cindy's Facebook page, we again see a problem concerning identity management. The page is a clear identity message, but she has little control over what kind of audiences access it or what gets posted. As a result, there is the potential for certain of her identity audiences to be taken aback by the identity they see.

This discussion of stage-appropriate behavior also highlights the relative difficulty of defining what constitutes a "back" stage. "Public" and "private" may capture part of what is meant by such a distinction, in that "front" stage is that area to which the particular audience in question has access, and the "back" stage is that area to which the audience presumably has little access. Thus, parents may be unaware that their teenage son or daughter swears with their peers because they have little or no access to that part of their child's communication network and performance.

Finally, it is important to mention the audience's role in the impression management process. When self-presentation is successful, the audience and "actor" interact to help each other validate and maintain their identities. After all, we can work hard to establish a certain identity, but it depends on the audience to accept or reject our self-presentation. In fact,

Goffman (1967) argued that the validation of another person's identity is a "condition of interaction" (p. 12). In other words, we expect other people to accept the identities we show them and to help us save face when we accidentally display an undesired image. We have all been in situations where we inadvertently said or did something embarrassing, and the last thing we wanted was for someone to emphasize the error or laugh at our mistake. In fact, Goffman (1967) called people who can watch another's "face" being damaged without feeling sorrow, hurt, or vicarious embarrassment "heartless" human beings. Moreover, research shows that people who fail to help others save face are often disliked and shunned (see Cupach & Metts, 1994; Schlenker, 1980). Most people know how it feels to be made fun of after an embarrassing event, so instead of laughing at them, they try to relieve the distress that the embarrassed person is feeling. This leads to the next theory of impression management that we discuss in this chapter—politeness theory.

Politeness Theory

As an extension of Goffman's work, Brown and Levinson (1987) developed **politeness theory**, which focuses on the specific ways in which people manage face using communication. A large portion of their theorizing revolved around a distinction they made between positive and negative faces.

Positive Versus Negative Face. **Positive face** is the favorable image that people portray to others and hope to have validated by others. It essentially reflects our desire to be liked by others. In contrast, **negative face** reflects our desire to "be free from imposition and restraint and to have control over [our] own territory, possessions, time, space, and resources" (Metts & Grohskopf, 2003, p. 361). Put another way, our positive face is the "best face" we put forward so that others like us, while our negative face is the part of us that wants to do what we want to do or say, without concern about what others would like us to do or say.

Politeness theory revolves around four general assumptions (see Brown & Levinson, 1987; Metts & Grohskopf, 2003). First, the theory is built on the assumption that threats to positive and negative faces are an inherent part of social interaction. People have to deal with a constant struggle between wanting to do what they want (which satisfies their negative face needs) and wanting to do what makes them look good to others (which satisfies their positive face needs). On some occasions, the same action can satisfy both aspects of face. For example, suppose your best friend asks you to help prepare food for a party he or she is giving. You might agree to help your friend, which supports your positive face needs because it makes you look good. But if you happen to love cooking, your negative face needs also would be satisfied because you are doing exactly what you wanted to do. However, it is much more likely that a behavior will fall somewhere between the two face needs or that supporting one face need may threaten the other. For example, you may agree to help a friend move despite your desire to relax at home. In this case, if you attend to your negative face needs by staying at home, you would come across as a poor friend and threaten your positive face needs. These examples reflect substantial decisions. Central to politeness theory is that positive and negative face needs are managed in every single interaction. If you need to go, at what point do you end a conversation, and how do you do it? In what tone of voice do you talk to your parents despite your desire to express displeasure? How do you respond to someone's question about what "you're doing this weekend?" in a way that is friendly but doesn't commit yourself to do something you don't want to do? These examples illustrate that every interaction involves communication decisions that have implications for both positive and negative face.

Second, and related to the first premise, is the assumption that people's positive and negative faces can be either validated or threatened during interaction. Identity is validated when a person's behavior and the audience's response to that behavior support the image the individual is trying to advance. For example, you may validate your identity as a caring partner by taking your significant other for an unexpected dinner date after he or she had a long week at work. In return, your partner may validate your identity as a caring partner by telling you or others how appreciative he or she is when you do nice things such as arranging special dinners out. In this example, both you and your partner have done things to validate *your* positive face.

A study by Albas and Albas (1988) examined how students validated their positive faces following receipt of a good exam grade. The researchers identified several strategies that "acers" (as they labeled them) used to reveal their grade to others as a way to bolster their positive faces without directly bragging. These strategies included "repressed bubbling" (nonverbal signals of elation), "accidental revelation" (leaving the test facing upward, with the grade in full display), and "question-answer chain" (asking other students how they did, which sets the stage for them reciprocating with a similar question). In these ways, students who performed well on the test could "publish" that fact to others, thereby supporting their identity as an intelligent person and good student. However, as mentioned previously, if the person appears to be bragging or fishing for a compliment, these strategies could backfire. That is, in addition to validating one's identity as an intelligent person, such strategies could threaten one's identity as a nice and modest person.

When a person's behavior is at variance with the identity he or she wants to convey, a face-threatening situation occurs. **Face-threatening acts** (FTAs) are behaviors that detract from an individual's identity by threatening either their positive or negative face desires (Brown & Levinson, 1987). For example, forgetting a dinner date with your significant other is a self-inflicted threat to your positive face—your identity as a caring partner. Your partner may further contribute to this face threat by publicly chiding you for getting stood up at the restaurant. Of course, not all behaviors are equally face threatening. Certain behaviors cause people to lose more face and lead to more negative personal and relational consequences than others.

The third assumption on which politeness theory is based is that both members of an interaction are typically motivated to avoid threatening either their own or the interaction partner's face needs. Given our desire to avoid face threats, we generally try to avoid making others look bad (i.e., threatening our positive face) and respect others who refrain from making us look bad. So interactions are typically dances where both partners understand the social expectations that help them maintain each other's face needs. Cindy might understand that it is important to respect Lindsay's time and space and not point out her flaws, and she might also expect Lindsay to do the same for her. Of course, you may know some people who enjoy negatively violating social expectations and embarrassing others. So how would politeness theory researchers respond to that? They would offer two explanations: The first is that those people are also often shunned, socially reprimanded, or disliked by a lot of people for their actions (e.g., seen as bullies, jerks, and so forth) even though some violations enhance the status of the person engaging in face-threatening behavior. Second, all threats to face are not equally bad; some are seen as much less severe than others. In fact, that issue forms the basis for the fourth assumption underlying politeness theory: that the severity of FTAs depends on several factors.

Research suggests that at least six factors affect the degree to which an FTA is perceived to be severe. The first three factors, identified by Schlenker and his colleagues (Schlenker, Britt, Pennington, Murphy, & Doherty, 1994; Schlenker & Weigold, 1992), focus on behaviors that threaten a person's own face. The remaining three factors, from Brown and Levinson's (1987) politeness theory, focus on behaviors that threaten either an individual's or his or her partner's face.

1. *The more important the rule that is violated, the more severe the FTA.* For example, forgetting your relational partner's birthday will be more of a rule violation than forgetting to call your partner to say you will be late coming home from work.

2. *The more harm the behavior produces, the more severe the FTA.* If you trip and lose your balance, you may feel some loss of face, but if you trip, fall to the ground, and scatter your paperwork, the loss of face will be much greater. Similarly, if you get caught telling a lie about something that has serious implications for your relationship, the loss of face will be greater than if you get caught telling a "little white lie."

3. *The more the actor is directly responsible for the behavior, the more severe the FTA.* If a store clerk refuses to accept your credit card because the

expiration date is past, it is much less face threatening than if the clerk phones in your card number and is asked to confiscate your card and cut it up because you are late on your payments.

4. *The more of an imposition the behavior is, the more severe the FTA.* For example, you would probably be more concerned about your negative face if someone asked you to help move furniture to a new house (which is quite an imposition on your time and energy) than if someone asked you to write down his or her new phone number (which is hardly an imposition).

5. *The more power the receiver has over the sender, the more severe the FTA.* If you make a silly comment that your boss could misconstrue as an insult, you will probably be more worried than if you make the same silly comment in front of a friend. With your boss you are more likely to worry about appearing incompetent.

6. *The larger the social distance between sender and receiver, the more severe the FTA.* For example, you will probably worry less about threatening the face of your best friend than that of an acquaintance, presumably because the foundation of the friendship is more solid and less susceptible to harm from face threats.

Although research has generally supported the validity of these factors, some research has shown that the sixth factor, which relates to the social distance between receiver and sender, may not always hold true. Work by Holtgraves and Yang (1990, 1992) suggests that in many cases, instead of being *less* concerned about threatening the identity of those close to us, we are actually *more* concerned about doing so. The context and purpose of the self-presentation strategy may make a difference here. Sometimes, we are particularly concerned about making a good impression and getting along well with a new acquaintance; other times, we are more concerned with protecting our close relationships from harm. The main point here is that identity management concerns become more salient as the consequences of impression management failure increase.

Facework Strategies. Given the importance of facework in people's everyday lives, it should come as no surprise that people use a variety of intricate strategies to manage face needs during interaction. In fact, most, if not all, interactions inherently include examples of facework that help people maintain or repair, or that strategically threaten, their own faces or those of others. Even simple requests ("Since we live so far apart, would you mind meeting at a restaurant that is somewhere halfway between us?") are phrased in a way that respects the positive and negative face needs of the other person. This fact becomes clear if you think of other ways in which these requests may be phrased ("I don't want to drive that far. You have to meet me halfway").

Given the many ways that concerns for facework influence our interactions, Brown and Levinson (1987) offered five options that individuals have when considering an FTA. The strategies differ in the degree of balance achieved between the goals of accomplishing a face-threatening task and managing face concerns (see Figure 2.2).

The **"bald on-record" strategy** is characterized by primary attention to task and little or no attention to helping the partner save face. It is the most efficient strategy but also the most face threatening. Brown and Levinson (1987) offered the examples of a mother telling her child to "Come home right now!" or someone in need of assistance telling a bystander to "Lend me a hand here!" Bald on-record strategies are typically used when maximum task efficiency is important or where there are large differences in power or status between actors.

The **"positive politeness" strategy** is intended to address the receiver's positive face while still accomplishing the task. It includes explicit recognition of the receiver's value and her or his contributions to the process, and couches the FTA (often a request) as something that does not threaten the identity of the receiver. For example, complimenting someone on her or his attire, haircut, or performance is an example of positive politeness that might precede a request. Similarly, if you want a friend to help you write a resume and cover letter, you might say, "You are such a good writer. Would you help me edit this?"

The **"negative politeness" strategy** is intended to address the receiver's negative face while still accomplishing the task. The key is that receivers do not feel coerced into doing something but instead feel that they are performing the act of their own volition. Often, negative politeness also involves deference on the part of the sender to ensure that he or she does not come across as coercive. For example, you might say to a friend, "I suppose there wouldn't be any chance of your being able to lend me your car for a few minutes, would there?" Brown and Levinson (1987) noted that requests phrased this way clearly emphasize the freedom of the receiver to decline.

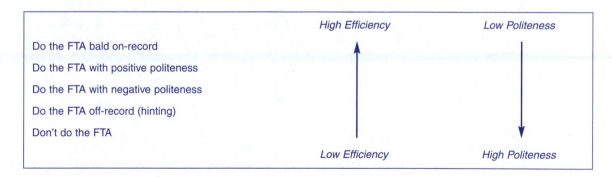

Figure 2.2   Options for Dealing With Face-Threatening Acts

SOURCE: We thank Sandra Metts for providing this graphic and granting us permission to use it in this book.

The **"going off record" strategy** is characterized by primary attention to face and little attention to task. As such, it is a relatively inefficient strategy for accomplishing tasks. However, given the importance of face, it may serve the participants well and so is often used. Examples include hinting, using an indirect nonverbal expression, or masking the request as a joke. For instance, if you want your partner to take you on a vacation, you might make comments such as "I've always wanted to go on a Caribbean cruise" or "It would be great to get away and go somewhere tropical."

Finally, people can make *the decision not to engage in the FTA*. Brown and Levinson (1987) noted that individuals often choose to forgo the face-threatening task completely in favor of preserving face. For example, even if you are upset because your roommate's partner always spends the night at your apartments, you might decide to say nothing for fear of embarrassing or angering your roommate (particularly if you do not want him or her to move out). According to Brown and Levinson (1987), people perform a cost-benefit analysis when deciding what type of strategy to use. Bald on-record strategies are the most efficient but also the most damaging to face, and as such may be most damaging to the relationship. However, by going off record people run a much greater risk that the receiver will not recognize the request or will simply ignore it.

Metts (1992) applied this logic to the predicament of breaking up with a romantic partner. The act of breaking up with someone is face threatening in many ways. For example, suppose Cindy tells her current boyfriend, Alex, that she wants to end their relationship but Alex does not want to break up. This act threatens Alex's negative face because he is being forced to do something he does not want to do. Alex's positive face also is threatened because Cindy's request suggests that he is no longer a desirable relational partner. Cindy's positive face may also be threatened if she worries that Alex (and perhaps other people) will see her as selfish, egotistical, or uncaring. Her negative face could also be threatened; she may change her relationship status on her Facebook, but feels it would be premature to do so without talking things over with Alex. According to Metts (1992), Cindy is likely to use different strategies depending on how face threatening she thinks the breakup will be for both herself and Alex. If she thinks the breakup will be highly distressing, she is likely to use an on-record-with-politeness strategy. Conversely, if Cindy thinks the breakup will cause little distress, she is likely to use an off-the-record strategy (such as avoiding the person) or a bald on-record strategy (such as blunt statements about wanting to break up).

Preventive and Corrective Facework. Certainly, people are sometimes task driven, and perform FTAs, with little attention to the consequences of threatening their own or another person's face. But people are more likely to avoid face threats and/or attempt to repair a damaged face. Research on preventive and corrective facework highlights other ways in which concerns for face affect our interactions (Cupach & Metts, 1994).

Preventive facework is characterized by efforts to avoid or minimize a potential face threat. Preventive strategies are like preemptive strikes that seek to prevent future damage by framing the message in friendlier, softer terms. Studies have identified different types of preventive facework in daily interaction. The most common form of preventive facework is **disclaimers**. Hewitt and Stokes (1975) outlined five general disclaimers that individuals use before saying or doing something that may be face threatening: (1) hedging ("I may be way off here, but . . ."), (2) credentialing ("I'm your father, so I'm going to be straight with you"), (3) sin license ("Well, since we're all disclosing embarrassing situations . . ."), (4) cognitive disclaimer ("I know you're going to think I've lost it, but . . ."), and (5) appeal for suspended judgment ("Hear me out before jumping to conclusions").

Other researchers have included the notion of **verbal self-handicapping** as a method of preventive facework (Higgins & Berglas, 1990). That is, people will sometimes offer an excuse that serves to minimize the face threat of a potential poor performance. For example, prior to an important dance competition, Cindy may inform her team captain of a knee injury she has suffered. This strategic precompetition disclosure serves two functions. If Cindy dances her routines well, she bolsters her identity as a "tough" professional who can perform with pain. But if she performs poorly, she has already a built-in excuse for her subpar performance. Unfortunately, research shows that these self-handicapping tactics often become self-fulfilling prophecies because they offer the individual a reason *not* to do as well as possible. In sum, the various disclaimers all serve to soften the potential face threat that might result from impending action and essentially ask the audience to consider that act within the perspective of the context.

Corrective facework is characterized by efforts to *repair* an identity already damaged by something that was said or done. Like preventive facework, corrective facework may be performed by the person whose face was threatened or by others who are assisting in the protection and/or repair of the person's face. Embarrassing moments are good examples of situations that often lead to corrective facework because they undermine a person's positive self-image. As Cupach and Metts (1994) argued, people become embarrassed when they are perceived to have acted incompetently—that is, when behavior is judged to be "inappropriate, ineffective, or foolish" (p. 18).

In a comprehensive review of embarrassment research, Miller (1996) outlined 10 types of embarrassing behaviors that typically threaten one's face. The two most common causes of embarrassment were "physical pratfalls or inept performance" and "cognitive errors." The former category includes instances in which people appear unnecessarily awkward or incompetent—for example, missing a pole on which you intended to lean, tipping a chair over after leaning back too far, and catching your hair on fire as you light the grill. The latter category includes mistakes in judgment (trying every key before realizing you are at the wrong door), forgetfulness (forgetting your phone number or people's names), lack of attention or "temporary stupidity" (saying something that gives away a secret you are trying to keep for others), or clumsy answers. One of the best sources for examples of clumsy answers is Petras and Petras's (1993) book *The 775 Stupidest Things Ever Said*. One example of clumsy answers in this book is a response that the then vice president of the United States George Herbert Walker Bush gave at a campaign rally: "For 7½ years I've worked alongside President Reagan. We've had triumphs. Made some mistakes. We've had sex . . . uh . . . setbacks" (p. 71).

People typically use corrective facework in response to embarrassing situations such as these, as well as to other situations involving FTAs. You can take the test in Box 2.1 to determine which types of corrective facework you are most likely to use in a particular situation. There are six general corrective strategies for repairing a damaged face (Cupach & Metts, 1994; Schlenker & Weigold, 1992):

1. *Avoidance:* The common thread underlying avoidance behaviors is the goal of distancing oneself or one's partner from the act. Often, distancing occurs when individuals pretend that the act never happened or otherwise ignore its occurrence. For example, continuing to walk down the aisle after knocking over a display in a grocery store and glossing over an obvious Freudian slip are instances of avoidance. The hope is that the audience may pay less attention to the act if the actor avoids reference to it.

2. *Humor:* When the consequences of the FTA are relatively small, people often resort to humor as a way to deal with the threat. By using humor after an FTA, people show poise and come across as competent communicators, thereby repairing their damaged faces. Sometimes, it is best to laugh at yourself so that others will laugh with you, not at you.

3. *Apologies:* Apologies are "admissions of responsibility and regret for undesirable events" (Schlenker & Weigold, 1992, p. 162). In that sense, they may help repair some of the damage to face by emphasizing the actor's nature as a moral individual who intends to take responsibility for her or his action. Unlike avoidance, where actors deny responsibility, apologies tie the incident directly to the actor and, as such, may further threaten face—especially if the apology is deemed insincere.

4. *Accounts:* Accounts, or attempts to explain the FTA, come in the form of excuses or justifications. Excuses are explanations that minimize the personal responsibility of the actor for her or his actions. For example, if you engage in a silly fraternity or sorority prank that causes you to lose face, you might excuse your behavior by saying that your friends pressured you into action or that

▨ BOX 2.1   Put Yourself to the Test

Attempts to Repair Face

Imagine yourself in the following situation. You are assigned to work in a group of four students to complete a class project. Midway through the semester, one of the other group members puts you on the spot by saying, "You haven't been doing your share, so I'm afraid that if we give you something important to do you won't get it done on time or you won't do it well." How would you likely respond to this face-threatening comment?

	Very Unlikely					Very Likely	
1. I would ignore it.	1	2	3	4	5	6	7
2. I would apologize.	1	2	3	4	5	6	7
3. I would explain why I hadn't be able to do my fair share.	1	2	3	4	5	6	7
4. I would say something sarcastic or rude to the person who made the comment.	1	2	3	4	5	6	7
5. I would promise to do more than my fair share in the future.	1	2	3	4	5	6	7
6. I would laugh it off and say that I've always been a procrastinator.	1	2	3	4	5	6	7
7. I would change the subject.	1	2	3	4	5	6	7
8. I would admit that I had not done my fair share.	1	2	3	4	5	6	7
9. I would tell everyone why I wasn't able put in my best effort.	1	2	3	4	5	6	7
10. I would say something to put down the person who made the comment.	1	2	3	4	5	6	7
11. I would take on a task no one else wanted to do to make up for my past actions.	1	2	3	4	5	6	7
12. I would poke fun at myself and my bad studying habits.	1	2	3	4	5	6	7

To obtain your results, add your scores for the following items:

Avoidance: Items 1 + 7   _____

Apology: Items 2 + 8   _____

Account: Items 3 + 9   _____

Aggression: Items 4 + 10   _____

Remediation: Items 5 + 11   _____

Humor: Items 6 + 12   _____

Higher scores indicate a stronger likelihood of using a particular type of corrective facework in this type of situation. How might your use of corrective facework differ on the basis of the situation or the relationship you share with the people around you?

you had consumed too much alcohol. With justifications, actors do not try to distance themselves from the act, but instead "reframe an event by downplaying its negative implications" (Cupach & Metts, 1994, p. 10). Arguing that your behavior at the fraternity or sorority party was "not that big of a deal" or that the prank did not really hurt anyone are examples of justifications for FTAs.

5. *Physical remediation:* This strategy involves attempts to repair physical damage. For example, you might quickly clean up a coffee spill on the table, or you might zip up your pants once you recognize that your fly is open. Relational partners, especially if sympathetic, often engage in physical remediation as well. For example, if you see a food smudge on your partner's chin, you might wipe it off before other people see it.

6. *Aggression:* In some cases, individuals feel the need to repair their damaged face by using physical force. For example, people sometimes start a physical altercation in response to a put-down or personal attack. In fact, research shows that dating violence often follows a perception of face threats (for a review of violence research, see Gelles & Cornell, 1990). People may also become aggressive when they are embarrassed or violate a norm. For example, if you feel clumsy when you trip over clutter in your house, you might angrily say to others in the room, "No one ever picks up around here but me!"

Of course, several of these strategies may be combined in efforts to repair a damaged face. For example, after spilling coffee on the boss's desk, you might say you are sorry (apology), explain that you were distracted by the boss's stimulating presentation (account), and then clean up the mess (physical remediation). Indeed, the more face threatening the act, the more energy will be expended in multiple repair attempts.

In other situations, people are more likely to ignore face threats or to respond with humor. This is especially likely when FTAs are expected. For instance, embarrassing and face-threatening actions are more expected and accepted at wedding and baby showers. Common activities at baby showers include having people guess how big the mom-to-be's stomach is or how much she weighs, and at wedding showers the bride-to-be often receives revealing lingerie. Braithwaite (1995) observed behavior at coed wedding and baby showers to investigate the tactics people used to embarrass others and the tactics people used to respond to face threats. She found that wedding and baby showers are contexts where some embarrassment is expected, so potentially embarrassing actions are not as face threatening as they would be in other contexts. Yet the dance between embarrassment-producing face threats and face-repairing responses was still evident. Other situations, such as "roasting" someone at a retirement party, may require this same delicate dance.

SUMMARY AND APPLICATION

Our desire to present particular images of ourselves shapes our social interactions and influences our relationships. In this chapter, we outlined the factors that influence identity and the ways in which we communicate this identity to others during initial encounters and in established relationships. A person's identity is based on a complex theory of self that incorporates expectations, self-fulfilling prophecies, and feedback from others. People project a certain identity to the world, and that identity is either accepted or rejected by the audience, causing the identity to be either reinforced or modified. In this chapter, we also emphasized the ways in which other people help us maintain our public identities.

It is important to note, however, that this chapter covered only a small portion of the literature on identity and impression management. Research looking at psychological processes such as self-esteem and self-concept is also relevant to identity and impression management. In this chapter, our focus was on identity management in social and personal relationships. Other researchers have studied self-presentation within different contexts, such as first impressions during employment interviews or self-presentation strategies used by teachers in classrooms. The information posted on Cindy's Facebook functions for both established and new relationships—the page serves to maintain relationships with friends who can click and see all Cindy's pictures in which they are featured, and the page also serves as an introduction for new friends, acquaintances, and classmates who don't yet know Cindy very well.

Interpersonal communication researchers have also studied identity and impression formation within the attraction process. People are attracted to those who convey a positive self-identity while appearing to be modest and approachable. Physical appearance, which plays a key role in impression management, is also one of several bases for attraction in close relationships (see Chapter 3). Cindy's Facebook reflects some of the characteristics that people find attractive, including sociability and popularity. The pictures she and others have posted also show viewers what she and her friends look like, as well as giving them an idea of what kinds of activities they enjoy. The people viewing Cindy's Facebook are likely to perceive her differently depending on how they evaluate the identity she has portrayed. Some people might have a positive impression of Cindy as a popular, outgoing person who is a talented dancer, speaks Italian, and has visited exotic places such as Rome. Other people, however, may perceive Cindy to be a superficial, nonserious person who is more concerned about having a large social network than developing high-quality close relationships. Viewers' perceptions would be influenced by their own identities and the characteristics that they value in themselves and others. If Cindy learns that some people she cares about have a negative impression of her when they view her Facebook, she might change some of her postings.

Finally, identity can be expanded and protected within close relationships. Self-expansion theory suggests that relationships provide a venue for one's broadening identity and growing as a person. Facework is also important to project one's own desired image and to protect the positive and negative faces of a relational partner. Indeed, an awareness of the importance of face can go a long way toward helping people understand the development and deterioration of relationships.

DISCUSSION QUESTIONS

1. What personal characteristics are most central to your theory of self?

2. In this chapter, we discussed some ethical issues related to identity management. Under what circumstances do you think that the techniques used to manage one's positive identity are unethical or deceptive?

3. Think about one of your most embarrassing moments. Did you do any facework? If so, what identity management techniques did you employ? Did people around you help you save face? If so, how?

3

DRAWING PEOPLE TOGETHER

Forces of Social Attraction

Julie is frustrated with her dating life. Even though she considers herself to be smart and pretty, she always seems to be the single one among her friends and she is tired of feeling like the third wheel all the time. It seems so easy for her friends to find long-term boyfriends, while she seems to struggle. When she does find a boyfriend, the relationship never lasts very long. At first, Julie thought her last boyfriend, Steven, was perfect for her. Steven was extremely good looking, and his personality was exactly the oppo-site of her shy self. He loved to socialize and was flirtatious and fun. Eventually, however, Julie got tired of trying to keep up with his fast-paced social life, and she became jealous of the women he hung out with even though Steven swore they were only friends. When they broke up, Julie wondered why she had been so attracted to him in the first place. She also wondered if she was attracted to the wrong type of men. After all, her friends often had good relationships with men whom she didn't find particularly attractive.

Attraction is a force that draws people together. It can occur as quickly as a flash of lightning or develop slowly over time. Sometimes, attraction is accompanied by a surge of arousal, with your heart pounding and palms sweating. Other times, attraction is accompanied by a warm, cozy, comfortable feeling. Of course, attraction is not always mutual; people are often attracted to individuals who are not attracted to them.

The reasons people are attracted to some individuals and not to others are complex and dynamic, and frequently attraction is hard to explain. Julie's concerns about being able to find the right person are understandable; she wonders why she always seems to be attracted to the wrong person. She also wonders

why her friends are attracted to certain people who she finds unappealing. After Julie and Steven break up, she realizes that the qualities that attracted her to him were not enough to sustain their relationship. After an experience such as Julie's, people some-times tell themselves that they will never again be attracted to a certain type of person, only to later find themselves dating the same type of person.

Although attraction is complex, and the charac-teristics that attract people to others vary widely, there are fundamental reasons why attraction develops. Social scientists have devoted considerable energy to determining the causes of social attraction. In this chapter, we review some of the research in this area. Specifically, we focus on how the personal attributes of two individuals work separately and together to affect attraction. We also look at the role that context and the environment play in the attraction process. This chapter will give you insight into the many factors that influence to whom you are attracted and why people are or are not attracted to you.

DEFINING ATTRACTION

There are many types of attraction. We can be attracted to someone physically, sexually, intellectually, or relationally. We might also be attracted to someone who can help us accomplish goals. Sometimes, we are even attracted to people who are "bad" for us, which is a tendency called "fatal attraction." In this section, we examine differences among these forms of attraction.

The Big Three: Physical, Social, and Task Attraction

Usually people are attracted to someone based on physical appearance, sociability, or ability to complete tasks (McCroskey & McCain, 1974). **Physical attraction** results when we are drawn to people's look, whether it is their body, their eyes, their hair, their attire, or other aspects of their appearance. **Social attraction** reflects the feeling that we would like to "hang out" and be friends with someone. When people are socially attractive, we also usually think that they would fit in well with our circle of friends and our family. Finally, **task attraction** refers to our desire to work with someone to fulfill instrumental goals, such as completing a project or making a presentation. Think of people with whom you would like to work on a group project; they are probably smart, hardworking, fair, and friendly. Box 3.1 lists some of the test items used to measure these three types of attraction.

Obviously, these types of attraction are related. In fact, both task and physical attraction can contribute to more general perceptions of social attraction. For example, if you meet someone who is physically attractive, you might decide that he or she is also charming and intelligent, and thus socially attractive. This tendency to perceive physically

attractive people as more sociable is part of the **halo effect**, which we will discuss later in this chapter. You also might be socially attracted to certain people, such as roommates and coworkers, because you find them task attractive. This is likely if you are the type of person who attends carefully to tasks and takes your work seriously.

Despite the similarities, these types of attraction are distinguishable. For example, the person you would like to be part of your group project may not always be the first person you would ask to a party. Engineers and accountants often get a "bad rap" for fitting that stereotypic mold of people who are respected for their knowledge but can be dull socially. In a similar vein, if you had a choice of partners for an important project, you would rarely use someone's physical appearance as the main criterion for selection. So, despite some overlap between these types of attraction, there are also definite differences.

Sexual Attraction

In many cases, physical attraction leads to sexual attraction. (In Chapter 7, we review literature related to sexual attitudes and behaviors, which includes the notion of sexual attraction.) **Sexual attraction** reflects the desire to engage in sexual activity with someone and is typically accompanied by feelings of sexual arousal in the presence of the person. Although people can be sexually attracted to those they find socially attractive, social attraction is not necessarily accompanied by sexual thoughts. For example, your attraction to others as friends (part of what defines social attraction) is often a platonic feeling that does not include a sexual component. Even if we think of attraction to a potential dating partner, the qualities that attract us sexually may not be the same qualities that attract us socially. Reyes et al. (1999) found that physical attractiveness is more closely related to sexual attraction than is social attractiveness. As this study suggests, physical and sexual attraction often occur together in romantic relationships. In other relationships, however, physical and sexual attraction may be unrelated. For instance, you might initially be physically attracted to someone because he or she dresses well and is about the same age. But this does not necessarily mean that you desire sex with this person.

▨ BOX 3.1 Put Yourself to the Test

What Types of People Attract You the Most?

To see what types of people attract you, try rating your closest friends and current and/or recent romantic partners using this scale. Think about the qualities that attracted you to them when you first met and rate them accordingly by circling the appropriate number. Perhaps you are more attracted to people based on their ability to help with tasks, their sociability, or their physical appearance, or perhaps all these types of attraction are important to you. You might also notice that different forms of attraction were present when you first met your close friends versus your romantic partners. Use the following scale to make your ratings: 1 = Strongly disagree, 7 = Strongly agree.

	Disagree ← → Agree						
Task attraction							
1. If I wanted to get things done, I thought I could probably depend on her/him.	1	2	3	4	5	6	7
2. I had confidence in her/his ability to get the job done.	1	2	3	4	5	6	7
3. I thought I would enjoy working with her/him on a task.	1	2	3	4	5	6	7
4. I thought this person would be an asset in any task situation.	1	2	3	4	5	6	7
5. I thought this person would take her/his work seriously.	1	2	3	4	5	6	7
Social attraction							
1. I thought she/he could be a friend of mine.	1	2	3	4	5	6	7
2. I wanted to have a friendly chat with her/him.	1	2	3	4	5	6	7
3. I thought she/he would be easy to get along with.	1	2	3	4	5	6	7
4. I thought she/he would be pleasant to be with.	1	2	3	4	5	6	7
5. I thought I could become close friends with her/him.	1	2	3	4	5	6	7
Physical attraction							
1. This person struck me as handsome or pretty.	1	2	3	4	5	6	7
2. I found her/him attractive physically.	1	2	3	4	5	6	7
3. This person looked appealing.	1	2	3	4	5	6	7
4. I thought she/he was good looking.	1	2	3	4	5	6	7
5. I thought she/he had an attractive face.	1	2	3	4	5	6	7

SOURCE: Adapted from McCroskey and Richmond's revised version of the Interpersonal Attraction scale. In Tardy, C. H. (ed.), *A Handbook for the Study of Human Communication Methods and Instruments for Observing, Measuring, and Assessing Communication Process*, copyright © 1988. Reproduced with permission of Greenwood Publishing Group, Inc., Westport, CT.

Relational Attraction

Another type of attraction, relational attraction, refers to the desire to have an intimate relationship with a person. Some scholars maintain that there are differences between initial feelings of social attraction and well-thought-out feelings of relational attraction, although relational attraction can be thought of as a subset of social attraction. Initially, you might feel social attraction to someone and think you would like to get to know her or him better. However, for other reasons you may think he or she would not make a good long-term relational partner. For example, some women might be socially attracted to Steven because he is outgoing, physically attractive, and fun to be around, but they might also think that Steven would be too flirtatious and fickle to be a serious boyfriend.

A study by Johnson, Afifi, and Duck (1994) found support for this difference between initial social attraction and long-term relational attraction. Specifically, in their study on attraction to partners after a first date (with the dates set up through a dating service), Johnson et al. distinguished between instant or "flashbulb attraction" and "expected relational course." Flashbulb attraction occurred when people felt a surge of immediate interest. Expected relational course was measured by asking participants to assess the potential for a future relationship with their date. Johnson et al. found that people who experienced flashbulb attraction did not always want to have a long-term relationship with someone.

Fatal Attraction

Regardless of whether we are initially attracted to individuals because of their winning personality, their ability to help us accomplish goals, or their good looks, we could eventually discover that the very qualities we once found attractive are not as desirable as first thought. Felmlee (1995, 1998) studied this phenomenon by conducting a number of studies on **fatal attraction**, which she defined as occurring when the very qualities that draw us to someone eventually contribute to relational breakup. That is, certain qualities may seem attractive initially but spell danger ahead. Felmlee asked people to think of the last romantic relationship they were in that ended and then to describe both what initially attracted them to the person and what ultimately led to the breakup.

Felmlee's analysis of the answers led her to some interesting conclusions. First, differences were consistently the most common type of fatal attraction. In other words, being attracted to someone because he or she is one's "opposite" might be exciting in the short term, but this novelty is likely to wear thin over time as it did for Julie in her relationship with Steven. Except for the sexes, opposites do not attract in the long run. Second, initially attractive qualities, such as being fun, exciting, or easygoing can also contribute to breakups, especially if someone has these qualities to an extreme. For example, if you are attracted to someone primarily because of her or his sense of humor, that attraction could turn to dislike if you realize that your partner can never be serious. Similarly, Steven's attractive, outgoing, flirtatious nature became distressing to Julie when she saw him socializing with other women and when she preferred to stay at home rather than go out.

A FRAMEWORK FOR UNDERSTANDING ATTRACTION

Unfortunately, few scholars have examined the subtle differences between forms of attraction to ascertain which types are most strongly associated with our relational decisions. Instead, most scholars define social attraction broadly as "a motivational state in which an individual is predisposed to think, feel, and usually behave in a positive manner toward another person" (Simpson & Harris, 1994, p. 47). This definition embraces many motivations for thinking, feeling, and behaving positively toward someone. For instance, such motivation could stem from wanting to work with someone, wanting to be someone's friend, wanting to be someone's lover, or thinking that someone is physically attractive. However, when most relationship researchers measure attraction, they focus on social and/or physical attraction. Thus most of the research reported in this chapter is most relevant to these two forms of attraction.

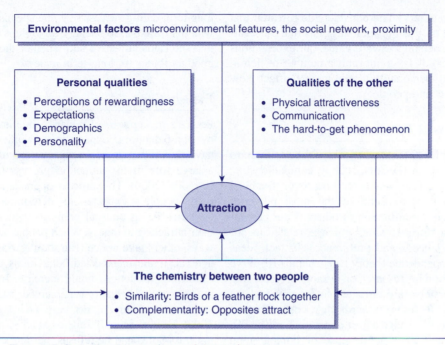

Figure 3.1 Factors Influencing Interaction and Attraction

In the rest of this chapter, we attempt to answer the question, What attracts us to others? As you will see, the answer to this question is complex. Indeed, researchers have found that many factors influence attraction. To organize these factors, we will use framework first presented by Kelley and colleagues in 1983. Our application of this framework to the attraction process is depicted in Figure 3.1. Kelley argued that four general factors influence how we behave during interactions:

1. personal qualities and preferences that we bring to the interaction, including our personality, interpersonal needs, expectations, mood, physical appearance, and level of communication skill, among other qualities;

2. qualities that the other person brings to the interaction, such as personality, looks, or communication style;

3. qualities that reflect the chemistry or synergy between two people, including similarities and

differences between relational partners across a range of characteristics, and that emerge only when the two of them are together; and

4. features of the physical environment or context in which the interaction takes place, called environmental variables, including details of the location in which the interaction is taking place (size, temperature, furniture, public vs. private setting, and so on) and feedback from friends and family.

These factors have been shown to be related to how interactions develop (see Kelley et al., 1983) and to whom people become attracted; therefore, we next review research relevant to each factor.

PERSONAL VARIABLES RELATED TO ATTRACTION

What personal preferences, personality traits, and perceptions do we possess that might influence our attraction to others? The considerable research that has focused on this question suggests that our evaluations of a person's reward value, our expectations about a person's behavior, and a number of demographic and personality variables all affect how attractive we find people.

Perceptions of Reward Value

When people enter relationships, they hope to obtain benefits or rewards, such as companionship, affection, sex, fun, and sometimes even financial resources. Therefore, one of the most powerful influences on our attraction to others is our perception of their reward value, which is related to our interpersonal needs and preferences. In fact, ideas from interdependence theory (see Chapter 10) serve as a foundation for research on attraction. According to this theory, we are attracted to others when we think they offer more rewards than costs. Thus, if someone seems to have a host of positive, rewarding qualities (such as a good sense of humor, good looks, a positive outlook, and a willingness to sacrifice for others) and only a few negative, costly qualities (such as being late all the time or being too possessive), attraction should be high. Furthermore, individuals will be perceived as especially attractive if they have more rewards to offer than other people.

Although many of these rewards can also be considered qualities possessed by the other person (such as the other person's physical attractiveness) or are associated with the chemistry between two people (such as similarity in beliefs and attitudes), it is people's own *perception* of these rewards that are relevant; if a person is perceived as rewarding or attractive to you, he or she is in fact rewarding or attractive. Because these perceptions are our own and may have no basis in objective reality, they reflect our personal preferences and biases. Anything that affects our perception of the rewards that others can offer plays a role in determining to whom we are attracted. Additionally, what qualifies as "rewarding" varies from one individual to another. For example, in the scenario that opened this chapter, Julie may find that the qualities she sees as initially rewarding in a prospective partner (e.g., he has a large social network) is actually something that may be harmful for

long-term dating success (e.g., he spends all his time with his friends). So one key for Julie is the qualities that she finds attractive and whether those jibe with good attributes for long-term mates.

Expectations

People's perceptions of reward value are influenced by our behavioral expectations. Numerous studies have shown that people's expectations of others play a large role in the attraction process (see Afifi & Burgoon, 2000). This process operates in two ways. First, people's expectations determine what they notice as being unusual or usual, which influences their attraction to others. When people act in unusual ways, others take notice (Burgoon & Hale, 1988). In general, if the unexpected behavior is perceived as rewarding, attraction should increase. In contrast, if the unexpected behavior is perceived as unrewarding, attraction is likely to decrease (Afifi & Burgoon, 2000). For instance, if Julie expects Tim to lend her his class notes and he refuses, her attraction for him will likely decrease. In the same vein, people are attracted to those who positively violate their expectations. Thus if Tim not only offers to lend Julie his notes but also tells her she can call him at home with questions, her expectations may be exceeded, and her attraction for him is likely to increase. So something that Julie should also consider is her expectations of potential dating partners and how those affect her attraction to others.

Second, people's expectations have a way of becoming reality, regardless of the other person's actual behavior, and in so doing, influence to whom people are attracted. This suggests that our expectations of other people lead us to treat them in ways that make it more likely that they will confirm our expectations. For example, if Julie thinks Philip is a friendly, considerate person, she is likely to treat him with respect, which in turn will make Philip more likely to treat Julie in a friendly, considerate manner. This also suggests that we tend to perceive people as acting in ways that fulfill our expectations, regardless of their actual behaviors. The extensive research on self-fulfilling prophecies supports these ideas. In one study, new teachers were told that certain students were "smart" and that other students were less smart (see Rosenthal & Jacobson, 1968). Although the two groups of students were actually no different from each other, by the end of the semester the teachers' expectations about the students' intelligence translated into different grades and even IQ scores for the two groups. The students whom the teachers expected to be smart received better grades and had higher IQs than the students saddled with lower teacher expectations despite the initial similarity in ability and intelligence between the two groups.

This important study was followed by a series of studies that investigated why the teachers' expectations resulted in different grades and performance. At least two explanations have been given. First, teachers treated student comments and essays differently. Specifically, when supposedly poor students gave good answers, teachers focused on superficial aspects of their answers and attributed the smart-sounding parts of the responses to luck. In contrast, when supposedly smart students gave poor answers, teachers tended to look for something positive in their responses. For example, if a student labeled as smart commented that a political candidate won a debate because he or she "was nicer," the teacher might interpret the student's answer to mean that viewers put too much weight on style compared with substance.

Second, the teachers' expectations led them to treat the two groups differently, which eventually influenced the actual quality of the students' work and their performance. Teachers gave mostly positive feedback to the supposedly bright students and mostly negative feedback to the supposedly poor students. Eventually, the students in the "poor group" simply stopped trying, while those in the "bright group" were encouraged to try harder (Rubovits & Maher, 1973).

After these studies on teacher-student interaction were published, numerous other studies showed a similar pattern across a range of contexts, including courtrooms, job interviews, and athletic fields. Expectancy effects have also been found in research on attraction. For example, Snyder, Tanke, and Berscheid (1977) tested the impact of men's perceptions of women's physical attractiveness on the women's behavior. The researchers found that, when interacting with men who found them physically attractive, women behaved in a more sociable, likable, and friendly manner than when interacting with men who found them unattractive. Thus, subtle interpersonal cues of men's expectations had the power to actually influence the women's behavior.

Research on beliefs about future interactions provides another example of how expectations influence attraction. When people expect to see someone again, they are more likely to find that person attractive, regardless of his or her behavior, than if they do not have expectations of future interaction (Kellermann & Reynolds, 1990). The expectation of future interaction motivates people to look for positive qualities in someone so that they will look forward to future interactions rather than dreading them and increases the chances that people will find the individual attractive. Conversely, when people interact with someone whom they do not foresee meeting again, they have little reason to search for positive qualities. In fact, doing so may be depressing given that they may not have the opportunity to get to know the person better in future interactions. Indeed, people are sometimes motivated to find negative qualities in individuals whom they do not expect to see again, thereby minimizing any attraction.

Demographic Characteristics

As we have seen, perceptions and expectations have a direct effect on who people find attractive. Sex, age, and other demographic variables also affect attraction, although the effects of such variables appear to be somewhat weaker than those connected to expectations. The demographic characteristic that has received the most attention in the attraction literature is biological sex.

One of the most frequently asked questions is whether men and women differ in what qualities they find attractive. The popular belief is that men are primarily attracted by looks, whereas women are more often attracted by personality; but is this belief supported by research findings? In fact, the majority of studies show that men are attracted to others based on physical appearance more than are women (see also Chapter 7). For example, Feingold (1991) reviewed results from seven studies conducted in the 1970s and 1980s and concluded that "men valued physical attractiveness more than did women, and that women valued similarity more than did men" (p. 357). Similarly, Sprecher (1998a) found that men rated physical attractiveness as a more important reason for attraction than did women, while women rated personality as a more important reason for attraction than did men.

One explanation for these sex differences, and others like them (see Hamida, Mineka, & Bailey, 1998), stems from evolutionary psychology (see also Chapters 7 and 10). Social evolutionary theorists argue that sex differences in attraction are consistent with our evolution as a species. A central idea in evolutionary psychology is that humans, like all mammalian species, are driven by a desire to advance the species. Because only the strong survive, people are attracted to those whom they consider to be the "strongest" (see Buss, 1994). Because men and women fulfill different roles in the evolutionary chain, they look for different qualities in their mating partners. Specifically, theorists argue that women "are looking for men who are willing to commit and who can provide security for them and their offspring" (Pines, 1998, p. 148), whereas men are simply looking for the most attractive (and most potentially fertile) women available.

Social evolutionary theories suggest that these specialized sex roles evolved over thousands of years and are responsible for many of the sex differences observed today. According to this view, women are attracted to older men with more resources, whereas men typically are drawn to younger women in their reproductive prime (Buss, 1994). Also, men are more easily influenced by physical appearance, whereas women attend more closely to personality, resources, and compatibility.

However, sex differences in attraction are not always as clear cut as these studies suggest. In fact, sex differences between men and women may be exaggerated in studies in which the researchers rely on data from questionnaires. In these studies, respondents rate the extent to which physical appearance is an important part of their attraction to others. Women appear to be more hesitant than men to report that physical attraction is an important part of their selection process. Indeed, when researchers use a different measure to test whether both men and women are more attracted to physically appealing others, they find that men and women are both influenced by physical attraction. Sprecher (1989) conducted a study in which men and women were given a wide range of information about someone of the opposite sex. Of all the information provided, that which was related to the person's physical attractiveness was found to be the most important determinant of attraction for both men and women. However, when Sprecher later asked them how much the person's physical attractiveness influenced their attraction, men were more willing than women to acknowledge its effect. In sum, as is typical in much of the research that we will discuss in this book, sex differences in this context may be overstated. Men and women seem more similar than different in terms of what they find attractive in others.

Rather than studying sex differences, several scholars argue that we need to think of everyone as varying on a continuum of masculine-feminine qualities labeled as "gender orientation" or "sex-role orientation" (Archer, 1989; Bem, 1974). For instance, you may know men whose beliefs and behaviors are relatively feminine and women whose beliefs and behaviors are relatively masculine. Many men and women display a mix of feminine and masculine behaviors and beliefs and are classified as **androgynous** (Bem, 1974). Clearly, much behavior is affected by socialization. Thus men who grow up in an environment that encourages emotional expression and that values personal qualities are not expected to behave similarly to or be attracted to the same types of partners as men who grow up in an environment in which emotional expression is discouraged or masculinity is defined by inattention to relationships. The same can be said for women. Mayback and Gold (1994) found that women who agree with "traditional" female roles are more attracted to aggressive, "macho" men than are women whose attitudes toward female roles are more unconventional. Thinking about differences between people based on their location on a masculine-feminine continuum, rather than based simply on their biological sex, may be a better way to understand differences and similarities between people.

Two other important demographic characteristics that have received little attention from scholars are sexual orientation and age. The few studies that have examined the impact of these variables suggest that they do not have much effect on the qualities that people seek in their mates. For example, gay men are attracted to many of the same qualities that heterosexual men and women are attracted to (Boyden, Carroll, & Maier, 1984). In a similar vein, scholars studying aging have found that people show remarkable consistency in whom they find attractive, regardless of age. In fact, people seem to find essentially the same qualities attractive whether they are in their preteen or teen years or in their 70s or 80s (Aboud & Mendelson, 1998; Webb, Delaney, & Young, 1989). In sum, although these studies did not find differences in attraction due to sexual orientation or age, given the small number of studies, it seems premature to dismiss the possibility that differences exist.

Personality

Many aspects of personality are important in relationships; one of the most important is attachment style (see Chapter 6). Considerable evidence suggests that people perceive their current relationships based on their past experiences in relationships, starting with the parent-child relationship. These views of relationships are represented by four "attachment styles" (Bartholomew, 1990): (1) secure individuals are comfortable both alone and in relationships, (2) dismissive individuals prefer to be alone and are unmotivated to develop and maintain relationships, (3) fearful avoidant individuals fear intimacy and lack self-confidence, and (4) preoccupied individuals want intimacy and fear being alone.

Likewise, attachment style influences people's behavior in relationships. It should come as no surprise that attachment style also influences to whom we are attracted. For example, Bartholomew (1990) argued that one way people maintain their attachment styles is through the unconscious process of selectively choosing interaction partners who confirm their sense of self and others. This may explain why people who are treated badly as children are attracted to romantic partners who also treat them badly. In a related vein, Sperling and Borgaro (1995) found that preoccupied individuals are more attracted to people who provide a hint of positive feedback than are securely attached persons.

Apparently, because preoccupied individuals strongly desire to be in relationships, they grab onto any potential opportunity suggested by someone giving them a compliment. Secure individuals, in contrast, are not so quick to jump at the potential opportunity; other factors influence their relationship choices. So an important piece of the attraction puzzle with which Julie is struggling resides in her attachment style and related relational behavior.

Self-esteem and mood are also related to whom we are attracted. Have you noticed that about yourself? When you are feeling down, are you attracted to the same type of people as when you are feeling good about yourself? If your answer is no, you are not alone. Several studies have shown that people's feelings about themselves strongly influences whom they find attractive. For example, Joshi and Rai (1987) found that a person's self-esteem is directly related to his or her level of attraction to others. That is, those who have high self-esteem consistently find others more attractive than those whose self-esteem is low.

Self-esteem can operate in even more subtle ways. In two studies, Hoyle, Insko, and Moniz (1992) assessed students' self-esteem, asked students to complete a bogus test of intelligence, and then provided them with either positive or negative feedback about their performance. After this feedback, the students talked briefly with another person and completed a survey about their attraction to the interaction partner. The students with low self-esteem were more attracted to the person if they talked to her or him after being told good news about their performance on the "intelligence test," as opposed to being told bad news about their performance. In other words, good news made them more attracted to others, perhaps because they associated the person with a rewarding situation, or perhaps because they were simply in better moods, felt confident, and were more receptive to their interaction partner's positive qualities.

These findings may also be explained in relation to how we view others in comparison to ourselves. If we have a poor image of ourselves and think that we lack intelligence, we are unlikely to consider others attractive. This is because finding them attractive but feeling we have no chance with them is just too threatening or discouraging. Instead, we convince ourselves that they are unattractive to shield ourselves from what we perceive to be their eventual rejection of us.

People with high self-esteem showed the exact opposite pattern in Hoyle et al.'s (1992) study. That is, they were more attracted to others after hearing bad news about their performance on the intelligence test than they were after hearing good news. Why would that be? One explanation is that people with high self-esteem recognize the need to boost their self-image after receiving bad news, and one way to do so is to view others as attractive and to interact with them. In contrast, receiving good news only bolsters their already high self-esteem, which may lead them to view most others as unworthy partners and thereby lower their attraction to them. The bottom line seems to be that people with high self-esteem are choosier about potential partners than are people with low levels of self-esteem. Even temporary doubts about one's abilities may cause people to be less choosy.

Many other personality-related variables have been studied in connection to attraction. Two of the most important are the degree to which we are aware of our surroundings (self-monitoring) and our level of narcissism. **Self-monitoring** is the extent to which people regulate their behavior to fit the social context. High self-monitors attend to the rules of their surroundings and follow accordingly, while low self-monitors rarely tailor their behavior to the context (Snyder & Gangestad, 1986; Snyder & Simpson, 1987). Given their greater concern for how they appear to others, it is not surprising that high and low self-monitors differ in what they find attractive in others. High self-monitors are typically first attracted to others based on their physical appearance, while low self-monitors are usually drawn by personality traits (Snyder, Berscheid, & Glick, 1985). High self-monitors do not also like being the "third wheel" in a social setting, which is how Julie feels when she is single and her friends are paired up. Thus, they enter into relationships more quickly than people who care less about showing up alone at social functions (Glick, 1985).

Narcissism is characterized by an extreme focus on oneself during interaction, to the exclusion of others (Vangelisti et al., 1990). Campbell (1999) conducted five studies to determine how individuals' degree of narcissism affects their attraction to others. He found big differences between the qualities that are attractive to narcissists and to non-narcissists. Most noticeably, narcissists are attracted to others who admire them, while non-narcissists are drawn to others who exhibit caring qualities. Not surprisingly, Campbell (1999) also found that narcissists are partly drawn to these admiring others because of their own need to improve their self-esteem. In other words, as you may have suspected, narcissists are often those who, despite their outward appearance, have relatively low self-esteem and who seek self-esteem boosts.

OTHER PEOPLE'S QUALITIES

So far, our discussion has focused on personal perceptions and predispositions you have when evaluating others' attractiveness. Of course, other people's qualities increase your likelihood of being attracted to them. As noted earlier, one view of attraction boils down to a perception that someone can offer us more rewards than costs relative to other potential partners. Thus, the key question becomes What qualities do people find especially rewarding? People seem to prefer those who are physically attractive and communicatively competent. Moreover, people who are perceived to be in high demand and moderately "hard to get" are also highly valued. In this section, we discuss these variables starting with the quality that has received the most attention— physical attractiveness.

Physical Attractiveness

Studies have consistently shown that physical attractiveness is one of the top two predictors of social attraction (Dion, 1986; Huston & Levinger, 1978). For example, Sprecher (1989) found that the more physically attractive the other person was the more attracted participants were to him or her. Similarly, Johnson et al.'s (1994) research on first dates among dating club members showed that more than any other quality, people's physical attractiveness determined whether their date found them socially attractive. These findings may not be surprising, but the

SOURCE: iStockphoto.com

SOURCE: Copyright: iStockphoto.com/Jacob Wackerhausen

Photo 3.1　How would you rate this man and woman on physical attractiveness? What facial features makes them attractive?

more interesting question may be—What specific "looks" do we find attractive?

The answer to that question is too complex to be fully addressed here and in some ways is culturally determined, but several studies have yielded some insights. One feature that has been shown to strongly influence women's attraction to men is height. In fact, studies have found that women tend to find very short men unattractive as potential mates even when the researcher assigns them a whole host of other rewarding qualities, such as a positive personality, intelligence, and high earning potential (Jackson & Ervin, 1992; Pierce, 1996). In contrast, evidence is mixed about whether height impacts perceptions of females' attractiveness (Hensley, 1994). Across many different cultures,

when men are being evaluated, a strong jawline, broad shoulders, and a waist-to-hip ratio of around .90 or 1.0 (in other words, a waist just slightly smaller than their hips) contribute to judgments of physical attractiveness. For women, a soft jawline and an hourglass figure (with the waist significantly smaller than the chest and hips) is preferred (Buss, 1989, 1994; Singh, 1995). Both men and women also value physical fitness and an athletic build in their dating partners.

You might think that preoccupation with looks is unfair and that people should be judged by their inner character rather than their outward appearance. This may be true, but the research suggests that, fair or not, people use outward appearances to make judgments about people's inner character.

Specifically, research has shown that people often associate good looks with a wide range of other positive qualities. This tendency, often called the halo effect or the what-is-beautiful-is-good stereotype, leads people to believe that physically attractive individuals are more likely to succeed, and they are more sociable, popular, intelligent, and competent than their less attractive counterparts (Dion, 1986; Dion, Berscheid, & Walster, 1972). The halo effect means that people are drawn to attractive individuals because most people are looking for someone who offers the "complete package." Because looks are a shortcut for other positive traits, physically attractive people receive more positive attention from others throughout life (Dion, 1972), often develop more positive self-esteem (Nell & Ashton, 1996), and may actually develop some of the skills people assume they have (Chaiken, 1979).

The halo effect helps explain why good looks are so important in the attraction process. Social evolutionary theorists offer a complementary explanation for why physical attractiveness matters. Specifically, they argue that people's attraction to particular physical traits is due to the genetic drive to mate with the fittest person possible (Buss, 1994). To that end, physically attractive individuals should be socially attractive to the greatest number of people because they are essentially the most highly evolved physical specimens in our species and so are highly prized. Physical fitness, especially body shape and size, is also an outward sign of health and fertility. Thus, although cultural standards for beauty vary, social evolutionary theorists predict that some preferences cut across cultures. For example, while dark hair is prized in some cultures and light hair is prized in others, physical attributes related to health and fertility, such as a clear complexion and a physically fit body, have been found to be valued by most cultures around the globe (Buss, 1994). In fact, Buss's now-classic 1989 study showed remarkable consistency across 37 cultures in what they found to be physically attractive. Langlois et al.'s (2000) summary of 130 samples showed the same results. Specifically, we seem to be unconsciously drawn to features such as body and facial symmetry, body proportionality, and particular waist-to-hip ratios, among many other attributes (for review, see Guerrero & Floyd, 2006).

See Box 3.2 for a summary of the literature on attributes rated to physical attractiveness.

Judgments of beauty, however, are not always objective. For example, people involved in romantic relationships tend to see members of the opposite sex as less physically attractive, perhaps as a way of maintaining their current relationship (Simpson, Gangestad, & Lerma, 1990). Research testing **interaction appearance theory** has also demonstrated that people perceive others as more physically attractive if they have warm, positive interactions with them (Albada, Knapp, & Theune, 2002). Thus, in some cases relationships and interaction can lead people to revise their initial impressions of people or to regard their relational partners as more physically attractive than an objective observer would judge them to be.

Finally, people may be drawn to physically attractive individuals because they hope to gain rewards through association. Think about when you are with your most attractive friends; perhaps you have more opportunities to meet people and feel more attractive yourself. Research suggests that, whether intentional or not, people benefit by interacting with more attractive others. Sigall and Landy (1973), for example, found that people were rated as more attractive when they were with comparatively more attractive individuals than when they were not. The idea here is that some of the attention that physically attractive people get spills over to their friends through what is called the **assimilation effect**.

In sum, most people are attracted to good-looking persons, but what other qualities do we find attractive in potential partners or friends? Is physical appearance all that matters? The answer is a resounding "no." People notice those who are physically attractive and are more likely to initiate communication with attractive people, but this does not guarantee that highly attractive people will continue to be valued after the initial attraction fades. In fact, they can be at a disadvantage in trying to live up to the high expectations imposed by the halo effect. For example, Hatfield (1984) wrote about a beautiful woman who was insecure because she worried that men would be disappointed if they saw her for what she really was, rather than what they dreamed a beautiful woman should be. Physical appearance only goes so far. Next, we examine other qualities that make people attractive.

BOX 3.2   Highlights

Is Beauty Really in the Eye of the Beholder?

Scholars have debated whether beauty is universal or in the eye of the beholder. Research suggests that some attributes are universally associated with beauty, whereas other attributes are evaluated differently on the basis of culture or social group.

Universal attributes of beauty include the following:

Body and Facial Symmetry: When two sides of a face or body mirror each other, a person is rated as more physically attractive.

Body Proportionality and the Golden Ratio: The ratio of ϕ (Phi), or 1 to 1.618, is an index of attractiveness (e.g., bodies are rated as more proportional if the distance from the navel to the bottom of the feet is 1.618 times the distance from the navel to the top of the head; faces are rated as more proportional if the width of the lips is 1.618 times the width of the nose, among other comparisons).

Waist-to-Hip Ratio: For women, the ideal ratio is .70 (the waist is 70% the size of the hips). For men, the ideal ratio is about 1.0 (hips and waist about the same size).

Koinophilia: Faces are rated as more attractive when they have "average" features, with studies showing that a computer composite of multiple faces is perceived as more attractive than any single face.

Facial Neoteny and Maturity: Faces are rated as more attractive when they are characterized by a combination of baby-like and mature features that represent youth and sexuality (e.g., a woman with large eyes, full lips, and high cheekbones or a man with large eyes, a small nose, and strong jawline).

SOURCE: Information compiled from Guerrero and Floyd (2006).

Interpersonal Communication Skills

Are we so drawn to physically attractive people that their interpersonal communication skills do not matter initially? For years, scholars ignored the role of interpersonal communication in favor of studying the impact of other variables on our attraction. Sunnafrank (1991, 1992) was among the first scholars to study how communication influences attraction. In the mid-1980s, he began a series of studies that added what was, until then, a novel element to studies of attraction—he actually had participants interact with the person they were rating on attraction! Most previous studies had only shown participants a picture or given them information about some fictitious character. Sunnafrank argued that, unless people communicated, experiments would not be representative of the real qualities that people consider when evaluating the attractiveness of others. In fact, he suggested that many of the factors that scholars had found to predict attraction, such as similarity and physical attractiveness, might not matter as much once people started talking to one another. Instead, he claimed, people would be influenced by another's communication style and behavior to determine how attracted they were to each other.

Many studies have supported Sunnafrank's contention. Reyes et al. (1999) had students view a still picture of an opposite-sex actor and had them answer several survey questions, including questions about their attraction to the actor. They then answered the questions a second time after watching an interaction in which the actor was either nice or acted like a jerk. The power of communication was evident. Although physical attractiveness was a primary quality that drew people to the actor prior to watching the interaction, the actor's behavior during the interaction, whether positive or negative, became a primary determinant of their attraction to the actor afterward; physical attractiveness hardly mattered. Thus, communication plays a key role in determining to whom we are attracted. But what specific communication styles do we find appealing? Some studies provide important clues as to the connection between communication and attraction.

One communication quality that seems to emerge relatively consistently in studies of attraction is warmth. Warmth typically is communicated verbally by a generally positive attitude and a show of concern for others (Folkes & Sears, 1977) and nonverbally by such behaviors as smiling, making eye contact, and showing interest in the other person (Andersen, 1985; Andersen & Guerrero, 1998a; Friedmann, Riggio, & Casella, 1988). In fact, Sprecher (1998a) conducted three studies, all of which revealed that warmth and kindness were rated as the two qualities of the interaction partner that were most responsible for the participants' attraction to him or her.

Sociability and competence are two other communication qualities that are shown to influence attraction (Krueger & Caspi, 1993). Here, sociability refers to one's ability to communicate easily among a group of people. People who are extroverted and expressive are perceived as highly sociable. Competence is determined by one's level of composure and knowledge. People are often evaluated as competent when they communicate without showing signs of nervousness and seem knowledgeable—although when people go out of their way to seem knowledgeable, they are often rated as unattractive (Vangelisti et al., 1990).

In contrast to these "softer" qualities of warmth, sociability, and competence, some people are drawn to potentially "darker" qualities. For example, several studies have shown that women in particular are attracted to men who show a certain degree of assertiveness or power. This is consistent with evolutionary psychology in that women should be attracted to behavioral expressions of dominance in men because it reflects a reproductive advantage. In other words, women should be subconsciously attracted to the strongest and fittest men, who will produce the best offspring. To test this idea, Sadalla, Kenrick, and Vershure (1987) created perceptions of dominance by having male actors take seats close to the subjects. The "nondominant" actors sat up straight and chatted quietly among themselves; the "dominant" actors sat in a very relaxed posture and showed a lack of interest in the women while talking loudly, quickly, and clearly. They found that the women were most attracted to the men who showed these signs of dominance.

Does this mean that women prefer dominant men over nice men? Jensen-Campbell, Graziano, and West (1995) attempted to address the question of whether "nice guys really finish last." They argued that from an evolutionary perspective women should also value altruism in men because they want partners who make sacrifices and invest considerable resources in the relationship. This is exactly what they found. First, women were attracted to altruistic men (men who were willing to do something boring so that the woman did not have to do it) much more than to nonaltruistic men (men who jumped at the opportunity to do something fun and left the boring task to the woman). The study was consistent with the research showing that people are attracted to individuals who are warm and caring. However, men who were altruistic but otherwise unassertive and weak were not very attractive. Men who were assertive/dominant and nonaltruistic were not attractive to the women either. Instead, women found the combination of assertiveness/dominance and altruism most appealing. Thus, strong but altruistic men may be perceived as most attractive.

Interestingly, the same results did not emerge with regard to men's attraction to women. That is, men's levels of attraction were unaffected by a woman's level of dominance but were much more attracted to altruistic women. So, again, the importance of communicating care in interactions shines through; nice men, and women, do not necessarily have to finish last.

Finally, the timing of positive versus negative behavior seems to influence attraction. Several studies have identified what has been called the **loss-gain effect** (Afifi & Burgoon, 2000; Aronson & Linder, 1965; Sharma & Kaur, 1996). This effect reflects what happens to attraction when a person's behavior moves from positive to negative or from negative to positive. For example, if someone seems very nice to you early in the interaction but then begins to act like a jerk, would you be more attracted to that person than if he or she was a jerk from the start? Studies suggest that you would not. In fact, people are more attracted to individuals who are consistently negative than to people who initially behave positively and then switch to negative behavior. People who start out being nice get our hopes up, so the letdown we experience when we discover that they are not nice makes it worse than if they had acted badly from the start. Of course, people are most attracted to those who are pleasant throughout an interaction.

The "Hard-to-Get" Phenomenon

In some situations, the person who acts somewhat hard to get is perceived as attractive. For example, Roberson and Wright (1994) put males in a situation in which they had to try to persuade a female stranger (who was actually working for the experimenters) to be their coworker on a project. The men were told that the woman either would be easy to convince, might be difficult to convince, or would be impossible to convince. Results showed that the men rated the woman whom they were told would be moderately difficult to convince as most attractive. The authors concluded that playing hard to get has its benefits but that it can backfire if the person is seen as unattainable.

These findings were consistent with prior research by Wright, Toi, and Brehm (1984). Wright et al. were interested in whether the amount of energy that people put into pursuing someone is related to how much people like the individual they are pursuing. In this study, Wright et al. told male participants that they could work with a female actor on a project if they could memorize a certain number of sentence combinations in 2 minutes. Before the researchers had the men try to memorize these combinations, they asked them to rate the actor. Participants were assigned to memorize either two (the easy condition), five (the moderately difficult condition), or eight (the very difficult condition) combinations. Remarkably, given that the task was all that differed, the men who were about to try memorizing five combinations rated the actor as more attractive than the men in either the easy or the very difficult condition.

Similarly, Wright and Contrada (1986) found that people rated members of the opposite sex as most attractive when they were portrayed as moderately selective rather than as very selective or nonselective. Why is that? Apparently, we are more attracted to individuals who present a bit of a challenge than to those whom we perceive to be too easily attainable or completely unattainable. One reason for this may be that, in our effort to shoot for the best possible "catch," we think that we are not shooting high enough if we are attracted to those who are not at least somewhat of a challenge. Consistent with this reasoning, research has shown that we are most likely to be attracted to hard-to-get people if they are easy for us to attract but difficult for others to attract (Walster, Walster, Piliavin, & Schmidt, 1973). One explanation is that when a person is hard for others to get but easy for you to get, people view you in a more positive light. In other words, people will likely perceive that you must have outstanding personal qualities if you were able to obtain such a high-quality partner. Another explanation is that scarcer resources, including people, are more valuable.

In sum, in addition to individuals' own personal qualities, many qualities of other people increase or decrease feelings of attraction. However, unique qualities emerge when two people interact with each other. These factors, which we call the "chemistry" or "synergy" between people, also affect attraction.

INTERPERSONAL CHEMISTRY BETWEEN PEOPLE

When two people interact, the synergy of their interaction creates a certain chemistry that determines their mutual interpersonal attraction. One of the strongest and most important aspects of interpersonal chemistry is the degree to which people are similar to one another. This conclusion is far from new. As early as 1870, Sir Francis Galton, the cousin of Charles Darwin and a scientist best known for his research on intelligence and heredity, concluded that spouses usually are similar on several characteristics. Over the next century, many studies showed that friends and spouses tend to be similar on everything from attitudes and beliefs to height and visual acuity (Byrne, 1992). These studies all reached the same conclusion: The more similar others are to us, the more we will be attracted to them.

Similarity: "Birds of a Feather Flock Together"

Do similar individuals really tend to hang out together as this saying suggests? Think about your friends and dating partners. Do most of them have a lot in common with you? Maybe you like to do the same things, think the same way, and/or have similar personalities. Or perhaps you come from similar backgrounds. This preference for similarity has been shown to hold true across a whole host of personal qualities, including demographic characteristics such as race, cultural background, educational level, socioeconomic status, and religion, among other demographic characteristics (Hill, Rubin, & Peplau, 1976; Kandel, 1978). However, similarity has been studied most extensively in the context of similarity among attitudes.

Attitudinal Similarity. When people are similar in their attitudes, beliefs, and values, they are said to share attitudinal similarity. People can have perceived similarity (thinking that they are similar to the other person) and/or actual similarity (actually being similar to the other person). Two people may think they share attitudes and beliefs but later find out that they have very different likes and dislikes. The importance of this distinction quickly became evident to researchers. In one of the first extensive studies of attitudinal similarity, Newcomb (1961) found important differences between actual and perceived similarity. Newcomb gave a group of male undergraduates room and board in exchange for their participation in a study on friendships. The participants were randomly assigned roommates and were given surveys throughout the school year. The results showed that roommates liked one another more when they were similar. Interestingly, at the beginning of the year, perceived similarity and actual similarity did not match. New roommates were often oblivious to the actual level of similarity they shared, so they relied heavily on their perceptions of similarity to determine liking. As the year went on, however, the actual degree of similarity between roommates gradually became evident. By the end of the year, those who were actually dissimilar did not like one another, even though their initial perceptions of similarity had led them to like one another at first. This distinction between actual and perceived similarity has continued to play an important role in studies of attraction.

Recently, Morry (2005) reminded us that both actual and perceived similarity have important relational implications. She studied the attraction-similarity in ongoing same-sex friendships. Like other researchers, she found similarity to be important but also showed that the happier people were in their friendships, the more similar they reported their friend to be. Importantly, she was able to show that the attraction came *before* the bias toward perceptions of similarity in her study. In other words, we tend to see people to whom we are attracted as being more similar to us than they really are. Relatedly, we see people we dislike as being less similar. This finding does not discount the importance of actual similarity, but it underscores that we also have biases that make us feel more similar to or different from what we actually are to others.

At about the same time that Newcomb's now famous experiment was taking place, Byrne (1961, 1971) began to research the impact of attitudinal similarity attraction, which has contributed greatly to our understanding of the relationship between similarity and attraction. One of his main methods for testing the effect of similarity on attraction was what he labeled the "bogus stranger" method. Byrne would first ask participants a series of questions assessing their likes and dislikes. He would then take the questionnaire to a different room and create answers on another, similar questionnaire that ranged from being almost identical to the participants' answers to very different from the participants' answers. Next, he took the "bogus" survey back to the participants, told them that the survey belonged to a participant who had already taken part in the study, asked them to read it over, and then rate the extent to which they would be attracted to this "bogus stranger." Byrne and his colleagues repeatedly found that participants were more attracted to bogus strangers who were similar to them (Byrne, 1997).

As you might suspect, the real-life applicability of this method has been challenged, with some scholars arguing that this similarity effect disappears when two people communicate with each other (Sunnafrank, 1991). Nonetheless, the remarkable consistency of the finding that people are attracted to attitudinally similar individuals is hard to dispute. Thus the question becomes, What is it that makes attitudinal similarity so important?

According to Byrne's (1971) **reinforcement model,** we are attracted to similar others because they reinforce our view of the world as the correct perspective. People do not like it when others challenge the correctness of their own attitudes and values. The best way to avoid such a challenge is to interact with individuals who think the same way as they do. Imagine disagreeing about everything with your friends or dating partner; that would get tiresome rather quickly, so you probably avoid people with whom you think that may happen. In contrast, when two people are similar, they usually have more in common to talk about and like to do the same things, which make interaction enjoyable. Similarities make people's lives much easier and also make people feel that their way is the "right" way since their views are shared by others. The disadvantage, of course, is that people fail to grow very much if all their friends are just like them.

Similarity in Communication Skill. People also have a preference for similarity in communication style. Burleson (1998) examined why people are attracted to others who have similar levels of communication skill and are happier with similarly skilled individuals than with those who are not similarly skilled. What intrigued Burleson was not that very good communicators are attracted to each other, but that poor communicators are also drawn to other poor communicators, perhaps explaining why many relationships are characterized by communication problems. Why might people with limited communication skill be attracted to others who are similarly limited? Burleson advanced four possible explanations:

1. *The differential importance explanation.* Communication may not be a very frequent or important activity for those with low communication skill. As a result, low-skill people may not care if their partner is unskilled. In other words, since low-skill people do not engage in communication very often, they may not be looking for a high-skill partner. Other factors affecting attraction may be more important to them.

2. *The "ignorance is bliss" explanation.* Low-skill individuals are not aware that some people communicate better than they do. Because they have relationships with similar others, most of their interactions have been with people with relatively low social skills. As a result, they are happy with the way their low-skill partner communicates.

3. *The "sour grapes" explanation.* People who have poor communication skills are painfully aware of their shortcomings in the social arena. Although they might like to have partners with better skills than they do, they perceive highly skilled communicators to be hopelessly out of their reach. As a result, they settle for partners with lower social skills, figuring these partners are as good as they can get, while downgrading more skilled people.

4. *The skill-as-culture explanation.* What some people consider to be poor communication might actually be seen as effective communication by others. Thus, individuals who are defined as low-skill communicators by researchers may be enacting communication behaviors that they and their partners consider to be quite competent. For example, low levels of expressiveness might be perceived as indicative of incompetence by some people, but an inexpressive dyad might feel most comfortable keeping their emotions hidden.

Similarity in Physical Attractiveness. A final form of similarity that has been studied extensively for its impact on attraction is similarity in physical attractiveness. Have you ever noticed how people who are dating tend to be similar in terms of physical attractiveness? In fact, people take notice when one member of a romantic couple is much better looking than the other. Fair or not, the automatic assumption is that the less attractive partner must have other exceptional qualities (such as a great personality, wealth, or high social standing) that led the more attractive partner to choose her or him over better-looking alternatives.

Our tendency to be attracted to people who are similar to ourselves in physical attractiveness has been called the **matching hypothesis** (Berscheid, Dion, Walster, & Walster, 1971). This does not mean that people search for partners who look similar to themselves in terms of physical features—for example, brown-eyed people looking for brown-eyed partners or people with high cheek bones and fair skin looking for partners who have similar bone structure and skin color. Instead, the matching hypothesis predicts that people look for partners who have roughly the same level of overall physical attractiveness as themselves. Thus, even though Julie is a petite, fair-skinned, green-eyed blonde and Steven is a tall, dark-skinned, brown-eyed brunet, because they are both good-looking they fit the matching hypothesis. In contrast, if you think you are fairly good-looking but not stunningly beautiful or devastatingly handsome, the matching hypothesis predicts that you will look for a partner who is somewhat above average but not extraordinarily attractive. Interestingly, the matching hypothesis has been shown to hold true across a wide variety of relationship types, from friendships to marriages, and cultures (Feingold, 1988).

However, this matching hypothesis appears to be inconsistent with the research on physical attractiveness. Those studies found that people are most attracted to individuals who are very physically attractive. In contrast, research on the matching hypothesis suggests that people are most attracted to individuals who are similar to them in physical attractiveness. In other words, less attractive people should be attracted to other similarly less attractive people rather than to the best-looking ones. These seemingly inconsistent findings lead to two questions: (1) Which of these hypotheses is right? and (2) Why would less attractive people be attracted to other less attractive individuals as opposed to more attractive ones?

The answer to both of these questions depends on people's sense of what is ideal and the realistic. Ideally, people want to date others who are more attractive than they are but realistically recognize that physically attractive individuals are likely to have many options and are somewhat selective about whom they date. Recall the research on the hard-to-get phenomenon. These studies showed that people are attracted to individuals who are somewhat hard to get but tend to shy away from individuals who are too selective because they do not want to waste their effort on people they see too selective, choosy, or conceited. Thus people may label someone who is much better-looking than themselves as conceited and instead select a dating partner who is similar to themselves in terms of physical attractiveness. In short, the matching hypothesis is based on the idea that people want to maximize the attractiveness of their partner by choosing someone who is at least as attractive as themselves while minimizing their chances for rejection by choosing someone who is attainable. Based on this reasoning, both the beautiful-is-good and matching hypotheses appear to have some basis in truth.

Similarity in Names and Birth Dates. Recent evidence suggests that our affinity for similar others may go to absurd lengths. Using the notion of **implicit egotism**, several scholars have shown that we are attracted to others based on similarity on the most arbitrary things. These scholars argue that even similarity in first or last names, in the size of earlobes, or in the date of birth, among other subtle similarities, activate liking for others because they are subconsciously associated with liking for ourselves (e.g., our name, our earlobe length, our birth date). If this sounds crazy, it is worth pointing out that several studies have observed that trend. For example, Jones, Pelham, Carvallo, and Mirenberg (2004) summarized seven studies they performed which systematically tested this implicit egotism effect. In the end, their studies showed that people are more attracted to others whose arbitrary experimental code assigned by the researchers shared similarities with their birth date or was subliminally connected to their name. Moreover, their investigation of marriage records showed that people are disproportionately likely to marry someone whose first or last name shares at least some similarity to their own (e.g., their first or last name starts with the same letter), even after accounting for ethnic similarities in names. More research is necessary to determine the extent to which implicit egotism plays a role in the attraction process. In particular, implicit egotism would probably be most relevant when a person has high self-esteem, but this possibility has not yet been tested. Also, researchers need to see if similarities in things such as names and birth dates are more or less important than similarities in other areas, such as physical appearance.

Complementarity: Sometimes Opposites Attract

Although the research discussed thus far shows that there is a strong similarity effect when it comes to attraction and liking, this does not mean that people are always similar on every valued characteristic. Sometimes, relational partners or good friends also complement one another in some areas. For example, Julie and her best friend, Brittany, might both be intelligent, have the same major in college, and enjoy winter sports such as ice skating and skiing, but Julie might be the better student, while Brittany might be the better athlete. Instead of envying each other's skills, they may be proud of each other's special talents and benefit from Brittany's contribution to their tennis team and Julie's help in studying for an exam. And they also might be completely different in some ways. For instance, Julie might be shy and reserved, carefully thinking before talking, while Brittany is extroverted and impulsive. Likewise, these qualities could complement one another; that is, Julie might appreciate having Brittany around to help her make new friends, while Brittany might appreciate it when Julie tells her to think before acting on certain impulses.

As this example suggests, the old saying that "opposites attract" can have some basis in truth. However, **complementarity** seems to be a much better predictor of attraction and liking when it is linked to behavior or resources, and not attitudes and values (Strong et al., 1988). When it comes to people's core attitudes and beliefs, similarity seems to be much more important than complementarity. Additionally, as noted previously, sometimes people are initially attracted to someone who is completely unlike them, only to discover that those "opposite" characteristics eventually drive them crazy. This happened in Julie's relationship with Steven, who was too much an extrovert and player for Julie. As Felmlee (1998)

suggested in her work on fatal attraction, "Be careful what you wish for," because sometimes you might get it and then regret it (p. 235)!

Similarity and Complementarity in Initial Versus Committed Relationships

The vast majority of studies on the similarity-attraction link have looked at the advantages or disadvantages of similarity during the initial stages of a relationship's development. But we know less about the role that similarity plays beyond that stage. Amodio and Showers (2005) examined this issue more closely by having undergraduate students who were in exclusive dating relationships for at least 3 months complete two surveys, 1 year apart. Their results suggest a very important role for commitment in our understanding of the way that similarity operates in ongoing relationships. Specifically, the benefit of similarity for liking and attraction seems to hold primarily for high-commitment couples. Those who reported being highly committed to their relationship benefited from their attribute similarity over time. However, those who reported having low relationship commitment were actually harmed by that similarity.

Amodio and Showers (2005) speculated that dissimilarity may actually be exciting for dating partners who we don't see as long-term mates. In essence, you can experience new things with this person, while knowing that this person is not someone who you'll be with forever. In contrast, being dissimilar to someone with whom you see yourself in a relationship with for a long time is likely to gnaw at you, eroding that liking over time.

So which characteristic is more attractive— similarity or complementarity? The answer may depend on the goals you have for a relationship with the person. If you hope for, or are in, a highly committed relationship with your partner, then similarity seems to be a key ingredient to success. But if instead, you are looking for a somewhat casual relationship experience without considerable commitment, then dissimilarity or complementarity may, in fact, be more what you should look for. Just keep in mind that those differences may come back to haunt you if your relationship goals change. For example, Julie may like the excitement of having an outgoing and physically attractive boyfriend like Steven, but if she is interested in pursuing a long-term committed relationship, she may be well-advised to look for someone who is more similar to her.

In sum, several studies have shown that similarities in attitudes, likes and dislikes, and physical attractiveness are related to attraction and liking. Some complementary features may also be related to attraction, especially when there is complementarity in behavior (such as a shy person paired with an outgoing person) or resources (such as a wealthy person paired with a beautiful person). The best relationships may be characterized by both similarity and complementarity, with similarity in important attitudes and values sustaining commitment, and complementarity sustaining excitement. The final influence on people's attraction to others is environmental features.

ENVIRONMENTAL FEATURES RELATED TO ATTRACTION

How does the environment or context influence people's attraction to others? As you read through this section, you might be surprised by all the ways the environment can affect attraction and liking. Environmental features, social networks, and proximity are all contextual elements that are associated with attraction.

Microenvironmental Features

Research suggests that the environment has subtle effects on attraction and liking (see Andersen, 1999). For example, research on room features and their effects has shown that room temperature (Griffit, 1970), the presence of music (May & Hamilton, 1980), and even such seemingly irrelevant characteristics as the size of the room, the presence of high ceilings, the linear perspective of the room, the type of couch material, the color of the walls and ceilings, and the lighting may influence whether people are attracted to one another (Andersen, 1999; Burgoon et al., 1996). For example, environments that encourage interaction by providing a cozy atmosphere can promote attraction. Similarly, low lighting and soft colors may make certain people look particularly attractive, while brighter lighting and bolder colors may make other people look appealing. Environments that put people face-to-face in close proximity also enhance attraction (Andersen, 1999).

Environmental effects on attraction have also been explained by Byrne and Clore (1970; see also Clore & Byrne, 1974) using the **reinforcement affect model,** according to which certain types of environments are more likely to make people feel good. For example, an intimate setting with comfortable chairs and couches, soft wall colors, low lighting, and soft music relaxes people. These environmentally induced positive emotions get transferred to the interactants in that environment. In other words, people unconsciously associate the feelings they experience in a particular environment with the individuals who are part of that environment.

Other studies have shown that under some circumstances, the emotions people experience due to the environment can also be related to attraction. Dutton and Aron (1974) conducted an unusual experiment to test the impact of environment cues on attraction. They had male participants cross either a stable or a relatively unstable bridge. To make matters worse, the stable bridge was low lying, while the unstable bridge spanned a steep ravine. After crossing the bridges, the participants were met by either a male or female research assistant and told to write a brief story, which was later coded for sexual imagery. The participants also were given the assistant's phone number and invited to call her or him at home if they wanted more information. Amazingly, the researchers found that the men who crossed the unstable bridge and met the female assistant included more sexual images in their stories and were more likely to call the assistant at home. Apparently, their misattributed fear and arousal increased their attraction to the female assistant.

It may seem odd that a negative emotion such as fear can lead to attraction. Why does this happen? Zillman (1978), an emotions theorist, identified the presence of a process called **excitation transfer.** What sometimes happens, Zillman argued, is that people mistake the cause of their emotional arousal. This is especially likely to happen when people experience arousal in response to two different sources in close proximity to each other. In those cases, people mix the two states of arousal together and attribute excitement to the second stimulus. In the Dutton and Aron (1974) study, participants experienced high arousal/anxiety after walking over an unstable bridge and then immediately experienced emotional arousal when they met the female research assistant. In doing so, they may have unconsciously and mistakenly attributed their rapid heartbeats and other signs of intense emotional arousal to the presence of the female assistant, leading them to believe that they were more attracted to her than they objectively might have been. Although this may sound far-fetched (and scholars have challenged the validity of excitation transfer; see Riordan & Tedeschi, 1983), other studies have confirmed this finding (White, Fishbein, & Rutstein, 1981). Apparently, in some cases, people who share scary experiences such as riding a fast rollercoaster or watching a horror film together, may be more likely to be attracted to each other due to excitation transfer.

Social Networks

Another factor that affects attraction is one's social network, including family and friends. Have you noticed that what you find attractive in others is often similar to what your friends find attractive? If so, you are not alone. In fact, hundreds of studies have shown that people's attitudes and intentions are strongly influenced by the attitudes of their friends and family (Sheppard, Hartwick, & Warshaw, 1988). Many scholars argue that the attitudes of members of our social circle, known as subjective norms, are the strongest predictor of our own attitudes and intentions. Given that attraction represents an attitude toward other people, the feedback we receive from friends and family certainly plays an important role in those whom we find attractive.

In most cases, approval by one's social network promotes attraction and liking. For example, if you meet someone you would like to date, and all your friends tell you how wonderful she or he is, you are likely to feel even more positively toward this potential dating partner. However, the reverse can also occur. Perhaps you find someone attractive, but after your friends question what you see in her or him and discourage you from pursuing a relationship, your attraction decreases. There is one notable exception to this phenomenon, however. Some research has supported the **"Romeo and Juliet" effect**, which predicts that parental interference can strengthen attraction between two people. Specifically, Driscoll, Davis, and Lipetz (1972) found that partners in dating couples reported more love for each other when their parents disapproved of their relationship. Driscoll et al. retested their hypothesis 10 months later using the same couples and found the same results, with parental interference still positively related to the amount of love couples reported.

There are at least four viable explanations for the "Romeo and Juliet" effect. First, rebellious young couples may exert their power by defying their parents and becoming romantically involved with their forbidden partner. These feelings of power and excitement may be attributed to their relationship, much as the excitation transfer process suggests. Second, some writers believe that autonomy is so important to young adults that every day is independence day and that differences with parent are a sign of their emerging maturity and independence. Third, as discussed earlier, people may be attracted to individuals who are somewhat challenging or hard to get yet attainable. Finally, if their love is especially strong, the partners can endure disapproval from the social network. Two people who are less in love might be quick to break up when parents and friends disapprove, making it unlikely that they would be together long enough to be in research study.

Keep in mind that the "Romeo and Juliet" effect does not always hold true. In Chapter 15, we report suggesting that some couples break up due to disapproval from parents and friends. Similarly, in Chapter 9, we report that involvement in each other's social network helps keep relational partners close. Sometimes, interference from others draws people closer together, but at other times, such interference tears them apart.

Proximity

Of all the environmental features that affect attraction, proximity has received the most research attention. This is not surprising. Proximity gives people the opportunity to meet and be attracted to one another. Have you ever thought that the perfect friend or romantic partner was somewhere out there but that you would never find her or him? If so, you were worried that lack of proximity would prevent you from meeting someone to whom you would be attracted.

Several studies have confirmed that proximity is extremely important in attraction and relationship development. The earliest set of studies was conducted by Festinger, who found that the location of college students' apartments affected who became friends (see Festinger, Schachter, & Back, 1950). Students who lived close to one another were much more likely to become friends than were students who lived in the same building but farther apart. Similarly, Newcomb's (1961) famous dormitory roommates study demonstrated a strong proximity effect during the second year, even though proximity did not affect attraction during the fist year. Newcomb's findings were especially intriguing because they suggested that proximity can outweigh similarity as a basis for attraction. Specifically, Newcomb paired half of the male undergraduates with similar others and the other half with dissimilar others (unbeknownst to the participants). Regardless of whether they were similar or dissimilar, the students were more likely to be friends with their roommates than with other dormitory residents.

The tendency for people to develop romantic relationships and friendships with individuals they meet in the workplace has also been attributed primarily to proximity. Indeed, 75% of the organizational members Dillard and Witteman (1985) surveyed could identify at least one workplace romance involving themselves or someone they knew. This statistic is not surprising given the amount of time most people spend in the workplace. As Westhoff (1985) puts it, "Corporate romance is as inevitable as earthquakes in California" (p. 21). Similarly, a *New York Post* article began with the declaration that the workplace is "the best dating service"

around ("The Best Dating Service," 1988, p. 14). Other times, work associates become close friends (Bridge & Baxter, 1992). Proximity is a major contributor to the development of these friendships, as is similarity and shared tasks (Sias & Cahill, 1998; Sias, Smith, & Avdeyera, 1999).

In sum, the effects of proximity are all around you. You are more likely to be friends with your neighbor than with someone who lives a few miles away, and you are more likely to marry someone you meet at work or school than someone you meet in a bar. This is because you have more opportunities to interact with and become attracted to people you see on a frequent basis.

SUMMARY AND APPLICATION

Many factors help determine your attraction to friends and romantic partners. Although knowledge of these factors does not guarantee that you will be attracted to the "right people," it should help you better understand why you are attracted to certain people and not others. You should also be aware of the ways you might stereotype people based on factors such as physical appearance, so that you will consider a more complete package of attributes when deciding whether to pursue a relationship with someone.

So what advice does the literature on attraction offer for individuals like Julie who are having trouble finding the right person? First, as the research on fatal attraction suggests, it is important to understand what is attractive to you over the long haul, rather than being lured by "flashbulb attraction." If you are attracted to someone only because he or she is opposite to you in some characteristics, research suggests, the attraction may not be lasting. People like Julie may find themselves in the same types of doomed relationships over and over again because they subconsciously choose partners based on initially attractive qualities that become fatal attractions rather than the more stable factors of social or relational attraction. Recognizing what qualities lead to fatal attraction in your relationships is the first step in breaking this cycle.

Second, it is important to recognize your own biases and preferences as well as common stereotypes such as the "what is beautiful is good hypothesis." For example, Julie may be attracted to especially good-looking men because she perceives them to have an array of positive attributes that they may or may not actually possess. When she discovers their negative attributes, she is likely to be disappointed. If she was less focused on physical appearance, she might find someone with whom she is more compatible on a social and relational level. Julie might also benefit from taking stock of what she would find rewarding in a long-term relationship. She might decide that qualities such as being able to spend quiet time together would be more rewarding to her than having a partner who likes to socialize all the time.

Third, it is important to remember that similarity and complementarity are important factors in the attraction process. Similarity in key characteristics that are important to you, such as family values or life philosophies, is a critical part of the recipe for relational success. Indeed, social attraction is only a starting point. After two people who are attracted to each other become initially acquainted, they usually have a long way to go before they develop a truly intimate relationship. Having core similarities will help sustain commitment over the long term. Complementarity can also be beneficial, especially when different abilities help partners get tasks done and different personality traits help sustain novelty. The key might be for differences to be helpful or exciting rather than distracting or distressing. In Julie and Steven's relationship, their personality differences in sociability were initially appealing but soon become distressing. Thus, this is an area where Julie might want to look for similarity rather than complementarity.

There is no magical way to determine if someone to whom you are attracted will be a true friend or a long-term romantic partner. There is also no magical formula regarding what to look for in a potential mate. However, the research presented in this chapter should help you better understand why you are more attracted to some people than others. Attraction can occur as quickly as a flash of lightning, or it can develop slowly over time. Either way, attraction often provides the initial stepping stone into new relationships that may become your closest encounters.

DISCUSSION QUESTIONS

1. Think about five people in your social network. What initially attracted you to these people? Do all the qualities you thought of fit into the framework discussed in this chapter, or are there factors you would add to the model?

2. In this chapter, we discussed an abundance of research on similarity as a force affecting attraction. Less research has been conducted on complementarity. Based on your own experiences, which old adage do you think is truer, "Birds of a feather flock together" or "Opposites attract"?

3. This chapter also discussed the importance of proximity in the attraction process. In long-distance relationships proximity is missing, which has led people to debate whether "absence makes the heart grow fonder" or "out of sight means out of mind." Based on your experiences, which of these sayings is truer?

4

MAKING SENSE OF OUR WORLD

Coping With Uncertainty and Expectancy Violations

Vish sat excitedly waiting for Serena to arrive for their Friday night date. He had spent all day cleaning his apartment and preparing dinner for her. This was going to be a special night that would draw Serena closer to him. She was supposed to arrive at 6:00, but 6:00 came and went and no Serena; 6:30, no Serena. That was odd; she had always been on time in the past. He called her cell, but there was no answer. 7:30 came and went, and still no Serena. By 8:00 he realized that she wouldn't be coming. He was really down. What was going on? Was Serena okay? Was this her way of ending the relationship before it became more intimate? Why would she do this to him? He went to bed feeling angry and confused and was surprised when Serena called in the morning. She sounded like nothing was wrong. "Hi! Vish," she said. "What's up? Did you do something fun last night?" Now, Vish was even more confused. "What?" he responded, with his frustration clear in his voice. "We had plans last night, and you blew me off, so no I didn't have fun last night."

Serena sounded genuinely surprised. "What do you mean?" she asked. "Our plans were for tonight, not last night!" Vish scanned his mind for any way he could have gotten the night wrong. Was she just trying to make something up to explain her absence last night? Or was it really just a misunderstanding?

This type of scenario may have happened to you. There are times in all relationships when expectations are violated and people experience uncertainty. For example, Vish expected Serena to show up on time (or at least not too late) for their date. When she violated this expectation he experienced uncertainty about her and their relationship.

Communication researchers have examined how both uncertainty and expectancy violations affect perceptions and behavior. In this chapter, we examine how uncertainty functions within initial interactions as well as established relationships. We also examine what happens when people's behavior deviates from expectations.

DEFINING UNCERTAINTY

Uncertainty has been studied in almost every discipline involving the investigation of human interaction. As a result, we know that our experience of the world is inextricably linked to our level of uncertainty. When we receive information that reduces uncertainty, we are more confident that we understand ourselves, other people, and the world around us. In most cases, the more information we have about someone, the more we feel we know that person. A lack of information, or information that violates expectations, often increases uncertainty. Given this book's focus on close relationships, our examination of uncertainty relates to relationships, but it is important to realize that uncertainty extends well beyond our relationships with others.

The first studies on uncertainty focused on understanding how strangers act in initial interaction, with **uncertainty** defined as the inability to predict or explain the attitudes and/or behaviors of someone (Berger & Calabrese, 1975). In other words, uncertainty is the extent to which someone believes that he or she does *not* know and understand someone. Berger and Calabrese theorized that information seeking helps people reduce uncertainty so that more information equates to less uncertainty. However, there are times when people have abundant information yet still feel uncertain (Brashers, 2001). Sometimes, the information people have is inconsistent. Other times, people feel uncertain because they "feel insecure in their own state of knowledge or the state of knowledge in general [about a topic]" despite having a lot of information (Brashers, 2001, p. 478). For example, part of Vish's uncertainty might stem from feeling that he doesn't understand women or relationships despite his many experiences with them. Thus, we define **high uncertainty** as feeling unsure or insecure about your ability to predict or explain someone's attitudes and behaviors. **Low uncertainty** occurs when people feel confident in their ability to predict and explain someone's behavior, often because they believe they know someone well. Note that *being confident and secure* about

one's explanations and predictions is the key feature in these definitions.

So far, our definition of uncertainty has focused on uncertainty about a partner. People also experience uncertainty about themselves and their relationships. Knobloch and Solomon have found that uncertainty in relational contexts revolves around three primary questions (for review, see Knobloch & Solomon, 1999, 2002a, 2005). First, sometimes people are uncertain about their own feelings and how involved they want to be in the relationship (self-uncertainty). For example, after Serena failed to show up, Vish may question how much he really likes her. Second, people may be uncertain about their partner's feelings and intentions (partner uncertainty), including whether their partner reciprocates their feelings (Knobloch & Solomon, 1999). Finally, people are uncertain about the state of their relationship, in general (relationship uncertainty). In particular, Knobloch and Solomon (1999) noted that people often experience uncertainty about relationship definitions (Are we casually dating, or is the relationship more serious?), the future of the relationship (Is this relationship likely to last? Will we eventually marry?), the types of behaviors that are acceptable versus unacceptable with a relationship (Vish may have initially wondered how tolerant he should be of Serena's tardiness), and other behavioral norms (Are we sexually exclusive? How much of our free time should we spend together versus apart?).

A person's level of relational uncertainty affects how we communicate with others. In a study by Knobloch (2006), university students came to a research lab and imagined that they were calling their romantic partner to make plans for a date. Knobloch then had them call a specified phone number and leave their message on a rigged answering machine. Students who reported elevated levels of relational uncertainty left messages that were less skilled and fluent than students who reported low levels of relational uncertainty. Moreover, the messages left by students who were low in relational uncertainty were rated as more effective. This study suggests that relational uncertainty unconsciously comes through in the way we talk to our partners.

UNCERTAINTY REDUCTION IN INITIAL ENCOUNTERS

The connection between uncertainty and communication is highlighted in Berger and Calabrese's (1975) **uncertainty reduction theory**. This was the first communication theory to focus on uncertainty and arguably the first interpersonal communication theory. Berger and Calabrese maintained that the driving force in initial encounters is obtaining information about the other person to get to know her or him better and, ultimately, to reduce uncertainty. Berger and Calabrese laid out a clear, testable theory, and Berger, among others, has conducted numerous studies to further test and modify the original theory (Berger, 1979, 1988, 1993; Berger & Douglas, 1981; Berger & Kellermann, 1983). Although the original theory offered 7 general predictions and 21 more specific predictions, in this chapter we will focus on three general principles that provide a foundation for the theory.

Information Seeking and Uncertainty Reduction

The first principle is that *people seek information to reduce uncertainty during initial encounters with others*. Berger and Calabrese argued that our reason for behaving the way we do during initial interactions with strangers is simple: We want to get to know them better. Not only do we *want* to get to know them, but also we *have* to get to know them better if we hope to reduce uncertainty, increase predictability, and create order in our world. In other words, they claimed that we dislike situations in which we are not sure about the outcome and act as "naive scientists" who gather information and sort through alternative explanations to better understand the people around us. In initial interaction, we ask one another basic questions to establish commonalities and gain understanding because this type of information helps us get acquainted and reduces uncertainty. As others tell us about themselves, we feel more confident in our ability to predict how they think and act. As a result, we feel more comfortable in the interaction. Initially, however, we ask

"superficial" questions and engage in small talk. But small talk is important because this type of communication helps give us a sense of how the other person acts and thinks. In addition, by sticking to superficial topics, we can keep some things about ourselves private until we know the other person better and feel more comfortable disclosing more information about ourselves.

According to uncertainty reduction theory, the more bits of information we have about someone, and the more we "know" her or him, the better we should be able to predict that person's attitudes and behaviors. Thus, as communication increases, uncertainty about the person with whom we are interacting should decrease. We should be more certain about someone after spending 20 minutes with that person than after spending 5 minutes because we will have had four times as much time to seek information about him or her. Indeed, several studies have confirmed that uncertainty is related to the number of questions people ask and the amount of time they spend interacting. Douglas (1990a) put unacquainted college students in same-sex pairs and asked them to interact for 2, 4, or 6 minutes. After the interactions, the participants completed a measure of confidence in their ability to predict the other person's behavior and attitudes. The uncertainty levels of those who interacted for 6 minutes were much lower than the levels of those who interacted for just 2 minutes. Douglas also found that the students who asked more questions were more confident, suggesting that the amount of communication (in terms of responses to questions) was related to decreases in uncertainty. Other researchers extended the interaction time to a maximum of 16 minutes and obtained relatively similar results for the first 6 minutes but did not find that uncertainty decreased significantly from the 8th to the 16th minute of interaction (Redmond & Virchota, 1994). Apparently, people gather information rather quickly during initial interactions and then stick with their initial impressions.

In another study, Douglas (1990b) had students interact with a same-sex stranger for 4 minutes, after which they completed a survey measuring their uncertainty. He analyzed their conversations for the amount of self-disclosure and found that the participants' uncertainty reduction was directly related to the amount of information disclosed by their interaction partner. As the amount of the first person's disclosure increased, the second person's uncertainty decreased. This study supports uncertainty reduction theory's prediction that communication decreases uncertainty.

Strategies for Reducing Uncertainty

The second principle is that *people can reduce uncertainty using passive, active, or interactive strategies.* According to uncertainty reduction theory, people often reduce uncertainty using strategies other than face-to-face or direct communication. Specifically, Berger and his colleagues identified three general ways people go about reducing uncertainty in initial encounters.

Passive Strategies. People who rely on nonintrusive observation of individuals are using passive strategies (Berger, 1979, 1987) that involve behaviors such as looking at someone sitting alone to see if a friend or date comes along, observing how a person interacts with others, or paying attention to the kinds of clothes a person wears. For example, on the basis of observation, you might make assumptions about someone's age, their relational status (Are they physically close to someone else? Are they wearing a ring?), and personality, among many other characteristics.

Passive observations are most likely to be effective and informative when they are conducted in an informal setting, like a party, rather than in a formal setting, like a classroom or business office (Berger & Douglas, 1981). Moreover, people usually make more accurate judgments when watching someone interact with others than when sitting alone. Most people are constrained in formal settings because behavioral rules in these situations are fairly strict. For example, it is unusual to see people behave inappropriately in a fancy restaurant or during a business meeting. In contrast, people act in unique, personal ways at an informal party because the "rules" are less rigid. When people are relaxed and interacting in an informal setting, their natural selves typically emerge. Therefore it is more informative, and consequently much more uncertainty reducing, to observe someone in an informal, as opposed to a formal, setting. When passive observation strategies become compulsive, stalking or relational intrusion is the result (see Chapter 13).

Active Strategies. Often, our strategies for uncertainty reduction are more active. Berger and Calabrese identified two forms of active uncertainty reduction strategy. One type involves purposefully manipulating the social environment in a certain way and then observing how someone reacts to this manipulation. The information seeker may not be part of the manipulated situation, although he or she sets the situation up. These tactics are like mini experiments conducted with the intent of seeking information about the target person. For example, one student of ours used an active strategy on her boyfriend by typing a letter phrased as if it had come from another female admirer of her boyfriend. The letter included a request that they meet at a certain place and time and was signed "your secret admirer." She then placed this letter on the windshield of her boyfriend's car. She had two goals in mind when she did this: (1) She wanted to see if her boyfriend would tell her that he received such a letter and (2) she wanted to check whether he would show up at the location in search of this fictitious person. (In case you are wondering, he did not tell her about the letter, but he also never showed up to meet the fictitious person.) Several other students in our classes have admitted to using similar active uncertainty reduction strategies with their dating partners (e.g., flirting with someone else to see how their partner reacts) or leaving your relational partner alone with your attractive roommate! Serena could also have been using a form of this strategy if she intentionally decided to stand Vish up to see how he would react, thereby reducing her uncertainty about his personality and his commitment. This type of information-seeking strategy is useful because it can help reduce uncertainty without the need to rely on more direct methods. Of course, such manipulative attempts could backfire in the long run, making the person look paranoid and/or communicating distrust to her or his partner.

The second type of active uncertainty reduction strategy involves asking third parties (friends, family members) about the person in question. We often ask friends if they have heard anything about a particular person of interest or ask for help in interpreting something that person did. In fact, one study found that 30% of the information we have about someone comes from asking others (Hewes, Graham, Doelger, & Pavitt, 1985). For example, before starting to see Serena, Vish may have asked her friends whether she was seeing anyone, whether she ever mentioned any interest in him, or whether she'd consider going out with him. Box 4.1 details one increasingly popular method of obtaining information about people.

Interactive Strategies. The third general type of uncertainty reduction strategy is interactive (Berger, 1979, 1987). Interactive strategies involve direct contact between the information seeker and the target. Common interactive strategies include asking questions, encouraging disclosure, and relaxing the target. We are especially likely to ask such questions the first time we meet someone. In studies of behavior during initial interactions, researchers have found that the frequency of question asking drops over time, coinciding with decreases in our level of uncertainty (Douglas, 1990a; Kellermann, 1995).

It is important to note, though, that the questions being asked in initial interactions are usually very general. Research suggests that we hesitate to ask questions about intimate issues until we have a close relationship with the person and even then may avoid asking direct questions (Bell & Buerkel-Rothfuss, 1990). Studies have also shown that people sometimes disclose information about themselves with the specific hope that their disclosure will encourage the other person to do the same (Berger, 1979). Note, however, that we use disclosure as an uncertainty reduction strategy only after we reach a certain level of comfort in being able to predict the other person's attitudes and behaviors

---

BOX 4.1   Highlights

"Hired Help": Today's Relationship Information Seekers

More and more, we hear stories of people hiring "relationship detectives" to check out their current or potential mates. Open the Yellow Pages or search the Web, and you will find long lists of agencies or people willing, for a fee, to investigate your significant other for anything from infidelity to use of a false identity. In essence, these agencies are offering you the opportunity to reduce your uncertainty without having to personally work at it. Their list of services is long. For additional fees, they can do a variety of "spy" activities, including videotaping the target (maybe catching him or her leaving a third party's residence or flirting with someone at a bar) and hiring a member of the opposite sex to approach him or her in a bar or restaurant and proposition him or her for a date and/or sex.

By hiring an agency to spy on your significant other, you are reducing uncertainty the easy way. The difficulties of interactive uncertainty reduction are replaced by passive (in the case of videotapes) or active (in the case in which they simply relay to you what they saw or have another individual flirt with him or her) strategies. More important, you don't have to do guesswork on the truthfulness of the information you are receiving from the third party, as typically is the case with the use of active uncertainty-reduction methods. Also, you don't have to decide whether the behavior you are observing is a reflection of the person's true character, because they videotape the person without his or her knowledge and do so in informal settings. Of course, the ethics of such practices and the implications of such distrust for the relationship's future are important issues for people choosing this tactic. But the fact remains that our need to reduce uncertainty in relationships has spawned a burgeoning industry of information seekers for hire.

and enough trust to disclose ourselves. This comfort level is typically reached through the general questions that are so common during initial interactions. Finally, people sometimes try to relax the target so that she or he feels comfortable revealing information. People sometimes offer drugs or alcohol to achieve this effect. However, examples of less manipulative strategies include creating a comfortable environment that is conducive to talking, smiling a lot, giving a deep massage, or acting interested to get the other person talking (Berger, 1979).

As these examples suggest, interactive strategies are not limited to verbal communication. We often reduce our uncertainty about someone through nonverbal cues (Kellerman & Berger, 1984). For instance, if you smile at and make eye contact with someone across a room and the person motions you to come over, a clear message has been sent and received. That one motioning gesture provides considerable information and uncertainty reduction. Vish communicated much of his feelings to Serena just through his voice—angry intonation and abruptness, both nonverbal components. In fact, nonverbal behaviors can be the primary method of communicating our thoughts and feelings about other people and our relationships with them (Andersen, 1999; Burgoon et al., 1996). For example, research on sexual behavior (see Chapter 7) has shown that the primary way we go about discovering whether a partner is interested in escalating the level of sexual activity— that is, reducing our uncertainty about the person's sexual desires—is through nonverbal cues. So although much of the research on interactive uncertainty reduction methods has focused on verbal strategies, we often engage in nonverbal interactions that are potentially uncertainty reducing.

Of course, people use multiple uncertainty reduction strategies during a single interaction. Let's imagine that Vish did this when he first met Serena. Suppose he spotted Serena in a bar. After observing her for a minute, Vish thought she was probably a fellow college student, seemed very outgoing, and did not have other males around her (passive strategy), so he sent over a drink in hopes of receiving positive feedback to his gesture (active strategy using manipulation of the environment). The waiter brought her the drink and pointed over to Vish.

Serena took the drink, glanced at Vish, and appeared to smile slightly. When the waiter walked back past Vish's table, Vish asked him if she said anything (active strategy using a third party). The waiter said that she didn't but that she looked pleased. Now that Vish had reduced his initial uncertainty somewhat, he felt confident enough to take the next step, so he approached Serena and started engaging in conversation with her (interactive strategy).

Uncertainty and Attraction

The third principle is that as *uncertainty decreases, attraction usually increases.* According to uncertainty reduction theory, knowledge about someone is directly tied to our uncertainty about him or her. So the more we know someone, the less our uncertainty. The theory also argues that this reduction in uncertainty generally leads us to like the person more. Remember that Berger and Calabrese argued that we are uncomfortable with uncertainty and will therefore be motivated to gain information so as to better predict and explain our partner's behavior. Therefore, it also makes sense that we would be less attracted to people whose behavior we can't predict and with whom we have high uncertainty.

Research generally supports this prediction. In most cases, we are more attracted to people when we can predict their behavior (for a review, see Douglas, 1990a, or Kellermann & Reynolds, 1990). This association between attraction and uncertainty also appears to hold for members of different cultures. In fact, Gudykunst and his colleagues have argued that elevated uncertainty is one reason that many people feel less attracted to members of other cultures (see, e.g., Gudykunst & Nishida, 1984). According to this perspective, you feel more uncertain and anxious around people from other cultures simply because you are unsure of their cultural norms and customs. This uncertainty could prevent you from developing an attraction for these people.

However, when uncertainty is reduced, people from different cultures are often attracted to one another. Gudykunst (1988, 1989), in his theory of **intergroup uncertainty reduction,** described several conditions that make it more likely that uncertainty will be reduced in intercultural interactions.

First, he argued that people who identify strongly with their own group identity feel more confident about interaction with someone from a different social or cultural group. Second, when people perceive members of another culture favorably, they are likely to look forward to interacting with them. These two factors combine to create a communication climate that makes information exchange and uncertainty reduction easier. For example, imagine visiting Brazil for the first time. If you are confident about your own cultural identity and are looking forward to communicating with Brazilians, you are likely to be comfortable and open during interactions, which will likely lead to uncertainty reduction and increased liking. In contrast, if you are unsure about your role as a person in a foreign country and you dread interacting with people who speak a different language, you are likely to avoid interaction and to remain uncertain and anxious.

Although getting to know people better often leads to attraction and liking, as both uncertainty reduction and Gudykunst's theory of intergroup uncertainty reduction predict, there are times when uncertainty reduction leads to less attraction and liking. Think about your own experiences in initial encounters. You can probably recall times when, as you found out more about someone, you decided that you disliked that person rather than liking her or him more. For example, you might learn that someone you just met is a liar and a cheat or has extreme political views. Such a discovery reduces your uncertainty about your new acquaintance, but it probably doesn't increase your attraction. Similarly, if someone makes a tasteless, offensive remark, it is likely to reduce your uncertainty about the kind of person he or she is, but it is also likely to decrease your attraction. This idea that uncertainty reduction does not always lead to attraction is among the important challenges that scholars have raised in theories about uncertainty. We will discuss others in more detail later in the chapter, but first, we will summarize a theory that was developed in response to uncertainty reduction theory's claims that the primary motivation in initial interactions is the reduction of uncertainty.

PREDICTED OUTCOMES IN INITIAL ENCOUNTERS

An alternative to uncertainty reduction theory, called **predicted outcome value theory** (Sunnafrank, 1986, 1990), is based on the idea that people are not driven by a need to reduce uncertainty in all cases. Instead, whether we seek more information depends on whether outcome values are positive or negative. In this theory, **outcome values** relate to our predictions about how rewarding or unrewarding future interactions with a particular person would be. People are judged as having a **high outcome value** when they are perceived to be more rewarding than other potential partners. For example, when Vish first met Serena he might have perceived her to be more self-confident and physically attractive than other women he could date. This perception of Serena's high outcome value would lead Vish to ask her out. When people have a **low outcome value**, they are perceived to be less rewarding than other potential partners. Suppose that when Vish first approached Serena she seemed cold and arrogant. Obviously, if Vish had perceived Serena this way, he would have little desire to reduce uncertainty with her, he would have been much less likely to ask her out, and he would have likely looked for a more rewarding partner.

According to Sunnafrank's theory, we initially reduce uncertainty as a way of finding out how we feel about a person or an interaction. After that, the positive or negative outcome value becomes the driving force behind whether we try to seek further information. Thus, when someone reveals negative information to us during an initial encounter, we are likely to predict negative outcome values and to cut off communication with that person. Put another way, when outcome values are positive, we will be motivated to seek information; when outcome values are negative, we will decrease communication and stop seeking information. Therefore, according to predicted outcome theory, the relationship between uncertainty reduction and attraction might be better stated as follows: When uncertainty is reduced by learning positive information about someone, attraction increases; when uncertainty is reduced by learning negative information about someone, attraction decreases. Although predicted outcome value theory focuses on initial interaction, this reasoning may apply to more developed or well-established relationships. Think back to the scenario with Vish and Serena. Vish's belief that Serena stood him up could dramatically affect his perception of how rewarding it would be to interact with Serena in the future. If Vish reduced uncertainty by concluding that a future relationship with Serena would be filled with late arrivals, forgotten dates, anxiety, and frustration, his feelings of attraction would decrease.

Research has supported the idea that predicted outcome values are an important predictor of communication in initial encounters. People are more likely to engage in positive communication when their partner has a high outcome value. They are also more likely to attempt to continue interaction and communicate in future. In contrast, people restrict information and work to discourage future interaction when a partner has a low outcome value (Sunnafrank, 1986). In one study, students engaged in brief first conversations with another student at the beginning of the semester (Sunnafrank & Ramirez, 2004). The level of outcome value the students associated with their conversational partner after these brief, early interactions predicted later communication and relationship development. Specifically, when a student evaluated the conversational partner as having high reward value, he or she was much more likely to develop a relationship with the partner over the course of the semester.

Uncertainty in Established Relationships

Although uncertainty reduction may be an especially prominent goal in initial encounters, uncertainty can pervade even the closest of our relationships. Indeed, Berger (1988, 1993) has argued that people feel a need to reduce uncertainty at various stages of a relationship's development and decline. Planalp and Honeycutt (1985) conducted a study to determine when people in established relationships experienced uncertainty. Specifically, they asked students whether they could recall a time when they learned something surprising about a friend, spouse, or dating partner that made them question the relationship. Ninety percent of the respondents in this study were able to recall such an instance, thus strongly supporting the claim that certain behaviors increase, rather than decrease, uncertainty, even in developed relationships. These data suggest that, contrary to the original theory, communication can increase as well as decrease uncertainty. The researchers then categorized the responses into six uncertainty-increasing behaviors:

1. *Competing relationships* included the discovery that a friend or dating partner wanted to spend time with someone else.

2. *Unexplained loss of contact or closeness* occurred when communication and/or intimacy decreased for no particular reason.

3. *Sexual behavior* included discovering that a friend or dating partner engaged in sexual behavior with another person.

4. *Deception* involved discovering that friends or dating partners had lied, fabricated information, or been misleading.

5. *Change in personality/value* occurred when people realized that their friends or dating partners were different from what they used to be.

6. *Betraying confidences* included instances in which people's friends or dating partners disclosed private information to others about them without their consent.

For all six types of behavior, the participants felt less able to predict their friend or dating partner's attitudes and behaviors following these events than they had before these events took place. In other words, they felt as if they "knew them less" following the behavior than they did prior to it. Studies confirm the high incidence of such uncertainty-increasing behaviors in close relationships. For example, one study found that 80% of marriages included uncertainty-increasing events (Turner, 1990).

The method that Planalp and Honeycutt (1985) used is worth noting. They asked participants to think about something "surprising." In fact, earlier, Berger (1979) suggested that unexpected (or surprising) behaviors increase uncertainty, and this study seems to support his claim. When people do something unexpected, we are sometimes *less* able to predict their attitudes and behaviors. For example, Vish's uncertainty about

Serena increased after his night alone waiting for her. If they had actually agreed to get together the next day, then Serena's uncertainty about Vish also would have likely increased because she may have been surprised by his absentmindedness and his anger.

These sorts of examples led Berger (1993) to claim that unexpected behaviors led to increases in uncertainty. But let's examine that claim. Think about behaviors that fit in any of the six uncertainty-increasing categories. It is easy to see how they might increase uncertainty, but might they not also

---

▨ BOX 4.2   Put Yourself to the Test

The Attributional Confidence Scale

Respond to the following questions by circling the appropriate number. When responding, think of a specific person, such as a good friend or romantic partner.

1. How confident are you of your general ability to predict how he/she will behave?

   Not confident at all   1   2   3   4   5   6   7   Very confident

2. How certain are you that he/she likes you?

   Not certain at all   1   2   3   4   5   6   7   Very certain

3. How accurate are you at predicting the values he/she holds?

   Not accurate at all   1   2   3   4   5   6   7   Very accurate

4. How accurate are you at predicting his/her attitudes?

   Not accurate at all   1   2   3   4   5   6   7   Very accurate

5. How well can you predict his/her feelings and emotions?

   Not well at all   1   2   3   4   5   6   7   Very well

6. How much can you empathize with (share) the way he/she feels about himself/herself?

   Not much at all   1   2   3   4   5   6   7   Very much

7. How well do you know him/her?

   Not well at all   1   2   3   4   5   6   7   Very well

Add up your scores for the seven items. The maximum score is 49, and the minimum score is 7. The closer your score is to 49, the more certain and confident you are. The closer your score is to 7, the more uncertain you are about your prediction. (You might want to re-answer these questions later in the semester to see if your certainty level changes.)

SOURCE: Adapted from Clatterbuck, G. W., Attributional confidence and uncertainty in initial interaction, in *Journal of Human Communication Research* (5). Copyright © 1979 by the International Communication Association. Reprinted with permission.

reduce uncertainty in some cases? Couldn't these behaviors sometimes make us feel as if we now know how the person *really* is? To illustrate, suppose a friend lied to you about his past. The fact that he lied about such an important issue may tell you a lot about the kind of person he is. Discovering that lie may not increase your uncertainty, but may actually reduce it. Similarly, Serena might think that she now knows the *real* Vish after she hears him react the way he did on the phone. These counterexamples leave us with the question of whether all surprising events increase uncertainty or whether some actually reduce uncertainty. Clearly, uncertainty is a complex and sometimes paradoxical concept. Sometimes, behaviors that initially increase our uncertainty might reduce uncertainty in the long run, and sometimes these unexpected behaviors may even cause us to like someone more. Box 4.2 contains a scale you can use to see how much certainty you perceive to exist in one of your relationships.

Secret Tests

Regardless of whether uncertainty-reducing events lead to more positive or negative evaluations of a relational partner, such events often provoke a desire to seek more information. For instance, it is natural to wonder *why* your partner is suddenly showering you with unexpected gifts or is constantly staying out late and forgetting to call you. In these situations, people in established relationships often use passive, active, and interactive strategies that are similar to those mentioned earlier in this chapter. But relational partners also have a number of other more specific strategies at their disposal. In a particularly insightful look at uncertainty reduction in ongoing relationships, Baxter and Wilmot (1985) described seven sets of "secret tests" that people use to reduce their uncertainty about their partner's commitment to the relationship:

1. *Asking-third-party tests.* This strategy relies on feedback from social network members. This test is virtually identical to one of the active strategies described earlier. For example, a week after the "date that never was," Serena might ask Vish's best friend if he is still mad at her.

2. *Directness tests.* This strategy involves direct interaction with the partner. This test is similar to the interactive strategies described earlier. Here, Serena would go directly to Vish and ask him if he is still angry with her.

3. *Triangle tests.* This strategy is intended to test the partner's commitment to the relationship by creating three-person triangles. Fidelity checks (such as seeing if the partner responds to a fictitious "secret admirer" note) and jealousy tests (such as flirting with someone else to see how the partner responds) are two examples of triangle tests.

4. *Separation tests.* This strategy relies on creating physical distance between relational partners. The two primary methods are having a long period of physical separation (such as seeing if your relationship can survive a summer of not seeing each other) and ceasing contact for an extended period of time to see how long it takes for your partner to call.

5. *Endurance tests.* This strategy increases the costs or reduces the rewards for the other person in the relationship. One such test, known as "testing limits," involves seeing how much the partner will endure. For instance, someone might dress down, become argumentative, start arriving late for dates, or fail to call at a designated time to see if the partner stays committed despite these irritations. Another test, known as "self-put-downs," involves putting yourself down to see if the partner responds by offering positive feedback. For example, Chan may say that he feels overweight in the hope that Hong will try to convince him that he looks great, thus indicating her support for him.

6. *Public presentation tests.* This strategy involves watching for the other person's reaction to the use of certain relational labels or actions. It is most commonly used in the early stages of a relationship. It is typified by the first public presentation of a partner as your "boyfriend" or "girlfriend" (whereas before, the partner may have been introduced only as a "friend"), or by holding hands on a date, then observing the partner's reaction. Public presentation tests that might occur later in the relationship include asking someone to wear

a ring or a varsity jacket, or asking someone to spend the holidays with your family.

7. *Indirect suggestion tests.* This strategy involves using hinting or joking to bring up a topic without taking direct responsibility. The partner's response then gives you insight into his or her feelings about the issue. For example, Allison might joke about moving in with Peter to check his reaction to the issue. Although Allison may have been truly thinking about moving in, the fact that she said it as a joke gives her an "out" that allows her to save face if Peter rejects the idea. Or Allison could say, "I wonder what color our kid's eye will be," and then observes Peter's reaction. These tactics allow Allison to seek information about Peter's attitudes toward cohabiting with her or his interest in marriage.

These categories of secret tests were derived from interviews with college students who were asked to discuss information acquisition strategies that they used in one of three relationship types: (1) a platonic opposite-sex friendship, (2) an opposite-sex friendship with romantic potential, or (3) a romantic relationship. Beyond identifying these secret tests, Baxter and Wilmot's (1985) study revealed an important point about our behavior in relationships—namely, the vast majority of uncertainty reduction strategies in relationships are indirect. The image of relationships as completely open and of partners as totally direct was refuted by this study. In fact, only 22% of the students who reported on a romantic relationship listed direct strategies as a tactic they used to reduce their uncertainty. In contrast, 34% said they used triangle tests and 33% reported using endurance tests in their romantic relationships. Especially interesting is the extent to which indirectness was used in friendships with romantic potential. Consistent with research showing these relationships to be ambiguous and uncertain (O'Meara, 1989), the students who were reporting on a relationship with romantic potential were more likely than those reporting on the other relationship types to mention separation tests and indirect suggestion tests as information-seeking strategies. Perhaps this is because relationships with romantic potential are still developing and are more prone to uncertainty than are stable friendships or romantic relationships.

Other researchers have shown that people are also more likely to use indirect secret tests in the early stages of dating relationships, when using direct information-seeking strategies may be riskier than they are later in the relationship (Bell & Buerkel-Rothfuss, 1990). For example, Emmers and Canary (1996) found that when romantic couples wanted to repair their relationship after encountering an uncertainty-increasing event such as deception or infidelity, they used direct or interactive strategies more often than passive or active strategies.

People use a variety of direct strategies in response to uncertainty-increasing events in established relationships (Bachman & Guerrero, 2006a; Emmers & Canary, 1996; Knobloch & Solomon, 2003). Sometimes, people use relationship talk or integrative communication, such as questioning the partner or discussing the state of the relationship. Other times, people try to maintain the relationship through closeness or being romantic. Some people engage in conflict or distributive communication, such as arguing or making accusations. People also use indirect strategies, such as avoidance (not talking about the issue or doing nothing about it), distancing (pulling away from the partner), or loyalty (passively waiting for the issue to be resolved).

People are more likely to use direct and positive strategies, such as integrative communication and displays of closeness or romance, when they are in an intimate relationship. Specifically, a study by Knobloch (2005) examined the strategies people used in response to uncertainty-increasing events in close relationships. Her results showed that our reactions are influenced by the existing level of relational intimacy and by our emotional responses to the event. When people reported high levels of intimacy, they were more likely to use positive and closeness-enhancing strategies and to refrain from using distancing behaviors. In contrast, anger and sadness were associated with harmful and avoidant responses, respectively.

These findings also raise interesting questions. For example, we know that the people who are closest to us have the greatest capacity to affect us emotionally. We also know that uncertainty-increasing events in close relationships are often negative in nature. So what happens when a partner with whom we feel a lot of intimacy (which seems to encourage closeness-enhancing responses to uncertainty-increasing events) does something that saddens or angers us (which encourages distancing responses)?

Research that has looked at how people respond to events such as deception, infidelity, and other forms of betrayal provides preliminary answers to this question. This research suggests that people are *most* likely to respond positively under the following four conditions: the relationship was previously satisfying, the partner was previously considered to be rewarding, the event produced low levels of uncertainty, and the event did not represent a highly negative violation of expectancies (Bachman & Guerrero, 2006a; Guerrero & Bachman, in press-b; see also Chapter 13). This suggests that people in highly intimate and satisfying relationships are more likely to use positive strategies to deal with uncertainty. However, even in satisfying relationships, if the event is regarded as especially negative and produces lots of uncertainty, people often respond with destructive communication or distancing.

Uncertainty Reduction and Relational Satisfaction

As discussed earlier, in initial interactions uncertainty reduction generally increases attraction as long as the information obtained is positive. Therefore, it is reasonable to suspect that uncertainty reduction might also be associated with satisfaction in established relationships. However, research suggests that high levels of either uncertainty or certainty can decrease relational satisfaction.

One study in particular (Parks & Adelman, 1983) showed that too much uncertainty may have a negative impact on relationships. In this study, Parks and Adelman surveyed students who were currently in romantic relationships for an average of 1½ years, about their attraction to and uncertainty about their partner, among other variables. They then contacted these students 3 months later and asked them similar questions. Their results confirmed the predicted negative link between uncertainty and both attraction and satisfaction in relationships. In fact, the respondents who reported being uncertain about their partner on the first questionnaire were more likely to have ended their relationship than were the respondents who had initially felt relatively low uncertainty.

Conversely, other research suggests that too much certainty can also have a negative impact on relationships. According to this line of reasoning, knowing someone too well can become boring or unstimulating. Relationships that stagnate are usually characterized by a lack of uncertainty, as well as lack of growth. Being able to predict everything that someone is going to do or say is not necessarily a good thing, and some uncertainty may help keep the relationship exciting (Livingstone, 1980). One of the reasons that many heterosexual individuals enjoy cross-sex friendships is that there is often a sense of uncertainty or mystery about where the relationship is going. But that sense of mystery and excitement may eventually fade if the friendship turns romantic. Similarly, some people thrive on roller-coaster-type relationships that are hot one day and cold the next. For these individuals, uncertainty keeps the relationship challenging and exciting. Even in more stable relationships it is important to keep things from becoming too predictable.

The importance of both stability and excitement is also captured in **dialectics theory** (Baxter, 1990; Baxter & Montgomery, 1996; see also Chapter 9). According to this theory, people have opposing interpersonal needs. For example, people want to be close and connected to others, but they also want to be independent. People want to tell others about themselves, but they also want to keep some information private. Similarly, scholars adopting the dialectical perspective believe that we want both certainty (predictability) and uncertainty (novelty) in our relationships. Too much certainty or uncertainty can erode a relationship over time. Indeed, there is considerable evidence to support this claim. We don't like to be in situations in which we know everything about our partner, to hear the same stories again and again, or go through the same intimacy routines, because it produces boredom. But we also don't like situations in which we can't predict what our partner is going to do from day to day, because that produces stress. Instead, we want a bit of both ends of this dialectic. As a result, people often swing back and forth between wanting more excitement/ novelty and wanting more stability/predictability in their relationships.

Uncertainty Across Relationship Stages

As dialectics theory suggests, uncertainty levels are likely to fluctuate throughout the course of a relationship. Such fluctuations may be especially likely at certain stages of relationship development. Solomon and her colleagues introduced a **model of relational turbulence** that revolves around the idea that the transition from causal dating to commitment is unsettled and fraught with uncertainty (Knobloch & Donovan-Kicken, 2006; Solomon & Knobloch, 2001, 2004; Theiss & Solomon, 2006). The "turbulent" nature of this period, they suggest, comes from the partners' efforts to renegotiate their level of interdependence (see Chapter 10). The process of spending more time together and renegotiating the nature of the relationship brings with it increases in irritations. These irritations also come at about the time that a decision is being made about whether to increase commitment—a time that increases relational uncertainty and is marked by turbulence.

The model of relational turbulence proposes a different conception of communication in relationships from the original version of uncertainty reduction theory. Specifically, Solomon and her colleagues argue that relational uncertainty peaks in the middle stages of relationships, with relational doubts highest when couples are deciding whether to escalate their casual relationship into a more committed relationship. This is in contrast to early work on uncertainty reduction, which assumed that uncertainty is highest in the initial stages of relationships. Of course, various types of uncertainty may characterize different stages of a relationship. Uncertainty about another person's general beliefs, attitudes, and behavior may dominate initial encounters, whereas uncertainty about the relationship and the partner's feelings and intentions may dominate the transition from a casual to more committed relationship.

It is also important to note that studies have shown mixed support for the model of relational turbulence (for review, see Knobloch, in press). One study showed the predicted upturn in uncertainty during the middle stage of relationships, but two other studies showed that uncertainty gradually decreased as relationships developed, much as the original uncertainty reduction theory would predict (i.e., the longer that you are with your partner, the less uncertainty you have about him or her). The findings for irritations across relational stages have been more consistent, with the middle stages of a relationship shown to be marked by increased irritation as predicted by the model of relational turbulence. Across studies, increased uncertainty was shown to accompany increased irritation. The inconsistency in these findings might suggest that some couples experience relatively smooth transitions from casual to committed relationships, whereas others experience considerable turbulence.

FACTORS AFFECTING MOTIVATION TO SEEK INFORMATION

All the research discussed so far in this chapter is rooted in the assumption that people have a strong need to reduce uncertainty by seeking information, particularly during initial encounters and the early stages of relationships. In fact, the basic idea underlying uncertainty reduction theory is that we have a need to predict people's behaviors and that this need drives our constant search for information. But is that a valid assumption? Are we always motivated to find out more information? Or, as dialectics theory suggests, are we sometimes happier with some uncertainty?

The past 10 years have seen a mushrooming of research about the connection between uncertainty and our motivation to seek information. We will start our summary by noting the three conditions that Berger (1979) discussed as influencing that motivation, then move to an elaboration of recent theories that speak to our motivation to seek information.

High Incentive Value

The first condition for uncertainty reduction to occur is that there must be high incentive value that (Berger, 1979). In other words, people are particularly interested in reducing uncertainty about individuals who can provide them with important rewards and/or satisfy important needs. Thus people are likely to have a lot of incentive to reduce uncertainty about a potential romantic partner, a boss, or someone who appears to have a great personality and would make a good friend; but they are likely to have little incentive to reduce uncertainty with strangers or other people who are likely to have little impact on their lives. This logic is similar to Sunnafrank's (1986) reasoning in predicted outcome value theory: People are most motivated to seek information when they see the partner as a rewarding and likable person.

But does this condition always hold? Sometimes we are motivated to seek information about people we dislike, especially if they can affect our lives in some way. Think about your enemies. Have you ever wanted to dig up some "dirt" about someone you really disliked? Have you ever wanted to get to know why someone you dislike did what she or he did? Conversely, sometimes we don't want to seek information about people we really like. For example, people sometimes seem to prefer staying blissfully ignorant about their partner's infidelities rather than seeking information. Afifi and Burgoon (1998) argued that we often avoid finding out whether that friend of ours who we'd like to start dating is interested in the same because of fears she or he doesn't share the sentiment. Think about Vish in the scenario that opened this chapter—Does he really want to know whether Serena purposefully stood him up? The answer might be too painful. In other words, even in cases where incentive is high, we may sometimes choose to avoid the reduction of uncertainty.

Deviations From Expected Behavior

The second condition focuses on deviations from expected behavior, which Berger (1979) predicted increase in information seeking. If someone behaves in an unexpected or unpredictable way, Berger argued, our curiosity and need for predictability will increase. According to this principle, then, Vish is likely to feel uncertain and seek information about Serena's unexpected behavior.

Again, some research has questioned whether this condition applies universally. Later in this chapter, we discuss other research related to expectancy violations. As you will see, unexpected behavior has been shown to sometimes decrease uncertainty as well as increase it, with differential impact on the motivation to seek information.

Anticipation of Future Interaction

The third condition for uncertainty reduction to occur involves whether or not we anticipate future interaction. Berger (1979) predicted that the anticipation of future interaction provides strong motivation to seek information. Our interest in reducing uncertainty about people is heightened when we expect to see them again. If we do not think that we will ever see the person again, we will have little interest in better getting to know her or him. Several studies confirm that anticipation of future interaction is an important influence on our motivation to reduce uncertainty and to seek information (Douglas, 1985, 1990a; Kellermann & Reynolds, 1990). Research has shown that we consider information seeking to be more important when we think we will need to predict and explain someone's future behavior.

Although the accuracy of two of these three conditions has been questioned, Berger's (1979) acknowledgment of factors that influence our motivation to seek information was the catalyst to take a closer look at this issue. Research since that time has dramatically influenced the way we view these issues. In particular, researchers have theorized that the valence of the information people expect to receive is a major predictor of how comfortable people are with uncertainty as well as how likely they are to seek information to resolve their uncertainty. **Valence** refers to how positive or negative a person expects the information to be.

The Anticipated Positive Versus Negative Content of the Information

Much of what we know about the motivation to seek information comes from health scholars. For example, work on **uncertainty in illness theory** (Mischel, 1981, 1988, 1990) showed that the people often prefer uncertainty to knowledge. In other words, in the context of diseases, when eliminating uncertainty might mean eliminating hope for recovery (by discovering that the disease is fatal), uncertainty is cherished because it keeps hope alive. In other words, we will avoid seeking information and will instead prefer to live with uncertainty if we fear that we might discover information about our health that makes us lose hope.

In support of this idea, Brashers (2001) advanced the **theory of uncertainty management**. The theory emphasizes three features: (1) the meaning and experience of uncertainty, (2) the role of emotion in our response to uncertainty, and (3) the various communicative and psychological strategies for managing uncertainty. First, he supports Mischel's contention that we sometimes experience uncertainty as hope, but as a negative state. He also reminds us that cultures differ in their perception of uncertainty—some are much more comfortable with uncertainty than others. Second, rather than assuming that people are always motivated to reduce uncertainty, Brashers (2001) argues that uncertainty motivates information seeking only when that uncertainty is anxiety producing. That only occurs, he suggests, when we feel that a lack of information could be harmful. Otherwise, uncertainty will produce either positive emotions (e.g., when not knowing is better than knowing that harm is inevitable) or neutral emotions (e.g., when it doesn't matter whether you know or don't know more about this issue). As a result, Brashers proposed a shift from thinking about the ways in which we seek to *reduce* uncertainty (the predominant way of thinking in uncertainty reduction theory) to thinking about the ways we *manage* uncertainty.

Indeed, there is considerable evidence supporting Brashers' logic. Take people's sexual behavior, for example. Despite the fact that hundreds of thousands of college students are at high risk of contracting a sexually transmitted infection (STI), only a very small percentage ever get tested for such infections. This pattern is even stronger if you consider fatal STIs, like AIDS. One of the reasons people give for not getting tested is that they would rather not know if they have an STI. For these people, the uncertainty is preferable to the potential knowledge that they have a stigmatized disease that may change their life or even lead to their death. This attitude is especially worrisome given

that many STIs are quite treatable, especially if diagnosed early. Research shows a similar pattern in tests for breast cancer and colon cancer. Only a very small percentage of the population most at risk for these types of cancer actually get regular checkups, again despite the fact that with early detection the consequences are relatively benign.

Similarly, research suggests that we sometimes prefer to keep a level of uncertainty in our relationships, especially if reducing uncertainty could reveal negative information or lead to negative relational consequences. For example, studies on "taboo topics" that people avoid discussing in relationships show that the future of the relationship is one of the most avoided topics among romantic partners (Baxter & Wilmot, 1985). Studies have shown that even couples who have been together for many years sometimes avoid seeking information and reducing uncertainty. For example, one study included long-term dating couples in which one of the partners would be graduating from college in a few months (Afifi & Burgoon, 1998). Many of these couples avoided having the "dreaded discussion" about their future. Perhaps many were worried about their future together and feared that the relationship might change after graduation. In this case, uncertainty might be perceived as a better alternative than finding out that the relationship could be at risk.

Studies on cross-sex friendships also suggest that uncertainty is sometimes accepted in ongoing relationships. Some cross-sex friendships are full of uncertainty and ambiguity regarding issues such as whether romantic potential exists (O'Meara, 1989). In these cross-sex friendships, "sensitive" topics—especially about the relationship—are typically avoided at all costs (Afifi & Burgoon, 1998; Baxter & Wilmot, 1985). In fact, the current and future status of the relationship is often the most commonly avoided topic in cross-sex friendships. Guerrero and Chavez (2005) found that individuals were especially likely to avoid discussing the status of the relationship when they were romantically attracted to their cross-sex friend but feared that he or she did not reciprocate their feelings. Thus people sometimes prefer uncertainty when they fear that information seeking might confirm their worst fears—such as that the relationship does not have a future. As we discussed earlier, in other cases people might prefer some uncertainty to keep their relationships unpredictable and exciting.

Afifi and Weiner (2004) summarized this body of research by offering the **theory of motivated information management** (TMIM). The theory starts by recognizing that individuals are only motivated to manage their uncertainty levels when they perceive a discrepancy between the level of uncertainty they have about an important issue and the level of uncertainty they want. In other words, someone may be uncertain about an issue but be comfortable with that state, in which case he or she would not deliberately engage in information management. TMIM proposes, though, that people who feel a discrepancy between actual and desired uncertainty will experience anxiety and a related motivation to reduce that anxiety. How they do so will depend on two

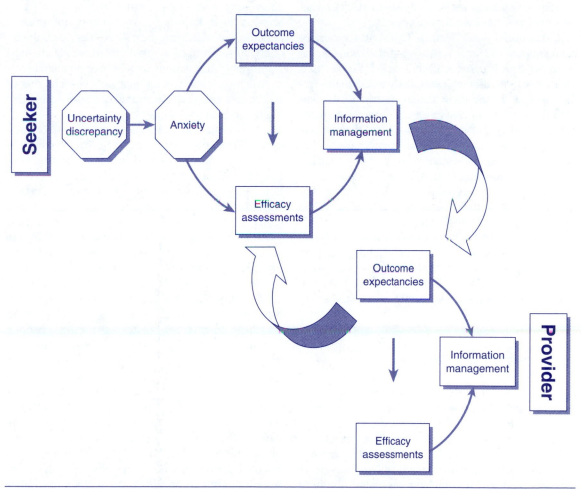

Figure 4.1   The Theory of Motivated Information Management

factors, according to Afifi and Weiner (2004): (1) Whether they expect the outcome of the information search to be positive or negative (i.e., the outcome expectancy) and (2) whether they feel they are able to gather the information for which they are searching and cope with it (i.e., the efficacy assessment). These two conditions will then determine whether they seek information directly, seek information indirectly, avoid information (either actively or passively), or reassess their level of uncertainty (see Figure 4.1). TMIM also explicitly notes the role of the information provider in this exchange, arguing that the provider goes through a similar process of information management in trying to decide what information to give and how to give it.

The initial work testing TMIM has generally been supportive (for review, see Afifi & Matsunaga, in press). Specifically, Afifi and Weiner (2006) used the theory to predict who was likely to ask their partner directly about their sexual health. Consistent with the theory and past research, some participants noted that they did not want to reduce their uncertainty on the matter. These participants were unlikely to seek information. In contrast, participants were most likely to seek information when they expected to receive positive information, felt they could talk to their partner honestly about it, and believed they could cope with the result.

What is clear from research in the past 15 years is that the process of uncertainty management is more complex than originally believed. Moreover, other studies show that personality may influence our decision to reduce uncertainty. These studies are reviewed next.

PERSONALITY DIFFERENCES

Several scholars have argued that some people have a greater need for uncertainty reduction than others. Social psychologists have suggested that instead of always needing to seek information, as uncertainty reduction theory originally suggested, or having this need vary according to specific circumstances as scholars such as Mischel have suggested, the need for information seeking varies from person to person. This construct is variously called need for closure (Kruglanski, 1990), tolerance for uncertainty (Kellermann & Reynolds, 1990), uncertainty orientation (Sorrentino & Short, 1986), tolerance for ambiguity (Martin & Westie, 1959), and coping style (Miller, 1987). Regardless of the label, these scholars essentially propose the same thing: Some people have a high need to reduce uncertainty while others are less concerned with predictability and certainty. You can think of people who are uncomfortable in new situations or with people about whom they know little, as well as people who thrive in such situations. Box 4.3 contains a scale to measure your own need for closure in relationships.

Uncertainty-oriented people are not afraid of uncertainty and, in fact, enjoy the opportunity to broaden their knowledge by seeking information regardless of whether it increases or decreases uncertainty. In contrast, certainty-oriented people are most comfortable in situations with little or no uncertainty, in which they can predict their behavior and that of others, and will find ways to ignore information that might increase uncertainty.

Studies have found that our uncertainty orientation influences us in a variety of ways. Not surprisingly, uncertainty-oriented individuals generally fare better than certainty-oriented ones in any situation of elevated uncertainty (Sorrentino, Short, & Raynor, 1984). The dating scene is full of uncertainty (What should I say? What does he mean? Does she like me? When should I call? Where should we go on the next date? When should I make my move?). As a result, if you are a certainty-oriented person, you are probably hesitant to initiate relationships with people and fare relatively poorly on first dates. But you also may be more satisfied in relationships than are uncertainty-oriented people. Certainty-oriented people have been shown to possess higher levels of trust for their partners (Sorrentino, Holmes, Hanna, & Sharp, 1995). Uncertainty-oriented people are adjusting their predictions about their partners with every new bit of information, which magnifies any inconsistency in the partner's behavior and hinders the achievement of complete trust in the partner. But certainty-oriented people are not as concerned with every piece of information about the partner (e.g., they would rather ignore information that increases uncertainty), so they find it easier to develop confidence in their partner.

BOX 4.3   Put Yourself to the Test

How Much Need for Closure Do You Have?

To determine your need for closure in relationships, mark the extent to which you agree or disagree with each of these statements using the following scale: 1 = Strongly disagree, 6 = Strongly agree.

	Disagree					Agree
1. I don't like situations that are uncertain. (A)	1	2	3	4	5	6
*2. I like to have friends who are unpredictable. (P)	1	2	3	4	5	6
3. When dining out, I like to go to places where I have been before so that I know what to expect. (P)	1	2	3	4	5	6
4. I feel uncomfortable when I don't understand why an event occurred in my life. (A)	1	2	3	4	5	6
5. I don't like to go into a situation without knowing what I can expect from it. (P)	1	2	3	4	5	6
6. When I am confused about an important issue, I feel very upset. (A)	1	2	3	4	5	6
*7. I think it is fun to change my plans at the last minute. (P)	1	2	3	4	5	6
*8. I enjoy the uncertainty of going into a new situation without knowing what might happen. (P)	1	2	3	4	5	6
9. In most social conflicts, I can easily see which side is right and which is wrong. (A)	1	2	3	4	5	6
10. I don't like to be with people who are capable of unexpected actions. (P)	1	2	3	4	5	6
11. I prefer to socialize with familiar friends because I know what to expect from them. (P)	1	2	3	4	5	6
12. I like to know what people are thinking at all times. (A)	1	2	3	4	5	6
13. I dislike it when a person's statement could mean many different things. (A)	1	2	3	4	5	6
14. It's annoying to listen to someone who cannot seem to make up his or her mind. (A)	1	2	3	4	5	6
15. I feel uncomfortable when someone's meaning or intention is unclear to me. (A)	1	2	3	4	5	6
16. I'd rather know bad news than stay in a state of uncertainty. (A)	1	2	3	4	5	6
17. I dislike unpredictable situations. (P)	1	2	3	4	5	6

Add together the scores for the questions that are *not* asterisked. Then subtract the scores for the questions that are asterisked. The maximum score is 81, and the minimum score is -4. The closer you are to 81, the stronger your need for closure. The questions marked with a (P) measure your preference for predictability, whereas the items marked with an (A) measure your discomfort with ambiguity.

So who is better off in relationships—someone who can ignore inconsistent information, thus maintaining trust in his or her partner, or someone who is always trying to figure out his or her partner? Neither type of orientation seems to have a clear advantage. Because of their information vigilance, uncertainty-oriented people are more likely to detect changes in their partner's moods and to react accordingly. Their awareness of inconsistencies also means that they will likely discover more deceptions by their partner than will certainty-oriented people. But certainty-oriented people may have smoother, more stable relationships because of their relative disinterest in focusing on every piece of information about their partners.

Miller and her colleagues (Miller, 1987; Miller, Brody, & Summerton, 1988) have shown in health behavior that some people tend to be information seekers (high monitors) and others information avoiders (blunters). Monitors tend to be more anxious in medical situations because they are always seeking information that might be threatening; Blunters tend to cope with stressful situations by distracting themselves and ignoring negative information. The advantage for blunters is that their coping mechanism allows for lower anxiety about their health; but at what cost? Because of their coping style, blunters may skip the diagnosis of a serious illness that, if discovered early, could have been addressed effectively. When applied to relational contexts, we would expect that Miller's distinction between monitors and blunters should operate similarly to Kruglanski's notion of difference on uncertainty orientation. Specifically, we would expect monitors to exhibit more distrust in their relational partner and more anxiety, just as uncertainty-oriented people do.

Finally, and most recently, Ickes and colleagues found that people differ in their motivation to acquire relationship-threatening information (MARTI; Ickes, Dugosh, Simpson, & Wilson, 2003). Consistent with the studies we've discussed, and others showing that knowing partners' relationally threatening thoughts and feelings creates personal and relational stress (see Simpson, Ickes, & Grich, 1999), four studies demonstrate that people differed in the degree to which they sought relationally threatening information and whether such differences affected their relational experiences. People consistently varied in their motivation to seek relationally threatening information, and that difference affected their level of partner trust and the degree of manipulative surveillance behaviors in which they engaged. This impact was especially noticeable in troubled relationships (i.e., those rated as not particularly close). Their results showed that people with high MARTI scores (i.e., those especially motivated to acquire relationally threatening information) who were in emotionally distant relationships were 30% more likely to have broken up 5 months later than those in similarly emotionally distant relationships but with low MARTI scores. In other words, people who are inclined to seek relationship-threatening information are more likely to have shorter relationships than those who are not so inclined. This research is important because it is focused on tendencies to seek relationally threatening information, not just any information, and it is the only work by personality scholars in this area that is specific to the relational context.

EXPECTANCY VIOLATIONS

As Berger (1979) suggested, behaviors that deviate from expectations are likely to increase a person's motivation to reduce uncertainty. This is because expectancy-violating behaviors make it more difficult for people to predict and explain someone's behavior. It is not surprising, then, that considerable research has been conducted on expectancy violations in both initial interactions and close relationships. In this section, we discuss Burgoon's (1978; Burgoon & Hale, 1988) expectancy violations theory, as well as related research on expectancy violations in close relationships.

Expectancy Violations Theory

How do people react when they encounter unexpected behavior? Burgoon has attempted to answer this question by developing and testing **expectancy violations theory** (Burgoon, 1978; Burgoon & Hale, 1988; Burgoon, Stern, & Dillman, 1995). In its earliest form, the theory focused on how people react to violations of personal space. Later, however, the theory was extended to encompass all types of behavioral violations, positive and negative. For example, a negative expectancy violation occurs when you expect your best friend to be smiling and happy for you when you win an award, but instead he or she frowns and looks envious. A negative expectancy violation also occurs when you expect someone to be honest and then you find out that she or he has lied to you. A positive expectancy violation occurs when you expect your significant other to be angry with you because you are late for a date, but instead he or she hugs you and expresses relief that you showed up. These examples show how commonplace expectancy violations are.

People build expectancies largely through interaction with others. By observing and interacting with others, people reduce uncertainty and form expectancies about how these others behave under different circumstances. These expectations can be either predictive or prescriptive. **Predictive expectancies** tell people what to expect in a given situation based on what normally occurs with a particular person or in a particular context (Burgoon et al., 1995). For example, based on Serena's past promptness, Vish would have been surprised had she been even 10 minutes late. His expectations for "on-time arrival" are very different for other people he knows, though—people who are consistently 30 minutes late, for example. Predictive expectancies are generally based on the norms or routines that typically occur within a given context and/or relationship. **Prescriptive expectancies**, in contrast, tell people what to expect based on general rules of appropriateness (Burgoon et al., 1995). So cultural norms would have led Vish to expect a call from Serena before the date had she known that she wasn't going to be able to make it.

According to expectancy violations theory, three factors affect expectancies: communicator characteristics, relational characteristics, and context. **Communicator characteristics** refer to individual differences, including age, sex, ethnic background, and personality traits. For instance, you might expect an elderly woman to be more polite than an adolescent boy, or you might expect your extroverted friend to be outgoing at a party and your introverted friend

to be quiet and reserved. **Relational characteristics** refer to factors such as how close we are to someone, what type of relationship we share (platonic, romantic, business), and what types of experiences we have shared together. Hearing "I love you" from a romantic partner might be an expected behavior but hearing the same words from a casual acquaintance might be highly unexpected. Similarly, certain types of intimate touch are usually expected in romantic relationships but not in platonic ones. Finally, **context** includes both the social situation and cultural influences. Clearly, there are different behavioral expectations depending on the situation. For example, if you are in church attending a funeral, you expect people to act differently than if you were at the same church attending a wedding. Behavioral expectations may also shift depending on whether you are at work or out for a night on the town with friends. Similarly, expectations differ based on culture. For example, you might expect someone to greet you by kissing your face three times on alternating cheeks if you are in parts of Europe but not if you are in the United States.

What happens when expectancies are violated? Maybe your platonic friend says "I love you" and touches you in an overly intimate fashion, or maybe you expect to be greeted affectionately by a European friend, but the friend offers only a stiff handshake. According to expectancy violations theory, your response will be contingent on at least two factors: (1) the positive or negative interpretation of the behavior and (2) the rewardingness of the partner.

The Positive or Negative Interpretation of the Behavior. When unexpected events occur, people often experience heightened arousal and uncertainty, leading them to search for an explanation (Burgoon & Hale, 1988). To do this, people pay close attention to their partner and the situation so that they can ascertain the meaning of the unexpected behavior and interpret it as positive or negative. As part of this process, the unexpected behavior is compared with the expected behavior. When the unexpected behavior is perceived to be more satisfying than the expected behavior, a positive violation has occurred. For example, if Serena had shown up on Friday night she may have been positively surprised by the care

Vish took in cleaning his apartment and preparing her dinner because he normally does not go to such trouble. In contrast, when the unexpected behavior is perceived to be less positive than the expected behavior, a negative violation has occurred (for review, see Floyd, Ramirez, & Burgoon, 1999). So, if Vish ends up telling Serena to forget about getting together over the weekend, Serena might be surprised because she expected Vish to be reasonable and understand that the mix-up was a simple mistake.

Expectancy violations can have positive or negative consequences for relationships. When positive violations occur people are likely to be happier and more satisfied with their relationships.

SOURCE: Copyright: iStockphoto.com/Bart Sadowski

Photo 4.1 Receiving a gift can constitute a positive or negative expectancy violation depending on what it is, how it compares with what was expected, and whom it's from.

When negative violations occur, however, people might become angry and dissatisfied with their relationships (Burgoon et al., 1995; Levitt, 1991; Levitt, Coffman, Guacci-Franco, & Loveless, 1994). It is not surprising that Vish became frustrated when Serena violated his expectations by failing to show up.

The Rewardingness of the Partner. Sometimes, people cannot determine the valence of a behavior simply by comparing the unexpected behavior with what they originally expected. This is because some behaviors are ambiguous; they can be positive in some circumstances and negative in others, depending on who enacts them. For example, imagine that you are working on a class project with several classmates. Because they are always together, you assume that two of the classmates, Terry and Alex, are a couple. However, Terry approaches you after the group meeting, smiles warmly, touches your arm, and asks you out on a date. You are surprised and ask, "Aren't you with Alex?" Terry replies, "Oh no, Alex and I are just really good friends."

How might you respond to Terry's unexpected behavior? The smile, touch, and request are not inherently positive or negative. Instead, the interpretation of these unexpected behaviors depends on how rewarding you perceive Terry to be. If you see Terry as attractive, charming, and intelligent, you will likely see the expectancy violation as positive and reciprocate by accepting the date. If, however, you see Terry as a deceitful person who is going behind Alex's back, you will probably see the expectancy violation as negative and refuse the date. In this case, it is not the behavior per se that is positive or negative; instead, it is the combination of the behavior and the rewardingness of the partner.

Interestingly, research and expectancy violations theory has shown that nonrewarding communicators are evaluated the most highly if they stay within the norms and avoid violating expectations (Burgoon & Hale, 1988). For example, suppose you have to work on a project with a coworker whom you dislike. The two of you do not talk to each other much but so far you have tried to keep your relationship civil. If the coworker suddenly starts asking you to go to lunch with her and telling you her life's story, you will probably evaluate her even more negatively because you will see her as pushy and overbearing. Similarly, if the coworker starts pointedly ignoring you and makes sarcastic remarks while you are speaking, you will likely evaluate her even more negatively as a mean, rude person. Note that whether the expectancy violation involves behaviors that are more friendly or less friendly, you might still perceive the coworker negatively. This is because people tend to interpret unexpected behavior as consistent with their initial impressions of someone. To produce a more positive result, the coworker would be better off remaining civil and gradually becoming less distant. Such behavior would confirm your expectations and perhaps lay a foundation for a better relationship.

With rewarding communicators, however, expectancy violations theory suggests that positive expectancy violations actually produce better outcomes than expectancy-confirming behaviors (Burgoon & Hale, 1988; Burgoon et al., 1995). When positive violations occur, people feel "bright emotions" such as joy, excitement, and relief. When expectancies are confirmed, people also feel bright emotions, but they are less intense. Finally, when negative violations occur, people feel "dark emotions," such as sadness, anger, and disappointment (see also Levitt, 1991). Positive violations are also met with reciprocity. In other words, the positive behavior that violated expectations will be met with positive behavior by the partner.

Clearly, positive expectancy violations can be beneficial in close relationships even though they sometimes create uncertainty and reflect a lack of predictability. As Floyd et al. (1999) summarized,

> How we evaluate and respond to unexpected behavior is largely dependent on our interpretation of the behavior itself and on our assessment of how rewarding the person is who enacted the behavior. In cases when the behavior is more desirable that what was expected, we may actually be more satisfied than if we had gotten what we expected. (p. 443)

The impact of unexpected behavior on uncertainty also varies. Afifi and Burgoon (2000) showed that unexpected behaviors that were generally consistent with past behavior (e.g., a kiss from someone who you suspected likes you) decrease uncertainty about the person while other violations increase uncertainty.

Types of Expectancy Violations in Close Relationships

Given that expectancy violations can be beneficial or harmful to relationships, a sensible next question to ask is, Do certain behaviors tend to function as positive or negative expectancy violations in people's day-to-day relationships? In past research, such as that by Planalp and Honeycutt (1985), researchers focused primarily on negative events. Afifi and Metts (1998) extended this research by asking people in friendships and romantic relationships to think about the last time their friend or partner did or said something unexpected. They emphasized that the unexpected event could be either positive or negative. Participants reported on events that had occurred, on average, 5 days earlier. Some of the behaviors reported were relatively mundane, and others were quite serious. The outcome was a list of nine general categories of expectancy violations that commonly occur in relationships:

1. *Criticism or accusation:* Actions that are critical of the person or that accuse her or him of some type of offense

2. *Relationship escalation:* Actions that confirm or intensify the commitment of the person to the relationship, such as saying "I love you" or giving expensive gifts

3. *Relationship de-escalation:* Actions that imply a desire to decrease the intimacy level in the relationship, such as reducing communication and spending more time apart

4. *Uncharacteristic relational behavior:* Actions that are not consistent with the way the person defines the relationship, such as members of cross-sex friendships asking their supposedly platonic friend for a sexual relationship

5. *Uncharacteristic social behavior:* Actions that do not have relational implications but that simply are not expected from that person in that context, such as a mild-mannered person raising her or his voice during an argument with a salesperson

6. *Transgressions:* Actions that are violations of taken-for-granted rules of relationships, such as

having an affair, being disloyal, sharing private information with other people, and being deceitful

7. *Acts of devotion:* Actions that imply that the person really views the partner and/or the relationship as being special, such as going "above and beyond the call of duty" to help that individual through a difficult time

8. *Acts of disregard:* Actions that imply that the person considers the partner and/or the relationship as unimportant, such as showing up late or being inconsiderate

9. *Gestures of inclusion:* Actions that show an unexpected desire to include the partner in the person's activities or life, such as disclosing something very personal or extending an invitation to spend the holidays with his or her family

In addition to varying dramatically in terms of severity, these reported violations differed tremendously in the extent to which they were seen as positive or negative and, most important, the extent to which they increased or decreased uncertainty. Unlike earlier researchers, Afifi and Metts (1998) found that many expectancy violations reduce uncertainty by providing important information about the actor. In other words, not all expectancy violations increase uncertainty, although a good number do.

This angle to the study of expectation violations in close relationships has been applied to our understanding of sexual activity in cross-sex friendships. Afifi and Faulkner's (2000) study of sexual contact with otherwise-platonic opposite-sex friends showed that participants generally rated those experiences as unexpected and that their impact depended on whether the event was seen as positive or negative and whether it increased or decreased uncertainty. Friends were most likely to perceive that their relationships were damaged when the sexual contact increased uncertainty and was evaluated negatively. Bevan (2003) followed up with an investigation that compared sexual resistance in cross-sex friendships and dating relationships. Her study revealed that resisting sexual attempts was perceived as more normative (less unexpected) and as a more relationally important expectation violation in

cross-sex friendships, as compared with dating relationships. The logic here is that such resistance essentially defines the relationship in the context of cross-sex friendships ("Okay, we're not going to move the relationship to that level"), making it important. In addition, because sexual activity is not typical in such relationships, resistance is more expected than in romantic relationships.

SUMMARY AND APPLICATION

Uncertainty reduction plays an important role in the way people communicate with others. In initial interactions with strangers and acquaintances, people feel motivation to reduce uncertainty. Even in close, developed relationships, people sometimes feel strongly motivated to reduce uncertainty. Behaviors that are unexpected, such as Serena not showing up for the date, are especially likely to lead to uncertainty. So people who are in situations like Vish's should recognize that their feelings of uncertainty are natural.

People use a variety of strategies to try to reduce uncertainty. They might passively observe others, manipulate the social environment, question third parties, or interact directly with the person. In established relationships, people also report using a variety of "secret tests" to help them determine how committed their partners are to the relationship. People in established relationships also have a number of direct strategies at their disposal, including using integrative communication, showing closeness or being romantic, and engaging in distributive communication or conflict. The strategies that Vish uses may, in part, be dependent on the type of relationship he shares with Serena. If, prior to Friday night, Vish had characterized his relationship with Serena as intimate and satisfying, he would be more likely to use direct and positive strategies to reduce uncertainty than distancing or avoidant strategies.

The stage of the relationship may also matter. The model of relational turbulence suggests that couples are especially likely to experience uncertainty and irritations during the transition from a casual to a committed relationship. Given that Vish had planned the date with the hope of bringing Serena close to him, their relationship may be at this transition point, which could intensify the frustration and uncertainty that Vish is experiencing. If Vish and Serena had a long-standing committed relationship, Vish might have more readily accepted her explanation of a misunderstanding about the day of the date.

The scenario between Vish and Serena illustrates another important point about uncertainty. Specifically, uncertainty reduction is most likely to lead to increased liking and attraction when people discover positive information about others. However, in some cases uncertainty reduction can decrease attraction and liking. This most likely occurs when people uncover negative information about someone, such as finding out that a new friend has been deceptive or disloyal. For Vish and Serena, there is a danger that the uncertainty they are both experiencing could seep into the fabric of their relationship and their feelings for one another. After their Saturday morning conversation, Vish may still not be convinced that Serena is telling him the truth about mixing up the night for the date. At the very least, this might lead Vish to question if he completely trusts Serena. For her part, Serena might be frustrated that Vish does not believe her and incredulous because he got the dates mixed up. As a result, Serena might reduce her uncertainty by reevaluating Vish as an unreasonable, forgetful, and paranoid person, thereby decreasing her attraction toward him.

Expectancy violations also often produce uncertainty. Interestingly, however, expectancy violations can be beneficial to relationships when they are interpreted positively. In other words, when unexpected behavior is perceived to be better than expected behavior, people experience positive outcomes despite the initial discomfort they might have felt at not being able to accurately predict their partner's behavior. This suggests that Vish's initial attempt to plan a special date may have been successful in positively violating Serena's expectations and promoting increased feelings of attraction and closeness even if it causes her some initial uncertainty. However, if Vish typically plans special dates, then they would become commonplace rather than unexpected.

As the situation between Vish and Serena illustrates, uncertainty-increasing events can be critical points in relationships. How partners cope with uncertainty, including whether or not they are motivated to manage uncertainty, affects the future course of the relationship. It is hoped that the research in this chapter gave you a clearer picture of why these experiences occur and how best to deal with them.

DISCUSSION QUESTIONS

1. According to uncertainty reduction theory, people are driven by the need to reduce uncertainty during initial encounters. Do you agree with this idea? Are there certain circumstances that make uncertainty reduction an especially salient goal?

2. Dialectics theory suggests that some level of uncertainty makes a relationship exciting. Do you agree or disagree?

3. Think about the last few times someone violated your expectations, either positively or negatively. Does expectancy violations theory help explain how you reacted to these expectancy violations? Why or why not?

5

GETTING CLOSER

Initiating and Intensifying Relationships

When Anne and Connor meet at a Sierra Club meeting, they discover they have a lot in common. They both have degrees in biology, love animals, and enjoy outdoor activities. Anne is a caretaker at the local zoo, and Connor teaches science at a middle school. For the first 2 months, their relationship goes smoothly. They have long talks on the phone and spend considerable time together. They decide to make their relationship exclusive. Connor assumes that Anne would want to spend Thanksgiving with him. When she says she'd rather be with her family, Connor becomes hurt and distant. After a week of silence, Connor calls Anne and apologizes. They resume their relationship, and a month later Connor tells Anne he loves her and hopes to marry her someday. She responds that she feels the same way. Six months later Anne suggests they move in together. Connor, however, hesitates. He worries that living together before marriage could cause them to take their relationship for granted. He has seen too many of his friends move in with their girlfriends and then break up 6 months later. Anne responds by saying that his friends are good examples of why two people should live together before marriage—to find out if they are indeed compatible.

The process of starting and developing relationships has interested communication researchers for decades. Researchers have tried to unlock the mysteries of how people can best use communication to help them get closer to one another and why some people are better at developing close relationships than others. In Anne and Connor's case, getting to know one another was easy. However, Connor has valid concerns about whether they should live together or not. If you were in Connor's place, would you have similar concerns? What possible paths might their relationship take next?

In this chapter, we discuss several different perspectives on the paths that relationships take as partners get to know one another and develop close relationships. First, we examine the concept of self-disclosure. Many researchers believe that intimate self-disclosure, which involves sharing personal information with another person, is a basic requirement for relationship development. Second, we discuss two models of relationship development: Altman and Taylor's social penetration theory and Knapp's coming-together stages. Third, we discuss relational turning points, which are events associated with changes in a relationship. The chapter ends with a discussion of two specific turning points that are highly relevant to relationship development in romantic relationships—date initiation and cohabitation.

Communication is the primary vehicle for developing relationships and creating feelings of connection and closeness. In fact, much of the research on relationship development has examined how a specific type of communication—self-disclosure—helps people move from being strangers to being close friends or lovers. **Self-disclosure** occurs when people reveal something about themselves to others. Some forms of self-disclosure, such as talking about where you grew up or what your major is, are fairly impersonal; other forms of self-disclosure, such as talking about your future hopes and childhood insecurities, are much more intimate. As relationships develop, communication is typically characterized by increases in intimate self-disclosure. This is not to say that other forms of communication are unimportant. Affectionate displays of nonverbal communication, such as loving gazes and comforting touches, can also help people develop their relationships, as can other forms of verbal communication, such as specialized and/or intimate nicknames such as "honeybunch" or "sweetheart" (see Chapter 8). However, most research on communication in the early stages of relationships has concentrated on self-disclosure and information sharing. This is probably because people typically increase self-disclosure before they begin using intimate forms of nonverbal communication, such as touch, and other forms of intimate verbal communication, such as calling each other by pet names.

Dimensions of Self-Disclosure

One of the first theoretical explorations of self-disclosure was developed by Altman and Taylor (1973). According to **social penetration theory,** self-disclosure usually increases gradually as people develop their relationships. Altman and Taylor

suggested that self-disclosure can be conceptualized in terms of three dimensions: depth, breadth, and frequency. **Depth** refers to how personal or deep the communication is, **breadth** refers to how many topics a person feels free to discuss, and **frequency** refers to how often self-disclosure occurs. Various types of encounters can be characterized differently based on these three dimensions. For example, when you have to work on a class project with someone you don't know well, you might talk a lot about school (a fairly superficial topic) but not about much else. However, you might need to get together with this person frequently in order to complete the class assignment. Your self-disclosure with this person could be described as low in depth and breadth but high in frequency. Of course, if you started to develop a close relationship with your classmate, the depth and breadth of your self-disclosure would probably increase, so that you'd be talking about more varied and more personal topics in addition to discussing the assignment.

As relationships develop, they tend to increase in depth and breadth. In fact, according to social penetration theory, it is helpful to visualize the process of self-disclosure during relationship development as the slow unpeeling of an onion, as Figure 5.1 shows. An onion has a rather thin and flimsy outer layer, but as you peel through the various layers, they get harder, with the core of the onion very tightly bound. Similarly, Altman and Taylor (1973) suggested that there are three basic layers of self-disclosure: (1) a superficial layer that is easy to penetrate, (2) a social or personal layer that is easy for most friends, family members, and lovers to penetrate, and (3) a very intimate layer, or core, that is seldom revealed, and then only to people whom we trust completely.

At the superficial layer, people reveal commonplace facts about themselves that are not threatening in any way. For example, telling someone your name, major, hometown, zodiac sign, and favorite color are benign self-disclosures. At the social/personal level, people typically reveal more about their likes and dislikes and hopes and fears, but they still keep their deepest hopes and fears a secret. For example, you might tell most of your friends that you'd like to marry a certain kind of person, that you had an unhappy childhood, or that you are worried about

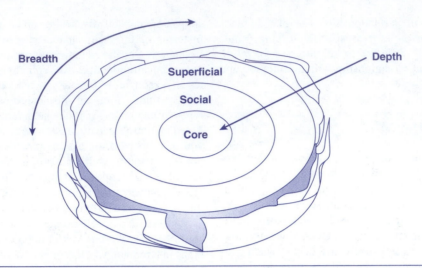

Breadth   Depth

Superficial

Social

Core

Figure 5.1   Depth and Breadth of Self-Disclosure

NOTE: Depth increases as people disclose about more intimate topics, while breadth increases as people talk about a wider range of topics. Different topics can be thought of as occupying different "wedges" of the onion.

getting a job when you graduate from college. But you might not tell them all the intimate details related to these topics. At the core, people share all the personal details that make them who they are. Within the core are people's most secret, intimate feelings. For example, you might disclose negative childhood experiences that you would normally prefer not to think about, and you might confess all your fears and insecurities about succeeding in your chosen profession. You might also reveal intimate, positive feelings about people by telling them how much they mean to you and how lost you would be without them.

In addition to depth, breadth, and frequency, research has uncovered two other dimensions relevant to self-disclosure: valence and duration (Gilbert, 1976; Tolstedt & Stokes, 1984). Although these two dimensions were not mentioned in the original social penetration theory, they appear to be critical for understanding the type of self-disclosure that characterizes a relationship.

Valence refers to the positive or negative "charge" of the self-disclosure. For example, if you disclose your dreams, your warm feelings for someone, or your happiest childhood memories, the

self-disclosure has a positive valence. In contrast, if you disclose your fears, your hostile feelings for someone, or your most unhappy childhood memories, the self-disclosure has a negative valence. Valence is a crucial dimension of self-disclosure because it helps determine how people feel about one another. Think about friends who call you all the time to complain about their lives. Their self-disclosure might be full of breadth and depth, but instead of feeling closer to your friend, you might end up feeling depressed and want to avoid such conversations in the future. Similarly, some research has shown that couples show an increase in depth of self-disclosure when they are continually arguing or when their relationship is in decline (Tolstedt & Stokes, 1984). The types of comments they typically make, however, are negatively valenced ("I wish I'd never met you," "Why don't you ever listen to me?" "You make me feel unimportant"). Thus high depth alone does not tell the whole story. Depth and valence work together to create the emotional climate of a self-disclosure. Of course, some negatively valenced self-disclosure can draw people closer. For example, when two individuals feel comfortable enough to reveal their deepest fears, worst failures, and most embarrassing moments, they probably have developed a particularly close relationship. The key is to limit the number of negatively valenced disclosures relative to the number of more positively valenced disclosures.

The other new dimension relevant to self-disclosure is **duration**, which reflects *how long* two people spend disclosing in a single conversation rather than *how often* they disclose (frequency). It is possible for people to have self-disclosures of limited frequency but long duration. A common example of this is the "stranger on the plane" (or train) phenomenon. When you sit down next to someone on a plane, you might chat with her or him for the entire duration of the flight. You might even disclose intimate details about your life to your seatmate, figuring that you probably won't see her or him again, so you are not really making yourself vulnerable. Thus it is the limited frequency of the interaction that allows you to confidently engage in self-disclosure that is high in both depth and duration. In other cases, you might have frequent self-disclosure with someone, but it is usually short in duration. For example, you might talk with a coworker every day, but only for limited amounts of time during a coffee break. One study showed that the duration of face-to-face interaction is more strongly related to closeness in friendships than the frequency of interaction (Emmers-Sommer, 2004). This same study showed that friendships that are regarded as especially close and intimate tend to be characterized by high levels of in-depth communication. Thus friends do not need to have frequent contact to stay close as long as they periodically have long, in-depth conversations.

Risks Associated With Self-Disclosure

Disclosing personal and intimate information can be risky. When we tell other people our innermost thoughts and feelings, we become vulnerable and open ourselves up to criticism. To see how willing you are to disclose information about sensitive topics to people in your social network, take the test in Box 5.1.

Several scholars have used a dialectical perspective to explain the costs and benefits of self-disclosure (Baxter & Montgomery, 1996; Petronio, 2000, 2002; Rosenfeld, 2000). According to this perspective, people have opposing needs in their relationships. For example, even though Anne wanted to spend a lot of time with Connor, she also wanted to spend time alone with her family on Thanksgiving. Such opposing needs can cause tension (see Chapter 9). When self-disclosure is considered, scholars adopting a **dialectical perspective** have noted that people have strong needs for both openness and secrecy. As Rosenfeld (2000) put it,

> I want to be open because I want to share myself with others and get the benefits of such communication, such as receiving social support, the opportunity to think out loud, and the chance to get something off my chest. I do not want to be open because I might be ridiculed, rejected, or abandoned. Open or closed; let others in or keep others out? Every interaction has the potential for raising the tension of holding both desires simultaneously. It is not that one desire "wins" and the other "loses." Rather, they exist simultaneously. Interpersonal life consists of the tension between these opposites. (p. 4)

Consistent with the dialectical perspective, scholars have delineated several risks associated with self-disclosure. Some of the most common reasons people avoid intimate self-disclosure include the following: (1) fear of exposure or rejection, (2) fear of retaliation or angry responses, (3) fear of loss of control, and (4) fear of losing one's individuality (Hatfield, 1984; Petronio, 2002).

Fear of Exposure or Rejection. Sometimes, people worry that too much self-disclosure will expose their negative qualities and cause others to think badly of them, like them less, and possibly even reject or abandon them. As Hatfield (1984) put it,

> One reason, then, that all of us are afraid of intimacy, is that those we care most about are bound to discover all that is wrong with us—to discover that we possess taboo feelings . . . have done things of which we are deeply ashamed. (p. 210)

▨ BOX 5.1   Put Yourself to the Test

Willingness to Disclose About Sensitive Topics

How willing would you be to disclose the following information to people in your social network (family, good friends, and your romantic partner)? Imagine yourself in the following situations. Whom would you disclose to? If you would be willing to disclose the information to everyone in your social network, circle 7. If you would tell no one, circle 1. The other numbers represent varying degrees of willingness to disclose (circling a 4 means that you would tell about half the people in your social network).

	No One ◄————————► Everyone						
1. I fail an important exam.	1	2	3	4	5	6	7
2. I am unmarried and discover that I (or my partner) is pregnant.	1	2	3	4	5	6	7
3. I am in love with someone who doesn't love me.	1	2	3	4	5	6	7
4. I get arrested and put in jail for a minor offense.	1	2	3	4	5	6	7
5. I cheat on an exam without getting caught.	1	2	3	4	5	6	7
6. I feel happy when something bad happens to an enemy of mine.	1	2	3	4	5	6	7
7. I find out I have a sexually transmitted infection.	1	2	3	4	5	6	7
8. I receive a negative performance evaluation at work.	1	2	3	4	5	6	7
9. I have a drug or alcohol problem.	1	2	3	4	5	6	7
10. I cheat on my long-term partner by having a one-night stand with someone I don't know.	1	2	3	4	5	6	7

Add up the numbers. A score of 70 or close to 70 suggests that you are highly willing to disclose sensitive information, perhaps to the point of being indiscriminant. A score of 10 or close to 10 suggests that you are unwilling to disclose sensitive information to others, perhaps because you fear vulnerability. Most people score somewhere in the middle, which would suggest that you are discriminating about whom you share sensitive information with. Taking this test can also help you recognize which members of your social network you tend to disclose to the most and the least, as well as which types of topics you perceive to be most sensitive.

Hatfield gave an excellent example of how exposing one's true qualities can lead to rejection and abandonment when she told the story of a graduate student with whom she had worked. This young European woman was beautiful, intelligent, and charming; in fact, many men were madly in love with her. Of course, she was not perfect—she had her insecurities and self-doubts, just as all of us do. But she put on a bright, charming facade to fit the perfect image that people had of her. The problem, however, was that whenever she got close enough to a man to admit her insecurities, she fell off the pedestal that he had put her on. It was impossible to meet all the high expectations of these men. When the perfect image was shattered, they lost interest and abandoned her.

Fear of Retaliation or Angry Attacks. People also worry that their partners might become angry or use what they disclose against them. For example, you might worry that your relational partner will retaliate if you confess to a one-night stand, admit telling a lie, or recount happy experiences you had with a former relational partner. One of our students once told us that he was secretly in love with his brother's fiancée. The two brothers had always had a very close but competitive relationship, and he worried that disclosing his feelings could lead to anger, suspicion, and even confrontation. He also worried that his brother's fiancée would end up hurt, confused, and maybe even angry. In other cases, people use the intimate information we share with them as ammunition against us. For example, if you tell your best friend that you sometimes only pretend to pay attention to people, your friend might later accuse you of being selfish and of not really listening when he or she is disclosing personal problems.

Fear of Loss of Control. People also worry that if they engage in too much self-disclosure, they won't be able to control their thoughts and feelings or the thoughts and feelings of others. For example, Connor fell in love with Anne after knowing her for only a couple of weeks, but he did not tell her he loved her then because he knew he might scare her away. Similarly, Anne might be afraid that if she starts talking to Connor about all the reasons that their relationship might not work, she will break down and cry. People may also fear losing control of information, especially if they think that the person to whom they disclose the information might share it with others (Petronio, 2002; Phillips & Metzger, 1976). Additionally, people may worry that if they disclose personal weaknesses to their partner, they will lose their ability to influence the partner (Petronio, 1991).

Fear of Losing Individuality. Some people fear losing their personal identity and being engulfed by the relationship. According to Hatfield (1984), one of the "most primitive fears of intimacy" is that we could "literally disappear" if we become too engulfed in a relationship (p. 212). Consistent with the dialectical perspective, this fear represents the push and pull that many people feel between the competing forces of wanting to be closely connected to others and wanting to be independent and self-sufficient. The idea here is that if we tell people too much about ourselves, they will know us so well that we risk losing our uniqueness and mysteriousness. Moreover, if we maintain high levels of self-disclosure, we may come to a point where there is nothing left to share. In this case, we may feel that we are part of a group or dyad rather than a unique individual with some private, secret thoughts and feelings. We may even feel a need to "escape" from our relational partner in order to find privacy and assert our independence.

Self-Disclosure and Liking

Because self-disclosure comes with considerable risk and yet also draws people together, the act of self-disclosure conveys both trust and closeness. Thus, according to social penetration theory, self-disclosure typically increases gradually as people get to know, like, and trust one another. If people do not develop trust or liking, self-disclosure will not progress very far, and the relationship will stagnate or terminate.

Many studies have examined the relationship between self-disclosure and liking. In a statistical review of 94 studies, Collins and Miller (1994) tested the **disclosure-liking hypothesis**, which predicts that, when a sender discloses to a receiver, the receiver will like the sender more. Collins and Miller's statistical review supported the disclosure-liking hypothesis, although this relationship appears to be stronger among acquaintances than strangers. Collins and Miller's statistical review also supported the **liking-disclosure hypothesis,** which predicts that people will disclose more to receivers they like. Thus, you are more likely to disclose to close relational partners and to people to whom you are attracted than to people you dislike.

In some cases, however, high levels of self-disclosure are not related to liking. Derlega, Metts, Petronio, and Margulis (1993) suggested that there are three reasons for this. First, when self-disclosure violates normative expectations, it will not lead to liking. Sometimes, people disclose too much information too quickly, or they disclose negative information that leads others to dislike them (Bochner,

1984; Parks, 1982). As Derlega and colleagues observed, "Highly personal, negative disclosure given too soon inhibits liking unless some strong initial attraction already exists" (p. 31). Second, self-disclosure is a better predictor of liking when receivers think that the sender discloses information only to certain special people. If senders are perceived to disclose information indiscriminately, the self-disclosure may be seen as less valuable, and liking may not result. Third, "disclosure will not lead to liking if it is responded to in a negative manner" (Derlega et al., 1993, p. 32). If a sender discloses sensitive information and the receiver dismisses the information or responds in an unkind or critical manner, both sender and receiver are likely to feel negatively about the interaction and about each other. Usually, however, receivers match the intimacy level of a sender's self-disclosure. Box 5.2 gives examples of the relationship between self-disclosure and liking.

Reciprocity of Self-Disclosure

For relationships to flourish in the initial stages, self-disclosure must also be reciprocated. Considerable research has focused on the reciprocity or matching of self-disclosure, starting with Jourard's (1959, 1964) pioneering work on patterns of self-disclosure. Jourard believed that reciprocal self-disclosure, which he termed the **dyadic effect**, is the vehicle through which people build close relationships (see also Altman & Taylor, 1973; Gouldner, 1960). Reciprocal self-disclosure occurs when one person reveals information and his or her partner responds by offering information that is at a similar level of intimacy. For example, if Connor tells Anne about his career ambition to get his Ph.D. one day and teach biology at a university, Anne might respond by telling Connor that she wishes she could go back to school and train to be a veterinarian. Jourard's work suggests that self-disclosure usually begets more self-disclosure. In other words, people are likely to respond to high levels of self-disclosure by revealing similarly personal information. Of course, there are exceptions to this rule. For example, you might not want to continue a conversation with someone because you don't want to "lead the person on," or

you might decide that the other person's level of self-disclosure is inappropriate and makes you uncomfortable. In these cases, you are less likely to reciprocate self-disclosure.

Nonetheless, research suggests that people typically feel a natural pull toward matching the level of intimacy and intensity present in their conversational partner's self-disclosure. In a statistical review of 67 studies involving 5,173 participants, Dindia and Allen (1995) concluded that the evidence overwhelmingly supports the tendency for people to reciprocate self-disclosure. Studies have shown that people typically match the intimacy level of their conversational partner's self-disclosure regardless of the context (face-to-face vs. via telephone or the Internet), the type of relationship (strangers vs. intimates), or the amount of liking or disliking (Derlega, Harris, & Chaikin, 1973; Dindia, Fitzpatrick, & Kenny, 1997; Henderson & Gilding, 2004; Hosman & Tardy, 1980; Janofsky, 1971; Levinger & Senn, 1967). Research also suggests that individuals who violate the norm of reciprocity are perceived as cold, incompetent, unfriendly, and untrustworthy (Bradac, Hosman, & Tardy, 1978; Chaikin & Derlega, 1974).

There are two primary theoretical explanations for the dyadic effect (Davis & Skinner, 1974; Rubin, 1974). According to the **social exchange explanation,** when self-disclosure is reciprocated, it is rewarding because it reflects mutual trust and liking. However, unreciprocated self-disclosure is costly because it unnecessarily makes a communicator vulnerable (Altman & Taylor, 1973; Hatfield, 1984). As Hendrick (1981) argued, "Self-disclosure can be seen as something that has both costs and benefits" (p. 1150). To balance these costs and benefits, individuals can respond to intimate self-disclosure by engaging in a similarly rewarding level of intimate verbal communication that signals trust and liking. As Derlega et al. (1993) put it, reciprocity helps "equalize both the rewards and the risks of self-disclosure" (p. 33). Indeed, research has shown that moderate to moderately high levels of positive self-disclosure are perceived as the most rewarding (see Gilbert, 1976; Gilbert & Horenstein, 1975) and that moderately intimate self-disclosure is most likely to be reciprocated (VanLear, 1987). Therefore, the highest levels of reciprocity may occur when the disclosure is the most rewarding.

BOX 5.2　Highlights

Examples of Relationships Between Liking and Disclosure

The Disclosure-Liking Hypothesis: Disclosure Leads to Liking

Hannah and Emily pair up to work on a school project. Although they have had a few classes together, they don't know each other well. However, one evening, after working on their project, they start talking about personal issues. Hannah tells Emily about her long-distance relationship with her boyfriend and confesses to really missing him. Emily tells Hannah about her 3-year-old son and confesses that it is difficult to concentrate on school when she is so busy as a single mom. The two women feel a new sense of connection to each other.

The Liking-Disclosure Hypothesis: Liking Leads to Disclosure

Patrick really likes his new neighbor, Spencer, who seems friendly, funny, and easygoing. Once in a while when they run into each other before work, Spencer tells Patrick a joke and makes him laugh. One day, Patrick wins a prestigious award at work. He doesn't talk about the award much at work because he does not want to appear boastful or conceited. But when he comes home after work, he sees Spencer out mowing his lawn. Spencer waves, and Patrick strides over to tell him the good news. Spencer shuts off the lawn mower, and the two men start to talk.

Too Much Disclosure Too Early Can Lead to Disliking

Madison and Joel are on a first date. They go out to dinner at a fancy restaurant and engage in chitchat. About halfway through dinner, Joel starts telling Madison his life story. He starts by telling her about how he was an unpopular kid in elementary school. Then he talks about how his dog died when he was 10 years old. He is just starting to get into the adolescent years when the waiter arrives to see if they want dessert. Madison says she is full and asks the waiter to bring the check, hoping that she can get out of the restaurant before Joel starts talking about his first sexual experiences.

Indiscriminant Disclosure Is Less Likely to Lead to Liking

Travis and Angela meet at a company party. Angela tells Travis about her dreams and career aspirations. She tells him, "I wouldn't tell just anyone this, but my secret ambition is to be a rock star. I know it is silly and probably will never happen, but it would be so much fun to turn on the radio and hear myself singing." Later she says, "Don't tell anyone, but I might be leaving the firm to concentrate on a possible music career." Travis feels honored that Angela told him those things until he runs into a coworker who says, "Hey, I saw you talking to that woman who wants to be a rock star. She's been saying she's going to quit for the last year. I doubt she ever will." Suddenly, Travis doesn't feel special anymore.

Negative Responses to Disclosure Reduce Liking

Amy's sister has been dating Diego for several months. Amy is very close to her sister and would like to get to know Diego better. One day, at a family picnic, Amy approaches Diego and says, "Hello." She asks him how he has been. He says, "Fine," and looks away from Amy and out at the lake. Undaunted, Amy continues the conversation: "My sister tells me that you just got a big promotion at work. What will you be doing?" "More of the same," he says, still looking at the lake. Amy tells him about her job, but he doesn't seem interested. Eventually, Amy gives up and walks away, wondering what her sister could possibly see in him.

The **uncertainty reduction/modeling explanation** predicts that people will feel high levels of uncertainty during initial interactions (see Berger & Calabrese, 1975; see also Chapter 4). Because of this uncertainty, individuals pay attention to their partner's behavior to determine the most appropriate way to respond. If one partner initiates intimate self-disclosure, the other will likely follow suit in an effort to be socially appropriate. Thus dyadic partners are likely to model each other's behavior. Recall that, according to uncertainty reduction theory (Berger & Calabrese, 1975), high levels of uncertainty also lead to information seeking and reciprocity, as conversational partners strive to learn more about each other. Once uncertainty is reduced, the need to seek information decreases, as does reciprocity. Thus, the uncertainty reduction/modeling explanation may work best when applied to initial interactions. The social exchange explanation, in contrast, may explain the dyadic effect in both initial and developed relationships.

It is also important to note that reciprocity may be delayed in long-term, close relationships. For example, a husband might disclose his social anxieties to his wife, who simply listens patiently. Subsequently, the wife might reciprocate by sharing some of her deepest fears while the husband assumes the listening role. In initial encounters between people, future interaction is often uncertain so immediate reciprocity is more important.

Not surprisingly, research has also shown that partners who believe they reciprocate self-disclosure tend to be more satisfied with their relationships, particularly when the self-disclosure is positively valenced (Chelune, Rosenfeld, & Waring, 1985; Rosenfeld & Welsh, 1985). Studies have found that spouses are usually dissatisfied with their relationships when there is a large discrepancy between the amount of personal information they share with their partner and the amount of personal information they receive from their partner (Davidson, Balswick, & Halverson, 1983; Hansen & Schuldt, 1984). Similarly, Afifi, Guerrero, and Egland (1994) found that perceived reciprocity of self-disclosure was the main predictor of relational closeness for male friends. These studies showed that self-disclosure is important not only in building relationships but also in maintaining them.

STAGE THEORIES OF RELATIONSHIP DEVELOPMENT

As you might suspect, self-disclosure, along with other patterns of communication, changes as a relationship progresses. Indeed, much of the research on relationship development focuses on the stages of people's relationships. In this section, we look at two popular stage theories of relational development. Both theories focus on how communication changes as people move from being strangers to being intimates.

Social Penetration Theory

To map out the progression of self-disclosure, Altman and Taylor (1973) described four stages that people can go through as they progress from being strangers to being intimates; Figure 5.2 shows the different stages. As discussed earlier, social penetration theory originally focused specifically on how the dimensions of depth, breadth, and frequency change; more recent research suggests that valence and duration may also change as relationships move through the different stages. Although the stages of social penetration suggest that relationships generally develop through the process of increased disclosure, Altman and Taylor noted that some couples move back and forth between the stages rather than progressing in a linear fashion.

Stage 1: Orientation. This stage includes the first time people meet and sometimes lasts for two or three more encounters, particularly if each meeting is short in duration. The orientation stage involves low levels of depth and breadth. The two people do not know each other, so they stay at the superficial level of the self-disclosure "onion" (see Figure 5.1). This helps them avoid becoming vulnerable. Bits of information, such as one's name, occupation, or major, may be exchanged in an effort to reduce uncertainty. The valence of the disclosure is usually positive, with participants trying to make a good impression by following rules of social politeness.

Most initial encounters are characterized by disclosure that is low in depth and breadth, and positive in valence. There are exceptions, however. One

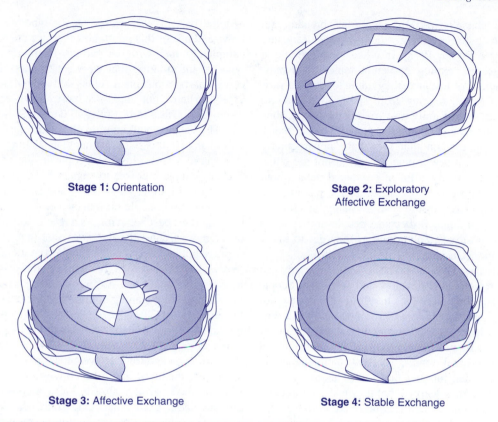

Stage 1: Orientation

Stage 2: Exploratory Affective Exchange

Stage 3: Affective Exchange

Stage 4: Stable Exchange

Figure 5.2 Changes in Depth and Breadth by Relational Stage

SOURCE: Adapted from Altman and Taylor (1973).

is the stranger-on-the-plane (or train) phenomenon mentioned earlier. This type of situation is special because of the potential for high duration and low frequency. In other words, we do not expect to see the other person again. And if we do see the other person sometime in the future, we might feel uncomfortable about the depth and breadth of our self-disclosure. For example, there is a scene in an old movie in which two people meet on a train. The woman is heading to the West Coast to marry her longtime boyfriend, but she has started to doubt her feelings for her fiancé. She discloses her misgivings to the stranger on the train, confessing that she thinks she is only going along with the marriage because the relationship is old and comfortable and that she no longer loves her fiancé. Later in the

movie, the stranger on the train appears again— as her fiancé's best man! Needless to say, she is extremely embarrassed and uncomfortable. Another exception to the orientation stage's general pattern of low breadth and depth is a first session between counselor and client. Often the client will discuss his or her problems and concerns in great depth because the environment is considered safe and the counselor is a professional.

Stage 2: Exploratory Affective Exchange. This stage is typical of acquaintances, casual friends, and casual daters. Sometimes, people move beyond this stage and develop closer relationships; at other times, they stay at this stage and simply remain acquaintances or casual friends. The exploratory affective exchange stage is characterized by increasing breadth and frequency but relatively low depth of self-disclosure (Altman & Taylor, 1973). In other words, people in this stage will "explore" potential topics by increasing breadth. For instance, they might touch on a variety of subjects, ranging from sports to politics to adventures with family and friends. However, they will not delve too deeply into any of these topics. They might explain that they have a particularly good relationship with one parent but not the other, but they won't give a lot of emotional detail about their innermost feelings about either parent. The valence of the disclosure is still, usually, much more positive than negative because people are trying to maintain positive impressions as they get to know one another (Guerrero & Andersen, 2000).

Increasing the breadth of self-disclosure can help a relationship develop and intensify. People often discover what topics they can talk about comfortably, what they have in common, and what they like (or dislike) about one another. During Connor and Anne's first few conversations, they talked about fairly superficial topics, such as their majors in school and their jobs. As they talked about these and other topics, they learned that they had a lot in common, which made them feel more comfortable self-disclosing more intimate information. Thus once partners have explored enough so that they begin to trust each other, they will begin to disclose in more depth. At this point, duration often increases because they want to know each other even better. Long phone conversations and face-to-face interactions are commonplace at the end of this stage, as partners try to learn as much about each other as they can. In some cases, though, people in the exploratory affective exchange stage decide that they do not have much in common and that they should either remain casual friends or terminate the relationship.

Stage 3: Affective Exchange. When relationships progress into the third stage, both breadth and depth of self-disclosure have increased significantly. This stage is usually reserved for people we consider to be good friends, as well as family members and romantic partners. Now, we feel a sense of closeness and connection to the partner, and we feel less vulnerable. We believe that we can trust the partner and

that the partner will accept us for who we are—flaws and all. At this point, however, we are still not completely open with our partner. There are certain types of information that we wish to keep hidden, certain parts of our inner selves that are still too private to share. For the most part, however, self-disclosure is high in breadth and depth.

The valence and duration of self-disclosure also may change in this stage. Rather than sticking mostly to positive self-disclosures, people in the affective exchange stage feel free to engage in negative self-disclosure. In some ways the "honeymoon period" has ended, and people no longer feel that they have to be on their best behavior. As a result, conflict may occur more frequently as people feel that they can express both positive and negative emotions more freely. The duration of the typical self-disclosive conversation may also lessen as people settle into this stage. The beginning of this stage, like the end of the exploratory affective exchange stage, is often marked by long, in-depth conversations as partners strive to get to know each other and then to show their affection and trust. However, as the relationship stabilizes, the need for long conversations diminishes because partners already know a considerable amount about each other. One study showed that although people disclose more intimate thoughts and feelings to their spouses than to strangers, they disclose more self-descriptive information (such as basic facts about themselves) to strangers (Dindia et al., 1997). This suggests that people's self-disclosure changes from an emphasis on self-description to an emphasis on sharing intimate thoughts and feelings as a relationship moves from the initial stages to the affective exchange or stable exchange stage.

Stage 4: Stable Exchange. The final stage in social penetration theory involves complete self-disclosure. In terms of breadth, every topic is fair game. In terms of depth, partners feel free to disclose their innermost thoughts and feelings and are completely open with each other about everything. In reality, however, achieving a true state of stable exchange is very difficult. Even in our closest relationships we tend to keep some secrets from our partner (Vangelisti, 1994a). In fact, Baxter and Wilmot (1984) found that 91% of the partners in romantic couples they surveyed said that there was at least one topic that they never discussed with their relational partner. Common taboo topics included the state of the relationship, past relationships, and sexual experiences. Thus although stable exchange may seem like a worthy goal, it is probably an unrealistic one. Partners in many couples exchange information on a regular basis, but very few actually share 100% of their thoughts and feelings.

In any case, complete self-disclosure is probably not the best prescription for a happy relationship. Elsewhere in this book, we emphasize that many people have strong needs for privacy and autonomy (see Chapters 9 and 12). As Hatfield suggested, too much self-disclosure may rob us of our sense of privacy and make us feel overly dependent on others. In addition, it can be nice to keep some mystery in our relationships. This is not to say that people should purposely hide important information from their close relational partners. They should, however, feel that they have the right to control private information and to keep certain innermost thoughts and feelings undisclosed (Petronio, 2002). This helps explain why a stable rate of exchange is difficult to achieve in relationships. Although close relational partners may engage in many conversations that are completely open, sometimes they may keep information private. Also, complete self-disclosure can require a lot of effort and energy. Thus, close relational partners often cycle back and forth between high and low levels of self-disclosure, even though the potential for high levels of self-disclosure is always there. Similarly, partners in stable relationships may go for a while without disclosing anything very intimate, but then "catch up" by engaging in a long, in-depth conversation.

Stages of "Coming Together"

A complementary stage model of relationship development was created by Knapp (Knapp & Vangelisti, 2005), who sought to describe the process of coming together by looking at a variety of communication behaviors beyond self-disclosure. Knapp's model was based on the same general idea as social penetration theory. That is, as relationships develop, communication will become more personal, and

people will worry less about managing their impressions. Knapp visualized the stages of relational development as a staircase leading upward, with each step or stage representing an increase in intimacy. Knapp also visualized stages of relational disengagement as a descending staircase, with each stage characterized by more avoidance and separation. In this chapter, we focus on Knapp's coming-together stages, or the ascending part of the staircase. In Chapter 15 on relational disengagement, we discuss Knapp's coming-apart stages. Like Altman and Taylor, Knapp recognized that although many couples follow the type of linear trajectory depicted in his model, other couples skip stages and move back and forth between stages.

The Initiating Stage. The first stage in Knapp's model is similar to the orientation stage in social penetration theory. Here, people are meeting each other for the first time. They are usually trying to make a positive impression, so they engage in polite, friendly, safe, and superficial communication. A greeting or question followed by a reply is typical of the initiating stage. For example, when Connor first met Anne he said, "Hi, I haven't seen you at our meetings before. Is this your first time coming?" Anne responded, "Yeah. Have you been coming for long?" Connor said he'd been to a couple of other meetings but was also fairly new. Then they exchanged names and continued talking about rather superficial topics, such as what happens at the Sierra Club, until the meeting was called to order. This short conversation helped Connor and Anne reduce uncertainty and set a foundation for future interactions. In some cases, however, people never progress beyond the initiating stage. Think of people with whom you work or take classes. You may recognize some of these people, but not spend time talking to them. When you see these types of casual acquaintances, you may exchange a quick greeting and reply ("Hi, how are you?" "Fine, thanks") but nothing more.

Initial interactions may play a key role in determining whether people like Anne and Connor develop their relationship further. Indeed, some researchers have argued that people determine their feelings for one another very quickly during initial encounters (Berg & Clark, 1986). They then communicate differently based on whether they like the person or not. According to **predicted outcome value theory**, during initial encounters people make decisions about how rewarding they expect a relationship to be (see Chapter 4). These initial impressions can have lasting effects on how a relationship develops. In one study, undergraduate students were paired with a stranger of the same sex to talk for between 3 and 10 minutes on the first day of class (Sunnafrank & Ramirez, 2004). After this initial interaction, students recorded their perceptions of how rewarding it would be for them to become involved in a relationship with the person they just met. The students were then surveyed again later in the semester. Students were much more likely to report developing a relationship with someone whom they initially perceived to be rewarding. They were also more likely to have sat near them during class, communicated with them frequently, and felt high levels of social attraction and liking. This study demonstrated that the first few minutes of initial encounters have a strong influence on if, and how, relationships develop.

The Experimenting Stage. The second stage in Knapp's model is similar to the exploratory affective exchange stage in social penetration theory. Impression management is still a goal, but the more salient goal is to get to know the other person better to determine whether to pursue a relationship. Here, people exchange a broad array of fairly superficial information as they try to identify each other's likes and dislikes, values, attitudes, and personal opinions. For example, Connor might ask Anne what she likes to do on the weekend, whether she has a family, and where her hometown is. Anne might ask Connor about his job, his education, and the reasons he decided to join the Sierra Club. Each is likely to reciprocate as well. Thus when Anne says she likes to play tennis and go biking or hiking on the weekends, Connor might say that he also enjoys the outdoors and has always wanted to learn to play tennis better. According to Knapp (Knapp & Vangelisti, 2005), this type of small talk is the key to understanding the experimenting stage. Both Anne and Connor are "experimenting" in that they are trying

to find out more about each other. Small talk allows them to fulfill a number of goals simultaneously, including discovering common interests, seeing if it would be worthwhile to pursue a closer relationship, reducing uncertainty in a safe manner that does not make them vulnerable, and allowing them to maintain a sense of connection with other people without putting themselves at much risk for hurt or rejection.

The Intensifying Stage. When experimenting leads people to pursue a closer relationship, they usually move into the intensifying stage. Typically, movement into this stage is gradual. Breadth and depth of self-disclosure increase slowly but steadily, and displays of affection begin tentatively. For example, in a romantic relationship, a peck on the lips is likely to precede a deeper kiss, which is likely to precede intimate touching. Other types of communication common in this stage include using nicknames or forms of endearment, making "we" instead of "I" statements ("We should go down to Mexico sometime"), and making statements that reflect positive regard and commitment, such as saying "I love you" or "You are my very best friend." Declarations such as these usually first occur in the intensifying stage and then continue into the next two stages as couples integrate and bond.

Work by Tolhuizen (1989) gives further insight into how people intensify their relationships. In his research, Tolhuizen found 15 different intensification strategies; Box 5.3 lists these strategies. The three most common strategies are increased contact, relationship negotiation (which involves talking about the relationship), and social support and assistance (which involves asking someone for advice and/or comfort). Nearly 40% of the people Tolhuizen surveyed described increased contact as an important intensification strategy, while 29% and 26% mentioned relationship negotiation and social support/assistance, respectively. Thus, these three strategies appear to be fairly common ways of intensifying various relationships. The other strategies listed in Box 5.3 appear to play more minor roles in the intensification process, but they still represent important means by which people escalate their relationships.

BOX 5.3   Highlights

Tolhuizen's Strategies for Intensifying Relationships

1. *Increased contact* includes seeing or calling the person more often (39.2%).

2. *Relationship negotiation* includes openly discussing the state of the relationship and the feelings the partners have for one another (29.1%).

3. *Social support and assistance* involves asking people for support, advice, and comfort (26.1%).

4. *Increased rewards* includes doing favors and making sacrifices for one another, such as helping someone move or helping with household tasks (17.6%).

5. *Direct definitional bid* involves asking the partner to make a definite commitment, such as seeing each other exclusively, moving in together, or getting married (16.1%).

6. *Tokens of affection* includes sending flowers, cards, and gifts, as well as exchanging rings (16.1%).

7. *Personalized communication* includes using idiomatic communication, such as special nicknames and inside jokes, as well as listening empathically (15.1%).

8. *Verbal expressions of affection* includes uttering declarations such as "I love you" and "I hope we are always this close" (14.1%).

9. *Suggestive actions* includes flirting, trying to get someone jealous, and playing "hard to get" (13.1%).

10. *Nonverbal expressions of affection* includes gazing at the partner lovingly, touching the partner, and smiling (12.1%).

11. *Social enmeshment* involves getting to know and spending more time with the partner's family and friends, sometimes through activities such as spending a holiday together (11.6%).

12. *Acceptance of definition bid* involves redefining the relationship through actions such as saying "yes" when the partner asks for more commitment or agreeing to date exclusively, move in together, or get married (9.5%).

13. *Personal appearance* involves changing one's physical appearance to please the partner by engaging in behaviors such as trying to lose weight, changing one's hairstyle, or dressing particularly well (9.5%).

14. *Sexual intimacy* involves engaging in increasingly intimate behavior, often including sexual relations (8%).

15. *Behavioral adaptation* involves changing one's behavior to please the partner, perhaps by trying to secure a better job or criticize the partner less and compliment the partner more (7.5%).

NOTE: The percentages in this box represent the percentage of people in Tolhuizen's study who described or reported using each strategy. Because people were allowed to describe as many strategies as they deemed relevant, the percentages add up to more than 100%.

The Integrating Stage. By the time two people reach the integrating stage, they have already achieved a high level of intimacy. Now, they are ready to show that intimacy to others by presenting themselves as a "couple." This type of presentation is not limited to romantic couples; friends often present themselves as a unified team as well. The key here is that the two people have developed a relational identity; they see themselves as part of a dyad with some aspects of their personalities and experiences overlapping (Knapp & Vangelisti, 2005). Once this coupling has occurred, people outside the relationship begin to see the partners as two halves of a whole. It is easy to see when this has taken place. For example, imagine that Connor attends a party alone and several people stop and ask him, "Where's Anne?" This indicates that people in Connor's social network regard Anne and Connor as a couple; they expect to see the two of them together. Connor and Anne may also start receiving joint invitations to parties or joint Christmas gifts, which shows that other people see them as a committed couple.

Other types of changes occur within the dyad in this stage. Close friends or romantic partners may be able to complete each other's sentences, and their tastes, attitudes, and opinions may merge. For example, in the movie *When Harry Met Sally*, the last scene shows Harry and Sally talking about their wedding. Sally starts to describe their wedding cake, including the rich chocolate sauce that they had "on the side." Harry concludes the description by saying that it is important to have the sauce on the side, because not everyone likes the same amount of sauce on their cake. This is a good example of coupling since Sally, not Harry, was originally the person who insisted on ordering the sauce on the side. Other signs of coupling include wearing similar clothing, opening a joint bank account, designating a favorite tune as "our song," and merging social networks.

The Bonding Stage. In the final stage of Knapp's model, partners find a way to publicly declare their commitment to each other, usually through the institutionalization of the relationship. Perhaps the most obvious way of institutionalizing a romantic relationship is through marriage. Getting married shows commitment and also makes it harder to leave the relationship. Most people cannot simply walk away from a marriage. There are possessions to divide, perhaps children to provide for, and a socially shared history that is hard to leave behind. Marriage can also be thought of as a social ritual, in that two people come together before family and friends to declare their love for each other. Such a public declaration cements their bond even further. Importantly, in states that do not allow gay and lesbian couples to marry, these couples often still have public commitment ceremonies uniting them as life partners in front of friends and family. These ceremonies underscore how important public commitment is to most couples.

Other types of relationships also reach the bonding stage, although the institutionalization of these relationships is more difficult. Friends and family members, however, can make public, enduring commitments to one another in many different ways. For instance, if you get married, the people you choose to stand up as your bridesmaids or groomsmen will be an important part of this critical life event, and they will hold that place in your memory forever. By choosing them, you are telling your social network that these people have a special place in your life. Similarly, if you have a child and choose godparents, these individuals will be part of a very important social ritual that publicly lets others know you value and trust them. Some friendship rituals, such as becoming blood brothers or getting matching tattoos, may also be ways to show a permanent bond.

The Ordering and Timing of Stages

When thinking about the two stage theories we have discussed, it is important to note that people do not always move through stages in an orderly manner. According to Altman and Taylor (1973), self-disclosure usually unfolds gradually, with people progressing through the various stages one at a time, in the "proper" order. However, they acknowledge that this is not always the case, as the stranger-on-the-plane phenomenon suggests. Similarly, Knapp has noted that his five stages show the typical pattern of relational development for many couples but that variations frequently take place (Knapp & Vangelisti, 2005). Couples might go through the stages in a different order, or they might skip some stages entirely. For example, some romantic couples meet, fall in love at first sight, and quickly get married. Other

SOURCE: Copyright: iStockphoto.com/Nicole Gawron

Photo 5.1   Wedding rings are an outward sign that a couple has reached the bonding stage.

couples move in together after only a few dates. However, a pattern of rapid escalation is atypical, and when people skip stages or move too quickly through them, they might later go back and engage in communication appropriate for that stage. Take a couple who meets and soon gets married as an example. Their friends and family might be surprised at the news of their marriage, and the newlyweds may need to work on merging their social networks and gaining acceptance as a couple. In this case, some of the processes that typically occur during the integrating stage would be occurring after the bonding stage.

THE TURNING POINT APPROACH

A turning point is "any event or occurrence that is associated with change in a relationship" (Baxter & Bullis, 1986, p. 469). Turning points can also be thought of as major relational events. Interestingly, most of the scenes in romantic movies and novels consist of significant relational events or turning points. This is probably because turning points help tell the story of relational change. Rather than focusing on the more mundane events that occur on a day-to-day basis, the turning-point approach emphasizes those events that stand out in people's minds as having the strongest impact on their relationships. Couples tell stories about turning points to their social networks (such as "how we met"), and turning points are often remembered through celebrations and mementos, such as anniversaries and pictures (Baxter & Pittman, 2001). This is not to say that mundane events are unimportant. Indeed, mundane events help shape the way people see their relationships, even if such events sometimes go unnoticed and unappreciated. These mundane events can be thought of as part of the regular road on which a relationship travels. Turning points, in contrast, are the detours relationships sometimes take.

The turning point approach is very different from stage approaches to relationship development and disengagement, even though turning points can mark entry into a new stage. Social penetration theory, for example, suggests that relationships develop fairly smoothly and gradually as people's communication becomes more personal. In contrast, according to the turning point approach, relationships can follow a choppier path, with both positive and negative events affecting their course. Research suggests that both the turning point approach and stage approaches have merit; some relationships follow a linear, gradual pattern of developing intimacy; other relationships are characterized by periods of extreme growth or decline, or by a random pattern of highs and lows. For example, Johnson and her colleagues examined how friendships develop and deteriorate (Johnson, Wittenberg, Villigran, Mazur, & Villigran, 2003; Johnson et al., 2004). They found that between 40% and 50% of friendships fit the linear pattern—closeness increased gradually as friends developed their relationships and closeness decreased gradually in friendships that ended. The other 50% to 60% of friendships developed and deteriorated in a nonlinear manner.

Various types of turning points are related to closeness and commitment in romantic relationships, family relationships, and friendships (Baxter, 1986; Baxter, Braithwaite, & Nicholson, 1999; Bullis, Clark, & Sline, 1993; Golish, 2000; Johnson et al., 2003, 2004). Next, we discuss some of the most common turning points that have been identified in the literature.

Communication-Based Turning Points

Although most turning points include some level of communication, the act of communication itself constitutes a turning point in some cases. For example, **get-to-know time** includes initial interactions and focuses on the quantity rather than the quality of communication and time spent together. First meetings and first dates typify this turning point (Bullis et al., 1993). In contrast, **quality communication** focuses on special times when two people have a high-quality interaction, such as having an especially long and intimate conversation. Both forms of communication are often integral to the story of romantic relationships. For instance, people often ask how a couple met. Connor might reply that "we met at a Sierra Club meeting and hit it off right

away." Anne might tell people, "I knew we had something special on our first date when we sat under the stars together wrapped in a blanket and talked for hours." Communicative events can also be turning points in family relationships. In a study on turning points in relationships between adult children and their parents, communication issues such as finally talking about something important or feeling listened to were identified as turning points that increased closeness (Golish, 2000). Friends also identify self-disclosure about feelings and discovery of positive personality traits as turning points that help develop closeness (Johnson et al., 2004).

Activities and Special Occasions

Other turning points involve engaging in activity and spending quality time with others. For romantic partners, occasions such as meeting the family and going on trips together are common turning points (Bullis et al., 1993). For family members, this turning point includes vacations, engaging in special activities together, holiday rituals, and special occasions such as graduations. A study on blended families showed that quality time together is strongly related to bonding (Baxter et al., 1999). Blended families occur when two previously separate families merge together into one family, as is often the case when divorced or widowed parents remarry. In the study by Baxter and her colleagues, turning points related to holidays and special events made people feel like the blended family was "more of a family," about two thirds of the time. Turning points involving activity, such as going on vacation together, were related to feeling more like a family 100% of the time. Similarly, turning points that involve engaging in special activities together are related to closeness in friendships. In fact, Johnson et al. (2003) found that activity sharing was the most common turning point identified in friendships.

Events Related to Passion and Romance

Some turning points mark particular junctures in the development of one's relationship based on the level of passion or romance that is present. **Passionate events** include the first kiss, the first time a couple exchanges the words "I love you," the first sexual encounter, and other passionate phenomena such as falling in love at first sight (Bullis et al., 1993). According to research by Metts (2004), the order in which passionate event turning points occur can affect relationship development; people were more likely to escalate their relationships and feel positively about one another when saying "I love you" preceded having sex. **Romantic relationship transitions** refer to the "point or period in time when a relationship changes from being either platonic or nonexistent to being romantic" (Mongeau, Serewicz, Henningsen, & Davis, 2006, p. 338). Some passionate events, such as love at first sight, qualify as romantic relationship transitions. At other times, friends or acquaintances turn their previously platonic relationships into romantic relationships.

Events Related to Commitment and Exclusivity

While some passionate events, such as saying "I love you," may imply some level of commitment, other turning points more directly reflect how committed two people are to each other and their relationship. **Exclusivity** occurs when people decide to date only each other and drop all other rivals. Somewhat related to exclusivity (or the lack thereof) is the turning point of **external competition**, which occurs when a person feels threatened by a third party or an activity that is taking up a lot of the partner's time. Sometimes, an ex-spouse or former girlfriend or boyfriend re-emerges; at other times a new rival starts to compete for the partner's affections; at still other times responsibilities related to work, school, or child care, or time spent with friends, interfere with the relationship. External competition can reinforce or threaten partners' levels of commitment toward one another. Finally, romantic couples can show **serious commitment** by events such as moving in together or getting married.

Changes in Families and Social Networks

While marriage can change the structure of a couple's relationship, other turning points often involve changes in a family's structure. For blended families, **changes in the household configuration** is a primary turning point (Baxter et al., 1999). Children may have to deal with a new stepparent, parents may have to deal with new stepchildren, and children may have to deal with new step-siblings. Contrary to the storyline in shows such as *The Brady Bunch*, the transition from one's family of origin to a blended family is often fraught with problems and confusion. **New family members** also constitute a turning point in other types of relationships. For example, a new baby changes the dynamics of a family for both the parents and any siblings. In Golish's (2000) study of adult children's relationships with their parents, some people said that a new baby brought them closer together. For example, a father and son may feel more emotionally connected when the son has his first baby and the father, as a consequence, has his first grandchild. At other times, sibling rivalry or jealousy may occur when a new baby becomes part of the family. In friendships, **interference from a romantic partner** can sometimes cause conflict and decreased closeness between friends (Johnson et al., 2004). As a case in point, imagine that Anne's best friend starts to feel increasingly left out and neglected as Anne spends more and more time with Connor.

Proximity and Distance

Another set of turning points deals with physical separation and reunion. In Bullis et al.'s (1993) study of romantic partners, **physical separation** was reported when people were apart, often involuntarily, due to vacations, business trips, and school breaks. **Reunions** occurred when the period of physical separation was over and the couple was together again. Adult children also report that **physical distance** is an important turning point in their relationship with their parents (Golish, 2000). Specifically, when children move out of the house, they sometimes feel that their relationship with their parents improves because the parent now perceives them as an adult. So far, the turning points under this category focus on physical distance. However, the desire for psychological distance and autonomy can also mark a significant turning point in parent-child relationships. In her study on parents and children, Golish identified **rebellious teenager** as a turning point that occurs when children express a need for autonomy from their parents. Friends also identify turning points related to proximity and distance. For example, friends often recall that **becoming roommates** was a significant turning point in their relationship that led to either increased or decreased closeness. Friends who ended their relationship often point to turning points such as **not living together anymore** and an **increase in distance** as markers of relationship decline (Johnson et al., 2004).

Crisis and Conflict

The challenges that people face are often significant turning points in their relationships with one another. Bullis and her colleagues identified **disengagement and conflict**, which includes a couple's first big fight, attempts to de-escalate or withdraw from the relationship, and actual relational breakups, as major relational turning points. Conflict is also a significant turning point in friendships (Johnson et al., 2004). Researchers examining turning points in both families and friendships have talked about **times of crisis** as a significant turning point (Baxter et al., 1999; Golish, 2000; Johnson et al., 2004). Times of crisis include illnesses, death, accidents, and major financial problems. In Baxter et al.'s study of blended families, 72% of the people reported that these crisis-related turning points brought the family closer together. A crisis situation can also lead to the turning point called **sacrifice or support**, which includes being there to support and comfort each other in crisis situations, such as dealing with the death of a loved one or helping one regain confidence after an embarrassing failure (Bullis et al., 1993; Johnson et al., 2004). Similarly, although conflict can decrease closeness and commitment, couples sometimes make up and feel more connected than ever. Thus, **making up** is another important turning point in many relationships. Baxter and Bullis (1986) noted that there is not always a perfect correspondence between conflict and making up. Sometimes, the conflict is viewed as more significant than the making-up session or vice versa.

Perceptual Changes

Sometimes people report that a turning point does not have a specific cause. Instead, they simply report that their attitudes toward the partner changed somehow, even though they cannot figure out exactly why. When attitudes and perceptions become more positive, the turning point is called **positive psychic change** (Bullis et al., 1993). For example, Anne might suddenly see Connor as more physically attractive and sexually appealing (a positive psychic change) without being able to pinpoint why. In other cases, labeled **negative psychic change**, attitudes and perceptions become more negative. A person might suddenly see the relationship as boring and the partner as dull even though nothing else has really changed.

Turning Points and Relationship Development

These turning points probably make sense to you. If you were asked to identify the events that had changed a relationship of yours in a significant way, you would likely list many of these events. In fact, you could create a map of your relationship, much like those that the participants in the Baxter and Bullis (1986) and Bullis et al. (1993) studies made. A sample of such a map, referred to as a **turning point analysis**, is shown in Figure 5.3. As you can see, the turning point approach does not depict a smooth, gradual increase in commitment. Instead, this approach reveals a rockier road that includes all the important ups and downs that influence the growth, and in some cases the demise, of close relationships.

Turning points are often related to tension about how much information to disclose or how close you want to be to someone. **Dialectical tensions** involve wanting two things that, on the surface, seem to be opposite (see Chapter 9). A study by Baxter and Erbert (1999) showed that many turning points are related to the dialectical tension of autonomy/connection. Autonomy involves wanting to be independent and self-sufficient, whereas connection involves wanting to be emotionally and physically close to someone. Turning points related to commitment

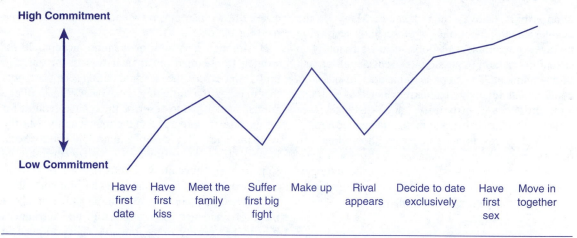

Figure 5.3   A Sample Turning Point Analysis

show closeness and connection. Other turning points, such as rebellious teenager and physical separation, may be related to wanting independence and autonomy. The dialectical tension of openness/closedness is also associated with many of the turning points (Baxter & Erbert, 1999). Openness refers to the desire to disclose information to others, whereas closedness refers to the desire to keep some information private. The communication-based turning points, such as get-to-know time and quality communication, reflect certain levels of openness and closedness. Baxter and her colleagues have argued that couples need to manage dialectical tensions such as these as they move through various turning points and develop their relationships.

Turning points also help explain the different paths that relationships take. One study looked at the first 4 years of blended families (Baxter et al., 1999). Many of these newly blended families (around 31%) followed an **accelerated trajectory**, with family members rapidly moving toward feeling like a family. People in the accelerated trajectory reported that positive turning points outweighed negative turning points by about 3.65:1, which enabled them to feel bonded as a family. The second most common pattern was a **prolonged trajectory**, which involved a slow but steady increase in feeling

like a family. The 27% of people in this trajectory reported more positive than negative turning points, with a ratio of about 3:1. The other fairly common pattern was the **turbulent trajectory**, which was characterized by a lot of highs and lows as reflected in both positive and negative turning points. This roller-coaster type of relationship development occurred in about 22% of blended families.

Two other types of trajectories were found for blended families. A **stagnating trajectory** was reported by around 14% of people. Families following this trajectory consistently felt low levels of connection. Their ratio of positive to negative turning points was about 2:1, but the positive turning points did not seem to improve their feelings of being a family. The last pattern, the **declining trajectory,** was reported by around 6% of people. These blended families started out with relatively high feelings of connection but felt less and less like a family over time. In fact, by the end of the 4 years, their level of feeling like a family was really low. The declining trajectory was the only trajectory characterized by more negative than positive turning points, with a ratio of 2 negative turning points for every 1 positive turning point.

The turning point approach is a useful perspective for understanding the different trajectories that relationships take as they develop. Many of the chapters in this book take a closer look at turning points. For example, this book includes chapters on sexual interaction (a passionate event), conflict, and disengagement. This book also includes discussions about events related to exclusivity (such as jealousy and infidelity), proximity, and distance (see Chapters 3, 12, and 13), and in this chapter we already discussed issues related to get-to-know time and quality in-depth communication. Next, we discuss two additional turning points that are especially germane to developing and escalating romantic relationships: first dates and cohabitation.

First Dates

First dates provide a starting point for many romantic relationships. Whether the individuals are strangers on a blind date, acquaintances who are physically attracted to one another, or friends who have decided to explore the romantic potential in their relationship, first dates mark the possibility of embarking on a new romantic adventure. The research on first dates has focused on a number of issues, including date initiation and the goals and expectations people have for first dates.

Date Initiation

The social norms that govern how men and women get acquainted have changed throughout history. Mongeau, Hale, Johnson, and Hillis (1993) noted that at the end of the 19th century courtship involved men "calling" on women at their homes. The "call" often involved the woman inviting the man over for dinner or tea in the presence of her family. Around the beginning of the 20th century, dating started to replace calling. Dating involved two people going somewhere outside the home together, often to have dinner out and go to a concert, play, or social event. This shift from calling to dating also entailed a change in who initiated the get-acquainted process. With calling, women largely controlled the situation— they could invite the man over and decide what food and home entertainment they would provide. With dating, men usually controlled the situation—they

asked the woman out, provided transportation, and paid for the date.

Although it is now much more acceptable for women to ask men out than it was in the early to mid-20th century, the standard dating script still puts the man in the initiating position. When college students are asked to describe the typical request for a first date, they report that the man usually asks the woman. They also describe dates in heterosexual relationships as following a fairly predictable sequence (Honeycutt & Cantrill, 2001; Laner & Ventrone, 2000): The man asks the woman out. If she agrees, he plans the date and picks her up at her place of residence. She greets him and introduces him to her family or roommates. They engage in small talk and then depart. During the date, they engage in more small talk as they try to get to know each other. The man takes the woman home, they thank each other, kiss, and in some cases the man suggests that he will call and/or that they should get together again soon. The man then departs.

Even though this scenario is still regarded as the typical first-date script, dates such as these are starting to be replaced by group activities, where potential partners meet amid interaction between groups of friends and then break off into dyads. In addition, although men still tend to initiate dates more than women, date initiation by women is fairly commonplace. In one of the first studies to examine this issue, 87% of men reported that they had been asked out by a woman at least once (Kelley, Pilchowicz, & Byrne, 1981). The men in this study reported having positive responses to date initiation by women, even though the relationships that these initiations started were often short-lived. A later study by Mongeau et al. (1993) found that 90% of men reported that they had been asked out on a date by a woman, and 83% of men had been asked out on a *first* date by a woman. These results suggest that women might feel freer to ask men on dates once a relationship has developed. Importantly, Mongeau and his colleagues also reported that almost all the men accepted dates initiated by women.

Because women-initiated first dates break the stereotypical dating script, researchers have investigated how women who initiate dates are perceived. Studies suggest that women who initiate dates are seen as more open, liberal, active, and extroverted, but less attractive than women who wait to be asked by the man (Mongeau & Carey, 1996; Mongeau et al., 1993). Some studies also show that men are likely to have higher sexual expectations for dates that are initiated by women, even though these expectations are not likely to be met (Mongeau & Johnson, 1995; Muehlenhard & Scardino, 1985). In other words, men might expect that there will be more sexual activity on dates initiated by women, perhaps because the woman is perceived to be more liberal, open, and attracted to the man, but in actuality, dates initiated by women tend to be characterized by the same amount of or less sexual activity than dates initiated by men.

Expectations and Goals on First Dates

Expectations related to sexual activity represent only one of several types of goals that people have on first dates. Moreover, the goals people have vary based on the type of relationship people had prior to the first date, as well as who initiated the date. The goals people have for first dates include the following: having fun, reducing uncertainty, investigating romantic potential, developing friendship, and engaging in sexual activity (Mongeau, Serewicz, & Therrien, 2004). Having fun and reducing uncertainty are the most common goals. **Having fun** simply refers to wanting to have a good time and enjoy oneself. **Reducing uncertainty about the partner** refers to wanting to find out more about the person, including her or his attitudes, goals, and interests. The goals of investigating romantic potential and developing friendship are also fairly common on first dates. **Investigating romantic potential** involves trying to determine if there are romantic feelings or chemistry between two people. **Developing friendship**, in contrast, focuses on trying to determine if two people have enough in common to be friends and do things together or if two people should strengthen an already existing friendship. Finally, **engaging in sexual activity**, such as kissing and having sex, was the least commonly reported of these five goals.

These goals likely influence the communication that occurs on first dates. When people have similar goals, the goals of both individuals are more likely to be fulfilled, leading to a "good" date. Take Connor and Anne as an example. Imagine that as they embark on their first date together, they both believe that they have already established intimacy at the friendship level. Their priority, then, is to determine if there is sexual chemistry and the potential for a romantic relationship. During their first date, they show affection to one another, share personal stories, and spend considerable time kissing, which helps them both decide that the relationship does indeed have romantic and sexual potential. On the other hand, imagine that Anne was still uncertain about Connor as a person and potential friend, whereas Connor's goal was to determine romantic potential and to engage in sexual activity. In this case, the different goals that Anne and Connor have could put them at cross-purposes, with both being frustrated that they could not reach their individual goals. As Mongeau et al. (2004) put it, "What constitutes a 'good' or 'bad' date, then, depends on the compatibility of partners' goals" (p. 143).

The goals that people have also depend on the type of relationship they share prior to the first date. Some people enter the first date as strangers or acquaintances, whereas others are already good friends. Strangers and acquaintances are more likely to have the goals of reducing uncertainty about the person and developing a friendship than friends. In contrast, friends are more likely to have the goals of investigating romantic potential and engaging in sexual activity than strangers or acquaintances (Mongeau et al., 2004). Friends are also more likely to expect high levels of intimacy and affection on first dates (Morr & Mongeau, 2004). The goal of having fun appears to be salient regardless of the type of relationship. These findings comport with ideas from social penetration theory and uncertainty reduction theory (see Chapter 4).

When people do not know one another well, their primary goal is to seek information. During the beginning stages of a relationship, people often exchange rather superficial information as part of the getting acquainted process. However, once people have developed a friendship and exchanged in-depth information with one another, their goal on a first date may be to focus on other forms of intimacy that are yet undeveloped, such as sexual intimacy. Having fun may be an important goal on first dates because it reflects the valence dimension of self-disclosure: People tend to like and build relationships with those with whom they have enjoyable interaction. Similarly, people are more likely to develop close relationships with people whom they regard as rewarding (Sunnafrank & Ramirez, 2004).

Finally, some research has examined sex differences in goals and expectations related to sexual activity on first dates. This research suggests that men expect and desire more sexual activity on first dates than women (Mongeau & Carey, 1996; Mongeau et al., 2004). However, the differences in sexual expectations for men versus women are not very large. College-age men tend to expect heavy kissing, whereas college-age women tend to expect light kissing (Mongeau & Johnson, 1995; Morr & Mongeau, 2004).

COHABITATION

Cohabitation, or living together without being married, is a turning point in many romantic relationships. Couples cohabit for a variety of reasons ranging from convenience and financial advantages to love and the desire to be together. Some people choose to live together rather than get married because they are afraid of commitment or want to retain their autonomy, but most couples initially view cohabitation as a transitional period that occurs between dating and marriage or as a sort of "trial marriage." This is how Anne seems to regard cohabitation. One study showed that 90% of cohabiting couples expected to get married someday to their current partner or to someone else (Cunningham & Antill, 1994). Many of these couples see cohabitation as an "optional stage in the courtship sequence that may or may not end in marriage" (p. 78). Yet studies suggest that less than half of cohabiting partners end up getting married to each other (Blumstein & Schwartz, 1983; Brown, 2000; Bumpass & Sweet, 1989).

Much of the research on cohabitation has focused on determining whether cohabitation is beneficial or harmful to long-term relationships. To answer this question, researchers have compared couples who married without cohabiting first with couples who cohabited before getting married. Researchers have also compared cohabiting couples who marry with those who do not. These studies have focused on a number of issues, including relationship stability, relational quality, and communication patterns.

Relationship Stability

In general, marital relationships are more stable than cohabiting relationships. Some scholars have argued that cohabitation represents a looser bond than marriage because cohabitation involves more autonomy, less commitment, and fewer social and legal barriers to dissolution than does marriage (Schoen & Owens, 1992; Thorton, Axinn, & Teachman, 1995). For instance, a cohabiting couple is less likely to share property than a marital couple, and cohabiting couples can break up without having to file any legal paperwork. The **selection effect** provides another explanation for the instability found in some cohabiting relationships (Lillard, Brien, & Waite, 1995). According to the selection effect, people who choose to cohabit rather than get married have certain personal characteristics and attitudes that make it less likely that their relationships will last. These attitudes include a greater acceptance of divorce and premarital sex, a stronger need for autonomy, and more negative feelings about marriage (Cunningham & Antill, 1994; Lillard et al., 1995). Cohabiting couples who plan to get married are more likely to stay together than those who have no concrete plans for marrying. However, couples who cohabit before marriage are more likely to get divorced than couples who moved directly to marriage (Bennett, Blanc, & Bloom, 1988; Brown, 2000; Bumpass & Sweet, 1989).

Relational Quality

Given that cohabiting couples are more likely to break up than married couples, you probably expect cohabiting couples to report less relational satisfaction than married couples. The research on this issue is mixed. Some studies have shown that married couples who do not live together prior to marriage are more satisfied with their relationships than cohabiting couples or couples who transition from cohabitation to marriage (DeMaris, 1984; DeMaris & Leslie, 1984; Nock, 1995; Stafford, Kline, & Rankin, 2004). Other studies have shown no difference (Yelsma, 1986). Brown and Booth (1996) found that cohabitants who planned to get married were just as satisfied with their relationships as married couples, whereas cohabitants who did not plan to marry were less satisfied.

Importantly, time in the relationship may be a much better predictor of relational satisfaction than whether a couple lived together before marriage. Satisfaction levels appear to decrease over time in marriages regardless of whether couples cohabited or not (Stafford et al., 2004; Yelsma, 1986). This same pattern has been found in relationships between cohabiting gay and lesbian couples. In one study, satisfaction dropped during the first year that gay and lesbian couples lived together, but then rebounded again after they had lived together 11 years or longer (Kurdek, 1989). Couples who move directly toward marriage may still be in the "honeymoon" phase of their relationships. Those who cohabited before marriage may have already moved beyond the honeymoon stage. Thus some of the differences that researchers have found may be due more to time in the relationship than whether a couple had cohabited (Stafford et al., 2004).

Communication Patterns

Time may also be a better predictor of communication patterns than whether a couple cohabited or not. Stafford et al. (2004) compared three types of couples at two points in time over a 5-year period: cohabiting couples who had not married; transitioned couples who had moved from cohabiting to marriage; and married couples. Across all three types of couples, people reported less satisfaction, less sexual interaction, more conflict, and more heated arguing over time. There were also some small differences in communication among the three types of couples. Cohabiting couples reported the most conflict, followed by transitioned couples. Married couples reported the least conflict. Cohabiting couples were also more likely to report violent

behavior, such as hitting or throwing something, than either transitioned or married couples.

Other studies have found similar results. Brownridge and Halli (2000) reported that couples who lived together before marriage were 54% more likely to engage in violent behavior than couples who did not live together prior to marriage. Another study showed that cohabiting couples have more conflict than married couples (Nock, 1995). However, these differences may be strongest when the comparison is between married couples and cohabiting couples who do not plan to marry. Cohabiting couples who plan to marry do not differ from married couples in terms of conflict or violence (Brown & Booth, 1996).

Together, these studies suggest that cohabiting relationships are most likely to be characterized by satisfaction and high-quality communication when the couple is planning to get married. Couples who cohabit because they fear commitment, want high levels of autonomy, or have negative attitudes toward marriage are less likely to be satisfied and more likely to use destructive communication. Communication is also an important ingredient in the recipe for whether a cohabiting relationship will be successful. Cohabiting relationships characterized by positive interaction and low levels of destructive conflict tend to be as stable and satisfying as many marriages (Brown, 2000).

SUMMARY AND APPLICATION

This chapter focused on some of the most influential theories of relationship development and intensification. Although some of these theories suggest that relationships follow a typical pattern, it is important to recognize that every relationship follows a unique trajectory. Social penetration theory and Knapp's coming-together stages give us an idea of what to expect, but the specific paths our relationships travel will usually be filled with unexpected turns. Some relationships are characterized by more linear development than others.

Connor and Anne's relationship provides a good example of how linear stage theories might work with the turning-point approach to explain the trajectory of a particular relationship. Their relationship develops smoothly and in a linear fashion for the first 2 months. Then, they have their first big fight followed by a period of withdrawal and then making up. When they resume their relationship, they follow a fairly linear path toward increasing closeness for a while. Then, a new turning point occurs when Anne raises the issue of cohabitation. This combination of gradually increasing closeness marked by some turbulence due to turning points is probably fairly common in developing relationships.

It is also important to keep in mind that one person may want to intensify a relationship while the other person may not; so two people could actually want to be in different "stages." One person may be trying to reach the intensifying stage of Knapp's model, while the other is content to stay at the experimenting stage. Similarly, two people might map the turning points in their relationship differently. Anne might see the night they spent talking under the stars as the beginning of their romantic relationship, whereas Connor might regard their first kiss as the start of their romance. Anne might also be more ready than Connor to move in together and reach a sort of prebonding stage. If partners hope to develop and sustain a successful relationship, they have to negotiate the path that works well for both individuals. This is especially true when couples reach important relational turning points.

Our fictional couple, Anne and Connor, have just reached such a turning point. Should they move in together now or wait until they get married or engaged? The studies we reviewed in this chapter suggest that the reasons Anne wants to cohabitate are important. If she wants to move in together because she is afraid of a stronger commitment (like marriage) and wants to "test" the relationship, research suggests that cohabitation may not be the best move. Cohabiting couples are most likely to be happy and stay together if they plan on marrying and if their relationship is characterized by positive rather than negative communication patterns. Of course, Connor has some valid concerns. Some research suggests that cohabiting has a negative impact on the long-term happiness and stability of relationships, and if Connor has reservations, Anne needs to respect them and not pressure him to cohabitate. Like so many other aspects of relationships, there is no "right" answer to Anne and Connor's dilemma; they need to decide as a couple what is best for them.

In closing, the relational development models provide a nice blueprint of how close relationships typically unfold over time. Yet every relationship follows a different path, and rarely will relationships progress smoothly as people move from being strangers to being close friends or lovers. The joy of discovering a new friend or developing a new romantic relationship, however, makes the journey worthwhile.

DISCUSSION QUESTIONS

1. Think about times when you felt uncomfortable because someone engaged in too much or too little self-disclosure. What circumstances caused you to feel uncomfortable? In other words, why is self-disclosure considered inappropriate in some contexts and appropriate in others?

2. Stage theories of relational development suggest that although there is some variation, most relationships follow a fairly predictable trajectory. Do you agree or disagree? Do your relationships typically follow the stages outlined by Altman and Taylor's social penetration theory or Knapp's coming-together stages, or do they take a different course?

3. Based on the research reported in this chapter as well as your own personal experiences and observations, what is your position regarding cohabitation before marriage? When do you think it might be harmful to a relationship, and when might it be beneficial? What other variables, besides those mentioned in this chapter, are likely to influence whether people live together before marriage?

6

MAKING A LOVE CONNECTION

Styles of Love and Attachment

Gabriela and Brian have been dating for months. Although they care deeply for one another, some problems have started to surface in their relationship. Brian wishes Gabriela would show him more affection. Every time they get really close, she seems to pull away. She also seems to put her career ahead of their relationship. Just last week, she cancelled their Saturday night date so she could spend extra time working on an advertising campaign. Sometimes Brian wonders if he cares more for Gabriela than she cares for him. Perhaps she likes him but doesn't love him. Gabriela, in contrast, wishes Brian would give her more space. She doesn't understand why he needs her to say "I love you" all the time. Shouldn't he understand how she feels without her having to tell him all the time? After all, she always makes sure to fit some quality time with Brian into her busy schedule, and they do all sorts of activities together, such as golfing, skiing, and watching old movies. Sometimes Gabriela wonders if she can devote enough time to the relationship to satisfy Brian. Maybe she's just not ready for the level of commitment he wants.

Who do you relate to more—Gabriela or Brian? Gabriela is focused on her career. She expresses love by engaging in activity, and she values her autonomy. Brian, on the other hand, is more focused on the relationship. He expresses his feelings by saying "I love you" and showing affection. Are Gabriela and Brian's attitudes toward love fairly common? What other attitudes do people have about love? How do they know if they are really in love? Finally, can two people such as Gabriela and Brian—who have such different needs, priorities, and styles of communication—be happy together? The literature on love and attachment helps answer some of these questions.

In this chapter, we examine different styles of love and attachment. Before doing so, we distinguish love from liking and discuss the situation of unrequited love. Next, we cover three major perspectives on love: (1) Lee's love styles, (2) Sternberg's triangular theory of love, and (3) Marston and Hecht's love ways. These three perspectives show that people experience love in different ways. Finally, we discuss attachment theory. Attachment is an important part of various loving relationships, including relationships between family members, romantic partners, and close friends.

LOVE, LIKING, AND UNREQUITED LOVE

Feelings such as love and liking are the foundation of close relationships. Sometimes these feelings surface quickly; at other times they develop over time as people get to know one another. In other cases, feelings of love or liking are not reciprocated. When love is shared, it is one of the most wonderful human experiences. When love is not returned, people feel rejected and miserable. Researchers have spent considerable energy investigating issues related to love, liking, and unrequited love. Some of this research has focused on answering basic questions such as the following: When does liking turn to love? Is love a distinctly different experience from liking? And how do people feel in situations involving unrequited love?

Loving Versus Liking

Loving is a complex concept that can refer to a set of feelings, a state of mind, or a type of relationship. Love is communicated in a variety of ways, such as by making sacrifices, disclosing one's innermost thoughts and feelings, showing nonverbal affection, or having sexual intercourse. Some researchers have tried to separate loving from liking. Rubin (1970, 1973, 1974) suggested that there are *qualitative* rather than *quantitative* differences between loving and liking. In other words, liking someone a lot does not always translate into love. Love is more than an abundance of liking, and loving and liking are related but distinctly different concepts. People can, in some cases, love others without liking them very much. In general, however, individuals tend to like the people they love. For example, Rubin (1970, 1973) found that people *like* their close friends and dating partners about equally but *love* their dating partners more than their friends. Partners in romantic couples who were "in love" and planned to marry also reported loving each other more than dating partners who did not have concrete plans for the future. Thus, romance and commitment appear to be important in many love relationships.

Liking and loving can be distinguished from each other by certain feelings and relationship characteristics. Rubin (1973) suggested that liking is characterized by affection and respect. **Affection** is based on having enjoyable interactions with someone, which make one feel good when around that person. Enjoyable interactions promote interpersonal warmth, or a feeling of cozy closeness, which helps cement the bond between two people (Andersen & Guerrero, 1998a). **Respect** is based on admiring a person's positive personal characteristics, such as a good sense of humor, a sense of integrity, or an inner strength. Loving, in contrast, is characterized by attachment, caring, and intimacy (Rubin, 1973). **Attachment** occurs when people feel an emotional connection to someone. When people are in need of comfort, they rely on others with whom they have formed such an attachment. **Caring**, in contrast, refers to giving (rather than receiving) support and comfort, as well as to showing affection. Finally, **intimacy** involves a sense of interdependence, whereby two people rely on each other to fulfill needs for attachment and caring.

A series of studies by Davis and colleagues also demonstrated that loving is qualitatively different from liking and, again, that loving is special because it often includes more caring and passion than liking (Davis & Roberts, 1985; Davis & Todd, 1982, 1985). In these studies, friendship was defined by characteristics such as enjoyment, acceptance, trust, and respect, as well as doing things for one another, disclosing information, understanding each other, and feeling comfortable together. Love was defined by all these friendship characteristics *plus* caring and passion. Caring includes making supreme sacrifices for the loved one and defending her or him to others; passion includes being fascinated by the loved one, feeling that the relationship is unique and exclusive, and experiencing strong sexual desire.

Unrequited Love

Sometimes the feelings of friendship, caring, or passion that characterize liking and loving are not reciprocated. Such is the case with unrequited love, whereby one person, **the would-be lover**, wants to initiate or intensify a romantic relationship, but the other person, the **rejector**, does not (Baumeister & Wotman, 1992; Baumeister, Wotman, & Stillwell, 1993; Bratslavsky, Baumeister, & Sommer, 1998). Unrequited love can characterize several types of situations. Sometimes the two people do not know one another well even though one of them feels "in love" with the other; at other times, they may be good friends, but one person wants to intensify the relationship further and the other person does not. Unrequited love may also occur in the initial stages of a relationship. For example, after going on a few dates, one person may fall in love, but the other might want to stop dating altogether. Unrequited love also occurs in established or de-escalating relationships when one partner ceases to love the other.

When unrequited love is perceived, the would-be lover has two options: (1) to keep quiet about his or her feelings or (2) to try to win the partner's love (Baumeister et al., 1993). Either way, there are considerable risks for the would-be lover. On the one hand, approaching the loved one could lead to rejection, humiliation, or, in the case of an established friendship, the de-escalation or termination of the relationship. On the other hand, keeping quiet could cost the person any opportunity to win the other person over.

Situations of unrequited love are difficult for both people, but perhaps surprisingly, Baumeister and his colleagues discovered that rejectors typically report experiencing more negative emotions than do would-be lovers. According to their research, would-be lovers perceive the situation as having either extremely positive or negative outcomes, whereas most rejectors perceive only negative outcomes. Although it is flattering to be the object of someone's affection, the rejector typically feels guilty for being unable to return the would-be lover's sentiments. If the would-be lover is persistent, the rejector may feel frustrated and even victimized (Baumeister et al., 1993). The appropriate way to communicate rejection is also unclear since it is difficult to reject the would-be lover's advances without hurting her or his feelings. Would-be lovers, in contrast, have a much clearer script for how to behave. As Baumeister et al. (1993) put it,

> The would-be lover's script is affirmed and reiterated from multiple sources; for example, one can probably hear a song about unrequited love in almost any American house within an hour, simply by turning on the radio. A seemingly endless stream of books and movies has portrayed aspiring lovers persisting doggedly to win the hearts of their beloveds. Many techniques are portrayed as eventually effective. If one is rejected in the end, the familiar script calls for heartbroken lovers to express their grief, perhaps

assign blame, accept the failure, and then go on with their lives. (p. 379)

The rejector, however, does not have a clearly defined cultural prescription for how to deal with the would-be lover. Movies and novels often portray rejectors as "aloof, casual, teasing, or sadistic heartbreakers," but most rejectors are actually quite concerned with helping the would-be lover save face (Baumeister et al., 1993, p. 391). Thus, many rejectors initially resist making harsh declarations such as "I'm not attracted to you" and instead rely on more polite or indirect communication strategies, such as saying that they value the friendship too much to ruin it by pursuing a romantic relationship or that they are too busy to date anyone at this time. Folkes (1982) found that rejectors try to let the other person down easily and avoid hurting her or his feelings.

Of course, the problem with polite or indirect messages is that they can be misinterpreted (Cupach & Metts, 1991). Would-be lovers may cling to the hope that since the rejector did not dismiss them directly, a love relationship is still possible. For example, would-be lovers who receive a message such as "I'm not interested in dating anyone right now, but I want to stay friends" might hear this as "There might be a chance of a love relationship in the future since I like you." Eventually, the rejector may have to resort to harsher and more direct messages if the would-be lover persists (Metts, Sprecher, & Regan, 1998). When clear sexual advances are made, women are likely to be verbally direct, and most men accept their refusals (Metts et al., 1998).

TYPES OF LOVE

Just as situations vary in the degree to which love is reciprocated, so too do people differ in their styles of loving. Two styles of love—companionate love and passionate love—appear to be the most common in the United States as well as other cultures (Hatfield & Rapson, 1987; Jankowiak & Fischer, 1992). **Companionate love** is "the affection we feel for those with whom our lives are deeply intertwined" (Walster & Walster, 1978, p. 9). This kind of love is commonly experienced in family relationships and friendships, as well as romantic relationships. Hatfield (1988) labeled companionate love as the "warm" type of love because it tends to develop gradually into a consistent, secure source of warmth that endures over time. **Passionate love** is based on arousal and intense emotion. When the beloved person returns our passionate love, we feel ecstasy; when this person rejects our love, we feel agony. Hatfield (1988) called passionate love the "hot" type of love because it is typically sexual and characterized by emotional highs and lows rather than a more consistent feeling of interpersonal warmth.

Although companionate and passionate love are the most common styles of loving, there are other types of love as well. For example, some people view love as practical, while others see it as more spiritual. Love is also communicated in a variety of ways, including through self-disclosure, emotional responses, and time spent together. In this section, we examine three perspectives on different styles of loving. As you proceed, keep in mind that companionate and passionate love are represented in each of these perspectives.

Lee's Love Styles

Lee's (1973, 1977, 1988) work on love styles began with the notion that there are three primary styles of loving, much as there are three primary colors. When mixing paint, the primary colors are red, blue, and yellow. By mixing these three colors, you can create any color in the rainbow. Lee conceptualized styles of loving in a similar manner. He proposed that the primary love styles are **eros** (physical love), **storge** (companionate love), and **ludus** (game-playing love). Just as the primary colors can be blended to create a multitude of different hues, Lee theorized that elements of the three primary styles of love can combine to create a vast number of love styles. Of the many possible combinations, Lee suggested that three are the most common: **mania** (possessive love), **agape** (unselfish love), and **pragma** (practical love). Figure 6.1 depicts Lee's love styles as a color wheel. As we shall see next, each style of love is defined by both positive and negative characteristics. The more strongly and exclusively a person identifies with a single style, the more likely he or she is to experience some of the negative characteristics. Most people, however, report identifying with

a combination of styles, with one or two styles experienced most strongly. Box 6.1 gives a scale by which you can determine your own love style.

Physical Love (Eros). Erotic lovers are attracted to people on the basis of physical attraction (Lee, 1988). They are eager to develop intense, passionate relationships, and they often experience intense emotional highs and lows. They also feel substantial arousal and desire physical contact. Because they possess strong feelings of attraction, erotic lovers develop a sense of intimacy and connectedness relatively quickly. These individuals are "intense communicators" who show high levels of self-disclosure, are able to elicit similarly high levels of self-disclosure from their partners, and display high levels of touch and nonverbal affection (Taraban, Hendrick, & Hendrick, 1998, p. 346). Erotic lovers want to be with each other, and they feel considerable distress when apart.

Eros is a central part of many love relationships. This type of love is common in the initial stages of romantic relationships and often leads to a more friendship-based and secure style of love (Hendrick, Hendrick, & Adler, 1988). Some level of eros also keeps relationships exciting and passionate.

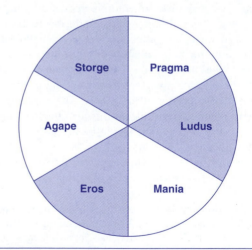

Figure 6.1 Lee's Love Styles Represented as a Color Wheel

NOTE: The primary styles are shaded; the secondary styles are composed of the aspects of the two primary styles adjacent to them.

BOX 6.1   Put Yourself to the Test

What Is Your Love Style?

To determine your dominant love style, rate yourself on each of these statements according to the following scale: 1 = Strongly disagree, 5 = Strongly agree.

	Disagree				Agree
1. My partner and I were attracted to each other immediately when we first met.	1	2	3	4	5
2. My partner and I have the right physical chemistry.	1	2	3	4	5
3. The physical part of our relationship is intense and satisfying.	1	2	3	4	5
4. My partner and I were meant for each other.	1	2	3	4	5
5. My partner fits my ideal standards of physical attractiveness.	1	2	3	4	5
6. I try to keep my partner a little uncertain about my commitment to her/him.	1	2	3	4	5
7. I believe that what my partner doesn't know about me won't hurt her/him.	1	2	3	4	5
8. I could get over my relationship with my partner pretty easily.	1	2	3	4	5
9. When my partner gets too dependent on me, I back off.	1	2	3	4	5
10. I enjoy playing the field.	1	2	3	4	5
11. It is hard for me to say exactly when our friendship turned into love.	1	2	3	4	5
12. To be genuine, our love first required caring.	1	2	3	4	5
13. Our love is the best kind because it grew out of a close friendship.	1	2	3	4	5
14. Our love is really a deep friendship, not a mysterious or mystical emotion.	1	2	3	4	5
15. Our love relationship is satisfying because it developed from a good friendship.	1	2	3	4	5
16. I considered what my partner was going to become in life before committing myself to her/him.	1	2	3	4	5
17. I tried to plan my life carefully before choosing a partner.	1	2	3	4	5
18. In choosing my partner, I believed it was best to find someone with a similar background.	1	2	3	4	5
19. An important factor in choosing my partner was whether she/he would be a good parent.	1	2	3	4	5
20. Before getting very involved with my partner, I tried to figure out how compatible our goals were.	1	2	3	4	5
21. If my partner and I broke up, I don't know how I would cope.	1	2	3	4	5
22. It drives me crazy when my partner doesn't pay enough attention to me.	1	2	3	4	5

(Continued)

▣ BOX 6.1 (Continued)

	Disagree ←——→ Agree

		Disagree	←——→			Agree
23. I'm so in love with my partner that I sometimes have trouble concentrating on anything else.		1	2	3	4	5
24. I cannot relax if I suspect that my partner is with someone else.		1	2	3	4	5
25. I wish I could spend every minute of every day with my partner.		1	2	3	4	5
26. I would rather suffer myself than let my partner suffer.		1	2	3	4	5
27. I am usually willing to sacrifice my own wishes to let my partner achieve her/his goals.		1	2	3	4	5
28. Whatever I own is my partner's to use as she/he pleases.		1	2	3	4	5
29. When my partner behaves badly, I still love her/him fully and unconditionally.		1	2	3	4	5
30. I would endure all things for the sake of my partner.		1	2	3	4	5

Add up the following items to get your score on each love style:

Eros: Items 1–5   _____
Ludus: Items 6–10   _____
Storge: Items 11–15   _____
Pragma: Items 16–20   _____
Mania: Items 21–25   _____
Agape: Items 26–30   _____

Higher scores mean that you possess more of a particular love style. The highest possible score for a given style is 25; the lowest possible score is 5.

SOURCE: Used with permission of Select Press.

However, too much eros can have negative effects. For example, if you are only interested in someone because of the person's beauty, the attraction may fade quickly. Also, some erotic lovers have trouble adjusting after the initial "hot" attraction begins to cool or after they discover that the partner, who seemed perfect at first, cannot possibly live up to their unrealistically high expectations. Still, research suggests that maintaining some degree of eros is beneficial in a relationship. Hendrick et al. (1988) found that dating couples were more likely to stay together if the partners were high in eros and low in the ludic, game-playing style of love. This finding supports the claim that passion and commitment are important in many love relationships.

Companionate Love (Storge). Storgic lovers have relationships based on friendship, shared values and goals, and compatibility (Lee, 1988). Physical attraction is not as important as security, companionship, task sharing, and joint activity. Although these relationships are not very exciting, they are dependable and stable. Love often is framed as a partnership or a lifelong journey. Thus it is important that the two individuals want the same things—perhaps a home and family or perhaps independence and the ability to travel together to exotic places. Storgic lovers feel extremely comfortable around each other, and emotions tend to be positive but muted. Unlike some of the other love styles, storgic lovers do not experience many intense emotional highs or lows.

Companionate love characterizes most long-term romantic relationships, as well as family relationships and close friendships. This type of love tends to be enduring. Because storgic lovers trust each other and do not require high levels of emotional stimulation and arousal, they are able to withstand long separations. For example, military couples may be better able to withstand their time apart if they are storgic lovers. Although they are likely to be sad when parted from each other, their trust and relational security keeps them from being highly distressed. Other types of lovers (e.g., erotic or manic lovers) feel much higher levels of distress because their relationships are fueled by physical attraction and the physical presence of the loved one. Of course, it is important to keep in mind that, although trust and security can provide a safety net for a relationship, too much stability can lead to predictability and boredom. Thus, bringing excitement and emotion to the relationship is often the biggest challenge for storgic lovers.

Game-Playing Love (Ludus). Ludic lovers see relationships as fun, playful, and casual; they view relationships as games to be played. They avoid commitment and prefer to play the field rather than settle down with one person (Lee, 1988). In fact, for the ludic lover, the challenge of pursuit usually is more rewarding than the actual relationship itself. Some ludic lovers are highly self-sufficient individuals who put their personal goals and activities ahead of their relationships—similar to Gabriela as described at the beginning of this chapter. They share relatively little personal information with their partners and are slow to develop intimate relationships (Hendrick & Hendrick, 1987). Many students and recent college graduates adopt the ludic style, especially if they feel they are not ready for a highly committed romantic relationship. Instead, they may feel that school or career takes precedence over relational involvements. When these individuals are ready and when they meet the right person, they are likely to move out of the ludic style and into a more committed style of loving.

In Margaret Mitchell's classic Civil War novel *Gone With the Wind*, the Scarlett O'Hara character provides a good example of an individual with a ludic love style. Scarlett is a notorious flirt. In an early scene, she is at a party surrounded by dozens of admirers; she is careful not to commit to any one man. Later, Scarlett marries men she does not love to fulfill personal goals. For example, she marries her sister's boyfriend, Frank, to help pay the taxes on the family plantation. Her ludic nature is also evident in her relationship with Rhett Butler. Scarlett and Rhett constantly compete with each other through glib and sarcastic remarks, and Scarlett often hides her warm feelings for Rhett. By the time she realizes she loves Rhett, it is too late. He has grown tired of her games and delivers the famous line, "Frankly, my dear, I don't give a damn."

Possessive Love (Mania). Manic lovers are demanding, dependent, and possessive (Lee, 1988). They often feel a strong need to "be in control" and to know everything that the partner is doing. The classic song "Every Breath You Take" by the Police exemplifies the manic lover's desire to monitor "every breath you take, every move you make, every smile you fake." In extreme cases, manic lovers are obsessive individuals who are addicted to love, much as a drug addict is dependent on heroin or cocaine (see Chapter 12). The obsessed lover cannot get enough; he or she wants to spend every minute with the partner, and any perceived lack of interest or enthusiasm by the partner, or any physical separation results in extreme emotional lows. In contrast, when the beloved person reciprocates affection, the manic lover experiences an emotional high. Manic lovers also become jealous easily. Of course, many people experience a mild form of mania: They feel jealous when their partners flirt with an ex-boyfriend or ex-girlfriend; they find themselves constantly thinking about the partner; and their happiness seems to depend, at least in part, on having a relationship with the person they love. When these thoughts and feelings become extreme, a more negative form of mania emerges.

According to Lee (1973), the manic style is a combination of eros and ludus. Manic lovers feel high levels of physical attraction and passion for their partners, which is consistent with the erotic style (Hendrick et al., 1988). However, manic lovers also play manipulative and controlling games with their partners, and they sometimes worry about committing to a relationship because they fear being hurt. To the manic lover, relationships embody a source of extreme joy and extreme pain. Manic lovers can quickly become infatuated with someone even though they do not know the person very well. Manic lovers often are willing to break off an old relationship to pursue a new, seemingly more attractive alternative before they really get to know the new love interest. If you have ever been hotly pursued by someone who barely knew you, chances are that you were dealing with a manic lover.

Unselfish Love (Agape). Agapic or compassionate love is unselfish, altruistic, and unconditional. The agapic lover is more focused on giving than receiving (Lee, 1988; Sprecher & Fehr, 2005). These lovers are motivated by an intense concern for their partner's well-being. They are willing to make sacrifices for their partner, even at the expense of their own needs and desires. For example, an agapic husband might decide not to pursue having a large family (even though he really wants one) if his wife had a difficult first pregnancy. Agapic love corresponds with the biblical description of love as patient, kind, and slow to anger and jealousy. Agapic or compassionate love is associated with prosocial behavior, love of humanity, and spirituality. Relationships between romantic partners, among family members (especially parents toward children), and between friends all can be characterized by agape.

The agapic style contains elements of both eros and storge (Lee, 1973). An agapic lover has a deep, abiding, highly passionate love for his or her partner—although not only in a physical sense. An agapic lover shows passion by giving gifts and making sacrifices for the partner or sometimes by granting the partner sexual favors even if such activity is not personally arousing. Physical intimacy may also be an important part of agapic love, with sexual contact viewed as something sacred that occurs between two people who love each other deeply. The storge side of agapic love stresses the enduring and secure nature of the relationship, which helps explain why agapic individuals are able to love their partners

unconditionally. Given all this, it might seem as if having an agapic lover would be an ideal situation. There are, however, some drawbacks to this style. Agapic lovers sometimes seem to be "above" everyone else. Their partners often have trouble matching their high level of unconditional love, which can lead to feelings of discomfort and guilt. In addition, agapic lovers sometimes put their partners on too high a pedestal, leading their partners to worry that they cannot live up to such an idealized image.

Practical Love (Pragma). Pragmatic lovers search for a person who fits a particular image in terms of vital statistics, such as age, height, religion, and occupation, as well as preferred characteristics, such as being a loyal partner or having the potential to be a good parent. Lee (1988) used a computer dating service metaphor to help describe pragma. If you went to a dating service, you might indicate that you are looking for a petite brunette who is Jewish, likes sports, and has a stable job. Or you might request a college-educated male who is older than you, has a good sense of humor, and loves children. In either case, you would have specified vital statistics that are most important to you. The pragmatic lover chooses these characteristics based on both personal preferences and compatibility issues. Overall, this style of love is characterized by a "common-sense, problem-solving approach to life and love" (Taraban et al., 1998, p. 346).

Pragma combines elements of both storge and ludus. As Lee (1988) explained, storge comes into play because pragmatic lovers are seeking a compatible partner. Furthermore, for pragmatic lovers, physical attraction usually is less important than shared values and goals (although attractiveness is often on the pragmatic lover's "laundry list" of vital characteristics). Undertones of the ludus style also are evident in many pragmatic lovers, who typically avoid emotional risk taking and commit to a relationship only after careful thought and considerable time. Finally, pragmatic love is highly rational, based on empirical knowledge. For example, when pragmatic lovers are considering marriage, they might make a list of pros and cons before deciding whether to "take the plunge." If love is based only on practical concerns, however, it can be lifeless and dull. Some level of intimacy and passion is required to put the spark into a relationship. For pragmatic lovers, intimacy and passion sometimes develop after realistic concerns have laid the foundation for the relationship.

Differences Due to Sex and Culture. Lee's original work, as well as subsequent research, suggests that the tendency to identify with the various love styles differs somewhat depending on sex and culture. Hendrick and Hendrick (1986) found women to score higher in storge, mania, and pragma than men, while men score higher in ludus. These findings for storge and pragma are in line with other research showing women to be more rational lovers, who are choosier about their partners. However, the finding for mania is somewhat contradictory to the research on jealousy, which has shown that men and women tend to feel similar levels of jealousy. The finding that men tend to identify more with ludus is consistent with research showing that men are generally less committed to relationships than are women. Yet studies have also found that men generally fall in love faster than do women (Huston, Surra, Fitzgerald, & Cate, 1981; Kanin, Davidson, & Scheck, 1970) and that they usually say "I love you" first in heterosexual romantic relationships (Owen, 1987; Tolhuizen, 1989). Together, these seemingly inconsistent findings suggest that although men may hesitate to make a strong commitment, when they do fall in love, they do it more quickly and emotionally than do women.

As noted previously, some types of love tend to be experienced similarly across different cultures. For example, Jankowiak and Fischer (1992) tested the idea that romantic (or erotic) love is a product of Western culture. Contrary to this idea, they found romantic love to exist in 147 of the 166 cultures sampled. Based on these data, Jankowiak and Fischer suggested that romantic love is nearly universal. Companionate love also appears to cross cultural boundaries, with many different peoples embracing the warmth and security that friendship-based love offers. There are some cultural differences in love styles, however. People from cultures that endorse arranged marriages believe more strongly in pragmatic love than do people in cultures where people marry for love alone. In arranged marriages, the parents and/or community often match their children based on perceived compatibility and an equitable exchange of resources.

Agapic love is also likely to differ across cultures. In the United States and other Western cultures, such as Australia, Great Britain, Canada, and the Netherlands, people are highly individualistic. In these cultures, individuals are more likely to strive for personal goals. As Lustig and Koester (2003) put it, individualism is characterized by the key words "*independence, privacy, self,* and the all-important *I*" (p. 120). For people in individualistic cultures, agapic love may be seen as too all-consuming, smothering, and other-oriented. However, people in collectivist cultures—such as parts of South America, including Venezuela and Colombia, and most of Asia, including Hong Kong and Taiwan (Hofstede, 1982)—are likely to be more amenable to agapic love. Individuals in collectivist cultures value interpersonal contact and togetherness. They prefer to engage in behavior that benefits the group or their partner rather than behavior that benefits only themselves.

Sternberg's Triangular Theory of Love

While Lee focuses primarily on stylistic differences in love, Robert Sternberg's (1986, 1987, 1988) triangular theory of love focuses on how three components of love—intimacy, passion, and commitment—work together to create different types of love. Sternberg also made predictions about how intimacy, passion, and commitment change as relationships develop, as well as the degree to which each component is under our control. Box 6.2 provides a scale by which you can determine what your love triangle looks like.

Intimacy: The "Warm" Component. Among the three sides of Sternberg's (1986) triangle, intimacy is seen as most foundational to love. This does not mean that intimacy is always a part of love, rather it is most often the central component within love relationships. Intimacy is based on feelings of emotional connection and closeness and has therefore been called the "warm" or "affectionate" component of love. The close, connected feelings that people experience when having intimate conversations or exchanging

■ BOX 6.2 Put Yourself to the Test

What Does Your Love Triangle Look Like?

To determine what your love triangle looks like, rate yourself on each of these statements according to the following scale: 1 = Not at all, 5 = Moderately, 9 = Extremely.

	Not at all	←					→	Extremely	
1. I view my relationship with my partner as permanent.	1	2	3	4	5	6	7	8	9
2. My relationship with my partner is very romantic.	1	2	3	4	5	6	7	8	9
3. I have a relationship of mutual understanding with my partner.	1	2	3	4	5	6	7	8	9
4. I am certain of my love for my partner.	1	2	3	4	5	6	7	8	9
5. I receive considerable emotional support from my partner.	1	2	3	4	5	6	7	8	9
6. I adore my partner.	1	2	3	4	5	6	7	8	9
7. I find myself thinking about my partner frequently during the day.	1	2	3	4	5	6	7	8	9
8. I am committed to maintaining my relationship with my partner.	1	2	3	4	5	6	7	8	9
9. My partner is able to count on me in times of need.	1	2	3	4	5	6	7	8	9
10. Just seeing my partner is exciting for me.	1	2	3	4	5	6	7	8	9
11. I find my partner very physically attractive.	1	2	3	4	5	6	7	8	9
12. I idealize my partner.	1	2	3	4	5	6	7	8	9
13. I have confidence in the stability of my relationship with my partner.	1	2	3	4	5	6	7	8	9
14. I feel emotionally close to my partner.	1	2	3	4	5	6	7	8	9
15. There is something almost magical about my relationship with my partner.	1	2	3	4	5	6	7	8	9
16. I expect my love for my partner to last for the rest of my life.	1	2	3	4	5	6	7	8	9
17. I give considerable emotional support to my partner.	1	2	3	4	5	6	7	8	9
18. I can't imagine ending my relationship with my partner.	1	2	3	4	5	6	7	8	9
19. I have decided that I love my partner.	1	2	3	4	5	6	7	8	9

To find the triangle for your relationship, add your responses to Items 3, 5, 9, 14, and 17, and divide by 5; this is your *intimacy* score. Next, add your responses to Items 2, 6, 7, 10–12, and 15, and divide by 7; this is your *passion* score. Finally, add your responses to Items 1, 4, 8, 13, 16, 18, and 19, and divide by 7; this is your *commitment* score. The closer each score is to 9, the higher the component.

SOURCE: Adapted from Acker, M., & Davis, M. E., Intimacy, passion, and commitment in adult romantic relationships: A test of the triangular theory of love, in *Journal of Social and Personal Relationships, 9*, 21–50. Copyright © 1992, Sage Publications, Inc.

hugs with loved ones exemplify this interpersonal warmth (Andersen & Guerrero, 1998a; Andersen, Guerrero, & Jones, 2006).

Sternberg theorized that intimacy is moderately stable over the course of a relationship. However, he made an important distinction between latent and manifest intimacy. **Latent intimacy** refers to internal feelings of closeness and interpersonal warmth, which are not directly observable by others. This type of intimacy is what we feel inside. **Manifest intimacy** refers to external behavioral manifestations of affection and closeness, such as disclosing intimate feelings to a partner or spending extra time together. This type of intimacy is what we show to others. According to Sternberg (1986), latent intimacy is likely to increase but then reach a plateau as a relationship develops. Manifest intimacy, in contrast, is likely to grow during the initial stages of a relationship but then tends to decline over time. Research has shown some support for Sternberg's predictions. Acker and Davis (1992) found that couples felt more intimacy and closeness as their relationships became more serious; however, behavioral (or manifest) intimacy decreased as the relationship progressed. Guerrero and Andersen (1991) found a similar pattern for touch in public settings. Their observations showed that couples in serious dating relationships touched more than married couples, yet spouses felt just as close to each other as did daters. Therefore, even though married couples used less touch to manifest intimacy, they still experienced very high levels of latent intimacy.

According to the triangular theory of love, intimacy is moderately controllable. This means that people have some power to manage their intimate feelings but not to a great extent. An example may help illustrate this point. Imagine that you have been on two or three dates with a fun, attractive person to whom you feel an emotional connection. However, you discover that this person has very different values than you do. Perhaps your date wants to move to New York City to pursue a career on Wall Street, whereas you prefer the simple country life and hate the big city. Perhaps your date is not interested in starting a family for a long time, whereas you want to settle down, get married, and raise a couple of children. Although you feel an emotional connection to this person, you may decide to spend less time with her or him so that you won't develop further attachment. Of course, it is hard to turn off one's emotions, so you might find yourself drawn to this person despite your intention to maintain an emotional distance.

Passion: The "Hot" Component. According to Sternberg (1986, 1988), passion is the "hot" component of love that consists of motivation and arousal. However, passion is not limited to sexual arousal. It also includes motivational needs for affiliation, control, and self-actualization. Thus, parents can feel a passionate love for their children that includes an intense desire for them to achieve success and happiness. In romantic relationships, however, passion is usually experienced primarily as sexual attraction and arousal.

Sternberg (1986) predicted that passion and romance would be high during the initial stages of relationships but would then decrease as the relationship became more predictable and less arousing. Passion requires energy and excitement and is draining and perhaps even stressful to maintain throughout a long-term relationship. This is not to say that long-term romantic relationships are devoid of passion. As Sternberg suggested, highly committed couples are likely to cycle back and forth in terms of passion. A romantic weekend away or a candlelight dinner followed by stargazing in a hot tub can provide an important passionate spark to a long-term relationship. Sternberg's point is that these types of events occur less often in developed relationships because it is hard to sustain a high level of passion all the time. Acker and Davis (1992) found that people feel and desire less passion as they grow older, which suggests that passion may be more characteristic of young romances and the reproductive years than mature relationships. However, Acker and Davis also found that while women were more passionate in new relationships than in established relationships, men showed fairly high levels of passion regardless of whether the relationship is new or old. In another study, Hatfield and Sprecher (1986a) found that college-aged couples reported an increase in passion during the early stages of relationships and then a leveling off, rather than a decline, as the relationship stabilized.

As this discussion suggests, it can be very hard to control the passionate aspect of love. Indeed, recent research shows that passionate, romantic love is accompanied by involuntary activation in parts of the brain (Aron et al., 2005). Because this type of love is based on arousal, and because arousal is a physiological response, passionate feelings are difficult to control. You may have experienced times when you wished you could feel passion for someone but could not muster anything more than feelings of friendship. For example, one of our students once told us about a time when she and her male best friend had sat together in her bed talking comfortably all night. At one point they wondered out loud why they had never gotten together romantically. After all, they had a great relationship; they always had fun together, never fought, found each other attractive, and had been friends for a long time. In fact, their friendship had lasted longer than any of their romantic relationships. After some further discussion, they decided that their relationship simply did not have a romantic spark. They felt more like sister and brother than lovers, and even though it would be great to have passion as well, it just wasn't there. You may have also experienced the opposite phenomenon— wanting to feel less passionate about someone. You might feel passion for someone who is happily married to another person, someone who has repeatedly rejected you, or someone who you know will be "bad" for you in the long run, but you cannot turn off those passionate feelings.

Commitment: The "Cool" Component. The third component of Sternberg's (1986, 1988) love triangle is commitment/decision. This component refers to the decision to love someone and the commitment to maintain that love. Because commitment is based on cognition and decision making, Sternberg referred to it as the "cool" or "cold" component. Commitment is undoubtedly an important part of love for many people. In a study by Fehr (1988), college-aged students rated how closely various words or phrases, such as "affection" and "missing each other when apart" relate to love. Of the 68 words and phrases Fehr listed, trust was rated as the most central to love. Commitment ranked 8th overall, suggesting that it is also highly central to love. The other two

components of the triangular theory of love were also important, although less central, with intimacy ranking 19th and sexual passion ranking 40th. Fehr also had college-age students rate words and phrases describing the concept of commitment. Loyalty, responsibility, living up to one's word, faithfulness, and trust were the top five descriptors of commitment, suggesting that commitment involves being there for someone over the long haul.

Of the three components of the love triangle, commitment is the most stable over time. In long-term relationships, commitment typically builds up gradually and then stabilizes (Acker & Davis, 1992). Commitment also appears to play an important role in keeping a relationship satisfying and stable. In Acker and Davis's (1992) study, intimacy, passion, and commitment were all related positively to satisfaction, but commitment, followed by intimacy, was the strongest predictor of satisfaction. Hendrick et al. (1988) conducted a study to determine whether commitment, relational satisfaction, or investment of time and effort was the best predictor of relational stability. They found that commitment was the best predictor of whether dating couples would still be together 2 months later. Thus, commitment is not only a stable factor within love relationships but also a stabilizing force within these relationships.

Commitment/decision is the most controllable component of the triangle (Sternberg, 1986). When people commit to a relationship, they have made a cognitive choice to maintain their love and build an enduring bond. Highly committed individuals are likely to devote much time and effort to their relationships, and these investments help keep the relationship going (Rusbult, 1983). If people decide that they are no longer committed to a relationship, these investments will stop. Thus, people have considerable conscious control over the commitment decision as well as the decision whether to engage in behaviors that reinforce commitment.

Different Types of Love. Sternberg (1986, 1988) theorized that the three components of the triangle can be combined to create six different types of love plus nonlove and liking. Box 6.3 shows how the types of love differ in passion, commitment, and intimacy, although of a number of research studies suggest they are inseparable.

Two types of love contain passion but not commitment and often occur in the early stages of romantic relationships (Sternberg, 1988). In some ways, these two types of love are similar to Lee's (1973) eros style. **Infatuation** is based on high levels of passion and low levels of both commitment and intimacy. When people become infatuated with someone, they usually are new acquaintances. Nonetheless, infatuated individuals idealize the objects of their affection and imagine that their lives would be wonderful if they could develop a relationship with that person. Because infatuation is based on the "hot" component of the love triangle, it is not surprising that infatuated individuals often fall in and out of love quickly as their passion heats up and then cools down. **Romantic love**, in contrast, is usually somewhat more enduring. In this type of love, passion and intimacy are high, but commitment is low. Romantic love often characterizes the initial stages of dating relationships, when two people are sexually attracted to each other and feel an intimate connection but have not yet fully committed themselves to the relationship.

Companionate love, like Lee's storge love, is based on high levels of intimacy and commitment but low levels of passion. Love for family members and friends fits this description, as does love between romantic partners who have been together for a long time. **Empty love**, in contrast, characterizes relationships high in commitment and low in both passion and intimacy. Some long-term relationships may also fall here. For instance, if partners no longer feel attached to each other but stay together for religious reasons or because of the children, their love might be characterized as empty. In other cases, empty love characterizes the beginning of a relationship. For example, spouses in arranged marriages or pragmatic lovers who chose one another based primarily on logical characteristics may begin their relationships with empty love. Intimacy and passion may, or may not, emerge later.

In the United States, **fatuous love**, which is characterized by high levels of passion and commitment but low levels of intimacy, is somewhat rare.

BOX 6.3   Highlights

Different Love Triangles

According to Sternberg's triangular theory of love, different types of love are based on the various combinations of intimacy, passion, and commitment. Using your scores from the love triangle test (see Box 6.2), you can determine what type of love best characterizes your present or past romantic relationship. A low score is represented by a minus sign; a high score is represented by a plus sign. Of course, your score may fall somewhere in between two or more types.

Types of Love	Intimacy	Passion	Commitment
Nonlove	−	−	−
Liking	+	−	−
Infatuation	−	+	−
Empty love	−	−	+
Romantic love	+	+	−
Friendship love	+	−	+
Fatuous love	−	+	+
Consummate love	+	+	+

Yet sometimes people meet, fall in love, and get married before really getting to know each other. Some long-term affairs can also be characterized by fatuous love. The individuals involved in the affair may feel more emotional intimacy with their spouses than with their lovers, yet sustain an exciting, passionate, committed relationship with each other. In Western cultures these types of arrangements were more acceptable in the past—especially for men. In fact, research reported in the History Channel's documentary *The History of Sex* shows that until the 20th century, men often were expected to have extramarital affairs. In Victorian England, for instance, women were taught that sex was something that good mothers and wives did not enjoy and that sex should be engaged in only occasionally for purposes of procreation with one's spouse. Men, in contrast, were allowed to enjoy sex and taught to distinguish the kind of relations they had with their wives from those with their mistresses.

These types of arrangements, as well as open marriages, in which both the wife and the husband can have extramarital affairs, are still accepted in some cultures today (Altman & Ginat, 1996). In fact, in some cultures, wives can easily disregard the importance of their husband's long-term mistresses because they know that the mistresses do not have the same intimate connection with their husbands that they do. In cultures that allow multiple husbands or wives, fatuous love may also surface fairly often. For example, when husbands have more than one wife, the wives often form very close, intimate relationships with one another rather than with the husband (Altman & Ginat, 1996), with fatuous love characterizing the husband-wife relationships. In the PBS series *The Human Sexes,* the anthropologist Desmond Morris reported that in some tribal cultures, women with high social and economic status act as the head of household, acquiring both husbands and wives and giving their name to all the children produced within their household. In this system, the female head of household is committed to all those in her domain, but she is likely to have stronger physical relationships with certain husbands and stronger emotional relationships with certain wives than others. Morris reported that in other cultures, fatuous love is common in male-female relationships because true intimacy (which is manifest through behaviors such as hugging, holding hands, and self-disclosure) is only believed to be possible in same-sex relationships.

While most Americans do not desire fatuous love, they believe strongly in **consummate love**. This type of love, which includes all three components of the triangle—intimacy, passion, and commitment—is held up as the ideal standard within American culture. Think about our fairy tales: Two people meet, fall madly in love, and live happily ever after; their relationship has it all! Some relationships can achieve this state, at least for a time, but this type of love may be hard to sustain. Most happy relationships are characterized by some degree of intimacy, passion, and commitment (Acker & Davis, 1992), but it is unrealistic to expect these components to be high all the time.

Different Perspectives on Triangles. Finally, to fully understand Sternberg's triangular theory of love, it is important to recognize that the love triangles can be viewed from different vantage points (Acker & Davis, 1992; Sternberg, 1987). First, every individual has her or his actual triangle, or perception of the type of love felt. Second, each person perceives that her or his partner sees their love in a particular way; this is the perceived partner triangle. Finally, both partners in any relationship have a desired triangle that represents what an ideal partner would think and feel. To illustrate, let's take another look at Gabriela and Brian's relationship. Gabriela might feel consummate love toward Brian (her actual triangle), yet Brian might think that Gabriela feels low levels of commitment and intimacy (his perceived partner triangle) because he wants her to express intimacy and commitment more openly (his desired triangle). In this case, there is a discrepancy between Brian's desired triangle and his perceived partner triangle, as well as a discrepancy between how Gabriela and Brian would describe her triangle. Inconsistencies such as these are bound to occur, and small deviations are usually not a problem. If these discrepancies are large, however, the relationship is likely to be dissatisfying (Acker & Davis, 1992; Sternberg, 1987). Thus it is important for partners to have realistic expectations about love and to understand that they might not always perceive each other's feelings correctly.

Marston and Hecht's Love Ways

In addition to thinking about love differently, Gabriela and Brian appear to have different styles of communicating love. Marston, Hecht, and colleagues developed a system for measuring different styles of communicating and experiencing love (Hecht, Marston, & Larkey, 1994; Marston et al., 1987; Marston & Hecht, 1994; Marston, Hecht, Manke, McDaniel, & Reeder, 1998). Specifically, they looked at physiological and behavioral responses to love, with behavior encompassing both verbal and nonverbal communication.

To identify different ways of loving, Marston et al. (1987) conducted interviews to determine the types of feelings and behaviors that occur when people experience love. First, they asked people to describe the physiological changes that occur when they are in love. The most common response was that people feel more energetic and emotionally intense when in love. People also reported feeling (1) beautiful and healthy; (2) warm and safe; (3) nervous, as manifested by butterflies or knots in the stomach; (4) stronger than normal; and (5) less hungry, with a marked loss of appetite. Next, the researchers asked, "How do you communicate love to your partner?" The top five responses were (1) saying "I love you" to the partner; (2) doing special things for the partner; (3) being supportive, understanding, and attentive; (4) touching the partner; and (5) simply being together. Of these, saying "I love you" was the most common response, with 75% of the respondents mentioning it. The researchers also asked, "How does your partner communicate love to you?" The top five responses were similar to those listed above. Saying "I love you" again emerged as the most common answer, with 70% of the participants mentioning this strategy. The next most common responses were showing love through touch and sexual contact, being supportive, doing favors or giving gifts, and engaging in behaviors that show togetherness. Other less frequently mentioned behaviors included communicating emotion, engaging in eye contact, and smiling. Together, these findings show that love is communicated and received in a variety of ways but that verbally telling our partners that we love them is a particularly important way of expressing love. This may explain why Brian wishes that Gabriela would tell him she loves him more often.

Marston and his colleagues argued that love consists of a set of interdependent thoughts, feelings, attitudes, and behaviors and that the subjective experience of love can change in importance throughout the relationship. They also suggested that relational partners can have similar or complementary styles and that the degree of similarity versus complementarity often changes as partners adapt to each other (Marston & Hecht, 1994). Therefore, love experiences are unique at any given time and for any given person or relationship. Nonetheless, Marston et al. (1987) found that the physiological and behavioral responses to love could be grouped into seven categories or love ways, with these **love ways** representing the experiences of over 90% of lovers:

1. *Collaborative love:* Love is seen as a partnership that involves mutual support and negotiation, increases energy, and intensifies emotion.

2. *Active love:* Love is based on activity and doing things together. It also involves feelings of increased strength and self-confidence.

3. *Intuitive love:* Love is a feeling that often is communicated through nonverbal behavior such as touch and gaze and experienced through physical reactions such as feeling warm all over, feeling nervous, and losing one's appetite.

4. *Committed love:* Love is based on commitment and involves experiencing strong feelings of connection, spending time together, and discussing the future.

5. *Secure love:* Love is based on security and intimacy. It is experienced through feelings of safety and warmth and communicated through intimate self-disclosure.

6. *Expressive love:* Love is shown through overt behavior. It involves doing things for the partner and saying "I love you" frequently.

7. *Traditional romantic love:* Love involves togetherness and commitment. When people are in love they feel beautiful and healthy.

Understanding each other's love style may help partners maintain a happy relationship. Marston and Hecht (1994) provided specific advice for managing love styles in ways that maximize relational satisfaction. First, they suggested that people recognize that their partner's love style might be different from their own. For example, if Brian expresses love through public affection, he should not necessarily expect Gabriela to do the same. In fact, Gabriela might dislike showing affection in public and prefer to cuddle in private or to show her love through shared activities. Second, people should be careful not to overvalue particular elements of their love way. For example, Gabriela seems to have an active love style. Therefore, she might worry if she and Brian start to develop different sports interests or argue about which old movies to watch. If this happens, Gabriela should recognize that other aspects of their relationship may still reflect their love for one another. Finally, people should avoid statements like "If you really loved me, you'd give me more space" (as Gabriela might say) or "If you really loved me, you'd tell me more often" (as Brian might say). Instead, Brian and Gabriela should focus on the various other ways that they express love for one another. Remember that any two people bring different expectations about love to the relationship. The key may be to appreciate what each partner brings to the table rather than wishing that the table was set in a different way.

ATTACHMENT THEORY

So far, we have shown that scholars classify love in many different ways. Lee's six styles of love are based largely on stylistic and perceptual differences. Sternberg's types of love are based on various combinations of intimacy, passion, and commitment. Marston and Hecht's seven love ways are based on how people experience and express love through verbal and nonverbal communication. Attachment theorists take yet another approach in studying love. According to attachment theorists such as Hazan

and Shaver (1987), love is best conceptualized as a process of attachment, which includes forming a bond and becoming close to someone. Attachment theory takes a social developmental approach, stressing how interactions with others affect people's attachment style across the life span. Children first learn to develop attachments through dependence on their caregivers. As children grow, they develop a sense of independence that is rooted in security. Finally, security in adulthood is based on being self-sufficient when necessary while also having the ability to provide care and support for another adult in a love relationship that functions as a partnership (Ainsworth & Bowlby, 1991).

The Propensity for Forming Attachments

Originally, attachment theory was studied within the context of child-caregiver relationships (Ainsworth, 1969; Ainsworth, Blehar, Waters, & Wall, 1978; Ainsworth & Wittig, 1969; Bowlby, 1969, 1973, 1980). Later, researchers extended the theory to include adult romantic relationships (Hazan & Shaver, 1987). Although parent-child and romantic relationships have received the most attention, attachment theory is applicable to all types of close relationships, including friendships and sibling relationships. Because people usually want to be part of a social group and to be loved and cared for by others, attachment theorists believe that people have a natural tendency to try to develop close relational bonds with others throughout the life span.

In childhood, the need to develop attachments is an innate and necessary part of human development (Ainsworth, 1991). According to Bowlby (1969, 1973, 1980), attachment is an essential component within a larger system that functions to keep children in close proximity to caregivers. This proximity protects children from danger and provides them with a secure base from which to explore their world. For example, a toddler may feel free to try the slides and swings at the playground because he or she knows that a caregiver is close by to act as a secure base if he or she gets hurt or needs help. Exploration of the environment eventually leads to self-confidence and autonomy. Thus one goal of the attachment system is to give children a sense of security and independence. Another goal is to help children develop a healthy capacity for intimacy.

In adulthood, attachment influences the type of relationship a person desires. For example, some people (like Gabriela) might want a relationship that is emotionally reserved, while others (like Brian) might desire a relationship that is emotionally charged. Bowlby (1977) and Ainsworth (1989, 1991), who pioneered research on child-caregiver attachments, both believed that attachment typifies intimate adult relationships, with Bowlby (1977) arguing that attachment is characteristic of all individuals from the cradle to the grave. The type of attachment individuals form depends on their cognitive conceptions of themselves and others. These cognitions, or internal working models, influence orientations toward love, intimacy, and interpersonal interaction in adult relationships.

Internal Working Models and Attachment Styles

According to attachment theorists, people develop different styles of attachment depending on how they perceive themselves and others. These perceptions, which are called **internal working models**, are cognitive representations of oneself and potential partners that reflect an individual's past experiences in close relationships and help him or her understand the world (Bowlby, 1973; Bretherton, 1988; Collins & Read, 1994). Models of both self and others fall along a positive-negative continuum. A positive self-model is "an internalized sense of self-worth that is not dependent on ongoing external validation" (Bartholomew, 1993, p. 40). Thus individuals who hold positive self-models view themselves as self-sufficient, secure, and lovable. Those holding negative self-models see themselves as dependent, insecure, and unworthy of love and affection. Positive models of others reflect expectations concerning how supportive, receptive, and accepting people are, as well as how rewarding it is to participate in an intimate relationship. Individuals with positive models of others see relationships as worthwhile and tend to possess "approach" orientations

toward intimacy. Individuals with negative working models of others see relationships as relatively unrewarding and tend to possess "avoidant" orientations toward intimacy.

Depending on individuals' configurations of internal working models—that is, the "mix" of how positive or negative their models of self and other are—they develop different "attachment styles." An **attachment style** is a social interaction style that is consistent with the type and quality of relationship one wishes to share with others, based on working models of self and others (Bartholomew, 1990). Attachment styles include one's own communication style, the way one processes and interprets others' behavior, and the way one reacts to others' behavior (Guerrero & Burgoon, 1996). Attachment styles are also associated with "relatively coherent and stable patterns of emotion and behavior [that] are exhibited in close relationships" (Shaver, Collins, & Clark, 1996, p. 25).

Attachment Styles in Childhood

Early interaction with primary caregivers shapes children's internal models of themselves and others and sets the stage for later attachments (Ainsworth et al., 1978; Bowlby, 1977). Although new interactions with significant others continue to modify the way people see themselves and relational partners, the first 2 to 3 years of life (and especially the first year) are critical in developing these internal models. By the time a baby is about 6 weeks old, he or she already shows a preference for the primary caregiver—usually the mother. For example, if a 2-month-old baby is crying, she might be best comforted by her mother. At around 14 to 20 months, toddlers are usually attached to their mothers and feel separation anxiety when they leave. At this time, babysitters may have trouble with their charges, who often become fairly distressed when they realize their mother, who functions as their secure base, is not around. One of us had an experience like this when babysitting a friend's child. The little boy, who was about 1½ years old, was fine right after his parents left. However, an hour later he began searching the house for his mother. When he could not find her, he stood at the window calling, "Mommy, Mommy!" and looking for her. Eventually, he settled down and watched a cartoon on television, but he clearly had experienced a bout of separation anxiety.

Most children emerge from the first 2 years of life with secure, healthy attachments to caregivers (Ainsworth et al., 1978; Bowlby, 1969). If this is the case, they have developed positive models of both themselves and others. Not all children are so lucky. About 30% of children develop insecure attachment styles because they have negative models of themselves or others. Bowlby's original work showed that children who were raised in institutions and deprived of their mother's care for extended periods of time were more likely to develop insecure attachments (Bowlby, 1969, 1973). Ainsworth and her colleagues later demonstrated that the type of care children receive at home influences their attachment style (Ainsworth, 1969, 1982, 1989; Ainsworth et al., 1978; Ainsworth & Eichberg, 1991; Ainsworth & Wittig, 1969). They delineated three types of infant attachment: secure, avoidant, and anxious ambivalent.

Secure Children. The majority of children fall into the secure category. Secure children tend to have responsive and warm parents, to receive moderate levels of stimulation, and to engage in synchronized interaction with their caregivers. The "goodness of fit" between the caregiver and the child is crucial. A caregiver may need to adjust her or his style of interaction to accommodate the child. Thus, one child may need a lot of cuddling and reassurance, while another may prefer to be left alone. This helps explain why children from the same family environment may develop different attachment styles. Children who develop secure attachments to a caregiver are more likely to feel free to explore, approach others, and be positive toward strangers than are insecure types. Secure children are also likely to protest separation and to show happiness when reunited with their caregivers. These children tend to develop positive models of self and others.

Avoidant Children. Some insecure children develop an avoidant attachment style (Ainsworth et al., 1978). Avoidant children tend to have caregivers who are either insensitive to their signals or trying

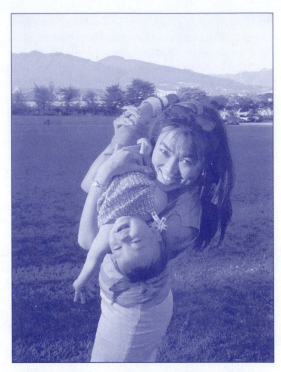

SOURCE: Copyright: iStockphoto.com/Ronnie Comeau

Photo 6.1   Affectionate play helps develop and strengthen the attachment bond between young children and caregivers.

too hard to please. In addition, avoidant children are often either over- or understimulated, which leads to physiological arousal and a flight response. When overstimulated, they retreat from social interaction to avoid being overloaded. When understimulated, they learn how to cope without social interaction. Because their caregivers are not able to fulfill their needs, they develop negative models of others. These children stay within themselves, seldom explore their environment, and are rarely positive toward strangers. They tend not to protest separation from caregivers and show little emotion when the caregiver returns.

Anxious-Ambivalent Children. Other insecure children develop anxious ambivalent attachment styles (Ainsworth et al., 1978). These children tend to be the product of inconsistent behavior by caregivers; sometimes the caregiver is appropriately responsive, at other times is neglectful or overstimulating. Anxious-ambivalent children often have caregivers who are preoccupied with problems of their own, such as relational conflict, divorce, or substance abuse. Instead of blaming the caregiver (or the caregiver's situation) for this inconsistency, they blame themselves and develop self-models of doubt, insecurity, and uncertainty. Anxious-ambivalent children often are tentative when exploring their environment in the presence of their caregivers and fearful of exploration if alone. They protest separation from caregivers vehemently, yet are both relieved and angry when the caregiver returns. This contradiction is reflected in their label—they are anxious when separated from the caregiver and ambivalent when the caregiver returns. Sometimes these children develop positive models of others because they do receive some comfort and security from caregivers.

Attachment Styles in Adulthood

Attachment styles are also relevant in adult relationships. Hazan and Shaver (1987) conceptualized love as an attachment process that is "experienced somewhat differently by different people because of variations in their attachment histories" (p. 511). Using Ainsworth et al.'s (1978) three attachment styles as a guide, Hazan and Shaver (1987) proposed that adults can have secure, avoidant, or anxious-ambivalent attachments to their romantic partners. **Secures** are comfortable getting close to and depending on romantic partners and seldom worry about being abandoned. They strive for a balance of autonomy and closeness in their relationships. **Avoidants** are uncomfortable getting close to or depending on romantic partners. They value autonomy over relational closeness. Finally, **anxious ambivalents** tend to be overinvolved, demanding, and dependent (Collins & Read, 1990; Feeney & Noller, 1991). They value relational closeness over autonomy. As Hazan and Shaver (1987) noted, anxious ambivalents "want to merge completely with another person, and this desire sometimes scares people away" (p. 515). Thus if interdependence is portrayed as a spider's web, secures would create intimacy webs

that are intertwined, avoidants would keep their webs relatively separate, and anxious ambivalents would build webs filled with heavy entanglements.

A few years after Hazan and Shaver published their groundbreaking work, Bartholomew (1990) proposed a four-category system of attachment. She argued that the working models a person holds about self and others combine to produce four, rather than three, attachment styles: secure, preoccupied, dismissive, and fearful (see Figure 6.2). Research has confirmed that people with these four kinds of attachment differ in important ways, including their communication styles.

Secure: The Prosocial Style. Secure individuals have positive models of themselves and others ("I'm okay and you're okay"). The secures in Bartholomew's system are essentially the same as those described by Hazan and Shaver. They feel good about themselves and their relationships, and they display "high self-esteem and an absence of serious interpersonal problems" (Bartholomew, 1990, p. 163). These individuals have the capacity for close, fulfilling relationships. They are likely to have realistic expectations, be satisfied with their relationships, and be comfortable depending on others and having others depend on them. Although they value relationships, they are not afraid of being alone.

Secure individuals have a communication style that displays social skill and promotes healthy relationships (Guerrero & Jones, 2005). They seek social support when distressed and know how to provide effective care and comfort to their relational partners (Kunce & Shaver, 1994; Weger & Polcar, 2002). In general, their communication tends to be pleasant, attentive, and expressive (Guerrero, 1996; Le Poire, Shepard, & Duggan, 1999), and they smile at, laugh with, and touch their romantic partners more than do individuals with other attachment styles (Tucker & Anders, 1998). When secures experience distress, they are usually able to express their negative feelings appropriately and seek support from others (Feeney, 1995; Simpson & Rholes, 1994). They cope with feelings of anger, jealousy, and sadness by behaving in ways that bolster their self-esteem and help maintain relationships (Guerrero, 1998; Guerrero, Farinelli, & McEwan, 2007; Sharpsteen &

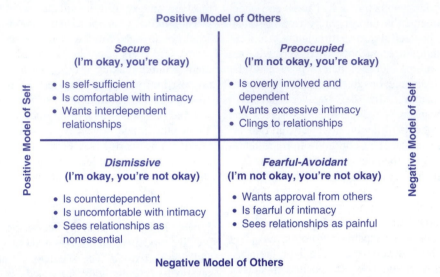

Positive Model of Others

Secure
(I'm okay, you're okay)

- Is self-sufficient
- Is comfortable with intimacy
- Wants interdependent relationships

Preoccupied
(I'm not okay, you're okay)

- Is overly involved and dependent
- Wants excessive intimacy
- Clings to relationships

Dismissive
(I'm okay, you're not okay)

- Is counterdependent
- Is uncomfortable with intimacy
- Sees relationships as nonessential

Fearful-Avoidant
(I'm not okay, you're not okay)

- Wants approval from others
- Is fearful of intimacy
- Sees relationships as painful

Positive Model of Self

Negative Model of Self

Negative Model of Others

Figure 6.2 Bartholomew's Four Attachment Styles

SOURCE: Adapted from Guerrero (1996).

Kirkpatrick, 1997). In conflict situations, secure individuals are more likely than individuals with other attachment styles to compromise and solve problems (Bippus & Rollin, 2003; Pistole, 1989). Secure individuals also engage in high levels of relational maintenance behavior, such as engaging in romantic activities, talking about commitment, and sharing activities (Bippus & Rollin, 2003; Guerrero & Bachman, 2006; Simon & Baxter, 1993). A study of married couples also showed that secure individuals were most likely to express positive emotions, such as love, pride, and happiness, to their spouses (Feeney, 1999).

Preoccupied: The Emotional Style. Preoccupied individuals, who are fairly similar to anxious ambivalents, have positive models of others but negative models of themselves ("You're okay but I'm not okay"). These individuals are overly dependent on relationships. As Bartholomew (1990) put it, preoccupied individuals are characterized by "an insatiable desire to gain others' approval and a deep-seated feeling of unworthiness" (p. 163). Their relational identities often are much stronger than their

self-identities; they need to have a relationship with someone to feel worthwhile. In fact, preoccupied individuals report feeling lost and unable to cope without a close relationship. They also are likely to cling to their relationships in times of trouble and to resist any attempts by a partner to de-escalate or terminate close relationships.

Preoccupied individuals exhibit mixed messages that reflect their high need for intimacy coupled with their low self-confidence. In everyday interactions, they often appear pleasant, attentive, and expressive (Guerrero, 1996). However, when they become anxious, their communication sometimes becomes unpleasant and self-focused. In one study, preoccupied individuals exhibited low levels of enjoyment when talking about relationship issues with their romantic partners (Tucker & Anders, 1998). In another study, preoccupied individuals were expressive but showed low levels of composure and altercentrism (with altercentrism representing a focus on the partner) when discussing a conflict issue (Guerrero & Jones, 2005). Preoccupied individuals are also overly sensitive and have trouble controlling their emotions (Guerrero & Jones, 2003). In their quest to develop intimacy, they sometimes disclose intimate information too quickly (Bartholomew & Horowitz, 1991; Mikulincer & Nachshon, 1991). Research has also shown that preoccupieds display demanding behavior in an attempt to hang onto their relationship or change their partners (Bartholomew & Horowitz, 1991; Guerrero & Langan, 1999). In conflict situations, they tend to engage in controlling behavior and to nag and whine (Creasey, Kershaw, & Boston, 1999; O'Connell-Corcoran & Mallinckrodt, 2000). Similarly, they tend to express anger, using aggressive or passive-aggressive behaviors (Feeney, 1995; Guerrero et al., 2007).

Fearful: The Hesitant Style. Fearful individuals have negative models of both themselves and others ("I'm not okay and you're not okay"). Some of the avoidants in Hazan and Shaver's system fall in this category, as do a few of the anxious ambivalents, particularly when they have negative views of both others and themselves. The key characteristic of fearful avoidants is that they are afraid of hurt and rejection, often because they have experienced painful relationships in the past. Fearful individuals usually want to depend on someone but find it difficult to open up to others. As Bartholomew (1990) put it, fearful individuals "desire social contact and intimacy, but experience pervasive interpersonal distrust and fear of rejection" (p. 164).

Fearful individuals tend to avoid social situations and potential relationships because they fear rejection. Even when in relationships, they tend to be hesitant to communicate emotions or to initiate escalation of the relationship. Bartholomew (1990) noted the paradoxical nature of fearful individuals' actions and desires: By refusing to open themselves up to others, they undermine their chances for building the very type of trusting relationship they desire. Their communication style reflects their fear and lack of trust. Guerrero (1996) found that fearful individuals were less fluent and used larger proxemic distances than individuals with other attachment styles. Other studies suggest that fearful individuals possess less social skill than people with other attachment styles. They tend to lack assertiveness (Anders & Tucker, 2000) and to appear uncomposed (Guerrero & Jones, 2005). They also have difficulty expressing their emotions and responding

to the emotions of others (Guerrero & Jones, 2003). Fearful individuals are both anxious and avoidant, and research has shown that people who possess these two characteristics report using less relational maintenance behavior (such as showing affection and being positive and cheerful) in their relationships (Guerrero & Bachman, 2006). Fearful individuals also have difficulty confronting conflict issues; instead, they tend to withdraw or accommodate the partner (Pistole, 1989).

Dismissive: The Detached Style. Dismissive individuals have positive models of themselves but negative models of others ("I'm okay but you're not okay"). Many of the avoidants in Hazan and Shaver's system would fall here. Dismissives can best be characterized as counterdependent. In other words, they are so self-sufficient that they shun close involvement with others. Some researchers suggest that counterdependence is a defensive strategy that allows people to feel good about themselves without opening themselves up to the criticisms and scrutiny of others. Dismissives neither desire nor fear close attachments but rather lack the motivation to build and maintain intimate relationships (Bartholomew, 1990). They place a much higher value on autonomy than on relationships and tend to focus on less personal aspects of their lives, such as careers, hobbies, and self-improvement (Bartholomew, 1990).

Not surprisingly, dismissive individuals possess a highly avoidant attachment style. Yet unlike fearful individuals, dismissives are composed and self-confident (Anders & Tucker, 2000; Guerrero & Jones, 2005). Dismissive individuals generally exhibit less disclosure, conversational involvement, and affection than do individuals with the secure or preoccupied style (Bartholomew & Horowitz, 1991; Guerrero, 1996). They report relatively low levels of relational maintenance behaviors, such as being romantic and giving assurances that they are committed to the relationship (Guerrero & Bachman, 2006; Simon & Baxter, 1993). Dismissives also are seen as fairly dominant. They tend to interrupt their partners more than do those with other attachment styles (Guerrero & Langan, 1999), and they report low levels of accommodation and tend to withdraw during conflict (Feeney, Noller, & Roberts, 2000). When dismissives experience emotional distress, they often deny their feelings and insist on handling their problems without help from others (Bartholomew, 1993). As Simpson and Rholes (1994) put it, dismissives "distance themselves from others emotionally. Over time they come to see themselves as fully autonomous and immune to negative events" (p. 184). For a summary of these attachment-style differences in communication, see Box 6.4.

BOX 6.4 Highlights

Attachment-Style Differences in Communication

	Secure	Preoccupied	Fearful	Dismissive
Conflict behavior	Most compromising and problem solving	Demanding, dominating behavior; nagging; whining	Accommodating, passive responses	Withdrawal, less accommodation, more interruptions
Maintenance behavior	Highest level of maintenance	High level of maintenance	Relatively low levels of maintenance	Less maintenance overall, especially less romance and assurances
Emotional expression	Readily express emotions in a direct, prosocial manner	Aggressive and passive-aggressive displays of negative emotion	Inhibit expression of negative emotion	Experience and express emotions (negative and positive) least
Self-disclosure	High levels of appropriate disclosure, able to elicit disclosure from others	High levels of disclosure that are sometimes inappropriate or indiscriminate	Low levels of disclosure, especially with strangers or acquaintances	Low levels of disclosure
Nonverbal intimacy	Relatively high levels of facial and vocal pleasantness, laughter, touch, and smiling	A mix of positive and negative nonverbal cues, depending on the situation	Relatively low levels of facial and vocal pleasantness, expressiveness, and smiling	Relatively low levels of facial and vocal pleasantness, expressiveness, and smiling
Social skill	Assertive, responsive to others, able to provide effective care and comfort	Overly sensitive, difficulty controlling emotional expression	Trouble expressing self and being assertive, exhibit anxiety cues such as lack of fluency and long response latencies	Trouble expressing themselves and comforting others

Stability and Change in Attachment Styles Across the Life Span

By now, you may be able to guess what attachment styles Brian and Gabriela have. Brian appears to be somewhat preoccupied. He worries that he might care more for Gabriela than she cares for him. He also appears to desire high levels of overt affection in his relationships. Gabriela, on the other hand, seems somewhat dismissive. She wonders if she can commit enough time and energy to her relationship, and her priority seems to be her personal goals. If Gabriela and Brian stay together, are their attachment styles likely to change or stay the same during the course of their relationship? Have they had these attachment styles since childhood or could they have developed these styles recently? Finally, do they have the same attachment style with their friends and family as they have with each other? Research investigating how stable attachment styles are across time suggests that the answer to all these questions is "it depends." Studies have shown that around 25% to 30% of adults experience changes in their attachment style toward romantic partners (Davila, Burge, & Hammen, 1997; Davila, Karney, & Bradbury, 1999; Feeney & Noller, 1996). Similarly, in a study on adolescent friendships, 35% of high school students reported a change in attachment style from one year to the next (Miller, Notaro, & Zimmerman, 2002). These studies suggest that although attachment styles are fairly stable, they can be modified by new experiences.

Explanations for Stability. At least two forces work to stabilize a person's attachment style. First, interactions with caregivers have an especially strong effect on a person's social development, including the attachment style a person develops. Bowlby (1969, 1973) believed that early interactions with caregivers provide a mental blueprint for thinking about oneself and others that carries into adulthood. So an avoidant child has many obstacles to overcome if she or he hopes to develop into a secure adult, including learning to trust others and being comfortable with closeness. Similarly, an anxious-ambivalent child needs to become self-confident and self-sufficient to achieve security. Such changes

are possible but require time, effort, and the cooperation and patience of others.

A second source of stability has been called **the reinforcement effect** (Bartholomew, 1993). According to this perspective, people communicate in cycles that reinforce their attachment style. For example, because secure individuals are self-confident and readily approach others, they are more likely to make friends and develop relationships, causing them to feel even better about themselves and others. Preoccupied individuals, in contrast, are continually reaching for higher levels of intimacy. Perhaps you have had a partner like this—someone who wanted to meet your family right away, told you how much she or he loved you on the third date, or wanted to move in with you after your first month together. A common reaction to these premature declarations of love and commitment is to try to de-escalate the relationship, which only makes the preoccupied person engage in more excessive intimacy and closeness. This process reinforces that individual's negative model of self ("My partner doesn't love me as much as I love her") and positive model of others ("Everything would be great if only I could get him to love me").

Fearful and dismissive individuals suffer from similarly paradoxical interaction patterns. More than anything else, fearful individuals need to build a secure, happy relationship to help them feel better about themselves and others. However, their fear of pain and rejection keeps them from reaching out to others and developing the kind of intimate relationship that would bring them out of their protective shells. Dismissives display similarly negative self-reinforcing patterns. If dismissives continually avoid highly committed relationships and refuse to ask others for help and support, they reinforce their view that other people are unnecessary and they should rely only on themselves. They miss the opportunity to discover ways in which committed relationships can enrich, rather than impede, personal satisfaction.

Explanations for Change. There are four primary explanations for change in attachment styles (Feeney et al., 2000). First, significant events such as divorce, marriage, reunion after a long separation, the development of a new relationship, or the death of a loved one may modify a person's attachment style. For example, a fearful man may become more secure after reuniting with his ex-wife, and a secure young woman may become somewhat dismissive when she heads off to college away from those who love her. Second, a person's attachment style may be affected by her or his partner's style, as several studies have shown (e.g., Guerrero & Bachman, 2006; Le Poire et al., 1999). In the case of Gabriela and Brian, their opposing needs could cause them to become more dismissive and preoccupied, respectively. When Gabriela expresses a need for more space, Brian might feel a lack of closeness and crave more intimacy. When Brian expresses a need for more affection, Gabriela might pull away and retreat into her personal activities.

Third, people may have different attachment styles depending on the type of relationship (Baldwin & Fehr, 1995; Cozzarelli, Hoekstra, & Bylsma, 2000; Pierce & Lydon, 2001). For example, Gabriela might have a dismissive attachment orientation toward Brian and her father but a secure attachment orientation toward her mother and her friends. The movie *Good Will Hunting* provides a good example of how attachment orientations sometimes vary on the basis of relationship type. Will exhibits classic fearful behavior with romantic partners—he avoids commitment because he is afraid of being hurt and abandoned as he was as a child in the foster care system. However, within his close-knit group of male friends, Will displays a secure attachment style. Finally, some researchers have suggested that stability (or instability) of attachment style is a personality characteristic, with some people more susceptible to change than others. So Brian's attachment style may be more likely to change based on life events (such as getting married) than Gabriela's.

Summary and Application

People approach loving relationships in a variety of ways. Every person has a unique set of perceptions, expectations, and preferences that contribute to her or his styles of loving and attachment. When two people's styles interact within the context of a close relationship, another unique relational pattern emerges. Partners should realize that what works in one of their relationships might not necessarily work in others and that it is difficult for two people to fully meet each other's expectations.

The attitudes Gabriela and Brian have about love and relationships are fairly common. From the description at the beginning of this chapter, Gabriela appears to have an active way of loving and a dismissive attachment style. Brian appears to have an expressive way of loving and a somewhat preoccupied attachment style. Of course, most people do not fall neatly into a love or attachment category. Take another look at Figure 6.2. Where would you fall on the dimensions representing positive versus negative models of self and others? You could fit squarely within a given category or you could fall in the border between categories. For instance, Gabriela might have an extremely positive model of self and only a slightly negative model of others, and Brian might be on the border between preoccupation and security. Moreover, the interaction between Brian and Gabriela's styles is likely to produce a unique set of behaviors. Styles of love and attachment reflect some important differences in how people approach and communicate in close relationships, but it is crucial to see ourselves and others as complex individuals who do not always fit a particular profile.

People with different relational needs and communication styles, like Brian and Gabriela, can often work together to build happy relationships. One key to a successful relationship is for relational partners to help each other grow as individuals. For example, preoccupied individuals like Brian may need to make an effort to give their partners more space, while dismissive individuals like Gabriela may need to work on showing more affection. At the same time, individuals in relationships with people who have insecure attachment styles should be patient and understanding rather than demanding more or less intimacy than their partners are comfortable giving. Relational partners should also understand and appreciate each other's ways of loving. For example, Brian may feel more secure if he realizes that Gabriela is showing that she cares for him when she plans activities for them to do together.

In the scenario at the beginning of this chapter, Brian also wonders if Gabriela really loves him. This is a difficult question to answer. Liking and loving differ in both quantitative and qualitative ways. Love is typically characterized by more attachment, caring, intimacy, and commitment than liking, and love between romantic partners is also usually characterized by feelings of passion. Yet it is hard to quantify love, and there is no simple answer to the seemingly straightforward question, What is love? Love is a complex, variable phenomenon that defies simple definition. Indeed, instead of simply asking what love is, it may be more appropriate to ask, What is love to me and to my partner, and how does love function in the unique relationship we share? Thinking about these issues may be especially helpful to relational partners, such as Gabriela and Brian, who have different styles of loving and attachment.

DISCUSSION QUESTIONS

1. How would you distinguish love from liking? Do you think the difference between loving and liking is more quantitative or qualitative?

2. Do you think people's love styles change throughout their lives? If so, what factors do you think account for this change? How might culture affect people's love styles?

3. According to attachment theory, parent-child interaction forms the basis for personality development, including the capacity to have close, intimate adult relationships with others. To what extent do you agree or disagree that early interaction with parents shapes a person's life? What other events and interactions have shaped your attachment style?

7

COMMUNICATING SEXUALLY

The Closest Physical Encounter

Although Brittany, Sarah, and Taylor are sisters in the same sorority, their sex lives could not be more different. Brittany has been seeing the same man for 4 years and has an active sex life. She believes her boyfriend Chris is completely faithful, but she insisted they both get tested to be sure that they do not have sexually transmitted infections (STIs). She is on the pill and tries to be as responsible about sex as possible, though she has never discussed her active sex life with her parents. Although she loves Chris, she is not completely sure he is the "one" for her. Sarah is deeply religious and has chosen to remain a virgin until after marriage. Sometimes she feels strange, because most of the girls in the house are not virgins. She enjoys sexual activity with her boyfriend but always makes sure that they stop well short of sexual intercourse. Occasionally, her sisters are a bit unkind and call Sarah frigid or prudish, which makes Sarah feel that her values are out of the mainstream. Taylor dated men in the past but recently admitted to herself and the world that she has always been more attracted to women. She announced to her sisters that she is a lesbian and is in a committed, monogamous relationship with her partner, Leslie. Most of the women in the house accepted her fully; however, she has heard a few homophobic comments and caught some of her sisters exchanging strange glances when she mentions Leslie.

Sex is one of the most rewarding and difficult issues people face. In this chapter, we focus on sexual behavior and its importance in human relationships. Additionally, we examine communication related to the development of sexual attitudes and beliefs, initiation and refusal of sexual activity, coercion and harassment, and safe sex in short- and long-term relationships for both heterosexuals and homosexuals. Though many intimate relationships are platonic, some of our closest encounters are sexual, including romances and marriages. Most of the research has focused on sexual relationships between men and women; therefore, despite our best efforts to include information about relationships between gay men and lesbians, there is a heterosexual bias evident in the research in general as well as in this chapter. Additionally, most studies focus on the attitudes and behaviors of couples living in the United States; in other countries, sexual attitudes and behaviors may be quite different. Finally, the physiology of sex and sexual desire per se is beyond the scope of this chapter, although excellent books on these topics are available if you would like more information (see Rathus, Nevid, & Fichner-Rathus, 1993; Regan & Berscheid, 1999).

SEX IN RELATIONSHIPS

Research has shown that sexual interaction, including physical contact such as intimate kissing and touching, and sexual intercourse, is a vital part of dating and marital relationships. Although people experience some ambivalence about sexual involvement in premarital relationships (O'Sullivan & Gaines, 1998), sexual involvement is typical in most dating relationships. For most people, sex, attraction, desire, romance, and love are closely intertwined. In this section, we examine differences in sexual interaction based on the type of relationship, sex and gender, and sexual orientation.

Sex in Short-Term and Early Dating Relationships

Short-term sex occurs when a couple has sex once or more without developing an emotionally intimate relationship. Most short-term sex takes the form of hookups or one-night stands. Contrary to the stereotype that only men seek short-term sexual relationships, research shows that women also engage in short-term mating strategies for many of the same reasons as men: sexual desire, sexual experimentation, physical pleasure, and alcohol or drug use. Men are likely to use short-term sex for status and sexual satisfaction, whereas women are more likely to use it as a means of trying to establish a long-term commitment or to enhance their economic status (Greitemeyer, 2005; Regan & Dreyer, 1999). For many men, the ideal short-term mate is physically attractive (Buunk, Dijkstra, Fetchenhauer, & Kenrick, 2002; Greitemeyer, 2005), but men are willing to compromise on traits such as intelligence and status. For women, the ideal short-term partner is physically attractive, somewhat older, more experienced, self-confident, and interpersonally responsive (Buunk et al., 2002; Regan, 1998b). Women are much less likely than men to compromise on these standards.

Situational variables affect short-term mating strategies as well. In a creative study, Pennebaker

and his colleagues (1979) showed that people in bars get more attractive as closing time nears. At three preselected times, researchers approached college students in bars and asked randomly selected men and women to evaluate the attractiveness of potential opposite-sex partners. Sure enough, as closing time neared, the perceived attractiveness of opposite-sex patrons increased while evaluations of same-sex patrons remained the same (Pennebaker et al., 1979).

Although one-night stands are not uncommon, premarital sex typically occurs in dating relationships between people who share some level of emotional intimacy. In these relationships, people seek to experience sexual attraction, sexual arousal, as well as relational closeness, and they often desire more relational intimacy (Mongeau et al., 2004; O'Sullivan & Gaines, 1998). Research also suggests that first sex is a turning point in relationships for better or worse (Metts, 2004). Situational factors, such as drinking alcohol, can also prompt sexual involvement (Laumann, Gagnon, Michael, & Michaels, 1994; Morr & Mongeau, 2004; Sprecher & McKinney, 1993), as can special occasions like going to the senior prom or anniversaries.

Research shows that among dating couples sexual satisfaction is an important component of relational satisfaction for both men and women (Byers, Demmons, & Lawrence, 1998), although many other factors contribute to relational satisfaction, such as commitment, love, and compatibility. If the relationship is satisfying and if neither partner feels coerced or obligated to have sex, their first experience of sexual intercourse usually has a positive effect on the relationship (Cate, Long, Angera, & Draper, 1993). This is not to say that sex always makes a relationship better, but high-quality sex can contribute to a good relationship.

Sex in Marriage and Other Long-Term Relationships

In long-term love relationships, physical contact, including touching, kissing, and sexual intercourse, is essential (Christopher & Kissler, 2004; Regan & Berscheid, 1999). It is in long-term romantic relationships, not in hookups or dating relationships, where most sexual activity takes place (DeLamater

& Hyde, 2004; Willetts, Sprecher, & Beck, 2004). Married people experience higher levels of sexual satisfaction than dating or cohabiting couples (Sprecher & Cate, 2004). Sexual intimacy is the sine qua non (essential component) of heterosexual love and evolved to keep mates interested in one another (Buss, 1988b; Hendrick & Hendrick, 2002). A couple's ongoing sexual interest promotes bonding, cooperation, a division of labor, and the establishment of a stable environment for child rearing (Buss, 1994; Sprecher & Cate, 2004). Sex is particularly satisfying and enhancing when it results from approach motives, such as feeling good about oneself, wanting to please one's partner, or promoting intimacy. Sex is not as pleasurable or relationship enhancing when it is prompted by avoidance motives such as preventing one's partner from getting upset, avoiding conflict, or preventing one's partner from losing interest (Impett, Peplau, & Gable, 2005).

Although men's sexual desire peaks in their 20s and women's in their 30s, the association between relational satisfaction and sexual satisfaction is high throughout life, even for seniors (Barr, Bryan, & Kenrick, 2002; Burgess, 2004; Lawrence & Byers, 1995). The amount of sex declines as couples age, but sexual satisfaction does not decline (Burgess, 2004; DeLamater & Hyde, 2004; Willetts et al., 2004). Lawrence and Byers (1995) reported that both men and women find a variety of sexual activities important to long-term sexual satisfaction.

Both men and women view sexual desire and satisfaction as vital to achieving true romantic love (Regan, 1998a; Regan & Berscheid, 1999; Sprecher & Cate, 2004; Sternberg, 1987). Studies show that people who report high levels of sexual desire in their relationships also tend to report high levels of excitement, connection, and love (Christopher & Kissler, 2004a; Hendrick & Hendrick, 2002; Sprecher and Regan, 1996). Indeed, when students in the United States were asked to list the persons whom they sexually desired and the persons with whom they were in love, 85% of the persons named appeared on both lists (Berscheid & Meyers, 1996). Interestingly, the positive association between sexual satisfaction and relational satisfaction also exists in China, suggesting the cross-cultural strength of this association (Reined, Byers, & Pan, 1997).

Selection criteria for a long-term romantic partner differ from those for a first date or short-term sexual encounter. Both men and women place a higher value on qualities such as interpersonal skill, emotional stability, responsiveness, and family orientation, and less value on physical attraction in long-term as opposed to short-term relationships, although for men physical attraction is always important (Buunk et al., 2002; Regan, 1998b). Women throughout the world prefer a long-term partner higher in social and economic status than themselves (Buunk et al., 2002). But sex itself is important; in long-term relationships, "sexual desire is a distinguishing feature and a prerequisite of the romantic love experience" (Regan & Berscheid, 1999, p. 126). In short-term sexual encounters, in contrast, sexual desire is often present without love or intimacy.

Sex and Gender Differences

Sex is an important part of a good relationship for both men and women, but they are not identical in their sexual inclinations and behaviors. The reproductive roles, sexual behaviors, and mate selection strategies of men and women are different. Biologically, women expend a much greater investment of time and resources in becoming a parent. For women, reproduction involves finding a mate, having sex, going through pregnancy and childbirth, nursing and nurturing the baby, and in most cases raising the child to adulthood; for men, only finding a mate and having sex are biological imperatives (Trost & Alberts, 2006). Of course, most men stay with their mate during pregnancy and help raise their offspring. But this is a choice made by responsible men. As the large number of single moms and deadbeat dads indicates, some men make little investment in their offspring.

Of course, having sex does not mean having babies. Indeed, most couples conscientiously avoid pregnancy during their sexual encounters. Having a baby is a huge commitment of time, money, and resources. Instead, sex is usually about pleasure, commitment, and closeness. The biological imperative of reproduction that makes humans sexual is deeply ingrained, and for most people, sexual desire leads to sexual encounters. Reproduction is far less necessary.

Men and women also think about sex differently. Men have greater expectations for sex on dates than do women (Mongeau & Johnson, 1995), and men think about sex more often than do women. Studies have shown that males think about sex every few seconds (Byers, Purden, & Clark, 1998; Vohs, Catanese, & Baumeister, 2004). Women are sexually attracted to men who are relationally oriented and emotionally connected and show tenderness and intimacy with them. Men are more likely to experience sexual desire in response to sexy looks, erotic situations, and friendly social behaviors (Buunk et al., 2002; Cupach & Metts, 1995; Greitemeyer, 2005; Regan, 2004). Studies consistently show that men have a stronger sex drive than women (DeLamater & Hyde, 2004; Vohs et al., 2004), are more motivated to date in order to have sexual relations, are less willing to live without sex (Mongeau et al., 2004; Regan & Berscheid, 1995), and have more sex partners (Willetts et al., 2004). Numerous studies show that women's sexual desire is more dependent on feelings, the type of relationship they share with the partner, the potential for intimacy and humor, and the status and intelligence of the man, whereas men's desire is more influenced by physical attraction, sexual pleasure, and erotic qualities (Buunk et al., 2002; Greitemeyer, 2005; Metts, 2004; Regan, 2004; Regan & Berscheid, 1995, 1999). Interestingly, the first act of sexual intercourse between two people usually has a much more positive effect on the relationship for women than men, assuming that the sex was a voluntary act reflecting love and/or commitment (Cate et al., 1993).

Research suggests that females exhibit erotic plasticity; their sex drive is more socially flexible, culturally responsive, plastic, and adaptable than the male sex drive, which is more predictable and consistent, less shaped by culture, and somewhat stronger (Baumeister, 2000; Vohs et al., 2004; Wells & Twenge, 2005). Some women seem to do fine without sex, while other women are highly sexual depending on circumstances (Baumeister, 2000). Numerous studies show individual women to vary in sex drive over time. For example, a woman may have a stronger sex drive when she is in an intimate relationship than when she is not involved with anyone. Men, in contrast, have a more consistent sex drive that operates regardless of their relational involvement with someone. Men masturbate more than women, are more likely to read pornography than women, and are more likely to approve of casual sex than women (DeLamater & Hyde, 2004). Of course, the popularity of Viagra and Cialis suggests that men's sex drive is also somewhat variable.

Female sexuality is also more varied across different sociocultural settings than male sexuality. Baumeister (2000) cited ethnographic studies that report much greater cross-cultural variation in sexual behavior for females than for males. For example, in some cultures women have premarital sex, while in others they do not. Studies show that women are less likely to reveal their true sexual attitudes than are men. This is part of a double standard that still exists, requiring women to hide their sexual interest to a degree so as to not appear "loose" (DeLamater & Hyde, 2004). On the other hand, women are more likely than men to fake sexual satisfaction to please their partners. Because the costs of pregnancy are great, women may have evolved to be more sexually selective than men, and hence they are more flexible and plastic in their sexuality (Vohs et al., 2004).

Sex in Gay and Lesbian Relationships

A significant minority of people are not attracted to members of the opposite sex, but rather have same-sex attractions. Like Taylor, whom we introduced in our opening, most homosexuals have early recollections of same-sex attraction and a clear sense that they were different from the majority as early as preschool (Rathus et al., 1993). Research suggests that throughout the world most gay men and lesbians experienced some degree of gender nonconformity as children (Crooks & Baur, 1999).

Because men and women differ in their sexual attitudes and behaviors, it is not surprising that relationships involving lesbians, gay men, and heterosexuals also differ. But there are major similarities between heterosexual, gay, and lesbian relationships as well. Like heterosexual couples, the vast majority of lesbians and gay men want long-term committed relationships (Peplau, Fingerhut, & Beals, 2004). Indeed, the vast majority of lesbians and gay men would marry their partner if gay marriage was legally sanctioned (Peplau et al., 2004).

Despite increasingly progressive attitudes about homosexuality and bisexuality in the United States, gay and lesbian relationships are still not readily accepted or understood by many segments of society (Peplau et al., 2004). Growing up gay in a heterosexual, homophobic world is not easy, and most problems for gay men and lesbians come from the adverse reactions of society. Adolescence is a tough time for all young people, as indicated by the high teenage suicide rate, and the rate is even higher for gay teens, who may need counseling as they adjust to their sexual orientation and to the attitudes of those around them.

Sex in Lesbian Relationships. Over 75% of lesbian couples are monogamous, and research suggests that fidelity is important to lesbians (Blumstein & Schwartz, 1983). Sexual activity for lesbians declines over time, leading to concerns and even jokes about the "lesbian death bed" (Peplau et al., 2004). Although the frequency of sexual relations is associated with increased satisfaction in lesbian couples (Peplau et al., 2004), they have sex less frequently than gay couples, heterosexual daters, or married couples (Blumstein & Schwartz, 1983). Women are taught to be selective in choosing sexual partners, to take a reactive as opposed to a proactive role in sexual situations, and to act as gatekeepers who decide whether sexual activity will take place. Lesbians must renegotiate these gender roles so that they feel comfortable initiating sex. Moreover, extensive evidence shows that women do not have as strong or consistent a sex drive as men (Baumeister, 2000; Julien, Bouchard, Gagnon, & Pomperleau, 1992), so with no man to initiate sex, it is less likely to occur. Finally, lesbians may be satisfied with nongenital sex since, like heterosexual women, lesbians value physical contact, like hugging and cuddling, and are likely to consider these ends in and of themselves rather than a prelude to sex (Blumstein & Schwartz, 1983).

Close to 25% of lesbians are actually married to men (Rathus et al., 1993). Some may be bisexual, others may be testing their heterosexual orientation, and still others may be concealing their homosexual orientation. According to Bell and Weinberg (1978),

relational satisfaction is low in such marital relationships, and almost all end in separation or divorce. Over 75% of lesbians have had at least one sexual encounter with a man (Reinisch & Beasley, 1990). Interestingly, research suggests that women are more sexually variable than men and have an easier time accepting various sexual orientations and conditions, including abstinence (Baumeister, 2000).

Sex in Relationships Between Gay Men. According to the latest Kinsey report, although about one third of all men have engaged in homosexual behavior at one time in their lives, about 8% have had exclusively gay relationships for 3 or more years, and only 4% have been exclusively gay throughout their lives. About two thirds of gay men have had sex with a woman, and 10% to 15% may be more accurately viewed as bisexual (Reinisch & Beasley, 1990).

On average, gay men have a higher number of sex partners than lesbians or heterosexuals, and gay men also engage in sex more often than any other group (Blumstein & Schwartz, 1983). Since women often act as sexual gatekeepers, the absence of a woman in a relationship probably reduces restraint and increases sexual frequency. Gay men are also more likely than lesbians or heterosexuals to be in non-monogamous relationships. In 1983, Blumstein and Schwartz reported that 82% of the gay men in their nationwide survey said they were non-monogamous. Despite this, long-term relationships among gay men are much more common than the media would have us believe. The Kinsey data suggest that virtually all gay men have had a steady, highly committed gay relationship that lasted 1 to 3 years (Reinisch & Beasley, 1990). Furthermore, some evidence suggests that gay men, like heterosexual men and women, have become more monogamous since the AIDS epidemic first emerged in the 1980s (Sprecher & Regan, 2000).

Gay men may have difficulty negotiating sexual initiation precisely because it is typically a male prerogative. In short, some gay men resent the other male's initiation and refuse sex, which can lead to conflicts. Gay men have more sex than other couple types since either partner can feel free to initiate sex (Blumstein & Schwartz, 1983) and most gay men are highly satisfied with their sexual relationships.

How to initiate sex may sometimes be difficult, since kissing is often the gateway to sexual relations, and kissing is a primarily female behavior and is more likely in lesbian relationships, moderately likely in heterosexual relationships, and least likely in gay relationships between men (Blumstein & Schwartz, 1983).

SEXUAL ATTITUDES AND BEHAVIORS

Deciding if and when to have sex is a personal choice that is influenced by many factors, including levels of commitment and passion, alcohol consumption, and moral values. Sexual behavior is strongly related to people's attitudes. People may be born with a number of sexual feelings, preferences, and proclivities, but virtually all their attitudes and beliefs about sex are learned. For example, a person might be physically aroused and curious when thinking about having sex, but moral attitudes and beliefs might stop her or him from acting on the impulse to have sex.

Developing Sexual Attitudes and Beliefs

Research has shown that sexual attitudes and knowledge come from a variety of sources, including culture, mass media, parents, peers, and past relationships (Andersen, 1993). Together, these factors influence not only sexual attitudes but also sexual behavior and communication about sex.

Culture. Culture influences relational and sexual attitudes. Andersen (1998a) argued that "the most basic force that molds and shapes human beings, other than our membership in the human race itself, is culture. Culture is such a pervasive influence it is often confused with human nature itself" (p. 48). Culture is resistant to change, and people usually adopt the values and attitudes of their parents and their culture unless very strong countervailing forces come into play. Children of immigrants, for example, are caught between two sets of cultural values: those of their parents and those of their peers. Sexual attitudes change slowly across each generation and still show cultural influences after a 100 or more years of cultural assimilation.

In the United States, African Americans have the most permissive sexual attitudes, followed by whites, while people from Asian, Latino, and Middle Eastern cultures have the most conservative sexual orientations (Sprecher & McKinney, 1993). Among white Americans, particularly women, and to a lesser degree among African Americans, talking about sexual intimacy is quite common and is believed to be the heart and soul of a good relationship (Crooks & Baur, 1999). In contrast, Asian Americans and Hispanic Americans tend to be more reluctant to discuss their sexual relationship. Among interethnic couples, these differences require considerable understanding and adaptation by the partners.

The Mass Media. Media are an important source of information about sex. According to Andersen (1993), "an abundance of mass media research has suggested that media—television in particular—provides prototypic family, sex-role, and relationship information that children imitate and incorporate into their cognitions and behaviors through the modeling process" (p. 5). These media effects are consistent and pervasive. Research has shown that 29% of interactions on prime-time television shows discuss sexual issues that emphasize male sexual roles and a recreational rather than a procreational orientation toward sex (Ward, 1995). Most of these interactions depict sex as a competition and equate masculinity with being sexual. The media also influence "sexual scripts" for communicating about sex, which we will discuss later in this chapter.

In addition to television and film, magazines are an important source of information about sex and sexual issues. Starting in 1953 with the publication of *Playboy*, Americans were introduced not only to open nudity on conventional newsstands but perhaps more important to the "playboy" philosophy, which rejected limits on sexual expression, condoned any form of consensual sex, and was critical of the institution of marriage (D'Emilio & Freedman, 1988). Similarly, the publication of Helen Gurley Brown's *Sex and the Single Girl* in the early 1960s urged young women to reconsider the taboo against premarital sex. These publications show the impact the media have on sexual attitudes.

Sexual material on the Internet is a more recent concern of parents, educators, and politicians. Cybersex may be a negative influence with increasingly bizarre or violent effects, or it may be a harmless form of safe sex with beneficial, cathartic effects.

Parents. Children learn about sex and relationships from their parents both indirectly and directly. Indirectly, parents serve as models for children. If parents are affectionate or sexual toward each other, children will expect their own romantic relationships to include affection or sex. Parents can also teach their children about sex directly, often by having the sometimes dreaded "sex talk." Direct parent-child communication about sex is important but rare (Fisher, 2004; Warren, 1995). As a result, parents are amazingly unaware of their teenage offspring's sexual behavior (Fisher, 2004). Studies have shown that children are more likely to delay sexual activity and to use contraception when their parents have talked with them about sex (Fox, 1981). Yet most research suggests that many teenagers are uncomfortable when their parents discuss sex with them, primarily because the parents issue orders or warnings rather than frankly discussing sexual thoughts and feelings (Brock & Jennings, 1993; Philliber, 1980; Rozema, 1986). On the rare occasions when sex talk occurs, it is more common with girls than boys (Fisher, 2004). It is extremely important for children to feel free to initiate discussions about sex when they are experiencing sexual feelings or have questions about sexuality. Within the family, teens report being most comfortable talking to a same-sex parent or older sibling about sex (Guerrero & Afifi, 1995b), and mothers and daughters are more likely to talk about sex than fathers and sons (Fisher, 2004; Philliber, 1980). Discussions about sex are most effective when they are integrated into family discussions well before a child is 16 years old (Warren, 1995).

Even when parents don't actively talk about sex, kids pick up attitudes about sex from their families through modeling and body language. People raised with more conservative family values are more erotophobic and have higher levels of sexual guilt and anxiety (Simpson, Wilson, & Winterheld, 2004). Family nudity during childhood is associated with less discomfort about sex and more comfort with physical affection, especially for boys, less adolescent sexual activity for both boys and girls, but a greater tendency to have casual sex for both males and females as adults (Fisher, 2004). Box 7.1 provides information about how parents can communicate effectively with their children regarding sex.

Peers. Rogers (1995) showed that most diffusion of information about a variety of topics, including sexually related ones, occurs interpersonally between people who are similar to one another. Sprecher and McKinney (1993) reviewed studies that showed that peers have a stronger influence on people's sexual standards than parents. Male adolescents are notorious for inculcating male attitudes regarding what constitutes a physically attractive woman, what is masculine behavior, and the importance of sexual conquests. Females share all manner of relational and sexual information with one another regarding male attractiveness, birth control methods, and the quality of individual males as potential mates. Although these stereotypes of heterosexual men and women are exaggerated, they illustrate that men and women talk about sex with their peers. Sexual attitudes and behaviors are modeled by friends and then imitated.

Past Relationships. Many attitudes about sex result from prior relational experiences. According to attachment theorists, people's past relationships help shape the way people think about current relationships. For example, people who have learned to trust others and to be comfortable with closeness tend to be more monogamous in their sexual relationships (Simpson & Gangestad, 1991). Moreover, having a partner who provides consistent, loving physical contact helps build an individual's self-esteem and sets up positive expectations for future relationships (Hazan & Zeifman, 1994). Some research also suggests that people who are uncomfortable with closeness and have had unsatisfying sexual relationships in the past will be more likely to desire short-term, casual sex than committed relationships (Brennan & Shaver, 1995; Stephan & Bachman, 1999). Additionally, people who have been hurt in past love relationships are less likely to experience highly passionate or obsessive love in the future (Stephan & Bachman, 1999). Together, these findings suggest that people who have had

BOX 7.1   Highlights

Ten Tips for How Parents Should Talk to Their Children About Sex

Clay Warren, a communication researcher who has conducted many studies on family sex communication, makes the following recommendations to parents who want to engage in effective communication about sex with their children.

1. **Start talking**. Most parents find it difficult to talk about sex with their children, but the more they initiate discussion about sex, the easier it becomes to talk about it.

2. **Continue talking**. Once discussions about sex are initiated, children expect to hear more. Parents should make an effort to continue talking about sex in more specific detail as their children mature.

3. **Start early**. Discussions about sex should start well before a young person is 16 years old. Early adolescence is often a good time to initiate sex talks. By their mid-teens, children may have outgrown the need to talk about sex with their parents and may instead rely more on peers.

4. **Involve both parents if the family has two parents**. If both parents are actively involved in the communication process, neither one should bear the pressure or responsibility alone. Also, teenagers may be more comfortable discussing certain issues with one parent and other issues with the other parent.

5. **Talk to both sons and daughters**. Some research suggests that parents are more likely to talk to their daughters than to their sons. This double standard needs to be broken so that girls do not always bear the sexual responsibility in teen relationships. It is important for both boys and girls to understand the consequences of sexual activity.

6. **Establish a mutual dialogue**. When parents talk *to* rather than *with* their children about sex, the children are less satisfied with the information they receive. It is important that children feel free to initiate discussions about sex and ask questions.

7. **Create a supportive environment**. Communication should be open and comfortable rather than defensive. Parents are often tense when discussing sex with their children. Instead, they should be relaxed and open.

8. **Use positive forms of nonverbal communication**. Nonverbal behavior is especially crucial in creating a supportive environment. Behaviors such as a relaxed posture, smiling, vocal warmth, and head nods can all help ease the tension.

9. **Remember that discussing sex does not promote promiscuity**. Knowing this fact might help ease some of the stress parents feel. Many studies have shown that talking about sex and sex-related topics such as contraception does not promote promiscuity. In fact, talking about these issues within the context of a broader discussion of sexual values might even reduce promiscuity.

10. **Don't leave the talking to someone else**. If parents are not successful in influencing their children's sexual attitudes, someone else will be. It might be a boyfriend, girlfriend, peers, teachers, or even the media. Adolescents have questions that need to be answered. If they cannot find the answers at home, they will seek them elsewhere.

SOURCE: Information compiled from Warren (1995).

positive sexual experiences in committed relationships are most likely to expect future relationships to be monogamous and sexually satisfying.

Past relationships affect sexual attitudes in other ways as well. Once people have sex for the first time, they are more likely to have sex on subsequent occasions—assuming that the sex was voluntary and enjoyable. Similarly, determining if and when to have sex for the very first time is a very difficult decision, and people often wait until they are in a committed relationship (Sprecher & McKinney, 1993). Before having sex, many people also deal with issues such as fear of STIs and pregnancy (Sprecher & McKinney, 1993).

Finally, past sexual relationships can affect attraction. Sprecher and Regan (2000) reviewed research on the association between a person's sexual history and her or his desirability as a long-term romantic partner. They concluded that

> in general, research indicates that low to moderate levels of current or past sexual activity and the restriction of sexual activity to committed relationships are more likely to increase one's desirability as a partner than is a history of many sexual partners or casual sexual activity. (p. 219)

Social Norms and Changing Sexual Attitudes

The social norms of one's culture also influence people's sexual attitudes. Attitudes toward sexuality, particularly premarital and female sexuality, became increasingly permissive and liberal in the United States during the 20th century (Sprecher & McKinney, 1993; Wells & Twenge, 2005). The best data on changes in sexuality come from a recent study by Wells and Twenge (2005) that aggregated over 500 studies that included over 250,000 participants. Throughout most of the century, premarital sex was considered unacceptable, particularly for women. But "premarital sexual activity has become normative for today's youth. Rates of sexual intercourse for teens have increased dramatically" since the early 1960s (Christopher & Roosa, 1993, p. 111). For males and particularly for females, both sexual activity and attitudes in favor of sexuality steadily increased from 1965 to 2005 (Wells & Twenge, 2005). In the 1950s, only 13% of teenage girls were sexually active, whereas by the 1990s, 47% were sexually active. Before 1970, the average age for first sexual intercourse for men was 18, and for women it was 19; by the late 1990s, this average had dropped to 15 years of age for both genders (Wells & Twenge, 2005). Similarly, before 1970, less than half of teenagers had engaged in oral sex, but by the 1990s, over two thirds of both men and women had engaged in oral sex. In the late 1950s, only 12% of young women approved of premarital sex; by the 1980s, about three quarters approved. The only variable of sexual behavior that has not increased is the number of partners, which has remained fairly constant over the years, especially since news of the AIDS epidemic in the 1980s (Wells & Twenge, 2005). But times have changed; today over 80% of men and women have had premarital sexual intercourse (Willetts et al., 2004).

The revolution in sexual attitudes that began in the 1960s was due to a number of factors. The 1960s was a revolutionary era for all types of values, including those associated with politics, music, the environment, civil rights, and women's rights. In the 1960s, images of sexuality were widely depicted in the mass media through magazines, books, and movies, and to a lesser degree, television. Perhaps the biggest factor was the birth control pill: the first simple and effective technology that permitted sex without reproduction. For the first time in human history, women could have sexual relationships without risking pregnancy. Several scholars suggest that the sexual revolution of the 1960s and 1970s was mainly a change in women's values, with men remaining much the same (Baumeister, 2000; Ehrenreich, Hess, & Jacobs, 1986). Today, teens and young adults are much more sexually active than they were before the sexual revolution of the 1960s.

Sex experts have identified three types of sexual attitudes held by people today (Sprecher & McKinney, 1993). Some people have a **procreational orientation**, which reflects the belief that producing offspring is the primary purpose of sexual intercourse. Other people have a **relational orientation**, which holds that sexual intercourse is a way of expressing love and affection, and developing greater relational intimacy. Still others have a **recreational**

orientation, viewing sex as a primary source of fun, escape, excitement, or pleasure. The procreational orientation, the position taken by most major religions, is associated with traditional, conservative cultural values. The relational orientation, which is equated with moderate sexual values, is widespread in the United States. People with this orientation disapprove of casual sex but usually approve of premarital sex in the context of a committed or loving relationship. The recreational orientation is a sexually liberal view holding that sex is appropriate between consenting adults.

Of course, these orientations are not mutually exclusive; many people's sexual attitudes are some combination of procreational, relational, and recreational. Indeed, most married couples in the United States embrace elements of all three values within their relationship at different times. In contrast, attitudes toward premarital sex vacillate between a relational orientation and a somewhat recreational orientation in the United States, but are rarely procreational. Research has shown that couples are more likely to endorse increased sexual activity, including sexual intercourse, as the relationship becomes closer (Sprecher, McKinney, Walsh, & Anderson, 1988). Judging by their behavior, for several decades, people in the United States have subscribed primarily to a relational orientation through the practice of **serial monogamy** (Christopher & Roosa, 1991; Rathus et al., 1993; Sorensen, 1973). In other words, couples are sexually active only with each other (monogamy) and do not engage in other sexual relationships until the current relationship ends. They may, however, move through a series of such relationships.

While a lot research has focused on the dark side of premarital sex, such as disease, pregnancy, and abortion, positive outcomes also occur. Most premarital sex takes place in an intimate and committed relationship that provides support and often leads to marriage (Christopher & Roosa, 1991). In fact, early research showed that serial monogamists overwhelmingly loved each other and had healthy, caring sexual relationships (Sorensen, 1973). Moreover, serial monogamists had the highest school grades, were most likely to use birth control, enjoyed sex more, and were generally better adjusted than either promiscuous adventurers or virgins.

Although most college students are sexually experienced, some choose to remain virgins. In a study of the sexual behavior of college students, Sprecher and Regan (1996) found that 11% of men and 13% of women were virgins, although virtually all the virgins reported experiencing sexual desire. Thus Sarah (whom we introduced at the beginning of this chapter) is not alone in her virginity. Women like Sarah give several reasons for being a virgin, including the absence of a long-term or love relationship, fear of negative consequences such as pregnancy or STIs, personal beliefs and values, and feelings of inadequacy and/or insecurity. All these reasons were stronger for women than for men. Virgins reported a mixture of pride and anxiety about their status, although positive emotions outweighed negative ones. Women were more likely to be proud and happy about keeping their virginity, while men were more likely to be embarrassed about it. The men and women who were virgins for deep religious or moral reasons, like Sarah, were the most positive about their status.

COMMUNICATION PATTERNS

Research on courtship patterns and flirtation provide insight into how romantic and sexual relationships develop. The literature on sexual scripts examines the communication people employ to initiate and refuse sex at various stages in relationships.

Courtship and Flirtation

When people flirt, they typically use indirect communication strategies to convey their interest and attraction, especially when they are in the early stages of a relationship. Nonverbal flirtation displays are more common than verbal cues. For example, gazes, smiles, warm vocal tones, and close distances are key flirtatious behaviors (Givens, 1978, 1983; Moore, 1985; Muehlenhard, Koralewski, Andrews, & Burdick, 1986). Indirect nonverbal cues are often used because they provide protection from potential rejection. The receiver can simply ignore these nonverbal cues without having to verbally reject the flirtatious person. The flirtatious person can deny that he or she was flirting and simply say that he or she was trying to be friendly. Sometimes, of course, direct verbal strategies are used, such as telling people they look sexy or talking about sex. These more direct strategies, however, are more likely to be used in an established romantic relationship.

Scheflen's (1965, 1974) model of the courtship process sought to explain how various nonverbal behaviors unfold over time to signal availability and sexual interest. Scheflen's model included five stages, with the earlier stages characterized by the most indirect communication. The courtship behaviors in this model often reflect attentiveness, approachability, and submissiveness. Thus potential partners must gain one another's attention and signal that they are available or approachable for communication. Submissive behaviors that communicate a desire for intimacy are particularly useful during the courtship process because they are seen as a non-threatening, playful way of conveying sexual interest. Some submissive behaviors, such as stroking someone's hair in a comforting way, also mirror those used in parent-child relationships to convey caring and intimacy.

The Attention Stage. The goal of the first stage in Scheflen's model is to get the other person's attention and to present oneself in the best possible light either strategically or accidentally. When Taylor met Leslie, she made sure she was in a good location to converse with her. At the table, she made sure that she was seated near her to encourage interaction. Throughout history, people have practiced the art of gaining attention as a precursor to courtship. In 19th-century America, it was common for women to drop something, such as a glove or handkerchief, in front of a man whom they wanted to get to know. The man, if polite, would be obliged to retrieve the dropped item and turn his attention to the woman. Similarly, men commonly asked to be formally introduced to a woman, often by a relative or friend, before pursuing a conversation. Any place where singles gather, we are likely to see a variety of attention-getting strategies, such as Taylor positioning herself in Leslie's view and trying to catch her eye. These behaviors are indirect, including demure glances, tentative smiles, anxious movement such as twisting the ring on one's

finger, and primping behavior such as fixing one's hair, applying lipstick, or straightening one's tie.

The Courtship Readiness Stage. In this stage, sometimes referred to as the "recognition stage," the initiator of the flirtation determines whether the other person is approachable for interaction. For example, if Taylor's eye contact and friendliness are met with Leslie's cold stare or annoyed glance or are ignored, the courtship process will end. Similarly, if Leslie is busy interacting with other people, Taylor will probably hesitate to approach unless she receives a fairly clear signal of interest. Typical flirting behaviors include sustained mutual gaze and smiling, raised eyebrows, more direct body orientation, head tilts in the direction of the other person, and nervous laughter. More grooming behavior also tends to occur in this stage, with people tucking in their stomachs, arranging their clothing and hair, and wetting their lips as they prepare to approach one another.

The Positioning Stage. If Taylor and Leslie are attracted to each other, they will engage in a series of positioning behaviors that signal availability for interaction while indicating to others that they are, at least temporarily, a "couple" and so should be left alone. Close distancing and face-to-face body orientation are typical at this stage, as is a forward lean. Partners gaze and smile at each other and show high levels of interest and animation through gestures and expressive voices. If the setting is quiet, Taylor and Leslie may lower their voices to draw each other closer. In this stage, communication becomes more synchronized; that is, turn-taking becomes smoother, and partners engage in similar behaviors such as crossing their legs. Although there is a marked increase in the intimacy of communication at this stage, some submissiveness and ambiguity still remain. For example, if Taylor and Leslie gaze for too long into each other's eyes, they might feel embarrassed, avert their eyes, and laugh nervously.

The Invitations and Sexual Arousal Stage. Taylor and Leslie are very attracted to each other and are moving into the fourth stage: sexual intimacy. The beginning of this stage is marked by the first implicit invitation for touch and sexual contact. For example, Taylor might put her hand on Leslie's knee to see how she responds. Other more subtle signs of intimacy include grooming the partner, performing carrying and clutching activities, and acting sexually provocative (Burgoon et al., 1996; Givens, 1978; Scheflen, 1965). Grooming behaviors include tucking the tag from someone's clothing back inside the collar and pushing a stray strand of hair out of someone's eyes. Carrying and clutching behaviors include carrying someone's bags or books, holding hands, and leaning on someone's arm for support. Sexually provocative actions include dancing in a suggestive way, revealing body parts by unbuttoning one's shirt or crossing one's leg to expose more thigh, and touching the partner in intimate places.

The Resolution Stage. If Taylor's invitation is accepted and sexual interaction occurs, Taylor and Leslie have reached the final stage. Of course, determining whether the invitation is accepted is not always easy, especially if the behaviors used in the sexual arousal/invitations stage were indirect and ambiguous. When people move through the courtship stages rapidly, the intent of both partners might be unclear. Perhaps Leslie was just being friendly, while Taylor was interested in a sexual relationship.

Some studies have shown that men are more likely than women to see flirtatious behaviors as seductive, whereas women often see these same behaviors as ways of being friendly and expressing innocent attraction (Abbey, 1982, 1987; Abbey & Melby, 1986). To complicate matters even further, research has shown that people flirt for a variety of reasons, only one of which is to signal sexual interest. For example, people may flirt because they see it as innocent fun, they want to make a third party jealous, they want to develop their social skills, or they are trying to persuade someone to do something for them (Afifi et al., 1994; Egland, Spitzberg, & Zormeier, 1996; Koeppel, Montagne-Miller, O'Hair, & Cody, 1993). Thus, when someone is flirting with you, he or she may or may not be showing sexual interest.

In longer courtships, couples may spend considerable time in the sexual arousal/invitations stage, with sexual intimacy increasing slowly over time. Partners are more likely to be direct about their intentions, but misunderstandings can still occur.

Sometimes one person is ready to have sex before the other, and one partner may view intimate touch as a way of expressing closeness while the other sees it as a prelude to sex. Partners must negotiate if and when sex occurs, often through both verbal and nonverbal communication. If one, or both, of the partners does not want to have sex, the first four of Scheflen's stages are referred to as **quasi-courtship** rather than courtship. Misinterpretation of flirtatious cues is likely, given that the first three of four stages often look the same regardless of whether they are quasi-courtship or true courtship stages.

It is important to note that these courtship stages provide only a rough guide for how people signal romantic interest and increased sexual involvement. Couples are unique and progress at different speeds. A relatively small number of couples have sex on a first date or shortly after the partners meet; most couples wait until some level of intimacy has developed before having sex. Christopher and Cate (1985) identified four types of couples. **Rapid-involvement couples** have high levels of physical arousal and have sex on the first date or shortly thereafter. For these partners, sexual intimacy often precedes psychological intimacy. **Gradual-involvement couples** let sexual involvement increase gradually as the relationship develops and becomes more psychologically intimate. Sexual involvement moves through stages and increases as the partners move from a first date to a casually dating relationship to a more serious, committed relationship. **Delayed-involvement couples** wait until the two people consider themselves to be a committed couple to become sexually involved. For them psychological intimacy precedes sexual intimacy. **Low-involvement couples** usually wait to have sex until the partners are engaged or married. Research suggests that most couples in the United States define themselves as falling under either the gradual-involvement (31%) or delayed-involvement (44%) category, with around 17% identifying themselves as low involvement and 7% classifying themselves as rapid involvement (Christopher & Cate, 1985; Sprecher & McKinney, 1993). These findings correspond with research showing that most people have a relational orientation toward sex.

SOURCE: Copyright: iStockphoto.com/
Simone van den Berg

SOURCE: iStockphoto.com

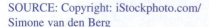

Photo 7.1   What nonverbal behaviors are these two people using to show their interest in each other?
Do the two pictures represent different stages in the courtship process? If so, which ones?

Sexual Scripts

Scripts are social information that is deployed in everyday interaction. Cultural forces define with whom, when, where, and in what relationships sexual behavior may appropriately be initiated and conducted (Regan & Berscheid, 1999). **Sexual scripts** most often revolve around the initiation and acceptance or refusal of sexual advances. The North American script casts men as initiators and women as gatekeepers who refuse or accept dates or sexual invitations, particularly in new relationships (Byers, 1996; Mongeau et al., 2004). As Hinde (1984) commented, men seek to propagate widely, while women seek to propagate wisely. Research indicates that both men and women are comfortable asking for dates and initiating sexual interaction (Kelley & Rolker-Dolinsky, 1987), although many women think their sexual initiatives might threaten men. However, women are more likely to initiate sexual interaction in well-developed relationships as opposed to developing relationships.

Negotiating sexual activity in a developing relationship can be difficult because both individuals have multiple goals, including managing impressions, providing relational definitions, satisfying their sexual desire, following their sexual standards or morals, and avoiding disease or pregnancy (Cupach & Metts, 1994). Most attempts to initiate sexual activity are indirect and communicated through nonverbal behavior and flirtation (Andersen, 1999). Sometimes, however, friendly behaviors, particularly those by women, are misinterpreted by men as sex-initiating behaviors. To avoid sexually coercive situations (discussed later in this chapter), individuals need to verbally articulate their disinterest, and their partners need to respect their wishes.

Initiation Strategies. Persuasive strategies and scripts are used by men and women to initiate dating and sexual relationships. These strategies typically fall into five categories: (1) hinting and indirect strategies, (2) expressions of emotional and physical closeness, (3) pressure and manipulation, (4) antisocial acts, and (5) logic and reasoning (Christopher & Frandsen, 1990; Edgar & Fitzpatrick, 1993, 1988).

Sexual relations are sensitive and ego threatening, so hinting and indirect strategies can be useful. Romantic conversations are full of indirect communication, such as compliments, sexual innuendo, hints, and nonverbal communication. Such ploys are safe because if the partner does not respond sexually, little face is lost. As Edgar and Fitzpatrick (1988) noted, when one person wants to have sex, the situation can be emotionally charged, and an opportunity to save face is welcome. Both men and women are most comfortable with sexual involvement if emotional and physical closeness is present; this is particularly true for women. Establishing a close relationship and sending reassuring relational messages can result in increased sexual activity (Christopher & Frandsen, 1990). For example, doing special things for your partner, telling your partner how much you like her or him, flattering your partner, and sharing time and space with her or him are important ways of enhancing emotional closeness and initiating sexual activity.

Another sexual influence tactic is logical reasoning that involves persuading someone that it is advantageous to become sexually involved. This strategy appeals to logic or compromises on the timing or degree of sexual involvement to overcome a partner's concerns (Christopher & Frandsen, 1990). For example, if Brittany is afraid of getting pregnant and/or contracting an STI, Chris might make reassuring statements about the effectiveness of condoms and/or suggest that they both get tested for STIs before having sex. These types of tactics are associated with greater sexual activity in a relationship over the long term, although they may limit or postpone sexual involvement in the short term (Christopher & Frandsen, 1990).

Not surprisingly, men are more likely to use pressure and manipulation to gain sexual compliance than are women (Christopher & Frandsen, 1990). These strategies encompass a wide variety of coercive tactics, such as repeated requests for sex, threats to break off or de-escalate the relationship, the use of drugs or alcohol to reduce resistance to sex, and outright deception. These tactics seldom increase the frequency of sexual activity in a relationship (Christopher & Frandsen, 1990) and can lead to relational dissatisfaction and/or de-escalation.

Evidence suggests that antisocial acts are similarly unsuccessful in initiating sex in a relationship (Christopher & Frandsen, 1990). These strategies encompass a wide assortment of tactics, including intentionally trying to make the partner jealous (Fleischmann, Spitzberg, Andersen, & Roesch, 2005), pouting or holding a grudge to try to get one's way, and sexual harassment. Such acts may lead to relational termination and even legal action in some cases.

Refusing and Accepting Sexual Invitations. The power to refuse and regulate sex is primarily a woman's prerogative. Throughout the world, women are more judicious and less casual in their choices about sex than men (Buss, 1994). Men are poor at turning down sex and have few refusal strategies in their repertoire; women tend to regard men's refusals as insincere, unexpected, and upsetting (Metts, Cupach, & Imahori, 1992). This does not imply that women have license to ignore men's refusals; men should be taken as seriously as women when they decline to have sex.

Research suggests that women are well prepared with sexual-compliance-resisting scripts and use multiple resistance strategies (Lannutti & Monahan, 2004; Metts et al., 1992). Women often use indirect strategies because these are perceived as polite; however, more direct strategies seem to be more effective for refusing unwanted sex. Moreover, most men have experience receiving sexual rejection messages and find them relatively predictable and not particularly disconcerting (Metts et al., 1992). This is useful information for women who use indirect strategies to refuse sex when they are worried about hurting the partner's feelings. Direct strategies are more effective, and thankfully, they are unlikely to be taken personally by men (Motley & Reeder, 1995).

In steady dating relationships, the majority of sexual initiations by both men and women are accepted by their partner (Byers, 1996). In Byers' study, only about 20% of initiations were refused by the partner with about the same percentage for men and women. These data suggest that sex in steady dating relationships is not adversarial and that, contrary to the stereotype, in developed relationships, women are more likely to be facilitators of sexual interaction than gatekeepers. In investigating sexual activity among heterosexual daters over a 1-month period, Byers and Lewis (1988) found that nearly half of the couples reported disagreements caused by the man's desire to increase sexual involvement. However, disagreements occurred during just 7% of all dates. Thus, although disagreements about sex did occur occasionally over the course of a month, most dates were free of such disagreements. When sex is refused from a long-term dating partner, the refusal is both unexpected and viewed negatively (Bevan, 2003).

Once sexual activity becomes fairly regular, shared dyadic scripts emerge to guide sexual interaction. In well-developed relationships, women feel freer to initiate touch, forms of affection, and sexual behavior (Cupach & Metts, 1991; Guerrero & Andersen, 1991). In fact, Brown and Auerbach (1981) found that wives increased their initiation of sexual activity by about 1% per year of marriage. Several studies have shown that stages of sexual involvement are fairly well scripted, starting with kissing, hand to breast, hand to genitals, oral sex, sexual intercourse, and orgasm in the ideal case (DeLamater & Hyde, 2004; Morris, 1977). This script is generally followed both within a single sexual encounter *and* across a series of dates with only occasional variation.

Saying no to sex in a long-term relationship is often difficult because partners do not want to hurt one another's feelings, but everyone has the right to refuse sex no matter how close their relationship is. It is important for long-term partners to say no in a tender and supportive manner with clear verbal communication. Research has shown that most refusals are done verbally and that the best refusals maintain both the relationship and the partner's face (Cupach & Metts, 1991). For example, telling your partner that you are "really tired" or "not feeling well" is better than saying that you are not feeling much sexual desire for her or him at the moment. When refusals are accompanied by assurances of future activity ("We'll have more time for each other this weekend"), they are also accepted more gracefully.

SEXUAL COERCION AND HARASSMENT

Most people associate sex with pleasure, intimacy, relational closeness, and desire. However, sex has its dark side as well. Negative aspects of sex include sexual dysfunction, sexual abuse, rape, sexual coercion, and sexual harassment. In this section, we focus on coercion and harassment because communication is at the heart of these types of problematic interactions.

Sexual Coercion

Sexual coercion occurs when an individual pressures, compels, or forces another to engage in sexual activity; these practices are considered unacceptable by most people, with verbal pressure the least unacceptable and physical force the most unacceptable (Struckman-Johnson & Struckman-Johnson, 1991). Verbal insistence is the most common method of coercion (Murnan, Perot, & Byrne, 1989). In general, women find sexual coercion to be less acceptable than do men (Christopher, Owens, & Strecker, 1993; Struckman-Johnson & Struckman-Johnson, 1991). Additionally, coercive strategies are generally unsuccessful in gaining sexual compliance (Christopher & Frandsen, 1990).

Sexual coercion is far too common. Research has shown that in the majority of sexually coercive situations a man is the perpetrator and a woman is the victim. For example, over 50% of college women report having been the victim of some form of sexual coercion (Byers, 1996), and over 95% of all women report having engaged in some form of unwanted sexual activity (Muehlenhard & Cook, 1988). Others studies have shown that 22% of college women report having been forced to engage in sexual intercourse, and 35% to 46% of women report having had unwanted sex as a result of sexual persuasion or coercion, typically from a partner the woman knew fairly well (Byers, 1996; Muehlenhard & Cook, 1988; Murnan et al., 1989). Women report experiencing sexual coercion on only about 7% of all dates (Byers & Lewis, 1988). In yet another study, 50% of college women reported that they had engaged in at least one unwanted sexual activity (ranging from hugs to sexual intercourse) over a 2-week period, with 20% of the women engaging in unwanted sexual intercourse (O'Sullivan & Allgeier, 1998). Sometimes women have unwanted sex to please their partners; at other times they are pressured or forced to have sex. Worst of all, almost two thirds of sexual assaults occur with regular relational partners (Christopher & Kissler, 2004b).

The most common reactions of women to sexual coercion are no response or a strong negative response. In most situations in which men pursue sex and women refuse, men halt their sexual advances (Byers, 1996). About 15% of the time, however, the man does not believe the woman's refusal really means no (Byers & Wilson, 1985). In these cases, the man perceives that the woman's saying no is only token resistance (Muehlenhard & Cook, 1988). Men should not try to second-guess a woman's motivation for saying no. As Andersen (1999) stated, "Sexual harassment or date rape can result from ignoring these explicit verbal cues in favor of nonverbal cues that seem positive and encouraging. We should all be aware: 'Stop' means stop and 'no' means no" (p. 210).

When token resistance is used, the situation is unclear, confusing, and dangerous. Both men and women use token resistance, although contrary to the stereotype, men are more likely to use it than women (O'Sullivan & Allgeier, 1994). As noted previously, a sexual initiator should not ignore a request to stop. If, however, an initiator has learned that stop does not really mean stop, "real" requests to stop may be ignored, leading to problems ranging from relational disagreements to sexual assault. Thus, it is best to stop and ask for clarification if you think your partner might be engaging in token resistance. Unless your partner explicitly changes the no into a yes, you should avoid further sexual activity. Similarly, research has shown that men often do not perceive indirect resistance messages on the part of women as real resistance (Motley & Reeder, 1995). Indeed, Motley and Reeder suggested that women need to be much more direct in communicating sexual resistance and that men should listen more carefully to understand women's resistance messages.

Women sometimes fail to send sexual resistance messages because they fear the relational consequences of turning down their partner (Motley & Reeder, 1995). But the reality is, men rarely disrupt or terminate a relationship because a woman resists sexual escalation. In fact, Motley and Reeder found that men are rarely hurt, offended, or angered when women use direct sexual resistance messages, although women erroneously think that men will be offended and de-escalate the relationship if they

resist. Because women seldom are turned down in their attempts to sexually escalate a relationship, they are more likely to be hurt and upset if they are turned down. They project these feelings onto men, who do not share their hurt and anger over being sexually rejected. Many men have considerable experience with sexual rejection and have learned coping strategies to deal with rejection short of relational de-escalation or breakup.

In about 10% of sexually coercive situations, the woman is the aggressor and the man is the target. Among college students, about one third of all men reported an episode of pressured or forced sex since the age of 16 (Byers, 1996; Struckman-Johnson & Struckman-Johnson, 1994), and in the vast majority of these cases, the perpetrator of coercion was a woman. O'Sullivan and Allegier (1998) reported that, during a 2-week period, 26% of college men engaged in an unwanted sexual act and almost 9% had unwanted sexual intercourse. Struckman-Johnson (1988) found that 16% of the men in her sample reported an incident of forced sexual intercourse. Muehlenhard and Cook (1988) studied over 1,000 men and women in introductory college psychology courses and found that more men (62.7%) than women (46.3%) reported having unwanted sexual intercourse. Although men generally have less negative reactions to being the target of coerced sexual encounters than do women, one fifth of the men in a study by Struckman-Johnson and Struckman-Johnson (1994) had a strong negative reaction to the experience.

Women are not very sensitive to male refusals to have sex. O'Sullivan and Byers (1993) found that, when met with a refusal to have sex, 97% of women still tried to influence the man to have sex. Women are not used to being refused, and they find such refusals unpredictable, constraining, and uncomfortable (Metts et al., 1992). Women get a lot of practice saying no and so develop good scripts to resist sexual persuasion and coercion. Men, in contrast, may have neither experience in nor well-developed scripts for saying no and believe it is unmanly to refuse sex (Metts et al., 1992). They also engage in unwanted intercourse due to peer pressure, inexperience, sex-role concerns, and popularity factors (Muehlenhard & Cook, 1988). Of course, both men and women often experience ambivalence about having sex, so some of these cases of unwanted sex probably represent situations in which mixed feelings were present.

Sexual Harassment

Sexual harassment occurs when inappropriate sexual comments, behaviors, or requests create a hostile work or school environment or when a person feels pressure to have sex to avoid negative consequences. Harassment is too common in the workplace, among some friends and acquaintances (Fairhurst, 1986; Keyton, 1996). Although men sometimes experience sexual harassment, research shows that women experience it far more. In fact, studies suggest that one out of every two working women is sexually harassed at some time (Swan, 1997). A study by Hesson-McInnis and Fitzgerald (1997) of 4,385 women employed by the federal government, found that 1,792 had been sexually harassed at least once in the past 2 years. This problem may be even worse for minority women. Hargrow (1997) found that over 80% of the working African American women she surveyed reported experiencing some form of sexual harassment. Sexual harassment is a serious problem that negatively affects job satisfaction, health, and psychological well-being (Glomb et al., 1997).

Describing the behaviors that constitute sexual harassment is complicated. What some people see as harassment, others might see as sexy or innocent fun. Moreover, women sometimes perceive behaviors to be more sexually harassing than do men, especially if they have recently entered the workforce (Booth-Butterfield, 1989). In any case, research suggests that certain kinds of verbal and nonverbal behavior should be avoided. Dougherty, Turban, Olson, Dwyer, and Lapreze (1996) noted that some behaviors, such as making lewd comments or grabbing someone's breasts or buttocks, are blatantly harassing. Gutek, Morasch, and Cohen (1983) found that touch behavior (operationalized as a pat on the bottom) and verbal comments about another person's body were perceived as harassing, although touch was perceived even more negatively than verbal comments. Similarly, Marks and Nelson (1993) found that potentially inappropriate touching by professors was seen as more harassing than inappropriate verbal

comments. Less sexually oriented forms of touch, such as on the shoulder or around the waist, are not perceived to be as harassing as verbal comments. Doughtery et al. (1996) compared people's interpretations of potentially harassing situations involving touch behavior (putting an arm around a female coworker's shoulder) and verbal behavior (asking a female coworker how her love life was and if she'd had any exciting dates lately). They found that the verbal comment was perceived as more harassing than the touch.

Lee and Guerrero (2001) compared types of touch to determine which were perceived as most harassing. They excluded blatantly harassing touches such as grabbing breasts or buttocks or kissing someone on the mouth and instead focused on more ambiguous forms of touch. Of the eight types of touch they studied, touching the face was perceived as most harassing, followed by arm around the waist. Lee and Guerrero theorized that these types of touch, which invade people's personal space, are particularly threatening. The face is an especially vulnerable part of the body, and letting someone touch it requires trust. Interestingly, not everyone saw these types of touch as harassing. In fact, while about one third of the participants "agreed strongly" that face touch was sexually harassing, another one third "disagreed strongly." This suggests that some forms of touch are seen as harassing by some people but not others, which leads to confusion and misunderstanding.

When people encounter sexual harassment, they can respond using passive, assertive, or retaliatory strategies. **Passive responses**, which are also referred to as indirect strategies, involve ignoring the harassment or appeasing the harasser. **Assertive responses** involve telling the harasser to stop the behavior with statements such as "Please stop bothering me," "I'm not interested in you that way," "I'm seeing someone else so I'd appreciate it if you'd stop asking me out," and "Your behavior is inappropriate and unprofessional." Assertive responses also involve issuing warnings, such as threatening to talk to the harasser's supervisor. Finally, **retaliatory responses** involve punishing or getting revenge on the harasser, usually by harassing her or him back, making derogatory comments about the harasser to others, or getting her or him in trouble.

Unfortunately, there is not always an effective way of responding to sexual harassment. Swan (1997) found that people who viewed sexual harassment experiences as highly upsetting were most likely to use coping strategies. When people used assertive strategies, they reported feeling better about their jobs and themselves. In contrast, when people used passive or retaliatory strategies, they reported feeling even worse. Retaliatory responses diminished job satisfaction, and passive responses diminished job satisfaction and psychological well-being. But some studies have also shown that assertive strategies can exacerbate the problem (Schneider, Swan, & Fitzgerald, 1997). Bingham and Burleson (1989) found that, although sophisticated verbal messages were more effective at stopping sexual harassment than unsophisticated ones, neither type of message was really effective. Because sexual harassment often involves a power imbalance, it is a particularly difficult situation. If the victim uses passive strategies, he or she remains powerless, and the harassment is likely to continue. But if the victim uses direct strategies, the powerful person might resent being told how to act and retaliate by demoting the victim or making the work environment even more unpleasant. Even so, research suggests that assertive strategies are most effective. If these strategies do not work, the victim may need to talk with the harasser's supervisor.

SEXUAL SATISFACTION: MISCONCEPTIONS AND REALITIES

People in the United States consider themselves sexually knowledgeable and skilled, but research paints a different picture. What people learn about sex is often haphazard, unreliable, stereotypic, and incomplete (Strong, DeVault, & Sayad, 1999). The Kinsey Institute tested the basic sexual knowledge of a representative sample of nearly 2,000 adults living in the United States (Reinisch & Beasley, 1990). Unfortunately, they failed miserably. Applying a standard grading scale, 55% would have failed, 27% would have received a D, and less than 1% would have received an A (Reinisch & Beasley, 1990). As this study suggests, most people think they know more about sex than they really do.

To be a good partner in a romantic sexual relationship, it is beneficial to understand sex and sexual interaction. A detailed description of the many aspects of human sexuality is beyond the scope of this book, so we recommend a college course in human sexuality if you want to supplement what you learn in this chapter. Here we will merely try to correct a few common misconceptions about the connections between sexual interaction and sexual satisfaction.

One misconception is that sexual intercourse is necessary for sexual satisfaction. While having an orgasm is related to sexual satisfaction (Sprecher & Cate, 2004), orgasms can be achieved through many forms of sexual interaction without sexual intercourse. Indeed, safe sex practices include a form of sexual interaction called "outercourse" that involves less intimate contact and no exchange of bodily fluids. Furthermore, for some people, sexual intercourse alone does not provide satisfaction. Shows of affection, such as holding hands, cuddling, and kissing, are just as important as, and in some cases even more important than, sexual intercourse for certain people.

A second misconception is that in an intimate heterosexual relationship women should not initiate sexual interaction because it may undermine the traditional male role and men will see them as too easy or unfeminine. The reality is that the vast majority of men, particularly those under age 40, think it is not only acceptable for women to initiate sex but desirable as well (Reinisch & Beasley, 1990). Nonetheless, as the misconception suggests, about half of all wives rarely or never initiate sexual interaction (Reinisch & Beasley, 1990). When women do initiate sex, they do it more subtly than men, so men need to tune in and respond to these understated cues. Of course, men should not assume that every indirect cue is a signal that the woman wants to have sex. Once partners learn each other's signals for sexual initiation, they can be nonverbal and implicit. If a woman (or a man) is not comfortable asking for sex, special signals can be used such as lighting a candle, drinking wine, or playing romantic music in the bedroom (Reinisch & Beasley, 1990). However, research suggests that men prefer clear, instrumental disclosure about sex because it leads to greater sexual understanding and in turn to more sexual satisfaction (MacNeil & Byers, 2005).

A third misconception is that heterosexual couples are more satisfied with sexual interaction than are gay or lesbian couples. In reality, although the sex lives of heterosexuals, gay men, and lesbians are different in some respects, all couple types generally report having satisfying sex lives. In fact, some studies have shown that gay and lesbian partners rate the *subjective* quality of their sexual experiences higher than do heterosexual couples, perhaps because they better understand each other's sexual needs (Crooks & Baur, 1999; Masters and Johnson, 1979; Peplau et al., 2004). In these studies, subjective quality was defined in terms of more psychological involvement, total body contact, enjoyment of sexual activities, and responsiveness to the sexual needs of the partner.

A fourth misconception is that men and women are equally aroused by the sight of nudity and touch. The reality is that, while each is potentially arousing to members of both sexes, men are visually aroused more than are women. Seeing one's partner in skimpy clothing is more of a turn-on for most men than for women. Conversely, women are much more aroused by touch than are men, particularly nongenital touch. Thus, cuddling and foreplay are important precursors to sexual intercourse for women. In sexual areas of the body, both men and women are highly arousable. Heterosexual couples, in particular, need to understand that what arouses each partner personally might not be as arousing for the other partner. Partners should adapt to each other's arousal needs.

A fifth misconception is that men enjoy sexual intercourse more than women. The reality is that heterosexual men and women both enjoy intercourse. Contrary to the stereotype, research suggests that women may actually enjoy intercourse more than men (Blumstein & Schwartz, 1983). In close, committed relationships, most women enjoy sexual intercourse because of the extreme intimacy and closeness it reflects. Although some women may not want to have sex as often as men, when they do have high-quality sex they report finding it extremely pleasurable.

A sixth misconception is that the most important predictor of sexual satisfaction is how often a couple has sex. Nearly 90% of married individuals report that they are sexually satisfied, with couples varying considerably in how often they have sex; indeed, most studies show little or no relationship between amount of sex and satisfaction (Blumstein & Schwartz, 1983; Laumann et al., 1994; Sprecher & Cate, 2004). Frequency of sex is not as important as the quality of sex and the match between two people's needs during sexual activity (Sprecher & Regan, 2000). When partners have similar attitudes about sex, they are happier with their sex lives. Thus if they believe that cuddling is more important than sex, they might have sex less often than a couple who believes that sex is the ultimate expression of intimacy; yet both couples would be satisfied. Some support for this line of reasoning also comes from studies comparing heterosexual couples to gay and lesbian couples. On average, gay men place a higher value on sex than do heterosexuals, and heterosexuals place a higher value on sex than do lesbians. These values are reflected in behavior. Rosenzweig and Lebow (1992) found that almost half of gay men reported having sexual relations at least three times a week, while only about one third of heterosexual couples reported having sex that often. Among lesbian couples only about one fifth reported having sex three times a week or more. According to other studies, lesbians spend more time cuddling than do heterosexuals or gay men (Blumstein & Schwartz, 1983). Yet, as discussed previously, relational partners in heterosexual, gay, and lesbian relationships report roughly equal levels of overall sexual satisfaction.

A seventh misconception is that sexual satisfaction is the only key to relational satisfaction. It is true that people who report being happy with their sex lives are also likely to report being happy with their relationships. However, sexual satisfaction is not the *best* predictor of relational satisfaction in most relationships. As Sprecher and Regan (2000) put it, "Neither the quality nor the quantity of sex might be as important as other nonsexual forms of intimacy in the prediction of relationship satisfaction including expressed affection and supportive communication" (p. 223). These authors note that sexual dissatisfaction and incompatibility alone are usually not enough to destroy an otherwise close, caring relationship. Only when these sexual problems are "symptomatic of other relational problems" are they likely to lead to conflict and relational termination. The message here is clear: Sexual satisfaction is an important part of romantic relationships, but other factors, such as love, supportiveness, and compatibility, are usually even more important.

In addition to being knowledgeable about sex, it is important for partners to communicate about sex. Some relational partners think sex is a taboo topic and so do not talk about their sexual desires and preferences with each other (Baxter & Wilmot, 1985). Yet studies suggest that communication about sex is very important. Frank, Anderson, and Rubinstein (1979) found that about one half of the husbands and three fourths of the wives they studied reported having some sexual difficulty in their marriages and that these difficulties were increased by poor communication skills. Cupach and Comstock (1990) examined the associations among sexual communication, sexual satisfaction, and overall relational satisfaction. They found that good communication about sex leads to greater sexual satisfaction, which in turn contributes to more relational satisfaction. An earlier study showed that couples are most satisfied with their communication about sex when they are in highly developed, committed relationships. In contrast, couples who are in the early stages of relationship development or who are in the process of disengaging from the relationship report being less satisfied with their communication about sex (Wheeless, Wheeless, & Baus, 1984). If you are currently in a sexual relationship, you can access your level of sexual communication satisfaction by taking the test in Box 7.2. As we discuss next, communication about safe sex is also critical.

COMMUNICATION AND SAFE SEX

The safest form of sex in relationships is no sex. Abstinence is the best way to avoid unwanted pregnancy, AIDS, and other STIs. But total abstinence from sex is unusual, unrealistic and precludes having romantic relationships or offspring. Thus additional safe sex practices are imperative. Unfortunately, close relationships inadvertently put partners at risk since trust is higher and, as a result, safe sex is practiced less in close relationships (Noar, Zimmerman, & Atwood, 2004). Worse yet, information and communication about STIs are far less common than they should be.

Most parents do not talk about safe sex with their children (Fisher, 2004) but many publications give excellent advice for safe sex and AIDS prevention (Centers for Disease Control and Prevention, 1996; Larkin, 1998; Rathus et al., 1993; Student Health Services, 1998). STIs are epidemic in America; 65 million Americans have an incurable STI such as genital herpes or HIV (Noar et al., 2004). For more information about HIV/AIDS, contact your campus health service or county health department.

Communication is an essential ingredient in promoting safe sex. Obviously, unsafe sex can occur with any partner, even one you know well. So it is always best to be proactive about safe sex with every partner. This requires communicating with partners about past sexual experiences and talking about safe sex practices, such as those discussed below. Unfortunately, many people are complacent when they have sex with someone they know well (Hammer, Fisher, Fitzgerald, & Fisher, 1996; Noar et al., 2004; Rosenthal, Gifford, & Moore, 1998). They believe that being well acquainted with someone means that they are free of STIs. Recent research suggests that 99% of one college sample were confident in their assessment that their partner did not have an STI, despite research showing that over one third of college students have an STI (Afifi & Weiner, 2006). Brittany, in our chapter opener, made an intelligent decision; before she got sexually involved with Chris, she insisted they both get tested for STIs. They waited to have sex until they were both found to be free of STIs.

Many sexually active people believe that they can tell if a partner is lying to them about safe sex behaviors. In actuality, research has shown that people cannot tell when someone is lying about sexual behavior or HIV status (Swann, Silvera, & Proske, 1995). Particularly dangerous is the truth bias, whereby individuals tend to assume that people they like are telling them the truth (see Chapter 13). Trust is important in relationships, but is it worth your life to trust someone who could be wrong about their HIV status?

Another danger is people's lack of condom use, even though they know that condoms help prevent

▨ BOX 7.2   Put Yourself to the Test

Sexual Communication Satisfaction

Think about a current sexual relationship and rate your communication about sex using the following scale: 1 = Strongly disagree, 7 = Strongly agree.

	Disagree ⟵					⟶ *Agree*	
1. I tell my partner when I am especially sexually satisfied.	1	2	3	4	5	6	7
2. I am satisfied with my partner's ability to communicate her or his sexual desires to me.	1	2	3	4	5	6	7
3. I let my partner know things that I find pleasing during sex.	1	2	3	4	5	6	7
4. I do not hesitate to let my partner know when I want to have sex with him or her.	1	2	3	4	5	6	7
5. I tell my partner whether or not I am sexually satisfied.	1	2	3	4	5	6	7
6. I am satisfied with the degree to which my partner and I talk about the sexual aspects of our relationship.	1	2	3	4	5	6	7
7. I am not afraid to show my partner what kind of sexual behavior I like.	1	2	3	4	5	6	7
8. I would not hesitate to show my partner what is a sexual turn-on for me.	1	2	3	4	5	6	7
9. My partner shows me what pleases her or him during sex.	1	2	3	4	5	6	7
10. My partner tells me when he or she is sexually satisfied.	1	2	3	4	5	6	7
11. I am pleased with the manner in which my partner and I communicate with each other about sex.	1	2	3	4	5	6	7
12. It is never hard for me to figure out if my partner is sexually satisfied.	1	2	3	4	5	6	7

Add up your answers. A score of 84 indicates maximum sexual communication satisfaction. A score of 12 indicates the lowest level of sexual communication satisfaction possible. Since research shows that sexual communication satisfaction increases as relationships develop, you might want to take this test later in the semester to see if your score changes.

SOURCE: "The Sexual Communication Satisfaction Scale," from Wheeless, Lawrence R., Wheeless, Virginia Eman, and Baus, Raymond (1984). Sexual communication, communication satisfaction, and solidarity in the development stages of intimate relationships, in Western *Journal of Speech Communication. 48* (3, Summer), 217–230. Used with permission of the Western States Communication Association.

STIs. Using condoms consistently, meaning *every time* you have sexual intercourse, is the only effective way to prevent getting STIs during intercourse (Noar et al., 2004). Studies show that only about one third of couples use any form of contraception during intercourse (Willetts et al., 2004). Many couples decline to use condoms because they limit spontaneity and reduce sensation (Hammer et al., 1996). Yet about one third of the males in Hammer et al.'s study reported that sharing the act of putting on a condom can actually bring the couple closer and is arousing.

Even though logic suggests that people should use condoms to prevent STIs, in real relationships, factors other than logic influence condom use. Managing identity, not wanting to seem promiscuous, not wanting to destroy a romantic moment, not liking the feel of condoms, and believing a partner is "safe"—are all important in making a decision as to whether to use condoms or not (Afifi, 1999; Galligan & Terry, 1993). Galligan and Terry (1993) found that knowledge of the risk-reduction effects of condom use was a major motivator for people to use them. However, women were less likely to want to use a condom when they feared it would destroy the romance of the moment. Afifi (1999) reported that, when attachment to a partner is high and partners worry that suggesting condom use will be perceived as reflecting a lack of trust, the probability of condom use is decreased. Of course, suggesting condom use may not always be perceived negatively by one's partner; rather, it may be seen as a sign of caring and of responsibility.

These findings underscore the importance of communication; partners should have a frank discussion about safe sex before becoming sexually involved. Interestingly, almost any communication strategy increases the likelihood of condom use, but discussing pregnancy prevention or suggesting condom use "just to be safe" are the most effective strategies, probably because talking about AIDS can make people uncomfortable (Reel & Thompson, 1994). Unfortunately, research has shown that general discussions about AIDS do not promote safe sex. In contrast, discussing the specific sexual history of the partners, negotiating monogamy, and requesting that the partner use a condom can promote safe sex (Cline, Freeman, & Johnson, 1990).

Cline et al. (1990), however, found that those who discuss safe sex are only a little more likely to engage in safe sex practices than those who do not. Therefore, it is crucial that partners do more than talk about safe sex practices; they must also take appropriate action to protect themselves. You have probably seen these before, but here are the rules to follow to avoid AIDS and other STIs:

1. *Practice abstinence.* Although complete abstinence is unlikely for most adults, about 12% of the college-age population are virgins who have had no high-risk sexual activity (Sprecher & Regan, 1996). Abstinence is the most effective policy when it comes to preventing STIs.

2. *Avoid high-risk sex.* HIV and other STIs are transmitted through the exchange of bodily fluids. Intercourse is particularly dangerous. A single episode of unsafe sex with an HIV-positive person puts you at risk for contracting the virus. Multiple unsafe sex episodes put you at even greater risk (Hammer et al., 1996).

3. *Use condoms.* During sexual intercourse, a new latex condom offers good protection against the transmission of HIV. Old condoms and "off brand" condoms offer poor protection because they may break or leak. Condoms made from animal membranes (skins) are porous and offer less protection against AIDS transmission. Although condoms do not offer complete protection, recent studies have shown that when condoms are used properly they are highly successful in preventing HIV/AIDS even with an infected partner (Centers for Disease Control and Prevention, 1996; Noar et al, 2004).

4. *Get tested.* If you are uncertain whether you have been exposed to HIV, get tested. Only about 1% of those who are tested show the presence of HIV, so the test is likely to relieve you of concern that you have the virus. If you are HIV positive, you need to get treated immediately. With the proper treatment, many people who are HIV positive live many symptom-free years and even decades. Your campus health center or county department of health typically does HIV tests that are either anonymous or confidential. You can also use an HIV home test kit.

5. *Limit your partners.* Another good preventive technique is to limit yourself to a single partner who was previously a virgin, has been strictly monogamous, or has been tested for HIV since her or his last sexual encounter, as Brittany and Chris did. Remember, when you have sex with your partner, you are exposing yourself to risk from every person who has had sex with your partner in the past. Having sex only in the context of a monogamous, infection-free sexual relationship provides you with protection and may be the healthiest form of sexual activity (Noar et al., 2004).

6. *Know your partners.* A partner whom you know, respect, and completely trust is the safest kind of person with whom to have a sexual relationship, but this can be misleading. There is great risk in having sex with a new acquaintance, with someone whose sexual history you do not know, or with a long-term partner who you do not trust. Research has also shown that people make flawed judgments about whom is a safe partner. Many people erroneously believe that having sex with healthy looking, physically attractive people, friends, or people similar to themselves is safe (Noar et al., 2004); but sometimes it is not. Research has also shown that many people find it difficult to bring up the topic of safe sex and condom use during a sexual encounter with a new acquaintance (Rosenthal et al., 1998). Of course, people who fail to communicate about safe sex are literally risking their lives.

7. *Avoid intoxication.* Research has shown that binge drinkers engage in more sexual activity with a wider variety of partners (Mongeau & Johnson, 1995) than do heavy drug users. Studies have also shown that people are most likely to lapse in their safe sex practices when they are under the influence of alcohol and other drugs. More than one third of the participants in one study said that they had failed to use condoms on one or more occasions due to the use of drugs or alcohol (Hammer et al., 1996).

8. *Be honest.* It is essential that you report any unsafe sex outside your relationship to your partner so that appropriate steps can be taken. Of course, telling your partner about past sexual experiences or recent infidelities can be uncomfortable and harm your relationship. However, in the long run, it is far better to warn your partner of possible dangers than to save yourself from potential discomfort or conflict.

SUMMARY AND APPLICATION

Sex is a vital part of most romantic relationships. Partners who have similar sexual attitudes and high-quality sexual interaction are likely to be satisfied with their sex lives. Sexual satisfaction is associated with relational satisfaction, although it is important to remember that other factors, such as affection, love, and compatibility, are more important. Similarly, partners who are knowledgeable about sex are generally happier with their sex lives.

The research discussed in this chapter can help people like Taylor, Sarah, and Brittany in at least two ways. First, research on sexual attitudes can help them better understand their sexual selves. Second, research on sexual communication can help them improve how they talk about sex with their partners. In terms of sexual attitudes, Taylor has accepted and embraced her homosexuality. Sex is important in lesbian relationships, but nonverbal affection may be even more important to Taylor and Leslie. When Taylor hears homophobic comments and sees strange looks on the faces of her sorority sisters when she mentions Leslie, she has every right to be upset. But Taylor might be consoled by recognizing that people have different attitudes and preferences regarding sex whether they are homosexual or heterosexual. For instance, Sarah sometimes struggles with derogatory comments that people direct at her because she is a virgin.

For her part, Sarah should be comforted by the fact that about 12% of college students (and 13% of women college students) are virgins and that people who remain virgins because of strong moral beliefs and values are usually happy and proud of their virginity. Indeed, if Sarah gave up her virginity for the sake of pleasing her boyfriend or conforming to social norms, she might very well regret her decision.

Research suggests that Sarah should refuse sexual advances in a direct manner, using clear verbal communication. Her boyfriend might use a wide variety of strategies to try to persuade her to have sex, including pressure, manipulation, or antisocial behaviors, but research suggests that these strategies are likely to backfire or result in less relational satisfaction, so they should be avoided. Research also suggests that Sarah's boyfriend will accept her decision.

Because she refuses to have sex, Sarah is in the position of being the sexual gatekeeper in her relationship with her boyfriend. Even in relationships that turn sexual, women tend to be in the gatekeeping position at the beginning of the relationship, with men cast in the role of sexual initiator. Socially accepted scripts for sexual communication are typically followed in the early stages of relationships. However, as the relationship develops, women usually feel freer to initiate sex. Unique, individual sexual scripts replace socially normative scripts in developed relationships.

Finally, communication plays an important role in promoting sexual satisfaction. Couples who tell each other their sexual preferences and communicate their needs, desires, and aversions are much more likely to be happier with their sex life. Communication is also critical for promoting safe sex and avoiding STIs or an unplanned pregnancy, as Brittany's communication with her boyfriend exemplifies. Although Brittany does not talk about her sex life with her parents, she learned how to be sexually responsible from them. Parents should talk to their children about sex in a supportive, nondefensive manner rather than issuing warnings. Partners like Brittany and Chris should also talk to each other openly and honestly about their past sexual experiences and the need to practice safe sex. However, it is important to remember that safe sex *talk* is not enough; safe sex *behaviors* save lives.

DISCUSSION QUESTIONS

1. In this chapter, we presented data suggesting that most couples wait until some emotional intimacy and/or commitment has developed before engaging in sex. We also reported a study indicating that around 11% to 13% of college students are virgins. Based on the conversations you have had with friends, do you think these numbers hold true for your school? Why might these estimates differ depending on the group of people responding?

2. Based on what you learned in this chapter, what strategies would you use to protect yourself from sexual coercion or harassment? Why do you think people misinterpret supposed sexual cues so often?

3. Why do you think people practice unsafe sex even though they know the risks involved? What communication strategies might partners use to ensure that they engage in safe sex?

8

COMMUNICATING CLOSENESS

Intimacy, Affection, and Social Support

Kevin treasures his close friendships. Among his dozens of friends, two are most special. His most roman- tic relationship is with his girlfriend Jennifer. He says that she brightens his day. They spend a lot of time together talking, touching, comforting, and listening. They play tennis and bicycle together. Jennifer says that she has never felt the same warmth and trust with another boyfriend. Best of all, she can tell him anything, and he listens! Kevin's other close relationship is with Dan. Kevin and Dan went through high school together, ran track, played football, and were on the debate team together. Today they still take ski trips and run together, and they have great conversations about everything—business, sports, politics, and life in general. Unlike with his other male friends, Kevin can talk to Dan about anything, even Jennifer. And importantly, he can count on Dan for anything.

Intimate interactions are a special type of communication that occur in our closest rela- tionships. These interactions transpire among close friends, within tightly knit families, in roman- tic relationships, and in many marriages. In everyday language, most people do not use the term *intimate* to describe their closest relationships. Instead, Kevin would be more likely to refer to his intimate relation- ships with Dan and Jennifer as close, friendly, warm, affectionate, cozy, caring, bonded, warmhearted, convivial, compassionate, and even loving. In fact, research shows that the most common term people use for intimate relationships is *close relationships* (Parks & Floyd, 1996). Dan and Kevin would never say they have an intimate relationship, even though by our definition they do; they would say they are "best" friends or "close" friends.

In their article on the "bright side of relational communication," Andersen and Guerrero (1998a) stated that intimate relationships are the foundation of our lives:

> Almost without exception, our relationships with friends and loved ones are the cornerstone of our lives and our emotional well-being. The warm feeling of an intimate conservation, a reassuring hug, seeing a close friend after a long absence, or sharing joy with one's family are experiences each of us has had. Indeed, the brightest side of life's experience often occurs in close intimate relationships during the exchange of warm, involving, immediate messages. (p. 303)

Kevin's close relationships with both Jennifer and Dan play vital roles in his life. Yet these two relationships are also likely to differ in important ways. If Kevin kept a diary of the behaviors that he used to communicate intimacy, affection, and social support to Dan and Jennifer, what types of behaviors would likely be similar across the two relationships? What behaviors might be more characteristic of his best friendship with Dan? Which might be reserved for his romantic relationship with Jennifer? To answer these and other questions, this chapter examines the feelings, behaviors, and relationships that comprise the experience of intimacy, as well as the related experiences of affection and social support. First, we help you recognize intimacy when you see and feel it and understand its importance in your life. Second, we discuss the nonverbal and verbal behaviors that communicate intimacy, affection, social support, and comfort. Third, we examine two interpersonal theories/models that focus on the exchange of intimate behavior: Reis and Shaver's intimacy process model and Andersen's cognitive valence theory. Finally, we examine sex differences and similarities in intimacy.

UNDERSTANDING INTIMACY

Intimacy refers to the special relational states and interactions that occur in close relationships, characterized by feelings of warmth, trust, and deep friendship. For many people, intimacy is synonymous with sexual involvement; however, that is *not* the meaning of intimacy we intend in this chapter. Sex can be intimate or impersonal, although the best sexual encounters certainly are intimate ones for most people. To use a thermal metaphor, if sexual encounters are hot, then intimate interactions are best characterized by warmth (Sternberg, 1987). And according to Sternberg (1987), "over the long term maintaining intimacy—communication, sharing, support and the like—is more important than maintaining passion" (p. 222). Thus having dinner with an old friend, going to your son's graduation, chatting with your significant other by the fireplace with a glass of wine, and telling your best friend about your new love are all intimate encounters.

These intimate encounters have a quality that is lacking in everyday interactions between strangers and acquaintances. Sternberg (1987) suggested that intimacy comprises feelings of warmth, trust, and happiness, which are present only in close relationships. Among the hundreds of people you meet at school, at work, in organizations, and through your family, acquaintances, and friends, you will build intimate relationships with only a few. Moving a relationship from impersonal to intimate is a fragile process (Andersen, 1998a). Many factors—such as cultural or personality differences, inappropriate behavior, loss of trust, lack of attraction, and lack of similarity, to mention just a few—can throw a relationship off track and prevent it from becoming a special, intimate one.

Locating intimacy is not easy; it comes in a variety of forms and contexts and can be found in feelings, interactions, and relationships (Acitelli & Duck, 1987; Andersen, 1999; Andersen et al., 2006; Prager & Roberts, 2004). However, researchers have argued that interaction plays the most central role in creating and sustaining intimacy (Andersen et al., 2006). This is because interaction is the means through which people share intimate thoughts and feelings. Intimate interaction is also the vehicle through which people develop and maintain close relationships. As shown in Figure 8.1, intimate thoughts and feelings lead to intimate behavior; intimate behavior then leads to more thoughts and feelings of intimacy. Both the experience and the expression of intimacy enhance the quality of relationships. As Prager (2000) observed, "If intimacy is one of the most often discussed aspect of personal relationship functioning, then there are good reasons. It is predictive of the highest levels of satisfaction, love, and trust as well as the primary reward of closeness" (p. 229).

Experiencing Intimacy

The experience of intimacy is rooted in internal processes related to feelings and thoughts. The feelings two people have for each other are the foundation of intimate relationships. These feelings are variously described as warmth, love, bondedness, emotional connectedness, and affection. Andersen and Guerrero (1998a) argued that the feelings of

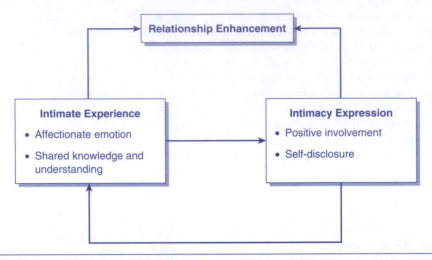

Figure 8.1 An Interaction-Centered Model of Intimacy Processes Related to Nonverbal Behavior

SOURCE: Adapted from Andersen, Guerrero, & Jones "An Interaction Centered Model of Intimacy Processes Related to Nonverbal Behavior." In Valerie Manusov & Miles L. Patterson (Eds.), *The SAGE Handbook of Nonverbal Communication.* Copyright 2006, Sage Publications.

warmth that occur in the presence of a friend, close relative, or relational partner are at the heart of intimate relationships. In marital relationships, emotional intimacy is connected to every other kind of intimacy: social, sexual, intellectual, and recreational (McCabe, 1999). These feelings may accompany a hug from a close friend, a talk with a lover, or a holiday celebration with the family. Statements that disclose one's vulnerable emotions are especially conducive to feelings of intimacy (Prager & Roberts, 2004).

Partners in close relationships feel numerous positive emotions when interacting with or thinking about each other. Guerrero and Andersen (2000) described a cluster of interpersonal emotions, including love, passion, warmth, and joy, that are related to affection. **Love** is an inherently relational emotion that is evoked in relationships and is associated with an intense desire to maintain closeness (Aron & Aron, 1986; Shaver, Morgan, & Wu, 1996). **Passion** is sometimes conceptualized as a part of love between romantic partners (Sternberg, 1986, 1988), although others see passion as encompassing feelings of attraction and sexual arousal. **Interpersonal warmth** is another inherently relational emotion that people experience as a sense of pleasantness, contentedness,

and intimacy during interactions with relational partners, such as friends, lovers, and family members (Andersen & Guerrero, 1998a). Finally, **joy** (or happiness) is an interpersonal emotion because it is commonly experienced after receiving praise from others or from being the object of love, affection, and/or admiration (Schwartz & Shaver, 1987). When partners frequently experience these types of emotions in connection with each other, they tend to feel closer and be happier with their relationship (Feeney, Noller, & Roberts, 1998; Prager & Buhrmester, 1998).

Thoughts and perceptions are also an important part of the intimacy experience. Prager and Roberts (2004) argued that intimacy is experienced through shared knowledge. This knowledge is gained through mutual self-disclosure, spending time together, and observing one another's behavior. These types of interactions help people reduce uncertainty so that they can predict and explain one another's feelings and behaviors (see Chapter 4). Think about your closest friends. You probably know a lot about them (and they about you) that other people do not know. Feelings of intimacy are also enhanced when people believe that their partners understand and value them (Prager, 2000).

Expressing Intimacy

If intimate feelings are not communicated, they remain internal processes that have little effect on a relationship (Andersen et al., 2006). Self-disclosure, which includes sharing personal information about oneself and expressing feelings, is essential for intimacy to develop (see Chapter 5). Intimacy is often communicated nonverbally through **positive involvement** behaviors, which represent the intersection of involvement and positive affect (Guerrero, 2004; Prager, 2000). Involvement behaviors show that a person is interested and engaged in an interaction. Positive affect cues show that a person is experiencing affectionate emotions, such as liking, joy, warmth, or love. As we discuss later in this chapter, positive involvement behaviors include a host of verbal and nonverbal messages that reflect intimacy and warmth. These behaviors have also been called **immediacy behaviors**—actions that signal warmth, communicate availability, decrease psychological and/or physical distance, and promote involvement (Andersen, 1985). Importantly, intimacy cannot be created or sustained if only one person expresses feelings of closeness to the other. Thus reciprocity is a critical part of intimate interaction; people must not only express intimate thoughts and feelings to each other, they must also respond positively to those expressions of intimacy.

As Andersen (1999) noted, "Immediacy behaviors are foundations by which intimate interactions and intimate relationships are created and sustained" (p. 219). However, immediacy behaviors, such as making eye contact, smiling, and using a pleasant tone of voice, are important in nonintimate relationships as well. Consequently, while immediacy behaviors are essential components of intimate relationships, they are not enough by themselves. Intimate relationships also (1) are unique, (2) contain depth, (3) exist over time in that they have a history and a future and are marked by rituals, (4) involve the exchange of very high levels of positive emotions, and (5) are characterized by high levels of listening and understanding. Intimacy is characterized by high levels of **interpersonal affection** in relationships (Floyd, 2006; Pendell, 2002). Affection, which is similar to intimacy, is characterized by liking and high regard for another and the communication of affectionate and immediate behaviors, and it is vital to mental and physical health (Pendell, 2002).

Uniqueness. Unlike many short-term relationships, interactions in intimate relationships are unique. Knapp (1983) argued that when we first meet people, our communication tends to be scripted. In other words, we use conventional language that is widely understood. However, as a relationship becomes close, Knapp suggested, two people develop an idiosyncratic style of communication that reflects the unique characteristics of their personalities and the relationship they share. A study by Hopper, Knapp, and Scott (1981) revealed that couples use unique forms of communication in their relationships. For example, one couple reported that twitching their noses signaled "You're special," while another reported that twisting their wedding rings meant "Don't you dare do or say that!" Every close relationship produces intimate interactions that have a unique flavor.

A close relationship, like Kevin and Jennifer's, is an irreplaceable and one-of-a-kind romance; it is unique. Hendrick and Hendrick (1992) maintained that intimacy "is characterized by genuineness and an absence of 'role' relationships" (p. 166). Thus, if someone can instantly replace one intimate relationship with another, it probably was not very intimate after all. But the intimate interactions individuals share with their boyfriend or girlfriend, their best friend, and their mother or father are unique. Intimate interactions use special forms of communication that individuals can share only with certain others with whom they share great trust and closeness. Think of a dark family secret, a sexual interaction you had with a relational partner, or a disclosure from a close friend about his or her sexual identity. With how many people could you share this information? Probably very few. Intimate relationships are special and relatively rare, although people often have numerous intimate interactions within their few special relationships.

Depth. Intimate interactions are deep rather than superficial connections. They are characterized by the sharing of time and space, touch, and in-depth self-disclosure not found in other relationships. Later in this chapter, we will explore some of the nonverbal and verbal behaviors that lead to deep interactions. In intimate relationships, partners "can communicate deeply and honestly . . . sharing innermost feelings" (Sternberg, 1987, p. 333). Self-revealing statements that convey vulnerable emotions are especially conducive to intimacy (Prager & Roberts, 2004). Self-disclosure plays a critical role in relationship development because as people become closer, they share their innermost thoughts and feelings (see Chapter 5). Only by sharing personal information, thoughts, and feelings can two people get to know each other well enough to develop a close, intimate relationship.

Comfort With Silence. Of course, self-disclosure is not the only way in which a couple can communicate depth. In the beginning stages of relationships, people often feel compelled to talk so as to prevent an awkward silence. In close relationships, however, silence can communicate comfort and connection. For example, a couple driving across town might hold hands and snuggle while listening to romantic music on the radio, and two close friends might smile and laugh together during certain scenes while watching their favorite movie (which they have seen together many times). Such interaction shows that nonverbal communication, and even silence, can indicate that two people share a deep connection with each other.

Time and Repeated Interaction. Intimate interactions rarely arise out of thin air. They typically occur in relationships that are well developed and between people who have sustained their relationship across multiple episodes and interactions. Intimate communication occurs in interaction sequences that may unfold over months, years, and even decades. Miller, Cody, and McLaughlin (1994) illustrated this point when they explained that intimate partners share more experiences and participate together in a wider range of situations than nonintimates. Rituals such as annual birthday celebrations, anniversaries, holidays spent together, and the renewal of wedding vows help people sustain intimacy and commitment in their relationships (Braithwaite & Baxter, 1995; Werner,

Altman, Brown, & Ganat, 1993). Total time spent together is also predictive of higher relational satisfaction and intimacy in both marital and dating relationships (Egland, Stelzner, Andersen, & Spitzberg, 1997; Emmers-Sommer, 2004). As Andersen (1999) stated, "Although many parents tell their children they love them, they proceed to spend time on dozens of activities while spending little time with their children. Not surprisingly, many of these children feel unloved despite their parents' words" (p. 64). Some researchers believe that quality of time is more important than quantity of time (Emmers-Sommer, 2004). This is probably true, although people have more opportunities to spend quality time together when they are in frequent contact with one another.

Positive Affect. High levels of positive affect characterize the most fulfilling and satisfying relationships for both men and women (Prager & Buhrmester, 1998). While negative communication is common in many intimate exchanges (see Chapters 13 and 14), in general, intimacy is fostered by a higher ratio of positive to negative behaviors. Feeney et al. (1998) reviewed several studies showing that happy couples report "higher rates of positive behaviors in their daily interactions with their partners" and that "more than three-quarters of couples . . . identified positive intimate behaviors as crucial to maintaining satisfaction in their relationships" (pp. 480–481). Using friendly, constructive forms of communication probably helps maintain relationships because it makes people feel good (Guerrero & Andersen, 2000). In another review of the literature, Kelly et al. (2003) observed that happy couples are not necessarily defined by the verbal content of their communication but rather by the positive emotions they "appear to be experiencing— the smiles, laughs, affection, and warmth" (p. 729). The expression of positive emotions such as love, passion, warmth, and joy is particularly important in communicating affection. Complimenting your partner, showering your partner with affection, and making sacrifices for your partner are maintenance behaviors that are likely to make your partner *feel* good and therefore strengthen the intimate bond that you share.

Listening and Understanding. Having a partner who listens and is understanding is very important for relational satisfaction and need fulfillment (Prager & Buhrmester, 1998). In fact, one study showed that among a large set of communication variables, perceived understanding was the best predictor of relational satisfaction (Egland et al., 1997). This study also found that a listener's ability to "backchannel" (saying "uh huh" and nodding in the appropriate places), actively listen, and show nonverbal immediacy were important predictors of perceived understanding. These types of behaviors validate the partner's thoughts and feelings. People who are understanding also tend to be more emotionally supportive and sensitive to the needs of their partners. As we shall discuss later in this chapter, being emotionally supportive is a key communication skill that helps people develop and maintain intimate relationships (Burleson, 2003).

THE IMPORTANCE OF INTIMACY AND AFFECTION

From infancy until death, intimate attachments are a vital part of life. Ainsworth (1989) described how intimate, secure attachments provide the basis for strong, trusting adult relationships (see Chapter 6 on attachment). Pendell (2002) suggested that "intimate relationships, pair bonding, and affection are basic human biological adaptations evolved for the purpose of reproduction and protecting the young" (p. 91). Having close, affectionate, and secure relationships is associated with happiness and both mental and physical health. Affection and intimacy also have benefits for relationships, including helping couples overcome relational turbulence and helping partners expand their identities.

Happiness

Intimate relationships are exceedingly beneficial in our lives. As Baumeister and Leary (1995) suggested,

> Happiness in life is strongly correlated with having some close personal relationships. Research suggests that it does not seem to make a great deal of difference what sort of relationship one has, but the absence of close bonds is strongly linked to unhappiness, depression and other woes. (p. 534)

In marriage, intimacy has been found to be highly beneficial in maintaining a satisfying relationship. Acker and Davis (1992) reported that intimacy was associated with higher levels of both passion and commitment in marital relationships. For most people, intimate relationships are the greatest source of satisfaction in their lives. In fact, according to Shaver, Schwartz, Kirson, and O'Connor (1987), people experience the most happiness when they feel loved and accepted and when they receive affection and praise from others. Research has even shown that babies are happiest when they are interacting with people who love and care for them. For example, Magai and McFadden (1995) summarized over a century of research on what causes infants to display joy. They reported that babies tend to look happiest when they see a parent's face, when their limbs are lightly and playfully shaken, when they are tickled or hear someone singing, and when someone opens the curtain around the cradle. Thus, for both children and adults, intimate social interaction is an essential ingredient in the recipe for a happy life.

Mental Health

Research also has shown that healthy, intimate relationships are vital to mental and emotional well-being (Guerrero, 2000). Children who grow up with parents who are "absent" emotionally due to mental problems, chemical dependency, or marital problems are unlikely to trust others, are more prone to mental problems, and are less likely to form healthy relationships (Vangelisti & Sprague, 1998). Offspring have a biological need for intimacy, affection, and support. Indeed, neglected children can become sick and even die (see Chapter 1). Recently, Floyd and Morman (2005) found that children from large families perceive receiving less affection than children from small families, suggesting the importance of maximization of parental affection to children. For adults, being rejected by others is related to depression; depression contributes to rejection and loneliness, but being rejected and lonely also contributes to depression (Segrin, 1998). A number of studies have shown that clinically depressed individuals often do not form intimate relationships and that other people view these individuals as somewhat hostile and/or difficult to be around (Segrin, 1998). Intimate relationships both promote mental health and are enabled by good mental health.

Affection is also related to better mental health. People who regularly receive affection are advantaged in almost every way compared with people who receive little affection; they are happier, more self-confident, less stressed, less likely to be depressed, more likely to engage in social activity, and in better general mental health (Floyd, 2002). Giving affection has similar benefits. In another study by Floyd et al. (2005), people who readily show affection to others reported more happiness, higher self-esteem, less fear of intimacy, less susceptibility to depression, and greater relational satisfaction.

Physical Health

Intimate relationships promote good health for a number of reasons. Studies have shown that married people live longer and suffer less ill health than do single people. Partners provide social support and get medical attention for their loved one. But the effect of intimate relationships goes beyond that. Prager (1995) observed that

> intimate relationships seem to buffer people against the pathogenic effect of stress. In the face of stressful life events, people who have intimate relationships have fewer stress-related symptoms, faster recoveries from illness, and a lower probability of relapse or recurrence than those who do not have intimate relationships. (p. 1)

Moreover, social networks that provide social support seem to have salutary effects on health (Cunningham & Barbee, 2000). People who feel accepted and supported by others are more likely to stay active and healthy than are people who are depressed or lonely, in part because they are more likely to engage in enjoyable activities with members of their social network (Guerrero, 2000). In sum, intimacy has many positive effects on people's lives.

An emerging body of research also suggests that *both* the giving and the receiving of affection are associated with better health. Floyd et al. (2005) showed that affection is associated with improved mental and physical health. Recently, he demonstrated a

physiological link between affection and bodily changes. Specifically, when people gave or received affection, secretion of adrenal hormones associated with stress tended to decrease, while secretion of oxytocin, a hormone associated with sexual satisfaction and lactation, tended to increase. The secretion of other hormones associated with positive moods and behaviors also tended to increase (Floyd, 2006). To see how affectionate you are, take the test in Box 8.1. Floyd's research has demonstrated that people who score higher on the affectionate communication index tend to be better off mentally and physically, even after controlling for the amount of affection they receive from others. The health benefits of affection include lower resting blood pressure, lower blood sugar (Floyd, Hesse, & Haynes, in press), lower heart rate, and a less exaggerated hormonal response to stress (Floyd, Mikkelson, et al., in press).

Researchers have also argued that affection is a basic biological need. Pendell (2002) stated that "intimate relationships, pair bonding, and affection are basic human biological adaptations evolved for the purpose of reproduction and protecting the young" (p. 91). **Affective exchange theory** suggests that affectionate communication is a biologically adaptive behavior that contributes to human viability and fertility by improving health and fortifying the body's flight-or-fight system (Floyd, in press). Consistent with affection exchange theory, Floyd and Morr (2003) found that people manifest the most affection in their marriages, less with their siblings, and least with their brother-in-law or sister-in-law.

Overcoming Relational Turbulence

Conflicts and troubles occur in every relationship. In Chapters 13 and 14, we discuss relational transgressions and conflict in more detail. For now, however, we want to suggest that a primary benefit of closeness and intimacy in relationships is that they help relationships survive challenges. When relationships begin to become intimate, it is often a turbulent time (Knobloch & Solomon, 2002b; Solomon & Knobloch, 2004). Getting close to another person creates uncertainty (see Chapter 4), a loss of independence, time pressures, and control issues. At high levels of intimacy, these issues subside because

BOX 8.1   Put Yourself to the Test

The Affectionate Communication Index

Circle the number that represents how much you agree that each statement describes you, with 1 representing strong disagreement and 7 representing strong agreement.

	Disagree						Agree
1. I consider myself to be a very affectionate person.	1	2	3	4	5	6	7
2. I am always telling my loved ones how much I care about them.	1	2	3	4	5	6	7
3. When I feel affection for someone, I usually express it.	1	2	3	4	5	6	7
4. I have a hard time telling people that I love them or care about them.	1	2	3	4	5	6	7
5. I am not very good at expressing affection.	1	2	3	4	5	6	7
6. I am not a very affectionate person.	1	2	3	4	5	6	7
7. I love giving people hugs or putting my arms around them.	1	2	3	4	5	6	7
8. I do not tend to express affection to other people very much.	1	2	3	4	5	6	7
9. Anyone who knows me well would say that I am pretty affectionate.	1	2	3	4	5	6	7
10. Expressing affection to other people makes me uncomfortable.	1	2	3	4	5	6	7

To calculate your score: First, give yourself 30 points. Second, add up your responses to Questions 1, 2, 3, 7, and 9, and put the total on the first line below. Third, add up your responses to Questions 4, 5, 6, 8, and 10, and put the total on the second line below. A score at or close to 0 means that you are highly unaffectionate; a score at or close to 60 means that you are highly affectionate.

My score: 30 plus _____ minus _____ = _____
          Line 1   Line 2

SOURCE: Adapted from Floyd, "Affectionate Communication Index," in *Communication Quarterly,* Vol. 50, copyright © 2002. Reproduced by permission of Eastern Communication Association, http://www.ecasite.org

they are outweighed by the high levels of closeness, trust, and warmth that characterize highly intimate relationships. At higher intimacy levels, couples are less uncertain and have fewer negative emotions, avoidance conflicts, and arguments (Knobloch & Solomon, 2002b). Similarly, research has shown that at higher levels of intimacy, people make fewer negative appraisals of their partner; in short, they have fewer unpleasant thoughts that can cause relational turbulence (Solomon & Knobloch, 2004).

Self-Expansion

Every relationship makes you more than you were or less than you were. Relationships have costs such as time, money, the exclusion of other relationships, conflict, and even hurt. But relationships have benefits as well: connection, fun, humor, expansion, sexuality, excitement, activity, and, of course, intimacy (see Chapter 10). Ideal relationships have more benefits than costs; you expand yourself and realize your full potential rather than contracting and stunting your personal growth. Research suggests that although intimacy is weakly associated with interference from partners, intimacy is strongly associated with facilitation from partners (Knobloch & Solomon, 2004). This means that the best and most intimate relationships facilitate and assist individuals in making plans, achieving goals, using time well, exercising, seeing other friends, studying, or just getting through the day (Knobloch & Solomon, 2004). This is consistent with self-expansion theory as discussed in Chapter 2, which suggests that people want to expand and enlarge themselves and that relationships are a primary means of self-expansion. Research has shown that people in close, intimate relationships describe themselves as more diverse, efficacious, motivated, and respected than those who do not have such intimate relationships (Aron & Aron, 1997). Kevin and Jennifer have a nearly ideal relationship; it allows them to be themselves and expand their potential via their intimate relationship with each other.

NONVERBAL INTIMACY

According to Montgomery (1988), "the nonverbal mode of expression appears to be more closely linked to relational quality than the verbal mode" (p. 348). Similarly, Prager (2000) suggested that

> nonverbal behavior contributes substantially to people's intimate experiences. The influence of nonverbal behavior is probably due to its relatively involuntary character. People's facial expressions, voice tones, postures and gestures can reveal unspoken emotions and intentions and can override efforts at impression management. (p. 232)

Clearly, nonverbal communication is an important component in close relationships. In this section, we focus on nonverbal behaviors that can be used to convey involvement, warmth, and affection.

Andersen (1985) referred to these behaviors as *nonverbal immediacy cues*; other scholars have referred to these behaviors as positive involvement cues (Prager, 2000). As you read this section, keep in mind that nonverbal behaviors are often processed as a **gestalt** (Andersen, 1985, 1999). In other words, rather than focusing on single behaviors, people usually take the whole package of nonverbal behaviors into consideration when assigning meaning. You should also realize that nonverbal communication is interpreted within a broader social context. For example, eye contact can reflect intimacy in one situation but intimidation in another situation. Similarly, a smile might be perceived as friendly in one context and condescending in another.

Visual or Oculesic Behaviors

Eye behavior, or oculesics, is essential in establishing interpersonal intimacy. The eyes have been said to be "the windows to the soul," and eye contact is generally regarded as an invitation to communicate (Andersen, 1999). Increased eye contact has been widely recognized as a sign of intimacy and attraction (Andersen, 1985; Exline & Winters, 1965; Ray & Floyd, 2006). People engage in the highest levels of eye contact with friends, dating partners, and people they like (Coutts & Schneider, 1976; Exline & Winters, 1965). Romantic partners, in particular, appear to use high levels of eye contact to communicate intimacy (Guerrero, 1997). During intimate interaction, eye contact is a sign of attentiveness and connection.

One interesting, although somewhat obscure, oculesic behavior is pupil dilation. You might be aware that pupils dilate in low light, but did you also know that pupils dilate in response to any stimuli people find interesting or attractive (Hess, 1965; Hess & Goodwin, 1974)? Moreover, people are more attracted to individuals with dilated pupils. In an imaginative study, Hess and Goodwin (1974) showed people two virtually identical pictures of a mother holding her baby; however, in one photo the eyes were retouched to appear dilated, while in the other photo they were constricted. Overwhelmingly, the subjects reported that the mother with the dilated pupils seemed to love her baby more. Interestingly, few subjects identified the eyes as the source of the attributions, which suggests that pupil dilation is processed as an intimacy cue but at very low levels of awareness. Of course, low light, candle-lit dinners, and dusk have always been associated with romance and intimacy, perhaps in part due to subtle cues such as pupil dilation.

Spatial or Proxemic Behaviors

The way people use space in interpersonal communication, or proxemics, signals how intimate the relationship is. Years ago, Hall (1968) identified four distance zones as a function of types of interpersonal interaction. He called the closest of these zones, from touch to 18 in., "intimate distance." The only people permitted into this zone are those with whom we have intimate relationships, such as our children, our closest friends, our family members, and our romantic partners. The other three zones—"personal" (1.5–4 feet), "social" (4–10 feet), and "public" (more than 10 feet)—are used for less intimate relationships. When our intimate zone is invaded by someone who is not a close friend or a romantic partner, we react with defensive or compensatory behaviors (Andersen, 1985, 1998b; Burgoon et al., 1995). These defensive behaviors include reducing eye contact, drawing back, using arms or objects as buffers, and literally giving the person the cold shoulder by turning away.

Intimacy is also communicated proxemically via body angle. Facing someone directly is intimate, while sitting or standing at a 45° angle is less intimate, and positioning oneself side by side with another person is even less intimate. Turning one's back on someone is the opposite of intimate. Interestingly, women are more likely to use a direct, face-to-face body orientation than men (Guerrero, 1997); this is one of several ways in which women seem to be more nonverbally intimate than men.

Face-to-face communication between people of very different heights is difficult. When a 6-foot adult communicates with a child, a person in a wheelchair, or a 5-foot person, he or she is attempting to communicate on a different physical plane. Research has shown that communicating on the same eye-to-eye plane increases perceptions of intimacy (Andersen, 1985; Brown, 1965). Andersen and Andersen (1982) suggested that getting into the same physical plane is essential to early elementary school teachers for creating rapport with their young students. Intimacy can be increased by sitting, reclining, or kneeling when height discrepancies inhibit interaction. Thus the 6-foot adult can increase intimacy simply by putting herself or himself on the same physical plane, and shorter individuals can engage in behaviors to raise themselves. For example, toddlers are often placed in high chairs so that they are face-to-face with the rest of the family at the dinner table.

Tactile or Haptic Behaviors

Physical contact, or haptics, is central to the notion of intimacy. People's most intimate relationships, such as those between parents and children, childhood friends, and romantic partners, are characterized by high levels of touch. Andersen (1985) observed that "although dependent on cultural norms and the interpersonal relationship, normative touch is usually perceived as a warm, intimate behavior" (p. 10). Touch is an important sign of relational intimacy. In a study of airport arrivals and departures, Heslin and Boss (1980) found a strong association between the amount of tactile intimacy, recorded by observers, and the intimacy of the relationship, as reported by couples. Another study found that observers perceived higher levels of intimacy for touching couples than for nontouching couples (Kleinke, Meeker, & LaFong, 1974). Similarly, Guerrero and Andersen's (1991) study of couples' tactile communication in theater and zoo lines revealed that high levels of touch were associated with an intimate and accelerating relationship. Emmers and Dindia (1995) found that this was true for private touch as well. Andersen (1999) concluded that "the highest frequency of touch occurs in intimate relationships at intermediate or escalating levels of acquaintance" (p. 48). Hugs and kisses are a particularly intimate, immediate, and affectionate form of communication, as is touch to the face (Andersen, 1999; Andersen et al., 2006; Guerrero & Floyd, 2006; Floyd, 2006).

A fundamental aspect of what people think of as intimate and affectionate interaction involves

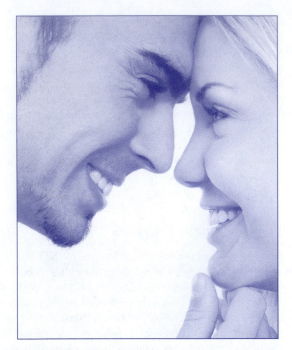

SOURCE: Copyright: iStockphoto.com/
Kateryna Govorushchenko

Photo 8.1   Face touch is an especially intimate
behavior. What other nonverbal cues
are this couple using to communicate
warmth and affection?

physical contact (Floyd, 2006; Monsour, 1992),
particularly for romantic partners and female friends.
This is also true for females in their closest cross-sex
relationships, even if their friend is not a romantic
partner. While same-sex touch is less common among
men in the United States, many men do express intimacy tactilely. For example, gay men who are
involved romantically touch each other frequently.
Although heterosexual men touch one another relatively infrequently, they still engage in roughhousing,
physical contact during sports and sports celebrations, high fives, and chest bumps—all of which
communicate intimacy with a masculine flavor.

Body Movement or Kinesics

Kinesics comprises body movements such as smiling, inclusive and expressive gestures, nodding, open

body postures, and bodily relaxation. Emotions
typically are revealed through facial expressions,
although they may also be manifested in the body or
voice. Research has shown that a primary component
of relational intimacy is emotional expressiveness
(Monsour, 1992). Relationships become more intimate when people express positive emotions about
themselves, their partner, and the relationship.

The smile is a primary vehicle for the establishment of close relationships. Over several decades,
researchers have found that the frequency and intensity of smiling is the single best predictor of interpersonal intimacy, liking, and warmth (Argyle,
1972; Bayes, 1970; Ray & Floyd, 2006; Reece &
Whitman, 1962). Smiles are a universal sign of positive affect that signal approachability and availability for communication.

Open body positions free of obstruction by
objects or limbs also are associated with greater intimacy. People are most likely to cross their arms,
hide their face, or stand behind objects when they
lack trust, feel vulnerable, and do not want to interact. Morris (1977) suggested that these "barrier
signals" communicate avoidance and defensiveness
in interpersonal interaction. Beier and Sternberg
(1977) reported that "close" couples used more open
leg positions than did couples who were less close
or who were experiencing conflict.

Like good dancers, intimate couples show high
levels of coordinated movement, called **body
synchrony**. The good "vibes" resulting from smooth
interaction with and adaptation to one's partner are
a vital part of relational intimacy (Guerrero &
Floyd, 2006; Morris, 1977). Andersen (1999) noted
that "although most synchronous patterns are reciprocal, some are not. Some are complementary: one
person gives a back rub, and the other receives it;
one person discloses, and the other listens and nods
attentively" (p. 223). It is not just reciprocity that
promotes intimacy; it is smooth synchronization of
behavior, whether complementary or reciprocal,
that creates relational intimacy. When confederates
in a recent study were asked to signal liking to
another person, one of the behaviors they employed
was postural matching (Ray & Floyd, 2006).
Although they are unaware of it, Kevin and his best
friend Dan frequently match postures; they lean forward together at a bar, both put their feet up while

watching a game, and both throw their heads back when they laugh.

Vocalic or Paralinguistic Communication

Words have meaning, but changes in pitch, volume, rate, and tone of voice may be more important than words. These nonverbal elements of the voice, called **vocalics** or **paralinguistics**, have important effects on intimacy. Studies have shown that shifts in vocal pitch, rate, amplitude, and duration are associated with interpersonal affect (Beebe, 1980; Scherer, 1979). For example, voices that are warm and expressive reflect interpersonal intimacy (Guerrero, 2004).

Certain vocalic behaviors, such as baby talk, produce uniquely high levels of intimacy. Adults frequently use baby talk, a high-pitched, highly varied imitation of children's speech, to communicate with infants and small children (Andersen, 1999). Baby talk includes real words ("You're a little sweetie") and nonsense sounds ("kutchy-kutchy-koo"). Such talk has been found to aid the development of conversational skills, as well as closer, more intimate parent-child relationships (Ferguson, 1964). Research also suggests that baby talk should be stopped once a child begins talking. Interestingly, lovers like Kevin and Jennifer sometimes privately employ baby talk during their most intimate interactions, perhaps because intimate behaviors related to courtship are often submissive, nonthreatening, and childlike (see Chapter 7).

Chronemic Behaviors

The way people use time, or chronemics, communicates a lot about their relationships. In North America and much of Europe, time is a precious commodity that is spent, saved, wasted, or invested as though it were money. Studies show that chronemic cues are part of the intimacy exchange process (Andersen, 1984). Spending time with another person sends the message that the person is important and reflects a desire for intimacy. Egland et al. (1997) found that the best way to signal closeness and intimacy in a relationship is by spending time with one's partner. Similarly, being on time, waiting for a late partner, sharing conversation time, and devoting time to work on the relationship all play a role in the communication of intimacy.

VERBAL INTIMACY

Humans are talkative creatures. Although nonverbal communication may be the essence of an intimate relationship, talk is extremely important as well. Several types of verbal behaviors are critical to intimate relationships, including self-disclosure, verbal responsiveness, relationship talk, and relational language.

Self-Disclosure

Communicating openly about one's feelings and beliefs is called self-disclosure (see Chapter 5). Among the many verbal behaviors that create and sustain relational intimacy, self-disclosure is probably the most important (Derlega et al., 1993). In fact, when Monsour (1992) asked people what intimacy meant to them, the most common response was self-disclosure. Research shows that most definitions of intimacy include verbal self-disclosure for males and females in both same-sex and opposite-sex relationships (Monsour, 1992; Parks & Floyd, 1996).

Self-disclosure figures prominently in all the basic theories of relational development and closeness, including social penetration theory and Knapp's coming-together stages (see Chapter 5). Studies consistently have found that self-disclosure is necessary for intimate relationships. As we will learn later in this chapter, although both females and males enjoy self-disclosure and find it important to the development of intimacy, females disclose more than males. But self-disclosure is extremely important in male *and* female friendships. Afifi and Guerrero (1995) reported that self-disclosure was the strongest predictor of relational closeness for both men and women friends. Couples' interpersonal needs are most likely to be satisfied when the partners disclose actively and listen to each other's self-disclosure (Prager & Buhrmester, 1998). When both males and females think intimacy is an important relational goal in a friendship, they engage in more self-disclosure and elicit more self-disclosure from their friend (Sanderson, Rahm, Beigbeder, & Metts, 2005).

Of course, self-disclosure is not always a positive thing. Studies have shown that excessive self-disclosure, too much negative self-disclosure, and poorly timed self-disclosure do not lead to intimacy (Bochner, 1984; Parks, 1982; see also Chapter 5). For example, revealing a history of psychological counseling on a first date and always disclosing negative health information are ineffective ways to develop an intimate relationship.

However, research also has shown that well-developed intimate relationships often are a good place to disclose negative emotions. Once people develop a highly intimate relationship, they feel safe to disclose negative feelings and emotions (Metts & Bowers, 1994). This is somewhat paradoxical because in the early stages of a relationship people tend to be cheerful and positive and tend to put on their "best face" (Guerrero & Andersen, 2000). As Metts and Bowers (1994) argued, "Intimacy is, by definition, a state of openness and familiarity. It is the domain in which the prescription for positive emotion is suspended. In theory, a sign of intimacy is that individuals can feel and express negative emotion" (p. 535). Ironically, too much expressed negative emotion can lead to relational dissatisfaction and loss of intimacy, but some expression of negative emotion indicates that a relationship is open and comfortable (Guerrero & Andersen, 2000). Particularly damaging to relational intimacy are reciprocal spirals of negative disclosure of emotion. Relationships in which partners reciprocate the disclosure of emotions such as dissatisfaction, anger, jealousy, insecurity, and loneliness can damage a relationship. Gottman (1982) has shown that the ability to de-escalate negative affect is important to relational satisfaction.

Verbal Responsiveness

Verbal or conversational responsiveness, or **altercentrism** (as opposed to egocentrism), is an important part of intimacy. When people are altercentric, they listen carefully to their partner rather than focusing on their own thoughts and needs. The behavior of the listener is vital to the creation of intimacy. For example, intimacy is assisted when you know your partner is listening to you, understands your feelings, and perhaps empathizes with you (Egland et al., 1997). Responsiveness also validates the discloser's thoughts and feelings. Indeed, responsiveness may be what makes the process of disclosure so intimate.

As Prager (2000) argued, in an intimate interaction "the behavior of the listener/responder is as important as that of the discloser" (p. 233). In an intimate interaction, the listener should be attentive to what the partner has said, respond appropriately and acceptingly, and show that she or he cares about the partner and her or his message.

Relationship Talk

People's communication about their feelings regarding the relationship is very important to the establishment of intimacy. Statements such as "I love you," "I value our friendship," "We always have a good time together," and "I hope our friendship never ends" are important symbols of relational intimacy (Andersen, 1998a; King & Sereno, 1984). Statements like these represent turning points that can lead to increased closeness and a more intimate relationship definition. But they can also frighten or intimidate a person who does not share that relationship definition or who is not ready for that level of intimacy. Direct statements about the relationship, such as telling people you like them, love them, value their friendship, or don't know what you would do without them are clear expressions of affection as well as intimacy (Andersen, 1998a; Floyd, 2006). Unlike nonverbal behavior and even the indirect use of language as forms of intimacy, directly conveying one's feelings verbally is clear and unambiguous. Similarly, talk about the future of the relationship can create perceptions of greater intimacy. For example, romantic partners might start making plans for the summer or talk about what they might name their future children. Such talk clearly implies a long-term commitment to the relationship, which reinforces intimacy. However, as with declarations of love or liking, talk about the future of the relationship can scare partners away if they do not share the same level of commitment.

Relational Language

Relational language, or **verbal immediacy**, is a function of several stylistic features of language used in close relationships (see Andersen, 1998a).

Inclusive pronouns ("we" as opposed to "you and I") are perceived by interactants as indicating more relational intimacy (Weiner & Mehrabian, 1968). Prager (1995) suggested that more immediate pronoun use ("this" and "these" vs. "that" and "those"), adverb use ("here" vs. "there"), and verb tense (present vs. past), as well as the use of the active voice as opposed to the passive voice, all contribute to greater verbal immediacy and relational intimacy. Bradac, Bowers, and Courtwright (1979) maintained that verbal immediacy builds positive relationships even as positive relationships lead to more verbal immediacy.

Casual forms of address ("Pat" as opposed to "Dr. Knight") also imply a more intimate relationship (King & Sereno, 1984), as do nicknames (Bell, Buerkel-Rothfuss, & Gore, 1987; Hopper et al., 1981). Using inappropriately informal names or disliked nicknames, however, is not a way to establish a positive intimate relationship. For example, calling your boss "Bud" when he prefers "Mr. Johnson" or calling your date by a derogatory nickname such as "big butt" or "booger" is not an effective way to build a strong relationship. Personal idioms, in contrast, can be a way to express intimacy and closeness in a relationship. Special greetings, secret nicknames, sexual euphemisms, mild teases, and unique labels for the relationship often are a source of intimacy (Bell et al., 1987; Hopper et al., 1981). Of course, the use of some of these terms in a public setting may be a source of embarrassment and cause a loss of relational intimacy.

The language partners use to refer to each other suggests a certain public, relational image that is an index of the intimacy between them. For example, cohabitators may describe themselves along a continuum that includes roommate, friend, boyfriend/girlfriend, and partner—which signals increasing levels of relational intimacy. Similarly, when you refer to someone as your "best friend" in public, this label sends a strong message of intimacy. The first time Kevin publicly referred to Jennifer as his "girlfriend" in public represented a turning point in their relationship. The intimacy level of the relationship is clear to both Jennifer and others, suggesting that Kevin and Jennifer are a "pair," have a special bond, and are dating each other exclusively.

COMFORT AND SOCIAL SUPPORT

Another important way in which people communicate intimacy and affection is by showing that they are there for relational partners in times of distress. As discussed in Chapter 9, making sacrifices for one another and providing social support are key ways of increasing intimacy and maintaining relationships. When people have the intention of establishing intimacy with a friend, they both give and receive more social support from that friend (Sanderson et al., 2005). People feel distress in reaction to a wide variety of situations. In S. M. Jones's (2000) study of distressing events among college students, the following were most frequently described as distressing: problems in a romantic relationship, college performance (grades), friend/roommate problems, family problems, work-related stress, family illness, death, and personal illness/injury.

Indirect Ways of Communicating Comfort and Social Support

Floyd (2006) has labeled social support as an indirect but powerful means of communicating affection. Verbal behaviors, such as saying "I care about you," are direct expressions of affection. Floyd also argues that many nonverbal behaviors, such as giving someone a hug, are direct expressions of affection because they are commonly interpreted as affectionate. In contrast, many forms of social support are indirect expressions of affection because they *imply* that a person feels affection for someone. To illustrate this, Guerrero and Floyd (2006) gave the following example of providing social support to a new mother: "The relatives and friends of the young mother might . . . show their affection by offering to babysit, bringing her meals, taking care of her yardwork, and sending her money to help with her financial needs" (p. 93). Although these types of actions would not directly communicate affection, they would let the young mother know that she was loved and cared for. These types of socially supportive behaviors send especially strong messages of affection even though they are indirect; they also tend to be used more commonly than direct messages in certain types of relationships, such as those between fathers and sons or male friends (Morman & Floyd, 1999). Thus you probably wouldn't be surprised to see Kevin (who is a math whiz) helping Dan with his calculus homework, but you probably would be surprised if you heard Kevin tell Dan "I love you" and then embrace him with a big hug.

Nonverbal Ways of Communicating Comfort and Social Support

Of course, many direct nonverbal behaviors communicate both affection and comfort. Although friends such as Dan and Kevin may not show much nonverbal affection to each other during their everyday interactions, during times of distress they would probably feel freer to comfort each other using behaviors such as hugs or pats on the arm. Dolin and Booth-Butterfield (1993) investigated nonverbal behaviors related to comforting by asking students how they would react nonverbally if their roommate was distressed because of a recent relational breakup. The students reported that they would use the following behaviors most frequently:

- *Hugs* (reported in 41.9% of the accounts): giving the person a whole-body hug or hugging him or her around the shoulder
- *Close proxemic distancing* (40.9%): sitting down next to the person or leaning closer
- *Facial expression* (38.7%): looking empathetic, sad, or concerned
- *Attentiveness* (37.7%): listening carefully and nodding as the person talked about the distressing event
- *Increased miscellaneous touch* (34.4%): using all forms of touch other than hugs or pats, such as holding the person's hand or stroking his or her hair
- *Pats* (26.9%): using short, repetitive movements such as patting the distressed person's arm or shoulder
- *Eye contact* (23.7%): looking directly at the distressed person, particularly while he or she is talking

In addition to these behaviors, Dolin and Booth-Butterfield (1993) found a few other nonverbal comforting strategies that were reported less often. Some students described behaviors related to weeping, such as crying with the distressed person or offering a "shoulder to cry on." Some said that they would engage in emotional distancing behavior, such as trying to remain uninvolved, getting comfortable, or fixing a cup of coffee. Presumably, these strategies would keep the individual from experiencing too negative affect while talking to the distressed person. Other students reported that they would engage in instrumental activities, such as getting the distressed person a tissue or something to eat. Still others indicated that they would show concern through warm vocal tones and empathetic gestures. For example, if the distressed person was angry, the individual in the comforting role might clench her or his fist to mirror the distressed person's anger.

Verbal Ways of Communicating Comfort and Social Support

Verbal strategies are important in the comforting process. In particular, messages that are person centered seem to help people alleviate emotional distress (Applegate, 1980; Burleson, 1982, 2003). **Person-centered messages** acknowledge, elaborate on, and validate the feelings and concerns of the distressed person. Comforting messages can be ranked as high or low in quality based on how person-centered they are (Applegate, 1990; Burleson, 1982, 1984; S. M. Jones, 2000). Highly person-centered messages help the distressed person gain a perspective on her or his feelings by placing them in a broader context. These messages also legitimize the distressed person's feelings. Suppose that Dan gets a C in his calculus exam even though he studied diligently. If Kevin used a highly person-centered message, he might say something like

> It sure must be frustrating to study hard for a test and then get a C. In fact, that really surprises me because you are smart. Don't you think you'll do better in the next test now that you know the type of questions your professor asks?

Notice that the highly person-centered response conveys understanding ("It sure must be frustrating") and support ("You are smart") while also helping the distressed person to think about the event in a different way (perhaps as a learning experience).

Moderately person-centered messages acknowledge the distressed person's feelings, but they do not help the distressed person contextualize or elaborate on her or his feelings as well as do highly person-centered messages. For example, Kevin might tell Dan, "I'll bet the test was really hard, and I'll bet most people got Cs or worse, so you shouldn't feel that bad." Or he might say, "It's only one test. You'll do better in the next one. Let's go see a good movie—that will help get your mind off this." Note that these messages provide neat, easy explanations and solutions that do not allow for much elaboration. These types of messages, which are frequently used by people in the comforter's role, provide comfort that is okay but not great.

Finally, messages that are low in person centeredness (sometimes called position-centered messages) implicitly or explicitly deny the legitimacy of the distressed person's feelings, sometimes by blaming the distressed person for the situation and other times by changing the topic or the focus. For example, Kevin might tell Dan, "It's only one test. You shouldn't make such a big deal out of it." Worse yet, he might say, "I'm sure some people got As, so you really don't have anyone to blame but yourself. I helped you as much as I could, but I guess calculus is just too hard for you to understand." Or Kevin might also start talking about himself: "I got a C in a test once too. It was a real bummer, but that's life. Hey, do you want to get some lunch or something?"

As you might suspect, several studies have shown that people who use highly person-centered messages provide the best comfort and are perceived the most positively (Burleson & Samter, 1985a, 1985b; Jones & Burleson, 1997; Jones & Guerrero, 2001). Highly person-centered messages are perceived as the most appropriate, effective, helpful, and sensitive. These messages are likely to be effective in expressing care and concern, but perhaps more important, they might help the distressed person reevaluate the situation so that the event seems less distressing (Burleson & Goldsmith, 1998; S. M. Jones, 2000).

Of course, when comforting someone, it is important to use both verbal and nonverbal strategies. Jones and Guerrero (2001) investigated whether both nonverbal intimacy behaviors and verbal person centeredness influenced the quality of comforting behavior. They trained people to enact high, moderate, and low levels of nonverbal intimacy and person centeredness and then had them listen and react to people's distressing stories. They found that both nonverbal intimacy behaviors and person centeredness had strong effects on comforting quality. When distressed people interacted with someone who used high levels of nonverbal intimacy and high levels of person centeredness, they reported feeling the best. When high person-centered messages were paired with low levels of nonverbal intimacy or, conversely, when low person-centered messages were paired with high levels of nonverbal intimacy, the overall comforting quality decreased. Not surprisingly, comforters who used low levels of both nonverbal intimacy and person centeredness were the least effective at alleviating distress. Recent studies have confirmed the importance of nonverbal intimacy and immediacy in high-quality, successful comforting (Jones, 2004; Jones & Burleson, 2003).

Thus if you want to do a good job of comforting someone, you should pay attention to both your verbal and your nonverbal behaviors. It is also important to let the distressed person talk rather than changing the topic or focusing the discussion on yourself. When people can freely disclose their distressing circumstances to others, it helps them vent their negative emotion and possibly think through and reassess the problem, which can contribute to psychological and physical well-being (Burleson & Goldsmith, 1998; Pennebaker, 1989; Pennebaker, Colder, & Sharp, 1990).

THEORIES AND MODELS OF INTIMATE INTERACTION

To truly understand how intimacy functions in close relationships, it is important to consider how partners initiate and respond to intimate behavior. Next, we focus on two theories that explain how intimacy is exchanged between two people: (1) the intimacy process model and (2) cognitive valence theory. Both these theories provide snapshots of the intimacy development process. That is, they freeze the interaction at a given stage, often referring to "Person A" and "Person B" in an effort to analyze the complex processes that occur during intimacy development. In actual communication, two interactants play both roles during the interactions, so keep this limitation in mind as you read about each of the theories.

The Intimacy Process Model

One model of the process of intimate transactions is Reis and Shaver's (1988) **intimacy process model**, shown in Figure 8.2. In this model, Person A is the individual who discloses intimate information or engages in intimate behavior, and Person B is the individual who receives and responds to the increased intimacy. To help illustrate the five components of this model, we will use best friends Jennifer and Kevin as an example, with Jennifer as Person A and Kevin as Person B.

The Motives, Fears, and Goals of Person A. Research has shown that two forces are independently related to how much intimacy behavior people show: approach and avoidance (Mehrabian & Ksionzky, 1974). It is perfectly possible to simultaneously feel *both* a strong motivation to increase intimacy (approach) and a need to avoid increased intimacy (Reis & Shaver, 1988). For example, at the beginning stages of their relationship, Jennifer may have felt attracted to Kevin but still feared the commitment and involvement that a close relationship could entail.

Verbal Disclosure or Emotional Expression by Person A. Although Jennifer has a mixture of motives, needs, goals, and fears, she begins the process of engaging in verbal disclosure and nonverbal involvement with Kevin. Early in their relationship, these intimacy behaviors are not entirely intentional, but they nonetheless begin the process of intimacy development. Particularly important is the disclosure of personal desires, fantasies, anxieties, and emotions rather then merely facts (Reis & Shaver, 1988). Such verbal disclosures and nonverbal expressions of emotion or social attraction are valuable because they get the intimacy process going and give Kevin a chance to validate and accept these emotions or expressions.

The Motives and Interpretive Filter of Person B. As they were getting acquainted, Kevin was in a position to respond to Jennifer's increase in intimacy, probably with a similar mixture of positive and negative emotions. Kevin was attracted to Jennifer but worried that a new relationship could disrupt his current circle of friends and interfere with his personal commitments to school and other activities. Kevin may also have worried about Jennifer rejecting him or about losing his independence. The list of possible negative emotions and concerns about starting a new relationship is virtually endless (Reis & Shaver, 1988). Kevin also has a set of personality and situational filters through which he interprets Jennifer's behavior. Expectations and schemata actively influence the perceptions and evaluations of the other person's behavior (see also Chapter 3).

Person B's Responses to Person A's Expression of Intimacy. According to Reis and Shaver's (1988) model, Kevin's response to Jennifer's behavior is as important as Jennifer's behavior itself. Appropriate and accepting responses enhance feelings of connectedness, whereas nonresponses or negative responses serve to maintain the distance between the interactants and thwart the intimacy development process. Thus intimacy involves two people. Kevin has the power to work with Jennifer to develop a close relationship, but he also has the ability to prevent the relationship from developing.

Person A's Interpretive Filter and Reactions to Person B's Response. Although researchers could objectively describe Kevin's response as accepting or rejecting, in real interactions the outcomes are never so simple (Reis & Shaver, 1988). Kevin's reaction passes through Jennifer's interpretive filter, including Jennifer's perception of whether Kevin valued her communication and was authentic in his response, as well as whether Jennifer has a general predisposition to see intimacy in others' behavior. Jennifer's reaction is crucial. If Jennifer responds positively to Kevin, then a cycle of intimacy has started. Of course, it may or may not be sustained through subsequent interactions. The final step of

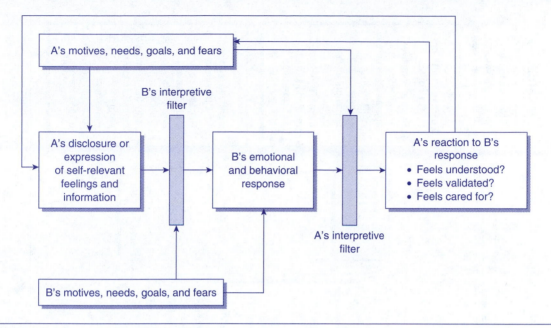

Figure 8.2   Intimacy Process Model

SOURCE: From Reis, H. T., & Shaver, P., "Intimacy as an Interpersonal Process." In Steve Duck (ed.), *Handbook of Personal Relationships,* copyright by John Wiley & Sons Limited. Reproduced with permission.

this model reinforces the idea that intimacy is created through a series of moves and countermoves and that the perceptions and interpretations of these moves are as important as the moves themselves.

Cognitive Valence Theory

Cognitive valence theory (CVT) focuses on explaining the intimacy process by combining verbal and nonverbal intimacy behaviors, interpersonal perception, physiological arousal, social cognition, and relational outcomes in a single unified theory (Andersen, 1985, 1989, 1998a). CVT is depicted in Figure 8.3. As with the intimacy process model, CVT emphasizes how people respond to increases in intimacy behavior. We will illustrate the components of the theory using Dan and Kevin as an example.

Behavior. All intimate relationships begin with one person increasing intimacy via nonverbal or verbal communication (see the Behavior column in Figure 8.3). As Andersen (1998a) explained, "Relationships do not occur in the absence of human contact. They begin, develop, thrive and disengage as communicative acts" (p. 40). Thus, Dan would try to develop a closer friendship with Kevin by increasing the intimacy level of an interaction through verbal or nonverbal communication. As noted previously, Dan would have a variety of verbal behaviors at his disposal, including self-disclosure, personal forms of address, and expressions of relational closeness, such as telling Kevin that he respects his athletic performance and is glad they are teammates. Usually, nonverbal communication plays a big role in the initiation of intimacy, so Dan also might engage in behaviors like smiling, making eye contact, touching, or hanging out with Kevin. CVT holds that all intimate relationships begin with the initiation of immediate or intimate communication behaviors by one or both people in a potential relationship.

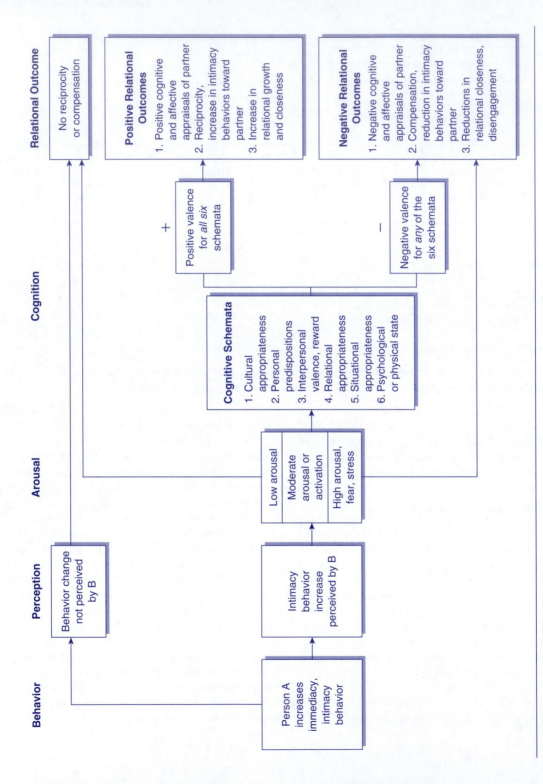

Figure 8.3 Cognitive Valence Theory

Perception. Such behaviors by themselves do not increase intimacy; behaviors must be noticed by one's partner (see the Perception column in Figure 8.3). According to Andersen (1989), "the expression of intimacy by one person has no communicative significance if it is not perceived by one's relational partner" (p. 8). Such perceptions do not need to be conscious, but they must register in the mind of the receiver. Words spoken to no ear and smiles perceived by no eye do not communicate and have no chance of increasing intimacy. So, Dan might smile and comment to Kevin that he enjoys being teammates. But if Kevin has his mind on something else, Dan's attempt to increase intimacy will fail.

Arousal. If Kevin notices Dan's intimacy behavior, he will respond physiologically and possibly cognitively and behaviorally. Nonverbal intimacy behaviors are stimulating and increase physiological arousal (see the Arousal column in Figure 8.3). In his summary of 24 studies on the relationship between immediacy behaviors and arousal, Andersen (1985) concluded that "the research generally supports a positive relationship between immediacy and increases in arousal" (p. 15). Increases in multichanneled immediacy behavior, such as more eye contact, smiles, and touch, increase physiological arousal (Andersen et al., 1998). Sometimes arousal change is accompanied by positive emotions and at other times by negative emotions. Take Kevin and Dan as an example. If Dan hugs Kevin after he scores a goal during a soccer game, Kevin might feel heightened arousal, joy, and pride because Dan's gesture affirms that he is highly valued as both a friend and a teammate. On the other hand, Kevin might experience a high level of arousal if he is embarrassed by Dan showing him high levels of intimacy in public, especially since heterosexual men are often homophobic and regard such displays of intimacy as unmasculine (Floyd, 2006).

Many studies have shown that rapid arousal increases are aversive and frightening (see Andersen, 1999, for a summary). For example, if a threatening-looking stranger stares at you with a menacing facial expression, you will likely experience very high arousal and look to flee. As a consequence, CVT predicts that negative relational outcomes will occur when arousal levels are very high. In contrast, if your best friend says "Hi!" to you on the way to class, no arousal will occur because this behavior is highly routine and represents no real increase in intimacy. The most interesting reactions occur in relation to moderate increases in intimacy. For example, when an attractive person in class smiles at you or when your friend discloses important information, moderate arousal occurs. Moderate arousal has been shown to stimulate cognitive processes, which in turn produce your reaction to your partner.

Cognition. For the sake of our example, let's imagine that Dan's friendly behavior leads Kevin to experience a moderate cognitive arousal increase. If this is the case, CVT predicts that Kevin's response to Dan's behavior will be contingent on how he cognitively appraises the situation. Specifically, CVT suggests that Kevin will employ knowledge structures called cognitive schemata to make sense of Dan's change in behavior. When this sense making leads people to perceive the change in intimacy as positive, the behavior is positively valenced. In contrast, when people interpret the change in intimacy negatively, the behavior is negatively valenced. Figure 8.3 shows six of the most commonly studied cognitive schemata (see Andersen, 1993, 1998a, 1999, for a detailed discussion of these schemata); the following list outlines the key features of each:

1. *Culture*: Andersen (1999) argued that "culture is such a basic and invisible force it is often confused with human nature itself" (p. 231). We determine if something is appropriate in our culture, and that gives us a basis for reacting to it. For instance, kissing the wife of a friend goodbye would often be appropriate in the United States but not in Arab countries. If a behavior is appropriate, it can be positively valenced; if the behavior is culturally inappropriate, it will be negatively valenced. Within U.S. culture, Dan's smile and self-disclosure would probably be perceived as appropriate and so would be positively valenced. However, if Dan's self-disclosure was too intimate for a male in U.S. culture, it could be valenced negatively.

2. *Personality*: Our personal predispositions make up our personality. People differ in their sociability, extroversion, and attitudes toward touch and the degree to which they approach or avoid new experiences or sensations (see Andersen, 1993, 1998a). A hug or an intimate disclosure may be appreciated by one person but not by another. Thus, people will valence the same behavior differently based on their personality. If Kevin is an outgoing, friendly person, he might welcome Dan's self-disclosure. However, if Kevin is shy and introverted, he might be nervous and uncomfortable hearing something personal about Dan. In the former case, Kevin would likely react positively to Dan's self-disclosure; in the latter, he would likely react negatively.

3. *Rewardingness*: The degree to which we find someone rewarding influences how we react to their increases in intimacy behavior. Rewardingness, which is also called interpersonal valence, refers to the degree to which we find someone attractive. Recall from Chapter 3 that people can be attractive based on physical attributes (such as how beautiful they are or what clothes they wear), social qualities (such as how friendly they are), and instrumental qualities (such as how good they are at performing certain tasks). In general, people who are physically attractive, have high social standing, possess positive personality traits, and are similar to us are highly rewarding. Thus, we react differently to changes in immediacy on the basis of who our partner is. Andersen (1993) noted that "positive perceptions of another person's values, background, physical appearance and communication style are the primary reasons why we initiate and maintain close relationships" (p. 25). For example, a touch from someone you dislike is judged very differently from a touch from your highly attractive date. Similarly, if Kevin likes Dan and thinks he is good buddy, he is likely to react positively when Dan increases intimacy. In contrast, if Kevin thinks Dan is a pest who is no fun to be around or has negative qualities like abrasiveness, he is likely to react negatively.

4. *The relationship*: The most important valencer of a person's intimate behavior is one's relationship (see Andersen, 1998a, 1999). People are able to easily classify their relationships with others as friend, coworker, best friend, lover, fiancée, parent, boss, roommate, and so on. Thus, too much touch or self-disclosure on a first date is usually a turnoff, yet the same amount of touch or self-disclosure from a fiancée would be warmly accepted. In the right relationship, almost any immediate behavior will be valenced positively. In the wrong relationship, such intimacy will be negatively valenced and cause negative relational outcomes. If Kevin and Dan have been close friends for years, Kevin will probably be open to a high level of intimate self-disclosure. But if Kevin does not know Dan at all and Dan suddenly starts disclosing information to him, Kevin will react negatively.

5. *The situation*: The situation or the context in which intimacy behavior occurs is vital to the relational outcome (Andersen, 1993). Intimacy in the classroom, boardroom, bathroom, and bedroom produces distinctly different reactions. Some settings, such as living rooms, jacuzzis, and hotel rooms, are highly conducive to intimacy. Some situations are highly formal, and intimacy would be limited to handshakes or polite smiles. Passionately kissing your date goodnight in a private place has entirely different connotations from engaging in the same behavior in front of your parents. The bottom line is this: "Intimacy must be situationally appropriate." If Dan increases intimacy with Kevin during a private conversation, his self-disclosure is likely to be regarded positively. But if he increases intimacy while Kevin is in the middle of an important conversation with Jennifer, his self-disclosure is likely to be regarded negatively.

6. *Temporary states*: Everyone has bad days and good days—intellectually, emotionally, and physically. Temporary states are short-term internal conditions that make individuals feel and react differently at various times (Andersen, 1993). Many things affect a person's temporary state or mood, including having a fight with the boss, being criticized (or complimented) by a friend, getting a bad night's sleep, partying too much, and receiving a pay raise. A classic example of negative-state valencing is a person's response to an affectionate spouse: "Not tonight, dear, I have a

headache." Negative physical or emotional states generally lead to negative valencing of intimate behavior, whereas positive states generally lead to positive valencing. Thus, Kevin is more likely to react positively to Dan's increase in intimacy if he is alert, feeling well, and in a good mood.

Relational Outcomes. Earlier, we noted that relationships are fragile and that few relationships reach intimacy. CVT provides one explanation for why this is so. Negative valencing for *any* of the six cognitive schemata can result in negative relational outcomes. When intimacy increases are valenced negatively, a host of negative outcomes follow, including appraising one's partner negatively, reducing intimacy behaviorally (perhaps by moving away), and perhaps even disengaging from the relationship. Positive valencing of the intimacy behavior, in contrast, results in more positive appraisals of one's partner, reciprocity of intimacy behaviors, and greater relational closeness and intimacy. Thus increasing intimacy behavior is not without risk, but the benefits can outweigh the potential costs if a more enjoyable, close relationship is desired. Dan's initial attempt to become friends with Kevin might result in rejection, but Dan could also end up developing a rewarding relationship with a new friend.

SEX DIFFERENCES IN INTIMACY AND AFFECTION

Sex differences can seem large when a man and a woman manifest dissimilarities. Yet it should not be presumed that men and women are completely different. Rather, men and women may achieve intimacy in somewhat different ways, but an important point of the research on intimacy is that men and women are far more similar than different in how they achieve intimacy in both same-sex and opposite-sex relationships.

Sex Differences in Relational Importance

Intimate relationships are extremely important to both men and women. However, a considerable body of literature suggests that relationships may be somewhat more important to women than to men. The landmark study of couples in the United States by Blumstein and Schwartz (1983) revealed that women are the primary keepers of the relationship. This means that women are more likely to do relational work such as performing relational maintenance behaviors and initiating discussion of relationship issues. In addition, men are less monogamous and are likely to have more sexual partners than women. Comparisons of heterosexual couples with gay male and lesbian couples confirm this fact by revealing that lesbians are the most loyal, heterosexuals are in the middle, and gay men are the least relationally loyal. In sum, men are more likely to "search for variety while women prefer a special relationship" (Blumstein & Schwartz, 1983, p. 279). In general, women are the keepers of fidelity and the protectors of the relationship (Blumstein & Schwartz, 1983). Women also cultivate more numerous and deeper relationships than do men. According to Verhoff, Young, and Coon (1993), "women more than men rely on and invest in relationships in addition to marriage for defining themselves" (p. 449). Perhaps this is due to a combination of the biological predisposition of women to bear, nurse, and nurture children (Andersen, 1998b, 2006) and the fact that men are socialized into task relationships and away from purely interpersonal ones.

Sex Differences in the Development of Intimacy

Certainly, both men and women have the potential to develop highly intimate relationships. Despite popular literature suggesting that men and women are from different planets, research has shown that men and women are far more similar than different. As noted in Chapter 9, according to Dindia, a more apt metaphor than "men are from Mars, women are from Venus" is "men are from North Dakota, women are from South Dakota" (Wood & Dindia, 1998). Even in the area of relational intimacy, men and women are far more similar than different. Males and females overwhelmingly believe that emotional communication is more important in the development of intimacy than are instrumental or task-oriented skills (Burleson, Kunkel, Samter, &

Werking, 1996). Perhaps surprisingly, this appears to be true in male-male relationships as well as male-female and female-female relationships. As Burleson et al. (1996) discovered, "Affectively oriented communication skills appear to be important for both genders in the conduct of intimacy—regardless of whether intimacy is realized in same-sex friendship or opposite-sex romances" (p. 218). Some studies have shown no difference in intimacy levels for men and women. A study of intimacy in married Canadian couples showed almost identical intimacy levels for males and females for all types of intimacy (McCabe, 1999).

Despite the considerable similarity in intimacy levels between males and females, some literature has reported that females are more intimate than males. For example, one study noted that girls have more intimate relationships than boys (Meurling, Ray, & LoBello, 1999). Others claimed that girls show more trust and loyalty, more dependence on friends, and a greater tendency to discuss their relationships with friends (Muerling et al., 1999; Sharabany, Gershoni, & Hoffman, 1981). Similarly, Floyd (in press) reports a series of studies that show that, in general, women express more affection than men in same-sex dyads but in opposite-sex dyads men increase their level of affection to nearly the same as women. Girls also are more understanding with their friends, offer more benefits to their friends, and are generally perceived as more rewarding to friends than are boys. But boys' friendships are more extensive than girls' friendships and often incorporate large play groups and playground activities and games rather than the closer, more intimate dyadic and small-group relationships that characterize girls.

The finding that females have more intimate relationships than do males may be due to the fact that researchers have employed a "feminine" definition of intimacy. Most of the data on the differences in intimacy between men and women come from research claiming that in the United States women disclose more than men (Floyd, 1995). But disclosure is only one type of intimacy. Parks and Floyd (1996) pointed out that for decades, scholars have thought of intimate relationships as emotional, feminine, and affectionate rather than instrumental, masculine, and logical. Because men's relationships are somewhat lower in emotional expression and self-disclosure, men were thought not to have very intimate relationships. However, there is little actual evidence for a sharp difference in male and female intimacy. Parks and Floyd (1996) found no support for the hypothesis that women are more likely than men to label their relationships as intimate.

Men may have somewhat different ways of communicating intimacy than women. Sharing adventures, telling stories, doing physical labor, working on a joint project, taking a fishing trip, serving in the army are all intimate experiences in their own way. We are not saying that women do not engage in these activities—they do, just not quite as often as men. Floyd (1995) suggested that men's intimacy primarily comes from shared interests and activities. These action-oriented behaviors may be just as valid a path to high levels of intimacy as self-disclosure or emotional expression. Research has found that males find intimacy in recreational activities such as playing or watching sports and by engaging in projects and task-related activities. Floyd (1995) found that among college students, males are more likely than females to create intimacy through shaking hands, drinking together, and talking about sex. Women, in contrast, are most likely to experience intimacy by sharing time, using expressive nonverbal and verbal communication during conversations, expressing liking or love for one another, hugging, discussing personal problems, talking about fears, and shopping (Floyd, 1995; Helgeson, Shaver, & Dyer, 1987; Monsour, 1992).

SUMMARY AND APPLICATION

As this chapter has emphasized, people communicate intimacy in a number of different ways. Kevin is very close to both Jennifer and Dan, but intimacy is communicated very differently in his two closest relationships. Kevin's relationship with Jennifer emphasizes deep conversations, lots of time spent together, long eye contact, and romantic touch as manifestations of intimacy. Kevin's relationship with Dan communicates intimacy in different ways, through playing ball and skiing, through debates about political issues and discussions about their careers, and through sharing a ball game and some refreshments on a Sunday afternoon.

To develop intimacy with Jennifer it is essential that Kevin do things that men sometimes forget to do, to listen during conversations and look at Jennifer when she is talking.

Real connection is impossible without communication, and communication requires both a sender and a receiver. If Kevin and Jennifer really tune into each other's nonverbal behavior, intimacy is far easier to achieve.

Real intimacy also means sharing activities. Kevin, like many men, thinks intimacy means sharing activity. Jennifer should remember to share in Kevin's activities, at least some of them, such as skiing or watching a ball game. She may need to try some activities that Kevin likes even though she has never attempted them herself. The same goes for Kevin and Dan. It is almost impossible to establish intimacy with someone who fails to share in the activities about which you are most passionate.

Kevin needs to be there for his closest friends even when Jennifer and Dan go through hard times. And they need to support Kevin as well. Kevin and Jennifer should avoid criticizing each other, avoid trying to "fix" each other, and avoid unsolicited evaluations. People like acceptance, not criticism, so keep judgments to a minimum, especially when comforting your partner.

Kevin and Jennifer need to talk about their relationship. As intimacy increases, it may be important for Kevin and Jennifer to define where they are in their relationship. Saying "I love you," giving rings, and planning a future together are important turning points. They should avoid making such moves too early in the relationship as they may scare their partner off, but they should not put off relational communication indefinitely.

In both his relationships, Kevin should remember to balance negative emotions and disclosure with positivity. Relationships are a safe haven where Kevin can reveal the negative side of his life to Jennifer and Dan, but negativity must be balanced with positivity, or an intimate friend might view you and the relationship in mostly negative terms. When Dan or Jennifer shares negative, distressing events with Kevin, he should respond with nonverbal intimacy behaviors and highly person-centered messages if he wants to provide high-quality comfort.

As the theories presented in this chapter suggest, intimacy is created by two people through a series of moves and countermoves. Kevin alone cannot create an intimate interaction: "It takes two to tango." It is also important to remember that intimate interaction occurs within a larger context. As cognitive valence theory predicts, Kevin needs to understand that factors such as Dan's or Jennifer's cultural background, the context or situation of their interaction, Dan's and Jennifer's temporary moods and states, their personalities, their level of rewardingness, and, of course, the stage of the relationship can all influence whether intimate communication is accepted or rejected. We hope that this chapter, as well as the chapters on relationship development and maintenance, will help you improve your intimate communication so that your attempts to develop new and closer relationships are more effective.

DISCUSSION QUESTIONS

1. Think about the five most intimate moments you have ever shared with others. What communication qualities made these moments special?

2. Which of the theories presented in this chapter do you think best captures the process of intimate interaction? What aspects of the intimacy process model and cognitive valence theory did you most like or dislike?

3. If you want to give friends and loved ones effective social support, what should you say and do? What might you avoid saying or doing?

9

STAYING CLOSE

Maintaining Intimate Relationships

After 3 years of serious dating, Michael proposes to Rachel, and she accepts. Although she is excited about the prospect of marrying Michael, she starts to worry that getting married could change things. When she was in middle school, her parents divorced after several years of bitter fighting. To add fuel to her worries, a good friend of hers recently announced that she and her husband were separating after only 2 years of marriage. Sometimes, it seems to Rachel that everyone is getting a divorce. Michael assures her that things will be different for them. After all, they love each other and have a great relationship. And Michael's parents have been happily married for nearly 30 years, so he has seen how two people can work together to maintain a successful relationship. Rachel wonders what their secret is. How do Michael's parents manage to keep their relationship so happy, and can she and Michael do the same?

In fairy tales, everyone lives "happily ever after," as if happiness was bestowed on them magically. In real life, however, there is no magic recipe for a happy relationship. So what can couples like Rachel and Michael do to keep their relationships happy? How might getting married change their relationship? Maintaining relationships requires effort and perseverance. The road to a successful relationship often contains rough spots and detours, but "staying on course" and maintaining important relationships is a worthwhile endeavor. In fact, research has shown that having a close relationship is a key determinant of overall happiness (Hatfield, 1984). People who have trouble maintaining close relationships with others are often lonely and depressed, and they may even doubt their self-worth (Segrin, 1998). Married people tend to report being happier and more satisfied with

their lives than do single people (Cargan & Melko, 1982); yet around half of first marriages in the United States end in divorce (Phillips, 1988; Teachman, 2000). Moreover, studies consistently show that marital satisfaction drops after parenthood, providing another maintenance challenge (Twenge, Campbell, & Foster, 2003). Given these facts, Rachel's concerns are certainly understandable.

The research on relational maintenance provides important information on behaviors that couples like Michael and Rachel can use to promote relational satisfaction and longevity. In this chapter, we look at three areas of research related to maintenance. First, we discuss specific types of behaviors people use to maintain a variety of close relationships, including those between romantic partners and those between friends. Second, we look at barriers to relational dissolution. Finally, we focus on dialectics theory, which describes how people cope with common relational tensions, such as the struggle between desiring intimacy while also wanting independence.

DEFINING RELATIONAL MAINTENANCE

People maintain things. They take their cars in for routine maintenance service and repair mechanical problems when they occur. They maintain their homes by keeping them clean, mowing the lawn, trimming the hedges, painting the walls, and so forth. They maintain their good images at work by trying to be punctual, professional, presentable, and well organized. Similarly, people usually try to maintain their relationships with others through contact and communication.

Maintaining a relationship is far more challenging than maintaining a car or a home. **Relational maintenance** has been defined in various ways. According to Dindia and Canary (1993), there are four common definitions. First, *relational maintenance involves keeping a relationship in existence.* Think of all the people to whom you send holiday cards once a year. Although you might not have much, if any, contact with many of these people over the course of a given year, the exchange of greeting cards helps you maintain your relationships with them.

Second, *relational maintenance involves keeping a relationship in a specified state or condition, or at a stable level of intimacy, so that the status quo is maintained* (Ayres, 1983). For example, friends might work to keep their relationship from becoming romantic, or sisters might try to keep their relationship as close as ever despite moving to different cities. Third, *relational maintenance involves keeping a relationship in satisfactory condition.* Dating and married couples often try to rekindle the romance in their relationships to keep them satisfying. Friends might plan a weekend ski trip together if they want to catch up with each other and have fun. Fourth, *relational maintenance involves keeping a relationship in repair.* The idea here is that the dyad works to prevent problems from occurring and correct problems when they do occur.

As Dindia and Canary (1993) stated, these four components of relational maintenance overlap. An important part of keeping a relationship satisfying is preventing and correcting problems, and an important part of keeping a relationship in existence is keeping it satisfying. In a broad sense, relational maintenance can be defined as *keeping a relationship at a desired level* (Canary & Stafford, 1994). Sometimes, this involves keeping a relationship from becoming too intimate; at other times, it involves keeping a relationship high in satisfaction and low in problems. Note that this definition does not necessarily mean that a relationship remains at the same level of intimacy over time. As people's desires change, the way they define and maintain their relationships also changes. Maintenance is a dynamic process that involves continually adjusting to new needs and demands.

BEHAVIORS USED TO MAINTAIN RELATIONSHIPS

Now that we have defined relational maintenance, you might be wondering *how* people maintain their relationships. Scholars began addressing this important question in the 1980s (Ayres, 1983; Bell, Daly, & Gonzalez, 1987; Dindia & Baxter, 1987; Duck, 1988; Shea & Pearson, 1986). Since then, much has been learned about behaviors people use to maintain various types of relationships.

Types of Maintenance Behaviors

Various researchers have come up with different lists of maintenance behaviors. Ayres (1983) focused on behaviors that function to keep a relationship at a given level of intimacy. He found three primary maintenance strategies: (1) **avoidance**, which involves avoiding talk or activities that might change the relationship; (2) **balance**, which involves reciprocating favors and emotional support levels; and (3) **directness**, which involves explicitly informing the person of a desire not to change the relationship. Dindia (1989) investigated maintenance strategies used by married couples. She found three general strategies: (1) **prosocial**, which refers to positive behaviors such as talking about the relationship and listening to each other; (2) **romantic**, which comprises behaviors that are affectionate, spontaneous, and fun, such as expressing affection nonverbally; and (3) **antisocial**, which includes behaviors that are coercive, such as trying to manipulate or control the partner.

Stafford and Canary (1991) asked dating and married couples what partners did to maintain their relationships and keep them satisfying. Five primary maintenance strategies emerged: positivity, openness, assurances, social networks, and task sharing. Research has found, however, that openness is not associated with maintaining a relationship (Stafford, 2003); so what people use as maintenance strategies may not actually maintain their relationships! Moreover, Canary and Stafford (Canary & Stafford, 1994; Canary, Stafford, Hause, & Wallace, 1993) later argued that these five behaviors may represent only *positive* strategies used by romantic couples. Thus they sought to develop a category system that would include *negative* behaviors (like Ayres's avoidance strategy and Dindia's antisocial strategy) and be applicable to other relationships, such as those between friends, family members, and coworkers. This led Canary and his colleagues (1993) to examine a number of additional strategies, including avoidance, antisocial behavior, supportiveness, joint activities, and mediated communication. Other researchers (e.g., Afifi, Guerrero, & Egland, 1994; Dainton & Stafford, 1993; Stafford, 2003) have also found that dating couples, married couples, and friends use these additional behaviors. A summary of the most common relational maintenance behaviors reported in the literature is found in Box 9.1. As this list clearly shows, people use a wide variety of routine and strategic behaviors to maintain their relationships, and communication plays an essential role in the maintenance process.

In addition to using the maintenance behaviors listed in Box 9.1, gay and lesbian couples use some unique strategies to maintain their relationships. In the first of two studies they conducted on maintenance behavior in gay male and lesbian relationships, Haas and Stafford (1998) found that partners in same-sex romantic relationships reported that it is important to live and work in environments that are supportive and not judgmental of their relationships. Similarly, gay and lesbian partners emphasized the importance of being "out" in front of their social networks. Spending time with friends and family members who recognize and accept their relationship was mentioned as a key relational maintenance behavior, as was being able to introduce each other as "my partner." Some gay and lesbian couples also reported modeling their parents' relationships. Gay and lesbian couples tend to see their relationships as similar to heterosexual relationships in terms of commitment and communication but dissimilar in terms of nonconformity to sex-role stereotypes. Finally, some people proposed that it would be helpful if gay and lesbian couples had the same legal rights as heterosexual couples.

In a second study, Haas and Stafford (2005) found that although same-sex romantic relationships were characterized by many of the same maintenance behaviors as opposite-sex marriages, there were subtle differences. Sharing tasks was the most commonly reported maintenance behavior for both types of relationships. However, gay and lesbian couples were more likely to report using maintenance behaviors that show bonding, such as talking about the commitment level in their relationships. Haas and Stafford argued that bonding communication may be more necessary in gay and lesbian relationships, because these relationships are not legally validated as marriages are.

Strategic and Routine Maintenance Behaviors

Maintenance behaviors can be distinguished on the basis of how strategic versus routine they are (Canary & Stafford, 1994; Dindia, 2003; Duck, 1986). **Strategic maintenance** involves behaviors that are intentionally designed to maintain your relationship. For example, if you have an argument with your best friend, you might call your friend with the intent of apologizing and repairing the situation. On Mother's Day, you might send your mom a bouquet of flowers so that she knows you are thinking of her. If you live far away from a loved one, you might call her or him twice a week at a designated time or send

BOX 9.1   Highlights

Maintenance Behaviors

Behavior	Definition and Examples
Openness and routine talk	Talking and listening to one another (e.g., self-disclosure, sharing secrets, asking how the partner's day went)
Positivity	Making interactions pleasant and enjoyable (e.g., giving compliments, acting cheerful)
Assurances	Giving each other assurances about commitment (e.g., assuring the other you still care, talking about the future)
Supportiveness	Giving each other social support and encouragement (e.g., providing comfort, making sacrifices for the partner)
Joint activities	Engaging in activities and spending time together (e.g., hanging out together, playing sports, or shopping together)
Task sharing	Performing routine tasks and chores relevant to the relationship together (e.g., sharing household chores, planning finances together)
Romance and affection	Revealing positive, caring feelings for each other (e.g., saying "I love you," sending flowers, having a romantic dinner)
Social networking	Spending time with each other's social network (e.g., going to family functions together, accepting each other's friends)
Mediated communication	Using cards, letters, phone calls, and technology (e.g., communicating via e-mail, sending photos)
Avoidance	Evading the partner in certain situations or on certain issues (e.g., planning separate activities, respecting each other's privacy)
Antisocial	Using behaviors that are coercive or unfriendly (e.g., making the partner feel jealous or guilty; crying or pouting to get attention)
Conflict management	Managing conflict in constructive ways that promote problem solving and harmony (e.g., listening to one another's positions, trying to come up with mutually acceptable solutions)
Humor	Using inside jokes, humor, and sarcasm (e.g., using funny nicknames, laughing together)
Balance	Keeping the relationship fair and equitable (e.g., putting similar levels of effort into the relationship, returning favors)

lots of e-mail to keep in touch. These types of actions are deliberate and intentionally designed to maintain a positive relationship with someone.

Routine behaviors are less strategic and deliberate. They are used without the express purpose of maintaining the relationship, yet they still help people preserve their bonds with one another. Behaviors such as task sharing and positivity are especially likely to be used routinely rather than strategically (Dainton & Aylor, 2002). For example, roommates might share household responsibilities as a routine or habit. One roommate might do grocery shopping, pay bills, and vacuum and dust the apartment, and the other might water the plants, clean the bathroom, and do the cooking. Similarly, Michael and Rachel might routinely engage in positivity by appearing happy when they first see each other at home after work and using polite communication, such as saying "thank you" when doing favors for one another. Duck (1994) argued that routine talk is at the heart of relational maintenance. Other researchers have demonstrated that routine maintenance is a somewhat better predictor of relational satisfaction and commitment than strategic maintenance (Dainton & Aylor, 2002). Thus, maintaining a relationship does not always require "work." Sometimes maintenance rests in seemingly trivial behaviors that people enact rather mindlessly on a day-to-day basis.

Of course, the line between strategic and routine maintenance behaviors is sometimes blurred. Additionally, many people cannot really tell if a given behavior is strategic or routine. Moreover, the same behavior can be strategic in some situations and routine in others. For example, holding your romantic partner's hand at the movie theater might be part of a habitual routine; you might always hold your partner's hand in this situation. After an argument, however, reaching for your partner's hand might be a strategic move designed to make things better by restoring intimacy to the relationship. Strategic maintenance behaviors may also be used when people try to prevent a relationship from becoming too intimate, escalate or de-escalate the level of intimacy in the relationship, or restore intimacy to or repair a relationship. Both routine and strategic behaviors can contribute to relational maintenance in terms of keeping the relationship close and satisfying.

Effects of Maintenance Behaviors

As you can see, people have a wide assortment of maintenance behaviors at their disposal. But how effective are these behaviors in maintaining relationships? There is no easy answer to this question. All relationships are different, and what works well for one relationship might be ineffective in another. However, research suggests that people in relationships characterized by high levels of maintenance tend to stay together longer and be more satisfied.

If relational partners use maintenance behaviors frequently, are they more likely to sustain their relationships? If they fail to use maintenance behaviors, will the relationship fall apart? A study by Guerrero, Eloy, and Wabnik (1993) addressed these questions by investigating whether prosocial maintenance strategies, such as positivity, assurances, openness, task sharing, and social networks, help predict whether a couple will stay together or break up. In this study, college-age daters were followed over an 8-week period. People who reported using more maintenance behaviors at the beginning of the study were more likely to have become more serious or stayed at the same intimacy level by the end of the 8 weeks. Those who reported using low levels of maintenance behavior were likely to have de-escalated or terminated their relationships by the end of the 8 weeks. This illustrates that high levels of maintenance behavior can help sustain relationships.

People who use high levels of maintenance behavior also appear to be more satisfied with their relationships. Vangelisti and Huston (1994) defined relational satisfaction as the "pleasure or enjoyment" that people derive from their relationships (p. 173). Positivity and assurances appear to have a particularly strong association with relational satisfaction (Dainton, Stafford, & Canary, 1994; Stafford & Canary, 1991). In one study, people reported being the most satisfied in their relationships when their partner used higher levels of positivity and assurances than they expected them to use (Dainton, 2000). In another study, couples who used high levels of positivity and assurances at the beginning of a year-long study were especially likely to be satisfied with their marriages at the end of the year (Weigel & Ballard-Reisch, 2001).

Positivity, which includes being cheerful and optimistic, and complimenting and encouraging the partner, is likely to enhance the atmosphere in the relationship. No one likes to be around someone who is always complaining and never has anything nice to say. People like to be around others who are usually fun and who make them feel good about themselves. Compliments and encouragement might even lead to higher levels of self-esteem, which could increase a person's satisfaction with herself or himself and with the relationship. Of course, no one can be cheerful and complimentary all the time. Everyone has bad moods and criticisms. The key is to make sure that pessimism and complaints are the exception, while optimism and praise are the rule (Gottman, 1994). Like positivity, assurances are likely to make a person feel good about herself or himself and the relationship. **Assurances** include behaviors such as telling people how much you love and care about them, and letting them know that you expect the relationship to be a lasting one. These types of assurances are likely to reduce uncertainty about the future of the relationship and thereby make people feel secure.

Several other maintenance behaviors are associated with relational satisfaction. These include joint activities, task sharing, and social networking. These maintenance behaviors all involve spending time together. The amount of time spouses and dating partners spend together is positively related to satisfaction, because time together creates feelings of companionship, and cohesion and opens lines of communication (Egland, Stelzner, Andersen, & Spitzberg, 1997; Reissman, Aron, & Bergen, 1993). Engaging in joint activities can promote feelings of togetherness and similarity. Likewise, when partners share tasks in a fair and equitable manner, they tend to feel closer and more satisfied with their relationships (Canary & Stafford, 1994; Guerrero et al., 1993). Social networking, which involves accepting and spending time with your partner's friends and family, appears to be especially important in marital and cohabiting relationships. In a yearlong study, married couples who reported engaging in high levels of social networking at the beginning of the year were more likely to be satisfied with their relationships at the end of the year (Weigel & Ballard-Reisch, 2001).

Important research by Vangelisti and Huston (1994) further demonstrated that maintenance behaviors such as social networking, joint activities, and task sharing are associated with relational satisfaction. In addition, this study showed that sexual compatibility, openness, and joint decision making are critical within marriage. Vangelisti and Huston examined data from a longitudinal study of newlyweds

over the first 2 years of their marriages. The newlyweds were contacted three times: after they had been married for 3 or fewer months and shortly after their first and second wedding anniversaries. Spouses generally became less satisfied over time, possibly due to unrealistic expectations at the beginning of their marriages. However, couples who were happy with certain areas of their married lives tended to be more generally satisfied with their relationships. For both husbands and wives, the areas of "communication" and "influence" were very important. Communication referred to how well spouses could talk to each other, while influence referred to the amount of input spouses had in making joint decisions. For wives, four other areas were related to satisfaction over the first 2½ years of their marriages: (1) sex, (2) fair division of labor, (3) time spent with the spouse, and (4) time spent with friends and family. These findings suggest that communication-related maintenance behaviors, such as being open and having a "voice" in the decision-making process, are strongly related to marital satisfaction. For wives, being sexually compatible, sharing tasks in an equitable manner, engaging in joint activities with their spouse, and social networking also appear to be particularly important.

MAINTENANCE BEHAVIOR IN VARIOUS TYPES OF RELATIONSHIPS

Although people generally use more maintenance behaviors in satisfying than unsatisfying relationships, some relationships require less maintenance behaviors than others. Furthermore, because relational maintenance involves keeping a relationship in a desired state, people use maintenance behaviors to accomplish different goals in various relationships. Maintenance behaviors reflect the type and degree of intimacy felt within a relationship at a given time. Therefore, you probably use different maintenance behaviors with friends than lovers, and with people you are extremely close to versus those whom you are just getting to know. You are also likely to use different maintenance behaviors at different stages in the same relationship because of your changing needs and goals. Most of the research on relationship-type differences in maintenance behavior has concentrated on romantic relationships and friendships. Therefore, in the next section we focus on these two types of relationships, as well as on how people in long-distance relationships (LDRs) maintain their relationships.

Maintenance Behavior in Romantic Relationships

Close romantic relationships are often high in both emotional and sexual intimacy, and the maintenance behaviors that romantic partners use reflect this special type of intimacy. Maintenance behaviors involving romance and affection are usually highest in romantic relationships, although people do show affection to their friends. Openness, assurances, and positivity also seem to be used more in romantic relationships than in other types of relationships (Canary et al., 1993). In addition, cohabiting romantic partners use many routine maintenance behaviors, including task sharing, joint activities, and routine talk, more than most friends do. Thus, when Rachel and Michael move in together after getting married, they may begin to use more routine maintenance behaviors.

Some studies have compared the maintenance behaviors of married and dating couples. For example, Dainton and Stafford (1993) found that spouses shared more tasks than daters, probably because they live together. Daters, however, engaged in more mediated communication, such as calling each other on the phone, exchanging cards and letters, and so forth. Again, this could be due to the fact that most married couples live together, while most dating couples do not.

Maintenance behavior also differs depending on the *stage* of the romantic relationship. Stafford and Canary (1991) compared couples at four stages: casually dating, seriously dating, engaged, and married. They found that (1) married and engaged couples reported using more assurances and task sharing than did dating couples, (2) engaged and seriously dating couples reported using more openness and positivity than married or casually dating couples, and (3) married couples reported using the most social networking. These results make sense.

As couples become more committed, partners may feel freer to provide assurances, and they may, by necessity, share more tasks. Similarly, couples may need to integrate social networks as the relationship becomes more committed and people come to view them as a "couple." However, openness and positivity may peak before romantic partners become fully committed. Once couples are married, the spouses may not feel the need to disclose their innermost feelings all the time, in part because they have already told each other so much about themselves. Spouses may also express more negativity once they have the security of marriage. When spouses are still in the "honeymoon stage," they are more likely to be on their best behavior and to "put on a happy face." Also, the daily interaction that comes from living together makes it difficult for married couples to be positive all the time. Complaints and conflicts are likely to occur, even in the best relationships.

In addition to varying across relationship stage, maintenance behaviors appear to change as a function of relationship length. A study of romantic relationships showed that couples used less openness as their relationships lengthened, but more social networking, task sharing, and conflict management (Dainton & Aylor, 2002). Presumably, partners disclose more information to their partners in early relationship stages as a way to get to know one another. As their relationships intensify, they begin to merge social networks and negotiate rules about managing conflict and sharing tasks.

In marriages, relational maintenance may follow a curvilinear pattern; in other words, spouses may use more maintenance behavior in the early and later years of marriage (Weigel & Ballard-Reisch, 1999). One explanation for this finding is that couples put considerable effort into their marriages when they are in the honeymoon stage. Imagine how Rachel might act during the early years of her marriage with Michael. Because being married is novel and exciting and because she is concerned about making her marriage a success, she may be especially likely to engage in maintenance behavior. As the marriage progresses, she and Michael may become preoccupied with their children and careers, leaving less time to devote to one another. Eventually, however, Weigel and Ballard-Reisch's research suggests, their level of maintenance will rebound, perhaps when their children are older or they settle into a comfortable work routine.

Finally, some evidence suggests that people put more effort into maintaining romantic relationships than into relationships with family or friends (see Canary et al., 1993). This may be because we expect the most from our romantic relationships (Phillips, 1988). Our romantic partners are supposed to excite us, comfort us, and love us unconditionally. We are also taught that romantic relationships require a spark to get started and that the spark needs to be rekindled from time to time if the relationship is to remain satisfying.

Maintenance Behavior in Friendships

Even though our friendships are extremely important, we don't work as hard to maintain friendships as we do to maintain romantic relationships (Dainton, Zelley, & Langan, 2003; Fehr, 1996). Perhaps this is because we take a more casual approach to our friendships. It would seem odd if Rachel was worried about maintaining a relationship with her best friend rather than with her future spouse. Research suggests that we often take our friends for granted (Fehr, 1996).

Fehr's (1996) book on friendship summarized how friends maintain their relationships. She suggested that three maintenance behaviors are particularly important in friendships: openness, supportiveness, and positivity. Afifi et al. (1994) found that all three of these behaviors are associated with relational closeness in friendships. Several studies have shown that openness, which includes both routine talk and intimate self-disclosure, is the cornerstone of good friendships (Canary et al., 1993; Rose, 1985; Rosenfeld & Kendrick, 1984). Other maintenance behaviors, such as joint activities and affection, differ depending on the type of friendship. As Dainton and her colleagues (2003) said, different types of friendships require different types of maintenance. Next, we take a look at research on maintenance in women's friendships, men's friendships, and various types of cross-sex friendships, including friends with benefits.

Same-Sex Friendships. Many studies have compared, directly or indirectly, how female versus male friends maintain their relationships. One common finding is that women tend to "talk" more, while men tend to "do" more (Barth & Kinder, 1988; Sherrod, 1989). Wright (1982) referred to women's friendships as "face-to-face," because of the focus on communication, and men's friendships as "side by side," because of the focus on activity. This sex difference, albeit small, appears early in life and extends to mediated communication, such as e-mail and phone calls. A study by Crockett, Losoff, and Peterson (1984), for example, found that 85% of eighth-grade girls reported talking to their friends on the phone every day as opposed to only 50% of the boys. In a study by the Annenberg Public Policy Center (APPC), researchers asked 10- to 17-year-old children what activity would be hardest to give up for a week (APPC, 1997). Over 35% of the girls said that it would be most difficult to give up talking on the telephone. In fact, giving up telephone talk was the top answer for girls, surpassing other activities such as listening to music, playing sports, and watching television. In contrast, over 41% of the boys reported that it would be most difficult to cease playing sports for a week. Only 6.5% of the boys felt that giving up telephone talk would be the most difficult.

However, the "talking" versus "doing" distinction does *not* mean that men are insensitive communicators who never share their thoughts and feelings with others. Nor does it mean that women sit around all day chatting endlessly. Research shows that both men and women value intimate talk in their relationships (Afifi et al., 1994; Floyd & Parks, 1995; Monsour, 1992; Parks & Floyd, 1996), but women disclose to one another a little more. Similarly, both men and women value spending time with one another, even though men tend to engage in more focused activities than do women. Fehr (1996) reviewed research showing that men and women spend similar amounts of time with their friends. The difference is that men engage in more activities, such as playing sports. In other words, women get together more often just to talk and spend time with one another, whereas men get together more often to do something specific, such as surf, play golf,

 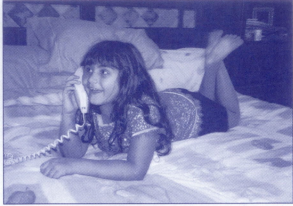

SOURCE: Photographs by Laura Guerrero

Photo 9.1   Studies have shown that boys like to bond through sports and other activities, whereas girls are especially likely to value one-on-one communication, such as talking on the phone.

or watch a movie. Of course, sometimes men get together just to talk, and sometimes women get together to play sports. In fact, one study found no difference in how much male and female friends reported engaging in shared activities (Floyd & Parks, 1995). The difference between men's and women's activities is more subtle than dramatic.

Friendships between men and women also differ somewhat in emotional supportiveness and affection. Fehr (1996) summarized research showing that women's friendships are characterized by more emotional support than men's friendships, although both men and women give one another social support at times. For example, female friends are more positive and supportive than male friends, although this sex difference is small (Afifi et al., 1994). Fehr (1996) summarized research showing that female friends are also generally more nonverbally affectionate than male friends (Andersen & Leibowitz, 1978; Fehr, 1996; Floyd & Morman, 1997). This is true for elementary school-age children (Thorne & Luria, 1986), university students (Hays, 1985), and elderly adults (Roberto & Scott, 1986). From a young age, girls are socialized to be more affectionate toward their friends than boys. Girls often comb one another's hair, sit so that their arms are touching, and hold hands while skipping or running. In contrast, except in the context

of sports, boys rarely touch one another. Similarly, adult women are more likely to hug one another and kiss cheeks than are male friends, especially in the United States and other Western cultures. Male friends show affection in other ways though, particularly through humor, roughhousing, and shared activities (Fehr, 1996).

Together, the research suggests that there are some sex differences in how men and women maintain their friendships. However, these differences are *not* dramatic; men and women are generally more similar than dissimilar, and when differences are found, they tend to be small (Andersen, 1998b; Canary & Hause, 1993). We all want friends with whom we can talk, do things with, and turn to in times of trouble, regardless of whether we are female or male. In fact, both men and women see their friendships as one of the most important sources of happiness in their lives (Fehr, 1996; Rawlins, 1992). Box 9.2 examines the issue of whether men and women really are from "different planets."

Cross-Sex Friendships. Cross-sex friendships can be very rewarding (Werking, 1997). Both men and women like to get the perspective of the "other sex," and many people perceive cross-sex friendships as fun and exciting. Often, however, cross-sex friendships

BOX 9.2   Highlights

Are Men and Women Really From Different Planets?

If you watch television talk shows or read popular books on relationships, you have probably been introduced to the idea that men and women are very different from each other and that these differences can cause relationship problems. For example, Deborah Tannen's popular 1990 book *You Just Don't Understand: Women and Men in Conversation* is built around the idea that boys and girls grow up in different cultures, with girls learning to communicate in ways that are confirming and create intimacy and boys learning to communicate in ways that enhance independence and power. According to Tannen, women and men have difficulty communicating with one another because of "cultural misunderstanding."

John Gray's 1992 best-seller *Men Are from Mars, Women Are from Venus* takes this argument a step further by conceptualizing men and women as inhabitants of different planets. As he puts it,

> Men and women differ in all areas of their lives. Not only do men and women communicate differently but they think, feel, perceive, react, respond, love, need, and appreciate differently. They almost seem to be from different planets, speaking different languages and needing different nourishment. (p. 5)

According to Gray, these "interplanetary differences" are responsible for all the problems that people have in their opposite-sex relationships.

Most relationship researchers, however, do not take a position as extreme as Gray's. Some take a position similar to Tannen's in that they believe a

different cultures perspective can help explain communication differences between men and women (see Wood, 1994, 1996). According to this view, boys and girls grow up primarily playing in same-sex groups. Therefore, they learn different sets of rules and values, leading to distinct communication styles.

Some researchers, however, disagree with the different cultures perspective (Dindia, 1997). Instead, they believe that men and women are remarkably similar and that sex differences are small. These researchers are quick to point out that boys and girls grow up in a similar cultural environment, interacting with a variety of people, including teachers and family members of both sexes. As Dindia has put it, "Men are from North Dakota, and women are from South Dakota."

What do you think? Andersen (1998b) summarized his take on the debate as follows:

> The actual research on sex differences has led to one major, overall conclusion: Men and women are far more similar than different. They are not from different metaphoric planets or cultures. They are all earthlings with goals, hopes, dreams, emotions, fears, and communication behaviors that are a whole lot more similar than they are different. Of course, South Dakotans probably believe that North Dakotans are from another planet. From close range, differences are more obvious than similarities and they are certainty more newsworthy and sensational! From any vantage point other than Dakota, North and South Dakotans look pretty similar. (p. 83)

can be confusing and ambiguous. Think about your friends of the opposite sex. Do you sometimes wonder if they are physically attracted to you? Do you wonder what it would be like to get involved with them romantically? If one or both of you are

heterosexual, these types of questions are likely to surface, even if only in your mind.

As a result of this ambiguity, cross-sex friends can face special challenges. O'Meara (1989) discussed four challenges that men and women face when they want to be "just friends" with one another. Three of these challenges—the emotional bond challenge, the sexual challenge, and the public presentation challenge—are especially relevant to maintaining cross-sex friendships. The **emotional bond challenge** is the result of men and women being socialized to see one another as potential romantic partners rather than platonic friends. This can lead to uncertainty regarding whether cross-sex friends have romantic feelings for each other. It may also be confusing to feel close to opposite-sex friends without also feeling romantic toward them. For example, people sometimes have trouble understanding why they can't seem to fall in love with that man or woman who is such a nice person and good friend.

The **sexual challenge** involves coping with the potential sexual attraction that can be part of some cross-sex relationships. In the movie *When Harry Met Sally*, Harry declares that men and women cannot be friends because the "sex thing" always gets in the way. Although Harry's statement is a bit extreme, it is true that cross-sex friends (particularly if both are heterosexual) are likely to think about sexual issues related to each other. This is especially true for men. Several studies have shown that men tend to see their cross-sex friends as potential sexual partners more often than do women (Abbey, 1982; Abbey & Melby, 1986; Shotland & Craig, 1988). Research has also shown that sex among platonic friends is not uncommon. In one study, nearly half of the college students surveyed admitted to having had sex with a nonromantic friend (Afifi & Faulkner, 2000). These students also reported having feelings of uncertainty following sex with their friend.

Finally, the **public presentation challenge** arises when other people assume there is something romantic or sexual going on in a cross-sex friendship. Cross-sex friends are sometimes careful about how they present their relationship to others and may be asked to explain the nature of their relationship to others. If you have a close cross-sex friend, you can probably relate to this. Have people ever asked you questions such as "Are you really just friends?" or Do you love her or him?" or "Have you ever slept together?" Romantic partners may also be suspicious and jealous of your close cross-sex friends.

Some scholars have criticized O'Meara's challenges for being applicable only to cross-sex friendships between heterosexuals. However, these challenges are also applicable to homosexual same-sex friends. In addition, when one friend is homosexual and the other is heterosexual, these challenges may apply regardless of whether the friends are of the same or of the opposite sex.

In cross-sex friendships that include at least one heterosexual partner, these challenges can make relational maintenance a complex and delicate matter (Werking, 1997). A study on relational maintenance by Guerrero and Chavez (2005) examined four types of cross-sex friendships that differ in terms of romantic intent. Individuals in the **strictly platonic** group said that neither they nor their partner wanted the friendship to become romantic. Individuals in the **mutual romance** group said that both they and their partner wanted the friendship to become romantic. Individuals in the **desires-romance** group said that they wanted the friendship to become romantic, but their partner wanted it to stay platonic. Finally, individuals in the **rejects-romance** group said that they wanted the friendship to stay platonic, but their partner wanted it to become romantic.

People in these four groups reported using different maintenance behaviors. Those in the mutual romance group said they used the most maintenance behaviors, which suggests that increases in maintenance behavior might mark a move from friendship toward romance. Those in the desires-romance group also reported relatively high levels of maintenance, with one notable exception: People who desired romance but believed that their friend did not were the least likely to report talking about the relationship with their friend, perhaps because they feared rejection and worried that confessing their feelings could jeopardize the friendship. Individuals in the rejects-romance group also reported relatively low levels of relationship talk, perhaps because they worried about having to hurt their friend's feelings.

Individuals in both the rejects-romance and strictly platonic groups reported using less joint activity and flirtation but more talk about outside relationships, such as their boyfriend or girlfriend. This suggests that individuals who want to keep the relationship platonic refrain from flirting with each other, so as not to lead each other on. They may also limit their public appearances by showing up at parties separately and engaging in less joint activity in public settings. This may be a way of managing O'Meara's public presentation challenge; if they limit the amount of time they spend together, others are less likely to see them as a potentially romantic couple. Finally, individuals in the rejects-romance and strictly platonic groups are especially likely to talk about their boyfriends, girlfriends, or spouses (assuming that they are already in another romantic relationship), perhaps as a way of signaling to their friend that they are already taken.

Although some cross-sex friends have to deal with the sexual and romantic challenges O'Meara proposed, most cross-sex friends define their relationships as strictly platonic (Guerrero & Chavez, 2005; Messman, Canary, & Hause, 2000). There are at least six reasons why people in cross-sex friendships want to maintain the status quo and keep their relationships platonic (Messman et al., 2000). First, people report that it is important to **safeguard the relationship**: People worry that a shift toward romance could hurt the quality of their friendship or result in a breakup. Second, people report that they are **not attracted** to their friend in a romantic or sexual way. Third, people report that there would be **network disapproval** if they became romantically involved with their friend. For example, people in their social network might get upset. Fourth, people report keeping friendships platonic because one or both members of the friendship are already involved with a **third party** in a romantic relationship. Fifth, people report **risk aversion**, which involves uncertainty about the partner's reaction coupled with worry about potentially being hurt or disappointed. Finally, people report taking a **time-out** from considering the possibility of moving a friendship toward romance when they do not want a serious romantic relationship with anyone at that particular point in time.

Of these six reasons, safeguarding the relationship was the most common, followed by lack of attraction and network disapproval. Risk aversion and time out were least common. Sex differences for keeping friendships platonic also exist. Women are more likely than men to want to safeguard the relationship and to say they are not attracted to their friend in a romantic way (Messman et al., 2000).

People also use different maintenance behaviors depending on their reason for keeping the friendship platonic. In particular, people who want to safeguard the relationship are most likely to report using openness, positivity, joint activities, and supportiveness in their friendships. People were most likely to report using avoidance when they reported risk aversion, network disapproval, and time out as reasons for keeping the relationship platonic. Finally, people who reported being unattracted to their friend reported that they avoided flirting as a way to maintain the relationship. To determine why you keep one of your friendships platonic rather than romantic, take the test in Box 9.3.

In contrast to platonic friendships, some friends decide to have sex but stay friends. This type of relationship, which has been called "friends with benefits" in television shows and the popular press, is fairly common on college campuses. In one study, 67.7% of the students on one campus and 48.5% of students on another campus reported that they had had at least one relationship characterized as friends with benefits (Mongeau, Ramirez, & Vorrell, 2003). Little research has been conducted on friends with benefits. However, a study by Hughes et al. (2005) provides some hints as to how this type of friendship is maintained. According to these researchers, friends with benefits often establish rules for maintaining their relationships. The most common rule involves staying emotionally detached. Friends with benefits often agree not to get jealous or fall in love with one another (Hughes et al., 2005). Other rules for maintaining these friendships include negotiations about the following: sexual activity (such as agreeing to use condoms), communication (such as making rules about calling one another and being honest about other relationships), secrecy (such as agreeing not to tell common friends that they have sex), permanence (such as agreeing that the sexual part of the relationship is only temporary), and the friendship (such as agreeing to value the friendship over the sexual relationship).

Although many of these maintenance rules help friends with benefits maintain the status quo, this type of relationship sometimes ends completely,

▨ **BOX 9.3   Put Yourself to the Test**

Why Do You Keep One of Your Close Cross-Sex Friendships Platonic?

Think about why you have kept a relationship with a good friend (of the opposite-sex if you are heterosexual or the same-sex if you are gay) platonic. Rate the following reasons using this scale: 1 = Disagree strongly, 7 = Agree strongly.

	Disagree	←			→	Agree	

I keep our friendship platonic because

1. My friend might reject me.	1	2	3	4	5	6	7
2. My friend and/or I are already dating someone else.	1	2	3	4	5	6	7
3. I do not want to risk losing our friendship.	1	2	3	4	5	6	7
4. My friend is not the kind of person I want to be involved with in a romantic way.	1	2	3	4	5	6	7
5. At this time, I am not ready for a romantic relationship with anyone.	1	2	3	4	5	6	7
6. My friend might end up hurting my feelings.	1	2	3	4	5	6	7
7. Other people would be upset if our relationship turned romantic.	1	2	3	4	5	6	7
8. I value this person as a friend too much to change things.	1	2	3	4	5	6	7
9. I think of this person *only* as a friend.	1	2	3	4	5	6	7
10. My friend and/or I are already romantically involved with someone else.	1	2	3	4	5	6	7
11. This person is not sexually attractive to me.	1	2	3	4	5	6	7
12. I don't want to date anyone at this time.	1	2	3	4	5	6	7
13. I am not sure that the romantic feelings I have for my friend are mutual.	1	2	3	4	5	6	7
14. Some of my friends or family would be upset with me if our friendship turned romantic.	1	2	3	4	5	6	7
15. My friend and/or I already have good romantic relationships with someone else.	1	2	3	4	5	6	7
16. Getting romantic could cause problems within our social network.	1	2	3	4	5	6	7
17. Getting romantic could ruin our friendship.	1	2	3	4	5	6	7
18. I'm not interested in a romantic relationship right now.	1	2	3	4	5	6	7

To obtain your results, add your scores for the following items:

1, 6, 13	(risk aversion)	_____
7, 14, 16	(network disapproval)	_____
3, 8, 17	(safeguard relationship)	_____
4, 9, 11	(not attracted)	_____
5, 12, 18	(time out)	_____
2, 10, 15	(third party)	_____

Higher scores indicate stronger reasons for keeping your friendship platonic.

SOURCE: Adapted from Messman, S. J., Canary, D. J., & Hause, K. S., Motives to remain platonic, equity, and the use of maintenance strategies in opposite-sex friendships, in *Journal of Social and Personal Relationships*, 17, 67–94. Copyright © 2000, Sage Publications, Inc.

returns to friendship only (no sex), or turns into a romantic relationship (Hughes et al., 2005). Although friends with benefits often keep the sexual aspect of their relationship private, Hughes and her colleagues found that these friendships are more likely to continue if one's social network is accepting of them. Of course, these types of friendships can be fraught with all kinds of challenges, including one friend wanting the relationship to turn romantic while the other person does not.

The Special Case of Long-Distance Relationships

Most people have been in at least one long-distance romantic relationship, and virtually everyone has been in an LDR of some sort, whether it be with a friend or family member. With more individuals pursuing higher education, more couples having dual professional careers, and more people immigrating to the United States, the number of romantic relationships separated by large distances is increasing. In 1987, Stafford, Daly, and Reske estimated that one third of dating couples in the United States were separated by sufficient distance to make frequent face-to-face interaction difficult. Within the college student population, between 25% and 40% of romantic relationships are long distance (Dainton & Aylor, 2001). If you have been in one of these relationships, you know the challenges that they pose, particularly in terms of relational maintenance. How can couples stay close if the partners are unable to engage in many of the maintenance behaviors discussed in this chapter? When separated, people in LDRs cannot show each other nonverbal affection, share activities or tasks, or engage in the same type of daily routine talk as do couples in proximal relationships. Indeed, studies show that people in LDRs generally use less maintenance behavior, such as openness, assurances, and joint activities, than people in geographically close relationships (Johnson, 2001; Van Horn et al., 1997). Yet many long-distance couples maintain happy relationships.

Indeed, contrary to the old adage "Out of sight, out of mind," most research suggests that LDRs may be just as satisfying, close, and nurturing as more proximal relationships (Rohlfing, 1995; Van Horn et al., 1997). In fact, some studies suggest that individuals in romantic LDRs are happier and more "in love" with their partners than are people in proximal romantic relationships (Stafford & Reske, 1990). Similarly, friends in LDRs report as much relational satisfaction as friends in geographically close relationships (Johnson, 2001).

Two specific aspects of the communication landscape of LDRs help account for continuing satisfaction in LDRs. First, staying in contact through mediated communication is a primary maintenance behavior in LDRs (Rabby & Walther, 2003; Rohlfing, 1995). People in LDRs rely on the phone and letters, and more recently e-mail and text messages, to communicate with each other. Keeping in touch through e-mail, text messaging (Rabby & Walther, 2003), greeting cards, or letters may be important maintenance behaviors in long-distance dating relationships and friendships. In fact, Internet messaging sites are marketed as a way to maintain relationships or to keep in touch with friends. Failure to answer an e-mail or even failing to send a greeting card for birthdays or holidays (Dindia, Timmerman, Langan, Sahlstein, & Quandt, 2004) may be perceived as a sign that you don't want to maintain the relationship. However, mediated communication may offer a skewed perception of the partners' communication styles. For example, a partner likely will pick up the phone when he or she feels like talking, something over which the partner has almost complete control. Moreover, if one partner calls but the other partner is not in the mood to talk, he or she can simply decline to pick up the phone or ask the partner if he or she can call back at another time. One of our students described how she sent videotapes to her long-distance boyfriend. She admitted to cutting out scenes in which she did not think she looked her best and to rehearsing her monologue so that she said exactly the right things. Such control over communication is unusual in proximal relationships, where relational partners communicate face-to-face on a regular basis. Similar behaviors have been found in Internet-based relationships (Wright, 2004). People who send electronic messages showing positivity and openness tend to be regarded favorably by their Internet partners.

Second, individuals in LDRs are typically on their best relational behavior when they are together.

Compared with those in geographically close relationships, people in LDRs tend to engage in less joint activities, task sharing, and social networking (Dainton & Aylor, 2001; Johnson, 2001), especially if they have limited contact with one another. However, when people in LDRs do get together, they often plan shared activities more carefully, work hard to treat each other in a fair and equitable manner, and have long, in-depth discussions. People in LDRs often prepare well in advance for the weekend visit and present an image of themselves that may not be consistent with the day-to-day reality of their lives. Dinner reservations are made, work calendars are cleared, and plans with friends and family are often suspended so that the partners can spend quality time alone. Partners in proximal relationships seldom make such accommodations for each other. As Johnson (2001) stated, it may be the quality rather than the quantity of communication that is most important when it comes to maintaining LDRs.

For romantic LDR partners, there is a third reason behind continuing satisfaction: idealization. Compared with dating partners in geographically close relationships, dating partners in LDRs idealize one another more and are more likely to believe that they will get married (Stafford & Reske, 1990). This may seem counterintuitive at first, but when you consider that people in LDRs usually care about each other a great deal before separating, these findings begin to make sense. Moreover, partners in romantic LDRs are likely to think about how great their lives would be if they could be with their partners, and when they do spend time together they are likely to engage in high-quality activities and communication, as described above. For these reasons, people in romantic LDRs are likely to idealize their partners (Stafford & Reske, 1990); in this case, "Absence indeed makes the heart grow fonder."

However, idealization can lead to difficulties when the relationship becomes proximal. Suddenly, the once seemingly perfect partner needs to study or write a report for work when the other partner wants to spend quality time together, and the sensitive issues that were never discussed over the phone lead to conflict in face-to-face interaction. Thus, partners in LDRs may need to work to keep their expectations realistic so that they are not disappointed once the relationship becomes proximal.

In sum, the good news is that LDRs are often as stable and satisfying as, and perhaps more emotionally intense than, proximal relationships (Van Horn et al., 1997). The bad news is that friends and romantic partners in LDRs sometimes get frustrated with their lack of face-to-face communication (Rohlfing, 1995). Romantic partners in LDRs also need to ensure that their positive perceptions of each other are not a function of idealization. Perhaps this is the biggest challenge facing long-distance partners who wish to maintain their romantic relationships.

BARRIERS TO RELATIONAL DISSOLUTION

Thus far, we have examined the various maintenance behaviors that people use to keep their relationships stable, satisfying, and rewarding. In this section, we explore how barriers keep relationships from falling apart. Barriers can be thought of as all the forces that stop people from terminating a relationship. As Johnson (1982) stated, "People stay in relationships for two major reasons: because they want to; and because they have to" (pp. 52–53). Attraction, relational satisfaction, love, and other rewards make people want to stay in relationships. Social pressures, financial considerations, and the fear of being alone are factors that make people feel that they have to stay in a relationship, whether they want to or not. Because these factors help keep people in long-term relationships, some scholars have argued that relationships are maintained unless something pulls them apart. Other researchers, however, have argued that people need to actively engage in the maintenance behaviors we discuss in this chapter if they hope to maintain healthy, happy relationships. Arguments related to this debate are presented in Box 9.4, which addresses the issue of whether relationships can go into "cruise control" and still prosper.

Researchers have identified many barriers to relational dissolution. Attridge (1994) grouped these barriers into two overarching categories: (1) internal psychological barriers and (2) external structural barriers. **Internal psychological barriers** are personal factors that keep people from ending a relationship; **external structural barriers** are outside forces that keep people in a relationship together.

BOX 9.4	Highlights

Can Relationships Go Into "Cruise Control"?

Once you are in a committed, long-term relationship, do you still have to work hard to maintain your relationship, or can you go on "cruise control"? This is a complicated question that relational maintenance researchers are still trying to answer: Some researchers take a centrifugal perspective, while others take a centripetal perspective (Canary & Stafford, 1994; Duck, 1988).

According to the **centrifugal perspective,** people must work actively to maintain their relationships. Without maintenance, relationships will deteriorate. Think of your car. It might be running great now, but if you never change the oil or check the coolant, it probably won't last very long. Researchers taking the centrifugal perspective see relationships the same way. If you don't put time and energy into maintaining them, they will eventually fall apart.

Researchers taking a **centripetal perspective** believe that people in close, committed relationships stay together unless something pulls them apart. According to this view, there are barriers that prevent people from leaving committed relationships. Unless some outside force makes it easier to break through the barriers or some problem becomes so big that the couples cannot handle it, people will stay with their current partners. It is almost like driving in cruise control. You can relax until something unexpected (like an animal running across the road) happens. For example, a married couple might be content together until one spouse finds a more appealing partner and has an affair. The affair forces the couple out of its routine and has the power to tear the relationship apart.

In this book, we take the position that highly committed relationships do run on cruise control some of the time but that periodic maintenance is necessary to keep them healthy and to adjust to changing needs and demands. Thus in this chapter we review literature on behaviors that help people stay together, as well as barriers that keep relationships from falling apart.

Internal Psychological Barriers

Commitment, obligation, and investments keep people together and act as internal psychological barriers. **Commitment** refers to how much a person feels attached to the partner and desires to remain in the relationship (Rusbult, Johnson, & Morrow, 1986). For example, because Rachel is highly committed to her relationship with Michael, she would be likely to try and work through problems. Longitudinal studies of relationships show that commitment, and specifically a long-term relationship orientation, is a key to relational maintenance (Rusbult, Arriaga, & Agnew, 2001). **Obligation** refers to the extent to which a person feels he or she owes something to the partner. For instance, Michael may feel a strong sense of personal obligation to Rachel. Perhaps

Rachel supported him—emotionally and financially— so he could finish school. As a result, he feels obligated to be there for her and make their relationship work. **Investments** are resources that have been deposited into the relationship and "would decline in value or be lost if the relationship were to end" (Rusbult, Drigotas, & Verette, 1994, p. 119). Since Michael and Rachel are in a long-term, committed relationship, they have likely made considerable investments in their relationship, including time, effort, and personal sacrifices. After they get married, their investment levels will likely increase.

Strong religious or moral beliefs might also act as barriers that keep people in relationships, especially in marriages. Some people believe that marriage is sacred and divorce is not an option. In fact, Attridge (1994) reviewed research showing that the more religious people were, the less likely they were to divorce. People who reported that they never attended church were two to three times more likely to divorce than people who reported attending church at least once a week. Thus, religiosity is one variable that might help explain why Rachel's parents got divorced while Michael's did not.

Another internal psychological barrier revolves around the **meshing of people's self- and relational identities**. Many people see their relationships as an important part of their self-identity. For example, after a few years of marriage, Michael may come to think of himself as a good husband and father. His roles as husband and father would become entwined within his broader image of himself as an accountant, son, Democrat, and so forth, but they are nonetheless likely to be central roles. If his marriage ended and he had to move out of the family home, he would have to adjust his view of himself. Self-identity is also connected to how partners reflect on each other. For example, Rachel might enjoy being married to a well-respected accountant, and Michael might be proud that his wife is a best-selling author of children's books. If they divorced, they would lose the "reflected glory" they gain from being married. The bottom line here is that the more central the relationship is to a person's self-identity, the more difficult it is to end the relationship.

The final internal psychological barrier identified by Attridge (1994) is **parental obligations**. The presence of children has been shown to help keep relational partners together even if marital satisfaction is lower. Attridge reviewed research showing that couples without children may be as much as six times more likely to divorce than couples with two children. Moreover, as the number of children increases, the likelihood of divorce decreases (see also Greenstein, 1990). Some couples may even postpone a divorce until they believe the children are old enough to handle it. Some couples with children are reluctant to divorce because the spouses remember how devastated they were when their own parents divorced. This may well be the case for Rachel. Interestingly, the presence of children also usually leads to an increased financial burden for divorced couples, which is related to one of the external structural barriers that we discuss next.

External Structural Barriers

Financial considerations are among the most important external structural barriers preventing breakups. Married couples, and many cohabitors, have to resolve myriad financial issues to end their relationships. Many couples cannot afford two separate mortgages, so they must sell their home and move into less luxurious homes. Couples also may have joint savings accounts and credit cards that need to be changed to separate accounts. Possessions can act as barriers. It is often difficult to decide who should keep joint property, such as furniture, exercise equipment, art, CD collections, computers, and so forth. Separation can also lead to increased financial obligations if alimony and/or child support payments must be made. And, of course, one spouse may be financially dependent on the other: typically the wife, because unfortunately, women still tend to earn less money than men, even for the same work (Greenstein, 1990). Greenstein reported that women are less likely to divorce if they are financially dependent on their husbands. Women who earned less than 25% of their household income were least likely to divorce, while women who earned more than 75% of their household income were most likely to divorce. All these considerations—household's income, possessions, alimony, child support, and financial dependency—make it costly, in more ways than one, to end the relationship.

For married couples, **the legal process** also acts as an external structural barrier to relational dissolution. Depending on the state where a couple resides, the legal process can be easy or difficult; but the fact remains that spouses have to go through a formal process to divorce. This process may cause them to stop and think before ending the relationship. In fact, some spouses go through marriage counseling en route to a divorce, only to find that they would rather stay together after all. Interestingly, some states have drafted legislation to try to make it more difficult to obtain a divorce. The reasoning is that, if the legal process is more time-consuming and draining, spouses might try harder to work their problems out before filing for a "quickie divorce."

Finally, a number of **social pressures** act as external structural barriers to ending relationships.

People's relationships are embedded in a larger social structure that includes their families and friends, and sometimes their communities and churches. The breakup of a long-term relationship often leads to disruption of the larger social network. For example, common friends may feel uncomfortable inviting both members of the estranged couple to a party. Members of the social network might also exert pressure on the couple to stay together. For example, if Michael and Rachel ever thought about divorcing, Michael's parents might be quick to urge them to try harder to work out their problems, to offer them advice, and to share their own stories about the problems they encountered and conquered in their long-lasting marriage.

THE DIALECTICAL PERSPECTIVE

Clearly, many factors are relevant to maintaining close relationships. The road to a happy relationship is not always smooth, and partners do not always travel in the same direction or at the same pace. Every relationship experiences ups and downs, and no relationship stays the same from start to finish. The dialectical perspective captures the dynamic nature of relationships and describes some of the common tensions, or ups and downs, that relational partners experience.

According to the **dialectical perspective** (see Baxter & Montgomery, 1996), relationships are never completely stable, but are constantly changing. As Baxter (1994) stated, "A healthy relationship is a changing relationship" (p. 234). Think about your close relationships. Wouldn't it be boring if they were always the same? Wouldn't you expect your partner to be somewhat different in several years from what he or she is today? Of course, you would. Relationships, like people, are constantly changing as goals and needs are reevaluated and redefined. The dialectical perspective holds that relationships are managed rather than simply maintained. Put another way, dialectical tensions are never solved; instead, successful couples learn how to best cope with these tensions within the ever-changing context of their relationships.

A **dialectical tension** can be thought of as a push-and-pull toward two seemingly contradictory needs.

In other words, people want two things that are both important yet are opposites. Fehr (1996) described the tug-of-war in dialectical tensions this way:

> We have to juggle our need for dependence with our need to be independent; wanting to be completely open versus wanting to protect ourselves by not revealing everything; wanting to have a lot in common, but not so much that the relationship feels boring and predictable. (p. 156)

If two people can manage these competing needs successfully, they will be more likely to sustain a happy and healthy relationship.

Baxter's Dialectics Theory

Baxter (1993) proposed three major dialectical tensions: integration-separation, stability-change, and expression-privacy. Each of these dialectical tensions has both an internal and an external manifestation, as Figure 9.1 shows. **Internal manifestations** refer to the tensions experienced between relational partners, including how they communicate with one another. **External manifestations** refer to the tensions between a couple and other dyads or society, including how the couple present themselves to others.

Integration-Separation. The dialectic of **integration-separation** refers to the tension between social integration and social division. That is, people want to feel a part of social groups, but they also want to be self-sufficient. The internal manifestation of this dialectic is the **connection-autonomy** tension. This is the tension between the desire to be close to a relational partner (connection) and the need to be independent (autonomy). Chances are, you have seen these tensions at work within your own relationships. You might have declared that you wanted more freedom or were feeling smothered. If so, you were experiencing the need for autonomy. Alternatively, you might have told your partner that you needed more attention and affection, which would indicate that you were not experiencing enough connection at a given time.

The external manifestation of the integration-separation dialectic is the **inclusion-seclusion**

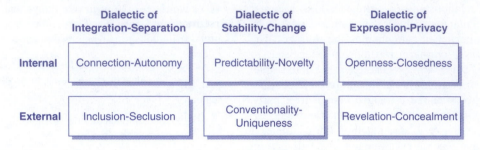

Figure 9.1 Baxter's Dialectical Tensions

SOURCE: From Werner, C. M., Altman, I., Brown, B. B., & Ganat, J., Celebrations in personal relationships: A transactional/dialectical perspective. In S. Duck (Ed.), *Social context and relationships* (pp. 109–138), copyright © 1993. Reprinted with permission of Sage Publications, Inc.

tension. This is the tension between the amount of time partners spend with other people in their social network (inclusion) and the amount of time they spend doing things only with each other (seclusion). One of our students gave a great example of this external contradiction. After graduation, she and her fiancé were moving to Boulder, Colorado, where she had landed a job. Neither of them knew anyone in Colorado, which scared them a little because they wouldn't have friends or family to rely on when they first got there. However, they both thought it would be nice to have some time alone for a while, without any interference from friends or family.

Stability-Change. The second major dialectical tension is **stability-change**. The idea behind this dialectic is that people want security and continuity on the one hand and excitement and discontinuity on the other. The internal manifestation of this dialectic is **predictability-novelty**. That is, people want some predictability in their relationships: They want to know that their partner will be there for them, and they necessarily establish routines and relational rules, such as eating dinner together in the evenings or making sure to call if they will be home late. However, people also want some novelty, excitement, and spontaneity in their relationships. As the saying goes, "Variety is the spice of life." Boredom is one of the top reasons couples give for breaking up (Hill, Rubin, & Peplau, 1976), suggesting that excitement is vital in relationships. In one study, couples who were told to engage in exciting activities

once a week reported more satisfaction than couples who engaged in pleasant but routine activities (Reissman et al., 1993).

The external manifestation of stability-change is **conventionality-uniqueness**. People want to be accepted by society, so they often act in conventional, predictable ways. However, couples also feel a need to be special and unique, and so they sometimes act in unconventional, unpredictable ways. For example, in the United States, many couples strive for the "American dream" of home ownership, children, and a good job, but a couple might decide to go against the norm by remaining childless. Couples can also show uniqueness in subtle ways, such as decorating a cactus instead of a traditional tree for Christmas.

Expression-Privacy. The third and final major dialectical tension is **expression-privacy.** This dialectic reflects the need to be heard by others versus the need to keep some information private. The internal manifestation of this dialectic, **openness-closedness**, refers to how much partners tell each other. Couples often feel a push-and-pull regarding how much information they should disclose to each other (Petronio, 2000). On the one hand, they have a natural inclination to share their thoughts and feelings with the person to whom they feel closest; on the other, they feel a need to keep some things private and to protect themselves from judgment or criticism. You have probably felt this tension in your own relationships. You might have wondered how many details about your past relationships you should divulge to your current romantic partner. Or you might have wondered whether you should tell your partner about some of your biggest faults.

The external contradiction, **revelation-concealment**, refers to what partners tell other people about their relationship. For example, you might feel torn between a desire to tell your best friend about the fight you had with your romantic partner and the need to keep the information to yourself. You would like to elicit support and comfort from your friend, but you would like to protect your romantic partner from the ill feelings that could result from your revelation.

Ways of Managing Dialectical Tensions. Baxter's theory also addresses how couples manage these dialectics. There are four general ways of managing dialectical tensions: selection, separation, neutralization, and reframing (Baxter, 1990). **Selection** involves valuing one side of the dialectic over the other. For example, Rachel and Michael might decide that it is important to be open and honest with each other and not keep any secrets. The potential problem with this type of strategy is that the partners sacrifice one need in favor of the other, and the other need does not go away.

Separation involves favoring each side of the dialectic at different times. There are two ways of accomplishing this. First, couples can use **cyclic alternation** by moving from one side of the dialectic to the other in a cyclical fashion. For example, if Michael and Rachel start feeling disconnected from each other, they might plan a romantic getaway. Conversely, if they start feeling smothered, they might spend a day apart. Another way of accomplishing separation is through **topical segmentation**, which involves emphasizing different sides of the dialectic depending on the topic or context. For example, Rachel and Michael might decide to reveal positive information about their relationship to others but conceal negative information. Rachel and Michael might decide to be open on most topics but to avoid talking about issues that tend to lead to conflict. Couples using topical segmentation might also decide to keep certain activities separate (such as playing golf or shopping with friends) while engaging in others together (such as going to a favorite restaurant).

Neutralization occurs when couples avoid fully engaging either side of the dialectic. There are two strategies for accomplishing neutralization. The first, **moderation**, involves striving to reach a "midpoint" such that couples engage both sides of the dialectic, but only to a certain extent. For example, Rachel and Michael might decide to be moderately open, affectionate, and conventional. Second, couples can use **disqualification**, which involves striving to be ambiguous so that neither side of the dialectic is engaged. This includes tactics such as changing the topic or avoiding an issue. For example, you might change the subject when someone asks you how your relationship is going. Or you might avoid engaging in behavior that is either too predictable or too novel.

The final general way of managing dialectical tension is through **reframing**, a sophisticated strategy that involves adjusting perceptions of dialectics so that they seem complementary rather than contradictory. For example, Michael and Rachel might realize that, if they share everything with each other all the time, soon there will be nothing new to share. They might also realize that, if their lives become too enmeshed, they will lose their individual identity and that, if they are always surprising each other, their novel behavior will eventually become predictable. For example, the first time you receive flowers or a gift from a romantic partner, it is probably a pleasant surprise. However, if your partner starts to bring you something every weekend, it will stop being a surprise and become dull and predictable. These examples illustrate that the different sides of the various dialectics do not necessarily have to be seen as opposing (Allen et al., 1995). All in all, reframing is an effective strategy because partners no longer need to worry if the other person temporarily seems unaffectionate, inattentive, or boring.

Other strategies are also effective, depending on the needs of a couple at a given time. The most frequent way in which couples manage the autonomy-connection dialectic is through cyclic alternation (Baxter, 1990). To manage the predictability-novelty and openness-closedness dialectics, couples often use topical segmentation. Baxter's study also showed that reframing and topical segmentation may be better strategies than selection or disqualification, perhaps because the latter two strategies don't allow relational partners to fulfill needs related to one or both sides of a given dialectic. For example, if you select the connectedness side of the dialectic, you are ignoring your need for autonomy. If you select disqualification, you are ignoring the needs on both sides of the dialectic. Ignoring these needs will not make them disappear.

The research on dialectics also suggests that relational partners who are satisfied with their relationships find a way to balance their needs for seemingly contradictory sides of each dialectic. Baxter and Simon (1993) found that when people saw their relationships as more autonomous than connected, they reported more satisfaction if their partners tried to increase contact. They also found that spontaneous, romantic efforts were especially appreciated when relationships were seen as predictable rather than novel. Finally, avoidance of relationship discussions was seen as particularly negative when people saw their relationships as closed rather than open. This research suggests that satisfied couples are able to adjust to the changing needs within their relationships.

Rawlins's Dialectical Tensions

Although applicable to a variety of relationships, Baxter's work on dialectics has focused primarily on romantic relationships. Researchers have also looked at dialectics within the context of friendships (Bridge & Baxter, 1992; Rawlins, 1989, 1992, 1994). In particular, Rawlins's (1992) investigation of friendship took a dialectical perspective. He argued that six main dialectical tensions characterize friendships as well as other types of relationships.

Two of Rawlins's dialectics—independent-dependent and expressive-protective—are similar to those identified by Baxter. The **independent-dependent** dialectic, like Baxter's connection-autonomy dialectic, refers to the tension between wanting the freedom to pursue individual activities and depending on someone for help and support. For example, you might want to ask your friend, who is a math major, to help you with your trigonometry homework, but you might also want to prove that you can do the work on your own. The **expressive-protection** dialectic is similar to Baxter's openness-closedness dialectic. After interviewing pairs of

close friends, Rawlins (1983a, 1983b) concluded that this was a central tension in many friendships. For a friendship to be close, people must disclose personal information. However, if friends disclose too much, they open themselves up to potential criticism and rejection (see also Chapter 5).

The remaining four dialectics differ from those proposed by Baxter. The **judgment-acceptance** dialectic involves being able to accept a friend for who he or she is versus feeling free to offer criticism and advice. This is a common tension. Imagine that a good friend of yours has been in a dead-end job for 2 years after graduation. Should you accept that your friend isn't very ambitious, or should you suggest that your friend go out and look for something better? You avoid insulting your friend if you do the former, but in the long run, you might help your friend if you do the latter. The choice is indeed a dilemma.

The **affection-instrumentality** dialectic refers to whether friends focus more on feelings of warmth or on instrumental tasks. When friendships are based only on instrumental goals (such as wanting help with homework), the relationship may seem too impersonal. On the other hand, when friendships are based on affection without any instrumental benefits, people might feel that some of their goals are not being fulfilled. Rawlins (1992) suggested that although both men and woman want both types of benefits, men value instrumentality more, while women value affection more.

The **public-private** dialectic involves how the relationship is negotiated in public versus private. Rawlins (1992) argued that all friendships are negotiated primarily in private, yet some aspects of the relationship are made public. For example, you might call your friend silly nicknames such as "bubblehead" or "monkey face" in private but not in public. In high school, if you invited an unpopular person to your house, you might not tell the other kids at school. But if the homecoming king and queen come over, you probably wouldn't mind if everyone knew. Cross-sex friends might show affection to one another in private, but not in public because they don't want other people to think they have romantic feelings for one another.

Finally, the **ideal-real** dialectic reflects the tension between what the friendship "ought to be" and what the relationship "really is." People wish for the ideal friendship, but most people also know that the ideal relationship is a fantasy and that no friend is perfect. In high school, some kids wish they could be friends with a particular student who is especially popular, athletic, talented, or beautiful. However, their "real" friends have a mix of positive and negative characteristics. There may also be tension between trying to live up to idealistic expectations and wanting to be oneself.

Although Rawlins's work focuses on friendships, his dialectical perspective can also be applied to relationships between coworkers, family members, and romantic partners. It is important to recognize that the dialectical tensions experienced by friends vary over the course of the life span. For example, the adolescent years are usually marked by tension in the private-public and acceptance-judgment dimensions because of the focus on popularity during this life stage.

SUMMARY AND APPLICATION

Keeping a relationship satisfying and preventing a relationship from ending are complicated processes, as anyone who has been through a relational breakup knows. People must put effort into their relationships if they want them to last. This involves engaging in constructive maintenance behaviors and managing dialectical tensions effectively. Forces such as investment, internal psychological barriers, and external structural barriers also help keep relationships together.

The literature on relational maintenance offers couples such as Rachel and Michael advice about how to keep their relationship strong. Both routine and strategic maintenance are related to satisfaction, but routine behavior may be a little more important. Therefore, it is essential that Michael and Rachel settle into a routine that includes positive maintenance behaviors, such as asking about each other's day and sharing tasks in a fair and equitable manner. For married couples, positivity and assurances appear to be especially effective maintenance behaviors. So Rachel might try to compliment Michael once in a while and act cheerful and optimistic. Rachel might

periodically offer Michael assurances that she loves him and is committed to their relationship. Michael should do the same. The couple should also focus on doing things together through maintenance behaviors such as joint activities and social networking. Engaging in these activities creates a partnership, reinforces similarity, and allows couples to have fun together. Social networking helps couples like Rachel and Michael integrate their social worlds, which may provide a barrier to breakup.

Rachel wondered if getting married would change their relationship. It likely would. Married couples have more barriers to relational dissolution. Their friends and families are more likely to object if they consider divorcing. Married couples are also likely to make more investments in their relationships, to have more financial dependency on one another, and to feel more morally obligated to one another than dating couples. The legal process of having to formally obtain a divorce is another barrier to dissolution. If Rachel and Michael have children, they would also be less likely to break up. The dialectical tensions in their relationship would also change. For instance, they might feel more constrained by the conventional rules associated with being married, and they may feel pressure to merge their social networks. It may also be harder to be novel and to keep things private because they have more daily contact with one another.

As the dialectical perspective suggests, relationships cycle through periods of highs and lows. The ebb and flow of relational closeness is a *normal* process (Wilmot, 1994). When things are not going well, it is a signal that a change needs to be made so that the relationship can be rejuvenated. This is comforting! An argument might help solve a problem, and a temporary feeling of being smothered by the relationship might lead to some valued time alone. Couples like Michael and Rachel should remember that maintenance behavior is likely to vary throughout the course of their marriage. As newlyweds, they may exert considerable energy maintaining their marriage; but after a while, they may become absorbed in their daily lives, including their careers and their children, leaving less time for strategic maintenance. This is why routine maintenance is so important: Routine patterns of positive behavior help sustain relationships even when couples have little time to focus on one another. Using maintenance behavior may be one of the secrets that helps couples like Michael's parents maintain a happy relationship across the years.

DISCUSSION QUESTIONS

1. In this chapter, we discussed sex differences in relational behaviors such as self-disclosure and sharing activities. Do you agree with our conclusion that, although some sex differences exist, they are actually quite small? What do your everyday experiences tell you about sex differences in relational maintenance behaviors?

2. Which of the following statements do you think is truer: "Relationships stay together unless something tears them apart" or "Relationships require effort or else they fall apart"?

3. Based on the information in this chapter, what five pieces of advice do you think would be most important to share with someone like Rachel, who wants to maintain a relationship? How might your advice change based on the type of relationship (friendship, romantic, long-distance vs. proximal) that people wish to maintain?

10

GETTING A FAIR DEAL

Interdependence and Equity

Brent and Garrett have been best friends since sixth grade. They share an especially close bond since they went through the sometimes turbulent adolescent years together. Throughout middle school and high school, their friendship seemed almost ideal. They enjoyed the same activities; they could talk to each other about almost anything; and, most of all, they knew they could count on each other through thick and thin. Now in college, the two men decide to share an apartment. Suddenly, their normally tranquil relationship is filled with tension. Brent thinks Garrett is a slob who never cleans up after himself. Garrett thinks Brent is a freeloader who never pays his bills on time. Both men feel that they are being treated unfairly. There is also tension about the "house rules," especially when it comes to having girlfriends over. Brent wonders why becoming roommates has wreaked such havoc on their friendship. Would it be better if he moved out, or should he stick it out and hope that things will change?

If you were in Brent's or Garrett's place, would you consider moving out? What other options do Brent and Garrett have for addressing the problems that have surfaced in their friendship? As this scenario illustrates, it is important that relationships be rewarding and fair. As with a seesaw that is too heavy on one side, if one partner is putting more effort into the relationship and still getting less out of it, this person will feel weighted down, and as a result, the relationship could come crashing down. Indeed, in some ways, relationships are like balancing acts. Both partners need to give and take in a fair manner. For partners to stay satisfied with their relationship, the scales also need to be tipped so that rewards outweigh costs.

In this chapter, we examine four social exchange theories that focus on this delicate balancing act. First, we discuss interdependence theory, which explains how costs and rewards work in conjunction with our expectations about relationships to affect satisfaction and commitment. Second, we look at the investment model, which is an extension of interdependence theory. The investment model emphasizes the role commitment plays in maintaining relationships. Third, we discuss equity theory, which focuses on whether rewards and costs are distributed fairly between relational partners. Finally, we review literature related to social exchange from a social evolutionary perspective, which predicts that sex differences in sexual attraction and mate selection have evolved due to the different roles that men and women play in reproduction and parenting.

INTERDEPENDENCE THEORY

Interdependence theory is based on the idea that interaction between partners is "the essence of all close relationships" (Rusbult et al., 1994). Through communication and the exchange of resources, relational partners become interdependent and committed to one another (Kelley, 1979). Every relationship has a unique pattern of interdependence that is based on the specific rewards and costs partners exchange, as well as the degree to which they are dependent on one another to reach their goals.

According to interdependence theory and other social exchange theories, people are motivated to be in relationships that provide them with high levels of rewards and low levels of costs. Using accounting as an analogy, people want to maximize their "profits" and minimize their "losses" in relationships (Blau, 1964; Homans, 1961, 1974; Thibaut & Kelley, 1959). Rewards and costs are weighed against each other, against people's standards and expectations for relationships, and against the alternative rewards and costs that people could have in other relationships or on their own. When these comparisons are favorable, people are generally satisfied with and committed to their relationships. In this section, we examine the various components of interdependence theory.

Rewards and Costs

Relationships are characterized by different types of rewards and costs. Sprecher (1998b) defined **rewards** as "exchanged resources that are pleasurable and gratifying" and **costs** as "exchanged resources that result in a loss or punishment" (p. 32). Rewards and costs play an important role in both friendships and romantic relationships. In one study, people rated their friendships as especially close when they felt they were receiving rewards such as affection and support (Tornblom & Fredholm, 1984). For romantic couples, exchanging love and information is related to increased intimacy and satisfaction (Lloyd, Cate, & Henton, 1982).

Most rewards and costs fall under one of four broad categories: emotional, social, instrumental, and opportunity. **Emotional rewards** include positive feelings such as love, warmth, happiness, and caring. **Emotional costs** include negative feelings such as anger, hurt, stress, and fear of abandonment. Examples of **social rewards** include engaging in fun activities with someone and meeting interesting or high-status people through your association with your partner. Examples of **social costs** might include having to attend your partner's boring company picnic and being embarrassed when your partner criticizes you in front of others. Prior to becoming roommates, Brent and Garrett's friendship appeared to be characterized by high emotional and social rewards.

Since becoming roommates, however, their friendship has become characterized by instrumental costs. **Instrumental rewards** and costs revolve around tasks. Your partner helps you get things done. For example, if you have a partner who manages the household finances well, you enjoy an instrumental reward. In contrast, **instrumental costs** are incurred when being in a relationship causes you more work or increased responsibility or when your partner impedes your progress in relation to a specific task. Having to do the majority of the housework, paying off your partner's debt, and helping your partner with a project are all examples of instrumental costs. Note, however, that what constitutes an instrumental cost for one partner often constitutes an instrumental reward for the other partner.

Finally, being in relationships provides people with some opportunities while taking away others. **Opportunity rewards** involve being able to do something that you could not otherwise do. For instance, by moving in together, Brent and Garrett can probably afford a nicer apartment than each of them could if they lived alone (assuming that Brent contributes enough financially). Similarly, pooling financial resources often gives married couples the opportunity to purchase a nicer home than either partner could afford individually. **Opportunity costs** involve having to give up something you want for the sake of the relationship. For example, if you have to quit your job and move across country to remain with your partner, you have given up the opportunity to advance in a particular organization, which is an opportunity cost. It is also important to note that when a romantic relationship is exclusive, both people give up the opportunity to pursue relationships with other people.

In every relationship, whether it is between friends, romantic partners, family members, coworkers, or employees and their supervisors, there are both rewards and costs. According to interdependence theory, people mentally account for rewards and costs so that they can evaluate the outcome of their relationship as either positive or negative. When rewards outweigh costs, the outcome is positive; when costs outweigh rewards, the outcome is negative. Put another way, **rewards minus costs equal the outcome**. To illustrate, suppose that Garrett perceives that he is receiving 20 rewards and 10 costs in his friendship with Brent. According to interdependence theory, Garrett will have a positive outcome ($20 - 10 = +10$). But if Garrett perceives that he is receiving 10 rewards and 20 costs, the outcome will be negative ($10 - 20 = -10$). Of course, rewards and costs are very hard to quantify, and some rewards and costs are more important than others. The critical point here is that people mentally compare costs and rewards to determine whether they are in a positive or negative relationship.

Certain rewards and costs may be weighted especially heavily. A good example of this is found in the television show *Friends* when Ross discovers that Rachel is romantically interested in him. Ross has had a crush on Rachel since high school, but he is currently in a happy relationship with a woman named Julie. To try to decide which woman to date, Ross makes a list of Rachel's and Julie's good and bad qualities. Even though he lists more rewards and fewer costs in the "Julie" column, Ross ultimately chooses Rachel. Complications occur, however, when Rachel finds the list, sees all the bad qualities Ross listed about her, and questions why someone would make such a list in the first place. This example illustrates two points. First, a single reward (or cost) can outweigh other rewards and costs. Second, trying to quantify one's feelings is difficult. In Rachel's case, she is insulted by Ross's list as well as the idea that he needs a "list" to decide if he prefers her to Julie. To get a general idea of how rewarding one of your relationships is, complete the scale found in Box 10.1.

Comparison Level

Knowing whether the relationship has a positive or a negative outcome is not enough. Some people expect highly rewarding relationships, so the outcomes have to be particularly positive for them to be happy. Other people expect their relationships to be unrewarding, so a slightly positive outcome, or even an outcome that is not as negative as expected, might be all that is needed to make them happy.

To account for the influence of expectations, interdependence theory includes the concept of **comparison level**, which involves the expectation of the kinds of outcomes a person thinks he or she should receive in a relationship (Thibaut & Kelley, 1959). This expectation is based on the person's past relational experiences and on her or his observations of other people's relationships. For example, if you have had really good relationships in the past and your parents and friends all tend to have happy relationships, you are likely to have a high comparison level. Thus you could be in a relationship in which the rewards outweigh the costs but not enough to exceed your comparison level, leading you to be dissatisfied. Consistent with the idea of comparison levels, one study demonstrated that women are less likely to rate their current relationship as committed and satisfying if their past relationships were especially close (Merolla, Weber, Myers, & Booth-Butterfield, 2004). The history of one's current relationship can also influence comparison levels. For example, based on how their friendship has operated in the past, Garrett might expect his rewards to outweigh his costs by about 4 to 1 in his relationship with Brent. However, since becoming roommates, he perceives that he is receiving only 2 rewards for every cost. Garrett's friendship still has a positive outcome because he is getting more rewards than costs. However, because the outcome does not meet his expectation, he is likely to be dissatisfied with his relationship.

The opposite can be true when a person has a low comparison level. For example, imagine that a friend of yours has a history of really bad relationships. Your friend's current relationship might have 5 rewards versus 10 costs, leading to a negative outcome (of -5 if we quantify it). However, if your friend expects to have to incur at least 20 costs to

BOX 10.1   Put Yourself to the Test

How Rewarding Is Your Relationship?

To determine how rewarding one of your current relationships is, answer the following questions using this scale: 1 = Very unrewarding, 7 = Very rewarding.

	Unrewarding ← → Rewarding						
1. How rewarding is your partner in providing you with affection and warmth?	1	2	3	4	5	6	7
2. How rewarding is your partner in contributing material goods such as gifts and possessions?	1	2	3	4	5	6	7
3. How rewarding is your partner in being comforting and supportive of you?	1	2	3	4	5	6	7
4. How rewarding is your partner in contributing money, such as letting you borrow money or paying for you?	1	2	3	4	5	6	7
5. How rewarding is your partner in helping you accomplish your goals related to work or school?	1	2	3	4	5	6	7
6. How rewarding is your partner socially, in terms of having common friends and liking to do things together?	1	2	3	4	5	6	7
7. When you think about everything that your partner has to offer you and your relationship (in the areas above as well as other areas), how rewarding is he or she?	1	2	3	4	5	6	7

To calculate your score, add the numbers you circled for each of the first six questions. Multiply your response to Question 7 by 2, and then add this to the sum. The total can range from 8 to 56. Higher scores mean that you perceive your relationship to be especially rewarding in a variety of ways.

SOURCE: Adapted from Sprecher, S., A comparison of emotional consequences of and changes in equity over time using global and domain-specific measures of equity, in *Journal of Social and Personal Relationships, 18*, 477–501. Copyright © 2001, Sage Publications, Inc.

receive 5 rewards, your friend's outcome of −5 would actually be better than his or her low comparison level of −15, so your friend should be fairly satisfied with the relationship.

As these examples suggest, people will be satisfied when their outcomes meet or exceed their comparison levels. This can be written as an equation: **Satisfaction equals the outcome minus the comparison level**. Thus the comparison level and

the outcome work together to predict how satisfied people are in their relationships (Sabatelli, 1984). Comparison levels also influence how much positive behavior people expect from their partners. Dainton (2000) conducted two studies looking at comparison levels, relational satisfaction, and maintenance behaviors. Maintenance behaviors included actions such as showing commitment to the partner, being positive and cheerful around the partner, and sharing tasks in a fair manner. These behaviors can be thought of as "rewards" within the context of the relationship. Dainton's research showed that people tended to be satisfied with their relationships when they perceived their partner to use high levels of rewarding maintenance behavior. Satisfaction was also higher when people reported that their partner used more maintenance behavior than they expected them to. In other words, people were happiest when their partner engaged in lots of rewarding behavior that met or exceeded their comparison level.

Quality of Alternatives

Although satisfaction and commitment often go together, it is possible for people to be in satisfying relationships that are uncommitted or in committed relationships that are unsatisfying. You can probably think of relationships that fit these categories. Perhaps you know someone who does not seem to want to commit to a relationship even though he or she seems happy. Perhaps you also know someone who seems to be stuck in a relationship that has no future and is unsatisfying. Quality of alternatives helps explain these situations.

Quality of alternatives refers to the types of alternatives that a person perceives he or she has outside a current relationship (Thibaut & Kelley, 1959). Alternatives might include pursuing other relationships or being on one's own. Some people perceive that they have several good alternatives. Perhaps many other attractive people would be interested in them, and perhaps they would be happier alone than in their current relationship. Other people perceive that they have poor alternatives. Perhaps they are dependent on their partner for financial support and cannot afford to leave the relationship, or they can envision no attractive alternative relationships, or they view themselves as unlovable and think that if they leave the partner they will be alone for the rest of their lives.

When people have good alternatives, they tend to be less committed to their relationships. In contrast, when people have poor alternatives, they tend be highly committed to their relationships (Crawford, Feng, Fischer, & Diana, 2003). A simplistic example of the way alternatives function might be observed during the month before the senior prom. Suppose that Rosa, a high school senior, has been dating Carlos for the past year. She is considering breaking up with him sometime before they both leave for college, but she is not sure when. If Rosa thinks that two or three boys she finds attractive are likely to ask her to the prom, she might break up with Carlos sooner (assuming that going to the prom is important to her). But if Rosa thinks that no one "better" than Carlos is going to ask her to the prom, she is likely to stay with him, at least temporarily.

On a more serious note, some individuals stay in unsatisfying and even abusive relationships because they have poor alternatives. For example, a man might decide that it is better to stay in his unhappy marriage rather than risk losing custody of his children. In a study on predictors of divorce, people reported being much more likely to leave their spouses when they had appealing alternatives (Black, Eastwood, Sprenkle, & Smith, 1991). Research also suggests that abused women who are dependent on their husbands for financial support are more likely to stay in their abusive relationships (Pfouts, 1978; Rusbult & Martz, 1995). These women, many of whom have little education, few work skills, and no means of transportation, often see their abusive relationships as a better alternative than being poor, hungry, and unable to support their children (Rusbult & Martz, 1995).

The Combined Influence of Comparison Level and Quality of Alternatives

Whereas the comparison level is a measure of satisfaction, the quality of alternatives is a measure of dependency and (at least temporary) commitment. These two factors combine to create different types of relationships, as shown in Figure 10.1. Here are examples for each of the boxes in Figure 10.1.

Box 1: The Committed and Satisfying Relationship. Joe perceives Darren to be the best relational partner he has ever had. He is more considerate and caring than all his past boyfriends, and they also have a lot in common. Therefore, Joe's relationship exceeds his comparison level, and he is very satisfied. Furthermore, Joe cannot imagine being with anyone

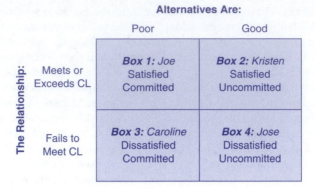

Figure 10.1 The Combined Influence of CL and CL-Alt

who makes him happier than Darren. When he considers his alternatives (which he rarely does), he thinks he is better off staying with Darren than pursuing a new relationship. Joe tells Darren, "I love you. Let's make our relationship exclusive."

Box 2: The Uncommitted but Satisfying Relationship. After her divorce, Kristen was really depressed. She thought dating would be really difficult, and she didn't think she'd ever find anyone she liked. Then she met Tim, who exceeded her expectations in nearly every way. He was easy to talk to, fun to be with, and very attractive. He definitely made her happy. Lately, however, several other attractive men have shown an interest in Kristen, and she wonders if it would be a mistake to "settle" for the first man to come along after her divorce. She tells Tim, "I really want to keep seeing you, but I think we should both see other people as well."

Box 3: The Dissatisfying but Committed Relationship. Caroline and Diana are partners who have been living together for almost a year. When they first moved in together, everything was great. But in recent months, they have started arguing more, and they seem to be drifting apart. Sometimes, Caroline dreads coming home at night because she is so worried that they will argue. Diana no longer meets her expectations; Caroline has been in happier relationships than this.

Yet Caroline feels trapped. She has not met anyone else she is remotely interested in dating, and she is terrified of being alone. She hopes that despite her unhappiness, things will eventually get better, so she says to herself, "I'll stick it out a little while longer—at least until something better comes along."

Box 4: The Dissatisfying and Uncommitted Relationship. Jose feels that his relationship with Cecilia is at a standstill. At first, Cecilia seemed like the perfect woman—intelligent, fun loving, easygoing, and beautiful. Six months into their relationship, however, Jose started focusing on Cecilia's flaws. Cecilia seems to use her intelligence to try to prove that she is always right, and she never wants to do anything fun anymore. In fact, Jose can think of many past girlfriends with whom he had much more fun. Lately, Jose has noticed that a coworker he finds more attractive than Cecilia has started to pay extra attention to him. He is sure she will accept if he asks her out. Jose tells Cecilia, "I'm sorry but I don't think this is working out anymore. I think we need to break up."

As these four types of relationships illustrate, the comparison level and the quality of alternatives shape the type of relationship people share. Some people stay in unhappy relationships because they do not have better alternatives, while others leave happy relationships to pursue even more appealing alternatives. Indeed, Donovan and Jackson (1990) argued that interdependence theory "may well be the theory most frequently used to explain the cause of divorce" (p. 24).

THE INVESTMENT MODEL

The investment model is an extension of interdependence theory. In the original **investment model,** Rusbult (1980, 1983) theorized that quality of alternatives, relational satisfaction, and investment size affect commitment. Commitment, in turn, determines whether people stay together or break up. Later, Rusbult and her colleagues developed an expanded investment model that focused on relational maintenance (Rusbult et al., 1994). According to this expanded model, commitment has a profound influence on whether people use positive, relationship-maintaining behaviors and survive the problems, conflicts, and temptations that threaten their relationships. In this section, we discuss both the original and the expanded versions of the investment model.

The Original Investment Model

Within the investment model, relational satisfaction is seen as a product of the choices and behaviors that both people in the relationship make. Consistent with other interdependence models, this model suggests that when relationships are characterized by behavior that is rewarding and fulfills expectations, satisfaction is likely. But satisfaction is only part of the story. According to the investment model, commitment is influenced not only by level of satisfaction but also by the quality of alternatives and the investments that people put into their relationships. Figure 10.2 depicts the components of this model.

Investments are "resources that become attached to a relationship and would decline in value or be lost if the relationship were to end" (Rusbult et al., 1994, p. 119). Investments can be classified as either intrinsic or extrinsic (Rusbult, 1983). **Intrinsic investments** are those that are put directly into the relationship, including time, effort, affection, and disclosure. **Extrinsic investments** are resources or benefits that are developed over time as a result of being in the relationship, such as material possessions, enmeshment within a common social system, and an identity that is attached to being in a relationship. People put more investments into relationships to which they feel a strong commitment (Matthews, 1986). These investments then make it difficult to walk away from a relationship, which strengthens commitment even more. If two people do end a highly invested relationship, they probably will feel

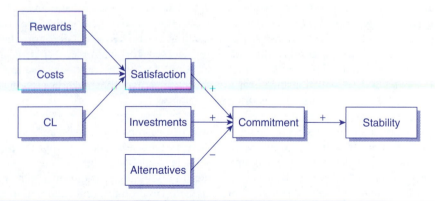

Figure 10.2 Rusbult's Original Investment Model

SOURCE: From Rusbult, C. E., Drigotas, S. M. & Verette, J., The Investment Model: An Interdependence Analysis of Commitment Processes and Relationship Maintenance Phenomena. In Daniel J. Canary & Laura Stafford (eds.), *Communication and Relational Maintenance.* Used with permission from Elsevier.

that all the time and effort they put into their relationship was a waste. They also might feel that they now have to start over, find someone new, and make adjustments to their identity and social image. These challenges make the prospect of ending a long-term, committed relationship a daunting one.

The basic idea behind the investment model is that satisfaction (which is influenced by rewards, costs, and comparison level), quality of alternatives, and investment size work together to produce commitment (as shown in Figure 10.2). When satisfaction and investments are high and the quality of alternatives is low, people are likely to be highly committed to their relationships. In contrast, when satisfaction and investments are low and the quality of alternatives is high, people are likely to be highly uncommitted to their relationships. Rusbult et al. (1994) noted that a high level of commitment can be good or bad. High commitment can keep a satisfying relationship strong, but it can also trap people in an unsatisfying relationship—especially if their alternatives are poor. Therefore, according to the investment model, satisfaction and commitment are related but distinctly different.

Several studies have supported the ideas behind the investment model (Le & Agnew, 2003). These studies have shown that investments, satisfaction, and the quality of alternatives determine whether people are committed to and stay in their relationships with friends and romantic partners (Drigotas & Rusbult, 1992; Duffy & Rusbult, 1986; Guerrero & Bachman, in press; Rusbult, 1980, 1983), as well as whether people stay at their jobs (Farrell & Rusbult, 1981; Rusbult & Farrell, 1983). For example, Rusbult (1983) looked at dating relationships over a 7-month period. She found that daters who reported increases in satisfaction and investment, as well as decreases in the quality of alternatives, were the most committed to their relationships. These people were also likely to be together at the end of the 7-month period. In contrast, daters who reported decreases in satisfaction and investment, as well as increases in the quality of alternatives, tended to experience less commitment and to voluntarily leave the relationship sometime during the 7-month period.

Another study examined abusive relationships by interviewing women at shelters (Rusbult & Martz, 1995). Women who went back to their abusive partners usually had large investments in the relationship and low-quality alternatives. Women in this situation may believe that it is better to stay in the relationship than to be alone or to move on to another, potentially worse, relationship. They may be dependent on their partner for financial resources and/or self-esteem. They also may not want to face the thought that they have put a lot of time and effort into a bad relationship. Therefore, they may work even harder to improve their relationship by trying to change their own and their partner's behavior. This continuous investment, however, keeps them trapped within the dissatisfying relationship. Thus, while high levels of investment keep people in relationships, it does not always ensure that relationships are satisfying.

Even partners in satisfying, highly committed relationships can go through periods of dissatisfaction, conflict, and interest in high-quality alternatives. Rusbult (1987; Rusbult & Zembrodt, 1983) suggested that people have four general options when dealing with negative events and dissatisfaction in their relationships: exit, neglect, voice, and loyalty. As Figure 10.3 shows, each of these responses is defined by whether it is constructive or destructive and whether it is passive or active.

The two destructive behaviors tend to exacerbate problems. **Exit** behaviors include actions such as threatening to break up, moving out of the house, and getting a divorce. **Neglect** behaviors involve standing by and letting conditions in the relationship get worse—for example, ignoring the partner, spending less time together, treating the partner poorly, and avoiding any discussion of relational problems.

The two constructive behaviors, in contrast, help people repair and maintain their relationships. Partners who use **voice** attempt to improve conditions in the relationship by engaging in activities such as discussing problems in a polite manner, seeking help from others, and changing negative behavior. Partners who use **loyalty** optimistically wait for positive change by hoping that things will improve, standing by the partner during difficult times, and supporting the partner in the face of criticism. Although voice and loyalty behaviors may help

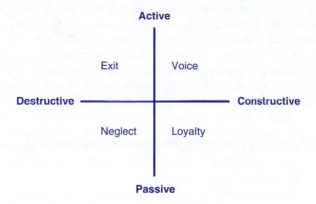

Figure 10.3 Rusbult's Model of Responses to Dissatisfaction

SOURCE: From Rusbult, C. E., Drigotas, S. M. & Verette, J., The Investment Model: An Interdependence Analysis of Commitment Processes and Relationship Maintenance Phenomena. In Daniel J. Canary & Laura Stafford (eds.), *Communication and Relational Maintenance.* Used with permission from Elsevier.

preserve the relationship, it is important to keep in mind that sometimes it is better to exit a bad relationship rather than work to improve it (Rusbult et al., 2001). Also, voice is a better strategy for repairing relationships than loyalty. Voice involves directly confronting issues and solving problems, whereas loyalty often leaves issues unresolved (Guerrero & Bachman, in press; Rusbult et al., 2001).

The Expanded Investment Model

An expanded version of the investment model (Rusbult et al., 1994) takes the original model a step further by suggesting that people in highly committed relationships get through difficult times by employing five types of prorelationship behavior, as shown in Figure 10.4: (1) deciding to remain in

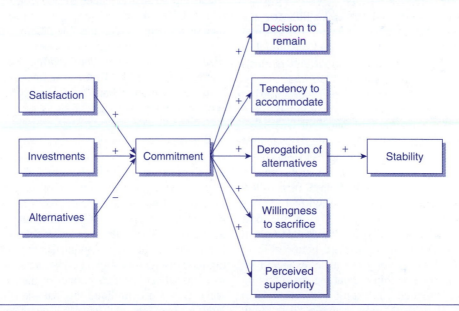

Figure 10.4 Rusbult's Expanded Investment Model of Relationship-Maintaining Behavior

SOURCE: From Rusbult, C. E., Drigotas, S. M. & Verette, J., The Investment Model: An Interdependence Analysis of Commitment Processes and Relationship Maintenance Phenomena. In Daniel J. Canary & Laura Stafford (eds.), *Communication and Relational Maintenance.* Used with permission from Elsevier.

the relationship, (2) accommodating the partner, (3) derogating alternatives, (4) being willing to sacrifice, and (5) perceiving relationship superiority.

Deciding to Remain. The first and perhaps most important step is the decision to remain in the relationship. People who choose the exit or neglect responses have usually stopped believing in their relationship. Without a commitment by the partners to stay in the relationship and work through problems, the relationship is unlikely to survive. In one study, couples who were committed to one another were less likely to report exiting the relationship following a relational transgression, such as their partner betraying or lying to them (Menzies-Toman & Lydon, 2005). In another study, couples were less likely to de-escalate their relationships following a transgression if they had reported high levels of satisfaction and investment earlier (Guerrero & Bachman, in press).

Accommodating the Partner. If the partners do decide to remain in the relationship, they must find a way to cope with their dissatisfaction and repair the relationship. To do this, they must resist the urge to engage in exit and neglect behaviors and instead use constructive responses such as voice (Rusbult et al., 1986). Rusbult and her colleagues use the term **accommodation** to refer to this process of using constructive behavior (voice and loyalty) rather than destructive behavior (exit and neglect) when responding to negative relational events. Accommodation helps partners repair a relationship after a negative event; however, accommodation can be difficult. When feeling hurt, angry, or frustrated, people's first reaction is often to retaliate against the partner. Rusbult and her colleagues (1994) put it this way: "Being treated in an inconsiderate manner generates a natural impulse to behave inconsiderately in turn (i.e., to fight fire with fire). . . . However, accommodation is clearly in the best interest of the relationship" (pp. 126–127). People in highly committed relationships are better able to resist the initial inclination to retaliate, especially if they have had time to think about the dissatisfying event in the broader context of the relationship (Rusbult et al., 2001). For example, one study

showed that people who are committed to their relationships tend to express jealousy by disclosing feelings and talking over problems in a calm manner (Bevan, in press). People are more likely to engage in constructive rather than destructive communication under three other conditions: (1) when they were satisfied with their relationships prior to the dissatisfying event, (2) when they have made considerable investments in their relationships, and (3) when their quality of alternatives is poor (Guerrero & Bachman, in press).

Derogating Alternatives. Commitment also leads people to derogate their alternatives. In other words, committed people tend to find reasons to downgrade potential alternative partners. For example, in a study by Johnson and Rusbult (1989), when highly committed individuals were matched up with attractive partners via computer-assigned dates, they found ways to derogate their computer dates, especially if they were highly attractive! Although derogating alternatives is probably most relevant to romantic relationships, people in friendships and work relationships might also derogate attractive alternatives. Imagine, for example, that Garrett and Brent work out the issues that have been causing tension in their friendship so that satisfaction and commitment are restored. If an acquaintance, Paul, who owns a nicer apartment and has a stable income, approaches Garrett about becoming roommates, Garrett would likely find fault with Paul's offer. For example, Garrett might think "Brent is a lot more fun than Paul," even though Paul is known to have a great sense of humor.

Willingness to Make Sacrifices. People in highly committed relationships are also more willing to make sacrifices for each other. Sacrifices can be thought of as special types of investments that involve putting aside one's own immediate self-interest and focusing on the best interests of the relationship. The willingness to make sacrifices has been found to be an important factor in maintaining high-quality relationships. People are more likely to make sacrifices for their partner or their relationship when they are committed and satisfied, have made large investments, and have low-quality alternatives

(Van Lange et al., 1997). Making sacrifices sometimes involves helping a relational partner through a crisis situation. One study showed that college students see their closest friends as a significant source of comfort, encouragement, and social support (Burleson & Samter, 1994). Willingness to sacrifice is also important because it is difficult for two people to get everything each one wants within the constraints of the relationship. For example, spouses have to make hard decisions regarding their careers, children, and so forth. If the wife's new promotion means that the family will have to move somewhere that is unappealing to the husband, the couple will have to make some type of compromise or sacrifice. Or, if the husband wants to have only one child and the wife wants at least three, one of them will have to give in, or they will both have to compromise. In short, because both people cannot always have everything their own way, it is essential that relational partners be willing to sacrifice their own preferences for the overall good of the relationship.

Perceiving Relationship Superiority. Relational partners who are highly committed to each other perceive their relationship to be superior to other relationships. This can be thought of as a "relationship-enhancing illusion" (Rusbult et al., 1994, p. 129). For highly committed relationships, "the grass is rarely greener" on the other side. People tend to see their own relationships as having more positive and fewer negative characteristics than the relationships of others. This bias is particularly strong in highly committed relationships (Rusbult, Van Lange, Wildschut, Yovetich, & Verette, 2000). People might say and think things such as "We give each other a lot more freedom than most couples do" and "Our relationship doesn't have as many problems as the average relationship has." This type of thinking leads to positive attitudes about the relationship and sets the tone for behaving constructively and making more sacrifices. In relationships that are low in commitment and satisfaction, such positive thinking is less likely; the "grass on the other side" may indeed seem greener!

The investment model has proven to be a powerful theory for explaining the role that commitment plays in the process of relational maintenance.

Two people are most likely to become committed to each other when they are satisfied with the relationship, have low-quality alternatives, and have made sizable investments. Once a couple is highly committed, the relationship is maintained through several types of prorelationship activities, including remaining in the relationship through good times and bad, accommodating the partner by resisting the urge to retaliate, derogating alternatives, being willing to sacrifice for the good of the relationship, and perceiving the relationship to be superior to the relationships of others. These forces combine to help maintain the relationship.

EQUITY THEORY

Like interdependence theory and the investment model, equity theory has been used to explain why some couples are more satisfied with their relationships than others. **Equity theory** focuses on determining whether the distribution of resources is fair to both relational partners (Deutsch, 1985). Equity is measured by comparing the ratio of contributions and benefits for each person. The key word here is *ratio*. Partners do *not* have to receive equal benefits (such as receiving the same amount of love, care, and financial security) or make equal contributions (such as investing the same amount of effort, time, and financial resources) as long as the ratio between these benefits and contributions is similar.

For example, Brent might put more effort into maintaining the roommate relationship than Garrett does. Brent might clean the house more, cook or bring home dinner nearly every night, and give Garrett and his girlfriend lots of time alone in the apartment on weekends. However, Brent may also get more substantial rewards from the arrangement than Garrett. Because Garrett works a lot and contributes more financially, Brent may have more time to pursue a challenging chemistry major. In this case, the balance of rewards and costs that each man receives in comparison with the other might be satisfactory. However, if Brent put more effort into the roommate relationship without receiving extra rewards, he would likely feel dissatisfied with their arrangement.

Principles of Equity Theory

As the example of Brent and Garrett illustrates, equitable relationships are usually characterized by more satisfaction and commitment than inequitable relationships, largely because people feel distress when inequity is perceived to exist (Adams, 1965; Walster, Berscheid, & Walster, 1973; Walster, Walster, & Berscheid, 1978). Five principles help explain why rewards and equity are associated with relational satisfaction and commitment (Canary & Stafford, 2001; Guerrero, La Valley, & Farinelli, 2006; Walster, Walster, & Berscheid, 1978):

1. Individuals try to maximize their outcomes so that relational rewards outweigh relational costs.

2. People in groups and dyads develop rules for distributing resources fairly.

3. Within groups and dyads, people will reward those who treat them equitably and punish those who treat them inequitably.

4. When individuals are in inequitable relationships, they will experience distress. This distress will lead them to try to restore equity, such that the more distress they experience, the harder they will try to alleviate that distress.

5. Individuals in equitable relationships experience more satisfaction. They also engage in more prosocial behavior than do individuals in inequitable relationships.

Around half of couples report that their marriages are equitable (Peterson, 1990). When relationships are inequitable, one individual is overbenefited, and the other is underbenefited (Walster, Walster, & Berscheid, 1978). The **overbenefited** individual receives more benefits and/or makes fewer contributions than does his or her partner, so that the ratio between them is unbalanced. In simple terms, this person is getting the "better deal." The **underbenefited** individual, in contrast, receives fewer benefits and/or makes greater contributions than does her or his partner, so that the ratio between them is not balanced. This person is getting the "worse deal."

When actual inequity exists, one person is always underbenefited, and the other person is always overbenefited. However, perception does not always match reality. Because people tend to overestimate their own contributions to relationships, both dyadic members might think they are underbenefited even though this is not actually the case. For example, in a classic study by Ross and Sicoly (1979), husbands and wives rated the degree to which they had responsibility for various activities, such as caring for the children, washing the dishes, and handling the finances, on a scale from 0 (no responsibility) to 150 (complete responsibility). Thus, if a husband and wife split the task of doing the dishes evenly, both should have rated their responsibility at the 75-point midpoint. However, the results suggested that 73% of the spouses overestimated the amount of work they did; when their ratings were summed and averaged across all the activities, they totaled over 150 points. Apparently, a lot of dishes were being cleaned twice! As this example illustrates, relational partners, like Garrett and Brent, might both perceive themselves to be underbenefited; but in reality, it would be impossible for each person to be getting a "worse deal" than the other. To see if you and a relational partner overestimate the extent to which you contribute to the relationship, take the test in Box 10.2.

Benefits of Equity. Partners who perceive equity tend to be satisfied with and committed to their relationships. Early work on equity theory showed that individuals who perceived their dating relationships to be equitable reported being happier and more content than those who perceived their dating relationships to be inequitable (Walster, Walster, & Traupmann, 1978). Later work on married couples showed that people who perceive equity or overbenefitedness are happier than those who perceive themselves as underbenefited (Buunk & Mutsaers, 1999; Guerrero et al., 2006). Couples who perceive equity also tend to report more commitment to their relationships (Crawford et al., 2003).

Communication patterns may contribute to the satisfaction that couples in equitable relationships experience. For instance, couples in equitable relationships report using more relational maintenance behavior than those in inequitable relationships

◼ BOX 10.2   Put Yourself to the Test

How Much Do You and Your Partner Contribute to the Division of Labor?

Think about a relationship you have with a person with whom you live. It could be a romantic relationship, a roommate relationship, or a family relationship. (If you are currently living alone, you can report on a past relationship.) Make two copies of this page so that you and your partner can each fill it out separately at first.

What percentage of time, from 0% to 100%, do you spend on the following things? If you and your partner do a particular chore separately, mark 50%. For example, you and your roommate might each do your own laundry. If something is not relevant to your relationship, leave it blank.

	% Time I Do This	% Time My Partner Does This	Total %
1. The dishes	_____	_____	_____
2. The household laundry	_____	_____	_____
3. Writing checks or using e-mail to pay the bills	_____	_____	_____
4. Contributing money to pay for bills and household expenses	_____	_____	_____
5. Cleaning the bathroom(s)	_____	_____	_____
6. Vacuuming the floors	_____	_____	_____
7. Cleaning noncarpeted floors	_____	_____	_____
8. Grocery shopping	_____	_____	_____
9. Dusting the furniture and other household goods	_____	_____	_____
10. Taking care of a pet or pets	_____	_____	_____
11. Taking out the trash	_____	_____	_____
12. Cooking meals	_____	_____	_____
13. Setting and clearing the table	_____	_____	_____
14. Going out and getting prepared meals (such as from a restaurant)	_____	_____	_____
15. Mowing lawns and landscaping	_____	_____	_____
16. Maintenance on cars (including washing and repairs)	_____	_____	_____
17. Helping children with homework	_____	_____	_____
18. Taking basic care of children, such as getting them dressed and brushing their teeth	_____	_____	_____
19. Driving children places	_____	_____	_____
20. Purchasing clothing and supplies for people in the household	_____	_____	_____

After each person fills out this form separately, add up the percentages and put them under the "Total %" column. Percentages over 100 indicate that one or both of you overestimate the extent to which you do a chore, whereas percentages under 100 indicate that one of both of you underestimate the extent to which you do a particular chore.

(Canary & Stafford, 2001; Messman et al., 2000). Maintenance behaviors help couples keep their relationship satisfying. Several specific maintenance behaviors have been found to be associated with equity, including positivity, openness, and assurances. **Positivity** involves making interactions pleasant and enjoyable by engaging in behaviors such as being cheerful and optimistic and complimenting the partner. **Openness** involves disclosing personal information, as well as engaging in more routine, mundane talk. **Assurances** involve making statements that show commitment to the relationship, such as talking about the partners' future together. (These and other maintenance behaviors were discussed in greater detail in Chapter 9.) Couples in equitable relationships also say that they express anger, guilt, and sadness in more constructive ways than do couples in inequitable relationships (Guerrero et al., 2006). For example, they talk about their anger in an assertive manner without restoring to aggression.

Consequences of Underbenefiting Inequity. According to equity theory, whether people are over-benefited or underbenefited, they experience increases in distress and decreases in satisfaction and happiness (Walster, Walster, & Berscheid, 1978). Of course, underbenefited individuals experience a different kind of distress than overbenefited individuals. As you might expect, underbenefited individuals are usually more distressed than overbenefited individuals (Canary & Stafford, 1994). They also report the least relational satisfaction (Buunk & Mutsaers, 1999; Guerrero et al., 2006). When people are underbenefited, they tend to feel cheated, used, and taken for granted, and they experience anger and/or sadness (Walster, Walster, & Traupmann, 1978). Men may be particularly likely to be angry when they are underbenefited, while women may be especially likely to be sad, disappointed, or frustrated (Sprecher, 1986, 2001). Both men and women report expressing anger more aggressively when they are in the underbenefited position (Guerrero et al., 2006).

Underbenefited individuals also report that both they and their partners use less relational maintenance. In one study, underbenefited husbands reported that their wives used less positivity, offered fewer assurances, and shared fewer tasks than did overbenefited husbands and husbands in equitable relationships (Canary & Stafford, 1992). Therefore, people may feel underbenefited if they do not receive adequate amounts of relational maintenance. On the other hand, people who feel underbenefited might not feel like exerting much effort into maintaining a dissatisfying relationship.

Consequences of Overbenefiting Inequity. Over-benefited individuals tend to experience less distress than their underbenefited counterparts but more distress than individuals who are in equitable relationships (Guerrero et al., 2006; Sprecher, 1986, 2001; Walster, Walster, & Traupmann, 1978). People who perceive themselves as overbenefited may also feel smothered and wish that their partner would spend less time doing things for them. One study showed that overbenefited wives tend to express guilt by apologizing and doing nice things for their husbands (Guerrero et al., 2006). When wives perceive themselves to be overbenefited, they might use these types of behaviors to try to balance their marriages by increasing their husband's rewards. Yet some research shows that women in overbenefiting relationships use less relational maintenance behavior (Canary & Stafford, 1992). These women may not feel much need to maintain their relationships because their husbands are already providing them with high levels of reward. However, if they feel guilty about something, they may be likely to engage in positive behavior that prevents the relationship from becoming too out of balance.

Of course, some overbenefited men and women feel quite content with their relationships and not guilty at all (Hatfield, Greenberger, Traupmann, & Lambert, 1982; Traupmann, Hatfield, & Wexler, 1983). One study even showed that the more over-benefited people are the happier they are (Buunk & Mutsaers, 1999). People may need to be highly overbenefited before they experience distress and guilt. In contrast, being even somewhat underbenefited can lead to anger and frustration. In any case, if people perceive inequity, feelings of anger, sadness, and guilt may pervade the emotional fabric of their relationship.

Combined Influence of Reward-Cost Ratios and Equity

Although equity is related to a host of positive processes in relationships, equity alone does not determine how interdependence affects a relationship. To be highly satisfied, a couple also needs to be in a relationship in which rewards outweigh costs. In fact, studies by Cate and his associates showed that the overall level of reward value associated with a relationship is more important than equity (Cate & Lloyd, 1988; Cate, Lloyd, & Henton, 1985; Cate, Lloyd, & Long, 1988). Some level of inequity might be inconsequential if both partners are receiving high levels of rewards. Thus relationships that are characterized by equity as well as positive outcomes (rewards outweigh costs) are most likely to be satisfying. Relationships that are inequitable with rewards outweighing costs should also be satisfying, especially if the rewards are high and the inequity is fairly small. In contrast, relationships that are equitable with costs outweighing rewards are likely to be perceived as fair but somewhat dissatisfying. Finally, inequitable relationships in which costs outweigh rewards are the least satisfying.

Let's take a look at some examples that illustrate how equity and reward-cost levels work together. Earlier, we introduced you to Joe and Darren, who are in a satisfied, committed relationship. Suppose that Joe receives 25 benefits for every 5 contributions he makes to his relationship with Darren. This means that Joe has a benefit-contribution ratio of 25:5. Darren has a ratio of 50:10. Is their relationship equitable or inequitable? Because both Joe and Darren are receiving 5 benefits per contribution, their relationship is equitable. Note that for the relationship to be equitable, Joe and Darren do not have to be receiving the same number of benefits, nor do they have to be making the same number of contributions. Instead, the ratios between each person's benefits and contributions must be the same. Note also that their outcome value (rewards minus costs) is positive. Thus, Darren and Joe's relationship is equitable and rewarding and, as a consequence, satisfying.

In other cases, relationships can be equitable without being particularly rewarding. Imagine one partner having a benefit-contribution ratio of 15:30, while the other partner has a benefit-contribution ratio of 10:20. Both individuals are getting 1 benefit for every 2 contributions they make, so the relationship is equitable. But would such a couple have a satisfying relationship? The answer seems to be yes and no. They might be satisfied in that both are getting a fair deal but dissatisfied because they are not maximizing their rewards, which, as discussed previously, is the first principle of equity theory.

Ways to Reduce Distress in Inequitable Relationships

So what happens when relational partners experience inequity and distress? According to Walster, Walster, and Berscheid (1978), they will be motivated to reduce inequity and the accompanying distress. There are three general ways to do this. First, people can attempt to restore **actual equity** through some behavioral change. For example, the overbenefited partner might contribute more to the relationship, whereas the underbenefited partner might do less. Alternatively, the underbenefited partner might ask the overbenefited partner to do more. Second, people can attempt to restore **psychological equity**. Recall that equity is "in the eye of the beholder" in that perceptions are as important as actions. To restore equity, people sometimes reassess their costs and benefits and decide that they are actually getting a fairer deal than they first thought. For instance, on reflection Garrett might realize that Brent actually does a lot for him and that it isn't his fault he is broke all the time. Sometimes, mental adjustments such as these represent the situation more accurately. However, there is also a potential danger. An individual might continually readjust her or his perceptions even though the situation has remained unchanged. If this happens, the person might remain stuck in the underbenefited or overbenefited position. Third, people can simply end the relationship. This option is most likely when people have made low investments in the relationship and have high-quality alternatives outside the relationship.

SOURCE: Copyright: iStockphoto.com/Maartje van Caspel

Photo 10.1   Sharing tasks in a fair and equitable manner is important for the entire family. Sometimes sharing chores can be fun, as demonstrated by this family cooking together.

Equity in the Division of Household Labor

Before leaving the topic of equity, it is important to discuss how issues of equity and fairness are related to the division of household labor. Couples who share tasks in a fair manner report being happier and more committed (Canary & Stafford, 1993, 1994). They also report giving and receiving more social support to one another (Van Willigen & Drentea, 2001). Yet research suggests that it is hard for many couples to achieve a fair division of labor (Steil, 2000). When it comes to household work, women are typically underbenefited and men are typically overbenefited. In fact, according to Steil's (2000) careful review of the literature, working women do about two thirds of the household chores and even more of the child care. You might think that the division of household chores would be more equitable for working than for nonworking women, since

working women's husbands might be expected to do more. However, Berk (1985) found that men in dual-career couples spend only 4 more minutes a day engaged in household tasks than do men in traditional single-career relationships. Even among dual-career partners who report splitting household tasks evenly, women still do far more in terms of caring for children (Rosenbluth, Steil, & Whitcomb, 1998). The situation is no better for wives who earn more than their husbands. In fact, Biernat and Wortman (1991) found that men actually do less household chores when their wives earn more than they do, perhaps because they see their wives as highly capable of handling multiple tasks or because they are resentful. On the basis of these results, it is not surprising that wives are more likely to feel underbenefited than husbands (e.g., Guerrero et al., 2006).

Ironically, although women usually air their relational grievances to their husbands (Gottman & Carrere, 1994), in the case of unfair division of household labor they are often silent (Thompson & Walker, 1989). Unless their share of household work exceeds the two-thirds mark, they typically do not perceive that the division of labor is unfair, nor do they complain. Instead, they deal with the inequity by adjusting their perceptions or comparing themselves with other women who have a worse situation than themselves (Himsel & Goldberg, 2003; Shelton & John, 1996). Steil (2000) labeled this problem "the paradox of the contented wife" (p. 127). Women want equality, yet even when they are aware that they do more household tasks than their husbands, they often end up reporting that their relationship is fair, equitable, and satisfying.

Even though women are fairly satisfied in marriages in which inequities (up to the two-thirds share mark) occur, working mothers become less satisfied as the gap between their husband's and their own share of the housework tasks widens (Barnett & Baruch, 1987; Staines & Libby, 1986). At this point, women begin to feel underbenefited. Based on these findings, Gottman and Carrere (1994) made the following recommendation: Most men need to do more housework, care for their children more, and show their wives more affection and appreciation if they want their wives to be truly happy.

Unlike their heterosexual counterparts, most gay and lesbian partners do roughly the same amount of household tasks. Peplau and Spalding (2000) provided a comprehensive review of the literature on the division of labor in homosexual households. In their review, they noted that most gay men and lesbians are in dual-career relationships, "so that neither partner is the exclusive breadwinner and each partner has some measure of economic independence. The most common division of labor involves flexibility, with partners, sharing domestic activities or dividing tasks according to personal preferences" (p. 117). Kurdek (1993a) compared the division of household labor in heterosexual, gay male, and lesbian couples. Consistent with other research, he found that women did a larger portion of household work than did men in heterosexual relationships. Gay men and lesbians were more likely to do an equal amount of household tasks. But whereas gay men divided the chores up so that each man routinely did certain tasks more

than the others, lesbians tended to share tasks, often by doing chores together. Thus, opposite-sex couples might take a lesson from same-sex couples when it comes to sharing household chores in a fair, equitable manner.

EVOLUTIONARY THEORIES OF SOCIAL EXCHANGE

All the theories we have reviewed so far in this chapter focus on the social exchange of rewards and costs within interdependent relationships. In the final section of this chapter, we take a look at how social evolutionary theorists have applied the principles of social exchange to attraction and mate selection (Buss, 1994; Buss & Kenrick, 1998; Trost & Alberts, 2006). Take a look at the personal advertisements in Box 10.3. Personal ads such as these, although typical, may appear quite superficial to you. However, they illustrate how social exchange operates in the dating marketplace. People look to exchange certain resources for other resources that they value. For some people, there are even minimum "resource requirements," such as being a nonsmoker, college educated, or a certain age or height. In a classic study, Cameron, Oskamp, and Sparks (1977) examined personal advertisements such as these and suggested that they read like the New York Stock Exchange, with potential partners seeking to "strike bargains which maximize their rewards in the exchange of assets" (p. 28).

According to the evolutionary perspective on social exchange, people's preferences for mates evolved in ways consistent with the biological imperative to reproduce. Because reproduction and child care involve different rewards, costs, and investments for men versus women, social evolutionary theorists argue that there are sex differences in the qualities people find attractive in long-term mates. Across various cultures, men appear to look for mates who are fertile and will be good mothers, whereas women tend to look for mates who have the necessary resources to be good fathers and providers. A woman, however, should be choosier than a man when it comes to a finding a mate because her investment, in terms of pregnancy and child care, will typically be higher than his (Trost & Alberts, 2006).

Social evolutionary theories of sexual attraction and mating also emphasize the importance of the **pair bond**, which is defined as a committed union between two people (Kenrick & Trost, 1987, 1989). The pair bond is important because throughout human history, children were more likely to survive and reach maturity if they had a mother and a father who worked together to protect, provide for, and nurture them. To provide the best prospects for having children and promoting their survival, social evolutionary theorists contend that men and women look for certain qualities in their mates. Kenrick, Groth, Trost, and Sadalla (1993) put it this way: Potential partners

> seek and value mates that would (in our ancestor's time) have been related to (a) the likely possession of adaptive genes that might directly promote the survival of offspring and (b) the capacity and inclination to contribute tangible resources that could help the offspring survive. (p. 951)

Thus according to evolutionary psychology, resource exchange involves trading assets that will help a couple ensure the survival of their children.

These evolutionary processes supposedly are driven by unconscious impulses that have evolved across the millennia.

Sex Differences in Sexual Attraction

Sexual attraction, which was defined in Chapter 3 as the desire to engage in sexual activity (which may or not include intercourse) with a person, is a ubiquitous human experience. According to evolutionary theories, the human sex drive is an innate, biological drive that serves to ensure reproduction and to maintain dyadic relationships between sexual partners. Although sexual desire and sexual attraction can be suppressed, most people experience sexual desire and are, at least occasionally, sexually attracted to other individuals. While some adults do abstain from sex for periods of time, most do not (Blumstein & Schwartz, 1983; Sprecher & Regan, 1996). There are important sex differences in sexual desire. Men's sex drive is often motivated by physical needs, whereas women's sex drive is more variable and contextually driven than men's (Baumeister, 2000). Women also tend to have more sexual disorders, such as low sexual desire, orgasmic disorder, and pain during intercourse (Laumann, Paik, & Rosen,

1999). Yet women who have these disorders often wish that sex was more pleasurable. These sex differences are consistent with evolutionary principles, in that women are usually choosier about when and with whom to have sex (Trost & Alberts, 2006).

A huge body of research has shown that similarity produces attraction. As discussed in Chapter 3 and as Box 10.3 suggests, similarities in wealth, age, physical attractiveness, political beliefs, educational level, personal habits, religion, and a host of other factors typically increase attraction. Research has even shown that romantic partners are more sexually similar than randomly paired individuals (Cupach & Metts, 1995). Social evolutionary theorists believe that men and women are also similar in that they are most attracted to potential mates who show signs of physical health, sexual maturity, and reproductive potential and who are therefore capable of passing "good" genetic material on to their offspring (Buss & Kenrick, 1998). However, because men and women play different roles in the reproductive process, they should also differ to some extent in the qualities they look for in a mate.

Evolutionary psychology predicts that men select sexually mature but youthful females to maximize their reproductive potential. Regardless of culture, men are theorized to prefer characteristics associated with high reproductive capacity such as good looks, an hourglass body shape, youthfulness, and chastity. Singh (1993), for example, showed that men preferred women of average to below average weight and with hourglass figures (waist-to-hip ratio of .70) across two cultural groups.

In contrast, women should prefer characteristics associated with resource acquisition in potential mates, such as a masculine body type, ambition, industriousness, and good financial prospects. In a study of 37 cultures, from Zulus to Poles and from Canadians to Japanese, Buss (1989) uncovered just such a pattern. Likewise, Singh (1995) showed that women prefer men with a masculine shape (a waist-to-hip ratio of .90 is best), moderate weight, and higher financial status. For whatever reason, resources such as status, dominance, and material possessions appear to be very important for women's attraction to men but less important for men's attraction to women.

Apparently, however, if they have to choose between the two characteristics, women value men with good personalities more than they value men with wealth. Cunningham, Barbee, Graves, Lundy, and Lister (1996), for example, found that women were more likely to report that they would have sexual intercourse with a nice, moral, wealthy man than with a nice, moral, middle-class man but would be unwilling to have sex with a man who was unfriendly and immoral regardless of his wealth. According to evolutionary theory, women should be attracted to men who will provide resources such as long-term emotional and financial support, so an unfriendly and immoral man would be unacceptable.

Evolutionary psychology has also been used to explain why men are usually attracted to younger women and women are usually attracted to older men (Kenrick & Keefe, 1992). Women tend to reach optimal fertility levels in their early to mid-20s. Therefore, the potential for a man to have multiple children is highest when he pairs with a young woman. For example, a 20 year-old woman usually has more reproductive years ahead of her than a 28-year-old woman. This logic also explains why young men are sometimes attracted to older women; an 18-year-old man would have a more immediate reproductive advantage if he paired with a woman his own age (or slightly older) than a girl younger than himself. As men age, they should prefer women progressively younger than themselves.

Because men do not experience the same dramatic decrease in fertility that women typically encounter by their mid-30s, women are less concerned with age per se and more concerned with the resources potential mates can offer them. However, men tend to gain greater resources as they age. For instance, a man in his 40s is more likely to have accumulated financial resources than a man in his 20s. Similarly, physical strength peaks later for men than for women. As a result, young women are more likely to be attracted to older men who have these types of resources. However, as women age, they show less age preference.

In a series of studies, Kenrick and Keefe (1992) tested the hypothesis that men prefer younger women and women prefer older men. Specifically, they looked at (1) want ads in singles' magazines and an elite intellectual publication, (2) the current marriage records in two U.S. cities, (3) marriage records from 1923, (4) personal ads in Germany and Holland, and (5) Philippine marital statistics prior to World War II. Across all these samples, Kenrick and Keefe confirmed this evolutionary hypothesis. When there is an age difference of 5 years or more between husband and wife, the wife is much more likely to be the younger spouse. However, it is important to note that many spouses are close in age (although the husband does tend to be older) and that *both* men and women are waiting longer to get married now than in previous decades. According to data on first marriages from the U.S. Census Bureau, in the 1950s and 1960s the average woman married before her 21st birthday, while the average man married at around age 23, often after finishing college and starting a career. In the 1990s, the average woman married at about age 24, and the average man married at about age 26. By 2005, these numbers inched up a bit more, with the average age at first marriage around 25 for women and 27 for men. It will be interesting to see if these ages continue to rise or if they stabilize, especially since most women hit their fertility peak in their mid-20s. An increasing number of couples in the United States experience problems of infertility; data from the National Center for Health Statistics of the Centers for Disease Control and Prevention (http:\womenshealth.gov) indicate that 12% of women in the United States (which equals 7.3 million women) had infertility problems in 2002. One reason for the surge in infertility rates is that women in the United States are waiting longer to have children. Indeed, 20% of women in the United States are 35 years old or older when they have their first child.

The Parental Investment Model

The evolutionary perspective also explains the influence of personality on long-term attraction. Having the ability to reproduce is not enough. Couples must also be able to care for their offspring to ensure survival. According to the **parental investment model,** men and women (like other mammals) fulfill different reproductive functions and make different investments in their children (Trivers, 1985). **Parental investment** refers to any resources that a parent

devotes to her or his children at the cost of investing the resource elsewhere (Daly & Wilson, 1983). As new parents find out, raising a child takes considerable time, effort, and sacrifice. Parents arrange their schedules around the needs of their children. Money that a couple could have spent on a vacation or a new car might be placed in a child's college fund, and romantic nights out might become scarce. Thus having a mate who is patient, willing to make sacrifices, and loyal to the family is a valued commodity.

According to the investment model, women make particularly costly investments in parenting because of pregnancy and nursing. Additionally, women are usually the primary caregivers for their children. Men, in contrast, have the option of investing minimally in their offspring simply by providing their genes. Although most men do invest heavily in their offspring, they still do not invest as much as women. As noted previously, among married couples with children, women typically handle more than two thirds of the child-care responsibilities. In addition, most single-parent families are headed by women, which underscores the increased parental investment that often is shouldered by women. Although some men remain heavily invested in their children's lives after a divorce, many men gradually reduce their investments once they move out of the family home (Pearson & Thoennes, 1990; Seltzer, 1991).

Kenrick and his colleagues extended this line of reasoning by proposing the **relationship-qualified parental investment model** (Kenrick et al., 1993; Kenrick, Sadalla, Groth, & Trost, 1990). According to this model, various stages of relationships are characterized by different configurations of rewards and costs. In casual dating relationships that do not involve sex, the partners will be relatively unconcerned about resources connected to parental investment. However, if the relationship becomes more serious, issues related to parental investment will become more salient for both men and women. However, women will be choosier than men when deciding whether to have a one-night stand or a brief sexual liaison with someone because women (at least historically) risk pregnancy and the resulting costs.

Based on the relationship-qualified investment model, Kenrick and his associates (1990, 1993) tested for sex differences in attraction at different relational stages. Specifically, participants in these studies rated the *minimum* levels of physical attractiveness, dominance, status, and intelligence (among other characteristics) that they would seek in a person they would go on a date with, have sex with, date steadily, and marry. Consistent with evolutionary psychology women were choosier than men on all characteristics except for physical attractiveness.

One of these studies (Kenrick et al., 1993) also included ratings of the minimum characteristics needed for people to engage in one-night stands. As noted previously, social evolutionary theorists predict that women will be particularly choosy when engaging in one-night stands because of the risks associated with getting pregnant and not having the emotional support of a committed partner. Men, in contrast, will be particularly unselective because they have a low-cost opportunity to have sex. Kenrick et al.'s (1993) study supported this sex difference in selectiveness. That is, when rating potential partners for one-night stands, women were nearly as choosy as they were when rating potential partners for committed relationships, whereas men's level of choosiness dropped to its lowest point in every category except for physical appearance. The difference here was particularly striking when the results for intelligence were analyzed. Women reported that a man would have to be above average in intelligence if they were to consider having a one-night stand with him. Men, in contrast, reported that they would consider having a one-night stand with a woman who was below average in intelligence. However, both men and women desired marital partners who were well above average in intelligence, suggesting that both sexes are the most selective when it comes to choosing a long-term mate.

In sum, evolutionary psychology predicts that potential mates exchange resources at least partially based on their drive to reproduce and to care for their offspring. These evolutionary processes have evolved over many millennia and continue to evolve today. In the 21st century, as men and women bring new resources to the "dating marketplace," it is likely that different attributes will be seen as attractive, and new socially adaptive preferences may slowly emerge as humans continue to evolve. Most women today are educated and capable of supporting themselves financially, so the need to find men who can provide economic security may not be as relevant now as it was for our female ancestors. Similarly, modern fertility treatment makes it less critical for men to mate with younger women. Nonetheless, if evolutionary psychology is correct, the genetic predispositions that guide people's mate choices are a function not of changing economic or social conditions but of thousands of years of evolution.

SUMMARY AND APPLICATION

People exchange resources with one another in all types of relationships. Parents provide children with love and a secure home, and children give their parents affection and feelings of self-worth. Friends exchange companionship and do favors for one another, and romantic partners exchange financial resources, household responsibilities, and love. Social exchange is also a part of work relationships, wherein employers provide rewards such as praise and raises, and subordinates contribute productivity and loyalty to the company (Farrell & Rusbult, 1981).

Certain circumstances can change the balance of rewards, costs, and equity in relationships. For Garrett and Brent, becoming roommates introduced a new set of costs into their friendship. Issues revolving around financial responsibility and the division of chores, which were once irrelevant to their relationship, now threaten to ruin their long-standing friendship. These types of shifts in reward-cost ratios can occur in all types of relationships. For instance, a new baby might change the division of labor for a married couple, and a wife's big promotion at work might alter how financial resources are distributed between spouses.

Whether relational partners experience a change in their reward-cost ratios or not, it is important for them to exchange resources in a fair and equitable manner. People report being happier in relationships characterized by equity, perhaps because partners in equitable relationships experience less distress and perhaps because they use more maintenance behaviors and express emotion in more positive ways. In contrast, people who are underbenefited tend to experience distress in the form of anger, frustration, and disappointment, whereas people who are overbenefited tend to experience distress in the form of guilt. Perceptions of equity are just as important as the actual balance of rewards and costs in a relationship. In Brent and Garrett's relationship, both men may be incurring similar levels of cost, but as long as they each think that they are in the underbenefited position, they will continue to experience distress.

Brent and Garrett have several options for relieving the distress they are feeling. They could negotiate new rules in their relationship so that Garrett picks up after himself more and Brent contributes more financially. Or they could recognize that they are in a sense trading costs—Brent could agree to continue doing more around the house in exchange for Garrett paying more rent. They could also decide that it is better to stop being roommates so they can preserve their friendship.

Although it is possible that the tension in their roommate relationship could end up destroying their friendship, there are several reasons to be optimistic for the future of Garrett and Brent's relationship. First, given their long history together, it would appear that Garrett and Brent have made considerable investments in their friendship. It would be difficult for either man to build the same kind of friendship with someone else, especially in the short term. Second, they are likely to evaluate the current state of their relationship in the context of their broader friendship. For years, they have been satisfied with their friendship and shown loyalty to each another. According to Rusbult's investment model, being invested and committed to someone provides a buffer against relationship termination. Although Garrett and Brent are experiencing some dissatisfaction in their relationship, they are likely to engage in accommodation and make sacrifices for one another. They are also likely to derogate alternatives (e.g., living with someone else would be worse) and to see their friendship as superior (e.g., our friendship is stronger than most so we can work this out).

Married and cohabiting couples often deal with some of the same issues that roommates such as Brent and Garrett have to cope with. The fair division of household labor is often a contentious issue in marriage, as are issues related to the distribution of financial resources (see Chapter 14). Couples with children also exchange resources related to parenting, and principles of social exchange help predict attraction in the early stages of dating relationships. Thus across various types and stages of relationships, the balance of rewards and costs plays a critical role in determining our feelings toward others. So we hope that the next time you think that one of your relationships has become unfair or less rewarding, this chapter will give you some insight into the causes of and possible remedies for your distress.

DISCUSSION QUESTIONS

1. People obtain various types of rewards and costs in their relationships, including those related to emotions, tasks, social needs, and opportunity. Based on your experience, which types of rewards do you think are most important within relationships? Are some costs especially detrimental to relationships? How might the importance of various rewards and costs differ by relationship type (e.g., married couples, roommates, siblings)?

2. Why do you think working women still do two-thirds of the household work, and perhaps more important, why don't most women complain until their share of the work exceeds this two-thirds mark?

3. According to the evolutionary perspective on social exchange, men and women have different preferences for mates because of the different rewards and costs they incur in their relationships. These preferences are believed to have evolved across thousands of years and may therefore have been more functional for our ancestors than for us. Imagine taking a relational communication class in the year 5010. How might the cultural and social influences of the 21st century be reflected in our descendants' genetic inheritance?

11

PLAYING WITH POWER

Dominance and Influence in Relationships

Tyler is a pretty laid-back individual who really loves his girlfriend Ashley. Ashley feels the same toward Tyler, although she would like him to get a better job and go back to school. Their love life is good in all respects except when Ashley hassles him about school and work. Tyler defends his lifestyle and his current job, but when Ashley's persuasion becomes more strident, Tyler withdraws, Ashley gets mad and shops excessively, and their sex life goes downhill. Ashley is smart and beautiful, and Tyler worries that she has better alternatives, especially since she is about to graduate with a communication degree from college and already has better job offers than his current entry-level position.

As illustrated by Ashley and Tyler's situation, many relationships are characterized by a struggle for power, with one or both partners striving to influence or change the other. Power is an important aspect of life as well as relationships. The philosopher Bertrand Russell (1938) once remarked, "The fundamental concept in social science is Power in the same sense that Energy is the fundamental concept in Physics" (p. 10). The historian Lord Acton (1887) famously observed, "Power corrupts and absolute power corrupts absolutely" (p. 335). It has also been said that power abhors a vacuum, and close relationships are no exception. Power exists in all relationships: Someone takes the initiative to start a relationship, or decides how to spend money, or

initiates sex, or accepts or rejects the initiation, or takes out the garbage and cleans the bathroom. At some level power exists in every friendship, romance, marriage, and family.

Power is so prevalent in relationships that some scholars have labeled dominance and submission as a basic dimension of interpersonal communication (Burgoon & Hale, 1984). When power imbalances exist, couples such as Ashley and Tyler need to find ways to communicate their needs in constructive rather than controlling ways. What options do they have for influencing one another? Are some forms of communication more effective than others? And perhaps most important, how can they achieve a more balanced, egalitarian relationship? This chapter addresses these and other questions by examining how issues of power, control, and influence play out in close relationships. First, we define power and outline six principles of power. Next, we review the literature on influence goals and examine specific verbal tactics and nonverbal power behaviors. Finally, we focus on issues of power and equality in families.

DEFINING POWER AND RELATED TERMS

Power refers to an individual's ability to influence others to do what he or she wants (Berger, 1985; Henley, 1977), as well as a person's ability to resist the influence attempts of others (Huston, 1983). People often exert power by controlling valuable resources (Ellyson & Dovidio, 1985). In relationships, people control resources in several ways. First, relational partners can grant or withhold resources, such as money and possessions, affection, sex, and time spent together (Fitzpatrick & Badzinski, 1994). For example, Ashley gives her partner extra affection as a way to reinforce his good behavior and withholds affection to punish his negative behavior. Second, power is part of the decision-making process when relational partners determine how to spend valuable resources such as time and money. Relational partners exercise power when they distribute tasks such as washing the dishes, balancing the checkbook, and doing the driving on a road trip. Relational partners also exercise power when they decide what type of car to buy, how to spend their time together, and where to go on vacation. In interpersonal relationships, power reflects the ability to affect the behavior, emotions, or decisions of one's partner (Berger, 1985).

Power is a basic feature of relationships because humans want to control their lives and be their own free agents. **Agency** is that unique, empowering quality of experience in which a person masters the surrounding environment, including social interaction and relationships (McAdams, 1985). This is why people often feel the need to "change" their relational partners so that they fit their conceptions of how a perfect partner should behave. Uncontrolled agency leads to dominance. Ideally, power motivates, energizes, and enables a person without diminishing or enslaving other people. Negative forms of power, such as harassment or coercion, usually destroy intimacy and produce unstable and dissatisfying relationships. The key to using power productively is for partners to use their influence for the good of the relationship and to keep the decision-making process fair and equitable. In other words, both people in a relationship should have a voice.

Dominance refers to the display or expression of power through behavior (Burgoon et al., 1996). As we will discuss in this chapter, dominant behaviors include verbal communication such as commands and other "one-up" messages ("WE are going to MY family's house for Thanksgiving this year"), as well as nonverbal communication such as using a loud voice while maintaining high levels of eye contact. However, using a particular type of behavior does not determine whether someone is dominant. Instead, "dominance is determined by the subservient or submissive responses of others. It is not dominance unless it works" (Burgoon et al., 1996, p. 306). So if the demand to spend Thanksgiving with your family is met with a response such as "I'm not going—you can go by yourself," or if the strategy of using a loud voice while maintaining steady eye contact fails to get your partner's attention, dominance has not occurred.

Social influence involves changing someone's thoughts, emotions, or behaviors (Burgoon et al., 1996). Sometimes social influence is the result of strategic communication, whereby one person actively uses communication to try to change the other person's attitudes, beliefs, feelings, or behaviors. In other cases, indirect influence occurs. Dominant behaviors can be part of the social influence process, although they do not necessarily have to be. The person who ultimately effects a change in the other person is influential and has exerted power, either directly or indirectly.

POWER PRINCIPLES

Whether power is exercised through dominance or more subtle forms of influence, it occurs within a social and relational context. In this section, we discuss six principles of power that describe how power functions within our interactions with others.

Power as a Perception

The first principle is that *power is a perception.* As suggested earlier, people can engage in powerful communication, but if others do not perceive them as powerful, their behavior is not dominant. Others are powerful only to the extent that we believe them to be powerful. Some people have objective power but still have trouble influencing others. **Objective power** is the authority associated with factors such as position, strength, weaponry, and wealth. For example, presidents, defensive linemen, nuclear powers, and millionaires have objective power, but they have real power only if other people perceive their power and are influenced by these perceptions. Of course, people who use power cues do tend to be perceived as powerful by others (Hall, Coates, & LeBeau, 2005). However, people's perceptions about power are more exaggerated than actual power cues because these stereotypes are important social knowledge, taught by culture even though they may contain only a "kernel" of truth (Hall et al., 2005). For instance, using direct gaze while talking is a powerful behavior, but people think it is more powerful than it really is.

The opposite can occur as well; some people become influential and dominant even though they do not engage in much powerful behavior. The lives of people such as Mahatma Gandhi, Martin Luther King, Jr., and Mother Teresa suggest that people of humble means and little objective power still can be very influential and wield real power when they stand for something in which large groups of people believe. Similarly, our relational partners are only as powerful (or as powerless) as we perceive them to be, regardless of their level of objective power.

The way people perceive themselves is also important. Thinking that you are powerful does not ensure that you will be powerful, but thinking you are powerless virtually guarantees powerlessness. People who are confident and appear self-assured are more likely to manifest more power and be able to influence others than are people who lack confidence (Burgoon et al., 1996; Dunbar & Burgoon, 2005). People who feel powerless sometimes get trapped in bad relationships because they do not have the confidence to assert themselves and try to change the situation.

Power as a Relational Concept

A second principle is that *power exists in relationships.* Power is always a relational concept; an individual cannot be powerful without someone else being less powerful. In relationships, the issue is often how much **relative power** a person has in comparison with one's partner. Most romantic relationships are characterized by small imbalances of power (Dunbar & Burgoon, 2005). In heterosexual relationships, men are more likely to be perceived as the more powerful partner (Felmlee, 1994; Sprecher & Felmlee, 1997). Research suggests that people are most happy in egalitarian relationships and least happy in relationships where the woman has considerably more power than the man (Gray-Little & Burks, 1983). However, the balance of power in relationships is often dynamic. Partners in close and satisfying relationships often influence each other at different times in various arenas. For example, in a single day a wife may influence her husband to invest in a certain stock and meet her at a particular restaurant for dinner, while he may decide what movie they see that night and which babysitter to call. Interestingly, men are more likely than women to perceive the world to be hierarchical and organized in pecking orders and power structures (Mast, 2005). Box 11.1 provides a way of determining how much relative power you have in one of your relationships.

In close relationships, influence is inevitable and even desirable. Partners who exercise little influence over each other may not really be a couple but simply strangers in the same household. Partners in close relationships are interdependent; the actions of one person affect the other. As we will see throughout this chapter, the way in which power is used and communicated is crucial. When partners perceive that power is fairly distributed and that they are receiving adequate resources from each other, they are more likely to experience relational satisfaction (see Chapter 10).

Power as Resource Based

A third principle is that *power usually represents a struggle over resources.* The more scarce and valued resources are, the more intense and protracted are

▨ BOX 11.1   Put Yourself to the Test

How Much Relative Power Do You Have?

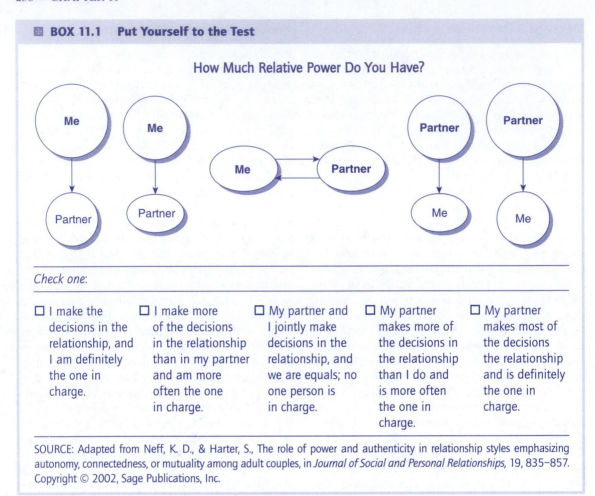

Check one:

| ☐ I make the decisions in the relationship, and I am definitely the one in charge. | ☐ I make more of the decisions in the relationship than in my partner and am more often the one in charge. | ☐ My partner and I jointly make decisions in the relationship, and we are equals; no one person is in charge. | ☐ My partner makes more of the decisions in the relationship than I do and is more often the one in charge. | ☐ My partner makes most of the decisions the relationship and is definitely the one in charge. |

SOURCE: Adapted from Neff, K. D., & Harter, S., The role of power and authenticity in relationship styles emphasizing autonomy, connectedness, or mutuality among adult couples, in *Journal of Social and Personal Relationships*, 19, 835–857. Copyright © 2002, Sage Publications, Inc.

power struggles. People bring a variety of resources to their relationships. Most early research on power focused on money and social standing as powerful resources (Berger, 1985), and when resources are defined in this way, men typically have more power than women. Of course, the gap between men's and women's earnings is narrowing. Today, more women than men are graduating from college, and most of these women are pursuing well-paying careers. As women bring more financial resources to relationships, their level of power is continuing to increase.

Income also appears to be an important source of power for gay men. Studies have shown that in gay relationships the man who is older and earns more money typically has more power (Blumstein & Schwartz, 1983; Harry, 1984; Harry & De Vall, 1978). For lesbians as well, some research has shown that the woman who earns more has more power (Caldwell & Peplau, 1984; Reilly & Lynch, 1990), but Blumstein and Schwartz's extensive study found no differences in power based on income. Instead, lesbians reported that it was important for both partners to earn money so that neither partner would be financially dependent on the other.

Of course, money is only one resource that people bring to relationships. The research on power in families has been criticized for focusing too much on income and social prestige (Berger, 1985; McDonald, 1981). Other resources, such as communication skill, physical attractiveness, advice, social support, a sense of humor, parenting ability, sexual rewards, affection, companionship, and love are exchanged in relationships (see Chapter 10).

When resources are defined as more than financial, women wield considerable power in their relationships. Gottman and Carrere (1994) argued that in public interactions, or interactions with strangers, men typically act more dominant and are more influential than women. However, in private interactions, especially with relational partners, women are typically more dominant and influential. As Gottman and Carrere put it, "Women's public tentativeness and deference, the acceptance of a subordinate role, and politeness in stranger groups does not hold in marriages" (p. 211). In close relationships, women have considerable influence in that they confront conflict more readily and are more demanding, expressive, and even coercive (Gottman, 1979). Thus, women are *not* passive in marriages, as gender stereotypes may suggest. Interestingly, in high-status positions men and women exhibit few power differences, but in low-status positions men are much more likely to employ power strategies than women (Keshet et al., 2006).

Women also tend to be more powerful during sexual interactions. The decision to escalate or not escalate a relationship sexually in almost all societies has been a women's prerogative (Byers, 1996). Virtually every theory, based on either biology or socialization, suggests that women have more negative attitudes toward casual sex than do men (Browning, Kessler, Hatfield, & Choo, 1999). Studies have shown that the more powerful partner can refuse sex, and this finding is true in gay, lesbian, and heterosexual romances (Blumstein & Schwartz, 1983). Thus, in dating relationships, sexual escalation and access are an arena where women exert considerable power. However, more submissive women were more likely to consent to casual sexual behavior, particularly unusual sexual behavior (Browning et al. 1999).

Some resources are scarcer than others in relationships. According to the **scarcity hypothesis**, people have the most power when the resources they possess are hard to come by or in high demand. For example, you may be attracted to several different people, but if you are in love with one of them, that person will have the most power. Of course, a scarce resource leads to power only if it is valued within a

relationship. For one person, money and position may be important; so a partner who is rich and successful is seen as possessing a scarce and valuable resource. For another person, religious beliefs and family values might be perceived as scarce and valuable resources for a relational partner to possess.

Power as Less Dependence and Interest

A fourth principle is that *the person with less to lose has greater power*. People who are dependent on their relationships and partners are in the less powerful position, especially if they know their partners are uncommitted and might leave them. This phenomenon has been termed **dependence power** (Samp & Solomon, 2001). Dependence power is also related to a person's alternatives. According to interdependence theory, **quality of alternatives** refers to the types of relationships and opportunities people could have if they were *not* in their current relationship (see Chapter 10). In the above example, if Ashley is attractive to many other men but Tyler is not as attractive to other women, Ashley is the scarcer resource and has more power than Tyler.

A similar idea, called the **principle of least interest**, suggests that if there is a difference in the intensity of positive feelings between partners, the partner who feels more strongly is at a disadvantage when it comes to power (Safilios-Rothschild, 1970; Waller & Hill, 1951). For example, if you are in love with your partner but your partner is not in love with you, your partner has more power. There is an inverse relationship between your interest in the relationship and how much relational power you have. When the least interested partner makes requests, such as requesting money or sexual favors, the more interested partner is likely to comply rather than risk losing the relationship. In contrast, when the more interested partner makes a request, the less interested partner knows that he or she does not have to give in to maintain the relationship.

Research on both heterosexual couples and lesbian couples confirms the principle of least interest (Caldwell & Peplau, 1984; Peplau & Campbell, 1989; Sprecher & Felmlee, 1997). Sprecher and Felmlee found that for both men and women the partner who was less emotionally involved in the relationship had greater power. They also found that men are generally less emotionally invested in their relationships than women, which suggests the balance of power favors men in most couples. In lesbian relationships, Caldwell and Peplau found that women who were more committed and involved in the relationship than their partners tended to have less power.

In line with the principle of least interest, when one person in a relationship values autonomy over closeness, that person usually has more relative power. Harter and her colleagues (1997) described three orientations toward relationships: self-focused autonomy, other-focused connection, and mutuality. People who emphasize autonomy value their independence over relational closeness. Those who emphasize connection do exactly the opposite—they value closeness over independence. Finally, people who have a mutuality orientation value balancing needs for independence with needs for relational closeness. Around 74% of people report having a mutuality orientation. Most of the other 26% of couples are characterized by one partner having a mutuality orientation and the other partner having either an autonomy- or connection-focused style.

Neff and Harter (2002) showed that people are more likely to be subordinate if their partner values self-focused autonomy. Conversely, people are more likely to be dominant if their partner values other-focused connection. Equality was most likely in relationships where both partners valued mutuality.

Power as Enabling or Disabling

A fifth principle is that *power can be enabling or disabling*. People can use power to hone their skills and to achieve success. Power is part of the human spirit that infuses us with agency and potency. However, excessive power or frequent power plays often cripple close relationships. Few people like being dominated or manipulated and usually respond to such power plays with resistance, stubbornness, and defiance (McAdams, 1985). As we will learn later, large power discrepancies in a relationship tend to be unhealthy. Overall, research has shown that men with very high power needs frequently have problems in love relationships, and

both men and women with high power needs have less intimate friendships (McAdams, 1985). Like powerful nations, powerful people must be careful not to overuse their power. Research has shown that people are more likely to have an enduring influence on others when they engage in dominant behavior that reflects social skill rather than intimidation (Guerrero & Floyd, 2006). People who communicate dominance through self-confident, expressive, energetic, and composed behavior tend to be successful in achieving their goals and maintaining good relationships.

In contrast, power can be disabling when it leads to destructive patterns of communication. Two such patterns are the chilling effect and the demand-withdrawal pattern. According to the **chilling effect**, the less powerful person often hesitates to communicate grievances to her or his partner (Roloff & Cloven, 1990). Researchers have identified the conditions that are conducive to the chilling effect, which are related to the power dynamics within the relationship. First, people are susceptible to the chilling effect when they are dependent on their relationship but perceive that their partner is uncommitted (Cloven & Roloff, 1993; Roloff & Cloven, 1990; Solomon, Knobloch, & Fitzpatrick, 2004). The chilling effect is less likely to occur in committed relationships. Second, people who are afraid of losing their partners are likely to respond to relationship problems by withdrawing support and withholding complaints (Roloff, Soule, & Carey, 2001). Third, partners are likely to withhold grievances to avoid negative relational consequences, such as conflict or partner aggression (Cloven & Roloff, 1993). These conditions are related to dependence power (Solomon & Samp, 1998). The chilling effect can have harmful effects on relationships; problems habitually stay unsolved, power differentials increase, and eventually relational satisfaction erodes.

Power dynamics can also lead to a **demand-withdrawal pattern**, which can be disabling and destructive (Christensen & Heavey, 1990; see also Chapter 14). This pattern occurs when one person makes demands and the other person becomes defensive and withdraws. When people feel powerless, they sometimes enact demanding behavior to try to change their partner's behavior. In the scenario at the beginning of this chapter, Ashley is portrayed as the

SOURCE: Copyright: iStockphoto.com/Rasmus Rasmussen

Photo 11.1 Patterns such as the chilling effect and demand-withdrawal sequences often reflect power imbalances in relationships. When couples stop talking, they are unable to solve problems and restore equality.

"demander." She is frustrated that Tyler lacks ambition, so she tries to get him to go back to school and find a better job. Tyler is portrayed as the "withdrawer" who unsuccessfully tries to defend himself and then withdraws, perhaps to avoid further conflict. Although Ashley might have other types of power in her relationship, she seems powerless when it comes to influencing Tyler on an issue. Research has demonstrated that people are most likely to be in the demanding position when, like Ashley, they are seeking compliance or change from their partner (Sagrestano, Heavey, & Christensen, 2006). Women are more likely than men to seek such change, as well as to be in a less powerful position; therefore, they are more likely to be in the demanding role. Patterns of demand-withdrawal are found in satisfying as well as dissatisfying relationships, but when such patterns occur repeatedly over time, they tend to erode relational satisfaction (Heavey, Christensen, & Malamuth, 1995).

Power as a Prerogative

The sixth principle is that the partner with more power can make and break the rules.

According to this **prerogative principle**, powerful people can violate norms, break relational rules, and manage interactions without as much penalty as powerless people. In fact, in many cases powerful individuals actually enhance their positive images when they engage in such actions (Guerrero & Floyd, 2006). In organizations, people with higher status and power can usually arrive at a meeting late without penalty, while subordinates may be reprimanded. Similarly, high-status individuals, such as presidents or CEOs, can dress casually if they want (Burgoon et al., 1996). In families, parents may be able to eat while sitting on the new leather sofa in the living room, but children might be told to eat their food at the table. In romantic relationships, the person who cares the least may be able to get away with arriving late for dates, forgetting birthdays or anniversaries, or even dating other people. These actions may reinforce the powerful person's dependence power; such actions show that one person is more dedicated to the relationship than the other.

The more powerful person also has the prerogative to manage both verbal and nonverbal interactions. As you will learn later in this chapter, powerful people can initiate conversations, change topics, interrupt others, and terminate discussions more easily than less powerful people. For instance, imagine that you are in a hurry to get to your next class and someone stops you and starts to initiate a conversation. Would you be likely to chat for a moment or to brush them off and rush to class? According to the prerogative principle, you would be much more likely to stop and chat with someone you found powerful and/or attractive (such as your professor or someone you want to date). Similarly, in high school the more popular kids get to decide where to go and what to talk about, with the less popular kids following their lead. In romantic relationships, the person with the most power may decide which relational topics can be discussed and which are taboo.

The power prerogative is evident in nonverbal behavior as well (Andersen, 1999; Burgoon et al., 1996). Take touch as an example. Think about interactions between teachers and students, superiors and subordinates, or lawyers and clients. Who has the prerogative to initiate touch in these relationships? Research suggests that the teachers, superiors, and lawyers will be most likely to initiate touch because they typically have more power in these relationships. In contrast, if the students, subordinates, or clients initiate touch, it will be perceived as inappropriate. Some research also suggests that in heterosexual romantic relationships men typically have more power in the initial stages of the relationship. As a result, they have the prerogative to ask the woman out and to initiate behavior such as handholding and sex. For example, Guerrero and Andersen (1994) found that men were more likely than women to initiate touch in casual dating relationships, but women tend to initiate touch more than men in married relationships.

Together these six principles suggest that power is negotiated by relational partners based on their perceptions of each other and the characteristics of their relationship. In close relationships, partners often share power, with each person exerting influence at certain times and accommodating the partner's wishes at other times. Thus designating one person as "powerful" and the other as "powerless" often can be misleading. Next, we examine some goals relational partners have when they are trying to influence each other.

INTERPERSONAL INFLUENCE GOALS

Most communication is influential. Thus when we ask someone to do us a favor, when we advertise a product, or when we campaign for a political office, we are trying to influence people's attitudes and change their behavior. Other times we try to resist such influence. This is particularly true in close relationships—for example, parents try to prevent their kids from smoking, dating partners initiate or refuse sexual involvement, and spouses influence each other about when and whether to have children or to buy a new house. As Dillard (1989) stated, "Close personal relationships may be the social arena that is most active in terms of sheer frequency of influence attempts" (p. 293). Most interpersonal influence attempts are goal driven. In other words, people enact influence attempts to try to achieve particular goals (Berger, 1985). Dillard's (1989) research suggests that most influence goals fall into the six categories described here.

Making Lifestyle Changes

The most frequent influence attempt in close relationships involves the desire to change the behavior patterns of a partner, friend, or family member, which Dillard (1989) called giving advice about lifestyles. Examples of these types of influence goals might include trying to prevent conflict between your partner and your friends, getting a close friend to terminate a romantic relationship that you think is bad for her, persuading your brother not to move to Ohio for a job, and persuading a friend to reconcile differences with his parents. In addition to being common in relationships, influence attempts that revolve around lifestyle changes are some of the most important. Dillard's (1989) research indicated that lifestyle-change messages are usually logical, positively presented, and direct.

Gaining Assistance

A more routine but important kind of influence attempt involves gaining assistance. Examples of these influence attempts might include getting your spouse to proofread your term paper, getting a friend to drive you to another city to see your girlfriend, borrowing money from your parents, and getting the university to accept your petition for readmittance. These influence attempts may be less significant than lifestyle changes, but they are personally and relationally important. For example, when romantic partners, friends, or family members assist you, their actions say something powerful about your relationship with them—namely, that they are willing to aid and support you. Messages designed to gain assistance are often indirect rather than direct. Thus when people attempt to gain assistance, they may do so through the use of hints or suggestions (Dillard, 1989). Instead of saying, "Get me a blanket and a bowl of popcorn," the person might hint by saying, "I'm kind of cold and hungry. A soft blanket and some warm popcorn would really feel good right now."

Sharing Activities

A critical type of relational influence attempt involves offers to share time and space (see Egland et al., 1997). As discussed in Chapter 9, shared activities play a critical role in maintaining relationships. Joint activities enable people to spend time together, show common interests, enjoy companionship, and develop a sense of intimacy. Shared activities may be a particularly important form of intimacy in male friendships because men disclose personal information to one another somewhat less often than do women. Examples of these influence attempts might include going out on a date together, running or biking together, taking a vacation together, or spending the night together. Many of these activities reflect serious attempts to increase

the closeness of a relationship, and if the other person agrees to the persuasive overture, the relationship can escalate. This is particularly true of activities that require people to spend time together, especially time alone together, and activities that signal commitment or exclusivity, such as going to a romantic partner's home for Thanksgiving. Sometimes requests for shared activity are direct, but more often they are indirect and appeal more to emotion than logic (Dillard, 1989).

Changing Political Attitudes

Some people are more political than others, but nearly everyone gets involved in political issues at one time or another. Persuading someone to take a stand, support a cause, or join a movement are all acts of political persuasion. Examples of these influence attempts might include talking someone out of joining a union, persuading someone to vote for a student initiative or political candidate, getting someone to register to vote, or convincing someone to boycott a sexist movie. By participating with you, friends or partners show their support for your cause and demonstrate that their attitudes are aligned with yours, which can contribute to relational satisfaction. When relational partners seek to change each other's political attitudes, they often use indirect appeals for involvement that are low in coerciveness so that they will not threaten each other's autonomy (Dillard, 1989).

Giving Health Advice

One important reason for exerting power and influence in close relationships is to help partners improve their mental and physical health. For example, we may want our romantic partners to get more exercise or to take vitamins. We may advise a friend to abandon abusive relationships or tell our teenage brother to drive carefully and to party safely. We tell a troubled colleague to seek counseling, and we recommend that a sick friend go to the doctor. Of course, the way people give health advice may make a difference in terms of whether the advice is followed. If the persuader is too judgmental or demanding, the receiver may resist exercising, refuse to seek help, or rebel by engaging in dangerous behavior. **Psychological reactance** or **boomerang effects** occur when a friend or a spouse is controlling or demanding (see Shen & Dillard, 2005). When this happens, one person's influence attempts cause the other person to become defensive and resistant. As a result, the person continues engaging in unhealthy behavior, or even worse, engages in more unhealthy behavior than before. For example, one study showed that wives' social control efforts on their husband's cancer treatments had no positive effects and some negative effects on his health behavior as well as negative effects on the couple's interactions (Helgeson, Novak, LePore, & Eton, 2004). Conversely, socially supportive communication had positive effects. Simple messages that express concern without being critical may be best. Dillard (1989) found that most messages aimed at giving health advice are direct and logical.

Changing Relationships

A common form of influence among close friends is relationship advice. You may suggest that a friend dump her unfaithful boyfriend, or ask a friend to join your church community, or suggest to a romantic partner that you "just be friends." Because the stakes are so high, such influence attempts can be problematic, and whether they are accepted or not, they signal major changes in a relationship. Think about times when you wanted to change either your own or a friend's relationship. Maybe you wanted a platonic friendship to turn romantic but were afraid that communicating your romantic desire might ruin your friendship (see Chapter 9). Or perhaps you were afraid to give relational advice to a friend because you thought you might get caught in the middle. The prototypical example of this is when you see a friend's romantic partner out with someone else. If you tell your friend what you saw, your friend might side with her or his partner and accuse you of being jealous or making things up. But if you keep silent, your friend might be more hurt in the long run. As these examples suggest, giving relational advice can be a tricky proposition. When people try to influence others to change their relationships, they usually use direct communication, logical appeals, and large amounts of positivity (Dillard, 1989).

VERBAL POWER PLOYS

Traditionally, power and persuasion have been thought of as verbal activities. But in reality communication that is powerful and persuasive consists of a combination of verbal and nonverbal cues. In this section, we examine aspects of verbal power ploys; in the next section, we consider power associated with nonverbal communication.

Verbal Influence Strategies

Research has shown that relational partners can choose from an assortment of strategies that help them influence each other. These strategies are often called compliance gaining (Miller & Boster, 1988; Miller, Boster, Roloff, & Siebold, 1977; Wiseman & Schenck-Hamlin, 1981) or influence (Falbo & Peplau, 1980) strategies. Skilled communicators have a diverse arsenal of strategies at their disposal. In given situations, they select the strategies that are most likely to be influential for particular people and purposes. However, research has shown that people in more stable and equitable relationships use fewer power strategies than do people in unstable and inequitable relationships (Aida & Falbo, 1991), presumably because there is less that they want to change. Research has also shown that powerful people are more likely to be persuasive than less powerful people, regardless of the strategies they use (Levine & Boster, 2001). For individuals who are low in power, the best strategy may be to phrase requests using a positive, polite tone (Levine & Boster). Next, we discuss some of the most common verbal influence strategies.

Direct Requests. One of the most obvious interpersonal influence strategies is the direct request (Wiseman & Schenck-Hamlin, 1981), also known as the simple request or asking (Falbo & Peplau, 1980). Research shows that this is the most common strategy for both men and women, most likely to be used by a person who feels powerful and supported (Levine & Boster, 2001; Sagrestano, 1992). Examples of direct requests include asking your boyfriend or girlfriend, "Could you turn down the stereo, please?" or saying, "I really wish you wouldn't swear in public." While they are not very sophisticated or strategic messages, they are usually effective, particularly in relationships with high levels of mutual respect and closeness. Indeed, in a study of unmarried heterosexual and gay couples, Falbo and Peplau (1980) found that the most satisfied couples typically use direct strategies. Similarly, in a study of married couples, Aida and Falbo (1991) found that satisfied couples used more direct and fewer indirect strategies than did unsatisfied couples.

Bargaining. This strategy involves agreeing to do something for someone if he or she does something for us. In addition to bargaining (Falbo & Peplau, 1980; Howard, Blumstein, & Schwartz, 1986), this type of influence attempt has been called promising (Miller et al., 1977; Wiseman & Schenck-Hamlin, 1981) and the quid pro quo strategy. For example, if one partner agrees not to watch football on Sunday if the other gives up smoking, each partner is giving up something in return for a concession by the other. Sometimes individuals using the bargaining strategy to persuade a partner will recall past favors or debts owed by the partner (Wiseman & Schenck-Hamlin, 1981). Other times people using the bargaining strategy reward their partner prior to a persuasive request; this is called pregiving (Miller et al., 1977). Howard et al. (1986) found that more occupationally and relationally equal couples tended to bargain more than unequal ones. In unequal relationships, the person with more power does not need to bargain to get compliance, while the person with less power does not have as many resources at her or his disposal to use in the bargaining process. However, less powerful people may be more likely to negotiate and bargain than more powerful people (Levine & Boster, 2001).

Aversive Stimulation. Also called the negative affect strategy (Falbo & Peplau, 1980), aversive stimulation (Miller et al., 1977; Wiseman & Schenck-Hamlin, 1981) involves whining, pouting, sulking, complaining, crying, or acting angry until the person gets her or his way. The idea here is that the receiver will get so tired of the aversive behavior that he or she will comply merely to stop it. This strategy is not very sophisticated and is often thought of as childish because it is so widely employed by toddlers and small children. Although this strategy is sometimes effective, individuals who use it may be seen as spoiled or immature, and other people will avoid them if they use this strategy frequently. In fact, Sagrestano (1992) reported that people perceived aversive stimulation as the second most negative and unpleasant power strategy among the 13 strategies she tested (withdrawal, which we will discuss shortly, ranked first).

Ingratiation. Often called positive affect (Falbo & Peplau, 1980), liking (Miller et al., 1977), ingratiation (Wiseman & Schenck-Hamlin, 1981), "kissing up," or "sucking up," this strategy involves using excessive kindness to get one's way. A husband buying his wife flowers before asking for forgiveness or an athlete continually complimenting her coach are examples of ingratiation strategies. The person using the ingratiation strategy wants to be perceived as friendly and likable so that the other person will want to be helpful and compliant. Of course, ingratiation strategies can backfire if the person using them is perceived as insincere. Canary and Cody (1994) discussed the concept of **illicit ingratiation**, which occurs when a person acts nice merely to gain compliance. Ingratiation can be persuasive only if it is seen as honest rather than manipulative.

Hinting. Called indirect requests, suggesting (Falbo & Peplau, 1980), or hinting (Wiseman & Schenck-Hamlin, 1981), this strategy involves implying a request without ever coming out and stating one. For example, Ashley might hint to Tyler that lots of people are returning to college this fall after taking a break from school. A wife who mentions to her husband how nice it would be to take a vacation might be hinting that she wants to go somewhere special for their anniversary. Although this is a polite strategy, its effectiveness depends on the perceptiveness of one's relational partner. If the partner does not pick up on the hint, this strategy will fail. In other cases, the partner might understand what the sender is hinting at but ignore the request nonetheless. When the request is made in such an indirect manner, the partner's responsibility for responding is diminished.

Moral Appeals. These compliance-gaining messages, which are also called positive and negative altercasting (Miller et al., 1977), take one of two forms. Positive moral appeals suggest that a good or moral person would comply with the request ("An understanding partner wouldn't nag me about school," says Tyler). Negative moral appeals suggest that only bad or immoral people would fail to comply ("Only an unambitious or unintelligent person would pass up the opportunity to complete his education," says Ashley). Both positive and negative moral appeals associate certain behaviors with the basic "goodness" of the receiver. Such a strategy also ties into an individual's identity as a basically good person. As discussed in Chapter 2, people generally prefer to act in ways that are consistent with their positive self-identities. So if Ashley sees herself as an understanding girlfriend and Tyler sees himself as an ambitious and intelligent person, they might be more likely to comply in response to the moral appeals just described. Of course, such appeals can also exacerbate conflict and lead to defensiveness, especially if interactants perceive that they are being attacked at a personal level (see Chapter 14).

Manipulation. This set of strategies involves attempts to make the partner feel guilty, ashamed, or jealous until the sender gets her or his way (Fleischmann et al., 2005; Wiseman & Schenck-Hamlin, 1981). Examples of this strategy might include making a relational partner feel guilty for going on vacation without you or feel ashamed for flirting with other people. Suggestions that alternative partners are available are also highly manipulative and threatening and can occasionally be an effective manipulation strategy if the person becomes jealous. For instance, if your partner is not spending enough time with you at a party, you might flirt with someone in the hope that your partner will get jealous and be more attentive to you. Of course, such strategies can backfire because people do not like to be manipulated. Manipulative strategies can also be thought of as a special kind of aversive stimulation. As mentioned earlier, strategies that cause people to experience negative affect often are seen as childish. Moreover, instead of stopping the offending behavior, some people avoid the person administering the aversive stimulation as a way of alleviating negative affect. So if you start flirting with someone at a party, your partner simply might

ignore you or leave with someone else rather than giving you the attention you want.

Withdrawal. Closely related to both aversive stimulation and manipulation are a set of strategies called distancing, avoidance (Guerrero, Andersen, Jorgensen, Spitzberg, & Eloy, 1995), withdrawal (Falbo & Peplau, 1980), or passive aggression, when people give partners the silent treatment, ignore them, or limit communication with them. A young woman in one of our classes gave a good example of how withdrawal can be used as an influence strategy. She had been dating her fiancé for 6 years and thought she would be getting an engagement ring for Christmas. When she failed to get a ring, she gave her fiancé the silent treatment until he asked what was wrong; eventually, he bought her the ring. This might not be the best way to become engaged. Over time, she might begin to wonder whether he would have proposed if she had not manipulated him in this way. Furthermore, this strategy does not always work. Sometimes the partner gets used to being ignored or grows tired of dealing with negativity and moves on. In fact, Sagrestano (1992) found that people perceived withdrawal as the most negative of the 13 power strategies she examined. Still, the withdrawal strategy can be effective in some situations. Sometimes people might be hesitant to bring up a sensitive subject, and by withdrawing, they let the partner be the one who initially asks, "What's wrong?" and starts the conversation. Other times people might miss their partner and appreciate them more after spending time apart.

Deception. Some people use lies and deception as a compliance-gaining strategy (Wiseman & Schenck-Hamlin, 1981). People may make false promises, such as saying that they will do something in exchange for compliance, when they actually have no intention of doing so. People may also exaggerate or make up information to try to gain compliance. For example, a teenager who wants his curfew extended might tell his parents that all his friends get to stay out past midnight when only a handful of them actually do. Aside from the ethical issues associated with this strategy, it is a risky relational maneuver. Discovery of deception may result in a loss of trust and the general deterioration of the relationship (see Chapter 13). Even if the relationship survives the discovery of deception, the partner may become suspicious and guarded, making it difficult for the deceiver to successfully gain compliance later.

Distributive Communication. With distributive strategies, people attempt to blame, hurt, insult, or berate their partner, sometimes, in an effort to gain compliance (Guerrero et al., 1995; Sillars, Coletti, Parry, & Rogers, 1982; Wiseman & Schenck Hamlin, 1981). These strategies are sometimes called bullying (Howard et al., 1986). Tactics such as these usually are ineffective and often lead to escalated conflict (see Chapter 14) and relational deterioration. Howard et al. (1986) reported that, contrary to some stereotypes, both men and women and both masculine and feminine people are likely to use distributive strategies.

Threats. Tactics such as threatening to walk out on the partner, failing to cooperate with the partner until he or she gives in, or promising to withhold resources such as money or information are usually ineffective. Howard et al. (1986) found that asserting authority through the use of self-serving threats was used equally by men and women. People also engage in mock violence or issue violent warnings, acting as if they are going to hurt their partner but then not doing so. For example, a girl might make a fist and shake it in front of her brother's face without hitting him to illustrate what might happen if he does not stop teasing her. People are more likely to use threats such as these when the partner is perceived to be low in power (Levine & Boster, 2001).

Relational Control Moves: One-Ups and One-Downs

A classic method of determining power and control in relational communication was developed by Rogers and her associates (Rogers & Farace, 1975; Rogers & Millar, 1988). In any conversation, messages can be coded as dominant and controlling (a one-up message), deferent or accepting (a one-down message), or neutral (a one-across message). The focus is on the *form* of the conversation rather than the content. Consider the following interaction between teenage sisters:

Marissa: You've been on the phone for an hour— get off! (one-up)

Nicole: Okay. (one-down)

Marissa: Now! (one-up)

[Nicole tells her friend she will call her later and hangs up.]

Marissa: Thank you. (one-down)

Nicole: Ask a little more nicely next time. (one up)

Coding a person's verbal behavior can reveal whether he or she is domineering or submissive. Researchers can also study how the behavior of one partner affects the relationship. For example, Rogers and Millar (1988) reported that when wives were domineering, both husbands and wives tended to experience less relational satisfaction. More significantly, by looking at patterns of one-up and one-down messages, we can determine the nature of the relationship between two people. This coding method represented a major conceptual breakthrough. A pair of utterances, called a **transact**, can be coded as symmetrical or complementary. If people engage in a pattern in which one person uses mostly one-ups and the other person uses mostly one-downs, the pattern is **complementary,** with one person in the dominant position and the other person in the submissive position. If both people use the same moves, it is **symmetrical**. When two people repeatedly use one-up moves, the pattern is termed **competitive symmetry**. When two people repeatedly use one-down moves, the pattern is termed **submissive symmetry**. A considerable portion of conversation is neutral in terms of control. When both partners exchange these one-across messages, the pattern is termed **neutral symmetry**. And when a one-up or one-down message is paired with a one-across message, a **transition** has occurred. Box 11.2 gives examples of these five patterns. Research has shown that spouses who report dyadic inequality in their marriages have higher proportions of competitive symmetry (Rogers & Millar, 1988).

Of course, some interactions do not fall neatly into one of these categories. Take the interaction between Marissa and Nicole. At the beginning of the interaction, Marissa is the dominant sister, but by the end of the interaction, Nicole asserts herself. It is also important to consider the nonverbal components and the context as well when interpreting one-up and one-down statements. A statement such as "You sure are in a good mood today" could be interpreted as a one-down message in some cases but as a one-up message if delivered using a sarcastic tone of voice.

BOX 11.2   Highlights

Examples of Transacts

Complementarity

Ashley: If you really don't want to go back to school, it's okay. (one-down)

Tyler: I won't go back no matter what you say. (one-up)

Marissa: We should pool our money together to buy something for Mom and Dad's anniversary. (one-up)

Nicole: Okay. How much do you think I should give? (one-down)

Competitive Symmetry

Tyler: Stop nagging me about school. (one-up)

Ashley: Then get off your butt and look for a better job. (one-up)

Submissive Symmetry

Nicole: What should we buy Mom and Dad for their anniversary? (one-down)

Marissa: I don't know. You decide. (one-down)

Neutral Symmetry

Marissa: They have been married for 23 years. (one-across)

Nicole: Grandma and Grandpa were married for over 50 years before Grandpa died. (one-across)

Transition*

Tyler: I wish you would stop talking about graduation all the time. (one-up)

Ashley: Hey, did you see *American Idol* last night? (one-across)

Nicole: I wonder if there are tickets left for that concert Mom said she'd like to go to. (one-across)

Marissa: If you want me to, I can check. (one-down)

* Transitions include all combinations of one-across messages paired with one-up or one-down messages, regardless of order.

Powerful and Powerless Speech

Researchers have also identified the characteristics associated with powerful speech. Speakers who use **powerful speech** focus mainly on themselves rather than others, dominate conversations, redirect the conversation away from topics others are discussing, and interrupt others (Fitzpatrick & Badzinski, 1994). Research suggests that men are somewhat more likely than women to use these forms of powerful speech (Kalbfleisch & Herold, 2006). Falbo and Peplau (1980) found that women used more indirect strategies such as hinting, whereas men used more direct strategies such as open communication. Moreover, women were more likely to use unilateral strategies such as pouting or negative affect, whereas men were more likely to use bilateral strategies such as debate or negotiation. Timmerman's (2002) review of 30 studies supported the claim that men use more powerful language than women, particularly when addressing other men. However, the effect of sex on powerful language tends to be small, which brings into question the practical importance of these differences. Nonetheless, research has shown that more powerful speech creates more credibility and persuasive power, enabling those who use it and hindering those that do not (Burrell & Koper, 1998).

It is also important to note that the differential use of strategies appears to be less a function of sex or gender than one of power or powerlessness. Cowan, Drinkard, and MacGavin (1984) found that both men and women use more indirect and unilateral strategies when communicating with a power figure. In contrast, both females and males tend to be more direct and bilateral when communicating with a power equal. Kollock, Blumstein, and Schwartz (1985) found that the more powerful person in the relationship tends to interrupt her or his partner more, regardless of sex or sexual orientation. Moreover, whether men or women use more powerful verbal behavior depends on the topic. A study by Dovidio, Brown, Heltman, Ellyson, and Keating (1998) revealed that on traditionally male topics, such as working on a car, men engage in more verbal power strategies, such as speech initiation and total time speaking. However, women use more of these verbal power strategies when discussing traditionally female topics such as cooking or raising children.

Some studies have also found that women use more **powerless speech** than men (Giles & Wiemann, 1987). Powerless speech occurs when people use tag questions and hedges. Tag questions involve asking people to affirm that you are making sense or that they understand you. For example, you might ask, "You know what I mean, don't you?" Hedges refer to statements that give the sender or receiver an "out." Statements such as "I'm not sure this is right but . . ." and questions such as "You did say you'd help me with this, didn't you?" exemplify hedges. Although studies show that women use these forms of powerless speech more often than do men, studies also suggest that these forms of speech are not always submissive. Sometimes women use tag questions and hedges in creative ways to get more information, accomplish goals, and improve their relationships (Giles & Wiemann, 1987). Speaking is a skill that can be taught, and many women have learned to use more powerful speech (Timmerman, 2002).

NONVERBAL POSITIONS OF POWER

Verbal communication carries messages of power, but nonverbal communication is an even richer source of power messages. The animal kingdom, which is a nonverbal world, is replete with dominance displays, power structures, and pecking orders. Competition for mates, food, and territory is fierce and can be deadly. Animals developed power cues that establish dominance hierarchies without the need for continual deadly combat, and these pecking orders are all established nonverbally. Humans have even more complex power structures, and these are mostly nonverbal in nature (Andersen, 1999). Power is communicated through various channels of nonverbal communication. As you read about nonverbal behavior, keep in mind that the context and the relationship between people help determine if these behaviors are perceived as powerful.

Physical Appearance

Before a word is even uttered, people make judgments about power from others' physical appearance. Formal, fashionable, and expensive dress is indicative of power (Andersen, 1999; Bickman, 1974; Morris, 1977). Similarly, expensive shoes, as well as the latest workout or basketball shoes, are major status symbols that connote power (Andersen, 1999). Women's clothing, once inflexibly prescribed, is now quite varied. Women can dress informally or formally, in modest or sexy attire, and in a feminine or masculine style. Men's clothing, in contrast, is prescribed more rigidly and generally must be modest, masculine, and appropriate to the occasion (Kaiser, 1997). Despite the variability of women's clothing, when women violate norms by dressing in attire that is perceived as too trendy, sexy, nerdy, or masculine, they are perceived more negatively than men when they violate clothing norms. Uniforms can convey the power associated with a task or occupation (surgeon, police officer), or they can convey powerlessness because they strip away individuality and other status symbols (fast food worker, exterminator) (Joseph & Alex, 1972). Clothing color also makes a difference. Black athletic uniforms, for instance, may be associated with power and aggression (Frank & Gilovich, 1988).

Studies have shown that the mesomorphic or muscular body is associated with power. Likewise, height is related to power and confidence (Andersen, 1999; Burgoon et al., 1996). This "principal of elevation" (Guerrero & Floyd, 2006) suggests that, fair or not, height or vertical position is associated with power. This is why powerful people are often seated in elevated positions. Kings and queens sit on thrones, and judges often sit above the courtroom. In contrast, people bow to show submission. In interpersonal interactions, people can exercise power by looming over someone who is seated (Andersen, 1999). Height differentials are also related to the use of space. For example, moving in close and simultaneously standing over someone is often perceived as intimidating. Interestingly, the greater height and muscle mass of men as compared with women is one explanation for the traditional dominance and oppression women have experienced at the hands of men. Traditional ideals of the tall, dark, and handsome man and the petite women have perpetuated this stereotype (Andersen, 2004). It is important to note that physical appearance is most important during initial interactions; once a relationship is established its effects diminish (Andersen, 1999).

Spatial Behavior

The study of interpersonal space and distance (proxemics) reveals that the way we use space reflects and creates power in interpersonal relations. Invading someone's space and "getting in someone's face" are powerful and intimidating behaviors. In the United States, most people interact at about arm's length, but powerful people, such as superiors communicating with subordinates, or parents talking to children, are afforded the right to invade another's space (Carney, Hall, & LeBeau, 2005; Henley, 1977; Remland, 1981). Subordinates, in contrast, must respect the territory of their superiors. As the prerogative principle suggests, powerful individuals can violate personal space norms by invading other people's space or by remaining spatially aloof. These violations, in turn, are viewed as dominance displays by others (Burgoon & Dillman, 1995; Hall et al, 2005).

A higher-status person can give someone the "cold shoulder" by adopting an indirect body orientation and not facing that person. For example, the husband who reads the paper during a conversation with his wife or the teenager who won't even look at his parents when they are talking to him might be seen as powerful but also rude. Body angle often interacts with another form of nonverbal communication, eye behavior, to create messages of power. Open body positions have been found to convey intimacy (see Chapter 8) but also are an indicant of confidence and power (Carney et al., 2005; Hall et al., 2005).

Eye Behavior

The study of eye behavior (oculesics) has revealed a number of behaviors associated with power, including staring, gazing while speaking, and failing to look when listening. People who are perceived as powerful are also looked at more by others, a principle we call **visual centrality**. Although eye contact is usually affiliative and friendly, staring is powerful, rude, and intrusive (LaFrance & Mayo, 1978). Looking less while listening is the prerogative of the powerful; low-status individuals must remain visually attentive. Direct eye contact while speaking is perceived as a highly dominant, even intimidating behavior (Andersen, 2004; Carney et al., 2005; Hall et al., 2005). Although eye contact while speaking is a dominant behavior, eye contact while listening is a submissive behavior. This finding led Exline et al. (1975) to develop the **visual dominance ratio**, which is a function of the time spent looking while speaking divided by the time spent looking while listening. A high score indicates interpersonal dominance. Shy, submissive people tend to break eye contact when confronted with direct gaze (Andersen, 2004). Similarly, excessive blinking is perceived as an indication of weakness and submission (Mehrabian, 1971).

Body Movements

The study of body movement (kinesics) has revealed that several different body positions, facial expressions, and gestures communicate power and status. Expansive body positions with arms and legs apart and away from the body, and the hands-on-hips positions convey considerable power and dominance (Andersen, 2004; Hall et al., 2005; LaFrance & Mayo, 1978; Remland, 1982). Superiors have the latitude to sprawl and even to get into another person's personal space (Andersen, 1999). Powerful people can lean back to relax or lean forward to make a point; submissive people usually must remain still and attentive. In short, relaxation rules (Andersen, 2004).

Gestures, especially grand, sweeping ones and those directed at other people, are perceived as powerful and create perceptions of dynamism and panache (Burgoon, Johnson, &. Koch, 1998; Carney et al., 2005; Hall et al., 2005). Purposeful gestures communicate power and confidence. Pointing at someone or wagging one's finger in the face of another person is a powerful but hostile move (Remland, 1981; Scheflen, 1972). Such gestures are intrusive acts, much like invading another person's space or, as we discuss next, brashly or rudely touching another person.

Some facial expressions, such as a deep frown or a scornful sneer, are dominant and threatening. A jutting jaw, narrowed eyes, and a face reddened with anger are facial expressions that communicate dominance (Andersen, 1999; Carney et al., 2005; Henley, 1977). Conversely, expressions of fear and sadness are believed to be signs of lower power (Carney et al., 2005). Overall facial expressiveness and skill at facial expressiveness are perceived as more dominant and powerful (Carney et al., 2005; Hall et al., 2005) and are associated with more power (Dunbar & Burgoon, 2005). Because smiling is sometimes designed to convey the absence of threat, it is often perceived as a submissive, appeasing gesture in both humans and other primates (Andersen & Guerrero, 1998b; Hall et al., 2005). Women smile more and by doing so send friendly, nonthreatening messages (Andersen, 1999). Smiling women are more likely to be interrupted by their interaction partner than are either unsmiling women or men (Kennedy & Camden, 1983). However, it is important to recognize that smiling can convey dominance in some situations. When smiling is used alongside other dominance cues, smiles convey confidence, power, and social skill (Burgoon & Bacue, 2003; Hall et al., 2005).

Touch

The study of interpersonal touch (haptics) has shown that while touch is usually an affectionate, intimate behavior, it can also be used to display one's power (Andersen, 1999). First, the initiation of touch is perceived as more dominant than receiving or reciprocating touch, because the person who initiates touch is controlling the interaction (Carney et al., 2005; Hall et al., 2005; Major & Heslin, 1982). Among casual daters, men are more likely to initiate touch, presumably because social norms dictate that men have the prerogative to try to escalate intimacy in the early stages of relationships. Women, however, initiate touch more often in marital relationships (Guerrero & Andersen, 1994; Stier & Hall, 1984). Guiding another person through a door, physically restraining an individual, and touching someone in an intimate place are all indicative of high power (Andersen, 1999). But caution is advised; charges of sexual harassment and even sexual assault can be the consequences of excessive or inappropriate touch (Lee & Guerrero, 2001). Even when the sender means to send a message of affiliation, touch can be perceived as inappropriate or harassing by the receiver. While early research (Henley, 1977) indicated that touch was a highly dominant, powerful behavior, more recent research suggests that touch is more affiliative than dominant (Andersen, 1999; Burgoon & Dillman, 1995; Hall et al., 2005; Stier & Hall, 1984).

The Voice

The content of spoken words is the subject of verbal communication, but voice tones and intonations are in the realm of nonverbal communication, called vocalics or paralinguistics. Social status can be detected from one's voice fairly accurately (Andersen, 1999), with higher-class speakers having clearer articulation and sharper enunciation of consonants. Similarly, fewer filled pauses, such as ahs and ums and other speech errors are associated with greater status and power (Carney et al., 2005; Hall et al., 2005). Listeners can make fairly accurate judgments about people's levels of dominance by listening to samples of their voices (Scherer, 1972). Vocal variation, which is perceived as an immediate, affiliative behavior (see Chapter 8), is also perceived as more powerful (Hall et al., 2005). Louder, deeper, and more varied voices are perceived as more dominant (Andersen, 1999; Hall et al., 2005). However, research suggests that for male speakers higher-pitched voices are sometimes rated as more dominant (Tusing & Dillard, 2000) and that for both men and women louder and slower speech rates are viewed as more dominant than softer or faster speech rates. More expressive speech was also rated as more dominant. When people are making an important point, they might vary their pitch and talk slowly but loudly and deliberately. Other research suggests that moderately fast voices are perceived as reflecting confidence and power because they suggest that the speaker knows what he or she is talking about and does not need time to think (Burgoon

et al., 1996; Hall et al., 2005). Together this research suggests that both slower and faster voices can be considered dominant under certain circumstances.

Time

The study of the interpersonal use of time (chronemics) has revealed that the way people employ time tells a lot about how powerful and dominant they are. Speaking time is related to dominance, especially for men (Mast, 2002). Powerful people are allowed to speak longer and have more speaking turns, which gives them more opportunity to influence others. Waiting time also reflects power; waiting is the fate of the powerless, as people are generally waiting for the powerful. The powerless wait in long lines for welfare checks and job interviews, while the rich and powerful have reservations and can relax in luxurious lounges on the rare occasions when they must wait (Henley, 1977). Doctors are notorious for exercising their power prerogative to keep patients waiting, and many executives let people "cool their heels" as a power ploy before negotiating a business deal. Keeping relational partners waiting may be a bad idea because it signals their lack of importance and could be perceived as inconsiderate.

Spending time with relational partners is one of the most meaningful signs of love. Time together shows that a relationship is valued. Egland et al. (1996) found that, among all the behaviors that convey understanding, equality, and intimacy, spending time together is the most important. Conversely, people who spend little time with children, friends, or spouses are communicating that the relationship is of little importance to them.

Artifacts

Artifacts are the ultimate status symbols. A big house, luxury cars, and expensive toys are signs of power, particularly in our status-conscious, materialistic society. Some status symbols are subtle, such as the largest office, the reserved parking space, and the most expensive and slimmest briefcase (Korda, 1975). Similarly, giving expensive, unique, or rare gifts to loved ones is a sign of their status and importance in your life.

POWER AND INFLUENCE IN FAMILIES

Power is part of the fabric of family relationships. Although equality is often the goal, parents sometimes have more knowledge than do their children, and one spouse sometimes has more financial resources than the other. In this section, we outline some of the main power issues that surface in parent-child relationship, in romantic relationships, and in marriage.

Parent-Child Relationships

Parents need power. No one believes that a 2-year-old is capable of making important decisions. Parents must control the behavior of their young children, but control should be inversely related to age. Clearly, the youngest children need the most control. Teenagers still need considerable control and guidance, but parents are kidding themselves if they believe they can start to become strong parents during the teen years. Attempts to crack down on an unruly teen who has no moral foundation will usually result in conflict and defiance. A strong foundation laid in early childhood helps children become good decision makers and responsible teens. Indeed, the whole enterprise of parenting involves the gradual relinquishing of authority, from total control over an infant or toddler to minimal control over a young adult. As Gibran (1923) famously said,

> Your children are not your children. They come through you but not from you. And though they are with you, yet they belong not to you. You are the bows from which your children as living arrows are sent forth. Let your bending in the archer's hand be for gladness. (pp. 18–19)

Gibran's quote highlights two junctures at which power can be especially important in parent-child relationships: (1) at the beginning, when parents are raising infants and very young children and (2) during the teenage years, when children often assert their independence. Although parents need to control young children, they are certainly not the only agents of influence in early parent-child interactions. As anyone who has seen a mother trying desperately to calm a crying infant or a father trying to get his toddler to eat her or his vegetables can attest, young children can have a huge impact on their parents' behavior. Yingling (1995) put it this way:

> That parents influence their infants is beyond dispute, but infants' influence on parents has begun to receive attention as well. . . . At some point in the first year, infants begin to recognize the power of their interactive behaviors to influence the primary relationship. However, interactive effects begin even before that recognition. (p. 35)

Without consciously intending to, newborns persuade parents to feed them in the middle of the night, change their diapers around the clock, and soothe them when they are upset. As infants get older, they learn to manage social interactions through crying, cooing, and smiling, and by the time they are toddlers, they are particularly good at using the word "no" to assert themselves (Lewis & Rosenblum, 1974).

Of course, parents use much more sophisticated influence strategies than their young children. Classic work by Baumrind (1971, 1991) suggests that there are three general approaches to parenting: authoritarian, permissive, and authoritative. **Authoritarian** parents are demanding, directive, and nonresponsive. They try to control their children's behavior so that it conforms to strict standards of order. They monitor their children's behavior carefully to ensure that they meet these standards. These parents are nonresponsive in that they expect their children to obey them without question. Authoritarian parents also believe that they do not need to explain the reasons behind their disciplinary action to their children—their word is "law" and is not to be questioned.

Permissive parents, in contrast, are undemanding, nondirective, and responsive. These parents relinquish most of their authority and let their children regulate their own behavior in most situations. If they punish their children, which happens rarely, they are lenient. Permissive parents try to be responsive to their children by showing them support and giving them encouragement. Unlike the authoritarian parent, who acts like a dictator, the permissive parent acts more like a friend, and the child is given considerable, often excessive, power.

The **authoritative** style blends aspects of the authoritarian and permissive styles. These parents are demanding and directive but also responsive. Authoritative parents have clear standards and expectations for how their children should behave, and these standards are communicated to the children in terms they can understand. These parents set limitations, but they also allow their children some freedom and privacy. Authoritative parents are responsive in that they generally avoid harsh punishments and focus instead on reasoning with their children and providing support. The authoritative parent is more like a benevolent teacher than either a dictator or friend. Although the parent has more power than the child, the child still has a voice in the decision-making process, and parents and children mutually influence each other.

Hoffman's (1980) work identified two similar styles of parenting: power assertion and induction. **Power assertion** is similar to the authoritarian style. Parents with the power assertion philosophy believe that they should be in complete control and so should be able to demand compliance without having to explain why. The prototypical dialogue that characterizes this style is when a parent issues a directive ("You cannot go to Olivia's party"), the child asks for an explanation ("Why not?"), and the parent asserts authority without giving an explanation ("Because your father and I say you can't go—that's why not"). Power assertion strategies can also include threats, spankings or other physical punishment, and harsh verbal reprimands (see Box 11.3).

The **inductive philosophy** of parenting is similar to the authoritative style. When parents use **induction**, they believe that it is critical that they provide their children with reasons for their disciplinary actions. They give their children explanations for their decisions in the hope that the children will eventually learn how to make good decisions on their own. For example, if Lauren was told that she could not go Olivia's party, her parents would explain why. Perhaps Lauren's parents know that Olivia's parents will not be home and that some of the kids are planning to bring beer, or perhaps Lauren had violated her curfew the last three times she went to a party. In any case, Lauren's parents would explain their thinking, and Lauren would have the opportunity to reason with them.

Inductive parenting strategies are effective because they involve explanation and reasoning.

BOX 11.3   Highlights

Discipline Strategies: To Spank or Not to Spank

When it comes to disciplining children, experts in the social science and medical fields mainly agree that explanation and inductive techniques are superior to power-assertion strategies. Here is the American Academy of Pediatrics position on spanking:

> [We strongly oppose] striking a child. If the spanking is spontaneous, parents should later explain calmly why they did it, the specific behavior that provoked it, and how angry they felt. They might apologize to their child for their loss of control, because that usually helps the youngster understand and accept the spanking. (Shelov, 1998, p. 286)

Eisenberg, Murkoff, and Hathaway (1996) took a similar stand, stating that spanking and other punitive measures have never been effective discipline strategies. Instead of learning to differentiate right from wrong, children merely learn how to avoid getting punished. Moreover, when children are disciplined using power strategies, it "denies them the chance to learn alternative, less hurtful, routes to dealing with anger and frustration" and "represents an abuse of power" (Eisenberg et al., 1996, p. 339). As these authors argue, there should be a fair distribution of rights in parent-child relationships, with parents teaching their children to make good choices rather than forcing them to act a certain way.

Burleson, Delia, and Applegate (1992) argued that such strategies are also **reflection enhancing** because they encourage children to think about their misconduct, including how their actions affect themselves and others over time. Numerous studies show that children, from preschoolers to teenagers, who are disciplined using the authoritative or inductive style have higher self-esteem, are more morally mature, engage in more prosocial and cooperative behavior, show greater communication competence, and are more accepted by their peers than are children who are disciplined using other styles (Baumrind, 1991; Buri, Louiselle, Misukanis, & Mueller, 1988; Burleson et al., 1992; Hart, DeWolf, Wozniak, & Burts, 1992; Hoffman, 1970; Kennedy, 1992).

Of course, authoritarian or power-assertive strategies might be necessary in some cases. Steinmetz (1979) found that power strategies often lead to more rapid compliance than to inductive strategies. Similarly, studies have shown that power-assertive strategies are efficient when parents are seeking immediate, short-term compliance (Grusec & Kuczynski, 1980; Kuczynski, 1984). Thus, when a mother is worried that her son might hurt himself by crossing the street without looking or by using drugs, an authoritarian strategy might be most effective in the short term, with inductive explanations given later.

Separation and Individuation. As children grow older and become more independent, a moral foundation based on explanations and reasoning rather than commands helps them make better decisions. Such a foundation is particularly important during the adolescence when teenagers become more independent and sometimes rebel against their parents' authority (Andersen, 2004). By their early teens, most children depend more on their friends than their parents when it comes to making decisions and asking advice (Steinberg & Silverberg, 1986). Similarly, they yield much less to their parents and insist on making their own decisions much more often when they reach mid-adolescence (Steinberg, 1981). The teen years are a transition between the time when children are heavily dependent on their parents and the time when teenagers become

responsible, independent young adults. Scholars have referred to this transition period as a process of **separation and individuation,** whereby teenagers distance themselves, to some degree, from their parents and develop an individual identity apart from the family structure (Guerrero & Afifi, 1995b).

During this transition period, some form of power struggle between parents and teenagers is almost inevitable. Teenagers are often ready to express their independence before parents are ready to relinquish authority or before the teens are ready to make responsible adult decisions. This can lead to a period of "storm and stress" characterized by emotional distance between parents and children, as well as increased conflict (Kidwell, Fischer, Dunham, & Baranowski, 1983; Paikoff & Brooks-Gunn, 1991; Steinberg, 1987). Researchers have found that parent-child interaction during the teen years is often marked by less warmth (Paikoff & Brooks-Gunn, 1991; Steinberg, 1981), more interruptions by the child (Jacob, 1974), and less open communication (Guerrero & Afifi, 1995b).

Of course, some adolescent-parent relationships are stormier than others. If children gradually show that they are responsible enough to make their own decisions and parents gradually relinquish authority, the transition from child to young adult can be marked by more cooperation and mutual respect than rebellion. Indeed, Hill and Holmbeck (1986) argued that adolescence is a time of family regrouping, as parents and teenagers renegotiate rules and role relationships. Hill and Holmbeck also argued that the process of separation and individuation does not preclude close relationships between parents and children. Instead, this period of transition often leads to a redefinition of the parent-child relationship from an authority-based relationship characterized by unequal power to one characterized by mutual friendship and respect. Indeed, Grotevant and Cooper (1985) found that by age 17, most teens had begun renegotiating relational rules and roles with their parents. The key to a successful transition lies partially with the parents, who need to let adolescents become more individuated while still providing a supportive and caring environment (Campbell, Adams, & Dobson, 1984; Papini, Sebby, & Clark, 1989; Sabatelli & Mazor, 1985).

Traditional Versus Egalitarian Marriages

Relationships are complex, and maintaining any long-term relationship is difficult (see Chapter 9). Although there is no one formula for an ideal romantic relationship, evidence suggests that peer relationships characterized by respect and relative equality are healthier, more satisfying, and more likely to succeed. This is true for both friendships and dating relationships (Roiger, 1993). However, equality may be harder to achieve in marriages than in many friendships or dating relationships because spouses typically share money and possessions and have to divide household chores. As discussed in Chapter 10, this division is not usually equitable; most working married women in the United States are still responsible for around two thirds of household chores and an even larger percentage of child care. Trying to find a fair way to share resources and divide labor can lead to power struggles within even the best of marriages.

When studying issues of equality, social scientists have described two different types of marriages: traditional and egalitarian (Steil, 2000). According to Steil,

> Traditional marriages are based on a form of benevolent male dominance coupled with clearly specialized roles. Thus, when women are employed, the responsibility for family work is retained by the women, who add the career role to their traditionally held family role. (p. 128)

Of course, some women in traditional marriages are not employed or work only part-time, so that they can devote considerable time to managing the house and raising the children.

Some couples are very happy in traditional marriages (Fitzpatrick, 1988). However, in the 21st century, most women are not satisfied with traditional gender roles, and dual-career households are the rule rather than the exception. In dual-career marriages (as well as other close relationships in which people live together), partners need to negotiate roles related to household responsibilities rather than relying on traditional gender roles. Thus although various types of marriages can be fulfilling, research suggests that today the best chance for happiness resides in marriages in which the balance of power is nearly equal (Aida & Falbo, 1991; Schwartz, 1994; Steil, 2000; Thompson & Walker, 1989). In egalitarian marriages, also called peer marriages or sharing marriages (Schwartz, 1994), "Both spouses are employed, both are actively involved in parenting, and both share in the responsibilities and duties of the household" (Steil, 2000, p. 128).

Egalitarian marriages are often more intimate than traditional marriages. Most egalitarian marriages are deep and true friendships, as well as romances. Emotionally bonded spouses are likely to achieve equality in their relationships. Research conducted in Scandinavia by Thagaard (1997) showed that "close emotional ties between spouses are linked to the interpretation of the relationship in terms of equality. The perception of equality is based on the ability to influence the relationship beginning with one's own values" (p. 373). Aida and Falbo (1991) found that partners in egalitarian marriages used fewer dominant power strategies than partners in traditional marriages, perhaps because they could influence each other without using power plays. When they want to influence each other, partners in equal, independent relationships use more diverse and egalitarian influence strategies than do traditional couples (Witteman & Fitzpatrick, 1986).

Partners in traditional, unequal couples, in contrast, are more likely to use blatant power strategies such as verbal aggression and less likely to use compliance-gaining strategies (Witteman & Fitzpatrick, 1986). They are also less likely to engage in open communication. One study compared couples in interdependent, egalitarian marriages with those in more separate, isolated marriages (Solomon et al., 2004). Those in egalitarian marriages were more likely to express complaints and talk about relational problems than those in separate or traditional style marriages.

Equality has also been associated with increased mental health, whereas inequality is sometimes associated with decreased mental health. Among couples with troubled marriages, inequality is likely to be associated with depression symptoms in the less powerful partner (Bagarozzi, 1990). Even people in troubled marriages who have an equal power structure are less likely to have severe mental or emotional problems. Halloran (1998) suggested that inequality in close relationships is a cause of both depression and low-quality marriages. Moreover, this pattern leads to a vicious cycle. As one spouse becomes depressed, the other spouse must take over more control of the family, leading to greater inequality.

Equality of marriage does not simply "happen." It takes commitment on the part of partners. As Schwartz (1994) observed, "Social forces and psychological processes tenaciously maintain marriage along the old guidelines. Women still look to men to provide larger and more predictable income that establishes the family's social class and creature comforts" (p. 8). Several forces conspire against equality. At the turn of the century, women in the United States still earned less than 80% of what men earn, creating a power discrepancy and dependence on the part of many wives. Childbearing typically affects a woman's career and earning power more than her husband's. Perhaps even more important, in terms of household labor, most so-called egalitarian relationships are not really so equal after all. As reported in Chapter 10, in heterosexual relationships women still tend to do more of the household work than men, even when both relational partners are working. Centuries of hierarchical relationships do not disappear overnight, nor do the power structures that exist in most families. While great progress has been made in elevating the status of women, sources of inequality still exist that will take additional years and effort to break down.

SUMMARY AND APPLICATION

Power and influence are present in almost every human relationship, including Tyler and Ashley's. Whether you are persuading your roommate to take out the trash, asking your child to be home at a certain time, or deciding if and when you should marry your dating partner, some level of interpersonal influence is present. Power is a perception. But people do not automatically have power; rather, power is granted to people. Resources such as money, social standing, and love give people the ability to be powerful, especially when these resources are scarce, but ultimately people are only as influential as others let them be.

In Tyler and Ashley's relationship, they can assert power and try to influence others using a variety of verbal and nonverbal strategies. Some are ineffective, like Tyler's withdrawal behavior where he refuses to discuss relationship issues, or like Ashley's constant nagging, which she knows does no good. Tyler and Ashley are at their best when they use a large assortment of influence strategies they have in their repertoire and when they know how to select appropriate strategies in a given situation are the most effective at persuasion. Power is tied to issues of authority and equality. Parent-child relationships are initially marked by child dependence and parental authority. Gradually, however, parents relinquish control and children assert their independence—a process that prepares children to be responsible young adults. In marriage, the husband typically has more concrete resources (such as income and occupational status) than the wife, which can reduce her power base. Ashley, however, has better job offers than Tyler and will be more independent and powerful as a result. In fact, Ashley's ambition and Tyler's laziness may create a power imbalance and threaten the equality and stability of the relationship. Ashley has dependence power that makes her more powerful in the relationship. It is hoped that they will resolve this power discrepancy because research shows that both men and women are usually happier and the relationship is stronger in egalitarian marriages than in traditional marriages where one partner is more powerful.

Power and equality are certainly important in relationships. As discussed in Chapter 10, relationships function best when people are experiencing more rewards than costs and when they feel that they are being treated fairly. Ashley feels that Tyler is not trying hard enough and that the relationship sometimes has a poor cost-benefit ratio. This is true not just in heterosexual relationships; gay men and lesbians also believe that it is important to have an egalitarian relationship. Achieving equality, however, is a difficult task. Ashley and Tyler need to value the different resources they bring to the relationship equally. One strength of Ashley and Tyler's relationship is that they have the power to influence decisions without getting their way at the expense of the partner. And if Tyler is less ambitious about his career, perhaps he can do more of the household tasks, such as cleaning and home repair, to provide balance between the partners.

It is important for Tyler and Ashley to realize some facts about power. Power is a perception that is a reality for a person. If Tyler believes that Ashley is too powerful or controlling in the relationship, they both have to deal with that perception, and either the perception or behavior must change to resolve that discrepancy.

Tyler is right to be concerned about the future of the relationship. People with considerable resources—Ashley has beauty, occupational status, and intelligence—have more power since they have more alternatives. And as with so many women today, who are graduating from college in greater numbers, her excellent job offers give her the ability to be self-sufficient and powerful in ways beyond typical sources of feminine power such as sex and beauty.

DISCUSSION QUESTIONS

1. Think about the three most powerful famous people you have heard of. Now, think about the three most powerful people you have known personally. What characteristics make (or made) these individuals powerful?

2. In heterosexual relationships, some scholars have proposed that men have more power than women. Do you agree or disagree? On the basis of what you have read in this chapter, how do you think relative power and sex differences in power influence relationship satisfaction and decision making?

3. In this chapter, we discussed a number of strategies people use to gain compliance in their relationships. Which persuasive strategies do you think are most effective? Why?

12

GETTING TOO CLOSE FOR COMFORT

Privacy and Secrets in Relationships

Khaled is secretly in love with his best friend's long-term girlfriend. He wishes he could tell her that he loves her and see if there is a chance that she might reciprocate these feelings, but he values his relationship with his best friend Steve too much to put their friendship in jeopardy. Samantha was sexually abused by her uncle as a child but has never told anyone; she just accepted her boyfriend's marriage proposal and is feeling guilty that even he doesn't know. She also hasn't told him that her family was on welfare when she was in elementary school, in part because she is embarrassed about it but mostly because it is a family secret that her mother and sisters don't like to talk about. She would feel as if she was betraying them if she told her fiancé. Tyrone and Suzanne suspect that their teenage son, John, is starting to experiment with drugs and alcohol. They sit down with John and have a long talk about the dangers of doing drugs and drinking. During the conversation, Tyrone carefully avoids telling John that he smoked pot in college, and Suzanne avoids telling him that she used to have a drinking problem—a topic she has never even disclosed to Tyrone.

These situations reflect disclosure and privacy decisions that people make every day. Who among these people is "right" in the decision to withhold information? Who, in your opinion, is "wrong"? The research in this area makes one thing clear—the popular idea that we should always be 100% open with our romantic partners, family, and friends is neither followed nor well-advised. Indeed, several studies have shown that the times people seek privacy and/or avoid sharing information with others are just as important to personal and relational health as disclosure and connectedness. Parks (1982) was one of the first scholars to recognize this. He argued that the ideology of complete intimacy is overrated— that too much openness can be smothering and that people need privacy. Altman, whose work on social penetration theory (see Chapter 5) helped popularize the notion that self-disclosure is essential for relationship development, has also touted the importance of balancing needs for expression with needs for privacy (Altman, Vinsel, & Brown, 1981). Rosenfeld (2000) echoed these sentiments when he stated, "Self-disclosure is a scary notion! It can explain our existence, reveal who we are to ourselves and others as we disclose and engage in an act of 'becoming,' and, more fundamentally, *allow* us to exist in the world" (p. 4). It is no wonder, then, that people value their privacy. Yet too much privacy can also be problematic. Most people also need some openness and connection with others.

In this chapter, we review some of the research on the importance of privacy in our relationships with others. First, we examine communication privacy management theory, which explains how people manage information in ways that maintain privacy (Petronio, 1991). Second, we discuss privacy violations, including obsessive relational intrusion. Finally, we discuss patterns of topic avoidance and secret keeping in relationships.

COMMUNICATION PRIVACY MANAGEMENT THEORY

Communication privacy management (CPM) theory helps explain how individuals cope with the need to maintain privacy boundaries (Petronio, 1991, 2002). The theory is rooted in the assumption that people set up **boundary structures** as a way to control the risks inherent in disclosing private information. These boundary structures are based on two elements associated with private information: ownership and permeability.

When people feel that they have **ownership** over information, they believe they also have the "right" to control who has access to it. For example, if Suzanne thinks that her past drinking problem is private information, she will be upset if one of her old college friends starts telling people about it. The courts are filled with cases in which this battle over information ownership is being waged. For example, movie stars and other celebrities have sued the tabloid press for using their words or images without permission.

The information people own also comes with varying levels of **permeability**. In other words, a strict set of rules governs who can access the information that we own. For example, Samantha may share certain information with her fiancé that she does not share with anyone else. Yet Samantha also keeps some family secrets from him. She doesn't tell him that her mother was on welfare when she was young because this is considered a family

secret—something that only members of her immediate family have the right to know. Samantha also keeps the information that she was abused by her uncle a secret from her fiancé and everyone else. As these examples show, pieces of private information differ in the extent to which the boundaries of access are permeable. Once boundary structures are set, rules are established for managing the information within the boundaries. These rules are guided by three principles (Petronio, 1991).

Influences on Rules for Boundary Management

The first principle specifies that the rules for communication boundary management are influenced by culture, personality, the relationship, sex/gender, and needs/motivation. First, each culture has different rules regarding privacy and self-disclosure. For example, some cultures have relatively loose rules regarding what topics are appropriate to discuss with strangers; other cultures are more restrictive. Cultures differ in terms of ownership of health information. In some cultures, physicians give information about a patient's health only to her or his family, who decide what, if anything, to tell the patient. Other cultures have strict laws that ensure that health information belongs only to the patient. Second, personality variables guide disclosure decisions. Some people are highly self-disclosive and expressive, whereas other people are much more private. Third, a host of relational factors, such as attraction, closeness, and relationship type (friends vs. coworkers), affect the dynamics of privacy and self-disclosures. As mentioned in Chapter 5, people tend to disclose more with individuals they like than with those they dislike. Fourth, sex and gender differences, although usually small, can nonetheless influence privacy boundaries. As discussed previously, women's rules for disclosing information sometimes differ from men's, and women tend to disclose somewhat more than men, particularly on intimate topics (see Chapter 9). Finally, individuals' needs and motivations can affect how they manage privacy boundaries. For instance, people who are motivated to make friends may disclose more than those who are motivated to accomplish a task, and people who worry about getting hurt or rejected might avoid self-disclosure that could make them vulnerable. These criteria for rule formation determine when, where, and to whom people disclose information.

Cooperation

The second principle is that *successful boundary management often requires cooperation between people*. People often must involve others in their information boundary management. For example, secrets held by an entire family (such as Samantha's family secret regarding welfare) require that all family members agree to keep the relevant information private, which means that they must coordinate their boundary structures and rules on that particular issue. In a similar vein, someone who cheats on her or his partner must either implicitly (and naively) assume or explicitly discuss a degree of boundary coordination with her or his sexual partner to keep the incident a secret. To help maintain coordinated boundary structures, people usually develop penalties for group or dyad members who violate the boundary structure (Petronio, 1991, 2002). Boundary coordination becomes especially salient when the information is revealed to someone who is not a part of the group with access to the secret. For example, Samantha's family secret about welfare may eventually be divulged to her fiancé when they marry and he officially becomes a member of the family. The addition of a new member into the secret-keeping group necessitates additional boundary structure coordination, and the rules must often be made explicit to the new member.

Boundary Turbulence

The third principle is that *stress creates boundary turbulence*. **Boundary turbulence** occurs when these structures come under stress or threat, forcing renewed boundary management (Petronio, 1991). There are situations in which old boundary structures may need to be either fortified or renegotiated. For example, when people's lives change, topics previously avoided (such as the future of the relationship) may become acceptable topics (such as after a marriage proposal). Similarly, once a previous boundary structure is violated (such as when a secret is first disclosed), a radical change in the nature of the new structure may occur (such as the once-secret information becoming a commonplace disclosure).

Petronio (2000) argued that people's need to maintain privacy leads them to create boundaries that guide their communication behavior. These boundaries are often revised to adjust to changing circumstances, but their continual management allows people to balance their needs for privacy with their coexisting needs for self-disclosure and connection. Next, we review research on privacy seeking, which further emphasizes the delicate balance that people attempt to strike between autonomy and connectedness.

NEGOTIATING PRIVACY BOUNDARIES IN RELATIONSHIPS

The central feature of CPM is its recognition that we cherish our rights to privacy and our ability to control information. But perhaps the most interesting questions revolve around information ownership issues. Ask yourself this: What information does your romantic partner (present or future) have a right to know? Your past dating history? Your financial status? Your job history? Whether you have a sexually transmitted infection? Your medical history? Details about your parents' relationship? Do you have the right to decide whether to disclose these types of information or not? Now ask yourself this: What information about your parents do you have the right to know? The quality of their relationship? Their health and well-being? Put yourself in John's shoes (see the examples at the beginning of this chapter). Does he have a right to know about his parents' past experiences with drugs and alcohol since they are judging him for engaging in similar behavior? or Do Tyrone and Suzanne have a right to keep this information private?

To address the real-world privacy right challenges facing people every day, Petronio, Sargent, Andea, Reganis, and Cichocki (2004) used CPM to study family and friends who serve as informal health care advocates for patients. Their results showed some of the privacy-related difficulties that physicians, patients, and extended family members face in these situations. Physicians are not always comfortable giving information to someone other than the patient, and advocates sometimes worry that the information they receive could depress or worry the patient and undermine the treatment. Advocates also struggled with the problem of whether to keep certain patient information private (by not divulging it to the physician) or reveal private information for the sake of the patient's health. In the end, most advocates put the patient's health needs over their privacy needs. Culture also plays a substantial role in defining privacy rights. In the health field alone, some cultures expect physicians to talk to family members, *not* the patient, about the patient's health status. It is then up to the family to decide whether to tell the patient.

This struggle for privacy emerges in many different relationships, including those between friends, romantic partners, and coworkers. Much of the research in this area, however, has focused on privacy in family relationships, particularly those between parents and children (Guerrero & Afifi, 1995b). Big "Keep Out" signs often adorn the doors of teenagers' rooms, sending a clear message of their desire for privacy. Frequently, parents and children view privacy issues quite differently. As they move closer to adulthood, teenagers may believe they have a right to be independent and to maintain their privacy, but parents may believe that their teens still need guidance and protection. In this sense, the boundary coordination rules in families can be complex, and their negotiation can be very difficult. What is considered private information and private behavior is a topic of heated debate in some families, especially those in which teenage sons and daughters are asserting their independence.

Children react to privacy violations in various ways depending on the circumstances, but they are particularly likely to be resentful of privacy violations once they are adults and have left home. Once children have "left the nest," privacy violations by the parents reflect a failure to recognize the children's "right" to independence at a time when their sense of autonomy is beginning to flourish (McGoldrick &

Carter, 1982). Indeed, the consequences of such privacy violations are potentially severe, but how common are they, and what form do they take?

To answer these questions, Petronio and Harriman (1990) asked students to describe ways in which their parents invade their privacy and their reaction to these privacy violations. All the students were able to describe at least one example, and 96% of them described at least three such incident, suggesting that privacy violations by parents are a fairly common occurrence for college students. Eight types of parental privacy violations were reported: (1) asking personal questions about the student's life, (2) giving unsolicited advice, (3) making unsolicited remarks about the student's life (4) opening the student's mail without permission, (5) going through the student's belongings without permission, (6) entering the bathroom without knocking, (7) eavesdropping on face-to-face conversations with others, and (8) using a second telephone line to listen in on a phone conversation without permission.

As you might suspect, some of these violations are more severe than others. Petronio and Harriman grouped the violations into two general types: (1) **subversive invasion tactics,** which violate children's privacy without their prior knowledge or permission (eavesdropping, opening mail, going through personal things), and (2) **direct invasion tactics,** which include more overt violations of privacy with no attempt by parents to hide their actions (giving unsolicited advice, asking personal questions). Not surprisingly, the students in Petronio and Harriman's study reported that subversive invasion tactics were considered worse violations of privacy than were direct tactics.

According to Petronio and Harriman (1990), young adults react to parental privacy invasions in at least seven ways: They (1) show disappointment, (2) ask the parents to stop invading their privacy, (3) make the parents feel guilty, (4) confront the parents with evidence, (5) use a pay phone to make personal calls, (6) hide belongings, and (7) meet friends outside the home. As you may already have noticed, these reactions differ along two general lines: They are either (1) confrontational, where the child openly challenges the guilty parent (asking the parent to stop the privacy violation, confronting the parent with evidence), or (2) evasive, where the child changes her or his behavior to protect privacy but does not discuss it directly with the parents. Petronio and Harriman found that students were more likely to react in a confrontational manner in response to subversive invasions. In other words, they were more likely to directly challenge their parents when they caught their parents secretly trying to invade their privacy than when their parents invaded their privacy by asking questions or giving unsolicited advice.

Privacy violations and related responses have a strong impact on parent-child relationships. Privacy invasion, especially when subversive and when followed by a confrontational response, was generally associated with less trust and a decrease in the perceived quality of the parent-child relationship (Petronio & Harriman, 1990). However, sometimes privacy violations increased openness in parent-child relationships (probably by forcing discussion of issues that would otherwise have been ignored). In sum, subversive boundary violations can have long-term effects on the parent-child relationship.

Privacy is important in other relationships as well. Our need to maintain privacy and to control information about ourselves is evident in many of our actions. Several scholars have studied the ways people try to create their private space and communicate their needs for privacy (Burgoon et al., 1996; Buslig, 1999). For example, people build fences around their houses, erect "No Trespassing" signs, and put partitions between office cubicles. Doors are perhaps the most obvious architectural way in which people regulate privacy. Think of the difference between professors who have "open-door policies" and those who do not. Those who have such policies are signaling a willingness to forgo some of their privacy needs and, in doing so, appear much more accessible than those who protect their privacy needs by closing their office doors.

People also signal their degree of privacy needs by the way they arrange furniture. Again, think about professors' offices. Some professors have their office set up so that during meetings students sit on one side of the desk and they sit on the other, thereby maximizing privacy boundaries. Other professors sit with no desk between them and their students, thereby minimizing privacy boundaries and creating a greater sense of closeness. Other forms of privacy management are less subtle. For example, Buslig

(1999) reported that college students sometimes hang markers on the outside of their doors (such as tying a scarf around the door knob) to indicate that they are "entertaining" a boyfriend or girlfriend and want privacy. A desire for privacy is communicated in other subtle nonverbal ways, such as reducing eye contact, increasing conversational distance, turning away, using body barriers such as folded arms, and displaying less alert or positive facial expression (see Burgoon et al., 1996). Indeed, we spend much of our time signaling to others, often unconsciously, the degree of privacy we need and, in so doing, managing our privacy boundaries.

Another study investigated how graduate student teachers react to privacy violations by professors and other graduate students (Koehler, 2005). This study identified four general types of reactions to privacy violations. **Verbal assertion** involves communicating with the person who violated one's privacy in a direct and cooperative manner (e.g., asking the person to stop engaging in the behavior). **Passive aggression and retaliation** involve trying to retaliate against a person through behaviors such as making the person feel guilty and getting revenge by violating her or his privacy. **Tempered tolerance** involves outwardly accepting the privacy violation through responses such as "grinning and bearing it" and "acting like the incident never happened." Finally, **boundary restructuration** occurs when people adjust their public boundaries to prevent future privacy violations. For example, the graduate students reported hiding personal belongings and making phone calls from home rather than from the office. Koehler's study showed that graduate students were more likely to use tempered tolerance with professors than with fellow graduate students, probably due to the power dynamics that characterize the student-professor relationship. However, graduate students were less likely to report feeling solidarity with their professor if they responded to privacy violations with tempered tolerance. This suggests that students who feel they cannot talk directly to their professors about privacy violations are less satisfied with the student-professor relationship. In contrast, in peer relationships between graduate students, boundary restructuration was related to less interpersonal solidarity, suggesting that people may resent having to restructure physical boundaries to prevent peers from violating their privacy. These types of strategies are also likely used in our relationships with friends, family, and romantic partners. To get an idea of which of these strategies you tend to use within a given relationship, take the test in Box 12.1.

▨ BOX 12.1   Put Yourself to the Test

How Do You React to Privacy Violations?

Think about the times that someone you know has violated your privacy by doing things such as listening to your conversations with others, asking you overly personal questions, or borrowing something of yours without permission. How do you typically react to these types of privacy violations? Mark a 7 if you almost always react a particular way and a 1 if you almost never react a particular way.

When a certain person violates my privacy, I	Almost Never ◄——► Almost Always						
1. ask this person to stop engaging in such behavior.	1	2	3	4	5	6	7
2. tell this person that her or his actions are inappropriate.	1	2	3	4	5	6	7
3. ask for an apology.	1	2	3	4	5	6	7
4. ask for assurances that it won't happen again.	1	2	3	4	5	6	7
5. make this person feel guilty.	1	2	3	4	5	6	7
6. give this person the silent treatment.	1	2	3	4	5	6	7
7. invade this person's privacy to get revenge.	1	2	3	4	5	6	7
8. get back at this person somehow.	1	2	3	4	5	6	7
9. act like the incident never happened.	1	2	3	4	5	6	7
10. try to forget about it.	1	2	3	4	5	6	7
11. just grin and bear it.	1	2	3	4	5	6	7
12. pretend that I'm not upset about it.	1	2	3	4	5	6	7
13. make sure not to have private conversations in front of this person.	1	2	3	4	5	6	7
14. hide personal belongings.	1	2	3	4	5	6	7
15. lock my door or otherwise prevent this person from entering my private space.	1	2	3	4	5	6	7
16. am careful not to talk about certain topics in front of this person.	1	2	3	4	5	6	7

Add up your responses:

Verbal assertion	(Items 1–4)	_____
Passive aggression and retaliation	(Items 5–8)	_____
Tempered tolerance	(Items 9–12)	_____
Boundary restructuration	(Items 13–16)	_____

Higher scores indicate that you use more of a particular response within a particular relationship. (The highest score possible is 21, the lowest is 4). You might want to try taking this test referencing different people to see if your privacy management strategies vary on the basis of the relationship.

SOURCE: Used with permission of Milissa Koehler

One of the most difficult aspects of maintaining privacy is that the need for privacy is often interpreted as a desire to separate from others (see Mehrabian, 1981). For example, it is sometimes hard to separate a partner's request for some time alone from a desire to distance herself or himself from you. Similarly, if your spouse or roommate retreats into another room for an extended period of time and refuses to talk to you about something that is bothering her or him, you might interpret this as a violation of marriage or friendship rules that call for openness. Of course, as discussed in previous chapters, the need for privacy is completely normal and, in fact, is critical to healthy relationships (Baxter & Montgomery, 1996). As dialectics theory suggests, people have needs for both autonomy and connection and for both privacy and interaction. Still, the reality is that communicating privacy needs, especially in relationships, can be difficult. Therefore, relational partners often do not express their privacy needs directly. For example, you may communicate that you are upset when your partner departs for a weekend trip, but note that you are also looking forward to the time alone afforded by your partner's absence.

OBSESSIVE RELATIONAL INTRUSION

In some cases, people continue to invade another person's privacy even when the other person clearly wants to be left alone. This is often the case when people engage in **obsessive relational intrusion (ORI)**, defined as repeated invasion of one's privacy boundaries (Cupach & Spitzberg, 1998). ORI occurs when someone uses intrusive tactics to try to get closer to someone else. For example, in Chapter 6 we discussed situations of unrequited love, wherein one person (the would-be lover) is interested in another person who does not return her or his affection (the rejector). Some would-be lovers use ORI, as do some people after a relational partner breaks up with them. Sometimes ORI is also used when one person wants the relationship to turn romantic and the other person wants to remain only friends (Cupach & Spitzberg, in press).

Cupach and Spitzberg (2004) developed the **relational goal pursuit theory** to help explain ORI.

According to this theory, people expend energy to develop or reinitiate relationships to the extent that they perceive a relationship is desirable and attainable. When a relationship is perceived to be unattainable, people abandon their original goal and seek an alternative. Unfortunately, however, people sometimes continue to believe that a relationship is unattainable even though it is not. In these cases, ORI is likely to occur.

In fact, episodes of ORI typically increase in intensity as the object of attention tries to fortify her or his privacy boundaries—for example, by taking pains to avoid the pursuer. At first, ORI behaviors are usually prosocial, indirect, and only mildly annoying (Cupach & Spitzberg, 2004, in press). The pursuer might act flirtatious, try to spend time with the desired partner, and telephone or e-mail a lot. If these ORI behaviors are unsuccessful, the pursuer will sometimes employ more invasive violations of privacy, such as surveillance, harassment, and infiltration into the desired person's social network. Such behaviors are typically perceived as aggravating and inconvenient. Finally, in some cases ORI becomes extreme, frightening, and creepy, with pursuers stalking their victims and engaging in coercive and even violent behavior (Cupach & Spitzberg, 2004). Cupach and Spitzberg (in press) report that 54% of stalking victims experience some type of threat, 32% experience physical violence, and 12% experience sexual violence. Box 12.2 contains a sample of ORI behaviors.

So why do some pursuers continue to use ORI behaviors rather than abandoning their goal and seeking an alternative relationship? Cupach and Spitzberg (1998, 2004, in press) suggest four general reasons: cultural scripts, the ambiguity of communication, rumination, and a shift in motivation. First, cultural scripts often portray people "playing hard to get." Cultural scripts also suggest that if people try hard enough, they will eventually win the affection of the person they love. Together, these cultural scripts work against the realization that a relationship is unattainable.

Second, communication patterns related to the initiation, reinitiation, and rejection of relationships are ambiguous. As noted in Chapter 7, during courtship people engage in ambiguous flirtatious

BOX 12.2   Highlights

Types of Obsessive Relational Intrusion

Cupach and Spitzberg surveyed 876 people to determine the types of ORI behaviors they had experienced. Some of the behaviors they found are listed below, along with the percentage of people who reported experiencing these types of ORI:

Called and argued with me (73%)

Called and hung up when I answered (70%)

Constantly asked for "another chance" (64%)

Watched or stared at me from a distance (62%)

Made exaggerated claims about her or his affection for me (61%)

Drove by my house or workplace (57%)

Used third parties to spy or keep tabs on me (55%)

Performed large favors for me without my permission (52%)

Spread false rumors about me to my friends (49%)

Left notes on my car windshield (45%)

Sent me unwanted cards or letters (42%)

Increased contact with my family members to stay connected to me (37%)

Went through private things in my room (34%)

Physically shoved, slapped, or hit me (32%)

Made obscene phone calls to me (30%)

Damaged my property or possessions (26%)

Forced me to engage in unwanted sexual behavior (16%)

Called a radio station and dedicated songs to me (15%)

Cluttered my e-mail with messages (11%)

Broke into my home or apartment (8%)

SOURCE: Adapted from Spitzberg and Cupach (1998).

behavior that is safe and helps them save face if they are rejected. Similarly, people often use indirect strategies to reject people because they worry about hurting their feelings. Rather than seeing these strategies as polite ways of rejecting them, pursuers continue to believe that the desired relationship is attainable.

Third, when people are having trouble obtaining a goal, they often ruminate about it, sometimes obsessively. Rumination leads to stress and arousal, with pursuers often redoubling their efforts to get close to the desired partner as a way of alleviating the negative affect they are feeling. Indeed, studies have shown that the combination of anger and jealousy leads to ORI behavior (Cupach & Spitzberg, in press). Finally, the motivation for ORI behaviors can shift from relationship pursuit to the desire for revenge if the pursuer feels humiliated. This shift sometimes marks the beginning of more aggressive ORI behaviors (Cupach & Spitzberg, in press).

ORI sometimes escalates to stalking, wherein someone repeatedly harasses another person in a way that threatens her or his safety (Meloy & Gothard, 1995). A recent summary of studies suggests that anywhere from 2% to 13% of men and 8% to 32% of women have been stalked in their lifetime (Cupach & Spitzberg, 2004). This wide range is likely a function of the various definitions given for stalking in different studies. For example, Kohn, Flood, Chase, and McMahon (2000) found that 15% of the women in their sample reported that they had been "stalked, harassed, or threatened with violence for more than one month by someone who would not leave [them] alone." In comparison, 45% of Elliott and Bradley's (1997) sample reported having been "stalked or harassed with obscene phone calls." Studies also suggest that the vast majority of stalkers (e.g., about 75%) have had a previous relationship with their victims (Cupach & Spitzberg, 2004). And strikingly, the average stalking episode lasts nearly *two* years! One individual described her experience as "pure hell" that "just kept going on and on and on and on" (Draucker, 1999, p. 478). Not surprisingly, the toll that this sort of constant threat takes on victims' psychological and physiological health is tremendous.

Even moderate forms of ORI can have devastating psychological consequences for the person being pursued (Cupach & Spitzberg, 2000). The most obvious consequence of ORI episodes is the extreme and repeated experiences of fear associated with the target's loss of control over his or her physical and psychological privacy (Mullen & Pathe, 1994). This fear often results in the target's making drastic attempts to regain this privacy, including equipping house and car with alarm systems, changing phone numbers and addresses, and even changing jobs. In fact, Wallace and Silverman (1996) argued that the effects

of stalking are often similar to those experienced by victims of posttraumatic stress disorder.

A key question, then, is how the desired person can thwart ORI behavior? Cupach and Spitzberg (in press) identified five general ways in which people cope with ORI behavior: **passive** (waiting for the pursuer to tire of you, lose interest, or give up), **avoidant** (not answering phone calls and staying away from the pursuer), **aggressive** (being mean or rude, threatening to harm the pursuer if she or he doesn't leave you alone), **integrative** (communicating disinterest directly, negotiating relationship rules and boundaries), and **help seeking** (asking others for assistance in preventing ORI behavior). Cupach and Spitzberg concluded that no one strategy is effective most of the time. In fact, victims of ORI sometimes use multiple strategies over long periods of time with no success. However, integrative communication that includes confrontation and negotiation is effective 5% to 40% of the time, which offers some hope to ORI victims.

TOPIC AVOIDANCE

So far, we have discussed how people react to privacy violations that are either mildly or highly intrusive in ways that are mostly reactive rather than proactive. One proactive way to maintain privacy is to engage in **topic avoidance**, which occurs when a person deliberately decides to avoid disclosing information on a particular subject. Topic avoidance may occur regardless of the context or the person with whom one is talking. For example, there might be certain topics that you keep completely private and do not disclose to anyone—perhaps a particularly embarrassing moment or a painful failure. More often, however, topic avoidance is specific to the situation or the person with whom one is talking. For example, there might be a topic that you refuse to discuss with your parents but would readily discuss with a friend. Conversely, you may keep some information about your family secret from your social network.

Indeed, research suggests that some topic avoidance is common in all types of close relationships. Baxter and Wilmot (1984) found that more than 95% of the college students in their study could name at least one topic that they considered to be "taboo" or off-limits in their friendships or dating relationships. Subsequent research has revealed that individuals use topic avoidance to maintain control over information across a wide variety of relationships, from stepfamilies (Golish & Caughlin, 2002), to sibling relationships (Guerrero & Afifi, 1995a), to same- and cross-sex friendships (Afifi & Guerrero, 1998).

Commonly Avoided Topics

Although people can avoid talking about almost anything, some topics are more likely to be avoided than others. Guerrero and Afifi's (1995a, 1995b) summary of the available research revealed six general topics that are commonly avoided in close relationships: **relationship issues** (e.g., relationship norms, the state and future of the relationship, the amount of attention given to the relationship), **negative experiences/failures** (e.g., past experiences that may be considered socially unacceptable or were traumatic), **romantic relationship experiences** (e.g., past or present romantic relationships and dating patterns), **sexual experiences** (e.g., past or present sexual activity or sexual preferences), **friendships** (e.g., current friendships with others, the qualities of the friendship, and the activities engaged in together), and **dangerous behavior** (e.g., behaviors that are potentially hurtful to oneself). Golish and Caughlin's (2002) study of avoidance between parents and their children led to the addition of six other topics— **everyday activities** (e.g., school, daily events), **other family members** (e.g., talking about the other parent/stepparent, siblings), **money**, **deep conversations**, **drinking/drugs**, and **religion**. Of course, no one study will likely capture all the possible issues that may be avoided in relationships, so it is best to think of these as ones that are commonly avoided. For example, given that most studies in this area used college students, adolescents, and young married couples, they likely underrepresent some of the topics avoided by older adults.

Some research suggests that some types of relationships may be more fraught with informational boundary management issues than others. Golish and Caughlin (2000) found that children in stepfamilies most often avoided discussing issues with their stepparent and least often with their natural mother.

Guerrero and Afifi (1995a) found that adolescents and young adults avoided discussing negative life experiences and dating experiences with their parents more than with their siblings and avoided sexual discussions with opposite-sex family members more than with same-sex ones. Thus, a teenage boy is more likely to talk about sex with his older brother or father than with his mother or sister, while a teenage girl is more likely to talk to her older sister or mother. Finally, Afifi and Guerrero (1998) found that individuals avoided discussions of negative life experiences and relationship issues with male friends more than with female friends and avoided topics related to dating and sexual experiences when with cross-sex friends more than when with same-sex friends. In sum, people do appear to have relationship-specific concerns that lead them to avoid particular issues most often in certain types of relationships.

Reasons for Topic Avoidance

Research has also examined why people avoid talking about certain topics. Afifi and Guerrero's (2000) summary of the literature suggests that there are three general motivations for topic avoidance, with specific motivations underlying each.

Relationship-Based Motivations. Paradoxically, people can use topic avoidance either to strengthen or to disengage from a relationship. In fact, contrary to research conducted in the 1970s and early 1980s that touted the benefits of complete openness and self-disclosure, more recent studies on topic avoidance suggest that one of the most important reasons for maintaining individual boundaries around information is a concern for maintaining the relationship (Afifi & Guerrero, 2000; Parks, 1982). Baxter and Wilmot (1985) found that the desire for **relationship protection** was the single biggest motivator leading to avoidance of a particular issue with a relational partner. Similarly, Hatfield (1984) and Rosenfeld (1979) noted that fear of abandonment often explained a person's decision to avoid certain topics. In other words, if people are worried that their current dating partner will disapprove of their revelations, they often avoid talking about topics that they think reflect negatively on them.

This motivation is not restricted to romantic relationships. Like Khaled, people sometimes withhold information that could harm their friendships. Although Khaled would like to see if Steve's girlfriend, Tara, shares his romantic feelings, he puts his friendship with Steve above his feelings for Tara. Afifi and Guerrero (1998) found that males were more likely than females to claim relationship protection as a reason for topic avoidance in their friendships and that people avoided certain topics with male friends more than with female friends because of this concern. In family relationships, Guerrero and Afifi (1995a) found that individuals were more likely to be driven by a desire to protect the relationship when avoiding topics with their parents as opposed to their siblings. In an extension of this research, Golish and Caughlin (2000) found that relationship protection was more often a reason underlying avoidance with stepparents than with fathers and with fathers than with mothers. So although relationship protection is an important reason underlying decisions to avoid disclosure, it seems especially relevant to some close relationships.

In contrast to the desire to protect and sustain the relationship, some people avoid discussing certain topics in the hope of destroying the relationship or preventing it from becoming closer. This motivation has been labeled **relationship destruction** or **relationship de-escalation** (Afifi & Guerrero, 2000). Although much less work has focused specifically on this motivation, several lines of research support the idea that people use topic avoidance to terminate a relationship or to prevent it from becoming more intimate. For instance, during the breakup stages of relationships, one of the partners may distance herself or himself from the other by shutting down communication and keeping information that was previously shared private (see Chapter 15). Another way to think about this motivation is how it works when someone you dislike wants to become friends with you. You might strategically avoid discussing personal topics with this person so that intimacy cannot develop.

As dialectics theory would suggest (see Chapter 9), people sometimes experience competing tensions to maintain a level of closeness in a relationship and also to prevent the relationship from becoming closer (see also Altman et al., 1981). For example, have you ever been in a relationship in which you wanted to remain just a friend but the friend wanted to become a romantic partner? One way of preserving the friendship is to avoid discussing any topics that may lead to "relational talks" or otherwise give the person an opportunity to express her or his interest in advancing the relationship. You might worry that discussing the relationship could harm your friendship by making communication awkward or by forcing you to reject your friend. Note that in this case, topic avoidance may actually serve a dual motivation: (1) preventing the friendship from turning romantic and (2) preserving the friendship itself.

Individual-Based Motivations. People also avoid discussing certain issues to protect themselves. In Chapter 2, we talked about the importance people place on protecting their public identities. Literally hundreds of studies have shown that people work hard to project and maintain a positive image. Not surprisingly, then, one of the main reasons people avoid discussing certain issues is that disclosure on certain topics may make them "look bad." Afifi and Guerrero (2000) labeled this motivation **identity management.** In fact, across four studies, spanning sibling, parent-child, stepparent-child, friendship, and dating relationships, the fear of embarrassment and criticism, fueled by feelings of vulnerability, was the leading reason given for topic avoidance (Afifi & Guerrero, 1998; Guerrero & Afifi, 1995a, 1995b; Hatfield, 1984). Together, these studies suggest that the primary reason people avoid discussing certain issues is the fear that disclosure will threaten their identities. Relationship protection is a close second. Apparently, people decide that it is better not to talk about something if it might make others perceive them negatively. If a person's identity is on the line, disclosure oftentimes is not worth the risk.

Besides this concern over public identity, people may avoid specific topics as a way to maintain privacy. This motivation, which Afifi and Guerrero (2000) termed **privacy maintenance**, is rooted in individuals' needs for privacy and autonomy. Earlier, we discussed the importance of privacy maintenance in people's lives. One way in which people maintain privacy is avoiding disclosure about certain topics. As we noted, this sort of privacy maintenance is especially common in families, where teenage sons and daughters largely create their own identity by refusing to share certain information about themselves with their parents. This enables the teenagers to maintain their privacy boundary. Of course, this desire for privacy exists in other relationships as well. For example, you may become annoyed with a friend who wants to know all the details about your romantic relationship or who is constantly asking you how well you did in exams or term papers. In response, you may refuse to answer your friend's questions and avoid bringing up any related topics in the future as a way to protect your privacy.

Information-Based Motivations. The final set of reasons why people choose to avoid disclosure is based on the information they expect to receive from the other person. In particular, people may choose to avoid disclosure because they suspect that the other person may find the disclosure trivial, not respond in a helpful way, or lack the requisite knowledge to respond. Afifi and Guerrero (2000) labeled these types of motivations **partner unresponsiveness.** For example, if you have a problem for which you need advice but think your friend will be unable to provide you with much help or will not care enough to really listen, you will likely avoid discussing that problem with your friend. Studies have found that people are especially likely to avoid discussing problems with men for this reason (Afifi & Guerrero, 1998; Guerrero & Afifi, 1995a, 1995b). In fact, a study by Burke, Weir, and Harrison (1976) found that 23% of wives, compared with only 10% of husbands, avoided disclosure because of a belief that their spouse would be unresponsive. This finding is consistent with research on social support, which shows that women generally are better listeners than men (Derlega, Barbee, & Winstead, 1994).

People also engage in topic avoidance when they believe that talking about a particular topic would be futile or a "waste of their time." Afifi and Guerrero (2000) labeled this motivation **futility of discussion**. Although this motivation has received less attention than the others, it may play an important role in people's decisions to withhold information. Believing that a partner or friend is so entrenched in her or his position as to make discussion meaningless certainly

will motivate topic avoidance, but it may also be especially detrimental to relational success.

Collectively, these motivations account for many of the reasons why people maintain strict information boundaries within their relationships; Box 12.3 gives real-life examples of each. It is also important to keep in mind that people often avoid topics for several reasons, not just one, and that the reasons are often related. Knobloch and Carpenter-Theune (2004) found that people who avoided topics with their partner because of concerns that discussion would damage their image also worried that talking about the issue would harm the relationship. Thus, these two motivations—identity management and relationship protection—are the most commonly cited reasons for topic avoidance, and they tend to work together to prohibit disclosure. Other research has uncovered more specific reasons why people avoid disclosure. For example, Golish and Caughlin (2002) found several specific reasons why parents and children use topic avoidance with one another, including **lack of contact** (especially in the case of divorced families), the **emotional pain** of discussion, and plain **dislike** for the person.

Consequences of Topic Avoidance

Early work on topic avoidance focused on identifying commonly avoided topics (sometimes called taboo topics) as well as the reasons why people avoid disclosure. More recent work focuses on *how* people engage in topic avoidance, *when* people are most likely to avoid topics, and at *what consequence* that avoidance occurs.

Most studies of topic avoidance involved asking people to rate how much they avoid discussing a certain topic with a certain target person on a scale that ranges from "I always avoid discussing this issue with this person" to "I never avoid discussing this issue with this person." Recently, however, scholars have started investigating the specific ways in which people practice topic avoidance rather than just measuring the degree of topic avoidance. Dailey and Palomares (2004) identified eight general strategies for avoiding disclosure, which varied in directness and politeness. Examples of avoidance tactics perceived as direct and impolite are abruptly saying

BOX 12.3	Highlights

Examples of Different Motivations for Topic Avoidance

Relationship-Based Motivations

Relationship Protection. A member of a cross-sex friendship discussed avoiding talk about the "state of the relationship" by stating that "if you bring that stuff back up, you don't know what it's going to cause, you know . . . so it's safer to just avoid it . . . safer on the relationship."

Relationship Destruction. A 15-year-old girl wrote the following account:

My mom remarried about a year ago. I don't like my stepdad at all. He is always trying to act like my real dad and boss me around. I resent this. He will never be my dad. I already have a dad. I really hate it when he tries to get all close to me by asking about my life. He'll try to cozy up to me and ask all about my friends and stuff like he's my buddy or something. I make sure I don't tell him anything but he never gets the hint.

Individual-Based Motivations

Identity Management. A college student wrote the following about her actions on a first date. "He asked about school and started talking about grades and stuff. I tried to switch the topic because I am not a very good student and I didn't want him to think I'm dumb or something."

Privacy Maintenance. A 17-year-old girl wrote this account:

My mom wants me to tell her everything. She thinks she has to know everything about me all the time. I get sick of it. Sometimes I want to tell her it's just not her business. I am almost an adult. I have my own life. I need my privacy.

Information-Based Motivations

Partner Unresponsiveness. A college student wrote this account:

My husband sometimes asks me about school, but I know that he is only asking out of politeness. He is not really interested and doesn't really understand what it is like to go back to school when you are in your 40s. Once when I was stressed out about a final, he told me it was "only an exam." Since then, I haven't talked about school with him much at all.

Futility of Discussion. A 17-year-old boy wrote the following:

It is a total waste of time to talk to my dad about my SAT scores. We have been over it a million times and no matter how much we talk about it, it doesn't change anything. My college applications are in and I'm going to have to live with my score.

These are actual accounts written by teenagers and college students who reported topic avoidance (see Afifi et al., 1994; Afifi & Guerrero, 2000).

something like "you should go" or simply leaving the conversation when a topic comes up. Other strategies for avoiding disclosure are more subtle and polite, such as using an idiom to avoid expressing true feelings (e.g., "that's the way the ball bounces") or giving a hesitant response to signal discomfort about the topic (hoping the other helps out by switching topics). In another study, college students who had frequent contact with their parents recalled their response the last time their parents asked them about a topic they wanted to avoid (Mazur & Hubbard, 2004). Participants offered 10 different avoidance strategies, ranging from telling a lie (i.e., avoiding through deception), to showing anger or irritation, to appearing disinterested or uncomfortable.

Researchers have also examined how relationship stage affects *when* people are most likely to avoid certain topics. The assumption for a long time was that people avoided disclosure most in the beginning stages of dating relationships, when intimacy was still somewhat low and topics were considered sensitive. Knobloch and Carpenter-Theune (2004), however, found that the most avoidance in dating relationships usually occurs in the middle stages of development, when intimacy is moderate. Their rationale is that people are most likely to fear that discussing a topic will harm the relationship, make them look bad, or have other negative consequences when a relationship is shifting from casual to serious. They also reasoned that this transition time is accompanied by increased uncertainty about the relationship and how one's partner might react to certain disclosures. Their findings supported these predictions: People who reported moderate levels of intimacy were the most uncertain about their relationships and also the most likely to avoid topics with their partner.

Studies of family communication have also shown that there are times in the parent-child relationship when avoidance is particularly high. Not surprisingly, young people are most likely to avoid topics with their parents during their middle teenage years (Guerrero & Afifi, 1995b). Midadolescence is a time when teens try to separate themselves from their parents. Keeping information private from parents is an important way for teens to develop a unique sense of self. Less avoidance occurs when children go to college and/or leave their parents'

home. Another time when avoidance is high is during and shortly after a divorce. Tamara Afifi (previously Golish) has conducted several studies of topic avoidance in divorced families and found that children from divorced families are more likely to avoid issues with their parents than those from intact families, *especially* if the child feels caught between loyalties to each of the parents. A common reaction in these cases is to shut down and avoid expressing one's feelings so as not to betray either parent (Afifi, 2003; Afifi & Schrodt, 2003).

Avoidance is common, but what about the consequences of avoidance? Can avoidance have positive consequences for individuals and relationships? As we mentioned earlier in the chapter, some scholars say "yes" (Altman et al., 1981; see also Dialectical Theory, Chapter 9), but many researchers still assume that avoidance is a symptom of a bad or unsatisfying relationship. Indeed, the general conclusion that emerges from the research is that avoidance is rarely associated with satisfaction in relationships but is not always harmful. Three conditions seem to influence how avoidance affects relational satisfaction: (1) the topics being avoided, (2) the strategies used to avoid them, and (3) the reasons for avoidance.

In terms of topics, Dailey and Palomares (2004) studied three different relationship types: dating relationships, mother-child relationships, and father-child relationships. Across all these relationships, people reported less relational satisfaction when they avoided discussing their concerns about the relationship with their partner. However, avoidance on the topic of failures was associated with less relational satisfaction only in mother-child relationships, and many other avoided topics were unassociated with relational satisfaction. Dailey and Palomares's study also found that people in satisfying relationships report using more polite avoidance tactics, whereas those in dissatisfying relationships tend to report using more impolite strategies. This suggests that the way people practice topic avoidance is critical; using polite strategies may help people maintain privacy boundaries without harming their relationships.

Caughlin and Afifi (2004) examined how reasons for avoidance are associated with relational consequences and found that avoidance was related to less relational satisfaction. However, an important caveat was that people who avoided discussing something with their dating partner or family member to protect their relationship did not suffer negative consequences. Imagine that Steve confronts Khaled when he suspects Khaled has feelings for Tara. Steve is likely to be upset, but he might also understand why Khaled kept his feelings secret and appreciate that Khaled did not act on his feelings for Tara because of their friendship. Caughlin and Golish (2002) also showed that satisfaction is influenced by the person's *perception* of how much the partner is avoiding. So regardless of how much you are actually avoiding, communicating in ways that make you look as if you're avoiding seems to be just as harmful as if you *are* avoiding. Communication also plays a central role in how people perceive and respond to secrets.

SECRETS

Secrets are a form of topic avoidance that have received considerable attention from researchers and therapists. At the start of this chapter, we gave examples of people keeping different sorts of secrets. **Secrets** are defined as the intentional concealment of information (Vangelisti & Caughlin, 1997). Research suggests that almost everyone keeps some information secret (Vangelisti, 1994a; Wegner, 1992), but not all secrets are relevant to the success of the relationship. Secrets differ dramatically in content and may have positive or negative effects on close relationships. For example, you may keep secret the surprise birthday party you are planning for your best friend, the vacation plans you made for yourself and your romantic partner, or a gift you purchased for your child. These are positive examples of secret keeping. But you may also conceal more dark and dangerous types of information, such as a one-night stand you had, a socially stigmatized illness you have, your alcoholic father's behavior, your violent past, or a wish for harm to come to someone you hate.

Researchers have addressed several questions relevant to secret keeping: (1) What are the types and features of family secrets? (2) Are there any benefits to keeping information secret, or are secrets always harmful to a relationship? (3) What leads people to tell secrets? (4) What are the consequences of doing so? In this section, we will review studies that provide answers to these and similar questions related to the impact of secrets on families and other relationships.

Features and Types of Secrets

Because family secrets typically involve multiple people, it is important to distinguish between forms of secrets in families. Karpel (1980) discussed three forms of secrets particularly relevant to family units that differ in the complexity of the required boundary coordination (to use CPM terminology). The first form of secrets are whole-family secrets, which are held by the entire family and kept from outsiders. For example, Samantha's family has agreed to keep information about her mother's previous welfare status from everyone outside the family. Indeed, Armstrong (1978) described a common tendency to keep a child's sexual abuse secret from all those outside the immediate family, assuming that the family is aware of the abuse.

Karpel's (1980) second form of secrets, labeled intrafamily secrets, occurs when some family members have information they keep from other members. For instance, John's brother may have known for a while that John drinks and smokes pot, but he may have intentionally concealed this information from their parents. Or Samantha's sexually abusive uncle may have originally told her to "keep it our little secret," thereby hiding the abuse from other family members (Cottle, 1980).

The third form of secrets, individual secrets, occurs when information is held by a single individual and kept secret from other family members, such as Suzanne hiding the fact that she is a recovered alcoholic from her husband, children, and other relations (Karpel, 1980). Individual secrets may or may not be shared outside the family. Suzanne's best friend from college and the cohort she attended Alcoholic Anonymous meetings with might know her secret, even though family members do not.

Another way to classify secrets is not by the degree of boundary coordination they necessitate but by the content of the information. Vangelisti (1994a) conducted the first investigation into the content of family secrets by asking undergraduates to describe any secrets they held in their family, including one whole-family secret, one intrafamily secret, and one individual secret. Amazingly, 97% were able to describe a whole-family secret, 99% had an intrafamily secret they could recount, and 96% had an individual secret they kept. Obviously, secret keeping is commonplace.

Later, Vangelisti and Caughlin (1997) conducted two additional studies that surveyed more than 700 students and again found that almost all (98%) could describe a family secret they were keeping. One of their goals was to determine which types of secrets were most often kept within family boundaries. Perhaps surprisingly, secrets involving finances, which include issues related to money, business holdings, and other assets owned by family members, were by far the secrets most often kept by families, followed by substance abuse, and then premarital pregnancy. While the latter two topics are the kinds of issues that often come to mind as secrets, many people may not think of family finances as secretive, yet they obviously are. Of course, though family finances were mentioned most often, they might not be very emotionally charged secrets. The high percentage of people identifying family finances as their family secret may reflect the fact that those individuals are not holding any family-related information that anyone would consider particularly threatening. Indeed, unless secrets about family finances involve problems such as bankruptcy, unemployment, or welfare (as is the case for Samantha's family), they may not be highly face threatening. Instead, family finances may be considered "no one else's business" and be avoided as a way to maintain family privacy. Still, the fact that family finances are such a common secret is worth noting and emphasizes the degree to which we consider financial affairs private.

Another study that investigated secrets in dating relationships and friendships (Caughlin, Afifi, Carpenter-Theune, & Miller, 2005) showed some overlap between the types of secrets found in those relationships and those found in family relationships. The three most common secrets were dating or sexual history (22% kept this secret from a dating partner or friend), an affair (held by 18% of the sample), and personality or opinion conflicts (held by 14% of

the people in the study). It is interesting to note that 40% of the sample listed a secret involving dating or sexual information. This may reflect the degree to which college students feel uncomfortable or ashamed about something they have done relationally or sexually. Of course, people may keep information private because they do not see it as anyone's business but their own and their partner's. For example, a person might not talk about private aspects of their romantic relationship with their friends.

Motivations to Keep Secrets

The motivations to keep secrets generally are the same as the motivations for people to avoid certain topics: the desire to protect the relationship, the self, or someone else and to maintain privacy (for a review, see Afifi, Caughlin, & Afifi, in press). In addition, Caughlin et al. (2005) noted that some people keep secrets because they don't think they have a good way to tell the secret or because they don't believe that the other person will know how to respond. The second of these reasons is related to partner responsiveness (discussed earlier in this chapter). If people do not perceive that their partner will react in a helpful manner, they are likely to avoid disclosure. These are communication-based concerns that speak volumes about the vital role that communication plays in maintaining secrets. Afifi, Olson, and Armstrong (2005) also found that people's sense of whether they had the skill to disclose a secret played a key role in their decision to reveal or conceal information.

Negative Consequences of Secrets

Besides examining what topics people keep secret, scholars have studied some of the consequences that secrets have and some of the reasons people maintain these secrets. Much of this research comes from family researchers looking to help professional counselors. Therapists often help families regarding which communication boundaries created by secrets have negatively affected family dynamics. Nevertheless, regardless of whether the secret is revealed or not, there are several ways in which secrets can harm the family or the individual. The consequence that has received the most attention is the rumination and mulling that typically accompanies secrets.

Research on the effects of secret keeping on individuals has focused on how keeping information secret influences people's thought patterns through a process called **hyperaccessibility** (Wegner, 1989, 1992; Wegner & Erber, 1992; Wegner, Lane, & Dimitri, 1994). Because secrets require people to avoid disclosing information to others, people often try to suppress the information and thoughts related to that secret. The reasoning here is that if people suppress thoughts about a secret, they will be less likely to disclose secret information because it will not be "on their minds." However, thought suppression is not usually successful, and it can even backfire. The strong impact of thought suppression can be illustrated by a simple example. Here it goes: DO NOT THINK OF PINK ELEPHANTS. Now that you have been asked not to think about pink elephants, you will probably have pink elephants on your mind as you read this section. The simple request that people suppress a thought about a particular thing, regardless of how innocent the request or how irrelevant the thing, has been shown to increase their thinking about it. In fact, that information is often all they can think about!

In their study of thought suppression, Wegner, Schneider, Carter, and White (1987) asked students not to think of a white bear and then had them ring a bell every time they thought of the bear. Rather than suppress the thought of the white bear, the students, on average, thought of the bear more than once per minute over a 5-minute period. Several subsequent studies have confirmed that the desire to suppress a thought does the exact opposite, bringing it to the forefront of our thoughts and thus making it "hyperaccessible."

Studies have also examined *why* thought suppression leads to hyperaccessibility. Think of Khaled, from the chapter opening. He is purposely concealing his feelings for Steve's girlfriend from everyone. Wegner's (1992) work helps explain how keeping such a secret might intensify Khaled's feelings. First, Khaled might try to distract himself from thoughts about Tara and his need to keep his feelings secret (attempts at thought suppression). Next, he might try to think of something else to talk to Steve about, such as how school and his new job are

going. So he starts thinking in earnest about those aspects of his life, but soon thoughts about Tara, his secret, and how it might affect his friendship with Steve pop into his head. Even though he is trying to suppress those thoughts, they are hard to get out of his head, so he tries to think about something else, such as his mother's birthday party next week. But whatever Khaled thinks about, the same cycle kicks in, and he thinks about how difficult it is to be around Steve when Tara is around. In sum, he keeps going back to the thought he is trying to ignore.

But is this hyperaccessibility permanent? Don't those thoughts eventually fade? According to Wegner et al. (1987), the hyperaccessibility of the suppressed thought decreases over time if you remove yourself from contact with the relevant information or secret. This makes Khaled's case doubly problematic since he wants to be around Steve but being around Steve reminds him of Tara. Even if Khaled distanced himself from Steve and Tara for a while, his thoughts about them and his secret would likely come back with a vengeance at first contact with anything that reminds him of them. This scenario can also be applied to Samantha's situation. Children who were sexually abused may eventually stop thinking about the "secret" if they are separated from the abusing adult for long enough, but the thoughts will come flooding back as soon as the possibility of seeing that adult surfaces.

This **rebound effect** may also make if difficult for infidelity to remain a secret in relationships. The unfaithful person may be away from her or his partner at work long enough to successfully suppress the thought of infidelity, but seeing the partner or lover will immediately serve as a reminder of the thought that he or she is trying to suppress. The hyperaccessibility of the thought will make it difficult for the unfaithful person to keep the infidelity a secret. As a result of repeatedly thinking about the affair, the unfaithful person may also experience more guilt about the affair and/or anxiety about being caught.

These effects can be explained by the **fever model of self-disclosure** (Stiles, 1987; Stiles, Shuster, & Harrigan, 1992). According to this model, people who are distressed about a problem or who think about a problem a lot are much more likely to reveal thoughts and feelings about the problem than are those who are not experiencing anxiety about an issue. If given the opportunity, people who are feeling highly anxious about something are likely to disclose more about it than people who are not. This model, when combined with Wegner's research on the hyperaccessibility of secrets, may explain why people so often reveal secrets to others. Their hyperaccessibility (especially during times when the secret information is "rebounding") makes the level of stress and anxiety so high that individuals have to find an outlet. The result frequently is the selection of someone they consider to be a confidant.

Afifi and Caughlin's (2006) research has shown another consequence of the secret keeping and rumination mix. At two points in time, they asked students about a secret they were keeping from a friend or a dating partner and found that secret keeping was harmful for self-esteem. Although it was the first study to show that link, the association makes sense, especially for individually held secrets, where the information being concealed is often something that people regret and something that makes them question themselves. Given the negative impact that low self-esteem has on individuals and relationships, the fact that secret keeping promotes rumination about a negative aspect of self may be of one of its most damaging consequences.

The maintenance of secrets has been shown to have additional negative consequences. First, keeping secrets negatively affects the quality of interactions with the person from whom the secret is being kept (e.g., Brown-Smith, 1998). For example, imagine that John and his brother vowed not to tell their parents that they recently smoked pot together after school. The brothers are likely to experience considerable anxiety when the family sits together at the dinner table, especially if their parents ask them what they have been doing after school lately. Any topic related to after-school activities or how they have been getting along is likely avoided, making for awkward family interactions. This, in turn, is likely to make the parents question their children, further leading to awkwardness and often promoting conflict.

Second, secrets encourage concealment of relational problems and related deception. Hiding a secret from others requires the secret keepers to put on an "air" that everything is fine and that the secret keepers share a happy relationship. This pretense can cause personal and relational stress (Karpel, 1980). For example, growing up, Samantha may have had to act as if she didn't fear her uncle when the extended family got together. Concealing her feelings would likely add even more stress to her life. In Khaled's case, he may feel he has to act indifferent yet polite when around Tara so as not to betray his true feelings. Obviously, the effort it takes to project these *fake* feelings can hinder development of healthy relationships and prevent partners from addressing problems in or outside their relationship. A related problem, of course, is that the maintenance of secrets often results in the spinning of lies to cover up the information. For instance, Khaled might pretend to be interested in another woman. The consequence often is a web of deception that must be continuously tended. If discovered, the deception is often considered a serious relational transgression that erodes trust (see Chapter 13). Of course, in some cases, such as Samantha's, uncovering a secret can be the first step toward recovering from a traumatic event. Her fiancé and parents would likely understand why she kept the information secret and help her deal with the scars left from the sexual and emotional abuse.

Family researchers have also uncovered the negative consequences of keeping secrets. Researchers in the Netherlands demonstrated that 10- to 14-year-olds who keep secrets from their parents suffer lower self-esteem; elevated levels of depression; and high levels of stress, aggression, and delinquency (Frinjs, Finkenauer, Vermulst, & Engels, 2005). Family-held secrets also interfere with family dynamics in important ways. First, such secret keeping can create power imbalances. Given that knowledge often is equated with power, family members who know the secrets have power over those who do not (Imber-Black, 1993). When children have secret information about their parents, the typical power structure in families is sometimes irreversibly altered, changing the family dynamics forever (Brown-Smith, 1998). For example, imagine a child having knowledge about a parent's adulterous affair and holding that parent hostage with that information. Any disciplinary power that the parent has over that child is undermined by the fear that the secret will be disclosed.

The power structure of families has been studied to better understand to whom children are likely to disclose individual secrets (see Chapter 11). Afifi and Olson (2005) found that children were least likely to disclose secrets to the parent whom they saw as having the greatest punitive power. So while holding a parent's secret may decrease the parent's power, children who hold individual secrets are especially likely to fear repercussions from powerful family members and, as such, continue concealment from those people.

Another possible consequence of family secrets is the development of what Karpel (1980) called a "split loyalty pattern." Secret keepers are often put in a bind of having to choose between being loyal to other secret holders and being loyal to friends or family members who may be hurt by not knowing the secret. Samantha is caught in this bind. She feels guilty that she keeps the family welfare secret from her fiancé, yet she would also feel guilty if she told her fiancé and betrayed the "family secret." Split loyalties can also occur outside the family. Imagine that you were a college friend of Suzanne's who knew that Suzanne was a recovering alcoholic. Another friend of yours, Jill, was going to drive with Suzanne to and from a party. You would have to decide whether to warn Jill about Suzanne's past drinking problem. Should you help maintain Suzanne's positive identity by keeping the alcoholism secret, or should you protect Jill by giving her information that might help her determine whether it is safe to drive with Suzanne? Split loyalties create lose-lose situations, ruin relational dynamics, tear families apart, and destroy friendships.

Positive Functions of Secrets

Although most of the research points to the negative effects of secrets, there are cases when secret keeping has positive consequences. Although studies have shown it to be harmful for early adolescents to keep secrets from their parents, other studies have found secret keeping to be beneficial in middle adolescence. Specifically, 14- to 18-year-olds are usually in the midst of developing their own identities. As we discussed while summarizing research on avoidance, an important developmental event is the ability of children of that age to form their own identities, separate from those of their parents. Keeping secrets seems to perform that function, and as such, some types of secret keeping may be developmentally advantageous for children of that age (Finkenauer, Engels, & Meeus, 2002).

Another way in which secret keeping may be beneficial is that it sometimes increases cohesion among holders of the secret. Secrets kept by a whole family, spouses, dating partners, or members of a group may bring the secret holders closer together because of the bond and trust they share. Research by Vangelisti (1994a) and Vangelisti and Caughlin (1997) seems to support this conclusion. Students in these studies reported that the existence of family-wide secrets often improved relationships, perhaps by creating a special bond between members who were trusted to keep secrets. Thus secret keeping can sometimes be beneficial rather than harmful to relationships.

Vangelisti's work also suggests that family members keep secrets for several reasons. Most of these motivations stem from a desire to maintain family connections or protect the family or individual family members from harm. First, secret keeping can promote bonding by increasing family cohesiveness. Second, secret keeping can protect people from negative evaluation. In this case, a secret is kept as a way to protect the family as a whole or individuals within the family from "looking bad." Third, secrets can function to maintain relationships by helping family members avoid stress. For example, talking about a family member's illness with people outside the family might be stressful, and this additional stress could spill over into the family environment. Fourth, secrets can function to preserve privacy. This motivation is fueled by the belief that the secret represents private information that is not relevant to outsiders, thereby motivating family members to keep the secret. For example, if you think that the amount of money your family has in the bank is no one's business but your family's, you are not likely to divulge this information to anyone. Finally, people keep secrets as a defense. People are motivated to defend the family or its members from malicious uses of information. For example, one good reason for keeping a family's bank balance

SOURCE: Photograph by Laura Guerrero.

Photo 12.1   Secrets can serve a bonding function. Even young children feel privileged and special when someone shares a secret with them.

a secret is to protect the family from requests to borrow money.

As these motivations illustrate, people keep secrets for reasons ranging from a desire to maintain the family bond to a desire to protect the family from harm—hardly the sort of negative image that people often associate with the maintenance of family secrets. In fact, much as research has linked identity management to topic avoidance, most studies have found that the most common reason given for keeping secrets is to protect someone else. In Vangelisti's (1994a) study, the desire to protect the family's image accounted for approximately 40% of the reasons that individuals gave for maintaining family secrets. People often believe that secrets are being kept for good reasons, although this does not preclude the fact that secret keeping often hurts relationships.

Revealing Secrets

We have discussed the consequences of keeping a secret, but what are the consequences of revelation? Derlega and Grzelak (1979) noted five reasons why people eventually reveal private information: (1) to achieve catharsis, (2) to clarify their own interpretation of events, (3) to get validation from others that they are still good persons, (4) to make the relationship closer, or (5) to control others. Each of these reasons has different consequences—positive and negative.

Positive Consequences of Revealing Secrets. Although it is impossible to say with certainty when someone should or should not disclose a secret, Kelly and McKillop (1996) made several recommendations for when to do so. Their research led them to identify three reasons why people might want to consider revealing secrets: (1) if it reduces psychological and/or physical problems, (2) if it helps deter hyper-accessibility, and/or (3) if it leads to resolution of the secret.

First, there is considerable evidence that secret keeping is stressful and wears on secret keepers psychologically and physiologically (see Pennebaker, 1990). Spiegel (1992) found that individuals with life-threatening illnesses who reveal private information in therapy sessions have a longer life expectancy than those who do not. Pennebaker's research on social support also suggests that the mere act of disclosing distressful information makes people feel better.

Second, as noted previously, keeping information secret makes secrets salient. As Wegner et al. (1994) put it, "The secret must be remembered, or it might be told. And the secret cannot be thought about, or it might be leaked" (p. 288), thus creating the two conflicting cognitive processes discussed earlier. Disclosing the secret frees the secret keeper from having to suppress it and makes it no longer hyperaccessible, thereby decreasing anxiety.

Third, without disclosing the secret, secret keepers cannot work toward a resolution of issues underlying the secret. Sharing the information may provide the individual with insight into the secret and allow her or him to regain a much-needed sense of control over life's events (see Pennebaker, 1990). The secret keeper often has an unbalanced view of the situation and may benefit from the perspective of the recipient of the disclosure. Silver, Boone, and Stones (1983) found that female victims of incest who were able to reveal the secret to a confidant were much more likely to feel better about themselves and their lives than those who were unable to do so. Afifi and Caughlin (2006) showed that those who revealed their secret across an 8-week period experienced a significant increase in self-esteem. It is also worth noting that Caughlin et al. (2005) found that those who revealed secrets often reported partner reactions that were less negative than they had originally feared. So one benefit of disclosing may be that one gains the advantages of catharsis

and resolution without the feared destruction of the relationship.

Negative Consequences of Revealing Secrets. The positive consequences of revealing a secret should be weighed against three possible negative consequences. Specifically, Kelly and McKillop (1996) suggested that people might consider keeping a secret if revelation would (1) elicit a negative reaction from the listener or (2) help a person maintain a privacy boundary; and Petronio (1991) suggested that people might decide to keep secrets if revealing private information (3) would be seen as a betrayal by others.

First, given the typically negative nature of secrets, there is always a possibility that the recipient of the information will react with disapproval or shun the discloser. In fact, Lazarus (1985) reported that confidants often distance themselves following the disclosure of a negative secret. Coates, Wortman, and Abbey (1979) showed that people who disclose secret problems to others are considered less attractive than those who suppress such disclosure. When people have kept negative information to themselves as a way to manage their identities, they are especially likely to put stock in the listener's reaction when they finally reveal the secret. Disconfirming reactions may worsen what is likely an already diminished sense of self.

Work on disclosure of abuse makes this point especially well. Dieckman (2000) interviewed female victims about their decision to tell others about their abuse. Her interviews highlighted the difficulty associated with disclosure and the importance of the response. Victims of abuse often are hesitant to tell others about their experience because they fear being perceived as "weak" or being ridiculed for staying in the relationship. Indeed, Crocker and Schwartz (1985) found that many people responded to disclosures of abuse by telling the discloser that they "would never put up with that kind of treatment" and asking them why they "didn't just leave." Since victims typically disclose past abuse for the purpose of self-expression or validation, responses like these can diminish the discloser's ability to cope with the situation. Rather than helping disclosers, such responses often lower their self-esteem and discourage future disclosure. Their already low sense of self falls even lower because the response they feared the most—ridicule—is the response they received. Worse yet, the discloser might decide to keep the information secret once again, rather than risking more ridicule. As this example illustrates, the listener's response to sensitive self-disclosure is of paramount importance. (See Chapter 8 for specific information on how you can give effective social support to others.)

Second, preserving personal boundaries is critical to people's identities. Indeed, it is the essence of the communication boundary management theory discussed in this chapter. To the extent that secrets make up part of the personal boundaries of individuals, secret keeping may help people maintain a sense of independence. Some scholars have even argued that secret keeping serves a developmental function by helping people manage their personal identity (Hoyt, 1978). In contrast, revealing the secret erodes the personal boundaries being held tightly by the secret keeper. In a related vein, keeping secrets greatly increases a person's control over the information. In contrast, the decision to disclose a secret requires boundary coordination and leaves the individual vulnerable to betrayal of confidences. The information is no longer solely the person's own, and he or she has less control over how the information is spread.

Third, sometimes secrets are shared between two or more people, and revealing the secret to someone outside the dyad or group will be seen as a betrayal. Indeed, research reported in Chapter 13 suggests that betraying confidences is one of the most common relational transgressions in friendships, romantic relationships, and family relationships. If a confidence has been betrayed, revealing a secret often has a significant cost. Trust is eroded, and future self-disclosures from the person who feels betrayed are less likely. As such, another negative consequence of revealing secrets may be severe sanctions by other secret keepers. To ensure that a member of a group of secret keepers is not tempted to disclose the secret, groups will often make explicit boundary rules or threaten individuals with severe penalties for revealing the secret (Petronio, 1991).

The diversity of potential positive and negative consequences makes it difficult to determine when to disclose a secret and when not to do so. Kelly and McKillop (1996) developed a decision-making model for revealing secrets that take into account the primary consequences associated with the revelation of individually held secrets; Figure 12.1 is an illustration of that model. In a similar vein, Petronio (1991) noted that the answers to five questions typically determine what people will disclose and to whom they will disclose it: (1) How badly do you need to reveal the information? (2) What do you think will be the outcome of the disclosure? (3) How risky will it be to tell someone the information? (4) How private is the information? (5) How much control do you have over your emotions? These questions reflect a variety of issues raised in this chapter, as well as capturing the essence of Kelly and McKillop's model. Clearly, then, issues of anxiety, hyperaccessibility, and informational control play a key role in determining whether the revelation of secrets is likely to produce positive or negative outcomes.

SUMMARY AND APPLICATION

This chapter started with examples from three people struggling with decisions to keep information from significant others. It is hoped that this chapter has given you the background to help you understand how needs for privacy operate in your relationship and the relationships of others.

Several factors influence people's decision to disclose or avoid sharing information. People practice topic avoidance for a variety of reasons. Understanding what those motivations are may be the first step in deciding whether to reveal a secret or not. For instance, Samantha might realize that when she was a child she avoided talking about the sexual abuse that she suffered because she was afraid of her uncle and was deeply ashamed. Now that she is an adult, however, Samantha may no longer fear her uncle, and she may understand that she was an innocent victim. She may also recognize that now her main motivation for keeping the abuse a secret is that she does not want to relive the emotional pain. Through these types of realizations, Samantha may come to believe that she can trust her fiancé with her secret and that he will support her

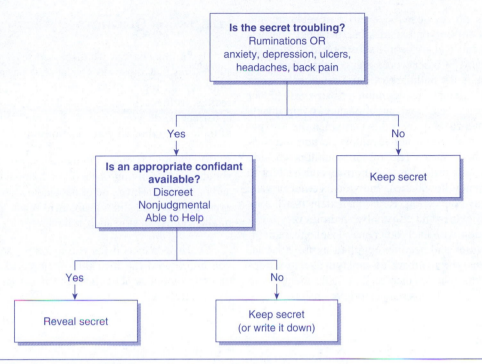

Figure 12.1 Decision-Making Model for Revealing Secrets

SOURCE: From Kelly, A. E., & McKillop, K. G., Consequences of revealing personal secrets, in *Psychological Bulletin, 120.* Copyright © 1996, the American Psychological Association. Reprinted with permission.

through the emotional pain and help her heal old wounds. However, if Samantha decides to keep this information a secret, it is her right to do so.

The research in this chapter also provides other helpful information about when to reveal a secret. If Khaled is feeling high levels of uncertainty and ruminating about his situation with Steve and Tara all the time, he might consider telling his secret to someone to help relieve his stress. Whether he decides to tell Steve or not may depend on how supportive and nonjudgmental he thinks Steve will be. If Khaled thinks that Steve's feelings for Tara will make it difficult for him to understand, he may talk to a trusted third party about his dilemma. Similarly, Tyrone's decision about whether to tell John that he smoked pot in college may come down to how he thinks John will react. If Tyrone believes that John will think he is a hypocrite who doesn't have any right to tell him what to do, he is likely to avoid disclosure about his

pot-smoking days. On the other hand, if Tyrone believes that John will think he better understands the allure and risk of smoking pot because he once did it himself, he would be much more likely to share his past experiences with his son.

As these examples illustrate, privacy dilemmas are common in relationships. Even in the closest relationships, people desire and defend their privacy. In this chapter, we reviewed many studies showing the impact of privacy boundaries on our relationships and day-to-day lives. In contrast, Chapter 5 highlighted the many ways in which loss of privacy through self-disclosure affects our relationships. Together, these chapters provide a peek into the dialectical struggles between openness and closedness that shape our lives. People need both privacy and expression (Altman et al., 1981). Managing privacy boundaries to accommodate both of these needs is a delicate process.

This process can be even more delicate and complex in the context of close personal relationships, because many people subscribe to an ideology of intimacy. In other words, many people think that openness is the hallmark of close relationships and that any attempts to maintain privacy will hinder the development and maintenance of intimacy. Samantha probably feels this way since she is experiencing guilt about not revealing certain information to her fiancé. The research in this chapter, however, suggests that it is normal and healthy to erect privacy boundaries. Individuals need privacy as well as connection. Relational partners who are always together and constantly sharing every bit of information with each other may lose their individual identities and become engulfed by the relationship. Thus, the hallmark of satisfying relationships may be the maintenance of individual identities in the midst of a close, connected relationship.

DISCUSSION QUESTIONS

1. In this chapter, we discussed several studies suggesting that most close relational partners consider certain topics to be "taboo" and keep certain secrets from each other. Based on your personal experiences, do you agree or disagree? What types of topics are taboo in your relationships?

2. On television and in the news, we often hear about cases involving obsessive relational intrusion and/or stalking. Have you or people you have known ever experienced this problem? What strategies might you use to stop such behavior?

3. How hard is it for you to keep a secret? Do you agree with the idea that attempts to suppress thoughts about it actually make it harder to keep the secret?

13

HURTING THE ONES WE LOVE

Relational Transgressions

Tia and Jamal are deeply in love and plan to marry after Tia finishes graduate school. During a conversation with a mutual friend, Jamal finds out that Tia had lunch with her ex-boyfriend, Robert, a week earlier. Jamal is flooded with negative thoughts and emotions. He always suspected that Robert regretted breaking up with Tia. Worse yet, Robert has become successful over the past couple of years, whereas Jamal's career has been stalled. Jamal can't help but wonder if Tia prefers Robert to him. And why hadn't she told him that they had lunch? Is she trying to hide something? Perhaps even an affair? When Jamal confronts Tia later that evening, she tells him that she is completely "over" Robert, that they met by chance and decided to have a quick lunch to "catch up," and that she didn't tell him because it didn't mean anything and she knew he'd get upset. Tia declares, "I told him that I love you and we are engaged." Tia's words provide Jamal with some comfort, but he still can't seem to stop worrying.

If you were in Jamal's place, would you still be worried about Robert? Research on the "dark side" of relationships suggests that Jamal's situation is not at all unusual. People commonly experience problems such as jealousy, deception, and infidelity in their close relationships (Cupach & Spitzberg, 1994; Spitzberg & Cupach, 1998). The question becomes, How can people cope with such situations most effectively? For example, should Jamal continue communicating his jealous feelings to Tia, or should he pretend that nothing is wrong? What about Tia? Was her explanation for not telling Jamal about her lunch with Robert plausible? And what can she do or say to convince Jamal that she loves him and has been faithful?

In this chapter, we focus on understanding how relational partners hurt one another, as well as how people respond to being hurt. First, we discuss hurt feelings in the context of relationships. Then, we review research related to three especially hurtful events: infidelity, jealousy, and deception. This is followed by a review of research on hurtful messages. The last part of the chapter focuses on communication and forgiveness following hurtful events.

HURT FEELINGS IN RELATIONSHIPS

Think about the last few times you felt emotional pain. Chances are that you had close relationships with the people who directly or indirectly inflicted that pain. In one study, people described a situation that led them to experience hurt feelings (Leary, Springer, Negel, Ansell, & Evans, 1998). Of the 168 participants in this study, only 14 described situations involving strangers or acquaintances; the other 154 all described situations involving close relational partners, such as romantic partners, family members, or good friends. Scholars have noted the paradoxical nature of hurt—the people with whom we share the strongest emotional connection have the power to hurt us in ways that other people cannot. As Dowrick (1999) put it,

> It is one of life's most terrible ironies that betrayal can be as connective as love. It can fill your mind and color your senses. It can keep you tied to a person or to events as tightly as if you were bound, back to back—or worse, heart to heart. The person you want to think of least may become the person you think of constantly. (p. 46)

The most intense hurt feelings arise when a partner's words or actions communicate devaluation (Feeney, 2005). **Devaluation** involves feeling unappreciated and unimportant. A person can feel devalued at the individual or relational level. For example, if a good friend says she's not surprised that you failed an exam because you're not very smart, you might feel hurt because your friend does not value your intellect. At a relational level, devaluation is a perception that one's partner does not perceive the relationship to be as close, important, or valuable as one would like (Leary et al., 1998). If someone betrays you, breaks up with you, or says that you are not that important in her or his life, you are likely to feel hurt because your partner does not value the relationship (Leary et al., 1998).

Communication researchers have studied relational transgressions and hurtful messages as forms of behavior that inflict hurt feelings. **Relational transgressions** occur when people violate implicit or explicit relational rules (Metts, 1994). For example, many people believe that romantic partners should be sexually faithful and that all close relational partners should be emotionally faithful, loyal, and honest. When people violate these standards of faithfulness, loyalty, and honesty, they also devalue

the partner and the relationship (Feeney, 2005). The top relational transgressions identified by college students are (1) having sex with someone else, (2) wanting to or actually dating others, and (3) deceiving one's partner about something significant (Metts, 1991). Other transgressions include flirting with or kissing someone else, keeping secrets from the partner, becoming emotionally involved with someone else, and betraying the partner's confidence (Jones & Burdette, 1994; Roscoe, Cavanaugh, & Kennedy, 1988). **Hurtful messages** are words that elicit psychological pain. As Vangelisti (1994b) argued, words

> have the ability to hurt or harm in every bit as real a way as physical objects. A few ill-spoken words (e.g., "You're worthless," "You'll never amount to anything," "I don't love you anymore") can strongly affect individuals, interactions, and relationships. (p. 53)

Indeed, studies have shown that hurtful words and events often have negative effects on relationships. In Jones and Burdette's (1994) study, 93% of people who had been betrayed by their partners said that their relationships had been harmed as a result of the transgression. Leary and his colleagues (1998) examined a wider variety of hurtful events than betrayals. Nonetheless, 42% of their participants said that the hurtful event had permanently damaged their relationships. In friendships, betrayal leads to less acceptance, trust, and respect (Davis & Todd, 1985). In fact, when people are betrayed by a friend, they often recast the friend's entire personality to frame her or him in a more negative light (Wiseman, 1986). To better understand some of the events that lead to hurt feelings and relational problems, the next part of this chapter provides a more detailed look at situations involving infidelity, jealousy, deception, and hurtful messages.

INFIDELITY

Infidelity is especially hurtful. Feeney (2004) studied a number of hurtful events and found infidelity to have a particularly strong negative effect on relationships. In another study, sexual infidelity, along with relationship breakup, was rated as the least forgivable of several hurtful events in dating relationships (Bachman & Guerrero, 2006b). The way people discover sexual infidelity also makes a difference. Afifi, Falato, and Weiner (2001) compared four methods of discovery: (1) finding out from a third party; (2) witnessing the infidelity firsthand, such as walking in on your partner with someone else; (3) having the partner admit to infidelity after you question her or him; and (4) having the partner tell you on her or his own. People who found out through a third party or by witnessing the partner's infidelity firsthand were the least likely to forgive their partners and the most likely to say that their relationships had been damaged. People were most likely to forgive their partners when they confessed on their own.

Sexual Versus Emotional Infidelity

Researchers have distinguished between two types of infidelity: sexual and emotional. Sexual infidelity refers to "sexual activity with someone other than one's long-term partner" (Shackelford & Buss, 1997, p. 1035). Although most people in the United States disapprove of sexual infidelity (Weinbach, 1989; Weis & Slosnerick, 1981), several studies indicate that extradyadic affairs are fairly common (see, e.g., Thompson, 1984). Estimates of sexual infidelity vary widely. When averaged, studies suggest that around 30% to 40% of dating relationships and 40% to 60% of marriages are marked by at least one incident of sexual infidelity (Guerrero, Spitzberg, & Yoshimura, 2004; Wiederman & Hurd, 1999). Men are more likely than women to have a sexual affair, regardless of whether they are in a married or dating relationship (Gass & Nichols, 1988; Hansen, 1987; Sprecher & McKinney, 1993). Gay men may be more likely than lesbians or heterosexual individuals to have sexual affairs. In Blumstein and Schwartz's (1983) classic study, 82% of gay male couples reported having nonmonogamous relationships, compared with around 28% of lesbian couples and 27% of heterosexual couples.

For individuals who value sexual monogamy, discovering a sexual affair is extremely hurtful. When sexual infidelity is coupled with emotional infidelity, the hurt is usually even more intense. **Emotional infidelity** refers to emotional involvement with another person, which leads one's partner to channel "emotional resources such as romantic love, time, and attention to someone else" (Shackelford & Buss, 1997, p. 1035).

Given the prevalence of infidelity, it is important to ask *why* people engage in acts of infidelity in the first place. Research on sexual infidelity suggests that dissatisfaction with the current relationship is the leading cause (Hunt, 1974; Roscoe et al., 1988; Sheppard, Nelson, & Andreoli-Mathie, 1995). Other common causes of infidelity include boredom, the need for excitement and variety, wanting to feel attractive, sexual incompatibility with one's partner, and trying to get revenge against the partner (Buunk, 1980; Elbaum, 1982; Fleischman et al., 2005; Greene, Lee, & Lustig, 1974; Johnson, 1972; Roscoe et al., 1988; Wiggins & Lederer, 1984). There has not been much research on the causes of emotional infidelity. It is likely, however, that emotional infidelity is related to feeling dissatisfied with the communication and social support a person is receiving in her or his current relationship.

Behavioral Cues to Infidelity

While any of the previous reasons might make people worry that their partner could be unfaithful sexually or emotionally, researchers have uncovered specific behavioral cues that trigger suspicion about infidelity. In particular, a study by Shackelford and Buss (1997) looked at cues to both sexual and emotional infidelity. In this study, undergraduate students were asked to describe the cues that would lead them to suspect that their partners were (1) being sexually unfaithful (sexual infidelity) and (2) falling in love with someone else (emotional infidelity). Fourteen types of behaviors were found to trigger suspicion. As can be seen in Box 13.1, some of these cues were associated more with suspicions of sexual infidelity, while others were associated more with suspicions of emotional infidelity. Still other cues were associated about equally with sexual and emotional infidelity.

Importantly, some of the behaviors that trigger suspicion about infidelity are the opposite of those that people use to maintain their relationships. For instance, apathetic communication involves shutting

BOX 13.1   Highlights

Cues to Infidelity

Behaviors Leading Primarily to the Suspicion of Sexual Infidelity

Behavior	Definition
Physical signs of disinterest in sexual exclusivity	You indirectly find out from your partner that she or he has had sex with someone else (examples: your partner smells like someone else or doesn't want to have sex with you anymore)
Revelations of sexual infidelity	You witness or are told directly that your partner is having sex with someone else (examples: your partner confesses or you walk in on your partner in bed with someone else)
Changes in routine and sexual behavior	You notice that your partner's actions are different from usual (examples: your partner starts trying new positions during sex or dresses differently)
Increased sexual interest and exaggerated displays of affection	You notice that your partner seems more interested in sex and shows more affection than usual, probably as a compensatory strategy (example: your partner says "I love you" more than usual)
Sexual disinterest/boredom	You notice that your partner seems less interested and excited about sex (example: your partner wants to end sex with you quickly)

Behaviors Leading Primarily to the Suspicion of Emotional Infidelity

Relationship dissatisfaction/loss of love	Your partner reveals that she or he is no longer in love with you and wants to pursue other alternatives (example: your partner wants a sexually open relationship)
Emotional disengagement	Your partner seems to be distancing herself or himself from you emotionally (examples: your partner forgets your anniversary or doesn't respond when you say "I love you")
Passive rejection/passive inconsiderate behavior	Your partner reveals her or his lack of emotional connection through acts rather than direct rejection (example: your partner is rude to you and your friends)
Angry, critical, and argumentative communication	Your partner is uncharacteristically angry, critical, or argumentative with you (example: your partner starts looking for reasons to argue with you)
Reluctance to spend time together	Your partner starts to spend less time with you and to separate her or his social network from yours (example: your partner stops inviting you to spend time with her/his family and friends)
Reluctance to talk about a certain person	Your partner seems reluctant or nervous to talk about a particular person (example: your partner changes the topic when a certain person's name comes up in conversation)

Guilty and anxious communication	Your partner acts like he or she has done something wrong (example: your partner is unusually apologetic)

Behaviors Leading to the Suspicion of Both Sexual and Emotional Infidelity

Apathetic communication	Your partner seems to be putting less effort into the relationship (examples: your partner stops trying to look attractive for you or stops sharing emotions with you)
Increased contact with and reference to a third party	Your partner seems to be focusing more time and attention on another person (examples: your partner accidentally calls you by someone else's name or starts wearing something belonging to someone else)

SOURCE: Information compiled from Shackelford and Buss (1997).

off communication and spending less time together. As discussed in Chapter 9, self-disclosure, routine talk, and time spent together are key behaviors that help keep a relationship satisfying. Another set of behaviors that triggers suspicion about infidelity—passive rejection—involves acting rude and inconsiderate, which is the opposite of the maintenance strategy of positivity, which focuses on being cheerful, optimistic, and polite to one's partner. Another infidelity cue is reluctance to spend time together, which involves keeping social networks separate rather than integrated. As discussed in Chapter 9, integrating networks is important to relational maintenance. Thus when people feel that their partners are no longer working to maintain the relationship, they may suspect this lack of effort is due to emotional or sexual infidelity. If Jamal notices changes in Tia's behavior that reflect a lack of effort and interest in their relationship, his worries about possible emotional or sexual infidelity might grow.

Responses to Infidelity

Now that you know about the different types of behavior that trigger suspicions about infidelity, you might wonder how people like Jamal act once they suspect that their partners might have been unfaithful. Buunk's (1995) research suggests that

people generally respond to sexual infidelity in one of the following three ways. First, people can use **angry retreat**. Here, individuals who suspect or confirm sexual infidelity might feel so much anger and betrayal that they turn away from their partner emotionally and physically, seek revenge (perhaps by having an affair of their own), or terminate the relationship. Second, people can use **accommodation**, which involves adapting to the situation by expressing loyalty, trying to understand the partner, and perhaps forgiving the partner. Third, people can use an **assertive response**, whereby they seek to protect themselves and voice their feelings and concerns. Examples of assertive responses include demanding that the partner stop seeing other people, having the partner tested for HIV, asking the partner to wear condoms during intercourse (Buunk & Bakker, 1997), and renegotiating relational rules and boundaries.

Sex Differences in Infidelity

Research has also examined sex differences in reactions to perceived and actual infidelity. Much of the research in this area takes a social evolutionary perspective (Buss, 1989, 1994; see also Chapter 10), suggesting that men and women react to emotional and sexual infidelity differently because they have different priorities related to reproduction. Women know they are the parent of a child, but men are sometimes uncertain about paternity and, therefore, are more concerned about sexual infidelity. Women, on the other hand, should be more worried about emotional infidelity, because they are more concerned with protecting their most important resource, their relationship (see Chapter 7).

Most research on sex differences in reactions to emotional versus sexual infidelity has supported this evolutionary hypothesis (Guerrero et al., 2004). Men show greater psychological and physiological distress when they imagine their partner engaging in sexual infidelity, whereas women display more distress when they imagine their partner in love with someone else (Buss, Larsen, Westen, & Semmelroth, 1992; Wiederman & Allgeier, 1993). Similarly, in studies where people are asked to choose which would make them more upset—their partner having a one-night stand or their partner falling in love with someone else—men identify sexual infidelity as more upsetting, whereas women identify emotional infidelity as more upsetting (Becker, Sagarin, Guadagno, Millevoi, & Nicastle, 2004; Trost & Alberts, 2006). Of course, both men and women get upset when their partners cheat on them—either emotionally or sexually—and the most devastating effects likely occur when people suspect or confirm *both* sexual and emotional infidelity.

There may also be sex differences in how people perceive possible cues to infidelity and how they respond to those cues. In Shackelford and Buss's (1997) study, women were more likely than men to see suspicious behaviors as indicative of infidelity (see Box 13.1). Perhaps this is because, in the United States, men are somewhat more likely than women to have extradyadic affairs (Sprecher & McKinney, 1993) or because women are better encoders of information than are men (Burgoon et al., 1996). Buunk and Bakker's (1997) study also revealed that women might respond to infidelity with angry retreat and assertion more than men. This study did not find a sex difference for accommodation, although other research has shown that women are more likely to forgive men for sexual infidelity than vice versa.

JEALOUSY

When people suspect or discover infidelity, jealousy is a common reaction. Interestingly, jealousy is often the *result* of a relational transgression, such as a partner having an affair or spending extra time with someone else. But jealousy is also seen as a transgression *in its own right* when a partner's suspicions are unwarranted (Metts, 1994). For example, if Tia has been completely emotionally and sexually faithful to Jamal but Jamal continues to act suspicious and possessive, Tia is likely to become upset by his behavior. To Tia, Jamal's lack of trust may very well be seen as a relational transgression.

Characteristics of Jealousy

This example highlights an important point about jealousy—that jealousy can be a reaction to an *imagined* threat or an *actual* threat. There are also different types of jealousy. **Romantic jealousy** occurs when a relational partner worries that a potential rival might interfere with the existence or quality of her or his romantic relationship, just as Jamal worries that Robert might interfere with his relationship with Tia. As White and Mullen (1989) put it, romantic jealousy "is generated by the perception of a real or potential romantic attraction between one's partner and a (perhaps imaginary) rival" (p. 9). **Sexual jealousy** is a particular form of romantic jealousy whereby an individual worries that a rival is having or wants to have sex with her or his partner. Bevan and Samter (2004) identified five additional forms of jealousy that can occur in romantic relationships, friendships, and family relationships: **friend jealousy** (feeling threatened by your partner's relationships with friends), **family jealousy** (feeling threatened by your partner's relationships with family members), **activity jealousy** (perceiving that the partner's activities, such as work, hobbies, or school, are interfering with one's relationship), **power jealousy** (perceiving that one's influence over the partner is being lost to others), and **intimacy jealousy** (believing that one's partner is engaging in more intimate communication, such as disclosure and advice seeking, with someone else).

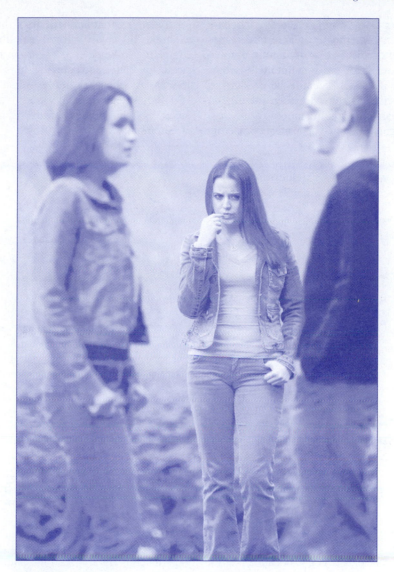

SOURCE: iStockphoto.com

Photo 13.1   Jealousy always involves at least three people. Jealousy also tends to involve multiple
emotions. What emotions do you think the woman in this photo is feeling?

Jealousy is different from two related constructs: envy and rivalry (Bryson, 1977; Guerrero & Andersen, 1998a; Salovey & Rodin, 1986, 1989). **Jealousy** occurs when people worry that they might lose something they value, such as a good relationship or high-status position, due to interference from a third party. The prototypical jealousy situation involves fearing that someone will "steal" a romantic partner away. **Envy**, in contrast, occurs when people want something valuable that someone else has. Prototypical envy situations involve feelings of resentment toward someone who seems to have a better life, often because he or she has stronger relationships, is better looking, intelligent, and talented, or has more stature, money, or possessions. **Rivalry** occurs when two people are competing for something that neither one of them has. A prime example of rivalry involves siblings who are competing to be seen as "best" in the eyes of their peers, parents, and other adults (Dunn, 1988a, 1988b). As these examples illustrate and Figure 13.1 shows, jealousy, envy, and rivalry are differentiated by who possesses the desired relationship or commodity.

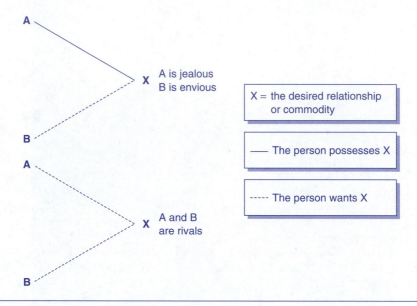

Figure 13.1 Differences Between Jealousy, Envy, and Rivalry Based on Possession of a Desired Relationship or Commodity

The triangle of Jamal, Tia, and Robert helps illustrate the differences between jealousy and envy. On the basis of the descriptions above, would you characterize Jamal as jealous or envious? It seems clear that Jamal is experiencing jealousy because he is worried that he might lose Tia to Robert. However, Jamal might also be experiencing envy because he wishes to possess some of the things Robert has, such as a successful career. Assuming that Robert is still in love with Tia, he might be envious of Jamal's relationship with her. Now, pretend that Tia is not currently in a relationship with either man and that they both want to date her exclusively. If this were the case, Jamal and Robert would be experiencing rivalry. As this example shows, jealousy, envy, and rivalry sometimes coexist within the same set of relationships. The remainder of this section will focus specifically on how people experience and express romantic jealousy.

Experiencing Romantic Jealousy

When people perceive a third-party threat to their romantic relationships, they are likely to experience a number of thoughts and emotions. On the cognitive side, jealous individuals typically make appraisals regarding the source and severity of the threat. On the emotional side, jealous individuals tend to experience a cluster of jealousy-related emotions.

Jealous Thoughts. White and Mullen (1989) described primary and secondary cognitive appraisals that tend to occur as jealous feelings develop. **Primary appraisals** involve general evaluations about the existence and quality of a rival relationship, including how much of a threat the third party is. For example, Jamal might ask himself questions such as "Has Tia been seeing Robert behind my back?" and "Could Tia love Robert more than me?" **Secondary appraisals** involve more specific evaluations of the jealousy situation, including possible causes and outcomes. White and Mullen described four types of secondary appraisals that people use to gather information and interpret the situation. First, jealous people assess motives ("Why did Tia have lunch with Robert?"). Second, they compare themselves with the rival ("Robert is more successful than I am, but I'm more intelligent and caring"). Third, they evaluate their alternatives ("If Tia dumps me for Robert, who would I want to date? Would I rather be on my own than date someone who has been unfaithful to me?"). These questions would help prepare Jamal, or anyone else dealing with jealousy and/or infidelity, for a possible breakup or reconciliation. Finally, jealous people assess their potential loss ("How devastating would it be to lose Tia?").

According to White and Mullen, jealous individuals like Jamal make appraisals so that they can plan coping strategies and assess outcomes. For example, if Jamal decides that Tia could be attracted to Robert because of his success, he might compensate by putting more effort into his own career. If Tia responded favorably to Jamal's intensified career pursuits, Jamal would likely continue those behaviors. But if Jamal's behavior change does not have the desired effect (perhaps Tia complains that Jamal is so focused on his career that he is ignoring her), he is likely to try a different strategy.

Jealous Emotions. In addition to making cognitive appraisals, jealous individuals usually experience combinations of emotions. The emotions most central to jealousy are probably fear and anger (see Guerrero & Andersen, 1998a, 1998b; Sharpsteen, 1991). People are jealous because they fear losing their relationship, and they are often angry at their partner for betraying them. Sometimes, jealous individuals are also angry at the rival, particularly if the rival is someone they know; at other times, they feel irritated or annoyed but not really angry (Guerrero, Trost, & Yoshimura, 2005).

Beyond fear and anger, jealousy is often marked by other aversive emotions such as sadness, guilt, hurt, and envy (Fitness & Fletcher, 1993; White & Mullen, 1989). Sadness occurs near the end of some jealousy episodes when people are feeling gloomy and lonely because a breakup seems inevitable or has just occurred (Sharpsteen, 1991). Sometimes, jealous individuals feel guilty because they wrongly accused their partners of misdeeds, as Jamal might feel if he discovers he mistakenly suspected Tia of any improprieties. At other times, people feel guilty because they think that their own negative qualities caused the partner to become interested in someone else. For example, Jamal might think that if he had paid more attention to Tia, she might not have become attracted to someone else. Envy can be part of the jealousy experience, especially when the rival has positive qualities that the jealous person does not possess.

Sometimes, jealousy leads to positive emotions, such as increased passion, love, and appreciation (Guerrero & Andersen, 1998b; Guerrero et al., 2005). Think about how you might feel if you saw someone flirting with your romantic partner. The fact that someone else sees your partner as attractive might make you feel more passionate and loving toward her or him (Pines, 1992; White & Mullen, 1989). Recent research shows that people sometimes intentionally induce jealousy to achieve two goals: to make their partner value the relationship more and to get revenge (Fleischmann et al., 2005). Pines (1992) also argued that jealousy can lead partners to appreciate their partners more, become more committed to the relationship, and work harder to maintain the relationship. Other researchers have argued that jealousy is closely related to love, because people would not get jealous if they did not care about their partners (Ciabattari, 1988; Salovey & Rodin, 1985). But inducing jealousy is a dangerous strategy because jealousy often leads to relationship dissatisfaction and sometimes even violence (Guerrero & Andersen, 1998a).

Communicative Responses to Jealousy

Just as jealousy can involve a wide range of thoughts and emotions, so too, can jealousy be expressed in many different ways. Guerrero and her colleagues have described 14 communicative responses to jealousy, which are summarized in Box 13.2 (Guerrero, 1998; Guerrero & Andersen, 1998b; Guerrero, Andersen, Jorgensen, Spitzberg, & Eloy, 1995). The most commonly reported responses are negative affect expression, integrative communication, and distributive communication.

Research suggests that people use various communicative responses to jealousy based on their goals and emotions (Bryson, 1977; Guerrero & Afifi, 1998, 1999; Guerrero et al., 2005). When people want to maintain their relationships and feel annoyance rather than anger, they report using integrative communication and compensatory restoration. People who are fearful of losing their relationships also tend to report compensatory restoration. In contrast, people who are more concerned with maintaining their self-esteem report denying their jealous feelings. When people are motivated to reduce uncertainty about their relationship, they report using integrative communication, surveillance, and rival contacts, all of which represent ways of seeking information. A number of retaliation tactics have also been reported, including manipulation attempts (such as counterjealousy and guilt induction), distributive communication, and active distancing (see Box 13.2). People tend to use these responses when they feel jealous anger and want revenge against their partners.

Jealousy and Relational Satisfaction

Although jealousy can be a sign of love and attachment, it can be both a symptom and a cause of relational distress. In fact, research has shown that jealous thoughts and feelings are generally associated with relational dissatisfaction (Andersen, Eloy, Guerrero, & Spitzberg, 1995; Buunk & Bringle, 1987; Guerrero & Eloy, 1992; Salovey & Rodin, 1989). However, jealousy is experienced in many relationships that remain satisfying. The trick seems to be to manage jealousy in a productive way, such that the jealous individual shows care and concern without seeming overly fearful, aggressive, or possessive.

Among the many communicative responses to jealousy listed in Box 13.2, only three appear to be associated with relational satisfaction: integrative communication, negative affect expression, and compensatory restoration. All the other responses usually make the problem worse, although some studies have shown that manipulation attempts such as counterjealousy induction can be effective in certain circumstances (Buss, 1988a; Fleischmann et al., 2005). Integrative communication involves talking about jealousy in a constructive manner, often by disclosing feelings and renegotiating relational rules and boundaries. Rusbult and Buunk (1993) suggested that this type of communication is critical for maintaining relationships after jealousy is felt. Similarly, Afifi and Reichert (1996) found a positive association between integrative communication and relational satisfaction when jealousy occurs.

Negative affect expression can also be an effective way to communicate about jealousy, but only if it is used in conjunction with integrative communication. Andersen et al. (1995) found that jealous individuals reported the most relational satisfaction when they used *both* integrative communication and negative affect expression. Integrative communication alone was not as effective as this combination, and negative affect expression could actually *reduce* relationship satisfaction when used alone or with other strategies, such as distributive communication or active distancing. Andersen and his colleagues concluded that people who engage in constructive communication about jealousy while expressing their emotions openly and honestly probably come across as sincerely hurt yet rational and in control. Furthermore, the honest expression of negative emotion may cause the partner to feel empathy for the jealous individual, which could lead to positive outcomes.

In some cases, compensatory restoration may also be associated with relational satisfaction. Individuals who try to improve themselves and their relationships may become more desirable to their

BOX 13.2   Highlights

Communicative Responses to Jealousy

Behavior	Definition and Examples
Negative affect expression	Nonverbal expressions of jealousy-related affect that the partner can see (examples: appearing hurt or anxious, crying)
Integrative communication	Direct, nonaggressive communication about jealousy with the partner (examples: disclosing feelings and trying to reach an understanding)
Distributive communication	Direct, aggressive communication about jealousy with the partner (examples: arguing, being sarcastic or rude)
Active distancing	Indirect, aggressive communication about jealousy with the partner (examples: giving the silent treatment, withdrawing affection and sex)
Avoidance/denial	Indirect, nonaggressive communication that focuses on avoiding the jealousy-invoking issue, situation, or partner (examples: decreasing contact, denying feelings)
Violent communication	Threats or actual physical violence against the partner (examples: threatening to harm the partner, hitting)
Signs of possession	Public relationship displays so that people know the partner is "taken" (examples: kissing the partner in front of rivals, telling rivals you have a relationship)
Derogating competitors	Negative comments about potential rivals to the partner and to others (example: telling the partner about the rival's bad traits)
Relationship threats	Threats to terminate or de-escalate the primary relationship or to be unfaithful (example: threatening to break up if the partner continues to see the rival)
Surveillance	Behavioral strategies designed to find out about the rival relationship (examples: checking the partner's cell phone or e-mail, spying on the partner)
Compensatory restoration	Behavior aimed at improving the primary relationship and/or oneself (examples: trying to look more physically attractive, giving the partner gifts or extra attention)
Manipulation attempts	Moves to induce negative feelings in the partner (examples: flirting with others, inducing counterjealousy, making the partner feel guilty)
Rival contacts	Direct communication with the rival about the jealousy situation or rival relationship (example: telling the rival the partner is already in a relationship)
Violent behavior toward objects	Violence toward objects, either in private or in the presence of others (examples: slamming doors, throwing the partner's possessions out of the house)

SOURCE: Adapted from Guerrero and Andersen (1998b); examples from actual accounts by jealous individuals, as reported in Guerrero et al.'s (1995) qualitative data.

partners. Indeed, Buss (1988a) reported that strategies such as demonstrating love and caring for one's partner were highly effective in keeping couples together after jealousy had occurred. However, it is important to recognize that too much compensatory restoration can make a person seem desperate and too eager to please, which can have detrimental effects on the relationship (Guerrero, 1998).

Sex Differences in Jealous Emotions and Communication

Research findings on sex differences in jealous emotions are mixed, but some studies suggest that women experience more hurt, sadness, anxiety, and confusion than men, perhaps because they blame themselves for the situation more often (Becker et al., 2004; Bryson, 1976). In contrast, men have been found to deny jealous feelings and focus on bolstering their self-esteem more than women (Buunk, 1982; White, 1981). These differences are small, but they suggest that women are somewhat more focused on the relationship, whereas men are more focused on individual concerns.

Sex differences in communicative responses to jealousy are more consistent, although relatively small. Jealous women report using integrative communication, expressing negative affect, enhancing their appearance, and using counterjealousy induction more often than do jealous men. In contrast, jealous men more often contact the rival, restrict the partner's access to potential rivals, and give gifts and spend extra money on the partner than jealous women (Buss, 1988a; Guerrero & Reiter, 1998). Jealous men also engage in dangerous behaviors, such as getting drunk or engaging in promiscuous sex with others, more often than do jealous women (see White & Mullen, 1989). These findings can be partially explained using an evolutionary perspective, which suggests that men focus on competing for mates and showing resources, whereas women focus on creating social bonds and showcasing their beauty (Buss, 1988a).

DECEPTION

Like jealousy, deception is a major relational transgression that often leads to feelings of betrayal and distrust (O'Hair & Cody, 1994). Deception violates both relational and conversational rules and is often considered to be a negative violation of expectancies (Aune, Ching, & Levine, 1996). Research suggests that most people expect friends and loved ones, as well as strangers, to be truthful most of the time. In fact, McCornack (1992) argued that expecting others to be truthful is a basic feature of conversations (see also Grice, 1989). If people do not expect that most conversations are truthful, talking to others would simply be too difficult and unproductive. Think about this for a moment: If you were always suspicious and had to question the veracity of every statement you heard, it would be virtually impossible to get to know people.

On a given day, however, it is highly likely that you or someone you are talking to will engage in some form of deception. In one study, people reported lying in about 25% of their daily interactions (DePaulo, Kashy, Kirkendol, Wyer, & Epstein, 1996). In another study, people were asked to keep a log of their conversations. Remarkably, only one third of these conversations were completely truthful (Turner, Edgley, & Olmstead, 1975). The other two thirds of conversations were characterized by some degree of lying, exaggeration, or intentional concealment of information. During a single interaction, people are more likely to tell lies to strangers and acquaintances than close relational partners, such as a good friend or spouse (DePaulo & Kashy, 1998). However, because people interact more often with close relational partners, most lies are told in the context of relationships. Studies comparing strangers, acquaintances, friends, and romantic partners suggest that the most lying occurs in romantic relationships (DePaulo & Kashy, 1998; Lippard, 1988). Moreover, romantic partners appear to "reserve their most serious lies for each other" (Cole, 2001, p. 107).

Types of Deception

Lying is only one way in which relational partners deceive each other. Deception includes all communications or omissions that serve to distort or omit the truth. Buller and Burgoon (1994) defined **deception** as intentionally managing verbal and/or nonverbal messages, so that a receiver will believe or understand something in a way that the sender knows is false. Note that *intentionality* is part of this definition. For example, if you truly believe that the big basketball game between your college and a rival school starts at 6:00 p.m. when it really starts at 7:00 p.m., it would not be deception if you told your friend the incorrect time. Instead, this type of misinformation might be termed a *mistake.* But when people intentionally mislead others or conceal or misrepresent the truth, deception has occurred.

Research suggests that there are five primary types of deception: lies, equivocations, concealments, exaggerations, and understatements. Lies, also called falsifications or fabrications, involve making up information or giving information that is the opposite of (or at least very different from) the truth (Ekman, 1985). For example, if you are single and someone you find unattractive approaches you at a bar and asks if you are married, you might say you are.

Another form of deception, **equivocation** or evasion (Bavelas, Black, Chovil, & Mullett, 1990; O'Hair & Cody, 1994), involves making an indirect, ambiguous, or contradictory statement. The prototypical example of equivocation involves people's physical appearance. Suppose your friend asks you how her new hairstyle (which you hate) looks. Instead of saying, "You look like a French poodle" (which is what you really think), you might equivocate by saying, "It's the latest style." In this case, your answer would be indirect even though it contains a kernel of truth. That is, you might really believe that your friend's new hairstyle is the latest fashion, even though your statement is designed to mislead your friend regarding your true feelings.

Concealment or omission is yet another form of deception (Buller & Burgoon, 1994; O'Hair & Cody, 1994; Turner et al., 1975). The key here is that people omit information they know is important or relevant to a given context. This is what Tia did. She decided not to tell Jamal about having lunch with Robert, even though she knew he might think the information was relevant to their relationship. At other times, concealment involves engaging in behavior that helps hide relevant information. For example, a teenager might leave her house in the morning with her backpack and books as if she were heading off to school, when in actuality she is going to meet her boyfriend and skip school.

The last two forms of deception are opposites. **Exaggeration** or overstatement involves stretching the truth a little—often to make oneself look better or to spice up a story (O'Hair & Cody, 1994; Turner et al., 1975). The prototypical example of exaggeration involves job interviews, in which people often make their skills and experiences sound better than they actually are. **Understatement** or minimization, on the other hand, involves downplaying aspects of the truth. As with exaggerations, people often use understatements to make themselves look better. People also use understatements when they want to avoid getting in trouble or taking too much blame. For instance, Tia might have told Jamal that she ran into Robert and they had a casual chat, when actually they had lunch together and talked for more than an hour about deep topics.

Motives for Deception

People engage in deception for many reasons. Metts (1989; Metts & Chronis, 1986) described three major motivations for deception in close relationships. First, relational partners have **partner-focused motives**, such as using deception to avoid hurting the partner, help the partner maintain his or her self-esteem, avoid worrying the partner, and protect the partner's relationship with a third party. For example, if you say that your best friend's new hairstyle looks great when you really think it looks awful, your deceptive behavior probably has a partner-focused motive. Sometimes, partner-motivated deception is seen as socially polite and relationally beneficial. Indeed, *not* engaging in deception when you hate your friend's new hairstyle might violate relational expectations and hurt your friend's feelings.

Second, people deceive due to **self-focused motives**, such as wanting to enhance or protect their self-image, or wanting to shield themselves from anger, embarrassment, criticism, or other types of harm. So if a job applicant exaggerates his qualifications during a job interview or a child avoids telling her mother that she failed an exam because she doesn't want to be punished, deception is based on self-focused motives. This type of deception is usually perceived as a much more serious transgression than partner-focused deception because the deceiver is acting for selfish reasons rather than for the good of the partner or the relationship.

Finally, people have **relationship-focused motives** for deceiving a partner. Here, the deceiver wants to limit relational harm by avoiding conflict, relational trauma, or other unpleasant experiences. For example, Tia might have concealed having lunch with Robert because she thought it would lead to an unnecessary argument or, at the very least, a misunderstanding. Note that in this case, as well as in other cases involving relationship-focused motives, partner- and self-focused motivations may also come into play. By not telling Jamal about her lunch with Robert, Tia might also be protecting herself from false accusations (a self-focused motive) while protecting Jamal from feeling hurt and jealous (a partner-focused motive). The key is whether someone is using deception primarily to protect the relationship, rather than only to protect either oneself or the partner.

Sometimes, relationally motivated deception is seen as beneficial within a relationship. At other times, however, such deception only complicates matters. Metts (1994) used the following excerpt from an advice column to illustrate how deception can make a bad situation even worse:

> Dear Abby: My husband and I were planning a 40th anniversary celebration, but I called it off 3 months ago when I learned from someone that my husband had had an affair with a young woman while he was stationed in Alameda, California, during World War II. The affair lasted about a year while he was waiting to be shipped out, but never was. When I confronted him with the facts, he admitted it, but said it was "nothing serious." . . . I am devastated. I feel betrayed, knowing I've spent the last 37 years living with a liar and a cheat. How can I ever trust him again? The bottom has fallen out of my world. (p. 217)

In this situation, even if the deception was motivated by relational concerns, such as wanting to avoid conflict and even divorce, it compounded the problem in the long run. As Metts (1994) observed, "In this case, the act of infidelity is only the first blow; the 37 years of omission is the second, and probably more devastating, hit" (p. 217). Jamal might feel the same. Even if Tia had a good motive for not telling Jamal about her lunch with Robert,

Jamal might feel betrayed because she didn't trust him enough to confide in him. Jamal may also question Tia's motivations and wonder if she didn't tell him because she really does have something to hide.

Deception Detection

As you read the letter about the husband who cheated on his wife, you might have wondered how he got away with deceiving her for so long. You might think that there must have been clues that he had had an affair or that he was concealing something from her. In reality, however, it is difficult to detect deception in everyday conversations with relational partners unless one partner says something that is blatantly false or that contradicts information the other partner knows. This is not to say that most people can successfully deceive their partners all the time. Indeed, it is difficult to hide serious relational transgressions such as infidelity over a long period. However, in day-to-day conversations about relatively minor issues, deception often occurs without one partner suspecting that anything is amiss.

Detecting deception is difficult because there are no completely reliable indicators of deception. Although deception is often accompanied by behaviors such as speech hesitations and body shifts, these behaviors can indicate general anxiety, shyness, or discomfort in addition to deception (Andersen, 1999; Burgoon et al., 1996). Also, stereotypic behaviors such as eye behavior are often controlled during deception. When people lie to you, they know to look you straight in the eye, which makes eye contact an unreliable cue for detecting deception (Hocking & Leathers, 1980). Perhaps the most reliable method for detecting possible deception is to compare a person's normal, truthful behavior with her or his current behavior. If the person's behavior is noticeably different— either more anxious or more controlled—*perhaps* deception is occurring. There is, however, *no* foolproof method for detecting deception.

People often assume that they are better able to detect deception by close relational partners than strangers or acquaintances. Research suggests that this is not the case. Although Comadena (1982) found that friends and spouses are better at detecting deception than acquaintances, he also found that friends are superior to spouses at uncovering deception, suggesting that the ability to detect deception does not increase as a relationship becomes closer. Other studies have shown that romantic partners have trouble detecting deception, with accuracy rates only slightly better than chance (Levine & McCornack, 1992; Stiff, Kim, & Ramesh, 1992). In one study, people reported that their romantic partners accepted about half of their deceptive messages as truthful (Boon & McLeod, 2001). Next, we discuss the advantages and disadvantages people in close relationships have when it comes to detecting deception.

Advantages of Relational Closeness. Because comparing "normal" behavior with deceptive behavior is important in the deception detection process, close relational partners have an advantage over strangers—they have knowledge of the partner's typical communication style. Burgoon and her colleagues (1996) called this type of knowledge **behavioral familiarity.** Close friends, family, and romantic partners are familiar with one another's honest behavior; therefore, deviations from this behavior can tip them off that something is amiss. Relational partners also have the advantage of **informational familiarity** (Burgoon et al., 1996). In other words, you know certain information about your relational partner, so your partner cannot lie to you about that information. You can tell a stranger that you have three children instead of one, but obviously you cannot get way with telling such a lie to family members or friends.

Disadvantages of Relational Closeness. Despite these advantages, deception is difficult to detect in close relationships for at least two reasons. First, people have a **truth bias**. In other words, people expect others to be honest, so they enter conversations without suspicion and do not look for deceptive behavior. Truth biases are especially strong within close relationships and with people whom we like. People who are socially attractive are generally seen as less deceptive, and when they are caught deceiving, people usually attribute their motives for deception to more benign causes (Aune et al., 1996). McCornack and Parks (1986) argued that the truth bias makes close relational partners overly confident of the truthfulness of each other's statements, causing them to miss much of the deception that occurs. Even in the face of seemingly deceptive information, relational partners can be influenced by the truth bias (Buller, Strzyzewski, & Comstock, 1991; McCornack & Parks, 1986).

The following example further illustrates the power of the truth bias. One of the authors of this book helped run an experiment on deception in which a friend who was assigned to be interviewed was instructed to lie in response to some questions and to tell the truth in response to others. The interviewer, who did not know that the interviewee had been instructed to lie on some questions, later rated the friend's answers on a variety of attributes, including truthfulness. The truth bias was evident in many of these interactions. As a case in point, one of the interviewees lied and said "no" when asked if he usually went out of his way to help other people in need. The interviewer looked at him in disbelief and said "Yes, you do. Just the other day you stopped and helped those teenagers who were stranded at the side of the road—you stopped and put the spare tire on their car." The interviewee paused and then said "Yeah, but I hadn't changed a tire in a while, and I wanted to make sure I could still do it." Amazingly, when the interviewer recorded how truthful he thought his friend's answer was, he marked "very truthful." This shows how the truth bias works. We expect and look for honesty in our friends and loved ones, even if it sometimes means having to reevaluate our initial suspicions of deception.

The second reason close relational partners might have trouble detecting deception is that the deceiver may exert **behavioral control**. In other words, people try to control their nervous or guilty behaviors to appear friendly and truthful. Several deception researchers have demonstrated that, regardless of whether deceivers are interacting with friends or strangers, they try to control their behavior so that they seem honest (see Ekman & Friesen, 1969; Zuckerman, DePaulo, & Rosenthal, 1981). However, this may be particularly true for close relational partners, who have more to lose if the deception is discovered. Buller and Aune (1987) found that when people deceived friends or romantic partners, they became friendlier and showed less anxiety as the interaction progressed than when they deceived strangers. In comparison with deceiving strangers, people tried harder to look truthful when deceiving relational partners, in part by "putting on a happy face" and hiding nervousness.

Effects of Deception on Relationships

Paradoxically, research shows that deception can help people develop and maintain relationships, but it can also lead to conflict and relationship breakup. Most people believe that honesty is a crucial part of close relationships. Yet people can identify situations where it is important, even ethical, to deceive their partner (Boon & McLeod, 2001). For example, if Jamal overhears someone saying something really negative about Tia, he might decide not to tell her because it would hurt her feelings too much. Partner-focused deceptions such as these are often regarded as acceptable and appropriate, and they can help maintain positive relationships.

Cole (2001) discussed two other ways in which deception is associated with the development and maintenance of relationships. First, deception may help couples avoid arguments, thereby promoting relational harmony. For example, a mother who is mediating an argument between her two sons may try to sound even-handed, even though she thinks one of the sons is more to blame. Similarly, your best friend might understate how hurt she feels when you receive an honor that she wanted, so you won't feel bad.

Second, deception allows people to downplay their faults and accentuate their virtues, which may help people develop and maintain relationships (Cole, 2001). Two lines of research support this idea. Work on the benefit of positive illusions (Murray, Holmes, & Griffin, 1996) suggests that people who hold idealized images of their partners (as well as their partner's perceptions of them) are most satisfied in their relationships. So if Tia exaggerates by telling Jamal "you are ten times more attractive than Robert," her exaggeration would contribute to his positive illusions and perhaps lead him to feel more secure about her having lunch with Robert.

Work in the area of date initiation supports the idea that people use deception to emphasize their positive qualities and minimize their negative qualities (Rowatt, Cunningham, & Druen, 1998, 1999). According to research reported in these studies, around 46% of men and 36% of women admit that they have lied to initiate a date with someone. In another study on deception in the early stages of dating (Tooke & Camire, 1991), men were more likely than women to exaggerate (or lie) about how successful they were and to act more committed and sincere than they actually were. Women, in contrast, were more likely to try to enhance their appearance by engaging in behaviors such as wearing clothing that made them look thinner and using makeup to exaggerate desirable facial features. People are most likely to lie when initiating dates with potential partners who are very physically attractive (Rowatt et al., 1999). People deceive prospective partners about many issues, including their appearance, personality traits, intelligence, income, and past relationships. With physically attractive partners, people are most likely to lie in ways that show similarity to the attractive partner (Rowatt et al., 1999). With Internet dating on the rise, people may have more opportunities than ever before to deceive dating prospects on these issues.

Of course, deceiving a partner about your positive versus negative qualities can backfire. Eventually, they are likely to see you for who you are, which may leave them disappointed and disillusioned. So it is important to remember that deception can have negative consequences for relationships. When people uncover a significant deception, they usually feel a host of negative emotions, including anxiety, anger, and distress (e.g., McCornack & Levine, 1990). People who use deception frequently in their relationships report lower levels of commitment, intimacy, and closeness. Similarly, when people perceive their partners as dishonest, they report less relational satisfaction and commitment (Cole, 2001). Deception is also a leading cause of conflict and relationship breakup (see Chapters 14 and 15). Finally, some deceptions are harmful not only to people's relationships but also to their health. Lucchetti (1999) found that one-third of sexually active college students avoided talking about their sexual history with their partners, even though many of them knew that doing so would help them have safer sex. Around 20% of these same college students reported that they had intentionally misrepresented their sexual history to their partner.

HURTFUL MESSAGES

Deception is one form of message that can be hurtful. Messages that imply a person or relationship is unimportant are especially hurtful and constitute a relational transgression and a violation of expectancies (Vangelisti, 1994b, 2001). People want and expect relational partners to regard them and their relationships positively. Messages that convey negative feelings or rejection are unexpected, leading to emotions such as hurt and anger (Vangelisti, 1994b).

Hurtful messages are associated with less satisfying relationships. Specifically, people report more distancing and less relational closeness when their partner frequently uses hurtful messages (Vangelisti, 1994b; Vangelisti & Young, 2000). Messages perceived to be intentional are especially hurtful and damaging to relationships (Mills, Nazar, & Farrell, 2002; Vangelisti, 1994b; Vangelisti & Young, 2000). If you think someone said something to purposely hurt your feelings, you are likely to be more upset than if you thought the comment was not intended to hurt you. Messages are also more or less hurtful based on the topic they address and the form of communication they take. One study showed that hurtful messages are less psychologically painful when they are lightened through humor (Young & Bippus, 2001).

Hurtful Message Topics

Vangelisti (1994b) examined the topics in hurtful messages. She had college students recall when someone said something hurtful to them and then write a script about the interaction as they remembered it. Most hurtful messages focused on relationships (both romantic and nonromantic), personality traits, and physical appearance. Messages of relationship devaluation were especially hurtful, such as being told, "I don't love you anymore," "I've been

sleeping with someone else," and "I decided we can only be friends" (p. 65). These types of messages, which focus on relationship issues, were even more hurtful than messages focusing on personality traits.

Types of Hurtful Messages

Vangelisti identified 10 types of hurtful messages (see Box 13.3) representing different forms of communication. The most common hurtful messages reported by college students are evaluations, accusations, and informative statements (Vangelisti, 1994b). Research has also examined hurtful messages between parents and children. In one study, children (aged 7 to 10) and parents were asked to describe a time when a hurtful message had occurred in the context of their parent-child relationship (Mills et al., 2002). Children described situations involving discipline or disregard, whereas mothers described situations involving misconduct or disregard. Under the category of "disregard," children mentioned issues such as sibling favoritism, teasing, criticism, rebuffs, and statements showing disrespect. Similarly, mothers wrote about times they felt criticized, rebuffed, or disrespected. Together, these studies demonstrate that feeling devalued is a central component of hurtful messages for young children as well as adults.

Responses to Hurtful Messages

Research has examined three general ways in which people respond to hurtful messages: active verbal responses, acquiescent responses, and invulnerable responses. These responses occur in adult relationships (Vangelisti & Crumley, 1998) and parent-child relationships (Mills et al., 2002).

Active verbal responses focus on confronting the partner about her or his hurtful remarks. Some active verbal responses are more positive than others. For example, questioning the partner and asking for an explanation are forms of active verbal responses that may help partners understand one another. Other active verbal responses, such as sarcasm and verbal attacks on the partner, can lead to an escalation of negativity. Active verbal responses are

BOX 13.3   Highlights

Hurtful Messages

Message Type	Definition and Examples
Evaluation	Negative judgments of worth, value, or quality (example: "This relationship has been a waste of my time")
Accusation	Charges about a person's faults or actions (example: "You are a selfish and rude person")
Informative statement	Disclosure of unwanted information (example: "I only dated you because I was on the rebound")
Directive	Directions or commands that go against one's desires or imply negative thoughts or feelings (example: "Don't call me anymore")
Expressions of desire	Statements about one's preferences or desires (example: "I wish you were more like your brother")
Threat	A declaration of intent to inflict punishment under certain conditions (example: "If you see him again I'll break up with you")
Question	An inquiry or interrogation that implies a negative judgment (example: "Aren't you finished with school yet?")
Joke	A witticism or prank that insults the partner (example: "I guess your wife wears the pants in the family and you wear the skirt")
Deception	A statement that is untrue or distorts the truth (example: your partner says "Trust me, I didn't do it" when you know he or she did)

SOURCE: Definitions adapted from Vangelisti (1994b).

the most frequently reported response in both adult relationships and parent-child relationships (Mills et al., 2002). People may be especially likely to use active verbal responses when they are in satisfying relationships (Vangelisti & Crumley, 1998). Couples in satisfying relationships may talk to one another more, which could help them repair the psychological damage caused by hurtful messages. Couples in happy relationships may also be better able to withstand the use of more negative active verbal responses than those in unhappy relationships.

Instead of talking about the hurtful message, people sometimes use acquiescent or invulnerable responses. **Acquiescent responses** involve giving in

and acknowledging the partner's ability to hurt you. For example, people might cry, apologize ("I'm sorry I make you feel that way"), or concede ("Fine, I won't see him anymore"). People use acquiescent responses when they are deeply hurt by something a close relational partner said (Vangelisti & Crumley, 1998). The quickest way for people to stop emotional pain may be to give in and acknowledge their feelings. **Invulnerable responses** involve acting unaffected by the hurtful remark. For instance, you might ignore the hurtful message, laugh it off, become quiet, or withdraw. Both acquiescent and invulnerable responses may be more likely than active verbal strategies when people become flooded with emotion and have difficulty talking about their feelings.

THE AFTERMATH OF HURTFUL EVENTS

As we discuss in Chapter 15, issues related to jealousy, infidelity, and deception, along with negative spirals of hurtful messages, often cause relational breakups. Yet many romantic couples and friends survive and even thrive after experiencing transgressions. Doing so, however, is a challenging enterprise. Fincham (2000) used the metaphor of "kissing porcupines" to describe this challenge:

> Imagine two porcupines huddled together in the cold of an Alaskan winter's night, each providing life-sustaining warmth to the other. As they draw ever closer together the painful prick from the other's quills leads them to instinctively withdraw—until the need for warmth draws them together again. This "kiss of the porcupines" is an apt metaphor for the human condition, and it illustrates two fundamental assumptions . . . humans harm each other and humans are social animals. (p. 2)

As Fincham put it, acceptance of these two assumptions results in the following challenge: "how to maintain relatedness with fellow humans in the face of being harmed by them" (p. 2). Next, we focus on this dilemma from the perspective of both the victim and the transgressor. Specifically, we look at forgiveness and communicative responses from the perspective of the victim and remedial responses from the perspective of the transgressor.

Victim Responses: Forgiveness and Communication

Forgiveness plays a critical role in repairing a relationship after a transgression occurs (Emmers & Canary, 1996). Forgiveness is a complicated process that does not occur immediately; instead,

> the decision to forgive starts a difficult process that involves conquering negative feelings and acting with goodwill toward someone who has done us harm. It is this process, set in motion by a decision to forgive that makes statements like "I'm trying to forgive you" meaningful. (Fincham, 2000, p. 9)

Forgiveness is a state of motivational change that involves inhibiting relationally destructive behavior and instead behaving constructively toward the person who committed the offense (McCullough, Worthington, & Rachal, 1997). As Freedman and Enright (1996) stated, "There is a decidedly paradoxical quality to forgiveness as the forgiver gives up the resentment, to which he or she has a right, and gives the gift of compassion, to which the offender has no right" (p. 983). Fincham (2000) made the key point that forgiveness is contingent not only on the hurt person's change in motivation but also on the offending person's change in behavior. If a person does not believe that her or his partner will change the hurtful behavior, that person is unlikely to be forgiving.

People communicate forgiveness in a variety of ways. Waldron and Kelley (2005) identified five specific ways in which people show forgiveness following a partner's relational transgression. **Explicit forgiveness** involves direct communication such as saying "I forgive you." **Nonverbal display** involves using touch or facial expressions to show forgiveness. **Conditional forgiveness** involves offering forgiveness with contingencies. **Minimization** involves downplaying the importance or seriousness of the transgression. Finally, **discussion** involves talking about the transgression with the partner. Explicit forgiveness is the most common of these strategies (Kelley, 1998), as well as the clearest way to let a transgressor know that he or she is forgiven and you want to repair the relationship (Scobie & Scobie, 1998). However, when a transgression is serious, victims are more likely to use conditional forgiveness (Waldron & Kelley, 2005). Minimization is most likely when the transgression is not so serious. So Jamal might be likely to use a minimization ("Okay, it doesn't seem like that big of a deal") if he believes Tia's lunch with Robert was innocent. If, on the other hand, he continues to be suspicious of Tia's motives, he might use conditional forgiveness ("It's okay, as long as you promise not to see him again"). To determine the strategy you used to grant forgiveness the last time you forgave someone after being hurt, take the test in Box 13.4.

Prior to forgiving a partner, victims often engage in avoidant and retaliatory forms of communication. However, once they forgive their partners, victims report engaging in more positive forms of communication,

BOX 13.4 Put Yourself to the Test

Forgiveness-Granting Strategies

Think about the last time you forgave a relational partner (such as a good friend, family member, or romantic partner) after he or she hurt your feelings. Use the following scale to determine which strategies you used the most: 0 = Not used at all, 4 = Used moderately, 7 = Used extensively.

	Not Used			⟵⟶				*Used Extensively*
1. I gave my partner a look that communicated forgiveness.	0	1	2	3	4	5	6	7
2. I told my partner I had forgiven him or her, but I really didn't forgive my partner until later.	0	1	2	3	4	5	6	7
3. I joked about it so my partner would know he or she was forgiven.	0	1	2	3	4	5	6	7
4. I initiated discussion about the transgression.	0	1	2	3	4	5	6	7
5. I told my partner I forgave her or him.	0	1	2	3	4	5	6	7
6. I gave my partner a hug.	0	1	2	3	4	5	6	7
7. I told my partner not to worry about it.	0	1	2	3	4	5	6	7
8. I discussed the transgression with my partner.	0	1	2	3	4	5	6	7
9. The expression on my face said, "I forgive you."	0	1	2	3	4	5	6	7
10. I told my partner I would forgive her or him only if things changed.	0	1	2	3	4	5	6	7
11. I told my partner it was no big deal.	0	1	2	3	4	5	6	7
12. I touched my partner in a way that communicated forgiveness.	0	1	2	3	4	5	6	7
13. I told my partner I would forgive her or him if the transgression never happened again.	0	1	2	3	4	5	6	7

To obtain your results, average your scores for the following items:

(1 + 6 + 9 + 12)/4 = _________ (Nonverbal display)

(2 + 10 + 13)/3 = _________ (Conditional forgiveness)

(3 + 7 + 11)/3 = _________ (Minimization)

(4 + 8)/2 = _________ (Discussion)

(5) = _________ (Explicit forgiveness)

Higher scores indicate that you used more of a particular strategy.

SOURCE: Adapted from Waldron, V. R., & Kelley, D. L., Forgiving communication as a response to relational transgressions, in *Journal of Social and Personal Relationships,* 22, 723–742. Copyright © 2005, Sage Publications, Inc.

such as talking over issues and calmly renegotiating relationships rules (Bachman & Guerrero, 2006b; McCullough et al., 1998). In contrast, when people do not forgive their partners, they tend to engage in more vengeful communication (such as arguing and name-calling), de-escalation (such as breaking up or dating others), and avoidance. A motivational shift toward forgiveness and positive communication is more likely if (1) a sincere apology is offered, (2) the seriousness of the transgression does not prohibit forgiveness, and (3) the relationship was of high quality prior to the transgression. Each of these conditions is discussed next.

Apologies and Empathy. Forgiveness is more likely when the transgressor sincerely apologizes for her or his actions (Darby & Schlenkler, 1982; Hargrave, 1994; McCullough et al., 1997; Weiner, Graham, Peter, & Zmuidinas, 1991). Sincere apologies can lead the victim to perceive the transgressor as a generally good and thoughtful person despite the hurtful event. In Kelley's (1998) study, 31% of the accounts indicated that people forgave their partners because they acted in ways that showed remorse and/or accepted responsibility, such as apologizing for their actions.

Apologies are most likely to be effective if the victim feels empathy for the transgressor. It may seem odd to you that a victim should feel empathy when he or she is the one who was hurt. However, if the transgressor expresses negative emotions—such

as guilt, remorse, and even fear of losing the partner—the victim might feel bad for the transgressor. As McCullough et al. (1997) put it, empathy can lead to "an increased caring" for the transgressor that "overshadows the salience" of the hurtful action and leads to forgiveness (p. 333). The relationships between apologies, empathy, forgiveness, and communication are depicted in Figure 13.2.

Sometimes, when victims experience empathy for the transgressor, they realize that the best way to restore their own peace of mind is through forgiveness. Kelley (1998) had people write descriptions of three situations where they forgave someone. In 21% of these descriptions, the reason for forgiving the partner was to restore well-being to themselves or the transgressor. Kelley gave the following excerpt from one of the narratives to illustrate this point: "I began to realize that this anger was not only torturing him, but myself as well. It was eating me up inside and making me more of an angry person. Why should I suffer for what he has done?" (p. 264).

The Seriousness of the Transgression. Of course, if the transgressor's offense was especially serious, empathy might not be forthcoming, and an apology might never be accepted (Worthington & Wade, 1999). Thus, people are less likely to be forgiving when the transgression is serious (Bennett & Earwaker, 1994; Girard & Mullet, 1997). In Kelley's study, 44% of the descriptions indicated that victims

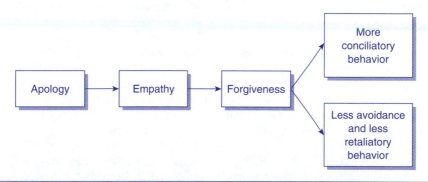

Figure 13.2 Model of the Forgiveness Process

SOURCE: From McCullough, M. E., Worthington, E. L., & Rachal, C., Interpersonal forgiving in close relationships, in *Journal of Personality and Social Psychology, 73,* p. 327. Copyright © 1997, the American Psychological Association. Reprinted with permission.

forgave their partners after reframing the situation, so that the transgression seemed less severe. For example, they came to understand why the transgressor had behaved in a certain way or realized that the transgressor had not intended to hurt them.

The seriousness of a transgression is also related to how much a behavior violates relationship expectations. For example, hurtful events vary in the extent to which you consider them unacceptable. When people consider a hurtful event to be a highly negative violation of their expectations, they are less likely to forgive their partner and less likely to engage in positive forms of communication (Bachman, 2002; Bachman & Guerrero, 2006a). Recall the situation between Jamal and Tia. Jamal might be upset that Tia concealed information from him, but he is unlikely to regard this transgression as one of the worst things Tia could do. Therefore, he would be more likely to forgive Tia for her deception. On the other hand, if she really was having an affair with Robert, Jamal would be much more likely to see that as a highly negative violation of a relationship rule, and as a consequence, he would be much less likely to forgive her.

Relationship and Partner Characteristics. People are also more likely to forgive their partners and engage in positive communication when they are in high-quality relationships with rewarding partners. In Kelley's study, 35% of the accounts indicated that forgiveness was granted because people wanted to repair their relationship. Love was a motivation behind forgiveness in another 15% of the accounts. People are also likely to evaluate transgressions as less serious, forgive their partners, and engage in more positive communication following transgressions by socially attractive and highly rewarding partners (Aune et al., 1996; Bachman, 2002; Bachman & Guerrero, 2006a). Similarly, people are more likely to report using positive communication following relational transgressions when their relationships are highly committed and emotionally involved (Guerrero & Bachman, in press; Menzies-Toman & Lydon, 2005; Roloff et al., 2001). People in committed, satisfying relationships also tend to evaluate their partner's transgressions as less serious than do those in less satisfying, less committed

relationships (Menzies-Toman, & Lydon, 2005; Young, 2004).

Consequences of Forgiveness. Finally, it is important to note that the consequences of forgiveness are not always positive. Although research has shown that partners who forgive each other are more likely to stay together and have happier relationships, this is not always the case. Kelley (1998) analyzed respondents who described relational consequences when they wrote about forgiving someone. Around 28% of the people indicated that their relationship had returned to "normal" after forgiveness was granted. Around 36% reported that their relationship had deteriorated, and around 32% reported that their relationship had strengthened. Relationships are more likely to deteriorate if the transgression is serious and the victim used conditional forgiveness. Relationships are more likely to strengthen if the victim used explicit forgiveness (saying "I forgive you") and nonverbal displays of forgiveness (showing affection to the partner). These findings suggest that forgiveness can help heal a relationship, but it cannot always save it. Of course, in some cases, it may be better *not* to save the relationship. For instance, people who forgive too readily might stay in abusive relationships (Katz, Street, & Arias, 1995).

The Transgressor: Remedial Strategies

Thus far, we have looked at repair from the victim's perspective by focusing on communication related to forgiveness. But what if you are the transgressor: Can you do something to save your relationship? The answer is far from simple; you cannot erase your offense with the wave of a magic wand, and your relationship might never again be the same even if your partner forgives you. However, research on discovered deception (Aune, Metts, & Hubbard, 1998), sexual infidelity (Mongeau, Hale, & Alles, 1994), social predicaments (Cupach, 1994), and forgiveness (Kelley, 1998) suggests that people use various remedial strategies when they have committed a transgression. **Remedial strategies** are attempts to correct problems, restore one's positive face, and/or repair the relationship. Some of the most common remedial strategies are discussed next.

Apologies/Concessions. Apologizing and admitting guilt is one of the most obvious and frequently used remedial strategies. As noted earlier, apologies can increase empathy while showing that the transgressor is willing to take responsibility for her or his actions. In fact, in Mongeau et al.'s (1994) study on responses to infidelity, concessions emerged as the most effective relational repair strategy. However, if an apology and accompanying confession are offered after someone is accused of a transgression, the apology is not as effective as it would have been if offered before accusations were made. Of course, many people do not want to apologize and admit guilt if their partner does not know about the transgression (Mongeau & Schulz, 1997). But if they wait until the partner accuses them (as would be the case if Tia apologizes), their apology might be seen as the result of being caught rather than a free admission of guilt. Apologies can vary from a simple statement, such as "I'm sorry," to more elaborate forms of apology that include expressing guilt and remorse, derogating oneself, promising to make up for the bad behavior, and promising never to engage in the transgression again (Cupach, 1994; Schlenker & Darby, 1981). When people have committed serious transgressions, elaborate apologies are more successful than simple ones (Darby & Schlenker, 1982, 1989).

Excuses/Justifications. When transgressors try to explain *why* they engaged in an untoward act, they are using excuses or justifications to account for their behavior. When transgressors use **excuses**, they try to minimize responsibility for their negative behavior by focusing on their inability to control their own actions or by shifting the blame to others (Aune et al., 1998; Cupach, 1994; Mongeau & Schulz, 1997). For example, Tia might offer an excuse by saying "I didn't know I was going to run into Robert; it just happened." Tia could also blame Robert by saying, "He insisted that we have lunch, and I was afraid of hurting his feelings." When transgressors use **justifications**, they try to minimize the negative implications of the transgression by denying their behavior was wrong or that the transgression was severe (Aune et al., 1998; Cupach, 1994; Mongeau & Schulz, 1997). Tia offers a justification when she says that having lunch with Robert didn't really

mean anything to her. The mutual friend who told Jamal she saw Tia and Robert having lunch together may also offer a justification by saying, "I didn't know you hadn't told Jamal" or "He probably would have found out eventually anyway."

Refusals. With excuses and justifications, the transgressor admits some responsibility for her or his actions. However, with refusals, transgressors argue that they should not be held accountable for their behavior or that a transgression never occurred. Some scholars believe refusals are a special type of excuse, one that is good enough that the transgressor feels that a relational rule has not been broken. The popular television show *Friends* provides a great example of refusal. Ross and Rachel have been dating for some time when they get into an argument and agree to "take a break." That night, Ross has sex with another woman. When Rachel finds out about Ross's one-night stand, she is very upset. Ross denies he has done anything wrong because they were "on a break." Ross refuses to take any blame because he does not see his behavior as a transgression. This example illustrates the complexity of relational transgressions: What is perceived as a transgression by one party might not necessarily be perceived as a transgression by the other. Not surprisingly, Mongeau et al. (1994) found refusals to be an ineffective remedial strategy; refusals are likely to aggravate the situation rather than repair the relationship.

Appeasement/Positivity. Different types of appeasement behaviors have appeared in the literature on remedial strategies. For instance, people who seek forgiveness often use ingratiation strategies, such as promising to make up for what they did (Kelley, 1998). When people are caught deceiving their partners, they sometimes use soothing strategies that are designed to appease the target. Specifically, Aune and his colleagues (1998) found that people used remedial strategies such as complimenting the partner, trying to be more attentive to the partner, spending more time with the partner, saying "I love you" more often, and buying the partner gifts and flowers. With all these strategies, the transgressor seeks to "make up" for the hurtful behavior by being particularly nice and helpful. Tia uses an indirect appeasement strategy when she says "I told him [Robert] that I love you and we are engaged." She might also show Jamal more affection to convince him that he is the one she loves.

Avoidance/Evasion. This strategy, which has also been called "silence," involves efforts to avoid discussing the transgression. Transgressors who use this strategy often report that talking about the problem only makes it worse and it is better to let the transgression fade into the background of the relationship and be minimized (Aune et al., 1998). Transgressors using this strategy might also refuse to give an explanation for their behaviors. If avoidance/evasion is used after an apology and forgiveness has been granted, it may be effective. But if avoidance/evasion is the primary strategy used, the problem might be left unresolved and could resurface in the future. Because relational transgressions often lead to relational change, which sometimes includes the altering of rules and boundaries, avoidance/evasion may not be a particularly effective strategy in the long run. Indeed, Mongeau et al. (1994) found that avoidance (or silence) was an ineffective strategy for repairing relationships after infidelity had occurred.

Relationship Talk. This strategy involves talking about the transgression within the larger context of the relationship. Aune et al. (1998) discussed two specific types of relationship talk. The first, which they called **relationship invocation**, involves expressing attitudes or beliefs about the relationship or using the qualities of the relationship as a backdrop for interpreting the transgression. For example, transgressors might say, "Our relationship is strong enough to survive this," or "I love you too much to lose you over something like this." In Tia's case, she might tell Jamal that their relationship is much better than Robert and hers ever was. The second type of relationship talk, **metatalk** (Aune et al., 1998), involves explicitly discussing the transgression's effect on the relationship. For instance, after conceding that she was wrong not to tell him about her lunch with Robert, Tia might say that she wants Jamal to trust her. This might lead Tia and Jamal into a discussion about rules of honesty in their relationship. They

might also discuss the future of their relationship and the type of marriage they want to have.

SUMMARY AND APPLICATION

In a perfect world, people would never hurt one another. But the world is full of imperfect people leading imperfect lives. Coping with relational transgressions and hurt feelings is a difficult challenge that many relational partners face. Sometimes, the damage from infidelity, deception, or other transgressions is too great, and the relationship ends. At other times, such as Fincham's kissing porcupines, people decide to draw back together despite the pain, hoping that they will not be "pricked" again.

So what advice can communication researchers give to people like Jamal, who are hurt because their partners engaged in relational transgressions? (At a minimum, Tia conceals the fact that she had lunch with Robert from Jamal. More seriously, she could be hiding an affair.) When coping with transgressions, it is important for partners to weigh the severity of the offense against how much they value the relationship. When a transgression destroys trust in a relationship, the relationship may not recover. However, many transgressions can be repaired by renegotiating the rules and boundaries of the relationship or by offering apologies and explanations for one's actions. For example, open discussion might reaffirm to Jamal that Tia is completely committed to him. Jamal may also learn that she concealed her lunch with Robert to protect him from hurt feelings. For her part, Tia might learn not to conceal such information from Jamal in the future. She might also apologize for not telling Jamal about her lunch with Robert, and she might use appeasement strategies and relationship invocation to show Jamal how much he and their relationship mean to her.

If Jamal continues to feel jealous, he should use integrative communication and negative affect expression rather than destructive responses such as distributive communication and violent behavior. He should also appraise the situation to determine the level of threat that Robert actually poses. Perhaps he is overreacting and should trust Tia rather than continuing to be suspicious. Or, perhaps, he has real reason to be jealous. In either case, it is important for people to remember that romantic jealousy can stem from a real or imagined (or sometimes exaggerated) relationship between a loved person and a rival.

If Jamal decides to forgive Tia for deceiving him, research suggests that he tell her explicitly, "I forgive you." If he regards her transgression as serious, he might add that it is important that she is honest with him when similar situations arise in the future. If the relationship is to be repaired, Jamal needs to move from feeling a need to retaliate against or avoid Tia, to using positive, conciliatory forms of communication. A transgression can be a bump in the relationship road or a detour sign; it depends on the seriousness of the offense, the strategies used to cope with the problem, and the willingness or unwillingness of the victim to forgive the transgressor.

DISCUSSION QUESTIONS

1. If your long-time relational partner were unfaithful, do you think you would leave your partner or try to work things out? If you think that "it depends," what does it depend on? Do you think men and women are socialized to react differently to sexual infidelity? Is there still a "sexual double standard" when it comes to infidelity?

2. Think about the last time you or someone you know was jealous. Which of the communicative responses to jealousy did you or the person you know use? Did these responses make the situation better or worse?

3. Under what circumstances, if any, do you think it is okay to deceive a friend or relational partner? When would you feel betrayed if your friend or partner deceived you?

14

COPING WITH CONFLICT

When Relational Partners Disagree

Mary and Doug catch their teenage daughter, Amanda, smoking after school with her friends. Because Mary is convinced that Amanda's friends are a bad influence on her, she wants to ground Amanda for a month, making her come home immediately after school. Doug, however, thinks grounding will be more of a punishment for the parents than Amanda, because she will be moping around the house complaining all the time and arguing with her twin sister, Megan. Instead, he proposes that they deduct the cost of a carton of cigarettes from Amanda's weekly allowance for the next 6 months. Mary objects, saying that she does not want Amanda to be motivated to change her behavior because of money. Each parent feels strongly that his or her punishment is the best, leading to a disagreement.

If you were Amanda's parent, how would you want to handle this situation? From Amanda's perspective, which punishment would be most likely to be effective? Are there other types of punishment—besides grounding or reducing Amanda's allowance—that might actually be more effective? What conflict styles might Mary and Doug use to deal with this situation, and are there any conflict behaviors that are especially destructive? The literature on interpersonal conflict demonstrates that people have a variety of options for dealing with conflict. Some of these options involve cooperating and managing conflict productively and effectively. Other options lead to distress, competition, and sometimes exacerbation of the problem.

In this chapter, we examine how relational partners cope with disagreement. First, we define conflict and discuss the role conflict plays in close relationships, including those between spouses, family members, friends, and romantic partners. Next, we turn our attention to how people communicate during conflict situations. We review six conflict styles—competitive fighting, compromise, collaboration, indirect fighting, avoiding, and yielding. We also discuss patterns of communication, such as negative reciprocity and demand-withdrawal sequences. The chapter ends with practical rules for constructive conflict management.

CONFLICT IN RELATIONSHIPS

Think about all the positive and negative experiences you have had with close friends, family members, and romantic partners. As you reflect on these experiences, can you think of a close relationship that has not included some conflict or disagreement? If you can, that relationship is the exception to the rule. Argyle and Furnham (1983) demonstrated that conflict is most likely to occur in the context of close relationships. In their study, people rated different relationships in terms of how much conflict participants had and how emotionally close and connected they were. Spouses reported the most closeness but also the most conflict. Family relationships, including between parents and children or siblings, were also high in both conflict and closeness. Conversely, relationships between neighbors were low in both conflict and closeness. Lloyd and Cate (1985) found that conflict increased as relational partners became more committed and interdependent. These studies make an important point: Conflict is a normal part of many close relationships.

Defining Conflict

When people think about "conflict" in their relationships, they imagine angry voices, name-calling, and relationship problems. However, people can engage in conflict by using positive forms of communication during disagreements, such as collaboration and compromise. Voices can be calm, positions can be validated, and relationships can be strengthened instead of weakened. Most scholars define **conflict** broadly as disagreement between two interdependent people who perceive that they have incompatible goals (Cahn, 1992; Hocker & Wilmot, 1998). Because the people are interdependent, lack of compatibility can interfere with each person's ability to reach personal goals. Of course, some forms of incompatibility are more important than others. Hocker and Wilmot (1998) argued that incompatibility will likely lead to a struggle when rewards are scarce. In short, conflict is most likely when incompatible goals are important to both people and hard for both people to obtain. Across the life span, conflict is more likely to occur within family and romantic relationships than friendships or work relationships (Sillars, Canary, & Tafoya, 2004). Next, we review research on conflict in four types of relationships: parent-child, sibling, friendship, and romantic.

Conflict in Parent-Child Relationships

For young children, conflict with parents is part of the learning process (Canary, Cupach, & Messman, 1995). Children develop social skills by learning appropriate ways to express disagreement, such as not raising their voices and asking politely. Conflict between parents and young children occurs frequently. One study showed that disputes between mothers and their 18- to 36-month-old children occurred around seven times per hour, with about half these disputes being brief and the other half lasting longer and being more competitive (Dunn & Munn, 1987). Disputes were most common with 2-year-olds, supporting the common belief that parents have to deal with more conflict when their children hit the "terrible twos."

Conflict between parents and children often revolves around issues of control, with the parent trying to assert authority and the child trying to assert independence. A study by Eisenberg (1992) showed that parents and young children typically argue about five issues: possession and rights (such as having to share a toy with a sibling or wanting to stay up late), caretaking (such as having to take a bath), hurtful behavior (such as not calling a sibling names), rules and manners (such as being polite and not talking back to one's parents), and assistance (such as demanding to be helped or left alone). In adolescence, conflict often intensifies as teenagers try to break free from parental control. Canary et al. (1995) discussed research suggesting that around 20% of parents and adolescents complain that they have too much conflict with one another. Adolescents and their parents argue most frequently about issues such as curfews, friends, dating patterns, privacy, and other lifestyle choices. When children reach late adolescence and early adulthood, conflict typically declines (Paikoff & Brooks-Gunn, 1991).

Conflict in Sibling Relationships

Like conflict between parents and children, conflict between siblings is often intense during early childhood and adolescence (Arliss, 1993). Same-sex siblings of about the same age are particularly likely to engage in frequent, competitive fighting. Many sibling relationships are characterized by emotional highs and lows, as well as cyclic patterns of friendly versus aggressive behavior (e.g., Stillwell & Dunn, 1985). Sibling relationships also tend to involve violence. Around 36% of siblings report engaging in acts of moderately severe violence, such as kicking and hitting with objects. Even more siblings (around 64%) report that they have engaged in less severe forms of violence, such as shoving and pushing (Straus & Gelles, 1990). Yet siblings also share a unique bond. They usually know each other most of their lives; the sibling relationship predates romantic relationships and typically outlives parent-child relationships. Many siblings not only survive stormy periods of conflict but also develop a close and special bond as adults.

Preschool-age siblings tend to argue over objects, such as toys and food, and privileges, such as who gets to choose which movie they will watch. As siblings reach elementary school, conflict over objects decreases, although arguments over possessions, such as clothing and DVDs, as well as space, still occur (Arliss, 1993). Not surprisingly, siblings who have to share space (such as a bedroom) have conflict more frequently than those with separate, private spaces. Studies on sibling conflict during the school-age years suggest that siblings compete for many resources but primarily for parental attention (Dunn, 1983). Privacy issues, such as having one's own territory and personal space, can be sources of contention for siblings when they reach their teens (Dunn & Kendrick, 1982). During adolescence, siblings have almost as much conflict with each other as with their parents. Adolescent siblings are also unlikely to compromise with one another. Instead, sibling conflict often ends in a standoff or in intervention by another family member or friend (Laursen & Collins, 1994).

Conflict in Friendships

Like siblings, preschool-age friends tend to argue about objects and possessions (Canary et al., 1995). By elementary school, however, friends tend to conflict over social conduct and norm violations. For example, Shantz (1993) found that conflict between 7-year-olds often started when one child teased the other, called the other names, or physically harmed

the other. In addition, conflict was often instigated when one child violated the rules of the friendship, such as not inviting a classmate to a birthday party. Some children in Shantz's study also reported conflict over facts and opinions, such as whose dad is stronger. Conflict between adolescent friends is more sophisticated. Common conflict issues include friendship violations, norms for sexual behavior, differences in opinions, teasing/criticism, and annoying behavior (Canary et al., 1995; Laursen, 1989).

Conflict between adult friends tends to be less severe and less protracted than conflict between family members or romantic partners (Sillars et al., 2004). Unlike romantic partners, who report experiencing high levels of both conflict and relational satisfaction, good friends typically report more satisfaction than conflict (Argyle & Furnham, 1983; Dykstra, 1990). Same-sex friends tend to have the most conflict when they are competing with each other over jobs, promotions, other friends, and dating partners, whereas cross-sex friends tend to have the most conflict over issues related to personal problems (Argyle & Furnham, 1983; Fehr, 1996). The most severe conflicts in friendships appear to revolve around acts of betrayal, such as violating confidences or deceiving a friend.

Conflict in Romantic Relationships

Disagreement appears to be common in romantic relationships. Most romantic couples have between 1 and 3 disagreements per week, with 1 or 2 disagreements per month being particularly unpleasant (Canary et al., 1995). Unhappy couples often experience much more conflict; one study found that distressed couples reported having 5.4 conflicts over a 5-day period (see Canary et al., 1995). Although most couples manage conflict without resorting to violent behavior, some disagreements escalate into violence. Research suggests that about 16% of married couples, 35% of cohabiting couples, and 30% of dating couples can recall at least one incidence of interpersonal violence in their relationship over the past year (Christopher & Lloyd, 2000). The most common types of interpersonal violence include pushing or shoving one's partner, forcefully grabbing one's partner, and shaking or handling one's partner roughly (Marshall, 1994).

SOURCE: iStockphoto.com

Photo 14.1   Violence is always unacceptable. Research suggests that people sometimes resort to violent behavior when they lack the interpersonal skills necessary to solve relational problems.

What do romantic couples argue about? The most serious disagreements reported by married and cohabiting couples tend to be over the fair division of household labor, jealousy and possessiveness, sex, work, money and possessions, social networks (including in-laws), and children (Blumstein & Schwartz, 1983; Gottman, 1994; Mead, Vatcher, Wyne, & Roberts, 1990). Although these are issues that commonly cause conflict in romantic relationships, they represent only a small piece of the pie when it comes to the topics about which couples disagree.

Rather than organizing conflict issues by topic, Braiker and Kelley (1979) discussed four levels of conflict. First, couples argue about **concrete behaviors**, such as whether to roll up the toothpaste container or how to properly clean the kitchen. Second, couples argue about **relational rules and norms**, such as forgetting a birthday or working late without informing the partner. Third, couples argue about **personality traits**. Perhaps Mary thinks Doug is being

selfish because he doesn't want to suffer if Amanda is at home whining and moping because she is grounded. Doug, on the other hand, might think Mary is old-fashioned in her approach to discipline. Finally, couples argue about the process of conflict itself, which can be termed **metaconflict**. People might accuse their partner of pouting, nagging, throwing a temper tantrum, not listening to them, fighting unfairly, and so forth. Because you are reading this book and learning about how to engage in constructive conflict, you might be at particular risk of using metaconflict. Keep in mind that if you start telling your partner how he or she *should* be acting during an argument, your partner may resent your advice!

Effects of Conflict on Relationships

Conflict that is accompanied by hostile communication, such as yelling, name-calling, sarcastic comments, and pointedly ignoring the partner, has a negative impact on relationships. Caughlin and Vangelisti (2006) summarized a substantial body of research showing that negative conflict is associated with relational dissatisfaction. Couples who argue frequently and in an aggressive manner also report less relational stability and reduced commitment (Knee, Patrick, Vietor, & Neighbors, 2004; McGonagle, Kessler, & Schilling, 1992).

Marital conflict can have harmful effects on children as well as spouses. Children who witness their parents engaging in frequent, aggressive conflict are more likely to have trouble interacting with their peers and performing at their full potential in school (Buehler et al., 1997; Sillars et al., 2004). Research on the **spillover effect** suggests that these negative effects arise because parents who engage in dysfunctional conflict are also likely to have dysfunctional parenting styles (Davies & Cummings, 1994). A **socialization effect** is also likely to occur, with children adopting conflict styles similar to their parents' conflict styles (Koerner & Fitzpatrick, 2002; Reese-Weber & Bartle-Haring, 1998). A study by Kitzmann and Cohen (2003) examined several aspects of interparental conflict: frequency (how often parents argue in front of them), intensity (how mad parents get when they argue with each other), perceived threat (how scared children get when their parents argue), and resolution (how long parents stay mad at each other beyond the actual argument). Their results showed that children in Grades 3 through 6 were less likely to report having a high-quality relationship with a best friend if their parents had trouble resolving their conflicts. Frequency, intensity, and threat were less predictive of poor friendship quality than resolution, underscoring how important it is for parents to manage conflict rather than holding grudges and remaining angry. Studies have also shown that children actually fare better when feuding parents divorce than when they stay together and engage in increasingly negative patterns of conflict communication (Caughlin & Vangelisti, 2006).

Despite these negative effects, conflict can be beneficial when it is managed productively. Gottman's (1979, 1994) research suggests that satisfied couples are more likely to discuss issues of disagreement, whereas dissatisfied couples are more likely to minimize or avoid conflict. By confronting issues of disagreement, relational partners can manage their differences in ways that enhance closeness and relational stability (Braiker & Kelley, 1979; Canary et al., 1995; Lloyd & Cate, 1985). A study by Siegert and Stamp (1994) that examined the effects of a couple's "first big fight" also underscores the important role that conflict can play in relationship development. Partners who stayed together after the fight gained a greater understanding of their feelings for each other, felt that they could solve problems together, and were confident that they would both be willing to make sacrifices for each other. In contrast, partners who broke up after the fight reported feeling confused or uncertain about their relationship. During the fight, many people discovered negative information about their partners, and many felt that future interactions would be tense and uncomfortable. More than anything, however, the way partners perceived and handled conflict predicted whether their first big fight would signal the end of their relationship or a new beginning. The way partners manage conflict is a better predictor of relational satisfaction than is the experience of conflict itself. Being able to resolve conflict so that both parties are satisfied with the outcome is also predictive of relational satisfaction (Cramer, 2002).

CONFLICT STYLES

Considerable research has focused on the strategies or styles that people use to deal with conflict in organizations (Blake & Mouton, 1964; Putnam & Wilson, 1982; Rahim, 1986; Rahim & Bonoma, 1979) and in relationships between friends, lovers, and roommates (Fitzpatrick & Winke, 1979; Klein & Johnson, 1997; Sillars, 1980; Sillars et al., 2004). Research in both of these areas suggests that conflict styles can be distinguished by two dimensions: cooperation and directness (Rahim, 1986; Sillars et al., 2004). Cooperative conflict takes the goals of both partners into account, whereas uncooperative conflict focuses on one person trying to win the argument. Direct conflict involves engaging in conflict and talking about issues, whereas indirect conflict involves avoiding discussion of conflict issues. Researchers have developed several typologies of conflict styles based on these dimensions, with some scholars identifying three styles (e.g., Sillars, 1980; Putman & Wilson, 1982), other scholars identifying four styles (e.g., Klein & Johnson, 1997; Sillars et al., 2004), and still other scholars identifying five styles (e.g., Blake & Mouton, 1964; Rahim, 1986). A review of the strategies in these typologies suggests that there are six styles of conflict: competitive fighting, compromising, collaborating, indirect fighting, avoiding, and yielding (see Figure 14.1). To determine your own conflict style, complete the scale in Box 14.1.

Competitive Fighting

Competitive fighting is characterized by an uncooperative orientation and a direct style of communication (Blake & Mouton, 1964). This style has also been called direct (Sillars et al., 2004), distributive (Sillars, 1980), dominating (Rahim, 1986), controlling (Putnam & Wilson, 1982), and contentious (Klein & Johnson, 1997; Pruitt & Carnevale, 1993). As these labels suggest, people with a competing style try to control the interaction so that they have more power than their partner. They attempt to achieve a win-lose situation, wherein they win and their partner loses. In their attempts to achieve dominance, individuals who engage in competing strategies use the following types of tactics: confrontational remarks, accusations, personal criticisms, threats, name-calling, blaming the partner, sarcasm, and hostile jokes (Sillars et al., 2004).

Imagine that Mary and Doug both use competitive fighting when trying to determine how to punish Amanda. They might cling stubbornly to their own perspectives, with each arguing that her or his method is superior to the other partner's. Mary might accuse Doug of being too selfish to put up with Amanda being at home all the time because she is grounded, and Doug might claim that Mary's past attempts at grounding Amanda have been unsuccessful and that "everyone knows" she is too lenient. The conflict could very well escalate, with Mary and Doug yelling at each other and calling each other names. Even if one of them eventually yields, the desired win-lose outcome likely will be only temporary (Kilmann & Thomas, 1977). In the long run, Mary and Doug's relationship could be harmed, leading to a lose-lose situation for both.

As this example illustrates, the competing strategy is usually associated with poor communication competence and reduced relational satisfaction (Canary & Spitzberg, 1987, 1989, 1990; Gross & Guerrero, 2000; Sillars, 1980). People who use competing strategies are typically ineffective in meeting their goals and inappropriate in their treatment of their partner. There are exceptions to this, however. In relationships where a power differential exists, such as those between managers and employees or between parents and children, strategies related to competitive fighting are sometimes effective. For instance, if a father wants to prevent his son from engaging in dangerous behavior, he might force him to stay home while his friends attend a rowdy party. The competing strategy is often useful when immediate compliance is necessary (Hocker & Wilmot, 1998). The competing strategy may also be useful

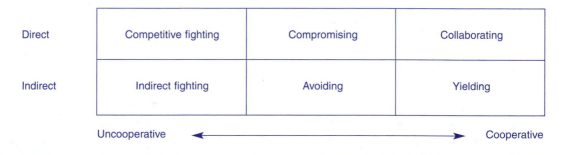

Direct	Competitive fighting	Compromising	Collaborating
Indirect	Indirect fighting	Avoiding	Yielding

Uncooperative ⟵———————⟶ Cooperative

Figure 14.1 Interpersonal Conflict Styles

▨ BOX 14.1   Put Yourself to the Test

What Is Your Conflict Style?

Think about the last few times you and a relational partner disagreed. How did you behave? Use the following scale to determine your typical conflict style: 1 = Disagree strongly, 7 = Agree strongly.

	Disagree ⟵				⟶ Agree		
1. I discuss the problem to try to reach a mutual understanding.	1	2	3	4	5	6	7
2. I keep arguing until I prove my point.	1	2	3	4	5	6	7
3. I show my partner that I am angry or upset without saying a word.	1	2	3	4	5	6	7
4. I sometimes sacrifice my own goals so my partner can meet her or his goals.	1	2	3	4	5	6	7
5. I try to find a new solution that will satisfy all our needs.	1	2	3	4	5	6	7
6. I usually try to win arguments.	1	2	3	4	5	6	7
7. I do not like to talk about issues of disagreement.	1	2	3	4	5	6	7
8. I am willing to give up some of my goals in exchange for achieving other goals.	1	2	3	4	5	6	7
9. I try to get my concerns and my partner's concerns all out in the open.	1	2	3	4	5	6	7
10. I try to get back at my partner by giving the silent treatment or holding a grudge.	1	2	3	4	5	6	7
11. I usually try to forget about issues of disagreement so I don't have to confront my partner.	1	2	3	4	5	6	7
12. I try to think of a solution that satisfies some needs of us both.	1	2	3	4	5	6	7
13. Sometimes I find myself attacking my partner.	1	2	3	4	5	6	7
14. I use facial expressions to let my partner know I am angry or upset.	1	2	3	4	5	6	7
15. It is important to get both our points of view out in the open.	1	2	3	4	5	6	7
16. Sometimes I criticize my partner to show that he or she is wrong.	1	2	3	4	5	6	7
17. I try to meet my partner halfway.	1	2	3	4	5	6	7
18. If the issue is very important to my partner, I usually give in.	1	2	3	4	5	6	7
19. I attempt to work with my partner to find a creative solution we both like.	1	2	3	4	5	6	7

	Disagree ←————————→ Agree

20. I tend to show negative feelings with facial expressions rather than talking about how I feel.	1	2	3	4	5	6	7
21. I usually let my partner take responsibility for bringing up conflict issues.	1	2	3	4	5	6	7
22. I would rather not get into a discussion of unpleasant issues.	1	2	3	4	5	6	7
23. I give in to my partner to keep my relationship satisfying.	1	2	3	4	5	6	7
24. I try to make my partner see things my way.	1	2	3	4	5	6	7
25. I avoid bringing up certain issues if my arguments might hurt my partner's feelings.	1	2	3	4	5	6	7
26. I might agree with some of my partner's points to make my partner happy.	1	2	3	4	5	6	7
27. I am likely to give my partner cold or dirty looks as a way of expressing disagreement.	1	2	3	4	5	6	7
28. I avoid talking with my partner about disagreements.	1	2	3	4	5	6	7
29. I try to find a "middle ground" position that is acceptable to both of us.	1	2	3	4	5	6	7
30. I believe that you have to "give a little to get a little" during a disagreement.	1	2	3	4	5	6	7

To obtain your results, add your scores for the following items:

4, 18, 23, 25, 26	(Yielding)	_____
7, 11, 21, 22, 28	(Avoiding)	_____
1, 5, 9, 15, 19	(Collaborating)	_____
2, 6, 13, 16, 24	(Competitive fighting)	_____
8, 12, 17, 29, 30	(Compromising)	_____
3, 10, 14, 20, 27	(Indirect fighting)	_____

Higher scores indicate that you possess more of a particular conflict style.

when it is important to deal with a particular conflict issue. For instance, if one partner does not want to talk about a critical problem (such as how to deal with the financial fallout of the wife being laid off from her job), the other partner may engage in competing behaviors to force the partner to confront the issue. In other cases (such as finding out one's partner flirted with an ex-lover all night at a party), people may be justified in expressing anger or leveling accusations at their partners. Usually, however, competitive fighting leads to an escalation of conflict and harms relationships, especially if such fighting is not counterbalanced by positive communication (Canary & Lakey, 2006).

Collaborating

The collaborating style involves having a cooperative orientation and using direct communication (Blake & Mouton, 1964). Collaboration also involves considering one another's goals and opinions. This style has been called integrating (Rahim, 1986; Sillars, 1980), solution oriented (Putnam & Wilson, 1982), problem solving (Klein & Johnson, 1997; Pruitt & Carnevale, 1993), and negotiation (Sillars et al., 2004). As these labels suggest, the collaborating style focuses on cooperative problem solving that leads to a win-win situation. Collaboration involves trying to find creative solutions to problems that incorporate the needs of both partners. This style opens lines of communication, increases information seeking and sharing, and helps maintain relationships for future interaction (Hocker & Wilmot, 1998). Specific tactics associated with the collaborating style include expressing agreement, making descriptive or disclosive statements, being supportive, accepting responsibility, brainstorming ideas, and soliciting the partner's opinions (Sillars et al., 2004).

So how might Mary and Doug use a collaborating style? A starting point would be to share their concerns and search for a creative way to teach Amanda about the dangers of smoking. By using collaborative tactics, Doug might discover that Mary's main motivation is to keep Amanda away from the "bad" crowd she has been spending time with lately. Mary might discover that Doug's main objection to grounding is that it will not teach Amanda anything about the negative consequences of smoking. Doug might also realize that reducing Amanda's allowance by the cost of several cartons of cigarettes will only teach Amanda about the monetary cost of smoking, not the health risks. They might agree that it would be better if they required Amanda to volunteer some time after school at the local hospital, where she can help patients with lung cancer. Such a disciplinary action will keep Amanda away from her new friends (meeting Mary's needs) while also teaching her about the risks associated with smoking (meeting Doug's needs). In fact, this new solution might address each of their concerns better than their original plans would have.

As you would expect, the collaborating style is evaluated as effective and appropriate in managing conflict (Canary & Spitzberg, 1987, 1989, 1990; Gross & Guerrero, 2000; Gross, Guerrero & Alberts, 2004). Couples who use collaborating styles and show positive affect during conflict are likely to be happier, and children benefit from having parents who use this conflict style (Caughlin & Vangelisti, 2006; Koerner & Fitzpatrick, 2006). Collaboration is related to perceptions of competence and relational satisfaction because it gives each individual access to the partner's views of incompatible goals, which allows disputants to reach an understanding and to co-construct meaning. When such understanding occurs, problems can be defined, and a solution that integrates the goals and needs of both parties can be reached (Tutzauer & Roloff, 1988).

Compromising

Like the competing and collaborating styles, the compromising style involves direct communication between partners. The compromising style is also moderately cooperative (Blake & Mouton, 1964; Kilmann & Thomas, 1977; Rahim, 1986). Compromise involves searching for a fair, intermediate position that satisfies some of both partners' needs. There is a key difference between collaboration and compromise. With collaboration, the solution is especially satisfactory because both people have met all their goals. With compromise, people need to give something up to reach a solution that will meet at least some of their goals and desires. Thus, compromise usually leads to a part-win/part-lose situation. Indeed, people who compromise talk about "splitting the difference" and "meeting the partner halfway." According to Hocker and Wilmot (1998), compromising behaviors include appealing to fairness, suggesting a trade-off, maximizing wins while minimizing losses, and offering a quick, short-term resolution to the conflict at hand.

Suppose that Mary and Doug are unable to come up with a better solution than either of them originally proposed. Maybe there is no hospital in their area. Or perhaps their goals are so radically different that a viable solution that will satisfy both their needs does not exist. In this case, compromise would be a good choice. They could decide to ground Amanda for 2 weeks instead of a month and deduct cigarette money from her allowance for 3 months instead of 6. This way, Mary and Doug both get to administer the punishment they perceive to be appropriate, but neither applies the punishment for the length of time they originally proposed. In short, they get to keep something, but they also have to give up something. Notice that compromising usually involves modifying preexisting solutions, whereas collaborating involves creating new solutions.

Research suggests that the compromising style is generally perceived to be moderately appropriate and effective (Gross & Guerrero, 2000). Although this style is not as effective or appropriate as collaborating, there are situations in which compromising is best. Suppose a couple is arguing over whom to ask to be godparents for their son. The husband wants his sister and brother to be godparents, while the wife prefers her favorite aunt and uncle. Assuming their son can only have two official godparents, the couple might decide to put names in a hat, with one slip of paper appointing the aunt and brother as godparents and the other designating the sister and uncle. Such a compromise is likely to be seen as fair by all parties. As Hocker and Wilmot (1998) stated, most people perceive compromising to be a reasonable, fair, and efficient strategy for managing conflict, even though it requires some sacrifice and hampers the development of creative alternatives. When a compromise is seen as unfair, it can lead to dissatisfaction. In one study, violent couples actually used more compromise than satisfied couples (Morrison, Van Hasselt, & Bellack, 1987). Thus, although compromise is usually a moderately effective conflict strategy, if couples have to compromise too often, they may feel that their needs are not being met and that their problems are never truly resolved.

Yielding

The yielding style is cooperative and indirect (Klein & Johnson, 1997; Pruitt & Carnevale, 1993; Sillars, 1980). People who use this style forgo their own goals and desires in consideration of the partner's (Kilmann & Thomas, 1977). This style has been labeled obliging (Rahim, 1986) and accommodating (Blake & Mouton, 1964). Papa and Canary (1995) noted that this type of response is adequate and comfortable; it does not cause further disagreement or escalations in conflict. However, the yielding style involves glossing over differences, playing down disagreements, and trivializing conflict, all of which make effective conflict management difficult. Hocker and Wilmot (1998) described several specific yielding tactics, including putting aside one's own needs to please the partner, passively accepting the decisions the partner makes, and making conciliatory statements.

Mary or Doug might engage in any or all of these tactics as part of a yielding response. Suppose Doug decides to give in to Mary and grounds Amanda. He might tell Mary that she is right, that he'll just have to deal with having Amanda at home, that he loves his family and hopes it all works out. Doug may yield for many different reasons. Perhaps he really does believe that Mary knows best when it comes to disciplining Amanda. Or perhaps he decides that it is not worth arguing over and he will simply let Mary have her way. Yet another possibility is that he feels threatened or coerced. In their research on **the chilling effect**, Cloven and Roloff (1993) found that people are likely to avoid voicing their opinions and complaints when they feel powerless or fear that their partner will act aggressively toward them (see also Chapter 12).

Yielding occurs for many different reasons, so it can be perceived as both competent and incompetent (Gross & Guerrero, 2000). Yielding behavior is cooperative and appropriate when one person feels strongly about an issue and the other person does not. In such cases, it is appropriate for the person who feels less strongly to give in to the partner's wishes. Yielding may also be an appropriate strategy when two people cannot agree but a decision needs to be made. For instance, if Mary and Doug are arguing over who is going to pick Amanda up after a party (each believes it is the other's turn), one of them might give in so that Amanda will have a safe ride home.

However, most research suggests that although the yielding style is sometimes appreciated by one's partner, it is generally ineffective (Gross & Guerrero, 2000; Papa & Canary, 1995). People who use the yielding style are unlikely to achieve their personal goals, which could strain their relationship. According to Hocker and Wilmot (1998), repeatedly yielding puts a person in a powerless position. Perhaps this is why people seldom report yielding when the conflict issue is important to them. Sillars (1980) examined how often roommates reported using yielding strategies. He had students recall the disagreements they had with their roommates and describe how they and their roommates communicated about the significant ones. Only 2% of the students reported using yielding strategies during their most significant disagreement with a roommate. In contrast, 33% of students perceived their roommates to have yielded during these same disagreements. Why the discrepancy? Sillars suggested that the students did not report yielding often because they were reporting on a disagreement that was significant to them. Their roommates, conversely, may not have seen these disagreements as significant and so were more willing to concede the issue. This finding suggests that yielding is more common when people do not care much about an issue.

Avoiding

Like accommodation (a cooperative strategy) and indirect fighting (an uncooperative strategy), avoiding is an indirect style of conflict. We regard avoiding as somewhat neutral in terms of how cooperative versus uncooperative it is. This style has also been called inaction (Klein & Johnson, 1997; Pruitt & Carnevale, 1993) and nonconfrontation (Putnam & Wilson, 1982). When using the avoiding style, people refrain from arguing and refuse to confront their partners in any meaningful way. Avoiding tactics appear to be fairly common. Studies have shown that roommates frequently report using the avoiding style in their conflicts (Sillars, 1980), and 63% of college students report withholding at least one complaint from their dating partners (Roloff & Cloven, 1990). People who use the avoiding strategy engage in tactics such as denying the conflict, being indirect and evasive, changing and/or avoiding topics, acting as if they don't care, making irrelevant remarks, and joking to avoid dealing with the conflict (Hocker & Wilmot, 1998).

Imagine that Mary and Doug deal with their disagreement through avoidance. Neither of them wants to confront the issue, so they avoid talking about how best to handle the situation with Amanda. Perhaps they both punish Amanda in their own way, without consulting the other, making Amanda suffer two punishments instead of one. Or perhaps they both decide not to do anything, letting Amanda "off the hook" for smoking. Either way, the use of avoidance would lead to a lose-lose situation, with little being accomplished. Consistent with this example, several studies have shown that the avoiding style is evaluated as inappropriate and ineffective (Canary & Spitzberg, 1987, 1989, 1990; Gross et al., 2004; Gross & Guerrero, 2000).

Occasionally, avoidance may be beneficial. Roloff and Ifert (2000) described five conditions that likely influence whether avoidance has a positive or a negative effect on relationships. First, avoidance may be an effective strategy for certain types of couples. Couples who find it difficult to engage in conflict without resorting to aggression may find avoidance preferable to engagement. Second, avoidance is more acceptable when it is accompanied by expressions of positive affect. So if Doug says, "I'm too tired to talk about this anymore, honey," in a warm voice and with a genuine smile, Mary might empathize with him rather than feeling dismissed. Third, people are most likely to respond positively to avoidance when the topic is of little importance to both people. As Hocker and Wilmot (1998) noted, the avoidant style can be used to acknowledge that a relationship is more important than a particular issue (Hocker & Wilmot, 1998).

Fourth, individuals are more likely to find avoidance acceptable if it is their decision to avoid discussion about a particular topic. When people feel their partners are pressuring them to keep quiet about relational issues that are bothering them, avoidance may have an especially harmful effect on the relationship. Finally, when people are socially skilled communicators, they may be able to recognize when avoidance is appropriate versus inappropriate. For example, imagine that Doug is staunchly conservative and Mary is extremely liberal. If they are socially skilled, they might be flexible enough to "agree to disagree" when it comes to political issues but to confront conflict issues revolving around Amanda and her twin sister, Megan.

Indirect Fighting

Sillars and his colleagues (2004) used the term *indirect fighting* to refer to conflict behaviors that are indirect and uncooperative. These behaviors have also been called passive aggression (Guerrero & La Valley, 2006) and active distancing (Bachman & Guerrero, 2006a) and are related to patterns of negative withdrawal (Gottman, 1994). Examples of indirect fighting include failing to acknowledge or validate the partner's concerns, ignoring the partner, holding a grudge, using a whiny voice, giving the partner cold or dirty looks, angrily leaving the scene, rolling one's eyes, and administering the silent treatment (Guerrero & La Valley, 2006; Sillars et al., 2004). Note that all these behaviors express aggression or disagreement in an indirect manner that could shut down discussion about the conflict issue.

For instance, rather than discussing optimal punishment in a calm manner that facilitates cooperation, Doug and Mary might show hostility through their use of indirect behaviors. Doug might try to explain his philosophy—that Amanda needs to learn there are consequences associated with smoking—in a condescending tone that makes Mary feel he is talking to her as if she is a child. Mary's response may be to sigh, roll her eyes, and cross her arms over her chest in a defensive manner. Doug might then complain, in a hostile voice, that Mary isn't even listening. Such tactics could result in one or both of the partners leaving the scene in frustration. Note that in this type of scenario, the indirect behaviors often provoke metaconflict, which we earlier defined as conflict about how people disagree. Mary might demand, "Stop talking to me as if I'm a child," and Doug might complain, "We never get anywhere because you don't listen to me." Metaconflict often sidetracks partners away from discussing the issue at hand—in this case, how best to teach Amanda a lesson about smoking.

Indirect fighting may be especially destructive when partners use these behaviors to avoid confronting problems (Sillars et al., 2004). Indirect fighting reflects a level of hostility that is not found in other indirect styles of conflict management. In comparison, yielding is much more cooperative, and avoiding is more neutral. Indirect fighting is related to many of the same negative outcomes as the competing style, including dissatisfaction with the relationship and a failure to resolve conflicts. However, indirect fighting may be even more detrimental to relationships than competitive fighting because it is an indirect strategy. At least, competitive fighting involves engaging in direct, verbal communication, which might bring important issues to the forefront. As you will learn later in this chapter, behaviors associated with indirect fighting, such as rolling one's eyes, sounding disgusted or fed up, and ignoring one's partner, have been identified as signs of unproductive conflict that can lead to relationship decline (Gottman, 1994). People who use indirect fighting are also perceived as less effective and socially appropriate than are those who use cooperative strategies (Guerrero & La Valley, 2006).

PATTERNS OF CONFLICT INTERACTION

Although people have a tendency to manage conflict in particular ways, many people use a variety of strategies depending on the situation and the type of conflict. Conflict strategies are not mutually exclusive. In other words, you can use more than one strategy during a single conflict interaction. For example, Doug and Mary may begin with the intention of communicating in a cooperative, direct manner but may then become increasingly competitive as they both stubbornly hang on to their original positions. They might also exhibit different conflict styles altogether. Perhaps Mary favors indirect fighting, whereas Doug prefers to yield. As these examples illustrate, understanding the various conflict styles in isolation does not give us a very good picture of how conflict interaction unfolds. This is why researchers have sought to understand common patterns of conflict within relationships. Next, we discuss four such patterns: negative reciprocity, the demand-withdrawal pattern, the four horsemen of the apocalypse, and patterns of accommodation.

Negative Reciprocity

Despite the fact that indirect fighting and competitive fighting usually have negative effects on relationships, people use these strategies more frequently than cooperative strategies (Canary et al., 1995; Sillars, 1980). This may be because of **the principle of negative reciprocity**, a pattern whereby aggression begets more aggression. Once one person uses competitive or indirect fighting, the other person is likely to follow suit. Hostile nonverbal behaviors tend to be reciprocated during conflict (Gottman, 1994; Krokoff, Gottman, & Roy, 1988). Relational partners also tend to reciprocate verbal communication such as complaints and criticisms. Alberts and her colleagues (Alberts, 1989; Alberts & Discoll, 1992) found that if a partner launches a complaint, the other partner is likely to fire back with a countercomplaint. Moreover, individuals in dissatisfying relationships were twice as likely as individuals in satisfying relationships to respond to complaints by denying the validity of the complaint or by escalating the hostility of the interaction (Alberts & Discoll, 1992). Patterns of negative reciprocity also distinguish couples who are dissatisfied and violent from those who are dissatisfied but nonviolent. Violent couples are most likely to engage in high levels of negative reciprocity and low levels of positive reciprocity (Smith, Vivian, & O'Leary, 1990).

In conflict interaction, negative reciprocity appears to be more common than positive reciprocity. In a classic study, Gaelick, Brodenshausen, and Wyer (1985) examined how perceptions of a partner's behavior influence patterns of reciprocity during conflict. They found that people enact positive behaviors when they perceive their partner is expressing affectionate emotions and negative behaviors when they perceive their partner is expressing hostile emotions. However, negative reciprocity was the main pattern for two reasons. First, people exhibit more negative than positive emotion in conflict situations. Second, and perhaps more important, people *perceived* that their partners were expressing hostility even when they were not. For instance, imagine that Mary offers her view using a neutral voice but Doug interprets her tone to be condescending. This could set off a chain of negativity, even though Mary's initial comment was not meant to be hostile.

Patterns of negative reciprocity can be set off by a variety of hostile behaviors, including sarcasm, personal criticism, name-calling, yelling, and unfair accusations. Three other tactics have been found to

be especially likely to divert attention away from the conflict issue while escalating negativity—gunnysacking, kitchen sinking, and bringing third parties into the argument. **Gunnysacking** occurs when people store up old grievances and then dump them on their partner during a conflict (Bach & Wyden, 1970). Rather than discussing each issue when it first surfaces, issues are placed in a metaphorical gunnysack and then all presented at once. **Kitchen sinking** is similar to gunnysacking. However, instead of storing up complaints, people rehash their old arguments when they get into a new argument (Bach & Wyden, 1970). Because gunnysacking and kitchen sinking involve multiple attacks, partners are likely to feel defensive and overwhelmed, making it difficult to discuss any of the issues productively.

Bringing third parties into an argument can also promote defensiveness. There are at least three ways in which people bring third parties into their arguments. First, people mention things that other people said as a form of evidence ("Your sister warned me that you can be really picky"). Such comments are particularly hurtful and hard for receivers to defend because they cannot immediately confront the person who supposedly made them. Second, people can bad-mouth the partner's friends or family by making comments such as "I guess your erratic behavior shouldn't surprise me—your whole family acts that way." Statements like these make people particularly defensive. Not only do they have to defend themselves, but they also have to defend their friends and/or family. Third, individuals compare their partner unfavorably with other people ("None of my other girlfriends ever complained about that"), which is an especially frustrating type of personal attack.

Couples who engage in patterns of negative reciprocity, such as joint gunnysacking and sequences of complaints followed by countercomplaints, report less relational satisfaction (Gottman, 1979). Dissatisfied couples also become increasingly hostile during the course of discussions about problems or conflict issues, while satisfied couples maintain a consistently lower level of hostility (Billings, 1979; Gottman & Levenson, 1992). This does not mean that couples in satisfying relationships never display negative reciprocity. On the contrary, research suggests that negative reciprocity is a fairly common pattern in conflict interaction. The difference lies in the percentage of behaviors that are negative versus positive. Gottman's (1994) research demonstrates that happy couples tend to engage in about five positive behaviors for every negative behavior, whereas the ratio of negative-to-positive behaviors is about 1:1 for unhappy couples.

The Demand-Withdrawal Pattern

Researchers have identified another common but dysfunctional conflict sequence called the **demand-withdrawal interaction pattern** (Gottman & Levenson, 1988; Sagrestano et al., 2006). This pattern occurs when one person uses demanding communication as a means of engaging in conflict, and the other person tries to avoid conflict by withdrawing. The person in the demanding position is likely to be in a less powerful position (relative to the partner) and tends to be dissatisfied with something. In contrast, the person in the withdrawing position is likely to be in a more powerful position and happy with the status quo. Married couples are more likely to engage in the demand-withdrawal pattern when one partner desires more closeness or involvement in the home and the other partner desires more autonomy (Sagrestano et al., 2006).

The demand-withdrawal pattern can move in both directions—increased demands can lead to more withdrawal, but increased withdrawal can also lead to more demands (Klinetob & Smith, 1996). In fact, couples who use the demand-withdrawal pattern may have problems of **punctuation** (Watzlawick et al., 1967), with each partner "punctuating" the cause of the conflict differently. One partner might say, "I have to nag you all the time because you always withdraw," whereas the other partner might say," I have to withdraw because you are always nagging me." Note that both partners blame the other for their behavior.

The demand-withdrawal pattern is most likely to occur when the conflict engager uses either competitive or indirect fighting. Engagers who use cooperative strategies are rarely perceived as demanding (Heavey et al., 1995). Because the demand-withdrawal pattern consists of uncooperative behavior, it is generally seen as a highly incompetent form of dyadic communication (Christensen & Shenk, 1991; Gottman & Levenson, 1988). Yet the effect this pattern of conflict communication has on relationships is not yet clear. Some studies have shown that couples characterized by the demand-withdrawal pattern are more likely to be dissatisfied with their relationships and, eventually, to break up. Yet other studies have shown that couples who use the demand-withdrawal sequence are likely to report increased relational satisfaction over time (Caughlin & Vangelisti, 2006). It may be that couples who break free from this sequence end up reporting more satisfaction because important changes were made in their relationships, whereas those who repeatedly follow this pattern become increasingly dissatisfied.

A more consistent finding is that women are more likely to do the demanding, whereas men are more likely to do the withdrawing (Caughlin & Vangelisti, 1999; Christensen & Shenk, 1991; Gottman, 1994; Heavey, Layne, & Christensen, 1993). Imagine the following scenario: Doug approaches Mary to discuss Amanda's punishment, but Mary tells him she does not want to talk about it anymore. Would this situation seem more believable if it were reversed—with Mary wanting to talk about the problem and Doug retreating? The research suggests that it would. However, this sex difference is reversed if the conflict involves something the man wants to change (Kluwer, de Dreu, & Buunk, 1998; Sagrestano, Heavey, & Christensen, 1998). For example, if Doug thinks it is unfair that he always ends up having to tell his daughters what their punishments are, he might be cast in the demanding role when he and Mary discuss who will tell Amanda that she must volunteer at the hospital. Women may be in the demanding role more often because they are more likely to want to institute change in their relationships. Finally, some evidence suggests that couples characterized by husband-to-wife violence are more likely than nonviolent couples to exhibit rigid patterns of husband demand and wife withdrawal (Caughlin & Vangelisti, 2006).

The Four Horsemen of the Apocalypse

Gottman's extensive research on the causes of divorce uncovered an especially destructive pattern of conflict, which he called the **four horsemen of**

the apocalypse. According to Gottman (1994), couples who divorce are more likely to exhibit a conflict pattern that includes the following four behaviors: (1) complaints/criticisms, (2) contempt/disgust, (3) defensiveness, and (4) stonewalling. Gottman proposed that the four horsemen of the apocalypse form a "cascade" or sequence, with complaining and criticizing leading to contempt, "which leads to defensiveness, which leads to listener withdrawal from interaction" (p. 110); Figure 14.2 depicts this process. For unhappy couples, the most common pattern is as follows: The wife's complaints are perceived as criticisms by the husband, then both husband and wife become contemptuous and defensive, followed by the husband stonewalling. Although this is the most common pattern in Gottman's work, this sequence can occur in various ways (e.g., the husband's complaint could start the process, and both husband and wife might end up stonewalling).

Complaints and Criticisms. The cascade starts when one person complains or criticizes. Gottman (1994) noted that some complaints can actually be healthy. If relational partners never complained, they would be unable to improve their relationships by changing problematic behavior. However, if complaints continue over long periods, if they turn into criticisms, or if they are perceived as criticisms, Gottman's research suggests, the partner will start to feel contempt.

There are at least five types of complaints (Alberts, 1988, 1989). The first and most common type of complaint is about **behavior**. For instance, Amanda might complain that her twin sister, Megan, is gloating because she got punished. This type of complaint focuses on the behavior rather than the person and is specific in terms of the kind of action a person has to take to remedy the problem—in this case Megan should stop gloating. The second most common type of complaint revolves around **personal characteristics** ("You are an inconsiderate and rude sister"). This type of complaint almost always constitutes a character attack and is likely to lead to negative reciprocity (Gottman, 1994). Third, people can complain about **performance**. In this case, they dislike the way something is done. For example, Amanda and Megan might complain that

Doug forgot to put oil in the pot when cooking spaghetti, leading the noodles to stick together. This type of complaint can be frustrating because it implies that someone is not doing something the proper way. (Indeed, Doug might respond by telling his daughters to cook themselves next time.) Fourth, people can complain about **personal appearance**. Alberts (1988) gave the following example of this type of complaint from her data: "You have a fat butt and better lose weight" (p. 188). Clearly, this kind of complaint is also a personal attack. Finally, people can make **metacomplaints**, which involve complaining about the partner's complaining behavior. For example, Doug might tell his daughter to "stop whining about the spaghetti and eat." Alberts (1988) found that satisfied couples were more likely than dissatisfied couples to use behavioral complaints. Dissatisfied couples, in contrast, were more likely to use personal characteristic complaints.

Contempt and Disgust. According to Gottman, when complaints are interpreted as criticism, they often lead to feelings of contempt and disgust, which are usually communicated to the partner. As Gottman (1994) put it, "Disgust typically is communicated by sounding fed up, sickened, and repulsed" (p. 25). For example, you might say, "I've had enough" or "I'm not going to take it anymore." When people who have been criticized feel disgust, they may be particularly prone to making both real and empty relational threats, such as threatening to leave the partner. Contempt is communicated in similarly negative ways. Gottman (1994) stated,

> Contempt is also easy to identify in speech. It involves any insult, mockery, or sarcasm or derision, of the person. It includes disapproval, judgment, derision, disdain, exasperation, mockery, put downs, or communicating that the other person is absurd or incompetent. Three types of contempt are hostile humor, mockery, or sarcasm. In this form of contempt, there may be derision, a put down, or cold hate. There is often a definite sense of distance, coldness, and detachment in this category of behavior. (p. 25)

Defensiveness. People become defensive when they feel a need to defend themselves and ward off personal attacks. Gottman listed several communicative

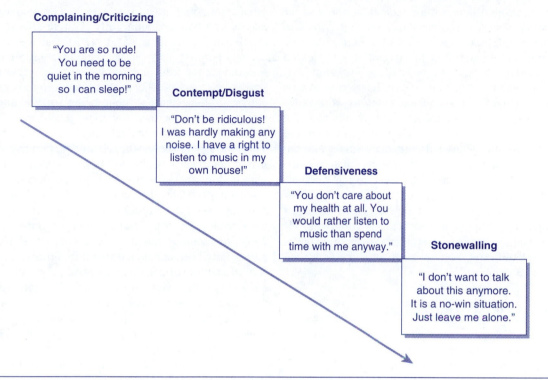

Complaining/Criticizing

"You are so rude! You need to be quiet in the morning so I can sleep!"

Contempt/Disgust

"Don't be ridiculous! I was hardly making any noise. I have a right to listen to music in my own house!"

Defensiveness

"You don't care about my health at all. You would rather listen to music than spend time with me anyway."

Stonewalling

"I don't want to talk about this anymore. It is a no-win situation. Just leave me alone."

Figure 14.2 Gottman's Cascade Process of Relational Dissolution: The Four Horsemen of the Apocalypse

behaviors related to defensiveness, including denying responsibility for a problem, issuing countercomplaints, whining, making accusations, and reading minds. According to Gottman (1994), when a person begins mind reading, it is a particularly good clue that he or she is becoming defensive.

Mind reading occurs when people assume that they know their partner's feelings, motives, and behaviors. Gottman (1994) gave the following examples to illustrate mind reading: "You don't care about how we live," "You get tense in situations like this one," and "You have to spend whatever we save" (p. 25). Gottman also noted that mind-reading statements often include words like "always" or "never." As such, mind reading violates two principles of fair fighting: (1) it often is based on jumping to conclusions and (2) it usually is based on overgeneralizations.

Mind reading is common in marital interaction, yet seldom accurate, and it usually escalates conflict (Gottman, 1994). Conversational data collected by Alberts and Driscoll (1992) on complaints illustrate this point. In the following example, Charles was upset because Cindy assumed that if he did a favor for her he would hold it against her in some way. He told her that he did not mind doing favors for her and would not expect anything in return. Eventually, Charles said to Cindy,

When you tell me what I was going to say, it's almost always wrong. I mean it's wrong, and it's infuriating and it drives me nuts. Like you really know me so well, that you know exactly what I'm going to say. And it's never ever true. It's never the correct answer. It's what you want to believe I'm going to decide. (p. 404)

Stonewalling. Stonewalling comes at the end of Gottman's cascade of negative conflict behavior. After people have been attacked, experienced contempt, and tried (often unsuccessfully) to defend themselves, they often stonewall, or withdraw from the interaction. At this point, interaction seems futile. Partners no longer are trying to work problems out, as disagreements escalate into negative conflict interactions, and both partners are hurt and defensive. As mentioned previously, however, men tend to stonewall more frequently than women (Gottman, 1994). This often leads to the demand-withdrawal cycle discussed earlier, with wives insisting on talking about problems and husbands refusing to engage in such a dialogue. If stonewalling persists, Gottman's research suggests that relationships become stagnant and couples are likely to break up.

Patterns of Accommodation

The conflict patterns we have discussed so far tend to increase negativity or avoidance rather than promoting positive, open communication about contentious issues. Rusbult's work on accommodation helps explain why some couples are more likely to break away from these patterns of negativity and avoidance than others (Rusbult, Bissonnette, Arriaga, & Cox, 1998; Rusbult, Verette, Whitney, Slovik, & Lipkus, 1991). **The accommodation principle** rests on three ideas. First, people have a tendency to retaliate when their partner engages in destructive behavior. Second, accommodation occurs when people are able to overcome this initial tendency and engage in cooperative rather than uncooperative communication to maintain their relationships. Third, couples in satisfying, committed relationships are more likely to engage in accommodation than couples in uncommitted or dissatisfying relationships (Rusbult, Olsen, Davis, & Hannon, 2001).

Several studies have supported the accommodation principle (e.g., Duffy & Rusbult, 1986; Guerrero & Bachman, in press; Rusbult & Zembrodt, 1983; Wieselquist, Rusbult, Foster, & Agnew, 1999). These studies demonstrate that accommodation is most likely to occur in relationships characterized by high levels of commitment, satisfaction, and trust. However, accommodation may not always have uniformly positive effects on relationships. Rusbult et al. (2001) noted that accommodation can cause relational problems, including power imbalances. As with the yielding strategy discussed earlier in this chapter, if only one person is doing the accommodating (or yielding), that person may be in a powerless position, which could eventually lead to relational dissatisfaction. Thus, the key to successful accommodation may be that it prompts a pattern of **positive reciprocity**, with both partners eventually engaging in cooperative strategies. This does not mean that all conflict behaviors need to be cooperative; indeed, it may be hard to refrain from using some uncooperative forms of communication when a conflict issue is particularly contentious. It does mean, however, that it is critical for partners to break escalating cycles of negativity by engaging in and responding positively to accommodation. Some research has even shown that couples who fail to reciprocate positive messages are more likely to report interpersonal violence (Smith et al., 1990).

There are many ways to accommodate a partner's negative behavior, including refraining from reacting angrily, using appropriate humor, or showing positive affect. Alberts and Driscoll's (1992) data on conversational complaints provide a nice example of accommodation that leads to a more productive interaction. They gave an example of a man (we'll call him Aaron) who complains to a woman (we'll call her Beth) that he cannot find his possessions because she always moves them when she cleans the house. The end of their conversation went this way:

Aaron: But, I mean, it's not like you do it on purpose. It's because you're absentminded.

Beth: Uh-huh. Yeah.

Aaron: And it's not like I don't do it either.

Beth: Yeah, I mean, I agree that things have to have their place . . . if you put them in their place, then you know where they are and it saves you a lot of worry.

Aaron: Well, then, there's really no disagreement.

Beth: Yeah, that's the way things should be. It's just that sometimes we do things that are contrary to the things we agree on.

Note that Aaron engaged in a personal attack when he called Beth "absentminded." Yet instead of reciprocating his hostility, Beth accommodated by expressing agreement (perhaps because she agreed that she did not do it "on purpose"). This led Aaron to admit that he sometimes does the same thing, which paved the way to ending the disagreement.

Being able to respond to negativity with positivity promotes relational satisfaction. In one study, couples in which people were nice only when the partner was nice were more likely to separate either 1½, 2½, or 5 years later than were couples in which the two people were nice regardless of whether their partners acted positively or negatively. As this study demonstrated, it is important for people to be positive when the partner is sad, angry, or inexpressive, as well as when the partner is happy. Gottman's (1994) recommendation that couples counterbalance every one negative statement with five positive statements appears to be very sound advice.

EXPLANATIONS FOR CONFLICT PATTERNS

You might wonder why patterns such as negative reciprocity and demand-withdrawal are common. If people care about their relationships, why don't they try to defuse a negative situation by accommodating and reacting with positivity? Sometimes people do respond positively, but often they find it hard to refrain from negativity because of the emotions they feel, the attributions they make, or their lack of communication skill. Each of these explanations is discussed next.

Emotional Flooding

During conflict situations, people often naturally experience aversive emotions, such as anger, hurt, and guilt (Guerrero & La Valley, 2006). Earlier in this chapter, we defined conflict as occurring when people have incompatible goals. Similarly, people feel negative emotion when someone or something blocks or disrupts their goals. So if Mary feels that Doug's plan for punishing Amanda is interfering with her goal to teach Amanda the "right" kind of lesson about smoking, Mary is likely to feel frustrated and perhaps even angry. Interestingly, moderate levels of emotion may be helpful during conflict situations (T. S. Jones, 2000). When people feel low levels of emotion, they are unlikely to put much effort into resolving conflict issues. On the other hand, especially intense emotion is counterproductive during conflict interactions.

During conflict situations, negative emotions may become so intense that people automatically resort to the fight-or-flight response. Gottman (1994) discussed the concept of **emotional flooding**, which occurs when people become "surprised, overwhelmed, and disorganized" by their partner's "expressions of negative emotion" (p. 21). When this happens, people typically experience high levels of physiological arousal (including increased heart rate and higher blood pressure), have difficulty processing new information, rely on stereotyped thoughts and behaviors, and respond with aggression (fight) or withdrawal (flight). Thus flooding contributes to negative patterns of communication that involve both uncooperative behavior and avoidance.

Several behaviors are associated with flooding. According to Gottman's (1994) research, if your partner becomes defensive, stubborn, angry, or whiny, you are likely to experience emotional flooding. Other behaviors act as buffers against emotional flooding. Specifically, if your partner expresses joy, affection, or humor during the course of a conflict interaction, you are less likely to experience emotional flooding. Situational variables may also play a role. For instance, Zillman's (1990) work on the excitation transfer suggests that people who are highly aroused (due to either stress or physical exertion) before engaging in conflict are more likely to react with aggression, presumably because they are experiencing emotional flooding. When people experience emotional flooding, they sometimes say things they don't really mean or wish they could take back. For example, relational partners who are experiencing intense emotion might call each other names and make statements such as "I hate you" or "I wish I'd never met you." At the moment, such statements may seem true because people are filled with negative emotion. However, when they calm down, they realize they actually care deeply for each other. At other times, people make these kinds of statements to get a kind of emotional revenge. They know that they don't really hate the partner, but by saying "I hate you," they hope to hurt the partner the way they themselves feel hurt.

When feeling hurt and uncertain, people sometimes lash out by engaging in button-pushing or making empty relational threats. When people engage in **button pushing**, they purposely say or do something they know will be especially hurtful to the partner. This could entail bringing up a taboo topic, insulting the partner with a name that he or she finds offensive, or looking away when the partner is talking. The key is that you know that your words or behavior will bother the partner.

Empty threats involve suggesting you will do something that you do not really intend to do. For instance, someone might say, "If you see her again, I'll break up with you" or "I can't stand this anymore; I want a divorce," although they actually have no intention of terminating the relationship. Empty threats have at least two negative consequences. First, if you do not follow through on these threats, you will lose face, and your partner might think you are bluffing sometime in the future when you are really serious. As the old fairy tale tells us, it is not wise to "cry wolf" too many times! Second, if you threaten to leave your partner when you do not really intend to, you could be planting the seed for relationship termination. Research suggests that people go through a cognitive process of psychological separation before terminating close relationships (Duck, 1988). So if you keep talking about leaving your partner, your partner might think about what he or she would do without you or about better alternatives, such as other relationship possibilities. If this happens, you have moved the possibility of breaking up to the forefront of your partner's mind. Thus, empty relational threats are more likely to backfire than to solve problems.

Because people tend to become defensive and/or aggressive when they are flooded with emotion, it is advisable to avoid discussing conflict issues until you and your partner are calm. Do not, however, put off conflict indefinitely. If necessary, you might have to schedule a time to talk about the issues that are bothering you. In the interim you might want to write down your feelings. One of our students once told us about a writing technique that she and her husband used when they were feeling really angry with each other. From their past experiences they knew there was a good chance that conflict would escalate if they confronted each other when their emotions were running high. So they decided to vent their negative emotions by going to different rooms and writing letters to each other. Later, after they had calmed down, they would each read the letters to themselves and decide whether to share them with the spouse. This student told us that neither of them ever ended up sharing the letters but instead always tore them up. The letters were usually filled with things they did not really mean, such as exaggerations, name-calling, or unfair accusations. But these letters helped our student and her husband put their conflict issues in perspective and enabled them to move on and discuss their problems in a calmer fashion.

Attributions

People like to be able to explain the behavior of others, particularly during significant events such as conflict episodes. To do this, people make attributions. In their book on interpersonal communication, Fisher and Adams (1994) defined an **attribution** as "a perceptual process of assigning reasons or causes to another's behavior" (p. 411). This definition is in line with Heider's (1958) conception of people as "naive scientists" who study one another's behavior and make judgments about why they act the way they do. People are especially likely to make attributions about negative behavior, including the uncooperative types of behaviors that often occur during conflict (Roloff & Miller, 2006).

Three specific types of attributions have been studied extensively (Kelley, 1973). First, people attribute a person's behavior to **personal versus situational** causes. When people make personal attributions, they believe that the cause of another person's behavior is rooted in that person's personality. In contrast, when people make situational attributions, they believe that the other person's behavior was affected by external factors, such as context or mood. For example, Doug might be upset because Mary ran out and got his birthday present at the last minute, causing them to be late for their dinner reservation. He could attribute Mary's behavior to personality factors (Mary is forgetful and disorganized) or to situational factors (Mary has been especially busy with work and has had to drive Amanda to the hospital every day after work).

Second, people make attributions about behavior being **stable versus unstable**. In other words, is Mary usually too busy to prepare for Doug's birthday? After many years of marriage, Doug might determine that her last-minute behavior is atypical and that she usually finds the time to buy him a nice gift no matter how busy she gets. Third, people make attributions about how **global versus specific** the cause of a behavior is. The more global a cause is, the more behaviors it applies to. For instance, the extra tasks with which Mary has been occupied might have caused her to put off doing things she normally does, or perhaps she just forgot about getting Doug a present.

Research on **the attribution hypothesis** has shown that certain patterns of attribution are related to conflict escalation and lower levels of satisfaction (Fincham, Harold, & Gano-Phillips, 2000). As Figure 14.3 shows, people in happy relationships tend to make *relationship-enhancing attributions* by attributing negative behavior such as complaints, whining, and nagging to causes that are external, unstable, and specific. In contrast, people in unhappy relationships tend to make *distress-maintaining attributions* by attributing negative behavior to internal, stable, and global causes (Bradbury & Fincham, 1990; Brehm & Kassin, 1990; Harvey, 1987; Holtzworth-Munroe & Jacobson, 1985). In general, people tend to make more positive attributions about their own behavior than their partner's behavior during conflict, but people in dissatisfying relationships are especially likely to blame their partners (Sillars, Roberts, Leonard, & Dun, 2000).

Since Doug and Mary are happily married, we would expect their pattern of attributions to be relationship enhancing. For instance, if Mary becomes aggressive when Doug doesn't agree with her, he might think, "She's just especially upset because her grandfather died of lung cancer and she's worried about Amanda. We can usually talk about disciplining our daughters without getting into a heated argument." On the other hand, if they were a dissatisfied couple, Doug might think, "Mary is so stubborn. She always thinks she's right! We never agree about how to discipline our daughters—or anything else for that matter!"

As these examples suggest, when people attribute negative behavior to internal, stable, and global causes (as people in dissatisfying relationships tend to do), they are more likely to respond using uncooperative conflict behaviors, such as indirect and competitive fighting (Davey, Fincham, Beach, & Brody, 2001; Schweinle, Ickes, & Bernstein, 2002). This can lead to negative spirals in dissatisfying relationships. Couples in dissatisfying relationships are also more likely to pay attention to negative behaviors than positive behaviors and to attribute positive behaviors to negative causes. In some cases, these attributions represent habitual but inaccurate ways of perceiving the partner's behavior. In other cases, negative attributions may be accurate. Amanda might resist her parents' advice about smoking because she is stubborn and rebellious (a personal cause), and Megan and Amanda might continually fight over family possessions, such as the phone and computer in the den, because they both want privacy and autonomy (a stable cause). In conflict situations such as these, identifying the causes may be essential for managing the conflict (Roloff & Miller, 2006). Therefore, it is essential (although difficult) to try to sort inaccurate attributions from accurate attributions so that the true causes of conflict can be identified.

Communication Skill Deficits

In addition to emotional flooding and cognitive attributions, some people simply do not have the communication skill necessary to engage in constructive conflict. These individuals are likely to feel helpless and defensive when attacked by others because they cannot respond effectively. Thus, they resort to aggressive behaviors or withdrawal, which can contribute to negative spirals of behavior. People with social skill deficits are also more likely to report

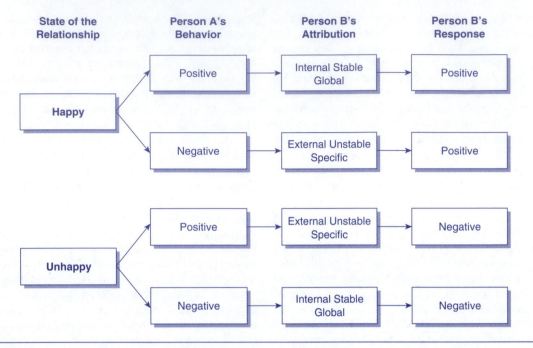

State of the Relationship	Person A's Behavior	Person B's Attribution	Person B's Response
Happy	Positive	Internal Stable Global	Positive
	Negative	External Unstable Specific	Positive
Unhappy	Positive	External Unstable Specific	Negative
	Negative	Internal Stable Global	Negative

Figure 14.3   Attribution Patterns in Happy Versus Unhappy Couples

being violent in their relationships (Christopher & Lloyd, 2000). The social skill deficits related to violence include having difficulties in the following areas: general emotional expression, anger management, social support seeking and giving, and problem solving. Men with communication skill deficits are also less likely to make relationship-enhancing attributions for their partner's behavior (Holtzworth-Munroe & Hutchinson, 1993; Holtzworth-Munroe & Smutzler, 1996).

Argumentativeness Versus Aggressiveness. Another important communication skill is the ability to engage in logical argument. Infante and his colleagues distinguished between argumentativeness and verbal aggressiveness (Infante, 1987; Infante, Chandler, & Rudd, 1989; Infante & Rancer, 1982). **Argumentativeness** refers to a conflict style that focuses on logical argument and reasoning: People with an argumentative style confront conflict directly by recognizing issues of disagreement, taking positions on controversial issues, backing up claims with evidence and reasoning, and refuting positions that go against their own viewpoint. Argumentativeness is an important social skill. People who are skilled in argument do not have to resort to name-calling, accusations, or other negative tactics. Instead, they can present their positions in a skilled and convincing manner. Rather than attacking their partner, they attack their partner's position.

Verbal aggressiveness involves attacking the other person's self-concept, often with the intention of hurting the other person. Verbally aggressive people engage in such tactics as teasing, threatening, and criticizing the partner's character or appearance (Infante, Sabourin, Rudd, & Shannon, 1990). Infante's research has shown that people resort to these types of tactics when they are unskilled in argumentation. Partners in violent marriages are more likely to report high levels of verbal aggression and low levels of argumentativeness than are those in nonviolent marriages (Infante et al., 1989, 1990).

The following example might help illustrate how difficult it is to deal with someone who is verbally aggressive. Amanda and Megan are starting to think about where to apply for college, so they watch a news report on admission requirements at various universities. After the report, the sisters begin discussing their differing opinions on affirmative action.

Amanda: I can't believe they are going to prohibit affirmative action at State.

Megan: If you ask me, it's about time they did.

Amanda: You mean you are against affirmative action?

Megan: Let's put it his way: I think people should be admitted to universities based on their qualifications rather than their skin color.

Amanda: So you are a racist who hates minorities.

Megan: That's not true. I don't like discrimination in any form. I just think universities should make exceptions based on factors other than race. Poor white students are also disadvantaged. Maybe a policy that admits students based on where they rank in their particular high school would be fairer. That way, all students who are economically disadvantaged, including minority students, would get help.

Amanda: And I suppose you think that white men are discriminated against too. I thought you were smarter than that. How can you be so gullible?

If you did not have a strong opinion about affirmative action policies in universities before reading Amanda and Megan's comments, you might have been swayed more by Megan's arguments because they focused on her position rather than attacking Amanda as a person. In short, Megan used argumentative communication. In contrast, Amanda used verbal aggression when she called Megan a racist, implied that she was unintelligent, and asked how she could be so gullible. If Amanda had used argumentative communication, you might have been persuaded by her argument. This example also illustrates how verbally aggressive communication can lead to negative spirals. Put yourself in Megan's place. If the conversation continued and you kept being attacked personally, would you be tempted to retaliate by using verbal aggression yourself? Most people have a hard time remaining neutral in the face of personal attacks, partly due to emotional flooding.

Effective Listening. The ability to listen to others is another critical skill for effective conflict management. When people practice effective listening, they are better able to understand their partner's thoughts and feelings and, ultimately, empathize with their concerns. Such understanding plays a vital role in collaboration and compromise. In fact, studies have shown that people with listening and decoding skills (the ability to figure out what the partner is feeling) tend to be more satisfied in their relationships (Guerrero & Floyd, 2006).

Active listening is particularly challenging during conflict situations. Think about the last heated argument you had with someone. How carefully did you listen to what the person had to say? If you felt attacked and/or became defensive, chances are that you did not really listen to the other person very carefully. Instead, you were probably thinking about what you would say next. Your mind may have been racing as you thought about ways to defend yourself, and your emotions may have been so turbulent that you became preoccupied with your own thoughts and feelings and "tuned the other person out." Ironically, if your partner was not practicing active listening either, all the counterarguments you spent so much time thinking about would not really have been heard.

Active listening requires effort and concentration. The experts on listening and negotiation give the following advice for improving your skill (Stark, 1994; Steil, Barker, & Watson, 1983; Stiff, Dillard, Somera, Kim, & Sleight, 1988):

1. *Let your partner speak.* Refrain from arguing your case or interrupting until your partner finishes stating her or his position. If you spend noticeably more time talking than your partner, this probably means that you need to talk less and encourage your partner to talk more.

BOX 14.2   Highlights

Ten "Rules" for Constructive Conflict Management

Based on the situation, there are various ways to manage conflict effectively. However, the research reviewed in this chapter suggests that the following 10 "rules" should serve people well in most conflict situations.

1. Avoid gunnysacking or bringing in everything but the kitchen sink.

2. Do not bring other people into the conflict unless they are part of the conflict.

3. Attack positions, not people (no name-calling, button pushing, or violence).

4. Avoid making empty relational threats.

5. If necessary, postpone conflict until your emotions cool down.

6. Try to understand your partner's position by practicing active listening and avoiding mind reading.

7. Use behavioral complaints rather than personal criticisms.

8. Try to accommodate rather than get defensive when you feel like you are being attacked.

9. Try to validate your partner's position by expressing agreement and positive affect rather than stonewalling or escalating the conflict.

10. For every one negative statement or behavior, use five positive statements or behaviors.

---

2. *Put yourself in your partner's place.* Enter a conflict situation with specific goals regarding what you would like to learn from your partner. As Gottman (1994) emphasized, if people want to understand and empathize with each other, they need to create **mental maps** of each other's thoughts and feelings. By listening actively, people can see things from their partner's perspective.

3. *Don't jump to conclusions.* Don't assume you know what your partner will say or why he or she will say it. Making such assumptions can lead you to interpret your partner's statements in a way that is consistent with your preexisting beliefs, even if your preexisting beliefs are wrong.

4. *Ask questions.* Ask questions that allow your partner to clarify and explain her or his position. Be sure to phrase these questions in a positive manner so that you don't sound sarcastic or condescending.

5. *Paraphrase what your partner says.* Paraphrasing helps confirm that you have really heard what your partner is trying to tell you. When partners paraphrase, they summarize each other's positions. This allows partners to give each other the opportunity to correct misinterpretations and to further clarify their positions.

SUMMARY AND APPLICATION

Conflict is inevitable in close relationships. The closer you are to someone, the more likely you are to encounter disagreements. Disagreements can have positive or negative effects on relationships. When differences are handled cooperatively, conflict can improve relationships by helping partners solve problems and understand each other. But when negative patterns of conflict communication become pervasive, relational partners are likely to become less satisfied and committed and feel less emotional closeness. When spouses argue, their conflict style can also affect their children's well-being. Children whose parents repeatedly engage in hostile patterns of conflict are less likely to have good peer relationships and more likely to use uncooperative conflict styles themselves. Conflict between parents and children also has a socializing effect on children. So if Amanda disagrees with her parents regarding her punishment, the way her parents communicate with her will likely influence how Amanda deals with conflict in other relationships in the future.

Doug and Mary have many options for dealing with conflict. They could engage in communication that is cooperative or uncooperative, direct or indirect. Although we described six styles of conflict separately in this chapter, Doug and Mary could use a variety of styles during the course of a conflict interaction, and each could use different styles of communication. Mary might be more direct than Doug, and Doug might be more cooperative than Mary. Conflict interaction is a two-way street. It takes two people to escalate conflict; it also takes two people to cooperate.

Engaging in cooperative conflict requires communication skill. Many people use uncooperative strategies such as competitive fighting and indirect fighting, which cause conflicts to escalate. Negative patterns of conflict communication can develop in relationships. For example, some relational partners get caught in patterns of negative reciprocity, demand-withdrawal, or the four horsemen of the apocalypse. If Doug and Mary notice that their conflict interactions are characterized by a lot of personal criticism, contempt, defensiveness, and/or stonewalling, their relationship could be in trouble. Patterns of accommodation, which involve responding to negative behavior with positive behavior, help defuse negativity and promote cooperation.

Using the collaborating style would provide Mary and Doug with the best option for disciplining Amanda effectively. Mary and Doug would be more likely to reach a collaborative solution if they avoided destructive patterns of conflict communication and remained focused on their goals. The studies reviewed in this chapter points to several rules for constructive conflict management, which Mary and Doug would be advised to follow. These rules are summarized in Box 14.2, and they provide a blueprint for communicating effectively during conflict situations.

Although these rules probably make sense to you, it may be hard for Mary and Doug (or any two people) to follow them all the time. Even if you have good intentions and know how you *should* act during a conflict situation, when your emotions are running high, it is difficult not to violate some of these rules. If you find yourself engaging in some destructive tactics during conflict situations, do not panic—even experts in negotiation make mistakes. Recognizing these mistakes is the first step toward managing conflict in ways that keep your relationship satisfying.

DISCUSSION QUESTIONS

1. Think about your long-term relationships. How often do you have disagreements with these relational partners? Did the number and types of conflict change as the relationship became more serious?

2. Do you tend to avoid or engage in conflict? Which of the six conflict styles discussed in this chapter best fits you? Does your style of communication remain fairly consistent, or does it vary a lot depending on the situation and the partner?

3. When people are in the midst of interpersonal conflict, they often are flooded with emotions. This makes it difficult to "fight fairly." Which of the rules for constructive conflict management do you think is the most difficult to follow? Do you have any additional suggestions that might help your classmates learn to manage conflict in more constructive ways?

15

ENDING RELATIONSHIPS

Disengagement and Termination

Katelyn is crushed. "I've never been hurt so badly in my life," she tells her friend Tamika. "I am a complete basket case since Sean left me. It was so out of the blue." Since Sean broke up with Katelyn last week she has suffered greatly. She can't sleep at night. She has missed work. She can't study. Worse, she left degrading, pleading messages on Sean's answering machine that must make him think she is psycho. For Sean, the breakup has been building for years. He thinks that Katelyn is too traditional, too religious, not spontaneous enough, and too preoccupied with money. He feels he has lost his "real self" in trying to be someone he is not, to please Katelyn. Finally, he decided to end the relationship despite the fact that he felt terrible about hurting someone he loved. Sean wished there had been a nicer way to break up. At first, he thought she'd get the hint when he spent more time with his friends and withdrew affection from Katelyn. When she didn't get the hint, he eventually had to tell her straight out that he wanted to break up. Katelyn insisted that they could work it out, but Sean was firm in telling her that his decision was made and it was definitely over.

In Paul Simon's classic song "Fifty Ways To Leave Your Lover," breakups sound so easy. We are told to "walk out the back, Jack, just make a new plan Stan, don't need to be coy, Roy, just set yourself free." Rarely is it that easy. For a person in either Katelyn's or Sean's position, breakups are some of the most difficult episodes in life. Relationship researchers who have been examining the ends of relationships for several decades have come to understand how and why relationships end and the central role played by communication before, after, and during relationship breakups.

In this chapter, our goal is to give you a better understanding of the relational disengagement process. Think about the relationships in your own life that have come to an end. Some of them probably ended abruptly, whereas others disintegrated slowly. You and your partner may also have had different perceptions of how and why the relationship ended, like Katelyn and Sean. It is also likely that it was painful to end some relationships and a relief to end others. Relational disengagement is a complex phenomenon. To help unravel this complexity, this chapter focuses on four areas of relational disengagement research.

First, we examine the reasons why relationships end. Second, we review models of the disengagement process. Third, we discuss 15 communication strategies people use to leave their partners. Finally, we take a look at the aftermath of relational disengagement.

WHY RELATIONSHIPS END

All relationships end. Regardless of whether they are brief or close encounters, last 50 days or 50 years, are friendships or marriages, all relationships end at one time or another, either voluntarily or involuntarily. Conville (1991) suggested that "disintegration is everywhere . . . Disintegration is a process that is triggered when the relationship is out of kilter" (p. 96). Baxter (1982) stated that "the breaking up of a relationship is a phenomenon known to most and dreaded by all. It accounts for some of our most intense and painful social experiences" (p. 223). The deep positive and negative feelings we experience in our relationships are connected: There are no highs without lows. Gibran (1923) described these two sides of love:

> When love beckons to you follow him, though his ways are hard and steep, and when his wings enfold you, yield to him, though the sword hidden among his pinions may wound you. And when he speaks to you believe in him, though his voice may shatter your dreams as the north wind lays waste the garden. Even as love crowns you so shall he crucify you. Even as he is for your growth so is he for your pruning. (p. 12)

The knowledge that relationships end, often painfully, prevents some people from developing meaningful relationships. By denying themselves the opportunity to feel both the joys and sorrows of relationships, these people miss an important secret of life: Not feeling anything at all may be worse than feeling bad. Avoiding relationships prevents them from experiencing the deepest involvements and emotions humans can have.

People become deeply enmeshed in their close relationships (Baxter, 1982). Relationships exist in a web of close ties, emotional involvements, financial arrangements, sexual relations, friendship networks, possessions, memories, identities, families, and sometimes offspring. When a relationship dies, many of these ties die as well. The emotional pain of relational loss is compounded by the loss of these other relationships, resources, and connections. Given how painful the end of relationships can be, you might wonder why relationships end. What are the common causes for relationship breakdowns? This section addresses this question.

General Pathways to Relational Endings

Relationships end in many ways, but research suggests that most couples, unmarried or married, straight or gay show more similarities than differences in the way they break up (Kurdek, 1991). However, in their massive study of American couples, Blumstein and Schwartz (1983) were surprised to find that lesbians were most likely to break up, followed by gay men, followed by heterosexual cohabitants. Married couples were the most stable of these four couple types, but when they did break up, they separated for many of the same reasons as did other couples. Interestingly, some variables that one would think are associated with relational breakups, such as self-esteem and positive self-beliefs, amount of conflict, and relational equity, show no relationship with breakups, as can be seen in the available research (Cate, Levin, & Richmond, 2002). What, then, does predict breakups?

Individual Choice. Most breakups are a rational or strategic choice by one partner. Research suggests that bilateral breakups are quite rare (Baxter, 1984; Hill et al., 1976; Tashiro & Frazier, 2003; Weber, 1998). The fact that most relationship breakups are driven by one partner is one reason breakups can be so painful. One person may desperately want the relationship to continue, while the other person may feel guilty for terminating the relationship. As the popular saying goes, it takes two people to develop a relationship, but only one to end it. Summaries of research on marriage show that the wife is the "dumper" in about two thirds of the cases (Braver, Whitley, & Ng, 1993). Similarly, Hill et al. (1976)

found that women were more likely to precipitate dating relationship breakups than men. Interestingly, most people attribute the "cause" of the relationship disengagements to situational factors that doomed the relationship rather than specific actions of either partner (Krahl & Wheeless, 1997).

Atrophy. Some relationships wither away (Metts & Cupach, 1986). This could be due to different interests, such as the dissimilarities between Katelyn and Sean discussed at the beginning of this chapter. Relationships also deteriorate due to decreased quality and quantity of communication, distance, reduced efforts to maintain the relationship, or competition from the hundreds of competing relationships in today's fast-paced world. Atrophy most commonly happens in friendships and, to a lesser extent, in dating relationships, especially long-distance relationships. Bonded and committed relationships are less likely to wither away, but research shows that even marriages can suffer from atrophy and that marital happiness slowly declines over time (Sternberg, 1987). Marital partners rarely just disappear the way casual friends and even lovers do, partially because of barriers to disengagement, such as children, intertwined social networks, and shared possessions and financial resources (see Chapter 9). Still, in marriages, as in other relationships, feelings of intimacy and passion may disappear as the relationship slowly atrophies. Owen (1993) found that many relationship breakups were characterized by atrophy or decay. Typical metaphors for relationship endings were, "It was like a flower that blossomed and then withered," "I could see the relationship rot each day," and "The relationship faded into the sunset" (pp. 271–272).

Separation. The history of the United States has been the history of movement. Our ancestors emigrated from other lands, and people in the United States have always moved from state to state, farm to city, city to suburb, and job to job. Many of you went away to college and will move to another place when you graduate. In their study of turning points in romantic relationships, Bullis et al., (1993) found that one of the most common turning points was physical separation, such as extended vacations, distant schools, or job transfers. Shaver, Furman, and Buhrmester

(1995) reported that moving away to college was the cause for the decline of 46% of precollege romances. In some cases, it seems, "Absence does not make the heart grow fonder." Instead, "Out of sight means out of mind." When people are separated from one another for extended periods, they often make new friends and discover new interests. In gay and lesbian relationships, Kurdek (1991) reported that frequent absence was the primary reason for breakups. The finding that separation often has negative effects on relationships corresponds with the attraction principle (discussed in Chapter 3), according to which geographical closeness and repeated interaction lead to liking and intimacy.

Death. Perhaps the most difficult relational ending is the death of a loved one; indeed the death of a child, a spouse, or primary partner is among the most devastating of human experiences. Because the average woman marries a man who is a couple of years older than she is and then lives 6 to 8 years longer than her husband, widows outnumber widowers by a 10:1 ratio. Research has shown that an important buffer in coping with the loss of a partner is a social support network (Prager, 1995). Likewise, research suggests that hospice workers are invaluable in providing comfort and support to the bereaved (Zimmerman & Applegate, 1994). Unfortunately, these authors found that hospice workers with more training provided fewer person-centered comforting messages than newer, untrained hospice workers, suggesting a need for more communication training among hospice workers. Nonetheless, most people's experiences with hospices are far superior to those with the traditional medical establishment. It appears to be most important, however, for widows and widowers to have a close circle of friends and family around them. Anticipation of one's own death appears to produce deliberate termination of many relationships, except for family and close social companions (Lang, 2000).

Specific Reasons for Relationship Termination

For several decades, scholars have been studying why and how relationships end. As Box 15.1 shows,

BOX 15.1 Highlights

The Top 10 Reasons for Breakups in Marriages and Dating Relationships

Marital Relationships	*Dating Relationships*
1. Communication breakdown	1. Becoming bored with the relationship
2. Loss of shared goals or interests	2. Differences in interests
3. Sexual incompatibility	3. Desire to be independent
4. Infidelity and jealousy	4. Differences in background
5. Boredom/lack of excitement	5. Conflicting ideas about sex
6. Money and financial issues	6. Conflicting ideas about marriage
7. Conflicts about children	7. Living too far apart
8. Alcohol or drug abuse	8. Interest in someone else
9. Women's equality issues	9. Differences in intelligence
10. Conflict with or about in-laws	10. Pressure from parents

SOURCE: Adapted from Safron (1979) and Hill et al. (1976).

relational researchers have repeatedly identified a number of themes or causes associated with relational breakups—both marital and dating. Poor communication is a common culprit. Indeed, several studies have found that the number one problem leading to divorce is poor communication (Bradford, 1980; Cleek & Pearson, 1985; Parker & Drummond-Reeves, 1993), including too much communication, too little communication, low-quality communication, communication that is too negative, and less mutually constructive communication. Many other factors, such as sexual incompatibility, money, and equality issues can also lead to relationship termination. These different causes are discussed next.

Withdrawal. Studies have shown that withdrawal is a common reason for relationship breakups. Baxter (1986) found that lack of supportiveness, particularly lack of listening, was a major factor in over one fourth of the relational breakups. As discussed in Chapter 14, stonewalling occurs when individuals fail to discuss important issues with their partners (Christensen & Shenk, 1991; Gottman, 1993; Gottman & Levenson, 1992). Males have been found to use this type of dysfunctional communication more often than females (Clements, Cordova, Markman, & Laurenceau, 1997). A number of studies have examined the demand-withdrawal sequence (also discussed in Chapter 14), which is associated with separation (Christensen & Shenk, 1991). This sequence occurs when one person (often the woman) makes a demand and the partner (often the man) withdraws from communication. Children of divorced parents are more likely to report that their mother and father engaged in demand-withdrawal patterns than are children of nondivorced parents (Afifi & Schrodt, 2003). Honeycutt, Cantrill, and Allen (1992) had disengaged couples recall and describe behaviors that aided in the process of relational disengagement. These behaviors included spending less time together, avoiding each other in public settings, and making excuses for not going out together.

Negative Communication. All couples have conflicts and disagreements. In fact, as dating partners become more loving and committed, conflict increases, presumably because of their increased interdependence (Lloyd & Cate, 1985). Research has shown that it is not primarily the presence or absence of conflict that determines whether a couple will be satisfied and stay together; it is how the partners deal with conflict that is more important (see Chapter 14). In a series of studies spanning 15 years, Clements et al. (1997) reported that, in their earliest interactions, partners who were destined to break up dealt with their disagreements in a destructive fashion characterized by fights, name-calling, criticisms, and accusations. Research by Filsinger and Thomas (1988) found that negative communication during interpersonal interaction was predictive of disengagement 1½ years later. In a major statistical summary of the research on divorce, Karney and Bradbury (1995) reported that one of the most prevalent factors leading to divorce was negative behavior. One study found that a common path to relational disengagement was rules violation, whereby one partner engages in behavior inappropriate to the relationship (Metts & Cupach, 1986). For example, if relational partners have agreed not to swear at each other and to call when they are going to be late, repeated violations of these rules can lead to dissatisfaction and, perhaps, disengagement.

Conflict increases as dating relationships become more committed; it rises even more sharply for partners contemplating a breakup or for those who have decided to terminate their relationships (Lloyd & Cate, 1985). Thus, there may be an optimal level of conflict in a committed relationship beyond which the relationship is threatened. In other words, some conflict may be normal and even healthy for relationships. But high levels of conflict may be detrimental, particularly if issues of contention keep resurfacing because they have not been discussed in a constructive manner.

Increased negative emotional expression and decreased positive emotional expression also put couples at risk for dissolution (Gottman, 1993; Gottman & Levenson, 1992; Karney & Bradbury, 1995). Karney and Bradbury (1995) found that the reciprocity of negative behaviors was the most detrimental factor in a marriage. Surprisingly, Gottman (1993) reported that husbands' anger was unrelated to divorce. However, husbands who became defensive, showed contempt, and used stonewalling were more likely to divorce. Similarly, wives who criticized, became defensive, and showed contempt were more likely to see their relationships end. Honeycutt et al. (1992) reported that couples recalled various forms of aversive communication, such as arguing about little things, disagreeing, verbally fighting, criticizing the partner, and making sarcastic comments, as sets of behaviors that led to the breakup of their relationships.

Lack of Openness and Intimacy. Even though couples need some degree of autonomy and privacy (see Chapter 12), open disclosure is still imperative for relationships. Partners who stayed together instead of breaking up reported much higher levels of self-disclosure early in their relationships (Berg & McQuinn, 1986). Sprecher (1987) found that dating couples who engaged in more self-disclosure were much more likely to be together 4 years later. Openness is particularly important to women's evaluation of their partners. In Baxter's (1986) study, 31% of the women, as compared with only 8% of the men, mentioned lack of openness as a major factor in relational termination. In a study on memories of relationship breakups, Honeycutt and his colleagues (1992) reported that many people remember decreases in verbal and nonverbal intimacy as the starting point for relational decline. Couples at risk for eventual disengagement may stop expressing intimate feelings and decrease acts of physical intimacy such as hugs, kisses, and touches.

Lack of Similarity. Despite the oft-repeated folk wisdom that "Opposites attract," a more valid cliche is "Birds of a feather flock together" (see Chapter 3). Dozens of studies show that the more two people have in common the more likely they are to stay together. Think of your close friends. Chances are that you have many things in common, including hobbies and interests, political opinions, and religious values. Similarities are also important in romantic relationships. Studies have shown that similarities in personality lead to longer relationships and fewer breakups. For example, spouses who are more alike in extraversion, attractiveness, and interest in art are less likely to divorce (Bentler & Newcomb, 1978). Similarly, Cody (1982) found personality incompatibility to be a major cause of relational breakups.

In Baxter's (1986) study of heterosexual dating relationships, the second most common reason for breakups was a discrepancy in beliefs, attitudes, and values, a factor mentioned by nearly one third of the respondents. Likewise, Metts and Cupach (1986) found that value dissimilarity commonly led to relational disengagement. In a major statistical summary of factors leading to divorce, Karney and Bradbury (1995) concluded that attitude dissimilarity was one of the most important factors leading to both relational dissatisfaction and divorce.

Although interethnic dating relationships and marriages can be very successful and rewarding, they are at greater risk for breakups. Lack of similarity in attitudes, activities, and interests, as well as differences in ethnic, religious, and socioeconomic backgrounds, can precipitate relational breakups (Cate et al., 2002; Felmlee, Sprecher, & Bassin, 1990). This may be primarily due to the prejudiced influences of family, friends, and society in general that put a greater strain on an interethnic couple (Williams & Andersen, 1998). In a classic study on dating relationships, Hill et al. (1976) found that the fourth most important factor leading to breakups was differences in background. Similarly, although age-discrepant relationships can be very happy, large age differences are statistically related to breakups (Bentler & Newcomb, 1978).

Differences in educational background and intelligence may pose problems for relationships. In Hill et al.'s (1976) study, differences in intelligence were among the top reasons for dating relationship breakups. Similarly, when one partner continues her or his education and the other partner does not, they sometimes find that they have less and less in common (Scott & Powers, 1978).

While some difference in interests is probably good for a relationship, common interests are more likely to lead to relational stability than are dissimilar interests. In Hill et al.'s (1976) study of dating relationships, the second biggest factor leading to breakups for both men and women was differences in interests. Similarly, Safron (1979) found that the second most important reason for marital breakups was loss of shared goals or interests.

Sexual Incompatibility. Sex is a central, personal feature of marriages, romances, and many dating relationships (see Chapter 7) that can lead to several types of relational problems. Relational partners may differ over the desired frequency of sexual relations, the type of sexual behaviors, the initiation of sex, and of course, fidelity issues. In dating relationships, engagements, marriages, and gay relationships, fighting about sex is associated with relational breakups (Blumstein & Schwartz, 1983), although there is little association between how much sex a couple has and how long the partners stay together. Apparently, frequency is not as important as compatibility. In other words, some couples may be satisfied with less sex than others.

Conflicting sexual attitudes was a common reason for premarital breakups in the Hill et al. (1976) study and for marital breakups in Safron's (1979) study. Sexual incompatibility was the fifth most important reason for divorce in Cleek and Pearson's (1985) study and the second most important reason for gay and lesbian separations in Kurdek's (1991) study. These studies show that sexual incompatibility is an important force that can lead to relationship breakups.

Sexual satisfaction is important in romantic relationships. In a major statistical analysis of the prior research on marital stability, Karney and Bradbury (1995) reported that sexual satisfaction was one of the most important factors in a stable marriage for both husbands and wives. Sexual dysfunction was a factor in the dissolution of 75% of marriages in one study (Bradford, 1980) and 60% of marriages in another (Parker & Drummond-Reeves, 1993).

For women, tenderness, communication, and intimacy are especially important parts of sexual satisfaction, and their absence during sex is associated with emotional dissatisfaction and relational termination. For men, physical attraction is an important part of sex, and absence of attraction may lead to male-initiated breakups. When men place great emphasis on physical attraction, their relationships are unlikely to survive past the first few years, because for these men the "Grass is always greener elsewhere" (Blumstein & Schwartz, 1983).

Extramarital or extrarelational sex is often detrimental to a relationship and may lead to termination, although the reverse is sometimes true: That is, unhappy relationships lead to extrarelational sex. For every type of couple, including gay and straight, the relationship is less likely to survive when one partner is having sex outside the relationship (Blumstein & Schwartz, 1983). Gagnon (1979) reported that nearly 40% of extramarital sexual relationships had an important effect on the decision to divorce, and 14% to 18% of the time these affairs had a major effect. Bradford (1980) reported that extramarital affairs were a factor in the breakups of 55% of the couples in his study. Parker and Drummond-Reeves (1993) reported that an extramarital affair was a factor for 25% of the divorced couples they studied. In Safron's (1979) study, infidelity was the fourth most common reason for divorce. Cupach and Metts (1986) found that, while extrarelational affairs were a problem associated with breakups for both married and unmarried couples, affairs were a more salient concern for women than for men. They suggested that for men an affair is a form of self-gratification, whereas women see affairs as a violation of the relationship and, thus, a more central cause of relationship disengagement. On the other hand, consistent with a social evolutionary hypothesis about sex differences between men and women, the type of the affair is critical. Men relative to women find it more difficult to forgive sexual infidelity than emotional infidelity and are more likely to terminate a relationship following a partner's sexual infidelity (Shackelford, Buss, & Bennett, 2002). The reverse was true for women, who were more likely than men to break up as a result of their partner's emotional infidelity. Of course, both forms of infidelity can be a reason for breakup for either men or women.

Autonomy and Independence. Studies have repeatedly shown that wanting to maintain one's autonomy is a major reason for relationship disengagement. People often complain that the relationship is "smothering" or "suffocating" them, and they need their "space" and "freedom." In Hill et al.'s (1976) study, the third most important reason for termination of a dating relationship was the desire to be independent. Baxter (1986) reported that the most frequent reason

for the breakup of a heterosexual dating relationship was the need for autonomy. Indeed, this was the primary reason for more than one third of the respondents. Men reported lack of autonomy 24% of the time, but women listed it as a primary reason 44% of the time. Similarly, one of the five most common general issues leading to relational breakups among gay and lesbian couples was excessive fusion, which is a loss of individuality due to the relationship (Kurdek, 1991).

Interest in Someone Else. Rivals can be threats to relationships. Perhaps this is why jealousy is such a widespread emotion and a major cause of relational violence (see Chapter 13). Hill et al. (1976) reported that one of the top 10 reasons for terminating a dating relationship for both men and women was interest in someone else. Similarly, Metts and Cupach (1986) reported that one of the most common disengagement themes was third-party involvement, particularly for women. Failure to maintain loyalty and fidelity was a primary reason for terminating relationships in 16% of the accounts in Baxter's (1986) study on breakups. The availability of attractive alternative partners makes relational breakups more likely (Felmlee et al., 1990; Rusbult, Zembrodt, & Gunn, 1982). Interestingly, when people have few good prospects as alternative partners, they are more likely to stay with their current partner (Simpson, 1987). These findings correspond with social exchange theory principles (see Chapter 10).

Boredom. The most important reason for relational breakups in Hill et al.'s (1976) study was boredom. Similarly, Safron (1979) found that boredom, or lack of excitement, was one of the top factors leading to divorce. In Safron's study, many people indicated that the fun or excitement had gone out of the relationship. Nearly 10% of the participants in Baxter's (1986) study noted the absence of magic and romance as a primary cause for relational termination. Interestingly, this was a factor for 19% of the men but only 5% of the women, suggesting that men are less practical partners who may disengage if the magic is no longer there. Honeycutt et al. (1992) also reported that one of the most common thoughts that disengagers have about a relationship is that it has become boring. Our interpersonal relationships are one of our greatest sources of joy and excitement. When they begin to bore us, the end may be near. This finding can also be explained by dialectics theory (see Chapter 9). People desire *both* novelty and predictability in their relationships. When predictability is emphasized to the detriment of novelty, boredom is the likely result. In healthy relationships, people's needs for both novelty and predictability are met.

Money. Money creates problems in many relationships. It was the sixth most important cause of divorce in Safron's (1979) survey of 730 marital counselors and one of the top causes of divorce (Bradford, 1980; Parker & Drummond-Reeves, 1993) and problems in gay and lesbian separations (Kurdek, 1991). Interestingly, few relational problems revolve around how much money a couple makes. Indeed, family income is not correlated with personal or relational satisfaction.

According to Blumstein and Schwartz (1983), money management and the values surrounding spending and saving produce considerable turmoil for couples. Even long-standing couples are likely to break up if arguments about money continue to occur. Partners who pool their money are much more likely to stay together than those who do not. Arguments about income are a factor only for heterosexual couples (particularly when there is inequity in the amount of money that two people are contributing to the relationship) and is less important than money management issues.

Women's Equality Issues. Because women experienced relational inequality for so many years, equality issues are particularly important to them. In Safron's (1979) study, women's equality issues were the ninth most common reason cited for marital breakups. Likewise, in Baxter's (1986) study of heterosexual dating relational breakups, equity was a primary factor in the breakup for 17% of the women but for only 5% of the men. In Blumstein and Schwartz's (1983) study, a major factor in relational breakups revolved around men's opinions about working women. Specifically, if the man objected to the woman working or if he was unhappy about her job, the couple was more likely to terminate their relationship.

Working women are also under considerable stress, especially if they have children and are trying to run a household. In the popular press, this problem is referred to as the "superwoman syndrome." Women are supposed to do their jobs and then go home and tend to their families and homes. Because women are expected to be the caregivers at home, they are always working—at the office and at home. Hochschild (1997; Hochschild & Machung, 1989), for example, has shown that women typically do about 70% of the household chores. Moreover, only 20% of dual-career couples report that a fair distribution of labor exists in their home. For the other 80% of couples, the woman is nearly always responsible for the majority of homemaking and child care chores. When this type of inequity exists, it is a primary source of tension in the relationship.

Alcohol and Drugs. Alcohol and drugs play a role in many relational breakups. These problems were cited as the eighth most prevalent reason for divorce in the Safron (1979) study. Similarly, alcohol and drugs were reported to be a factor in 45% of the divorces in Parker and Drummond-Reeves's (1993) study. Alcohol and drugs may lead to violence, addiction, problems with the law, the squandering of money, and problems at work, any of which can greatly strain a relationship.

Research suggests that alcohol and drugs can also lead to codependency in relationships. Le Poire, Hallett, and Giles (1998), for example, argued that the partners of alcoholics and drug addicts often become **codependent**, letting their partner's behavior greatly affect their own behavior. Many codependents become obsessed with controlling their partner's negative behaviors and with nurturing the partner. According to Le Poire et al. (1998), codependents often show a mix of punishing and reinforcing behaviors. Sometimes, they try to get their partner to stop using drugs or alcohol through punishment (verbal confrontation, threats to leave the relationship). At other times, however, they reinforce the partner's behavior by doing things such as keeping the children out of the way and taking care of the partner when he or she is ill. Although codependency may keep people in relationships for a while, in the long run, codependent behavioral patterns may put considerable strain on relationships.

Social Networks. When friends and family disapprove of one's partner, it puts pressure on the relationship. Felmlee et al. (1990) reported that the likelihood of a relational breakup increased as people's social networks became more disapproving of the partner. Sprecher and Felmlee (1992) found that parental support of dating relationships is important, especially for women; when parents were supportive, the stability of the relationship increased; when they were unsupportive, a breakup was more likely. There is little evidence of the "Romeo and Juliet" effect, whereby parental prohibitions on the relationship actually increase relational strength and stability (see Chapter 3).

Developing new social networks that displace an existing network or strain the relationship is another common theme in relational disengagements (Metts & Cupach, 1986). Vaughn (1986) claimed that in many relationships, partners separate physically by developing separate friendship networks that do not intermix. In Safron's (1979) study, in-laws were a major factor in the breakup of marriages. Likewise, in the Hill et al. (1976) study, pressure from both the woman's and the man's parents regarding the relationship was a common cause of relational breakups. The lesson here seems clear: The more the social network disapproves of and interferes with the relationship, the harder it is for the couple to build and maintain a stable relationship.

Chronic Dissatisfaction. Research has shown that temporary dissatisfaction may cause couples to attempt to repair and maintain their relationship (see Chapter 9). However, a couple with a long history of dissatisfaction is more likely to be at risk for marital dissolution and divorce (Kurdek, 1993b). Similarly, dating couples experiencing chronic dissatisfaction are more likely to employ exit and neglect strategies that are detrimental to the relationship (Rusbult et al., 1982; see also Chapter 9). Exit strategies include breaking up, moving out, and getting a divorce, whereas neglect strategies include ignoring the partner, initiating new romantic relationships, and spending less time with the partner. Of course, chronic dissatisfaction may be related to the other factors (negative communication, inequity) discussed earlier in this section.

Disillusionment. Chronic dissatisfaction is also related to disillusionment. **Relationship disillusionment** occurs when people's positive illusions about their partners and their relationships start to fade (Niehuis & Bartell, 2006). During courtship, people often see their partners and their relationships through "rose colored glasses." For example, some researchers have suggested that people have positive illusions about their partners during courtship and early marriage but that it is hard to maintain those idealized images once the honeymoon stage is over (Murray, Holmes, & Griffin, 1996; Swann et al., 1994). The process of disillusionment has been shown to predict divorce and dating relationship breakup (Niehuis & Bartell, 2006; Niehuis & Huston, 2002). Disillusionment is accompanied by decreases in affection and caring, loss of emotional attachment, and disappointment in the relationship and the partner. Disillusionment is especially strong when people have unrealistic expectations and perceptions about their relationship during courtship or early marriage. In fact, Neihuis and Huston (2002) found that people were most likely to experience disillusionment during the first 2 years of marriage, when they had reported particularly high levels of premarital affection and passion. To see if your relationship is characterized by disillusionment, you can take the test in Box 15.2.

MODELS OF THE DISENGAGEMENT PROCESS

Now that you are aware of factors that contribute to relational breakups, you might be wondering *how* people end their relationships. Researchers have tackled this question in two ways: (1) They have examined the general process by which relationships end and (2) they have uncovered specific communication strategies that people use to terminate their relationships. We will examine the research in both these areas, starting with the overall process of disengagement.

Researchers have created several models of how relationships come apart. Most of the thinking in this area has suggested that relationships pass through several phases—as if descending a staircase on their way from close, bonded relationships to breakups.

⊞ **BOX 15.2   Put Yourself to the Test**

Relationship Disillusionment Scale

Circle the number that best represents how much you agree or disagree with each statement, with 7 representing strong agreement and 1 representing strong disagreement.

	Disagree ←					→	*Agree*
1. I am very disappointed in my relationship.	1	2	3	4	5	6	7
2. I am very disappointed in my partner.	1	2	3	4	5	6	7
3. My partner used to be my best friend, but now I sometimes don't like her/him as a person.	1	2	3	4	5	6	7
4. This relationship is not at all what I expected it to be; I feel very disappointed.	1	2	3	4	5	6	7
5. I used to think I was lucky to be with someone like my partner; now I'm not so sure that I am so lucky.	1	2	3	4	5	6	7
6. I used to love spending time with my partner, but now it is starting to feel like a chore.	1	2	3	4	5	6	7
7. I feel tricked, cheated, or deceived by love.	1	2	3	4	5	6	7
8. The relationship is not as enjoyable as I had expected it to be.	1	2	3	4	5	6	7
9. If I could go back in time, I would not have gotten involved with my partner.	1	2	3	4	5	6	7
10. My partner used to be on her or his best behavior when with me, but now he or she doesn't bother trying to impress me.	1	2	3	4	5	6	7
11. My partner seems to be an entirely different person now.	1	2	3	4	5	6	7

Add up your responses. A score of 11 represents a lack of disillusionment, whereas a score of 77 represents the highest possible level of disillusionment.

SOURCE: From Niehuis, S., & Bartell, D., The marital disillusionment scale: Development and psychometric properties. *North American Journal of Psychology 8*, 69–83, copyright © 2006. Reprinted and adapted with permission of the North American Journal of Psychology and the author.

NOTE: This scale is an abbreviated version of their Marital Disillusionment Scale. We modified the scale to be applicable to both dating and marital relationships.

These are stage model approaches to disengagement. Alternatively, many relationships go through sudden changes more akin to falling off a balcony than descending a flight of stairs. These are catastrophe theory approaches to disengagement. The leading stage models are Duck's phase model of relational dissolution and Knapp's reversal hypothesis.

Duck's Phase Model of Relational Dissolution

One of the foremost stage models of relational breakups is Duck's (1982, 1988) **phase model of relational dissolution**, depicted in Figure 15.1. The model conceives of breakups as a set of distinct but connected phases. It is important to note that couples can go through several of these stages (particularly the first two) without proceeding to relational breakup. In fact, many couples recognize and resolve relational problems during Duck's first two phases. But as couples reach and then proceed through the third phase, relationship dissolution becomes more likely.

One of the most elegant features of Duck's model is that it blends cognitive and behavioral factors. Each of the dissolution phases is preceded by a cognitive threshold (see Figure 15.1). These thresholds can be thought of as statements that represent the culmination of a person's thoughts at the end of each phase. These cognitive thresholds then propel the individual into the next phase. Sometimes, of course, partners do not reach these cognitive thresholds, but instead repair their relationships and return

to a state of satisfaction. Duck's phases are described in more detail in what follows.

The Intrapsychic Phase. If people are dissatisfied with a relationship and reach the conclusion that they just "can't stand it anymore," they enter the intrapsychic phase. In this first stage of relational dissolution, a relational partner begins to reflect about the negative aspects of the relationship and contrasts these flaws with the cost of leaving the relationship. In some ways, this phase involves determining one's own feelings about the relationship, as well as preparing to talk to the partner about problems. Sometimes, individuals in this phase realize that their problems are not as bad as they originally thought. At other times, however, mulling about relational problems makes them worse rather than better (Cloven &

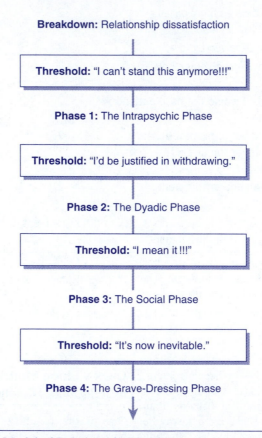

Figure 15.1 Duck's Phase Model of Relationship Dissolution

SOURCE: From "Personal Relationships 4: Dissolving Personal Relationships." In Steve Duck, *A typology of relational disengagement and dissolution,* copyright © 1982. Used with permission from Elsevier.

Roloff, 1993). Vaughn (1986) claimed that "uncoupling begins with a secret. One of the partners starts to feel uncomfortable with the relationship" (p. 11). This is exactly what happened to Sean, whom we introduced at the beginning of this chapter. He felt that the relationship was changing him in ways that made him uncomfortable. Dissatisfied partners face the dilemma of whether to discuss these feelings and thoughts with their relational partner. They may hint about the problems to the partner, but more often they confide in a third party (Duck, 1988). A breakup is certainly not inevitable at this phase; often the partner is seeking to resolve the problems and maintain the relationship. However, when people begin to believe that withdrawing from the relationship would be justified, they move into the next phase.

The Dyadic Phase. In this phase, dissatisfied partners begin to communicate about negative thoughts and feelings with each other. They attempt to negotiate and sometimes reconcile the differences to avert a relationship breakup. Fights, arguments, and long discussions often characterize this phase. According to Duck (1988), partners display uncertainty, oscillation, and hesitancy during this phase because of doubts over which path to take and because of the guilt, distress, and unpleasantness that would accompany a full-fledged breakup. In addition, some partners decide to use avoidance and withdrawal rather than communicating with each other during this phase, as Sean did initially. At the end of this phase, if people conclude that they are serious about the possibility of breaking up ("I mean it!"), they move into the third phase.

The Social Phase. In this phase, people begin talking to their social networks and investigating alternatives to the current relationship. They attempt to save face and receive support by telling their side of the story to friends and family members, as Katelyn did when she turned to Tamika for comfort. They are also likely to develop a story to convince their network, and themselves, that they are doing the right thing (Duck, 1982). Often nonverbal behaviors such as looking depressed or sounding upset reveal to others that something is wrong in the relationship. Thus the breakup initiator not only starts to complain publicly but also displays discontentment about the partner to others (Vaughn, 1986). Initially, the individual's network may try to prevent a breakup, but when the

outcome seems inevitable, they help facilitate the breakup by providing interpersonal and emotional support and taking her or his side in any disputes. When members of the person's social network take their friend's side, it helps convince the breakup initiator that he or she is making the right decision. A word of caution is in order here, though: If people complain too loudly about their partners to others, the social network may have a hard time accepting them back into the fold if the partners change their minds and get back together. If, however, the partners decide to proceed ("It is now inevitable"), they move on to the final phase.

The Grave-Dressing Phase. After the breakup, emotional repair and relational realignment must occur. Often, there are property to divide, children to deal with, and reputations to repair. Duck (1982, 1988) drew an analogy between erecting a burial monument and giving a eulogy, and the story that the separated parties begin to construct to help them save face and justify the breakup. Often, the story is that, despite how good the two people were, the relationship was flawed from the start. Of course, not all former relational partners are this gracious toward each other. Sometimes partners continue to harbor ill will toward one another and to smear each other's names. Still, stories are a vital part of the psychology of breakups and the movement toward new relationships.

Knapp's Reversal Hypothesis: The "Coming-Apart" Stages

One of the earliest and most creative stage models of disengagement was Knapp's (1978) model of interaction stages, which later became known as the **reversal hypothesis**. Knapp posited that five stages characterize the "coming-apart" process: differentiating, circumscribing, stagnating, avoiding, and terminating. These stages are essentially the reverse of Knapp's stages of coming together discussed earlier in the book (see Chapter 5). Hence these phases of Knapp's model comprise the reversal hypothesis.

Differentiating. This stage occurs when people begin to behave as individuals rather than as a couple and emphasize difference at the expense of similarities. Partners may start doing things separately, and they may also argue about their differences. Sean, for example, started noticing that he and Katelyn had radically different opinions regarding religion. Of course, many relational partners go through the differentiation phase without proceeding toward relational termination. Sometimes people simply need to assert their individuality and autonomy. Extended differentiation, however, can lead couples to feel disconnected.

Circumscribing. This stage occurs when communication becomes constricted in both depth and breadth. In some ways, the superficial communication that takes place during this stage is similar to small talk, except that the communicators are using talk (and avoidance of talk) to distance themselves from each other instead of to learn more about each other. Communication can be constricted at any stage of a relationship. However, when partners begin to feel that they have nothing to talk about, it could be a sign that the relationship is declining.

Stagnating. During the third stage, the relationship seems to be at a standstill. Communication becomes tense and awkward, and the relationship is itself virtually a taboo subject. At this point, people often feel that they already know what their partner will say or that the outcome of interaction will always be negative. Therefore, communication is seen as unproductive and unpleasant. Some couples who reach this stage eventually find a way to revive the relationship. Others, however, give up hope and, quickly or gradually, move to the next stage.

Avoiding. This stage is best characterized by physical separation. If possible, relational partners move into separate physical environments and try not to encounter each other. If physical separation is not possible, the partners simply ignore each other. For example, spouses who have young children and cannot afford to live apart might move into separate bedrooms until a more permanent solution can be reached. In any case, the goal in the avoidance stage is to achieve as much physical and psychological distance as possible.

Terminating. In this final stage, relational partners end contact, and the relationship is over. Although the partners may quickly be able to separate from each other physically, it might take longer to separate psychologically. Individuals develop their own self-interests and social networks as a way of distancing themselves from their past relationship and moving on with their lives. If communication does occur at this stage, it is usually tense, awkward, and hesitant.

Knapp's model makes intuitive sense, but it has not been tested extensively. One study partially supported Knapp's reversal prediction regarding self-disclosure. Tolstedt and Stokes (1984) found that during breakups self-disclosure decreased in breadth and became more negatively valenced, consistent with Knapp's model. However, contrary to the reversal hypothesis, depth of disclosure actually increased. This may be because some couples have intense arguments and discussions as they move toward relational termination. Other critics have argued that Knapp's model fails to accurately represent most breakups, because it focuses almost exclusively on patterns of avoidance and distancing rather than on conflict and relational discussion.

A study of the breakup scripts of undergraduates by Battaglia, Richard, Datteri, and Lord (1998) suggests most breakups cycle and recycle through a 16-step sequence: lack of interest, noticing other people, acting distant, trying to work things out, avoidance, lack of interest, considering a breakup, communicating feelings, trying to work things out, noticing other people, acting distant, dating other people, getting back together, considering breaking up, moving on, breaking up.

Catastrophe Theory

Catastrophe theory is an alternative to the stage models of relational disengagement. Critics of stage models believe that stages are artificial conceptualizations that fail to capture the actual nature of relational dissolution. First, many relational breakups skip steps. For instance, not every relationship goes through the stages of circumscribing or stagnation; some go straight to avoidance or termination. In the later versions of the model (see Knapp & Vangelisti,

2005), the researchers address the process of skipping steps. Second, stages may occur nonlinearly, in various orders. For instance, termination may be followed by reconciliation, temporary bonding, stagnation, and then avoidance. Derlega et al. (1993) contended that cyclical movements characterize most relationships, as they swing between periods of stability and change. Likewise, couples may go in and out of a stage several times before entering a stable period. Third, the stages of dissolution cannot simply be the reverse of the acquaintance process. Derlega et al. (1993) argued that during dissolution partners cannot "unknow" each other and are still very capable of predicting each other's behavior.

The **catastrophe model** of disengagement suggests that relationship breakups occur in a radically different way; relationships do not gradually unwind through stages of relational dissolution, but instead are characterized by sudden death (Davis, 1973). Like earthquakes along a silent fault line or like the violent wall next to the quiet eye of a hurricane, the stability of a relationship is shattered by a sudden cataclysmic event. Of course, fault lines are never completely silent, and impending hurricanes are accompanied by subtle signs such as falling air pressure and increased humidity. There are always signs of an impending relational catastrophe as well, but people fail to see them or deny them, as did Katelyn in the vignette at the opening of this chapter. As Vaughn (1986) stated, "Partners often report that they are unaware, or only remotely aware, even at the point of separation, that the relationship is deteriorating. Only after the other person is gone are they able to look back and recognize the signals" (p. 62).

Many relationship breakups are precipitated by a critical incident that led to rapid disengagement (Baxter, 1984; Bullis et al., 1993; Cupach & Metts, 1986; Rosen & Stith, 1995). These incidents ranged from the discovery of infidelity to big arguments and physical violence to a discovery of basic differences in values, such as the mundane reality that one partner hates pets and the other person loves them. In about 25% of the relationships in Baxter's (1984) study, partners reported that a single critical incident led to a breakup. Interestingly, Bullis et al. (1993) reported that few disengagements were intentional.

Instead, disengagements often represented a nonstrategic turning point in relationships that happened relatively quickly, which is more in line with a catastrophe model of breakups than a stage model.

Even when no critical incident can be singled out, relationships sometimes dissolve rapidly. Wilmot (1995) discussed the "point of no return" in every relationship, at which one or both the partners know for sure that it is over. Wilmot maintained that in these cases "sometimes people just disappear, without any warning or indication of their discomfort with the relationship" (p. 119). Similarly, Davis (1973) talked about sudden relational death, which occurs when a person abruptly decides the relationship is over, falls in love with someone else, or suffers a trauma like partner abuse. According to Wilmot (1995), sudden death can be likened to an execution rather than a slow death of the relationship. The breakup often occurs without direct, face-to-face communication, but the person initiating the breakup may enlist the help of a friend to tell the partner the relationship is over or may terminate the relationship via a letter or phone call.

Many events in nature are explained by catastrophe theory. This theory posits that events are discontinuous rather than following linear patterns (Isnard & Zeeman, 1977; Tesser & Achee, 1994). Sometimes, human behavior, including behavior in relationships, will flow along a smooth, geometric plane. However, like hikers on a path next to a cliff, the relationship can slip off the edge of the trail to a lower level, with catastrophic discontinuities for the relationship. Catastrophe theory has been successfully applied in many contexts, including mood changes, conflict during arguments, stock market behavior, and hostilities among nations (Zeeman, 1977). Relational researchers could benefit from catastrophe theory to predict sudden deaths of relationships.

FIFTEEN WAYS TO LEAVE YOUR PARTNER

People separate from relationships in a variety of ways. Although there may not be 50 ways to leave your lover, as in the Paul Simon song, research has found at least 15 strategies by which people terminate relationships, which can be differentiated based on whether they are direct or indirect and whether they are unilateral or bilateral (Baxter, 1982, 1984). Direct strategies rely mainly on face-to-face verbal communication, whereas indirect strategies employ more subtle, less direct forms of communication, including nonverbal communication. Unilateral strategies involve one person deciding to break up, whereas bilateral strategies are a joint decision to terminate the relationship.

More breakups are unilateral than bilateral, and more people end their relationships using indirect rather than direct strategies. Baxter (1979b) found that 71% of all disengagement strategies reported in her study were indirect and implicit. Similarly, in her study of disengagement accounts, Baxter (1984) found that 76% of couples employed indirect as opposed to direct communication strategies. In another study, Baxter (1979a) found that, when direct strategies were used, they were more commonly unilateral "dumps" than negotiated dialogues. While most sex differences regarding breakups are minimal or nonexistent, Wilmot, Carbaugh, and Baxter (1985) reported that females are more likely to use direct strategies than males.

Although indirect strategies are often used to end both casual and close relationships, they are particularly likely to be used in casual relationships when couples have less to negotiate (Baxter, 1979b, 1984, 1993; Perras & Lustig, 1982; Thieme & Rouse, 1991; Wilmot, Carbaugh, & Baxter, 1985). Breakups are stressful, and disengagers try to minimize their pain and anxiety through indirect rather than direct communication. In light of the fact that "ending a relationship is perhaps one of the most face-threatening situations we encounter" (Cupach & Metts, 1994, p. 81), people are most likely to use indirect strategies that seem to minimize guilt and embarrassment.

Unfortunately, indirect strategies send neither clear nor kind messages. In Baxter's (1984) study, only 22% of the recipients of indirect disengagement messages believed that the relationship was over. Worse, relational partners were most likely to express regrets about the relationships when indirect rather than direct relational disengagement strategies were employed (Baxter, 1979b). Baxter (1979b) suggested

that "hints" and other indirect relational disengagement strategies may actually create uncertainty, prolong the termination process, and be more painful for the participants.

Individuals can terminate their relationships using a single strategy or a complex array of both direct and indirect strategies. For people such as Sean, who are concerned about hurting their partner, finding a strategy that is both effective and sensitive can be challenging. As you read through the following strategies, you will likely recognize some of them from your own relational breakups. We do not intend this section to be a "how-to" guide for breaking up with relational partners. As the research presented in this chapter shows, breakups can be very emotionally distressing, and the strategies you use to end a relationship can contribute to that distress. We hope, however, that by learning about the ways in which people break off relationships, you will be better able to understand the disengagement process—and perhaps will be a little more sensitive the next time you find yourself initiating a breakup.

Strategies That Are Unilateral and Indirect

Avoidance. The most common and least direct relational disengagement strategy is avoidance, whereby people literally "just slip out the back, Jack." A number of studies have reported avoidance as a primary disengagement strategy (Baxter, 1982; Cody, 1982; Emmers & Hart, 1996; Perras & Lustig, 1982), which can range from complete evasion to decreased contact. Baxter (1979a) found decreased frequency of contact with a partner to be one of the two most common indirect disengagement strategies. In Baxter's (1984) study of disengagement accounts, 66% of the couples using indirect strategies reportedly used avoidance-based withdrawal strategies. Research has shown that avoidance tactics are likely when there is little likelihood of maintaining a friendship in the future, when intimacy is low, when there are fewer formal ties, and when the perceived faults of the partner are high (Banks, Altendorf, Greene, & Cody, 1987).

Not surprisingly, research shows that the avoidance strategy is a fairly ineffective way to end a relationship. Both parties experience a loss of face (Metts, 1997), and it is difficult for the former relational partners to experience closure. When avoidance strategies are used, "the breakup is particularly dissatisfying for the disengager and the partner," even in short-term or relatively casual relationships (Metts, 1997, p. 387). Several studies have found that avoidance strategies are the least effective, most protracted, and most distressing way to end a relationship (Baxter & Philpott, 1980). Sean's initial use of this strategy may have unwittingly extended the breakup process, because Katelyn failed to recognize his indirect attempts to end their relationship.

Relational Ruses. Unfortunately, disengagers sometimes resort to strategies that are downright unethical or manipulative. Relational ruses are a group of such strategies. In one of Baxter's (1982) studies, a common indirect communication strategy was labeled "manipulation attempts" and included behaviors such as leaking the impending breakup to a friend and asking a third party to break the news of the disengagement. Other forms of manipulation include having a third party reveal infidelity, pretending to be interested in someone else, and asking friends to persuade the partner to end the relationship before you do. Manipulation is less likely to be used as a disengagement strategy in close relationships (Baxter, 1982). Research also has shown that relationships that are ended through manipulation are unlikely to evolve into cordial postromantic relationships, such as a friendship (Metts, Cupach, & Bejlovich, 1989).

Withdrawal of Supportiveness and Affection. A common disengagement strategy in romantic relationships is to withdraw positive forms of communication, such as social support, emotional support, affection, and immediacy. In terms of social support, the disengager is less available to talk to, discuss problems with, and provide comfort and compassion. One study reported that the withdrawal of social support was the most common relationship disengagement strategy in relationships of less than 2 years (Baxter, 1979b). As noted in Chapters 9 and 10, social support is an important part of close relationships. We expect our friends and loved ones to be there when we need them. If they are unavailable or make no effort to help us, they send an indirect but clear message that they do not value the relationship. Likewise, we expect our close friends and romantic partners to provide us with positive, affectionate communication. During relational disengagement, nonverbal communication becomes less warm, involving, and immediate (Wilmot et al., 1985). In healthy interpersonal relationships, relational partners touch, engage in eye contact, employ positive facial expressions and maintain close interpersonal distances (see Chapter 8). Conversely, a lack of these behaviors provides a powerful, implicit message that psychological distance is widening. Increasingly, nonimmediate behavior is a virtually certain sign of relational distress and movement toward disengagement. Unfortunately, Katelyn did not see these signs and was surprised at what she considered the "suddenness" of the breakup with Sean.

Pseudo De-escalation. This strategy is a false declaration to the other party that the relationship would profit from some distance that masquerades as de-escalation but is really disguised relational breakup (Baxter, 1985). A person might say, "Let's just put a little space into the relationship" or "Let's just be friends for a while," when really meaning that "this relationship is over." The intent is often to let the other party down easily. However, even though this strategy may be more humane than the relational ruses described above, pseudo de-escalation is essentially a deceptive, unethical behavior that shows little regard for one's partner. Baxter (1984) found this strategy comprised 22% of indirect breakup strategies; but pseudo de-escalation was highly ineffective, since only 9% of the receivers of such a message got the clue that the relationship was actually over. The rest of the participants harbored false hope that the relationship would eventually be revitalized.

Cost Escalation. Also called Machiavellianism (Baxter, 1979c; Perras & Lustig, 1982), cost escalation (Baxter, 1984; Emmers & Hart, 1996; Thieme & Rouse, 1991) is an attempt to make the relationship unattractive to one's partner. Disengagers may drink or smoke excessively, or may be deliberately messy, obnoxious, rude, argumentative, demeaning, or disloyal, so that the partner comes to dislike them and becomes more amenable to a breakup. In one account of a breakup, the dumper stated that "I thought I would be an 'asshole' for a while to make her like me less" (Baxter, 1985, p. 249). In another study, cost escalation was found to be the most commonly used disengagement strategy, employed by 31% of the respondents (Thieme & Rouse, 1991). However, in Baxter's (1984) study, cost escalation was employed by only 12% of the couples using indirect strategies. Ironically, cost escalation can be beneficial in some breakups, especially if the "dumpee" is happy to break off the relationship after the costs have been escalated.

Strategies That Are Unilateral and Direct

The Direct Dump. The most common direct communication strategy is the simple statement that the relationship is over (Baxter, 1984; Thieme & Rouse, 1991). This strategy is sometimes called the open-and-honest approach, whereby someone forthrightly communicates her or his desire to end the relationship (Baxter, 1982; Perras & Lustig, 1982). Most commonly called the "fait accompli" approach (Baxter, 1979b, 1984), this tactic typically gives the partner no choice and little chance for a response. Often, this strategy emphasizes the negative consequences of not breaking up, which helps the partner accept the breakup. Baxter (1984) reported that fait accompli resulted in 81% of the receivers of such messages accepting the breakup and offering no resistance, probably because of the perceived futility of countering such a direct message. Of course, it can also be disconcerting to be the recipient of the direct dump—to be suddenly told that the relationship is over and there's nothing you can do about it. This is what Katelyn perceived to have happened, when in actuality Sean had been trying to signal that he wanted to break up for sometime. As the scenario between Katelyn and Sean illustrates, people sometimes use the direct dump after other, more subtle strategies have failed.

Dates With Other People. Sometimes, rather than break up completely, a disengager recommends dating other people. This strategy, which is sometimes called negative identity management (Banks et al., 1987; Cody, 1982; Metts, 1997), imposes one person's solution on the other person, at the expense of the recipient's feelings. For example, the person initiating the breakup might say, "I told him that I was going to date other people and that he should also date other people." In this strategy, the dumper at least has the class to communicate directly to her or his partner. However, even though this strategy is direct, its underlying meaning is less clear. Sometimes dating other people represents a temporary hiatus from an intense, intimate relationship that will rekindle. Often, however, this announcement is a disengagement message.

Justification. This strategy includes explanations for why the relationship is ending and why the partner is dissatisfied, and/or listing what changes have occurred in the individuals or in the relationship (Banks et al., 1987; Cody, 1982). Unlike the direct dump, this strategy acknowledges the need to provide some rationale for the breakup to one's partner. It is an attempt to protect the face of both partners. This strategy is most likely to be used in highly intimate and committed relationships in which the friendship networks of the partners are highly overlapping (Banks et al., 1987). Justification is also more likely when the disengager feels that the rejected partner has many faults.

Research has shown that justifications are important to the rejected partner's ability to accept the end of the relationship. Thieme and Rouse (1991) found a significant association between the number of reasons given for a breakup and the rebuffed person's ability to accept the end of the relationship. Of course, if the justification focuses on the rejected individual's personal faults, hurt feelings and lowered self-esteem are likely to follow. But when justifications focus on the initiator of the breakup and general relationship issues, more positive outcomes are likely.

One common type of justification in dating relationships revolves around the desire for autonomy. Sometimes, people feel they are becoming too dependent on each other and are losing their independence and individuality. As a result, they de-escalate or disengage from the relationship using a strategy that

Cody (1982) called "relationship faults" or "appeals to independence." Often, young lovers give this reason because they are not sure they are ready to settle down with one person just yet. Partners may also point to external factors, such as needing to concentrate more on school or one's career, as reasons for decreasing interdependence. This strategy is often less threatening than others, because it centers on the needs of the breakup initiator (for more space or freedom) and/or external events (such as school or work) rather than on the faults of the person who is being left. Often, the reason for leaving the relationship is framed in situational terms: "At this point in my life I'm not ready to settle down yet" or "Right now I only have time for school."

The Relationship Talk Trick. Some disengagers talk about "problems" in the relationship as a guise for a relationship breakup. Baxter (1984) found that this strategy was incorporated in 27% of direct breakups. Sometimes, this strategy is an honest attempt to discuss and solve problems in the relationship. More often, however, it is an insincere attempt to discuss problems and solutions in a manner that leads to the conclusion that the problems are insurmountable and justify a breakup. In other words, the breakup initiator intentionally structures the "relational talk" to show that the partners are better off going their separate ways. Like cost escalation, this strategy can be hurtful in some instances but beneficial in others. If the person initiating the breakup can convince her or his partner that the relationship is not worth saving, both partners can walk away feeling that although they tried the relationship just could not be saved.

Threats and Bullying. Another direct and unilateral strategy involves threatening the partner. Baxter (1984) identified threats and bullying as manipulation attempts that people use to get a partner to break up with them. Sometimes, people use these strategies when the partner refuses to break up with them. For example, if a wife wants a divorce and her husband stubbornly refuses, she might threaten to take the children out of state if he doesn't comply with her wishes. Sometimes, threats are also part of the fabric of the breakup itself, with people telling their soon-to-be former partner not to divulge certain information about them or the breakup to others and threatening to get revenge against them if they do. Obviously, these types of breakup strategies are very destructive. Threats and bullying can make the "dumped" person feel powerless at a time when her or his self-esteem is likely to be very fragile. These types of strategies are also likely to destroy any chances a couple might have of remaining friends following the breakup.

Positive Tone. Sometimes unilateral breakups are accomplished using a positive tone strategy that is designed to lessen the "dumped" person's hurt feelings and make them feel better about the breakup (Banks et al., 1987; Baxter, 1982; Cody, 1982; Perras & Lustig, 1982). For instance, Sean could have told Katelyn that even though their relationship is ending, he has no regrets about the time he spent with her. He might also have appealed to fatalism by saying things such as, "It's nobody's fault; it just wasn't meant to be." At other times, the fairness approach is adopted. Sean might have said something such as, "If I stayed in this relationship it wouldn't be fair to you. You deserve someone who loves you the way you deserve to be loved." Apologies and compliments can also be part of a positive tone strategy. Sean might tell Katelyn that he is sorry and doesn't want to hurt her, but his heart simply isn't in the relationship anymore. He might also tell her that he still thinks she is a beautiful and intelligent woman and wishes that it could have worked out. Like some of the indirect strategies we discussed earlier, one danger of using the positive tone strategy is that the person being dumped may hold onto hope that the relationship might somehow still survive—or at least rebound. Thus, it is important to emphasize that the breakup is imminent for this strategy to be both effective and sensitive.

De-escalation. These strategies avoid a complete breakup, at least initially, by proposing that the relationship de-escalate. Unlike pseudo de-escalation, these strategies involve an honest attempt to improve the relationship by de-escalating it (Cody, 1982; Banks et al., 1987) Usually, the de-escalator recommends breaking off the relationship for a while or recommends that "we just be friends" (Cody, 1982), a strategy most people, especially men, hate to hear

(Hill et al., 1976). Other options include a trial separation, moving out of the same living space, or spending less time together. Sometimes, people think that if they spend some time away from each other they will miss and appreciate each other more. At other times, they think they would get along better if they didn't live together. Although de-escalation can provide a new starting point for some relationships as couples transition from being romantic partners to friends or from being cohabitants to dating partners who no longer live together, research suggests that de-escalation is usually nothing but a giant step along the path of a complete disengagement. Indeed, most married couples who obtain a legal separation end up getting a divorce.

A Strategy That Is Bilateral and Indirect

The Fadeaway. In Baxter's research, only one strategy emerged as both bilateral and indirect. This strategy is called fading away. Sometimes, both people in a relationship recognize that the relationship is at a standstill, and they gradually drift apart and lose contact. This is very common in the case of friends who lose touch over the years (Baxter, 1979b) and when relational partners are separated from each other for long stretches of time. In long-distance relationships, people sometimes come to feel like strangers due to the limited contact they have with one another. Words may not be necessary to end the relationship; instead, the couple may simply sense that it is over. For example, one of our students told the following story of her relational breakup:

> We only saw each other a couple of times since moving away from our hometown to attend different colleges. At first, we called each other frequently, but over time the calls slowed down, and we seemed to have less and less to say to each other. After spending some awkward time together during Thanksgiving weekend, he drove me to the airport. When I left to board the plane, we hugged briefly, and it was clear that the relationship was not the same—it was over.

In some ways, fading away is the antithesis of breakups that occur in a catastrophic fashion. Fading away has no dramatic incident leading to the breakup but is rather a slow and gradual descent.

Strategies That Are Bilateral and Direct

The Blame Game. In some cases, dissatisfaction leads to a competitive blaming game that eventually results in relational breakup. Cycles of negativity become a common pattern, with both partners dissatisfied and the relationship charged with negative emotion. When the partners try to talk about their problems, they end up complaining and blaming each other rather than taking responsibility for their own actions. Eventually, when they agree to break up, they argue over the reasons and blame each other for the relationship's demise (Cody, 1982). Both may claim that the impending breakup is the other's fault, and both may feel justified in ending the relationship. In fact, partners who use the blaming strategy may set each other up so that leaving the relationship is the option that best helps them save face. This type of strategy can be beneficial in that it provides both partners with a good reason to exit the relationship. However, breakups of this kind can be particularly messy, since conflict and disagreement are likely to prevail to the bitter end.

The Negotiated Farewell. Another common method of relational disengagement, particularly for long-term couples, is negotiation, which is related to the strategies of integrative communication (Metts, 1997) and directness (Emmers & Hart, 1996). People using this strategy often have been together for a relatively long time but realize that problems cannot be resolved and that they would be better off if they parted. Some of these couples may also need to divide up possessions, negotiate child custody and financial issues, and determine how they can both reside comfortably within a joint social network. The key to the negotiated farewell is that both parties are willing to try to be fair to each other during the disengagement process (which is in direct contrast to the attitude of those playing the blame game). The goal of the negotiated farewell is to leave the relationship "well" rather than on a sour note. This strategy is most often used when there are high levels of relational intimacy and commitment

SOURCE: Copyright: iStockphoto.com/Peter Finnie

Photo 15.1   During the disengagement process, some couples play the "blame game." Deflecting responsibility for relationship problems by blaming each other makes reconciliation less likely.

and the partners' interpersonal networks are overlapping (Baxter, 1982; Cody, 1982). When negotiating the breakup, couples using this strategy may also use the positive tone strategies we discussed earlier. As you might suspect, this is one of the least distressing ways to end a relationship. Figure 15.2 summarizes the various disengagement strategies.

Relational Redefinition: Let's Be Friends

Some romantic relationships are able to shift from a romance to a friendship. If there is a great deal of mutual respect and admiration between relational partners, a friendship may serve to preserve the relationship while recognizing it does not have romantic potential any longer. Traditional relational dissolution models have failed to explain relationships that remain after the romance has ended, although some researchers have studied postdissolution relationships (Lannutti & Cameron, 2002; Masheter, 1997). Lannutti and Cameron's research on gay, lesbian, and heterosexual couples demonstrated that all

three couple types employ relational redefinition, and many are able to transition to nonsexual relationships. Gay and lesbian couples report high levels of satisfaction, contact, and emotional intimacy with their former partners, whereas heterosexual couples report only moderate satisfaction and closeness, and low contact with their former partners. Research shows that even 10 years after divorce, half of all divorced couples report contact with their former spouse (Fischer, De Graaf, & Kalmijn, 2005). Contact is especially likely if the couple had joint children, had a relatively longer marriage, and held more liberal social values.

The relationship that former spouses develop can take many different forms, including being co-parents without being friends and having a unilateral friendship (with only one of the former spouses regarding the other as a friend). Many former spouses stay connected through a social network that includes joint children and family get-togethers. Some former spouses become (or remain) good friends after their divorce. Ahrons (1994) uses the concept of *perfect pals* to describe postdivorce friendships that are close

	Unilateral	Bilateral
Indirect	• Avoidance • Relational ruses • Withdrawal of support and affection • Pseudo de-escalation • Cost escalation	• The fade-away
Direct	• The direct dump • Dates with other people • Justification • The relationship talk trick • Threats and bullying • Positive tone • De-escalation	• The blame game • The negotiated farewell

Figure 15.2   Disengagement Strategies

and satisfying. Most of these couples who described themselves as perfect pals reported that although their divorces were not amicable, they had also not been adversarial. Many of these couples also said that they grew closer in some ways after the divorce. They reported confiding in and doing favors for each other, regularly talking, and actively co-parenting their children, and they saw their friendship as close and irreplaceable. According to Ahrons, about 12% of co-parents describe themselves as having this type of friendship 5 years after their divorce. Masheter's (1997) research showed that some former spouses without children also develop or maintain close friendships after divorce.

OUTCOMES: THE RESULTS OF RELATIONSHIP ENDINGS

Losing a relational partner can be a devastating experience. During the breakup the world looks bleak and hopeless. While the experience is usually negative, most people do move on with their lives and, eventually, may find positive outcomes associated with the loss. In this section, we discuss the emotional and

relational outcomes that often follow the breakup of close relationships such as marriages.

Negative Outcomes of Relational Breakups

Most relational breakups are usually characterized by some degree of distress. In fact, most short-term reactions to relationship breakup are negative. Relational partners often feel as if the world is about to end. Even some long-term negative consequences may persist.

Negative Emotions. A common result of a relational breakup is the presence of negative emotions. A relational breakup is one of the most distressing, traumatic events we experience, particularly for the unwilling partner in the breakup. As Duck (1988) stated, "There is very little pain on earth like the pain of a long-term personal relationship that is falling apart" (p. 102).

Studies have shown that depression, anger, hurt, guilt, confusion, and frustration are common feelings during a relational breakup. In one-sided breakups, a sizable majority of partners experience negative emotions, regardless of whether they initiated the breakup and whether they are female or male (Kurdek, 1991; Simpson, 1987; Ugbah & DeWine, 1986; Wilmot et al., 1985). In Owen's (1993) study of relationship accounts, respondents described breakups as emotional injuries: "He left a huge hole in my heart," "My heart felt like a dart board," and "I was torn to shreds." Contrary to intuition, research has found that men experience more emotional trauma than women after an unwanted breakup (Hill et al., 1976). This is not to minimize women's distress after breakups. Studies have found that *both* sexes experience emotional distress following an unwanted breakup (Wilmot et al., 1985); men simply seem to do so a little more intensely.

Several factors predict how much distress people experience after a relational breakup. Social support, connectedness to other people, especially peers, and economic resources can cushion the distress (Moller, Fouladi, McCarthy, & Hatch, 2003; Vangelisti, 2002). People are more depressed by a breakup when their love for their partner was deep, they were highly committed to the relationship, their partner was physically attractive, they didn't want the relationship to end, and their partner did want the relationship to end (Mearns, 1991; Sprecher, Felmlee, Metts, Fehr, & Vanni, 1998). Additionally, people in a romantic relationship who felt emotionally close to their partner, had high levels of relational satisfaction, had been in the relationship for a long time, and had little control over the breakup were likely to experience the most distress following the breakup (Frazier & Cook, 1993; Simpson, 1987; Sprecher et al., 1998).

While distress is typically greater for the victim of an unwanted breakup, we should never underestimate the emotional distress experienced by the initiator of the breakup. Like Sean, many people feel bad about having to initiate a breakup. Initiators may feel guilt, shame, embarrassment, stress, and ambivalence about the breakup. Also, they may repeatedly be reminded of the breakup by their social network and may have to provide numerous accounts and justifications for their actions.

Loneliness. The loss of a relationship is very likely to produce intense feelings of loneliness. In a study of gay and lesbian relationships, Kurdek (1991) found that loneliness was the second most common emotional reaction following a breakup. Moreover, a breakup is a double whammy: Not only have the partners lost one of the most important people in their lives, but they have also lost the person they would normally have turned to for comfort following such a loss.

It is natural for people to feel lonely after the breakup of a significant relationship. According to Segrin (1998), loneliness is the result of a discrepancy between one's actual and desired level of social interaction with others. When an intimate relationship ends, this discrepancy may increase. Suddenly, there is a wider gap between how much intimacy someone wants and how much intimacy he or she is receiving. However, individuals are likely to feel less lonely after a breakup if they are surrounded by friends and family members who care about them (Segrin, 1998).

Interestingly, loneliness can also be a motivation for breaking off a relationship. As discussed previously, people sometimes initiate breakups because they are dissatisfied or bored with their relationships. They long for the connection that they felt early in their relationships when they were first getting to know each other and everything was exciting and new. Breaking up an old relationship and searching for a new one that better fulfills one's needs are often an impetus for breakup. Indeed, one reason for divorce is the hope of finding a happier relationship, and most divorced people do remarry. Unfortunately, a divorce is even more likely in a second marriage (Argyle & Henderson, 1988).

Financial Consequences. Divorce or separation commonly becomes a financial disaster. The costs of maintaining dual residences, paying lawyers, and selling a home quickly, to mention but a few problems, make divorce one of the worst things a person can experience financially. Single moms and "deadbeat dads" are a major source of poverty in this country. And men who pay alimony and child support often feel financially trapped (Hendrick & Hendrick, 1992); it is difficult to start a new family when the financial burdens of another family are still on one's shoulders.

Unfortunately, one factor keeping many long-term partners in negative and even abusive relationships is financial dependency (see Chapter 9). Just as with married couples, Kurdek (1991) found that one of the problems facing gay and lesbian couples after a breakup involved finances. Cohabitants, regardless of their sexual orientation, are particularly likely to experience financial difficulties as they move out of each other's homes and lives. Like emotional dependency, financial dependency often traps people in unhealthy relationships.

Effects on Children. What effect does the breakup have on the children of the divorcing couple? Sadly, children seem to fare worse in divorced families than in families in which their parents were continuously and happily married. Amato and Keith (1991) published a statistical summary of prior research on the effects of parental divorce on children's well-being as adults. Based on information from 81,000 people, they reported that divorce is generally associated with a host of negative consequences. Adults from divorced homes are more likely to be depressed, less satisfied with life, less likely to have satisfying relationships, more likely to get divorced themselves, and more likely to have lower socioeconomic status, less income, and poorer physical health than adults from nondivorced families. The authors concluded, "These results lead to a pessimistic conclusion: the argument that parental divorce presents few problems for children's long-term development is simply inconsistent with the literature on this topic" (Amato & Keith, 1991, p. 54). The bad news is that these negative effects are consistent across dozens of studies. The good news is that the effects tend to be small, and when both parents maintain positive relationships with their children, the effects are smaller still. There is also some evidence that boys cope better if they live with their father and that girls cope better if they live with their mother (see Hendrick & Hendrick, 1992 for a summary). These gloomy findings notwithstanding, research suggests that it is often better for a child to suffer through a divorce than to live with parents who are constantly fighting (Booth & Edwards, 1989; see also Chapter 14).

Research has also supported *the intergenerational transmission of divorce*, which refers to the fact that children of divorced parents are about 1½ to 2 times more likely to get divorced than are children of nondivorced couples (Amato, 1996; Segrin, Taylor, & Altman, 2005; Wolfinger, 1999). Segrin and his colleagues (2005) summarized some of the reasons why this occurs. First, children of divorced parents may have negative attitudes toward commitment and marriage; they may learn that "marriage is a miserable experience, and . . . therefore avoid the behavior" (p. 362). Second, children of divorced parents are likely to have witnessed negative, dysfunctional conflict, which only adds to the perception that marriage is a stressful experience. Third, some research suggests that couples who divorce are less likely to have effective communication skills than are couples who stay together. Certainly, this is not always the case. Some couples are communicatively competent and simply realize they are not compatible. Nonetheless, children of divorced parents may not have learned as many skills related to successful marital communication, making them more susceptible to divorce and other failed relationships. Although all three of these explanations—negative marital attitudes, dysfunctional parental conflict, and lack of communication skills—have been shown by various researchers to relate to the intergenerational transmission of divorce, the study by Segrin and his colleagues suggests that negative attitudes toward marriage and commitment may be the most important.

Research also suggests that "feeling caught" between one's parents leads to negative outcomes, such as anxiety and depression (Buchanon, Maccoby, & Dornbusch, 1991, 1996). As Afifi and Schrodt (2003) explained, "children who feel caught between their parents often describe themselves as being 'put in the middle,' 'torn,' or forced to defend their loyalty to each of their parents" (p. 142). Children are more likely to feel caught in the middle when their parents argue in front of them and disclose negative information about one another to them. When children feel caught in the middle of two divorced parents, they are likely to avoid talking about the state of their family in front of their parents (Golish & Caughlin, 2002), presumably because they do not want to start a conflict or appear to be supporting one parent over the other. Children who feel caught in the middle also report less satisfaction and closeness in their relationships with their parents (e.g., Afifi & Schrodt, 2003). These findings suggest that it is critical for parents to avoid having their children take sides. Parents who talk to and about one another in a respectful, positive manner are likely to foster a postdivorce environment that is more comfortable for both themselves and their children.

Health Consequences. Studies have also shown that separation and divorce threaten people's health. Divorced people have a higher incidence of heart problems, cancer, liver disease, pneumonia, and a host of other diseases (Argyle & Henderson, 1988). Divorce has also been linked to a variety of emotional and physical disorders, psychiatric illness, suicide, and interpersonal violence (Hendrick & Hendrick, 1992). The breakup of a dating relationship can also lead to psychological stress. Monroe, Rohde, Seeley, and Lewinsohn (1999) found that relational breakups were predictive of the onset of a major depressive disorder during adolescence. Najib, Lorberbaum, Kose, Bohning, and George (2004) documented changes in brain activity after a romantic relationship breakup consistent with the pattern associated with chronic depression. Similarly, the death of a partner can affect the grieving person's physical health. When people are depressed, stressed, or grieving, their bodies may be more susceptible to physical ailments, such as ulcers, heart problems, and even the common cold.

Healing After a Separation

Because relationship loss can be personally devastating, it is important to understand what factors influence recovery from the distress, loneliness, and depression that often accompany a breakup. Mutually negotiated breakups result in the fewest bad feelings (Wilmot et al., 1985) and, generally, are the easiest to recover from. Recovery from a unilateral breakup, when one person wants the relationship to continue, is difficult or impossible (Frazier & Cook, 1993). Thus if a relationship is really over, it is important to stop dwelling on it and to move on with one's life. Of course, this is more easily said than done. Research also suggests that breakups are more protracted and distressing when more indirect termination strategies are employed (Baxter & Philpott, 1980). It is more humane and honest to tell someone, in direct and positive terms, that the relationship is over, as Sean eventually did. Only then can the recovery process begin. Research suggests that disclosing your feelings to

others or even writing about them is a therapeutic activity that can aid recovery from a breakup (Lepore & Greenberg, 2002; Pennebaker, 1990). Therefore, Katelyn is taking a step in the right direction by talking with Tamika about her feelings.

Positive Outcomes of Relational Breakups

Despite the trauma associated with breakups, it is not unusual for one or both partners to actually have positive feelings about a separation (Wilmot et al., 1985). One of the most common outcomes in Kurdek's (1991) study of gay and lesbian relationships was increased happiness following the breakup. Indeed, often it is a relief to be out of a bad or dangerous relationship. Sometimes, a breakup can provide relief from relational ambiguity or conflict. Not infrequently, a person moves on to a more satisfying relationship following a breakup. Kurdek (1991) reported that relief from conflict was one of the most common outcomes of separation in gay and lesbian relationships. In addition, Kurdek found that personal growth was the most commonly cited positive outcome of relational breakups. Of course, some relationships continue to be problematic after the breakup, especially if one person cannot let go. For example, in our opening scenario, Katelyn leaves pleading messages on Sean's answering machine. Such messages are highly unlikely to change the situation. Instead, they make Sean feel guiltier and Katelyn feel even worse about herself.

One positive outcome of relationship breakups is personal growth that can occur in the relationship's aftermath. Tashiro and Frazier (2003) discovered several kinds of postrelational growth, including **personal positives**, such as increased self-confidence and being able to handle life on one's own, **relational positives**, such as having learned how to communicate in a relationship and the importance of not jumping into a relationship too quickly, **environmental positives**, such as concentrating more on school or work or relying on friendship networks more; and **future positives**, such as knowing what one wants in a relational partner. Eventually, Katelyn may gain some of these benefits. She may learn that she can cope temporarily without a romantic partner, and perhaps she'll devote more time to other activities that she finds personally rewarding.

Ending any relationship, especially a bad relationship, also represents an opportunity to form a new relationship. But many people make the mistake of leaping head first into a new relationship, which can land them in another relationship destined to fail. Thus rapid expressions of love and affection in a new relationship are often a turnoff, because people think that you cannot possibly like them that much yet (Sternberg, 1987) and that you are just using them to recover from your loss. Let any new relationships evolve slowly and naturally.

SUMMARY AND APPLICATION

Relationships end for a variety of reasons. Sometimes people make a conscious choice to take their lives in a new direction. At other times, relationships slowly wither away, partners physically separate from each other due to school or career choices, or death occurs. In each case, coping with the loss of a significant relationship is difficult. Both Katelyn and Sean will feel bad that their relationship has ended. Sean is likely to feel guilty since he initiated the breakup, but he may also feel relief because Katelyn finally got the message that the relationship is over. Katelyn is likely to have a more difficult time, in part because the breakup seemed sudden to her. Seeking social support from friends such as Tamika is a first step toward understanding the breakup and moving forward.

Understanding why you broke up can also be helpful. Researchers have identified various specific reasons for relationship breakups. Often, communication is the culprit. Avoidance, negative communication, and lack of openness are three common communication problems that cause breakups. Gottman's research shows that stonewalling (or avoidance) is an especially strong harbinger of divorce. Katelyn or Sean may have noticed some of these communication patterns in their relationship. If they had worked on their communication, it is possible (although not at all certain) that their relationship could have improved. Dissimilarity and sexual incompatibility can also precipitate relational breakups, as can financial issues, inequity, disillusionment, and alcohol or drug abuse. The most common reason for the termination of dating relationships is boredom. People simply miss the excitement that once was present in their relationships but that somehow dimmed over time. Sometimes, this boredom leads people to look elsewhere and develop an interest in alternative partners. Still others feel smothered by their relationships and break up to achieve autonomy and independence.

Regardless of why a relationship ends, research has shown that people usually experience a host of negative outcomes following relational termination, including emotional, physical, and financial distress. If a person did not want the relationship to end, he or she might feel rejected and fearful of starting a new relationship. If a person initiated the relational breakup, he or she often feels guilt. The strategy that people use to end their relationships can make a difference. Direct strategies are usually preferred, especially if they include positive communication. Thus, the best way for Sean to break up may have been to use the positive tone strategy. He could have told Katelyn that their relationship meant a lot to him, he could have complimented her, and he could have told her how sorry he was that it wasn't going to work out. Of course, for this strategy to be effective, Sean would need to communicate his desire to break off the relationship—despite his positive regard for her—very clearly. Direct, definitive statements delivered with a positive tone may be the best strategy when breakups are unilateral. The negotiated farewell is the optimal strategy when breakups are bilateral. Such strategies allow a person to get over the breakup more quickly, which opens up the possibility of finding new partners and exploring uncharted relational territory.

DISCUSSION QUESTIONS

1. How are the stage models developed by Duck and Knapp similar and different? Which of these models describes the disengagement process better? Why?

2. Of the 15 specific breakup strategies mentioned in this chapter, which do you think are the least pleasant and/or ethical? Why?

3. How might you help a friend get over a relationship breakup or the death of a loved one?

REFERENCES

Abbey, A. (1982). Sex differences in attributions for friendly behavior: Do males misperceive females' friendliness? *Journal of Personality and Social Psychology, 42,* 830–838.

Abbey, A. (1987). Misperceptions of friendly behavior as sexual interest: A survey of naturally occurring incidents. *Psychology of Women Quarterly, 11,* 173–194.

Abbey, A., & Melby, C. (1986). The effects of nonverbal cues in gender differences in perceptions of sexual intent. *Sex Roles, 15,* 283–298.

Aboud, F. E., & Mendelson, M. J. (1998). Determinants of friendship selection and quality: Developmental perspectives. In W. M. Bukowski & A. F. Newcomb (Eds.), *The company they keep: Friendships in childhood and adolescence* (pp. 87–112). New York: Cambridge University Press.

Acitelli, L. K., & Duck, S. W. (1987). Intimacy as the proverbial elephant. In D. Perlman & S. W. Duck (Eds.), *Intimate relationships: Development, dynamics, and deterioration* (pp. 297–308). Newbury Park, CA: Sage.

Acker, M., & Davis, M. E. (1992). Intimacy, passion, and commitment in adult romantic relationships: A test of the triangular theory of love. *Journal of Social and Personal Relationships, 9,* 21–50.

Acton, L. (1887/1972). *Essays on freedom and power.* Gloucester, MA: Peter Smith.

Adams, J. S. (1965). Inequity in social exchange. In L. Berkowitz (Ed.), *Advances in experimental psychology* (Vol. 2, pp. 267–299). New York: Academic Press.

Afifi, T. D. (2003). "Feeling caught" in stepfamilies: Managing boundary turbulence through appropriate privacy coordination rules. *Journal of Social and Personal Relationships, 20,* 729–756.

Afifi, T. D., Caughlin, J., & Afifi, W. A. (in press). The dark side of avoidance and secrets in interpersonal relationships: Reasons to question the ideology of openness. In B. Spitzberg & B. Cupach (Eds.), *The dark side of interpersonal relationships.* Mahwah, NJ: Lawrence Erlbaum.

Afifi, T. D., & Olson, L. (2005). The chilling effect and the pressure to conceal secrets in families. *Communication Monographs, 72,* 192–216.

Afifi, T. D., Olson, L., & Armstrong, C. (2005). The chilling effect and family secrets: Examining the role of self protection, other protection, and communication efficacy. *Human Communication Research, 31,* 564–598.

Afifi, T. D., & Schrodt, P. (2003). "Feeling caught" as a mediator of adolescents' and young adults' avoidance and satisfaction with their parents in divorced and non-divorced households. *Communication Monographs, 70,* 142–173.

Afifi, W. A. (1999). Harming the ones we love: Relational attachment and perceived consequences as predictors of safe-sex behavior. *Journal of Sex Research, 36,* 198–206.

Afifi, W. A., & Burgoon, J. K. (1998). "We never talk about that": A comparison of cross-sex friendships and dating relationships on uncertainty and topic avoidance. *Personal Relationships, 5,* 255–272.

Afifi, W. A., & Burgoon, J. K. (2000). The impact of violations on uncertainty and the consequences for attractiveness. *Human Communication Research, 26,* 203–233.

Afifi, W. A., & Caughlin, J. P. (2006). A close look at revealing secrets and some consequences that follow. *Communication Research, 33,* 467–488.

Afifi, W. A., Falato, W. L., & Weiner, J. L. (2001). Identity concerns following a severe relational transgression: The role of discovery method for the relational outcomes of infidelity. *Journal of Social and Personal Relationships, 18,* 291–308.

Afifi, W. A., & Faulkner, S. L. (2000). On being "just friends": The frequency and impact of sexual activity in cross-sex friendships. *Journal of Social and Personal Relationships, 17,* 205–222.

Afifi, W. A., & Guerrero, L. K. (1995, June). *Maintenance behaviors in same-sex friendships: Sex differences, equity and associations with relational closeness.*

Paper presented at the meeting of the International Network on Personal Relationships, Williamsburg, VA.

Afifi, W. A., & Guerrero, L. K. (1998). Some things are better left unsaid II: Topic avoidance in friendships. *Communication Quarterly, 46,* 231–249.

Afifi, W. A., & Guerrero, L. K. (2000). Motivations underlying topic avoidance in close relationships. In S. Petronio (Ed.), *Balancing the secrets of private disclosures* (pp. 165–180). Mahwah, NJ: Erlbaum.

Afifi, W. A., Guerrero, L. K., & Egland, K. L. (1994, June). *Maintenance behaviors in same- and opposite-sex friendships: Connections to gender, relational closeness, and equity issues.* Paper presented at the annual meeting of the International Network on Personal Relationships, Iowa City, IA.

Afifi, W. A., & Matsunaga, M. (in press). Theories of uncertainty management. In D. Braithwaite & L. Baxter (Eds.), *Engaging theories in interpersonal communication.* Thousand Oaks: Sage.

Afifi, W. A., & Metts, S. (1998). Characteristics and consequences of expectation violations in close relationships. *Journal of Social and Personal Relationships, 15,* 365–392.

Afifi, W. A., & Reichert, T. (1996). Understanding the role of uncertainty in jealousy experience and expression. *Communication Reports, 9,* 93–103.

Afifi, W. A., & Weiner, J. L. (2004). Toward a theory of motivated information management. *Communication Theory, 14,* 167–190.

Afifi, W. A., & Weiner, J. L. (2006). Seeking information about sexual health: Applying the theory of motivated information management. *Human Communication Research, 32,* 35–57.

Ahrons, C. R. (1994). *The good divorce.* New York: HarperCollins.

Aida, Y., & Falbo, T. (1991). Relationships between marital satisfaction, resources, and power strategies. *Sex Roles, 24,* 43–56.

Ainsworth, M. D. S. (1969). Object relations, dependency, and attachment: A theoretical review of the infant-mother relationship. *Child Development, 40,* 969–1025.

Ainsworth, M. D. S. (1982). Attachment: Retrospect and prospect. In C. M. Parkes & J. Stevenson-Hinde (Eds.), *The place of attachment in human behavior* (pp. 3–30). New York: Basic Books.

Ainsworth, M. D. S. (1989). Attachments beyond infancy. *American Psychologist, 44,* 709–716.

Ainsworth, M. D. S. (1991). Attachments and other affectional bonds across the life cycle. In C. M. Parkes, J. Stevenson-Hinde, & P. Marris (Eds.), *Attachment across the life cycle* (pp. 33–51). New York: Tavistock/Routledge.

Ainsworth, M. D. S., Blehar. M. C., Waters, E., & Wall, S. (1978). *Patterns of attachment: A psychological study of the strange situations.* Hillsdale, NJ: Erlbaum.

Ainsworth, M. D. S., & Bowlby, J. (1991). An ethological approach to personality development. *American Psychologist, 46,* 333–341.

Ainsworth, M. D. S., & Eichberg, C. (1991). Effects of infant-mother attachment of mother's unresolved loss of an attachment figure, or other traumatic experience. In C. M. Parkes, J. Stevenson-Hinde, & P. Marris (Eds.), *Attachment across the life cycle* (pp. 160–186). New York: Tavistock/Routledge.

Ainsworth, M. D. S., & Wittig, B. A. (1969). Attachment and the exploratory behaviour of one-year-olds in a strange situation. In B. M. Foss (Ed.), *Determinants of infant behavior* (pp. 113–136). London: Methuen.

Alain, M. (1985). Help-seeking and attractiveness in cross-sex dyads. *Canadian Journal of Behavioral Science, 17,* 271–275.

Albada, K. F., Knapp, M. L., & Theune, K. E. (2002). Interaction appearance theory: Changing perceptions of physical attractiveness through social interaction. *Communication Theory, 12,* 8–40.

Albas, D., & Albas, C. (1988). Aces and bombers: The post-exam impression management strategies of students. *Symbolic Interaction, 11,* 289–302.

Alberts, J. K. (1988). An analysis of couples' conversational complaints. *Communication Monographs, 55,* 184–197.

Alberts, J. K. (1989). A descriptive taxonomy of couples' complaint interactions. *Southern Communication Journal, 54,* 125–143.

Alberts, J. K., & Driscoll, G. (1992). Containment versus escalation: The trajectory of couples' conversation complaints. *Western Journal of Communication, 56,* 394–412.

Allen, M., Berchild, J., Bernhart, K., Domain, M., Gilbertson, J., Geboy, L., et al. (1995, November). *Dialectical theory: Testing the relationships between tensions and relational satisfaction.* Paper presented at the annual meeting of the International Communication Association, Chicago.

Altman, I., & Ginat, J. (1996). *Polygamous families in contemporary society.* New York: Cambridge University Press.

Altman, I., & Taylor, D. A. (1973). *Social penetration: The development of interpersonal relationships.* New York: Holt, Rinehart & Winston.

Altman, I., Vinsel, A., & Brown, B. B. (1981). Dialectical conceptions in social psychology: An application to social penetration and privacy regulation. In L. Berkowitz (Ed.), *Advances in experimental social psychology* (Vol. 14, pp. 107–160). New York: Academic Press.

Amato, P. R. (1996). Explaining the intergenerational transmission of divorce. *Journal of Marriage and the Family, 58,* 628–640.

Amato, P. R., & Keith, B. (1991). Parental divorce and adult well-being: A metaanalysis. *Journal of Marriage and the Family, 53,* 43–58.

Amodio, D. M., & Showers, C. J. (2005). "Similarity breeds liking" revisited: The moderating role of commitment. *Journal of Social and Personal Relationships, 22,* 817–836.

Anders, S. L., & Tucker, J. S. (2000). Adult attachment style, interpersonal communication competence, and social support. *Personal Relationships, 7,* 379–389.

Andersen, J. F. (1984, April). *Nonverbal cues of immediacy and relational affect.* Paper presented at the annual convention of the Central States Speech Association, Chicago.

Andersen, P. A. (1982, November). *Interpersonal communication across three decades.* Paper presented at the annual convention of the Speech Communication Association, Louisville, KY.

Andersen, P. A. (1985). Nonverbal immediacy in interpersonal communication. In A. W. Siegman & S. Feldstein (Eds.), *Multichannel integrations of nonverbal behavior* (pp. 1–36). Hillsdale, NJ: Erlbaum.

Andersen, P. A. (1989, May). *A cognitive valence theory of intimate communication.* Paper presented at the International Network on Personal Relationships Conference, Iowa City, IA.

Andersen, P. A. (1991). When one cannot communicate: A challenge to Motley's traditional communication postulates. *Communication Studies, 42,* 309–325.

Andersen, P. A. (1993). Cognitive schemata in personal relationships. In S. Duck (Ed.), *Individuals in relationships* (pp. 1–29). Newbury Park, CA: Sage.

Andersen, P. A. (1998a). The cognitive valence theory of intimate communication. In M. T. Palmer & G. A. Barnett (Eds.), *Progress in communication sciences: Vol. 14. Mutual influence in interpersonal communication: Theory and research in cognition, affect and behavior* (pp. 39–72). Stamford, CT: Ablex.

Andersen, P. A. (1998b). Researching sex differences within sex similarities: The evolutionary consequences of reproductive differences. In D. J. Canary & K. Dindia (Eds.), *Sex differences and similarities in communication* (pp. 83–100). Mahwah, NJ: Erlbaum.

Andersen, P. A. (1999). *Nonverbal communication: Forms and functions.* Mountain View, CA: Mayfield.

Andersen, P. A. (2004). *The complete idiot's guide to body language.* New York: Alpha.

Andersen, P. A. (2006). The evolution of biological sex differences in communication. In K. Dindia & D. J. Canary (Eds.), *Sex differences and similarities in communication* (2nd ed., pp. 117–135). Mahwah, NJ: Lawrence Erlbaum.

Andersen, P. A., & Andersen, J. F. (1982). Nonverbal immediacy in instruction. In L. L. Barker (Ed.), *Communication in the classroom: Original essays* (pp. 98–120). Englewood Cliffs, NJ: Prentice Hall.

Andersen, P. A., Eloy, S. V., Guerrero, L. K., & Spitzberg, B. H. (1995). Romantic jealousy and relational satisfaction: A look at the impact of jealousy experience and expression. *Communication Reports, 8,* 77–85.

Andersen, P. A., & Guerrero, L. K. (1998a). The bright side of relational communication: Interpersonal warmth as a social emotion, In P. A. Andersen & L. K. Guerrero (Eds.), *Handbook of communication and emotion: Research, theory, applications, and contexts* (pp. 303–329). San Diego, CA: Academic Press.

Andersen, P. A., & Guerrero, L. K. (1998b). Principles of communication and emotion in social interaction. In P. A. Andersen & L. K. Guerrero (Eds.), *Handbook of communication and emotion: Research, theory, applications, and contexts* (pp. 49–96). San Diego, CA: Academic Press.

Andersen, P. A, Guerrero, L. K., Buller, D. B., & Jorgensen, P. F. (1998). An empirical comparison of three theories of nonverbal immediacy exchange. *Human Communication Research, 24,* 501–535.

Andersen, P. A., Guerrero, L. K., & Jones, S. M. (2006). Nonverbal intimacy. In V. Manusov & M. L. Patterson (Eds.), *The handbook of nonverbal communication* (pp. 259–277). Thousand Oaks, CA: Sage.

Andersen, P. A., & Leibowitz, K. (1978). The development and nature of the construct, touch avoidance. *Environmental Psychology and Nonverbal Behavior, 3,* 89–106.

Applegate, J. L. (1980). Person-centered and position-centered teacher communication in a day care center. *Studies in Symbolic Interactionism, 3,* 59–96.

Archer, J. (1989). The relationship between gender-role measures: A review. *British Journal of Social Psychology, 28,* 173–184.

Argyle, M. (1972). Non-verbal communication in human social interaction. In R. A. Hinde (Ed.), *Non-verbal communication* (pp. 248–268). Cambridge, UK: Cambridge University Press.

Argyle, M., & Dean, J. (1965). Eye contact, distance, and affiliation. *Sociometry, 28,* 289–304.

Argyle, M., & Furnham, A. (1983). Sources of satisfaction and conflict in long-term relationships. *Journal of Marriage and the Family, 45,* 481–493.

Argyle, M., & Henderson, M. (1984). The rules of friendship. *Journal of Social and Personal Relationships, 1,* 211–237.

Argyle, M., & Henderson, M. (1985). The rules of relationships. In S. Duck & D. Perlman (Eds.), *Understanding relationships: An interdisciplinary approach* (pp. 63–84). London: Sage.

Argyle, M., & Henderson, M. (1988). *The anatomy of relationships.* London: Penguin Books.

Arliss, L. P. (1993). *Contemporary family communication: Messages and meanings.* New York: St. Martin's Press.

Armstrong, L. (1978). *Kiss daddy goodnight: A speak-out on incest.* New York: Doubleday.

Aron, A., & Aron, E. N. (1986). *Love as the expansion of self: Understanding attraction and satisfaction.* New York: Hemisphere.

Aron, A., & Aron, E. N. (1996). Self and self-expansion in relationships. In G. J. O. Fletcher & J. Fitness (Eds.), *Knowledge structures in close relationships: A social psychological approach* (pp. 325–344). Mahwah, NJ: Erlbaum.

Aron, A., & Aron, E. N. (1997). Self-expansion motivation and including other in the self. In S. Duck (Ed.), *Handbook of personal relationships* (2nd ed., pp. 251–270). Chichester, UK: Wiley.

Aron, A., Aron, E. N., & Smollan, D. (1992). Inclusion of other in the self scale and the structure of interpersonal closeness. *Journal of Personality and Social Psychology, 63,* 593–612.

Aron, A., Fisher, H., Mahek, D. J., Strong, G., Haifang, L., & Brown, L. L. (2005). Reward, motivation and emotional systems associated with early-stage intense romantic love. *Journal of Neurophysiology, 94,* 327–337.

Aron, A., Paris, M., & Aron, E. N. (1995). Falling in love: Prospective studies of self-concept change. *Journal of Personality and Social Psychology, 69,* 1102–1112.

Aron, E. N., & Aron, A. (1996). Love and expansion of the self: The state of the model. *Personal Relationship, 3,* 45–58.

Aronson, E., & Linder, D. (1965). Gain and loss of esteem as determinants of interpersonal attraction. *Journal of Experimental Social Psychology, 1,* 156–171.

Attridge, M. (1994). Barriers to dissolution of romantic relationships. In D. J. Canary & L. Stafford (Eds.), *Communication and relational maintenance* (pp. 141–164). San Diego, CA: Academic Press.

Aune, R. K., Ching, P. U., & Levine, T. R. (1996). Attributions of deception as a function of reward value: A test of two explanations. *Communication Quarterly, 44,* 478–486.

Aune, R. K., Metts, S., & Hubbard, A. S. E. (1998). Managing the outcomes of discovered deception. *Journal of Social Psychology, 138,* 677–689.

Ayres, J. (1983). Strategies to maintain relationships: Their identification and perceived usage: *Communication Quarterly, 31,* 62–67.

Bach, G. R., & Wyden, P. (1970). *The intimate enemy: How to fight fair in love and marriage.* New York: Avon Books.

Bachman, G. F. (2002). *An expectancy violations analysis of factors affecting relational outcomes and communicative responses following hurtful events in dating relationships.* Unpublished doctoral dissertation, Arizona State University, Tempe.

Bachman, G. F., & Guerrero, L. K. (2006a). An expectancy violations analysis of relational quality and communicative responses following hurtful events in dating relationships. *Journal of Social and Personal Relationships, 23,* 943–963.

Bachman, G. F., & Guerrero, L. K. (2006b). Forgiveness, apology, and communicative responses to hurtful events. *Communication Reports, 19,* 45–56.

Bagarozzi, D. A. (1990). Marital power discrepancies and symptom development in spouses: An empirical investigation. *American Journal of Family Therapy, 18,* 51–64.

Baldwin, M. W., & Fehr, B. (1995). On the instability of attachment style ratings. *Personal Relationships, 2,* 247–261.

Bandura, A. (1986). *Social foundations of thought and action: A social cognitive theory.* Englewood Cliffs, NJ: Prentice Hall.

Banks, S. P., Altendorf, D. M., Greene, J. O., & Cody, M. J. (1987). An examination of relationship disengagement: Perceptions, breakup strategies and outcomes. *Western Journal of Speech Communication, 51,* 19–41.

Barnett, R., & Baruch, G. (1987). Mothers' participation in child care: Patterns and consequences. In F. Crosby (Ed.), *Spouse, parent, worker: On gender and multiple roles* (pp. 63-73). New Haven, CT: Yale University Press.

Barr, A., Bryan, A., & Kenrick, D. T. (2002). Sexual peak: Socially shared cognitions about desire, frequency, and satisfaction in men and women. *Personal Relationships, 9,* 287-299.

Barth, R. J., & Kinder, B. N. (1988). A theoretical analysis of sex differences in same-sex friendships. *Sex Roles, 19,* 349–363.

Bartholomew, K. (1990). Avoidance of intimacy: An attachment perspective. *Journal of Social and Personal Relationships, 7,* 147–178.

Bartholomew, K. (1993). From childhood to adult relationships: Attachment theory and research. In S. Duck (Ed.), *Learning about relationships* (pp. 30–62). Newbury Park, CA: Sage.

Bartholomew, K., & Horowitz, L. M. (1991). Attachment styles among young adults: A test of a four-category model. *Journal of Personality and Social Psychology, 61,* 226–244.

Bateson, G. (1951a). Conventions of communication. In J. Ruesch & G. Bateson (Eds.), *Communication: The social matrix of psychiatry* (pp. 212–227). New York: Norton.

Bateson, G. (1951b). Information and codification: A philosophical approach. In J. Ruesch & G. Bateson (Eds.), *Communication: The social matrix of psychiatry* (pp. 168–211). New York: Norton.

Battaglia, D. M., Richard, F. D., Datteri, D. L., & Lord, C. G. (1998). Breaking up is (relatively) easy to do: A script for the dissolution of close relationships. *Journal of Personal and Social Relationships, 15,* 829–845.

Baumeister, R. F. (1982). A self-presentational view of social phenomena. *Psychological Bulletin, 91,* 3–26.

Baumeister, R. F. (Ed.). (1986). *Public self and private self.* New York: Springer-Verlag.

Baumeister, R. F. (2000). Gender differences in erotic plasticity: The female sex drive as socially flexible and responsive. *Psychological Bulletin, 126,* 347–374.

Baumeister, R. F., & Leary, M. R. (1995). The need to belong: Desire for interpersonal attachments as a fundamental human motivation. *Psychological Bulletin, 117,* 497–529.

Baumeister, R. F., & Wotman, S. R. (1992). *Breaking hearts: The two sides of unrequited love.* New York: Guilford Press.

Baumeister, R. F., Wotman, S. R., & Stillwell, A. M. (1993). Unrequited love: On heartbreak, anger, guilt, scriptlessness, and humiliation. *Journal of Personality and Social Psychology, 64,* 377–394.

Baumrind, D. (1971). Current patterns of parental authority. *Developmental Psychology Monographs, 4*(1, Pt. 2), 1–103.

Baumrind, D. (1991). Parenting styles and adolescent development. In R. M. Leder, A. C. Petersen, & J. Brooks-Gunn (Eds.), *Encyclopedia of adolescence* (Vol. 2, pp. 746–758). New York: Garland.

Bavelas, J. B., Black, A., Chovil, N., & Mullett, J. (1990). *Equivocal communication.* Newbury Park, CA: Sage.

Baxter, L. A. (1979a). Self-disclosure as a relational disengagement strategy. *Human Communication Research, 5,* 215–222.

Baxter, L. A. (1979b, February). *Self-reported disengagement strategies in friendship relationships.* Paper presented at the annual convention of the Western Speech Communication Association, Los Angeles, CA.

Baxter, L. A. (1979c, November). *Relational closeness, relational intent and disengagement strategies.* Paper presented at the annual meeting of the Speech Communication Association, San Antonio, TX.

Baxter, L. A. (1982). Strategies for ending relationships: Two studies. *Western Journal of Speech Communications, 46,* 223–241.

Baxter, L. A. (1984). Trajectories of relationship disengagement. *Journal of Social and Personal Relationships, 1,* 29–48.

Baxter, L. A. (1985). Accomplishing relational disengagement. In S. Duck & D. Perlman (Eds.), *Understanding personal relationships: An interdisciplinary approach* (pp. 243–265). London: Sage.

Baxter, L. A. (1986). Gender differences in the heterosexual relationship rules embedded in breakup accounts. *Journal of Social and Personal Relationships, 3,* 289–306.

Baxter, L. A. (1988). A dialectical perspective on communication strategies in relationship development. In S. Duck (Ed.), *Handbook of personal relationships* (pp. 257–273). New York: Wiley.

Baxter, L. A. (1990). Dialectical contradictions in relationship development. *Journal of Social and Personal Relationships, 7,* 69–88.

Baxter, L. A. (1993). The social side of personal relationships: A dialectical perspective. In S. Duck (Ed.), *Understanding relationship processes* (pp. 139–165). Newbury Park, CA: Sage.

Baxter, L. A. (1994). A dialogic approach to relationship maintenance. In D. J. Canary & L. Stafford (Eds.), *Communication and relational maintenance* (pp. 233–254). San Diego, CA: Academic Press.

Baxter, L. A., Braithwaite, D. O., & Nicholson, J. H. (1999). Turning points in the development of blended families. *Journal of Social and Personal Relationships, 16,* 291–313.

Baxter, L. A., & Bullis, C. (1986). Turning points in developing romantic relationships. *Human Communication Research, 12,* 469–493.

Baxter, L. A., & Erbert, L. A. (1999). Perceptions of dialectical contradictions in turning points of development in heterosexual romantic relationships. *Journal of Social and Personal Relationships, 16,* 547–569.

Baxter, L. A., & Montgomery, B. M. (1996). *Relating: Dialogues and dialectics.* New York: Guilford Press.

Baxter, L. A., & Philpott, J. (1980, November). *Relational disengagement: A process view.* Paper presented at the annual meeting of the Speech Communication Association, New York, NY.

Baxter, L. A., & Pittman, G. (2001). Communicatively remembering turning points of relationship development in heterosexual romantic relationships. *Communication Reports, 14,* 1–17.

Baxter, L. A., & Simon, E. P. (1993). Relationship maintenance strategies and dialectical contradictions in personal relationships. *Journal of Social and Personal Relationships, 10,* 225–242.

Baxter, L. A., & Wilmot, W. W. (1984). "Secret tests": Social strategies for acquiring information about the state of the relationship. *Human Communication Research, 2,* 171–201.

Baxter, L. A., & Wilmot, W. W. (1985). Taboo topics in close relationships. *Journal of Social and Personal Relationships, 2,* 253–269.

Bayes, M. A. (1970). An investigation of the behavioral cues of interpersonal warmth (Doctoral dissertation, University of Miami, 1970). *Dissertation Abstracts International, 31,* 2272B.

Becker, D. V., Sagarin, B. J., Guadagno, R. E., Millevoi, A., & Nicastle, L. D. (2004). When the sexes need not differ: Emotional responses to the sexual and emotional aspects of infidelity. *Personal Relationships, 11,* 529–538.

Beebe, S. A. (1980). Effects of eye contact, posture and vocal inflection upon credibility and comprehension. *Australian Scan: Journal of Human Communication, 7–8,* 57–70.

Beier, E. G., & Sternberg, D. P. (1977). Marital communication: Subtle cues between newlyweds. *Journal of Communication, 27,* 92–97.

Beland, N. (2005, October). Catch her eye. *Men's Health, 8,* 164, 166–167.

Bell, A. P., & Weinberg, M. A. (1978). *Homosexualities: A study of diversity among men and women.* New York: Simon & Schuster.

Bell, R. A., & Buerkel-Rothfuss, N. L. (1990). S(he) loves me, S(he) loves me not: Predictors of relational information-seeking in courtship and beyond. *Communication Quarterly, 38,* 64–82.

Bell, R. A., Buerkel-Rothfuss, N. L., & Gore, K. E. (1987). "Did you bring the yarmulke for the cabbage patch kid?" The idiomatic communication of young lovers. *Human Communication Research, 14,* 47–67.

Bell, R. A., Daly, J. A., & Gonzalez, C. (1987). Affinity-maintenance in marriage and its relationships to women's marital satisfaction. *Journal of Marriage and the Family, 49,* 445–454.

Bem, S. L. (1974). The measurement of psychological androgyny. *Journal of Consulting and Clinical Psychology, 42,* 155–162.

Bennett, M., & Earwaker, D. (1994). Victims' responses to apologies: The effects of offender responsibility and offense severity. *Journal of Social Psychology, 134,* 457–464.

Bennett, N. G., Blanc, A. K., & Bloom, D. W. (1988). Commitment and the modern union: Assessing the link between premarital cohabitation and subsequent marital stability. *American Sociological Review, 53,* 127–138.

Bentler, P. M., & Newcomb, M. D. (1978). Longitudinal study of marital success and failure. *Journal of Consulting and Clinical Psychology, 46,* 1053–1070.

Berg, J. H., & Clark, M. S. (1986). Differences in social exchange between intimate and other relationships: Gradually evolving or quickly apparent? In V. J. Derlega & B. A. Winstead (Eds.), *Friendship and social interaction* (pp. 101–128). New York: Spring-Verlag.

Berg, J. H., & McQuinn, R. D. (1986). Attraction and exchange in continuing and noncontinuing dating relationships. *Journal of Personality and Social Psychology, 50,* 942–952.

Berger, C. R. (1979). Beyond initial interaction: Uncertainty, understanding, and the development of interpersonal relationships. In H. Giles & R. N. St. Clair (Eds.), *Language and social psychology* (pp. 122–144). Oxford: Basil Blackwell.

Berger, C. R. (1985). Social power and interpersonal communication. In M. L. Knapp & G. R. Miller (Eds.), *Handbook of interpersonal communication* (pp. 439–499). Beverly Hills, CA: Sage.

Berger, C. R. (1986). Uncertain outcome values in predicted relationships: Uncertainty reduction theory then and now. *Human Communication Research, 13,* 34–38.

Berger, C. R. (1987). Communicating under uncertainty. In M. E. Roloff & G. R. Miller (Eds.), *Interpersonal processes: New directions in communication research* (pp. 39–62). Newbury Park, CA: Sage.

Berger, C. R. (1988). Uncertainty and information exchange in developing relationships. In S. Duck (Ed.), *Handbook of personal relationships* (pp. 239–256). Chichester, UK: Wiley.

Berger, C. R. (1993). Uncertainty and social interaction. In S. A. Deetz (Ed.), *Communication yearbook 16* (pp. 491–502). Newbury Park, CA: Sage.

Berger, C. R., & Calabrese, R. J. (1975). Some explorations in initial interactions and beyond: Toward a developmental theory of interpersonal communication. *Human Communication Research, 1,* 99–112.

Berger, C. R., & Douglas, W. (1981). Studies in interpersonal epistemology III: Anticipated interaction, self-monitoring, and observational context selection. *Communication Monographs, 48,* 183–196.

Berger, C. R., & Kellermann, K. (1983). To ask or not to ask: Is that a question? In R. N. Bostrom (Ed.), *Communication yearbook 7* (pp. 342–368). Beverly Hills, CA: Sage.

Berk, S. (1985). *The gender factory.* New York: Plenum Press.

Berscheid, E., Dion, K., Walster, E., & Walster, G. W. (1971). Physical attractiveness and dating choice: A test of the matching hypothesis. *Journal of Experimental Social Psychology, 7,* 173–189.

Berscheid, E., & Meyers, S. A. (1996). A social categorical approach to questions about love. *Personal Relationships, 3,* 19–43.

Berscheid, E., & Peplau, L. A. (1983). The emerging science of relationships. In H. H. Kelley, E. Berscheid, A. Christensen, J. H. Harvey, T. L. Huston, G. Leaving, et al, (Eds.), *Close relationships* (pp. 1–19). New York: Freeman.

Berscheid, E., & Walster, E. H. (1969). *Interpersonal attraction.* Reading, MA: Addison-Wesley.

Berscheid, E., & Walster, E. H. (1974). A little bit about love. In T. L. Houston (Ed.), *Foundations of interpersonal attraction* (pp. 355–381). New York: Academic Press.

The best dating service? Try the workplace! (1988, February 12). *New York Post,* p. 14.

Bevan, J. L. (2003). Expectancy violation theory and sexual resistance in close, cross-sex relationships. *Communication Monographs, 70,* 68–82.

Bevan, J. L. (in press). Experiencing and communicating romantic jealousy: An application of the investment model. *Southern Journal of Communication.*

Bevan, J. L., & Samter, W. (2004). Toward a broader conceptualization of jealousy in close relationships: Two exploratory studies. *Communication Studies, 55,* 14–28.

Bickman, L. (1974). The social power of a uniform. *Journal of Applied Social Psychology, 4,* 47–61.

Biernat, M., & Wortman, C. B. (1991). Sharing of home responsibilities between professionally employed women and their husbands. *Journal of Personality and Social Psychology, 60,* 840–860.

Billings, A. (1979). Conflict resolution in distressed and nondistressed married couples. *Journal of Consulting and Clinical Psychology, 47,* 368–376.

Bingham, S. G., & Burleson, B. R. (1989). Multiple effects of messages with multiple goals: Some perceived outcomes of responses to sexual harassment. *Human Communication Research, 16,* 184–216.

Bippus, A. M., & Rollin, E. (2003). Attachment style differences in relational maintenance and conflict behaviors: Friends' perceptions. *Communication Reports, 16,* 113–123.

Black, L. E., Eastwood, M. M., Sprenkle, D. H., & Smith, E. (1991). An exploratory analysis of the construct of leavers versus left as it relates to Levinger's social exchange theory of attractions, barriers, and alternative attractions. *Journal of Divorce and Remarriage, 15,* 127–139.

Blake, R. R., & Mouton, J. S. (1964). *The managerial grid.* Houston, TX: Gulf.

Blau, P. M. (1964). *Exchange and power in social life.* New York: Wiley.

Blumstein, P., & Schwartz, P. (1983). *American couples: Money, work, sex.* New York: Morrow.

Bochner, A. P. (1984). The functions of human communication in interpersonal bonding. In C. C. Arnold & J. W. Bowers (Eds.), *Handbook of rhetorical and communication theory* (pp. 544–621). Boston: Allyn & Bacon.

Bochner, A. P. (1992). On the efficacy of openness in closed relationships. In M. Burgoon (Ed.), *Communication yearbook 5* (pp. 109–124). New Brunswick, NJ: Transaction Books.

Boon, S. D., & McLeod, B. A. (2001). Deception in romantic relationships: Subjective estimates of success at deceiving and attitudes toward deception. *Journal of Social and Personal Relationships, 18,* 463–476.

Booth, A., & Edwards, J. N. (1989). Transmission of marital and family quality over the generations: The effect of parental divorce and unhappiness. *Journal of Divorce, 13,* 41–58.

Booth-Butterfield, M. (1989). Perceptions of harassing communications as a function of locus of control, work force participation, and gender. *Communication Quarterly, 37,* 262–275.

Bowlby, J. (1969). *Attachment and loss: Vol. 1. Attachment.* New York: Basic Books.

Bowlby, J. (1973). *Attachment and loss: Vol. 2. Separation.* New York: Basic Books.

Bowlby, J. (1977). The making and breaking of affectional bonds. *British Journal of Psychiatry, 130,* 201–210.

Bowlby, J. (1980). *Attachment and loss: Vol. 3. Loss, sadness, and depression.* New York: Basic Books.

Boyden, T., Carroll, J. S., & Maier, R. A. (1984). Similarity and attraction in homosexual males: The effects of age and masculinity-femininity. *Sex Roles, 10,* 939–948.

Bradac, J. J., Bowers, J. W., & Courtwright, J. A. (1979). Three language variables in communication research: Intensity, immediacy and diversity. *Human Communication Research, 5,* 257–269.

Bradac, J. J., Hosman, L. A., & Tardy, C. H. (1978). Reciprocal disclosures and language intensity: Attributional consequences. *Communication Monographs, 45,* 1–14.

Bradbury, T. N., & Fincham, F. D. (1990). Attributions in marriage: Review and critique. *Psychological Bulletin, 107,* 3–33.

Bradford, L. (1980). The death of a dyad. In B. W. Morse & L. A. Phelps (Eds.), *Interpersonal communication: A relational perspective* (pp. 497–508). Minneapolis, MN: Burgess.

Braiker, H. B., & Kelley, H. H. (1979). Conflict in the development of close relationships. In R. L. Burgess & T. L. Huston (Eds.), *Social exchange in developing relationships* (pp. 135–168). New York: Academic Press.

Braithwaite, D. O. (1995). Ritualized embarrassment at "coed" wedding and baby showers. *Communication Reports, 8,* 145–157.

Braithwaite, D. O., & Baxter, L. A. (1995). "I do" again: The relational dialectics of renewing marriage vows. *Journal of Social and Personal Relationships, 12,* 177–198.

Bramlett, M. D., & Mosher, W. D. (2002). *Cohabitation, marriage, divorce, and remarriage in the United States* (Vol. 23). Hyattsville, MD: National Center for Health Statistics.

Brashers, D. E. (2001). Communication and uncertainty management. *Journal of Communication, 51,* 477–497.

Bratslavsky, E., Baumeister, R. F., & Sommer, K. L. (1998). To love or be loved in vain: The trials and tribulations of unrequited love. In B. H. Spitzberg & W. C. Cupach (Eds.), *The dark side of close relationships* (pp. 307–326). Mahwah, NJ: Erlbaum.

Braver, S. L., Whitley, M., & Ng, C. (1993). Who divorced whom? Methodological and theoretical issues. *Journal of Divorce and Remarriage, 20,* 1–19.

Brehm, S. S., & Kassin, S. M. (1990). *Social psychology.* Boston: Houghton Mifflin.

Brennan, K. A., & Shaver, P. R. (1995). Dimensions of adult attachment, affect regulations, and romantic relationship functioning. *Personality and Social Psychology Bulletin, 21,* 267–283.

Bretherton, I. (1988). Open communication and internal working models: Their role in the development of attachment relationships. In R. A. Thompson (Ed.), *Nebraska symposium on motivation* (pp. 57–113). Lincoln: University of Nebraska Press.

Bridge, K., & Baxter, L. A. (1992). Blended friendships: Friends as work associates. *Western Journal of Communication, 56,* 200–225.

Brock, L. J., & Jennings, G. H. (1993). Sexuality education: What daughters in their 30s wish their mothers had told them. *Family Relationships, 42,* 61–65.

Brown, M., & Auerbach, A. (1981). Communication patterns in the initiation of marital sex. *Medical Aspects of Human Sexuality, 15,* 105–117.

Brown, P., & Levinson, S. (1987). *Politeness: Some universals in language usage.* Cambridge, UK: Cambridge University Press.

Brown, R. (1965). *Social psychology.* New York: Free Press.

Brown, S. L. (2000). Union transitions among cohabitors: The significance of relationship assessments and expectations. *Journal of Marriage and the Family, 62,* 833–846.

Brown, S. L., & Booth, A. (1996). Cohabitation versus marriage: A comparison of relationship quality. *Journal of Marriage and the Family, 58,* 668–678.

Browning, J. R., Kessler, D., Hatfield, E., & Choo, P. (1999). Power, gender and sexual behavior. *The Journal of Sex Research, 36,* 342–347.

Brownridge, D. A., & Halli, S. S. (2000). "Living in sin" and sinful living: Toward filling a gap in the explanation of violence against women. *Aggression and Violent Behavior, 5,* 565–583.

Brown-Smith, N. (1998). Family secrets. *Journal of Family Issues, 19,* 20–42.

Bryson, J. B. (1976, September). *The nature of sexual jealousy: An exploratory paper.* Paper presented at the annual meeting of the American Psychological Association, Washington, DC.

Bryson, J. B. (1977, September). *Situational determinants of the expression of jealousy.* Paper presented at the annual meeting of the American Psychological Association, San Francisco, CA.

Buchanon, C. M., Maccoby, E. E., & Dornbusch, S. M. (1991). Caught between parents: Adolescents' experience in divorce homes. *Child Development, 62,* 1008–1029.

Buchanon, C. M., Maccoby, E. E., & Dornbusch, S. M. (1996). *Adolescents after divorce.* Cambridge, MA: Harvard University Press.

Buehler, C., Anthony, C., Krishnakumar, A., Stone, G., Gerard, J., & Pemberton, S. (1997). Interparental conflict and youth problem behaviors: A meta-analysis. *Journal of Child and Family Studies, 6,* 233–247.

Buller, D. B., & Aune, R. K. (1987). Nonverbal cues to deception among intimates, friends, and strangers. *Journal of Nonverbal Behavior, 11,* 269–290.

Buller, D. B., & Burgoon, J. K. (1994). Deception: Strategic and nonstrategic communication. In J. A. Daly & J. M. Wiemann (Eds.), *Strategic interpersonal communication* (pp. 191–223). Hillsdale, NJ: Erlbaum.

Buller, D. B., Strzyzewski, K. D., & Comstock, J. (1991). Interpersonal deception: I. Deceivers' reactions to receivers suspicious and probing. *Communication Monographs, 58,* 1–24.

Bullis, C., Clark, C., & Sline, R. (1993). From passion to commitment: Turning points in romantic relationships. In P. J. Kalbfleisch (Ed.), *Interpersonal communication: Evolving interpersonal relationships* (pp. 213–236). Hillsdale, NJ: Erlbaum.

Bumpass, L. L., & Sweet, J. A. (1989). National estimates of cohabitation. *Demography, 26,* 615–625.

Burgess, E. O. (2004). Sexuality in midlife and later. In J. H. Harvey, A. Wenzel, & S. Sprecher (Eds.), *The handbook of sexuality in close relationships* (pp. 427–454). Mahwah, NJ: Erlbaum.

Burgoon, J. K. (1978). A communication model of personal space violations: Explication and an initial test. *Human Communication Research, 4,* 129–142.

Burgoon, J. K., & Bacue, A., (2003). Nonverbal communication skills. In B. R. Burleson & J. O. Greene (Eds.), *Handbook of communication and social interaction skills* (pp. 179–219). Mahwah, NJ: Erlbaum.

Burgoon, J. K., Buller, D. W., & Woodall, W. G. (1996). *Nonverbal communication: The unspoken dialogue* (2nd ed.). New York: McGraw-Hill.

Burgoon, J. K., & Dillman, L. (1995). Gender, immediacy and nonverbal communication. In P. J. Kalbfleisch & M. J. Cody (Eds.), *Gender, power, and communication in human relationships* (pp. 63–81). Hillsdale, NJ: Erlbaum.

Burgoon, J. K., & Hale, J. L. (1984). The fundamental topoi of relational communication. *Communication Monographs, 51,* 193–214.

Burgoon, J. K., & Hale, J. L. (1987). Validation and measurement of the fundamental themes of relational communication. *Communication Monographs, 54,* 19–41.

Burgoon, J. K., & Hale, J. L. (1988). Nonverbal expectancy violations: Model elaboration and application to immediacy behaviors. *Communication Monographs, 55,* 58–79.

Burgoon, J. K., Johnson, M. L., & Koch, P. T. (1998). The nature and measurement of interpersonal dominance. *Communication Monographs, 65,* 308–335.

Burgoon, J. K., & Langer, E. (1995). Language, fallacies, and mindlessness-mindfulness. In B. R. Burleson (Ed.), *Communication yearbook 18* (pp. 105–132). Thousand Oaks, CA: Sage.

Burgoon, J. K., & Newton, D. A. (1991). Applying a social meaning model to relational message interpretations of conversational involvement: Comparing observer and participant perspectives. *Southern Communication Journal, 56,* 96–113.

Burgoon, J. K., Parrott, R., Le Poire, B. A., Kelley, D. L., Walther, J. B., & Parry, D. (1989). Maintaining and restoring privacy through communication in different types of relationships. *Journal of Social and Personal Relationships, 6,* 131–158.

Burgoon, J. K., Stern, L. A., & Dillman, L. (1995). *Interpersonal adaptation: Dyadic interaction patterns.* New York: Cambridge University Press.

Buri, J. R., Louiselle, P. A., Misukanis, T. M., & Mueller, R. A. (1988). Effects of parental authoritarianism and authoritativeness on self-esteem. *Personality and Social Psychology Bulletin, 14,* 271–282.

Burke, R. J., Weir, T., & Harrison, D. (1976). Disclosure of problems and tensions experienced by marital partners. *Psychological Reports, 38,* 531–542.

Burleson, B. R. (1982). The development of comforting communication skills in childhood and adolescence. *Child Development, 53,* 1578–1588.

Burleson, B. R. (1984). Comforting communication. In H. Sypher & J. L. Applegate (Eds.), *Communication by children and adults* (pp. 63–104). Beverly Hills, CA: Sage.

Burleson, B. R. (1998). Similarities in social skills, interpersonal attraction, and the development of personal relationships. In J. S. Trent (Ed.), *Communication: Views from the helm for the twenty-first century* (pp. 77–84). Boston: Allyn & Bacon.

Burleson, B. R. (2003). The experience and effects of emotional support: What the study of cultural and gender differences can tell us about close relationships, emotion, and interpersonal communication. *Personal Relationships, 10,* 1–23.

Burleson, B. R., Delia, J. G., & Applegate, J. L. (1992). Effects of maternal communication and children's social-cognitive and communication skills on children's acceptance by the peer group. *Family Relations, 41,* 264–272.

Burleson, B. R., & Goldsmith, D. J. (1998). How the comforting process works: Alleviating emotional distress through conversationally induced reappraisals. In P. A. Andersen & L. K. Guerrero (Eds.), *Handbook of communication and emotion: Theory, research, contexts, and applications* (pp. 246–275). San Diego, CA: Academic Press.

Burleson, B. R., Kunkel, A. W., Samter, W., & Werking, K. J. (1996). Men's and women's evaluations of communication skills in personal relationships: When sex differences make a difference—and when they don't. *Journal of Social and Personal Relationships, 13,* 201–224.

Burleson, B. R., & Samter, W. (1985a). Consistencies in theoretical and naive evaluations of comforting messages. *Communication Monographs, 52,* 104–123.

Burleson, B. R., & Samter, W. (1985b). Individual differences in the perception of comforting messages. *Central States Speech Journal, 36,* 39–50.

Burleson, B. R., & Samter, W. (1994). A social skills approach to relationship maintenance: How individual differences in communication skills affect the achievement of relationship functions. In D. J. Canary & L. Stafford (Eds.), *Communication and relational maintenance* (pp. 61–90). San Diego, CA: Academic Press.

Burrell, N. A., & Koper, R. J. (1998). The efficacy of powerful/powerless language on attitudes and source credibility. In M. Allen & R. Preiss (Eds.), *Persuasion: Advances through meta-analysis* (pp. 203–216). Creskill, NJ: Hampton.

Buslig, A. L. S. (1999). "Stop" signs: Regulating privacy with environmental features. In L. K. Guerrero, J. A. DeVito, & M. L. Hecht (Eds.), *The nonverbal communication reader: Classic and contemporary readings* (2nd ed., pp. 241–249). Prospect Heights, IL: Waveland Press.

Buss, D. M. (1988a). From vigilance to violence: Tactics of mate retention in American undergraduates. *Ethology and Sociology, 9,* 291–317.

Buss, D. M. (1988b). Love acts: The evolutionary biology of love. In R. J. Sternberg & M. L. Barnes (Eds.), *The psychology of love* (pp. 100–117). New Haven, CT: Yale University Press.

Buss, D. M. (1989). Sex differences in human mate preferences: Evolutionary hypotheses tested in 37 cultures. *Behavioral and Brain Sciences, 12,* 1–49.

Buss, D. M. (1994). *The evolution of desire: Strategies of mating selection.* New York: Basic Books.

Buss, D. M., & Kenrick, D. T. (1998). Evolutionary social psychology. In D. T. Gilbert, S. T. Fiske, & G. Lindsay (Eds.), *The handbook of social psychology* (4th ed., Vol. 2, pp. 982–1026). New York: McGraw-Hill.

Buss, D. M., Larsen, R. J., Westen, D., & Semmelroth, J. (1992). Sex differences in jealousy: Evolution, physiology, and psychology. *Psychological Science, 3,* 251–255.

Buunk, B. P. (1980). Extramarital sex in the Netherlands: Motivations in social and marital context. *Alternative Lifestyles, 3,* 11–39.

Buunk, B. P. (1982). Strategies of jealousy: Styles of coping with extramarital involvement of the spouse. *Family Relations, 31,* 13–18.

Buunk, B. P. (1995). Sex, self-esteem dependency, and extradyadic experience as related to jealousy responses. *Journal of Social and Personal Relationships, 12,* 147–153.

Buunk, B. P., & Bakker, A. B. (1997). Responses to unprotected extradyadic sex by one's partner: Testing predictions from interdependence and equity theory. *Journal of Sex Research, 34,* 387–397.

Buunk, B., & Bringle, R. G. (1987). Jealousy in love relationships. In D. Perlman & S. Duck (Eds.), *Intimate relationships: Development, dynamics, and deterioration* (pp. 123–147). Newbury Park, CA: Sage.

Buunk, B. P., Dijkstra, P., Fetchenhauer, D., & Kenrick, D. T. (2002). Age and gender differences in mate selection criteria for various involvement levels. *Personal Relationships, 9,* 271–278.

Buunk, B. P., & Mutsaers, W. (1999). Equity perceptions and marital satisfaction in former and current marriage: A study among the remarried. *Journal of Social and Personal Relationships, 16,* 123–132.

Byers, E. S. (1996). How well does the traditional sexual script explain sexual coercion? Review of a program of research. *Journal of Psychology and Human Sexuality, 8,* 7–25.

Byers, E. S., Demmons, S., & Lawrence, K. (1998). Sexual satisfaction within dating relationships: A test of the interpersonal exchange model of sexual satisfaction. *Journal of Social and Personal Relationships, 15,* 257–267.

Byers, E. S., & Lewis, K. (1988). Dating couples' disagreements over the desired level of sexual activity. *Journal of Sex Research, 24,* 15–29.

Byers, E. S., Purden, C., & Clark, D. A. (1998). Sexually intrusive thoughts of college students. *Journal of Sex Research, 35,* 359–369.

Byers, E. S., & Wilson, P. (1985). Accuracy of women's expectations regarding men's responses to refusals of sexual advances in dating situations. *International Journal of Women's Studies, 4,* 376–387.

Byrne, D. (1961). Interpersonal attraction and attitude similarity. *Journal of Abnormal and Social Psychology, 62,* 713–715.

Byrne, D. (1971). *The attraction paradigm.* New York: Academic Press.

Byrne, D. (1992). The transition from controlled laboratory experimentation to less controlled settings: Surprise! Additional variables are operative. *Communication Monographs, 59,* 190–198.

Byrne, D. (1997). An overview (and underview) of research and theory within the attraction paradigm. *Journal of Social and Personal Relationships, 14,* 417–431.

Byrne, D., & Clore, G. L. (1970). A reinforcement model for evaluative responses. *Personality: An International Journal, 1,* 103–128.

Cahn, D. (1992). *Conflict in intimate relationships.* New York: Guilford Press.

Caldwell, M., & Peplau, L. A. (1984). The balance of power in lesbian relationships. *Sex Roles, 10,* 587–600.

Cameron, C., Oskamp, S., & Sparks, W. (1977). Courtship American style: Newspaper ads. *Family Coordinator, 26,* 27–30.

Campbell, E., Adams, R., & Dobson, W. R. (1984). Familial correlates of identity formation in late adolescence: A study of the predictive utility of connectedness and individuality in family relationships. *Journal of Youth and Adolescence, 13,* 509–525.

Campbell, W. K. (1999). Narcissism and romantic attraction. *Journal of Personality and Social Psychology, 77,* 1254–1270.

Canary, D. J., & Cody, M. J. (1994). *Interpersonal communication: A goals-based approach.* New York: St. Martin's Press.

Canary, D. J., Cupach, W. R., & Messman, S. J. (1995). *Relationship conflict.* Thousand Oaks, CA: Sage.

Canary, D. J., & Hause, K. G. (1993). Is there any reason to research sex differences in communication? *Communication Quarterly, 41,* 129–144.

Canary, D. J., & Lakey, S. G. (2006). Managing conflict in a competent manner: A mindful look at events that matter. In J. G. Oetzel & S. Ting-Toomey (Eds.), *The SAGE handbook of conflict communication* (pp. 185–210). Thousand Oaks, CA: Sage.

Canary, D. J., & Spitzberg, B. H. (1987). Appropriateness and effectiveness perceptions of conflict strategies. *Human Communication Research, 14,* 93–118.

Canary, D. J., & Spitzberg, B. H. (1989). A model of perceived competence of conflict strategies. *Human Communication Research, 15,* 630–649.

Canary, D. J., & Spitzberg, B. H. (1990). Attribution biases and associations between conflicts strategies and competence outcomes. *Communication Monographs, 57,* 139–151.

Canary, D. J., & Stafford, L. (1992). Relational maintenance strategies and equity in marriage. *Communication Monographs, 59,* 243–267.

Canary, D. J., & Stafford, L. (1993). Preservation of relational characteristics: Maintenance strategies, equity, and locus of control. In P. J. Kalbfleisch (Ed.), *Interpersonal communication: Evolving interpersonal relationships* (pp. 237–259). Hillsdale, NJ: Erlbaum.

Canary, D. J., & Stafford, L. (1994). Maintaining relationships through strategic and routine interaction. In D. J. Canary & L. Stafford (Eds.), *Communication and relational maintenance* (pp. 3–22). San Diego, CA: Academic Press.

Canary, D. J., & Stafford, L. (2001). Equity in the preservation of personal relationships. In J. Harvey & A. Wenzel (Eds.), *Close romantic relationships: Maintenance and enhancement* (pp. 133–151). Mahwah, NJ: Lawrence Erlbaum.

Canary, D. J., Stafford, L., Hause, K. S., & Wallace, L. A. (1993). An inductive analysis of relational maintenance strategies: Comparisons among lovers, relatives, friends, and others. *Communication Research Reports, 10,* 5–14.

Cappella, J. N. (1988). Personal relationships, social relationships and patterns of interaction. In S. Duck (Ed.), *Handbook of personal relationships: Theory, research and interventions* (pp. 325–342). Chichester, UK: Wiley.

Cargan, L., & Melko, M. (1982). *Singles: Myths and realities.* Beverly Hills, CA: Sage.

Carney, D. R., Hall, J. A., & LeBeau, L. S. (2005). Beliefs about the nonverbal expression of social power. *Journal of Nonverbal Behavior, 29,* 105–123.

Cate, R. M., Levin, L. A., & Richmond, L. S. (2002). Premarital relationship stability: A review of recent research. *Journal of Social and Personal Relationships, 19,* 261–284.

Cate, R. M., & Lloyd, S. A. (1988). Courtship. In S. Duck (Ed.), *Handbook of personal relationships* (pp. 409–427). New York: Wiley.

Cate, R. M., Lloyd, S. A., & Henton, J. M. (1985). The effect of equity, equality, and reward level on the stability of students' premarital relationships. *Journal of Social Psychology, 125,* 715–721.

Cate, R. M., Lloyd, S. A., & Long, E. (1988). The role of rewards and fairness in developing premarital relationships. *Journal of Marriage and the Family, 50,* 443–452.

Cate, R. M., Long, E., Angera, J. J., & Draper, K. K. (1993). Sexual intercourse and relational development. *Family Relations, 42,* 158–164.

Caughlin, J. P., & Afifi, T. D. (2004). When is topic avoidance unsatisfying? Examining moderators of the association between avoidance and dissatisfaction. *Human Communication Research, 30,* 479–513,

Caughlin, J. P., Afifi, W. A., Carpenter-Theune, K. E., & Miller, L. E. (2005). Reasons for and consequences of revealing personal secrets in close relationships: A longitudinal study. *Personal Relationships, 12,* 43–60.

Caughlin, J., & Golish, T. (2002). An analysis of the association between topic avoidance and dissatisfaction: Comparing perceptual and interpersonal explanations. *Communication Monographs, 69,* 275–296.

Caughlin, J. P., & Vangelisti, A. L. (1999). Desire for change in one's partner as a predictor of the demand/withdraw pattern of marital communication. *Communication Monographs, 66,* 66–89.

Caughlin, J. P., & Vangelisti, A. L. (2006). Conflict in dating and marital relationships. In J. G. Oetzel & S. Ting-Toomey (Eds.), *The SAGE handbook of conflict communication* (pp. 129–157). Thousand Oaks, CA: Sage.

Centers for Disease Control and Prevention. (1996). *Condoms and their use in preventing HIV infection and other STDs.* Rockville, MD: Author.

Chaiken, S. (1979). Communicator physical attractiveness and persuasion. *Journal of Personality and Social Psychology, 37,* 1387–1397.

Chaikin, A. L., & Derlega, V. J. (1974). Liking for the norm breaker in self-disclosure. *Journal of Personality, 42,* 117–129.

Chelune, G. J., Rosenfeld, L. B., & Waring, E. M. (1985). Spouse disclosure patterns in distressed and nondistressed couples. *American Journal of Family Therapy, 13,* 24–31.

Christensen, A., & Heavey, C. L. (1990). Gender and social structure in the demand/withdrawal pattern of marital conflict. *Journal of Personality and Social Psychology, 59,* 73–81.

Christensen, A., & Shenk, J. L. (1991). Communication, conflict, and psychological distance in nondistressed, clinical, and divorcing couples. *Journal of Consulting and Clinical Psychology, 59,* 458–463.

Christopher, F. S., & Cate, R. M. (1985). Premarital sexual pathways and relationship development. *Journal of Social and Personal Relationships, 2,* 271–288.

Christopher, F. S., & Frandsen, M. M. (1990). Strategies of influence in sex and dating. *Journal of Social and Personal Relationships, 7,* 89–105.

Christopher, F. S., & Kissler, T. S. (2004). Exploring marital sexuality: Peeking inside the bedroom and discovering what we don't know—but should. In J. H. Harvey, A. Wenzel, & S. Sprecher (Eds.), *The handbook of sexuality in close relationships* (pp. 371–384). Mahwah, NJ: Erlbaum.

Christopher, F. S., & Lloyd, S. A. (2000). Physical and sexual aggression in relationships. In C. Hendrick & S. S. Hendrick (Eds.), *Close relationships* (pp. 331–343). Thousand Oaks, CA: Sage.

Christopher, F. S., Owens, L. A., & Strecker, H. L. (1993). An examination of single men's and women's sexual aggressiveness in dating relationships. *Journal of Social and Personal Relationships, 10,* 511–527.

Christopher, F. S., & Roosa, M. W. (1991). Factors affecting sexual decisions in premarital relationships of adolescents and young adults. In K. McKinney & S. Sprecher (Eds.), *Sexuality in close relationships* (pp. 111–133). Hillsdale, NJ: Erlbaum.

Ciabattari, J. (1988, December). Will the '90s be the age of envy? *Psychology Today, 20*(5), 47–50.

Cialdini, R. B. (1988). *Influence: Science and practice* (2nd ed.). New York: HarperCollins.

Clatterbuck, G. W. (1979). Attributional confidence and uncertainty in initial interaction. *Human Communication Research, 5,* 147–157.

Cleek, M. G., & Pearson, T. A. (1985). Perceived causes of divorce: An analysis of interrelationships. *Journal of Marriage and the Family, 47,* 179–183.

Clements, M. L., Cordova, A. D., Markman, H. J., & Laurenceau, J. (1997). The erosion of marital satisfaction over time and how to prevent it. In R. J. Sternberg & M. Hojjat (Eds.), *Satisfaction in close relationships* (pp. 335–365). New York: Guilford Press.

Cline, R. J. W., Freeman, K. E., & Johnson, S. J. (1990). Talk among sexual partners about AIDS: Factors differentiating those who talk from those who do not. *Communication Research, 17,* 792–808.

Clore, G. L., & Byrne, D. (1974). A reinforcement-affect model of attraction. In T. L. Huston (Ed.), *Foundations of interpersonal attraction* (pp. 143–170). New York: Academic Press.

Cloven, D. H., & Roloff, M. E. (1993). The chilling effect of aggressive potential on the expression of complaints in intimate relationships. *Communication Monographs, 60,* 199–219.

Coates, D., Wortman, C. B., & Abbey, A. (1979). Reactions to victims. In I. H. Frieze, D. Bar-Tal, & J. S. Carroll (Eds.), *New approaches to social problems* (pp. 21–52). San Francisco: Jossey-Bass.

Cody, M. (1982). A typology of disengagement strategies and an examination of the role intimacy and relational problems play in strategy selection. *Communication Monographs, 49,* 148–170.

Cole, T. (2001). Lying to the one you love: The use of deception in romantic relationships. *Journal of Social and Personal Relationships, 18,* 107–129.

Collins, N. L., & Miller, L. C. (1994). The disclosure-liking link: From meta-analysis toward a dynamic reconceptualization. *Psychological Bulletin, 116,* 457–475.

Collins, N. L., & Read, S. J. (1990). Adult attachment, working models, and relationship quality in dating couples. *Journal of Personality and Social Psychology, 58,* 644–663.

Collins, N. L., & Read, S. J. (1994). Cognitive representations of attachment: The structure and function of working models. In K. Bartholomew & D. Perlman (Eds.), *Attachment processes in adulthood: Advances in personal relationships* (Vol. 5, pp. 53–90). Bristol, PA: Kingsley.

Comadena, M. E. (1982). Accuracy in detecting deception: Intimate and friendship relationships. In M. Burgoon (Ed.), *Communication yearbook 6* (pp. 446–472). Beverly Hills, CA: Sage.

Conville, R. L. (1991). *Relational transitions: The evolution of personal relationships.* New York: Praeger.

Cooley, C. H. (1922). *Human nature and the social order.* New York: Scribner.

Cottle, T. J. (1980). *Children's secrets.* Reading, MA: Addison-Wesley.

Coutts, L. M., & Schneider, F. W. (1976). Affiliative conflict theory: An investigation of the intimacy equilibrium and compensation hypothesis. *Journal of Personality and Social Psychology, 34,* 1135–1142.

Cowan, G., Drinkard, J., & MacGavin, L. (1984). The effects of target, age, and gender on power use strategies. *Journal of Personality and Social Psychology, 47,* 1391–1398.

Cozzarelli, C., Hoekstra, S. J., & Bylsma, W. H. (2000). General versus specific mental models of attachment: Are they associated with different outcomes? *Personality and Social Psychology Bulletin, 26,* 605–618.

Cramer, D. (2002). Linking conflict management behaviours and relational satisfaction: The intervening role of conflict outcome satisfaction. *Journal of Social and Personal Relationships, 19,* 431–438.

Crawford, D. W., Feng, D., Fischer, J. L., & Diana, L. K. (2003). The influence of love, equity, and alternatives on commitment in romantic relationships. *Family and Consumer Sciences Research Journal, 13,* 253–271.

Creasey, G., Kershaw, K., & Boston, A. (1999). Conflict management with friends and romantic partners: The role of attachment and negative mood regulation expectancies. *Journal of Youth and Adolescence, 28,* 523–543.

Crocker, J., & Schwartz, I. (1985). Prejudice and ingroup favoritism in a minimal intergroup situation: Effects of self-esteem. *Personality and Social Psychology Bulletin, 11,* 379–386.

Crockett, L., Losoff, M., & Peterson, A. C. (1984). Perceptions of the peer group and friendship in early adolescence. *Journal of Early Adolescence, 4,* 155–181.

Crooks, R., & Baur, K. (1999). *Our sexuality.* Pacific Grove, CA: Brooks/Cole.

Cunningham, J. D., & Antill, J. K. (1994). Cohabitation and marriage: Retrospective and predictive comparisons. *Journal of Social and Personal Relationships, 11,* 77–93.

Cunningham, J. D., & Antil, J. K. (1995). Current trends in marital cohabitation: In search of the POSSLQ. In J. T. Wood & S. Duck (Eds.), *Understudied relationships: Off the beaten track* (pp. 148–172). Thousand Oaks, CA: Sage.

Cunningham, M. R., & Barbee, A. P. (2000). Social support. In C. Hendrick & S. S. Hendrick (Eds.), *Close relationships: A sourcebook* (pp. 171–183). Thousand Oaks, CA: Sage.

Cunningham, M. R., Barbee, A. P., Graves, C. R., Lundy, D. E., & Lister, S. C. (1996, August). *Can't buy me love: The effects of male wealth and personal qualities on female attraction.* Paper presented at the annual meeting of the American Psychological Association, Toronto, Ontario, Canada.

Cupach, W. R. (1994). Social predicaments. In W. R. Cupach & B. H. Spitzberg (Eds.), *The dark side of interpersonal communication* (pp. 159–180). Hillsdale, NJ: Erlbaum.

Cupach, W. R., & Comstock, J. (1990). Satisfaction with sexual communication in marriage: Links to sexual satisfaction and dyadic adjustment. *Journal of Social and Personal Relationships, 7,* 179–186.

Cupach, W. R., & Metts, S. (1986). Accounts of relational dissolution: A comparison of marital and non-marital relationships. *Communication Monographs, 53,* 311–334.

Cupach, W. R., & Metts, S. (1991). Sexuality and communication in close relationships. In K. McKinney & S. Sprecher (Eds.), *Sexuality in close relationships* (pp. 93–110). Hillsdale, NJ: Erlbaum.

Cupach, W. R., & Metts, S. (1994). *Facework.* Thousand Oaks, CA: Sage.

Cupach, W. R., & Metts, S. (1995). The role of sexual attitude similarity in romantic heterosexual relationships. *Personal Relationships, 2,* 287–300.

Cupach, W. R., & Spitzberg, B. H. (Eds.). (1994). *The dark side of interpersonal communication.* Hillsdale, NJ: Erlbaum.

Cupach, W. R., & Spitzberg, B. H. (1998). Obsessive relational intrusion and stalking. In B. H. Spitzberg & W. R. Cupach (Eds.), *The dark side of close relationships* (pp. 233–264). Mahwah, NJ: Erlbaum.

Cupach, W. R., & Spitzberg, B. H. (2000). Obsessive relational intrusion: Incidence, perceived severity, and coping. *Violence and Victims, 15,* 357–372.

Cupach, W. R., & Spitzberg, B. H. (2004). *The dark side of relationship pursuit: From attraction to obsession and stalking.* Mahwah, NJ: Lawrence Erlbaum.

Cupach, W. R., & Spitzberg, B. H. (in press). "Thanks, but no thanks . . ." The occurrence and management of unwanted relationship pursuit. In S. Sprecher, A. Wenzel, & J. Harvey (Eds.), *The handbook of relationship initiation.* Mahwah, NJ: Lawrence Erlbaum.

Dailey, R. M., & Palomares, N. A. (2004). Strategic topic avoidance: An investigation of topic avoidance frequency, strategies used, and relational correlates. *Communication Monographs, 71,* 471–496.

Dainton, M. (2000). Maintenance behaviors, expectations for maintenance, and satisfaction: Linking comparison levels to relational maintenance strategies. *Journal of Social and Personal Relationships, 17,* 827–842.

Dainton, M., & Aylor, B. (2001). A relational uncertainty analysis of jealousy, trust, and maintenance in long-distance versus geographically close relationships. *Communication Quarterly, 49,* 172–188.

Dainton, M., & Aylor, B. (2002). Routine and strategic maintenance efforts: Behavioral patterns, variations associated with relational length, and the prediction of relational characteristics. *Communication Monographs, 69,* 52–66.

Dainton, M., & Stafford, L. (1993). Routine maintenance behaviors: A comparison of relationship type, partner similarity and sex differences. *Journal of Social and Personal Relationships, 10,* 255–271.

Dainton, M., Stafford, L., & Canary, D. J. (1994). Maintenance strategies and physical affection as predictors of love, liking, and satisfaction in marriage. *Communication Reports, 7,* 88–98.

Dainton, M., Zelley, E., & Langan, E. (2003). Maintaining friendships throughout the lifespan. In D. J. Canary & M. Dainton (Eds.), *Maintaining relationships through communication: Relational, contextual, and cultural variations* (pp. 79–102). Mahwah, NJ: Lawrence Erlbaum.

Daly, J. A., Hoggs, E., Sacks, D., Smith, M., & Zimring, L. (1983). Sex and relationship affect social self-grooming. *Journal of Nonverbal Behavior, 7,* 183–189.

Daly, J. A., & Kreiser, P. O. (1994). Affinity seeking. In J. A. Daly & J. M. Wiemann (Eds.), *Strategic interpersonal communication* (pp. 109–134). Hillsdale, NJ: Erlbaum.

Daly, M., & Wilson, M. (1983). *Sex, evolution, and behavior* (2nd ed.). Boston: Willard Grant Press.

Darby, B. W., & Schlenker, B. R. (1982). Children's reactions to apologies. *Journal of Personality and Social Psychology, 43,* 743–753.

Darby, B. W., & Schlenker, B. R. (1989). Children's reactions to transgressions: Effects of the actor's apology, reputation, and remorse. *British Journal of Social Psychology, 28,* 353–364.

Davey, A., Fincham, F. D., Beach, S. R. H., & Brody, G. H. (2001). Attributions in marriage: Examining the entailment model in dyadic context. *Journal of Family Psychology, 15,* 721–734.

Davidson, B., Balswick, J., & Halverson, C. (1983). Affective self-disclosure and marital adjustment: A test of equity theory. *Journal of Marriage and the Family, 45,* 93–102.

Davies, P. T., & Cummings, E. M. (1994). Marital conflict and adjustment: An emotional security hypothesis. *Psychological Bulletin, 116,* 387–411.

Davila, J., Burge, D., & Hammen, C. (1997). Why does attachment style change? *Journal of Personality and Social Psychology, 73,* 826–838.

Davila, J., Karney, B. R., & Bradbury, T. N. (1999). Attachment change processes in the early years of marriage. *Journal of Personality and Social Psychology, 76,* 783–802.

Davis, J. D., & Skinner, A. E. G. (1974). Reciprocity of self-disclosure in interviews: Modeling or social exchange? *Journal of Personality and Social Psychology, 29,* 779–784.

Davis, K. E., & Roberts, M. K. (1985). Relationships in the real world: The descriptive approach to personal relationships. In K. J. Gergen & K. E. Davis (Eds.), *The social construction of the person* (pp. 144-163). New York: Springer-Verlag.

Davis, K. E., & Todd, M. J. (1982). Friendship and love relationships. In E. E. Davis (Ed.), *Advances in descriptive psychology* (Vol. 2, pp. 79–122). Greenwich, CT: JAI Press.

Davis, K. E., & Todd, M. J. (1985). Assessing friendships: Prototypes, paradigm cases, and relationship description. In S. Duck & D. Perlman (Eds.), *Understanding personal relationships: An interdisciplinary approach* (pp. 17–38). London: Sage.

Davis, M. (1973). *Intimate relations.* New York: Free Press.

DeLamater, J., & Hyde, J. S. (2004). Conceptual and theoretical issues in studying close relationships. In J. H. Harvey, A. Wenzel, & S. Sprecher (Eds.), *The handbook of sexuality in close relationships* (pp. 7–30). Mahwah, NJ: Erlbaum.

DeMaris, A. (1984). A comparison of remarriages with first marriages on satisfaction in marriage and its relationship to prior cohabitation. *Family Relations, 33,* 443–449.

DeMaris, A., & Leslie, G. R. (1984). Cohabitation with the future spouse: Its influence upon marital satisfaction and communication. *Journal of Marriage and the Family, 46,* 77–84.

D'Emilio, J., & Freedman, E. B. (1988). *Intimate matters: A history of sexuality in America.* New York: Harper & Row.

DePaulo, B. M. (1992). Nonverbal behavior and self-presentation. *Psychological Bulletin, 111,* 203–243.

DePaulo, B. M., & Kashy, D. A. (1998). Everyday lies in close and casual relationships. *Journal of Personality and Social Psychology, 74,* 63–79.

DePaulo, B. M., Kashy, D. A., Kirkendol, S. E., Wyer, M. M., & Epstein, J. A. (1996). Lying in everyday life. *Journal of Personality and Social Psychology, 70,* 979–995.

Derlega, V. J., Barbee, A. P., & Winstead, B. A. (1994). Friendship, gender, and social support: Laboratory studies of supportive interactions. In B. R. Burleson, T. L. Albrecht, & I. G. Sarason (Eds.), *Communication of social support: Messages, interactions, relationships, and community* (pp. 136–151). Thousand Oaks, CA: Sage.

Derlega, V. J., & Grzelak, J. (1979). Appropriateness of self disclosure. In G. L. Chelune (Ed.), *Self-disclosure: Origins, patterns, and implications of openness in interpersonal relationships* (pp. 151–176). San Francisco: Jossey-Bass.

Derlega, V. J., Harris, M. S., & Chaikin, A. L. (1973). Friendship and disclosure reciprocity. *Journal of Personality and Social Psychology, 9,* 277–284.

Derlega, V. J., Metts, S., Petronio, S., & Margulis, S. T. (1993). *Self-disclosure.* Newbury Park, CA: Sage.

Deutsch, M. (1985). *Distributive justice: A social-psychological perspective.* New Haven, CT: Yale University Press.

Dieckman, L. E. (2000). Private secrets and public disclosures: The case of battered women. In S. Petronio (Ed.), *Balancing the secrets of private disclosures* (pp. 275–286). Mahwah, NJ: Erlbaum.

Dillard, J. P. (1989). Types of influence goals in personal relationships. *Journal of Social and Personal Relationships, 6,* 293–308.

Dillard, J. P., & Witteman, H. (1985). Romantic relationships at work: Organizational and personal influences. *Human Communication Research, 12,* 99–116.

Dindia, K. (1989, May). Toward the development of a measure of marital maintenance strategies. Paper presented at the annual meeting of the International Communication Association, San Francisco, CA.

Dindia, K. (1997, November). *Men are from North Dakota, women are from South Dakota.* Paper presented at the annual meeting of the Speech Communication Association, Chicago.

Dindia, K. (2003). Definitions and perspectives on relational maintenance communication. In D. J. Canary & M. Dainton (Eds.), *Maintaining relationships through communication: Relational, contextual, and cultural variations* (pp. 1–28). Mahwah, NJ: Lawrence Erlbaum.

Dindia, K., & Allen, M. (1992). Sex differences in self-disclosure: A meta-analysis. *Psychological Bulletin, 112,* 106–124.

Dindia, K., & Baxter, L. A. (1987). Strategies for maintaining and repairing marital relationships. *Journal of Social and Personal Relationships, 4,* 143–158.

Dindia, K., & Canary, D. J. (1993). Definitions and theoretical perspectives on relational maintenance. *Journal of Social and Personal Relationships, 10,* 163–173.

Dindia, K., Fitzpatrick, M. A., & Kenny, D. A. (1997). Self-disclosure in spouse and stranger interaction: A social relations analysis. *Human Communication Research, 23,* 388–412.

Dindia, K., Timmerman, L., Langan, E., Sahlstein, E. M., & Quandt, J. (2004). The function of holiday greetings in maintaining relationships. *Journal of Social and Personal Relationships, 21,* 577–593.

Dion, K. K. (1972). Physical attractiveness and evaluations of children's transgressions. *Journal of Personality and Social Psychology, 24,* 207–213.

Dion, K. K. (1986). Stereotyping based on physical attractiveness: Issues and conceptual perspectives. In C. P. Herman, M. P., Zanna, & E. T. Higgins (Eds.), *The Ontario symposium: Vol. 3. Physical appearance, stigma, and social behavior* (pp. 7–21). Hillsdale, NJ: Erlbaum.

Dion, K. K., Berscheid, E., & Walster, E. (1972). What is beautiful is good. *Journal of Personality and Social Psychology, 24,* 285–290.

Doelger, J. A., Hewes, D. E., & Graham, M. L. (1986). Knowing when to "second-guess": The mindful analysis of messages. *Human Communication Research, 12,* 301–338.

Dolin, D. J., & Booth-Butterfield, M. (1993). Reach out and touch someone: Analysis of nonverbal comforting responses. *Communication Quarterly, 41,* 383–393.

Donald, M. (1991). *Origins of the modern mind: Three stages in the evolution of culture and cognition.* Cambridge, MA: Harvard University Press.

Donovan, R. L., & Jackson, B. L. (1990). Deciding to divorce: A process guided by social exchange, attachment, and cognitive dissonance theories. *Journal of Divorce, 13,* 23–35.

Dougherty, T. W., Turban, D. B., Olson, D. E., Dwyer, P. D., & Lapreze, M. W. (1996). Factors affecting perceptions or workplace sexual harassment. *Journal of Organizational Behavior, 17,* 489–501.

Douglas, W. (1985). Anticipated interaction and information-seeking. *Human Communication Research, 12,* 243–258.

Douglas, W. (1990a). Uncertainty, information-seeking, and liking during initial interaction. *Western Journal of Speech Communication, 54,* 66–81.

Douglas, W. (1990b, November). *Uncertainty, information exchange, and social attraction during initial interaction.* Paper presented at the annual meeting of the Speech Communication Association, Chicago.

Dovidio, J. F., Brown, C. E., Heltman, K., Ellyson, S. L., & Keating, C. F. (1988). Power displays between men and women in discussions of gender-linked tasks: A multichannel study. *Journal of Personality and Social Psychology, 55,* 580–587.

Dowrick, S. (1999, March–April). The art of letting go. *Utne Reader,* no. 92, 46–50.

Draucker, C. B. (1999). "Living in hell": The experience of being stalked. *Issues in Mental Health Nursing, 20,* 473–484.

Drigotas, S. M., & Rusbult, C. E. (1992). Should I stay or should I go? A dependence model of breakups. *Journal of Personality and Social Psychology, 62,* 62–87.

Driscoll, R., Davis, K. W., & Lipetz, M. E. (1972). Parental interference and romantic love. *Journal of Personality and Social Psychology, 24,* 1–10.

Duck, S. (1982). A topography of relational disengagement and dissolution. In S. Duck (Ed.), *Personal relationships 4: Dissolving personal relationships* (pp. 1–30). London: Academic Press.

Duck, S. (1988). *Relating to others.* Monterey, CA: Brooks/Cole.

Duck, S. (1994). Steady as (s)he goes: Relational maintenance as a shared meaning systems. In D. J. Canary & L. Stafford (Eds.), *Communication and relational maintenance* (pp. 45–60). San Diego, CA: Academic Press.

Duck, S. W. (1986). *Human relationships.* London: Sage.

Duffy, S. M., & Rusbult, C. E. (1986). Satisfaction and commitment in homosexual and heterosexual relationships. *Journal of Homosexuality, 12,* 1–21.

Dunbar, N. E., & Burgoon, J. K. (2005). Perceptions of power and dominance in interpersonal encounters. *Journal of Social and Personal Relationships, 22,* 207–233.

Dunn, J. (1983). Sibling relationships in early childhood. *Child Development, 54,* 787–811.

Dunn, J. (1988a). Connections between relationships: Implications of research on mothers and siblings. In R. A. Hinde & J. Stevenson-Hinde (Eds.), *Relationships within families: Mutual influences* (pp. 168–180). New York: Oxford University Press.

Dunn, J. (1988b). Relations among relationships. In S. W. Duck (Ed.), *Handbook of personal relationships* (pp. 193–209). New York: Wiley.

Dunn, J., & Kendrick, C. (1982). *Siblings: Love, envy, and understanding.* Cambridge, MA: Harvard University Press.

Dunn, J., & Munn, P. (1987). Development of justification in disputes with another sibling. *Developmental Psychology, 23,* 791–798.

Dutton, D. G., & Aron, A. P. (1974). Some evidence for heightened sexual attraction under conditions of high anxiety. *Journal of Personality and Social Psychology, 30,* 510–517.

Dykstra, P. A. (1990). *Next of (non)kin.* Amsterdam: Swets & Zeitlinger.

Edgar, T., & Fitzpatrick, M. A. (1988). Compliance-gaining and relational interaction: When your life depends on it. *Southern Speech Communication Journal, 53,* 385–405.

Edgar, T., & Fitzpatrick, M. A. (1993). Expectations for sexual interaction: A cognitive test of the sequencing of sexual communication behaviors. *Health Communication, 5,* 239–261.

Egland, K. L., Spitzberg, B. H., & Zormeier, M. M. (1996). Flirtation and conversational competence in cross-sex platonic and romantic relationships. *Communication Reports, 9,* 105–118.

Egland, K. L., Stelzner, M. A., Andersen, P. A., & Spitzberg, B. H. (1997). Perceived understanding, nonverbal communication and relational satisfaction. In J. Aitken & L. Shedletsky (Eds.), *Intrapersonal communication processes* (pp. 386–395). Annandale, VA: Speech Communication Association.

Ehrenreich, B., Hess, E., & Jacobs, G. (1986). *Remaking love: The feminization of sex.* Garden City, NY: Anchor/Doubleday.

Eisenberg, A., Murkoff, H. E., & Hathaway, S. E. (1996). *What to expect the first year.* New York: Workman.

Eisenberg, A. R. (1992). Conflicts between mothers and their young children. *Merrill-Palmer Quarterly, 38,* 21–43.

Ekman, P. (1985). *Telling lies.* New York: Norton.

Ekman, P., & Friesen, W. V. (1969). Nonverbal leakage and clues to deception. *Psychiatry, 32,* 88–106.

Elbaum, P. L. (1982). The dynamics, implications, and treatment of extramarital sexual relationships for the family therapist. *Journal of Marital and Family Therapy, 7,* 489–495.

Elliott, L., & Bradley, C. (1997). *Sex on campus: The naked truth about the real sex lives of college students.* New York: Random House.

Ellyson, S. L., & Dovidio, J. F. (1985). Power, dominance, and nonverbal behavior: Basic concepts and issues. In S. L. Ellyson & J. F. Dovidio (Eds.), *Power, dominance, and nonverbal behavior* (pp. 1–27). New York: Springer-Verlag.

Emmers, T. M., & Canary, D. J. (1996). The effect of uncertainty reducing strategies on young couples' relational repair and intimacy. *Communication Quarterly, 44,* 166–182.

Emmers, T. M., & Dindia, K. (1995). The effect of relational stage and intimacy on touch: An extension of Guerrero and Andersen. *Personal Relationships, 2,* 225–236.

Emmers, T. M., & Hart, R. D. (1996). Romantic relationship disengagement and coping rituals. *Communication Research Reports, 13,* 8–18.

Emmers-Sommer, T. M. (2004). The effect of communication quality and quantity indicators on intimacy and relational satisfaction. *Journal of Social and Personal Relationships, 21,* 399–411.

Exline, R. V., Ellyson, S. L., & Long, B. (1975). Visual behavior as an aspect of power role relationships. In P. Pliner, L. Krames, & T. Alloway (Eds.), *Nonverbal communication of aggression* (pp. 21–52). New York: Plenum Press.

Exline, R. V., & Winters, L. C. (1965). Affective relations and mutual glances in dyads. In S. Tomkins & C. E. Izard (Eds.), *Affect, cognition, and personality* (pp. 319–350). New York: Springer.

Fairhurst, G. T. (1986). Male-female communication on the job: Literature review and commentary. In M. McLaughlin (Ed.), *Communication yearbook 9* (pp. 83–116). Beverly Hills, CA: Sage.

Falbo, T., & Peplau, L. A. (1980). Power strategies in intimate relationships. *Journal of Personality and Social Psychology, 38,* 618–628.

Farrell, D., & Rusbult, C. E. (1981). Exchange variables as predictors of job satisfaction, job commitment, and turnover: The impact of rewards, costs, alternatives, and investments. *Organizational Behavior and Human Performance, 27,* 78–95.

Feeney, J. A. (1995). Adult attachment and emotional control. *Personal Relationships, 2,* 143–159.

Feeney, J. A. (1999). Adult attachment, emotional control, and marital satisfaction. *Personal Relationships, 6,* 169–185.

Feeney, J. A. (2004). Hurt feelings in couple relationships: Toward integrative models of the negative effects of hurtful events. *Journal of Social and Personal Relationships, 21,* 487–508.

Feeney, J. A. (2005). Hurt feelings in couple relationships: Exploring the role of attachment and perceptions of personal injury. *Personal Relationships, 12,* 253–271.

Feeney, J. A., & Noller, P. (1991). Attachment style and verbal descriptions of romantic partners. *Journal of Social and Personal Relationships, 8,* 187–215.

Feeney, J. A., & Noller, P. (1996). *Adult attachment.* Thousand Oaks, CA: Sage.

Feeney, J. A., Noller, P., & Roberts, N. (1998). Emotion, attachment and satisfaction in close relationships. In P. A. Andersen & L. K. Guerrero (Eds.), *Handbook of communication and emotion: Research, theory, applications and contexts* (pp. 273–505). San Diego, CA: Academic Press.

Feeney, J. A., Noller, P., & Roberts, N. (2000). Attachment and close relationships. In C. Hendrick & S. S. Hendrick (Eds.), *Close relationships: A sourcebook* (pp. 185–201). Thousand Oaks, CA: Sage.

Fehr, B. (1988). Prototype analysis of the concepts of love and commitment. *Journal of Personality and Social Psychology, 58,* 281–291.

Fehr, B. (1996). *Friendship processes.* Thousand Oaks, CA: Sage.

Feingold, A. (1988). Matching for attractiveness in romantic partners and same-sex friends: A meta-analysis and theoretical critique. *Psychological Bulletin, 104,* 226–235.

Feingold, A. (1991). Sex differences in the effects of similarity and physical attractiveness on opposite-sex attraction. *Basic and Applied Social Psychology, 12,* 357–367.

Felmlee, D. H. (1994). Who's on top? Power in romantic relationships. *Sex Roles, 31,* 275–295.

Felmlee, D. (1995). Fatal attractions: Affection and disaffection in intimate relationships. *Journal of Social and Personal Relationships, 12,* 295–312.

Felmlee, D. H. (1998). "Be careful what you wish for . . .": A quantitative and qualitative investigation of "fatal attraction." *Personal Relationship, 5,* 235–254.

Felmlee, D. H., Sprecher, S., & Bassin, E. (1990). The dissolution of intimate relationships: A hazard model. *Social Psychology Quarterly, 53,* 13–30.

Ferguson, C. A. (1964). Baby talk in six languages. *American Anthropologist, 66,* 103–114.

Festinger, L., Schachter, S., & Back, K. (1950). *Social pressures in informal groups: A study of human factors in housing.* New York: Harper.

Filsinger, E. E., & Thomas, S. J. (1988). Behavioral antecedents of relational stability and adjustment: A five-year longitudinal study. *Journal of Marriage and the Family, 50,* 585–595.

Fincham, F. D. (2000). The kiss of the porcupines: From attributing responsibility to forgiving. *Personal Relationships, 7,* 1–23.

Fincham, F. D., Harold, G. T., & Gano-Phillips, S. (2000). The longitudinal association between attributions and marital satisfaction: Direction of effects and role of efficacy expectations. *Journal of Family Psychology, 14,* 267–285.

Finkenauer, C., Engels, R. C. M. E., & Meeus, W. (2002). Keeping secrets from parents: Advantages and disadvantages of secrecy in adolescence. *Journal of Youth and Adolescence, 31,* 123–136.

Fischer, T. F. C., De Graaf, P. M., & Kalmijn, M. (2005). Friendly and antagonistic contact between former spouses after divorce: Patterns and determinants. *Journal of Family Issues, 26,* 1131–1163.

Fisher, B. A., & Adams, K. L. (1994). *Interpersonal communication: Pragmatics of human relationships* (2nd ed.). New York: McGraw-Hill.

Fisher, T. D. (2004). Family foundations of sexuality. In J. H. Harvey, A. Wenzel, & S. Sprecher (Eds.), *The handbook of sexuality in close relationships* (pp. 385–409). Mahwah, NJ: Erlbaum.

Fitness, J., & Fletcher, G. J. O. (1993). Love, hate, anger, and jealousy in close relationships: A prototype and cognitive appraisal analysis. *Journal of Personality and Social Psychology, 65,* 942–958.

Fitzpatrick, M. A. (1988). *Between husbands and wives: Communication in marriage.* Newbury Park, CA: Sage.

Fitzpatrick, M. A., & Badzinski, D. M. (1994). All in the family: Interpersonal communication and kin relationships. In M. L. Knapp & G. R. Miller (Eds.), *Handbook of interpersonal communication* (2nd ed., pp. 726–771). Thousand Oaks, CA: Sage.

Fitzpatrick, M. A., & Winke, T. (1979). You always hurt the one you love: Strategies and tactics in interpersonal conflict. *Communication Quarterly, 27,* 3–11.

Fleischmann, A. A., Spitzberg, B. H., Andersen, P. A., & Roesch, S. (2005). Tickling the monster: Jealousy induction in relationships. *Journal of Social and Personal Relationships, 22,* 49–73.

Floyd, K. (1995). Gender and closeness among friends and siblings. *Journal of Psychology, 129,* 193–202.

Floyd, K. (2002). Human affection exchange: V. Attributes of the highly affectionate. *Communication Quarterly, 50,* 135–152.

Floyd, K. (2006). *Communicating affection: Interpersonal behavior and social context.* Cambridge, UK: Cambridge University Press.

Floyd, K. (2006). Human affection exchange: XII. Affectionate communication is associated with diurnal variation in salivary free cortisol. *Western Journal of Communication, 70,* 47–63.

Floyd, K., Hess, J. A., Mizco, L. A., Halone, K. K., Mikkelson, A. C., & Tusing, K. J. (2005). Human affective exchange: VIII. Further evidence of the benefits of expressed affection. *Communication Quarterly, 53,* 285–303.

Floyd, K., Hesse, C., & Haynes, M. T. (in press). Human affection exchange: XV. Metabolic and cardiovascular correlates of trait expressed affection. *Communication Quarterly.*

Floyd, K., Mikkelson, A. C., Tafoya, M. A., Farinelli, L., La Valley, A. G., Judd, J., et al. (in press). Human affection exchange: XIV. Relational affection predicts resting heart rate and free cortisol secretion during acute stress. *Behavioral Medicine.*

Floyd, K., & Morman, M. T. (1997). Affectionate communication in nonromantic relationships: Influences of communicator, relational, and contextual factors. *Western Journal of Communication, 61,* 279–298.

Floyd, K., & Morman, M. T. (2005). Fathers' and son's reports of fathers' affectionate communication: Implications of a naïve theory of affection. *Journal of Social and Personal Relationships, 22,* 99–109.

Floyd, K., & Morr, M. C. (2003). Human affective exchange VII: Affectionate communication in the sibling/spouse/sibling-in-law triad. *Communication Quarterly, 51,* 247–261.

Floyd, K., & Parks, M. R. (1995). Manifesting closeness in the interactions of peers: A look at siblings and friends. *Communication Reports, 8,* 69–76.

Floyd, K., Ramirez, A., & Burgoon, J. K. (1999). Expectancy violations theory. In L. K. Guerrero, J. A. DeVito, & M. L. Hecht (Eds.), *The nonverbal communication reader: Classic and contemporary readings* (2nd ed., pp. 437–444). Prospect Heights, IL: Waveland Press.

Folkes, V. S. (1982). Communicating the causes of social rejection. *Journal of Experimental Social Psychology, 18,* 235–252.

Folkes, V. S., & Sears, D. O. (1977). Does everybody like a liker? *Journal of Experimental Social Psychology, 13,* 505–519.

Fox, G. L. (1981). The family's role in adolescent sexual behavior. In T. Ooms (Ed.), *Teenage pregnancy in a family context* (pp. 73–130). Philadelphia: Temple University Press.

Frank, E., Anderson, C., & Rubinstein, D. (1979). Marital role strain and sexual satisfaction. *Journal of Consulting and Clinical Psychology, 217,* 1096–1103.

Frank, M. G., & Gilovich, T. (1988). The dark side of self- and social perception: Black uniforms and aggression in professional sports. *Journal of Personality and Social Psychology, 54,* 74–85.

Frazier, P. A., & Cook, S. W. (1993). Correlates of distress following heterosexual relationship dissolution. *Journal of Social and Personal Relationships, 10,* 55–67.

Freedman, S. R., & Enright, R. D. (1996). Forgiveness as an intervention goal with incest survivors. *Journal of Consulting and Clinical Psychology, 64,* 983–992.

Friedmann, H. S., Riggio, R. E., & Casella, D. F. (1988). Nonverbal skill, personal charisma, and initial attraction. *Personality and Social Psychology Bulletin, 14,* 203–211.

Frinjs, T., Finkenauer, C., Vermulst, A. A., & Engels, R. C. M. E. (2005). Keeping secrets from parents: Longitudinal associations of secrecy in adolescence. *Journal of Youth and Adolescence, 34,* 137–148.

Gaelick, L., Brodenshausen, G. V., & Wyer, R. S., Jr. (1985). Emotional communication in close relationships. *Journal of Personality and Social Psychology, 49,* 1246–1265.

Gagnon, J. H. (1979). *Human sexualities.* Glenview, IL: Scott, Foresman.

Gaines, S. O. (1995). Relationships between members of cultural minorities. In J. T. Woods & S. Duck (Eds.), *Understudied relationships: Off the beaten track* (pp. 51–88). Thousand Oaks, CA: Sage.

Gaines, S. O., Jr., & Liu, J. H. (2000). Multicultural/ multiracial relationships. In C. Hendrick & S. S. Hendrick (Eds.), *Close relationships: A sourcebook* (pp. 97–108). Thousand Oaks, CA: Sage.

Galligan, R. F., & Terry, D. J. (1993). Romantic ideals, fear of negative implications and practice of safe sex. *Journal of Applied Social Psychology, 23,* 1685–1711.

Gass, B. Z., & Nichols, W. C. (1988). Gaslighting: A marital syndrome. *Contemporary Family Therapy, 10,* 3–16.

Gelles, R. J., & Cornell, C. P. (1990). *Intimate violence in families* (2nd ed.). Newbury Park, CA: Sage.

Gibran, K. (1923/1970). *The prophet.* New York: Knopf.

Gilbert, S. J. (1976). Self disclosure, intimacy, and communication in families. *The Family Coordinator, 25,* 221–230.

Gilbert, S. J., & Horenstein, D. (1975). The dyadic effects of self-disclosure: Level vs. Valence. *Human Communication Research, 1,* 316–322.

Giles, H., & Wiemann, J. M. (1987). Language, social comparison, and power. In C. Berger & S. H. Chafee (Eds.), *Handbook of communication science* (pp. 350–384). Newbury Park, CA: Sage.

Girard, M., & Mullet, E. (1997). Propensity to forgive in adolescents, young adults, older adults, and elderly people. *Journal of Adult Development, 4,* 209–220.

Givens, D. B. (1978). The nonverbal basis of attraction: Flirtation, courtship, and seduction. *Psychiatry, 41,* 346–359.

Givens, D. B. (1983). *Love signals.* New York: Crown.

Glick, P. (1985). Orientation toward relationships: Choosing a situation in which to begin a relationship. *Journal of Experimental Social Psychology, 21,* 544–562.

Glomb, T. M., Richman, W. L., Hulin, C. L., Drasgow, F., Schneider, K. T., & Fitzgerald, L. F. (1997). Ambient sexual harassment: An integrated model of antecedents and consequences. *Organizational Behavioral and Human Decision Processes, 71,* 309–328.

Goffman, E. (1959). *The presentation of self in everyday life.* Garden City, NY: Anchor/Doubleday.

Goffman, E. (1967). *Interaction ritual: Essays on face-to-face behavior.* New York: Pantheon Books.

Goffman, E. (1971). *Relations in public.* New York: Basic Books.

Golish, T. D. (2000). Changes in closeness between adult children and their parents: A turning point analysis. *Communication Reports, 13,* 79–97.

Golish, T. D., & Caughlin, J. (2002). "I'd rather not talk about it": Adolescents' and young adults' use of topic avoidance in stepfamilies. *Journal of Applied Communication Research, 30,* 78–106.

Goodman, P. (1960). *Growing up absurd: Problems of youth in the organized society.* New York: Vintage Books.

Gottman, J. M. (1979). *Marital interaction: Experimental investigations.* New York: Academic Press.

Gottman, J. M. (1982). Emotional responsiveness in marital conversations. *Journal of Communication, 32,* 108–120.

Gottman, J. M. (1993). A theory of marital dissolution and stability. *Journal of Family Psychology, 7,* 57–75.

Gottman, J. M. (1994). *What predicts divorce? The relationship between marital processes and marital outcomes.* Hillsdale, NJ: Erlbaum.

Gottman, J. M., & Carrere, S. (1994). Why can't men and women get along? Developmental roots and marital inequities. In D. J. Canary & L. Safford (Eds.), *Communication and relational maintenance* (pp. 203–222). San Diego, CA: Academic Press.

Gottman, J. M., & Levenson, R. W. (1988). The social psychophysical of marriage. In P. Noller & M. A. Fitzpatrick (Eds.), *Perspectives on marital interaction* (pp. 182–200). Philadelphia: Multilingual Matters.

Gottman, J. M., & Levenson, R. W. (1992). Marital processes predictive of later dissolution: Behavior, physiology, and health. *Journal of Personality and Social Psychology, 63,* 221–233.

Gouldner, A. W. (1960). The norm of reciprocity: A preliminary statement. *Sociological Review, 25,* 161–178.

Gray, J. (1992). *Men are from Mars, women are from Venus: A practical guide to improving communication and getting what you want in your relationships.* New York: HarperCollins.

Gray-Little, B., & Burks, N. (1983). Power and satisfaction in marriage: A review and critique. *Psychological Bulletin, 93,* 513–538.

Greene, B. L., Lee, R. R., & Lustig, N. (1974). Conscious and unconscious factors in marital infidelity. *Medical Aspects of Human Sexuality, 8,* 87–91.

Greenstein, T. N. (1990). Marital disruption and the employment of married women. *Journal of Marriage and the Family, 52,* 657–676.

Greitemeyer, T. (2005). Receptivity to sexual offers as a function of sex, socioeconomic status, and intimacy of the offer. *Personal Relationships, 12,* 373–386.

Grice, H. P. (1989). *Studies in the way of words.* Cambridge, MA: Harvard University Press.

Griffit, W. (1970). Environmental effects on interpersonal affective behaviors: Ambient effective temperature and attraction. *Journal of Personality and Social Psychology, 15,* 240–244.

Gross, M. A., & Guerrero, L. K. (2000). Managing conflict appropriately and effectively: An application of the competence model to Rahim's organizational conflict styles. *International Journal of Conflict Management, 11,* 200–226.

Gross, M. A., Guerrero, L. K., & Alberts, J. K. (2004). Perceptions of conflict strategies and communication competence in task-oriented dyads. *Journal of Applied Communication Research, 32,* 249–270.

Grotevant, H. D., & Cooper, C. R. (1985). Patterns of interaction in family relationships and the development of identity exploration in adolescence. *Child Development, 56,* 415–428.

Grusec, J. E., & Kuczynski, L. (1980). Direction of effect in socialization: A comparison of the parent's versus the child's behavior as determinants of disciplinary techniques. *Developmental Psychology, 16,* 1–9.

Gudykunst, W. B. (1988). Culture and the development of interpersonal relationships. In J. A. Anderson (Ed.), *Communication yearbook 12* (pp. 315–354). Newbury Park, CA: Sage.

Gudykunst, W. B. (1989). Uncertainty and anxiety. In Y. Y. Kim & W. B. Gudykunst (Eds.), *Theories in intercultural communication* (pp. 123–156). Newbury Park, CA: Sage.

Gudykunst, W. B., & Nishida, T. (1984). Individual and cultural influences on uncertainty reduction. *Communication Monographs, 51,* 23–36.

Guerrero, L. K. (1996). Attachment-style difference in intimacy and involvement: A test of the four-category model. *Communication Monographs, 63,* 269–292.

Guerrero, L. K. (1997). Nonverbal involvement across interactions with same-sex friends, opposite-sex friends, and romantic partners: Consistency or change? *Journal of Social and Personal Relationship, 14,* 31–59.

Guerrero, L. K. (1998). Attachment-style differences in the experience and expression of romantic jealousy. *Personal Relationships, 5,* 273–291.

Guerrero, L. K. (2000). Intimacy. In D. Levinson, J. Ponzetti, & P. Jorgensen (Eds.), *The encyclopedia of human emotions* (pp. 403–409). New York: Macmillan Reference.

Guerrero, L. K. (2004). Observer ratings of nonverbal involvement and immediacy. In V. Manusov (Ed.), *The sourcebook of nonverbal measures: Going beyond words* (pp. 221–235). Mahwah, NJ: Lawrence Erlbaum.

Guerrero, L. K., & Afifi, W. A. (1995a). Some things are better left unsaid: Topic avoidance in family relationships. *Communication Quarterly, 43,* 276–296.

Guerrero, L. K., & Afifi, W. A. (1995b). What parents don't know: Topic avoidance in parent-child relationships. In T. J. Socha & G. H. Stamp (Eds.), *Parents, children, and communication: Frontiers of theory and research* (pp. 219–246). Mahwah, NJ: Erlbaum.

Guerrero, L. K., & Afifi, W. A. (1998). Communicative responses to jealousy as a function of self-esteem and relationship maintenance goals: A test of Bryson's dual motivation model. *Communication Reports, 11,* 111–122.

Guerrero, L. K., & Afifi, W. A. (1999). Toward a goal-oriented approach for understanding communicative responses to jealousy. *Western Journal of Communication, 63,* 216–248.

Guerrero, L. K., & Andersen, P. A. (1991). The waxing and waning of relational intimacy: Touch as a function of relational stage, gender, and touch avoidance. *Journal of Social and Personal Relationships, 8,* 147–165.

Guerrero, L. K., & Andersen, P. A. (1994). Patterns of matching and initiation: Touch behavior and avoidance across romantic relationship stages. *Journal of Nonverbal Behavior, 18,* 137–153.

Guerrero, L. K., & Andersen, P. A. (1998a). The dark side of jealousy and envy: Desire, delusion, desperation, and destructive communication. In B. H. Spitzberg & W. R. Cupach (Eds.), *The dark side of relationships* (pp. 33–70). Mahwah, NJ: Erlbaum.

Guerrero, L. K., & Andersen, P. A. (1998b). The experience and expression of romantic jealousy. In P. A. Andersen & L. K. Guerrero (Eds.), *The handbook of communication and emotion: Research, theory, applications, and contexts* (pp. 155–188). San Diego, CA: Academic Press.

Guerrero, L. K., & Andersen, P. A. (2000). Emotion in close relationships. In C. Hendrick & S. S. Hendrick (Eds.), *Close relationships: A sourcebook* (pp. 171–183). Thousand Oaks, CA: Sage.

Guerrero, L. K., Andersen, P. A., Jorgensen, P. F., Spitzberg, B. H., & Eloy, S. V. (1995). Coping with the green-eyed monster: Conceptualizing and measuring communicative responses to jealousy. *Western Journal of Communication, 59,* 270–304.

Guerrero, L. K., & Bachman, G. F. (2006). Associations among relational maintenance behaviors, attachment-style categories, and attachment dimensions. *Communication Studies, 57,* 341–361.

Guerrero, L. K., & Bachman, G. F. (in press). Communication following relational transgressions in dating relationships: An investment model explanation. *Southern Communication Journal.*

Guerrero, L. K., & Burgoon, J. K. (1996). Attachment styles and reactions to nonverbal involvement change in romantic dyads: Patterns of reciprocity and compensation. *Human Communication Research, 22,* 335–370.

Guerrero, L. K., & Chavez, A. M. (2005). Relational maintenance in cross-sex friendships characterized by different types of romantic intent: An exploratory study. *Western Journal of Communication, 69,* 341–360.

Guerrero, L. K., & Eloy, S. V. (1992). Jealousy and relational satisfaction across marital types. *Communication Reports, 5,* 23–31.

Guerrero, L. K., Eloy, S. V., & Wabnik, A. I. (1993). Linking maintenance strategies to relationship development and disengagement: A reconceptualization. *Journal of Social and Personal Relationships, 10,* 273–283.

Guerrero, L. K., Farinelli, L., McEwan, B., & Jones, S. M. (2007, November). *Attachment and relational satisfaction: The mediating effect of emotional expression.* Paper presented at the annual meeting of the National Communication Association, Chicago.

Guerrero, L. K., & Floyd, K. (2006). *Nonverbal communication in close relationships*. Mahwah, NJ: Lawrence Erlbaum.

Guerrero, L. K., & Jones, S. M. (2003). Differences in one's own and one's partner's perceptions of social skills as a function of attachment style. *Communication Quarterly, 51,* 277–295.

Guerrero, L. K., & Jones, S. M. (2005). Differences in conversational skills as a function of attachment style: A follow-up study. *Communication Quarterly, 53,* 305–321.

Guerrero, L. K., & La Valley, A. G. (2006). Conflict, emotion, and communication. In J. G. Oetzel & S. Ting-Toomey (Eds.), *The SAGE handbook of conflict communication* (pp. 69–96). Thousand Oaks, CA: Sage.

Guerrero, L. K., La Valley, A. G., & Farinelli, L. (2006, November). *The experience and expression of anger, guilt, and sadness in marriage: An equity theory explanation.* Paper presented at the annual meeting of the National Communication Association, San Antonio, TX.

Guerrero, L. K., & Langan, E. J. (1999, February). *Dominance displays in conversations about relational problems: Differences due to attachment style and sex.* Paper presented at the annual meeting of the Western States Communication Association, Vancouver, BC.

Guerrero, L. K., & Reiter, R. L. (1998). Expressing emotion: Sex differences in social skills and communicative responses to anger, sadness, and jealousy. In D. J. Canary & K. Dindia (Eds.), *Sex differences and similarities in communication* (pp. 321–350). Mahwah, NJ: Erlbaum.

Guerrero, L. K., Spitzberg, B. H., & Yoshimura, S. M. (2004). Sexual and emotional jealousy. In J. Harvey, A. Wenzel, & S. Sprecher (Eds.), *The handbook of sexuality in close relationships* (pp. 311–345). Mahwah, NJ: Lawrence Erlbaum.

Guerrero, L. K., Trost, M. L., & Yoshimura, S. M. (2005). Emotion and communication in the context of romantic jealousy. *Personal Relationships, 12,* 233–252.

Gutek, B. A., Morasch, B., & Cohen, A. G. (1983). Interpreting social-sexual behavior in a work setting. *Journal of Vocational Behavior, 32,* 30–48.

Haas, A., & Sherman, M. A. (1982). Reported topics of conversation among same-sex adults. *Communication Quarterly, 30,* 332–333.

Haas, S. M., & Stafford, L. (1998). An initial examination of maintenance behaviors in gay and lesbian relationships. *Journal of Social and Personal Relationships, 15,* 846–855.

Haas, S. M., & Stafford, L. (2005). Maintenance behaviors in same-sex and marital relationships: A matched sample comparison. *Journal of Family Communication, 5,* 43–60.

Hall, E. T. (1968). Proxemics. *Current Anthropology, 9,* 83–109.

Hall, J. A., Coats, E. J., & LeBeau, J. A. (2005). Nonverbal behavior and vertical dimension of social relations: A meta-analysis. *Psychological Bulletin, 131,* 898–924.

Halloran, E. C. (1998). The role of marital power in depression and marital distress. *American Journal of Family Therapy, 26,* 3–14.

Hamida, S. B., Mineka, S., & Bailey, J. M. (1998). Sex differences in perceived controllability of mate value: An evolutionary perspective. *Journal of Personality and Social Psychology, 75,* 953–966.

Hammer, J. C., Fisher, J. D., Fitzgerald, P., & Fisher, W. A. (1996). When two heads aren't better than one: AIDS risk behavior in college-age couples. *Journal of Applied Social Psychology, 26,* 375–397.

Hansen, G. L. (1987). Extradyadic relations during courtship. *Journal of Sex Research, 23,* 382–390.

Hansen, J. E., & Schuldt, W. J. (1984). Marital self-disclosure and marital satisfaction. *Journal of Marriage and the Family, 46,* 923–926.

Hargrave, T. D. (1994). *Families and forgiveness.* New York: Brunner/Mazel.

Hargrow, A. M. (1997). Speaking our realities: From speculation to truth concerning African American women's experiences of sexual harassment. *Dissertation Abstracts International, 57* (7-B), 4707.

Harry, J. (1984). *Gay couples.* New York: Praeger.

Harry, J., & De Vall, W. B. (1978). *The social organization of gay males.* New York: Praeger.

Hart, C. H., DeWolf, D. M., Wozniak, P., & Burts, D. C. (1992). Maternal and paternal disciplinary styles: Relations with preschoolers' playground behavioral orientations and peer status. *Child Development, 63,* 879–892.

Harter, S., Waters, P. L., Pettitt, L. M., Whitesell, N., Kofkin, J., & Jordan, J. (1997). Autonomy and connectedness as dimensions of relationship styles in men and women. *Journal of Social and Personal Relationships, 14,* 148–164.

Hartill, L. (2001). A brief history of interracial marriage. *Christian Science Monitor, 93,* 15.

Harvey, J. H. (1987). Attributions in close relationships: Recent theoretical developments. *Journal of Social and Clinical Psychology, 5,* 420–434.

Hatfield, E. (1984). The dangers of intimacy. In V. J. Derlega (Ed.), *Communication, intimacy, and close relationships* (pp. 207–220). New York: Academic Press.

Hatfield, E. (1988). Passionate and companionate love. In R. J. Sternberg & M. L. Barnes (Eds.), *The psychology of love* (pp. 191–217). New Haven, CT: Yale University Press.

Hatfield, E., & Rapson, R. L. (1987). Passionate love: New directions in research. In W. H. Jones & D. Perlman (Eds.), *Advances in personal relationships* (Vol. 1, pp. 109–139). Greenwich, CT: JAI Press.

Hatfield, E., & Rapson, R. L. (2000, March 15). *Rosie.* Pittsburgh, PA: Sterling House.

Hatfield, E., & Sprecher, S. (1986a). Measuring passionate love in intimate relationships. *Journal of Adolescence, 9,* 383–410.

Hatfield, E., & Sprecher, S. (1986b). *Mirror, mirror . . . The importance of looks in everyday life.* Albany: State University of New York Press.

Hatfield, E., Cacioppo, J. T., & Rapson, R. L. (1994). *Emotional contagion.* New York: Cambridge University Press.

Hatfield, E., Greenberger, E., Traupmann, J., & Lambert, P. (1982). Equity and sexual satisfaction in recently married couples. *Journal of Sex Research, 18,* 18–32.

Hays, R. B. (1985). A longitudinal study of friendship development. *Journal of Personality and Social Psychology, 48,* 909–924.

Hazan, C., & Shaver, P. (1987). Conceptualizing romantic love as an attachment process. *Journal of Personality and Social Psychology, 52,* 511–524.

Hazan, C., & Zeifman, D. (1994). Sex and the psychological tether. In K. Bartholomew & D. Perlman (Eds.), *Advances in personal relationships* (Vol. 5, pp. 151–177). London: Kingsley.

Heavey, C. L., Christensen, A., & Malamuth, N. M. (1995). The longitudinal impact of demand and withdrawal during marital conflict. *Journal of Consulting and Clinical Psychology, 63,* 797–801.

Heavey, C. L., Layne, C., & Christensen, A. (1993). Gender and conflict structure in martial interaction: A replication and extension. *Journal of Consulting and Clinical Psychology, 61,* 16–27.

Hecht, M. L. (1993). 2002—A research odyssey: Toward the development of a communication theory of identity. *Communication Monographs, 60,* 76–82.

Hecht, M. L., Collier, M. J., & Ribeau, S. (1993). *African American communication: Ethnic identity and cultural interpretations.* Newbury Park, CA: Sage.

Hecht, M. L., Marston, P. J., & Larkey, L. K. (1994). Love ways and relationship quality in heterosexual relationships. *Journal of Social and Personal Relationships, 11,* 25–43.

Hecht, M. L., Warren, J., Jung, J., & Krieger, J. (2004). Communication theory of identity. In W. B. Gudykunst (Ed.), *Theorizing about intercultural communication* (pp. 257–278). Thousand Oaks, CA: Sage.

Heider, F. (1958). *The psychology of interpersonal relations.* New York: Wiley.

Helgeson, V. S., Novak, S. A., Lepore, S. J., & Eton, D. T. (2005). Spouse social control efforts: Relations to heath behavior and well-being among men with prostate cancer. *Journal of Social and Personal Relationships, 21,* 53–68.

Helgeson, V. S., Shaver, P., & Dyer, M. (1987). Prototypes of intimacy and distance in same-sex and opposite-sex relationships. *Journal of Social and Personal Relationships, 4,* 195–233.

Henderson, S., & Gilding, M. (2004). "I've never clicked this much with anyone in my life": Trust and hyperpersonal communication in online friendships. *New Media & Society, 6,* 487–506.

Hendrick, C., & Hendrick, S. S. (1986). A theory and method of love. *Journal of Personality and Social Psychology, 50,* 392–402.

Hendrick, C., & Hendrick, S. S. (1990). A relationships-specific version of the love attitude scale. *Journal of Social Behavior and Personality, 5,* 239–254.

Hendrick, S. S. (1981). Self-disclosure and marital satisfaction. *Journal of Personality and Social Psychology, 40,* 1150–1159.

Hendrick, S. S., & Hendrick, C. (1987). Love and sex attitudes: A close relationship. In W. H. Jones & D. Perlman (Eds.), *Advances in personal relationships* (Vol. 1, pp. 141–169). Greenwich, CT: JAI Press.

Hendrick, S. S., & Hendrick, C. (1992). *Liking, loving, and relating* (2nd ed.). Pacific Grove, CA: Brooke/ Cole.

Hendrick, S. S., & Hendrick, C. (2002). Linking romantic love with sex: Development of the perceptions of love and sex scale. *Journal of Social and Personal Relationships, 19,* 361–378.

Hendrick, S. S., Hendrick, C., & Adler, N. L. (1988). Romantic relationships: Love, satisfaction, and staying together. *Journal of Personality and Social Psychology, 54,* 980–988.

Henley, N. M. (1977). *Body politics: Power, sex, and nonverbal communication.* Englewood Cliffs, NJ: Prentice Hall.

Hensley, W. E. (1994). Height as a basis for interpersonal attraction. *Adolescence, 29,* 469–474.

Heslin, R., & Boss, D. (1980). Nonverbal intimacy in arrival and departure at an airport. *Personality and Social Psychology Bulletin, 6,* 248–252.

Hess, E. H. (1965). Attitude and pupil size. *Scientific American, 212,* 46–54.

Hess, E. H., & Goodwin, E. (1974). The present state of pupilometers. In M. P. Janisse (Ed.), *Pupillary dynamics and behavior* (pp. 209–246). New York: Plenum Press.

Hesson-McInnis, M. S., & Fitzgerald, L. F. (1997). Sexual harassment: A preliminary test of an integrative model. *Journal of Applied Social Psychology, 27,* 877–901.

Hewes, D. E., Graham, M. L., Doelger, J., & Pavitt, C. (1985). "Second-guessing": Message interpretation in social networks. *Human Communication Research, 11,* 299–334.

Hewitt, J., & Stokes, R. (1975). Disclaimers. *American Sociological Review, 40,* 1–11.

Higgins, R. L., & Berglas, S. (1990). The maintenance and treatment of self-handicapping: From risk-taking to face-saving—and back. In R. L. Higgins (Ed.), *Self-handicapping: The paradox that isn't* (pp. 187–238). New York: Plenum Press.

Hill, C. T., Rubin, Z., & Peplau, L. A. (1976). Breakups before marriage: The end of 103 affairs. *Journal of Social Issues, 32,* 147–168.

Hill, J. P., & Holmbeck, G. (1986). Attachment and autonomy during adolescence. In G. Whitehurst (Ed.), *Annals of child development* (Vol. 3, pp. 145–189). Greenwich, CT: JAI.

Himsel, A., & Goldberg, W. A. (2003). Social comparisons and the division of housework among dual-earner couples: Implications for satisfaction and role strain. *Journal of Family Issues, 24,* 843–866.

Hinde, R. A. (1984). Why do the sexes behave differently in close relationships? *Journal of Social and Personal Relationship, 1,* 471–501.

Hochschild, A. (1997). *The time bind: When work becomes home and home becomes work.* New York: Metropolitan Books.

Hochschild, A., & Machung, A. (1989). *The second shift: Working parents and the revolution at home.* New York: Viking/Penguin.

Hocker, J. L., & Wilmot, W. W. (1998). *Interpersonal conflict* (5th ed.). Dubuque, IA: Brown & Benchmark.

Hocking, J. E., & Leathers, D. G. (1980). Nonverbal indicators of deception: A new theoretical perspective. *Communication Monographs, 47,* 119–131.

Hoffman, M. L. (1970). Power assertion by parents and its impact on the child. *Child Development, 31,* 129–143.

Hoffman, M. L. (1980). Moral development in adolescence. In J. Adelson (Ed.), *Handbook of adolescent psychology* (pp. 295–343). New York: Wiley.

Hofstede, G. (1982). *Culture's consequences* (abridged ed.). Beverly Hills, CA: Sage.

Hogg, M. A., & Abrams, D. (1988). *Social identifications: A social psychology of intergroup relations and group processes.* London: Routledge.

Holtgraves, T. (1988). Gambling as self-presentation. *Journal of Gambling Behavior, 4,* 78–91.

Holtgraves, T., & Yang, J. (1990). Politeness as a universal: Cross-cultural perceptions of request strategies and inferences based on their use. *Journal of Personality and Social Psychology, 59,* 719–729.

Holtgraves, T., & Yang, J. (1992). Interpersonal underpinnings of request strategies: General principles and differences due to culture and gender. *Journal of Personality and Social Psychology, 62,* 246–256.

Holtzworth-Munroe, A., & Hutchinson, G. (1993). Attributing negative intent to wife behavior: The attributions of maritally violent versus nonviolent men. *Journal of Abnormal Psychology, 102,* 206–211.

Holtzworth-Munroe, A., & Jacobson, N. S. (1985). Causal attributions of married couples: When do they search for causes? What do they conclude when they do? *Journal of Personality and Social Psychology, 48,* 1398–1412.

Holtzworth-Munroe, A. & Smutzler, N. (1996). Comparing the emotional reactions and behavioral intentions of violent and nonviolent husbands to aggressive, distressed, and other wife behaviors. *Violence and Victims, 11,* 319–340.

Holtzworth-Munroe, A., Smutzler, N., & Stuart, G. L. (1998). Demand and withdraw communication among couples experiencing husband violence. *Journal of Consulting and Clinical Psychology, 66,* 731–743.

Homans, G. C. (1961). *Social behavior.* New York: Harcourt, Brace & World.

Homans, G. C. (1974). *Social behavior: Its elementary forms* (2nd ed.). New York: Harcourt, Brace & World.

Honeycutt, J. M., & Cantrill, J. G. (2001). *Cognition, communication, and romantic relationships.* Mahwah, NJ: Lawrence Erlbaum.

Honeycutt, J. M., Cantrill, J. G., & Allen, T. (1992). Memory structure of relational decay: A cognitive test of the sequencing of de-escalating actions and stages. *Human Communication Research, 18,* 528–562.

Hoobler, G. D. (1999, June). *Ten years of personal relationships research: Where have we been and where are we going?* Paper presented at the annual meeting of the International Network on Personal Relationships, Louisville, KY.

Hopper, M. L., Knapp, M. L., & Scott, L. (1981). Couples' personal idioms: Exploring intimate talk. *Journal of Communication, 31,* 23–33.

Hosman, L. A., & Tardy, C. H. (1980). Self-disclosure and reciprocity in short- and long-term relationships: An experimental study of evaluational and attributional consequences. *Communication Quarterly, 28,* 20–30.

Howard, J. A., Blumstein, P., & Schwartz, P. (1986). Sex, power, and influence tactics in intimate relationships. *Journal of Personality and Social Psychology, 51,* 102–109.

Hoyle, R. H., Insko, C. A., & Moniz, A. J. (1992). Self-esteem, evaluative feedback, and preacquaintance attraction: Indirect reactions to success and failure. *Motivation and Emotion, 16,* 79–101.

Hoyt, M. F. (1978). Secrets in psychotherapy: Theoretical and practical considerations. *International Review of Psycho-Analysis, 5,* 231–241.

Hughes, M., Morrison, K., & Asada, J. K. (2005). What's love got to do with it? Exploring the impact of maintenance rules, love attitudes, and network support on friends which benefits relationships. *Western Journal of Communication, 69,* 49–66.

Hunt, M. (1974). *Sexual behavior in the 1970s.* New York: Playboy Press.

Huston, T. L. (1983). Power. In H. H. Kelley, E. Berscheid, A. Christensen, J. H. Harvey, T. L. Huston, G. Levinger, et al. (Eds.), *Close relationships* (pp. 169–219). New York: Freeman.

Huston, T. L., & Levinger, G. (1978). Interpersonal attraction and relationships. *Annual Review of Psychology, 29,* 115–156.

Huston, M., & Schwartz, P. (1995). The relationships of gay men and lesbians. In J. T. Wood & S. Duck (Eds.), *Understudied relationships: Off the beaten track* (pp. 89–121). Thousand Oaks, CA: Sage.

Huston, T. L., Surra, C. A., Fitzgerald, N. M., & Cate, R. M. (1981). From courtship to marriage: Mate selection as an interpersonal process. In S. Duck & R. Gilmour (Eds.), *Personal relationships: Developing personal relationships* (Vol. 2, pp. 53–88). London: Academic Press.

Ickes, W. I., Dugosh, J. W., Simpson, J. A., & Wilson, C. L. (2003). Suspicious minds: The motive to acquire relationship-threatening information. *Personal Relationships, 10,* 131–148.

Imber-Black, E. (1993). Secrets in families and family therapy: An overview. In E. Imber-Black (Ed.), *Secrets in families and family therapy* (pp. 3–28). New York: Norton.

Impett, A., Peplau, L. A., & Gable, S. L. (2005). Approach and avoidance sexual motives: Implications for personal and interpersonal well-being. *Personal Relationships, 12,* 465–482.

Infante, D. A. (1987). Aggressiveness. In J. C. McCroskey & J. A. Daly (Eds.), *Personality and interpersonal communication* (pp. 157–192). Newbury Park, CA: Sage.

Infante, D. A., Chandler, T. A., & Rudd, J. E. (1989). Test of an argumentative skill deficiency model of interpersonal violence. *Communication Monographs, 56,* 163–177.

Infante, D. A., & Rancer, A. S. (1982). A conceptualization and measure of argumentativeness. *Journal of Personality Assessment, 46,* 72–80.

Infante, D. A., Sabourin, T. C., Rudd, J. E., & Shannon, E. A. (1990). Verbal aggression in violent and nonviolent marital disputes. *Communication Quarterly, 38,* 361–371.

Isnard, C. A., & Zeeman, E. C. (1977). Some models from catastrophe theory in the social sciences. In E. C. Zeeman (Ed.), *Catastrophe theory: Selected papers 1972–1977.* Reading, MA: Addison-Wesley.

Jackson, L. A., & Ervin, K. S. (1992). Height stereotypes of women and men: The liabilities of shortness for both sexes. *Journal of Social Psychology, 132,* 433–445.

Jackson, R. L., II. (1999). *The negotiation of cultural identity: Perceptions of European Americans and African Americans.* Westport, CT: Praeger.

Jacob, T. (1974). Patterns of family conflict and dominance as a function of child age and social class. *Developmental Psychology, 10,* 1–12.

Jankowiak, W. R., & Fischer, E. F. (1992). A cross-cultural perspective on romantic love. *Ethnology, 31,* 149–155.

Janofsky, A. I. (1971). Affective self-disclosure in telephone versus face-to-face interviews. *Journal of Humanistic Psychology, 11,* 93–103.

Jellison, J. M., & Oliver, D. F. (1983). Attitudinal similarity and attraction: An impression management approach. *Personality and Social Psychology Bulletin, 9,* 111–115.

Jensen-Campbell, L. A., Graziano, W. G., & West, S. G. (1995). Dominance, prosocial orientation, and female preferences: Do nice guys really finish last? *Journal of Personality and Social Psychology, 68,* 427–440.

Johnson, A. J. (2001). Examining the maintenance of friendships: Are there differences between geographically close and long-distance friends? *Communication Quarterly, 49,* 424–435.

Johnson, A. J., Wittenberg, E., Haigh, M., Wigley, S., Becker, J., Brown, K., et al. (2004). The process of relationship development and deterioration: Turning points in friendships that have terminated. *Communication Quarterly, 52,* 54–68.

Johnson, A. J., Wittenberg, E., Villigran, M., Mazur, M., & Villigran, P. (2003). Relational progression as a dialectic: Examining turning points in communication among friends. *Communication Monographs, 70,* 230–249.

Johnson, D. J., & Rusbult, C. E. (1989). Resisting temptation: Devaluation of alternative partners as a means of maintaining commitment in close relationships. *Journal of Personality and Social Psychology, 57,* 967–980.

Johnson, M. L., Afifi, W. A., & Duck, S. (1994). *Social attraction on first dates: Is communication underrated?* Unpublished manuscript.

Johnson, M. P. (1982). Social and cognitive features of the dissolution of commitment to relationships. In S. Duck (Ed.), *Dissolving personal relationships* (pp. 51–73). New York: Academic Press.

Johnson, R. E. (1972). Attitudes toward extramarital relationships. *Medical Aspects of Human Sexuality, 6,* 168–191.

Jones, E., & Gallois, C. (1989). Spouses' impressions of rules for communication in public and private marital conflict. *Journal of Marriage and the Family, 51,* 957–967.

Jones, E. E., & Wortman, C. (1973). *Ingratiation: An attributional approach.* Morristown, NJ: General Learning Press.

Jones, J. T., Pelham, B. W., Carvallo, M., & Mirenberg, M. C. (2004). How do I love thee? Let me count the Js: Implicit egotism and interpersonal attraction. *Journal of Personality and Social Psychology, 87,* 665–683.

Jones, S. M. (2000). *Nonverbal immediacy and verbal comforting in the social process.* Unpublished doctoral dissertation, Arizona State University, Tempe.

Jones, S. M. (2004). Putting the person into person-centered and immediate emotional support: Emotional change and perceived helper competence as outcomes of comforting in helping situations. *Communication Research, 32,* 338–360.

Jones, S. M., & Burleson, B. R. (1997). The impact of situational variables on helpers' perceptions of comforting messages: An attributional analysis. *Communication Research, 24,* 530–555.

Jones, S. M., & Burleson, B. R. (2003). Effects of helper and recipient sex on the experience and outcomes of comforting messages: An experimental investigation. *Sex Roles, 48*(1/2), 1–19.

Jones, S. M., & Guerrero, L. K. (2001). The effects of nonverbal immediacy and verbal person-centeredness in the emotional support process. *Human Communication Research, 27,* 567–596.

Jones, T. S. (2000). Emotional communication in conflict: Essence and impact. In W. Eadie & P. Nelson (Eds.), *The language of conflict and resolution* (pp. 81–104). Thousand Oaks, CA: Sage.

Jones, W. H., & Burdette, M. P. (1994). Betrayal in relationships. In A. L. Weber & J. H. Harvey (Eds.), *Perspectives on close relationships* (pp. 243–262). Needham Heights, MA: Allyn & Bacon.

Joseph, N., & Alex, N. (1972). The uniform: A sociological perspective. *American Journal of Sociology, 77,* 719–730.

Joshi, K., & Rai, S. N. (1987). Effect of physical attractiveness upon the inter-personal attraction subjects of different self-esteem. *Perspectives in Psychological Research, 10,* 19–24.

Jourard, S. M. (1959). Self-disclosure and other cathexis. *Journal of Abnormal Social Psychology, 59,* 428–431.

Jourard, S. M. (1964). *The transparent self.* New York: Wiley.

Julien, D., Bouchard, C., Gagnon, M., & Pomperleau, A. (1992). An insider's view of marital sex. A dyadic analysis. *Journal of Sex Research, 29,* 343–360.

Kahneman, D., Slovic, P., & Tvesky, A. (Eds.). (1982). *Judgment under uncertainty: Heuristics and biases.* Cambridge, UK: Cambridge University Press.

Kaiser, S. B. (1997). *The social psychology of clothing: Symbolic appearances in context* (2nd ed.). New York: Fairchild.

Kalbfleisch, P. J., & Herold, A. L. (2006). Sex, power, and communication. In K. Dindia & D. J. Canary (Eds.), *Sex differences and similarities in communication* (2nd ed., pp. 299–313). Mahwah, NJ: Lawrence Erlbaum.

Kandel, D. B. (1978). Similarity in real life adolescent friendship pairs. *Journal of Personality and Social Psychology, 36,* 306–312.

Kanin, E. J., Davidson, K. D., & Scheck, S. R. (1970). A research note on male-female differentials in the experience of heterosexual love. *Journal of Sex Research, 6,* 64–72.

Karney, B. R., & Bradbury, T. N. (1995). The longitudinal course of marital quality and stability: A review of theory, method, and research. *Psychological Bulletin, 118,* 3–34.

Karpel, M. (1980). Family secrets. *Family Process, 19,* 295–306.

Katz, J., Street, A., & Arias, I. (1995, November). *Forgive and forget: Women's responses to dating violence.* Paper presented at the annual meeting of the Association for the Advancement of Behavior Therapy, Washington, DC.

Kellermann, K. A. (1995). The conversation MOP: A model of patterned and pliable behavior. In D. E. Hewes (Ed.), *The cognitive bases of interpersonal communication* (pp. 181–224). Hillsdale, NJ: Erlbaum.

Kellermann, K. A., & Berger, C. R. (1984). Affect and the acquisition of social information: Sit back, relax, and tell me about yourself. In R. N. Bostrom (Ed.), *Communication yearbook 8* (pp. 412–445). Beverly Hills, CA: Sage.

Kellermann, K. A., & Reynolds, R. (1990). When ignorance is bliss. The role of motivation to reduce uncertainty in uncertainty reduction theory. *Human Communication Research, 17,* 5–75.

Kelley, A. E., & McKillop, K. J. (1996). Consequences of revealing personal secrets. *Psychological Bulletin, 120,* 450–465.

Kelley, D. (1998). The communication of forgiveness. *Communication Studies, 49,* 255–271.

Kelley, H. H. (1973). The processes of causal attribution. *American Psychologist, 28,* 107–128.

Kelley, H. H. (1979). *Personal relationships: Their structures and processes.* Hillsdale, NJ: Lawrence Erlbaum.

Kelley, H. H. (1986). Personal relationships: Their nature and significance. In R. Gilmour & S. Duck (Eds.), *The emerging field of personal relationships* (pp. 3–19). Hillsdale, NJ: Erlbaum.

Kelley, H. H., Berscheid, E., Christensen, A., Harvey, J. H., Huston, T. L., Levinger, G., et al. (1983). Analyzing close relationships. In H. H. Kelley, E. Berscheid, A. Christensen, J. H. Harvey, T. L. Huston, & G. Levinger (Eds.), *Close relationships* (pp. 20–67). New York: Freeman.

Kelley, K., Pilchowicz, E., & Byrne, D. (1981). Responses of males to female-initiated dates. *Bulletin of the Psychonomic Society, 17,* 195–196.

Kelley, K., & Rolker-Dolinsky, B. (1987). The psychosexology of female initiation and dominance. In D. Perlman & S. Duck (Eds.), *Intimate relationships:*

Development, dynamics and deterioration (pp. 63–87). Newbury Park, CA: Sage.

Kelly, A. B., Fincham, F. D., & Beach, S. R. H. (2003). Communication skills in couples: A review and discussion of emerging perspectives. In J. O. Greene & B. R. Burleson (Eds.), *Handbook of communication and social skills* (pp. 723–751). Mahwah, NJ: Lawrence Erlbaum.

Kennedy, C. W., & Camden, C. (1983). Interruptions and nonverbal gender differences. *Journal of Nonverbal Behavior, 8,* 91–108.

Kennedy, J. H. (1992). Relationship of maternal beliefs and childrearing strategies to social competence in preschool children. *Child Study Journal, 22,* 39–55.

Kenrick, D. T., Groth, G. E., Trost, M. R., & Sadalla, E. K. (1993). Integrating evolutionary and social exchange perspectives on relationships: Effects of gender, self-appraisal, and involvement level on mate selection criteria. *Journal of Personality and Social Psychology, 64,* 951–969.

Kenrick, D. T., & Keefe, R. C. (1992). Age preferences in mates reflect sex differences in human reproductive strategies. *Behavioral and Brain Sciences, 15,* 75–113.

Kenrick, D. T., Sadalla, E. K., Groth, G., & Trost, M. R. (1990). Evolution, traits, and the stages of human courtship: Qualifying the parental investment model. *Journal of Personality, 58,* 97–116.

Kenrick, D. T., & Trost, M. R. (1987). A biosocial theory of heterosexual relationships. In K. Kelley (Ed.), *Females, males, and sexuality: Theories and research* (pp. 59–100). Albany: State University of New York Press.

Kenrick, D. T., & Trost, M. R. (1989). Reproductive exchange model of heterosexual relationships: Putting proximate economics in ultimate perspective. In C. Hendrick (Ed.), *Review of personality and social psychology* (Vol. 10, pp. 92–118). Newbury Park, CA: Sage.

Kesher, S., Kark, R., Pomerantz-Zorin, L. Koslowsky, M., & Schwarzwald, J. (2006). Gender, status and the use of power strategies. *European Journal of Social Psychology, 36,* 105–117.

Keyton, J. (1996). Sexual harassment: A multidisciplinary synthesis and critique. In B. R. Burleson (Ed.), *Communication yearbook 19* (pp. 92–155). Thousand Oaks, CA: Sage.

Kidwell, J., Fischer, J. L., Dunham, R. M., & Baranowski, M. (1983). Parents and adolescents: Push and pull of change. In H. I. McCubin & C. R. Figley (Eds.),

Stress in the family: Coping with normative transitions (pp. 74–89). New York: Brunner/Mazel.

Kilmann, R. H., & Thomas, K. W. (1977). Developing a forced-choice measure of conflict-handling behavior: The "MODE" instrument. *Education and Psychological Measurement, 37,* 309–325.

King, S. W., & Sereno, K. K. (1984). Conversational appropriateness as a conversational imperative. *Quarterly Journal of Speech, 70,* 264–273.

Kitzmann, K. M., & Cohen, R. (2003). Parents' versus children's perceptions of interparental conflict as predictors of children's friendship quality. *Journal of Social and Personal Relationships, 20,* 689–700.

Klein, R. C. A., & Johnson, M. P. (1997). Strategies of couple conflict. In S. Duck (Ed.), *Handbook of personal relationships: Theory, research, and interventions* (2nd ed., pp. 267–486). New York: Wiley.

Kleinke, C. L., Meeker, F. B., & LaFong, C. (1974). Effects of gaze, touch, and use of name on evaluation of "engaged" couples. *Journal of Research in Personality, 7,* 368–373.

Klinetob, N. A., & Smith, D. A. (1996). Demand-withdraw communication in marital interaction: Tests of interspousal contingency and gender role hypotheses. *Journal of Marriage and the Family, 58,* 945–957.

Kluwer, E. S., de Dreu, C. K. W., & Buunk, B. P. (1998). Conflict in intimate vs. nonintimate relationships: When gender role stereotyping overrides biased self-other judgment. *Journal of Social and Personal Relationships, 15,* 637–650.

Knapp, M. L. (1978). *Social intercourse: From greeting to goodbye.* Boston: Allyn & Bacon.

Knapp, M. L. (1983). Dyadic relationship development. In J. Wiemann (Ed.), *Nonverbal interaction* (pp. 179–197). Beverly Hills, CA: Sage.

Knapp, M. L., & Vangelisti, A. L. (2005). *Interpersonal communication and human relationships* (5th ed.). Boston: Allyn & Bacon.

Knee, C. R., Patrick, H., Vietor, N. A., & Neighbors, C. (2004). Implicit theories of relationships: Moderators of the link between conflict and commitment. *Personality and Social Psychology Bulletin, 30,* 617–628.

Knobloch, L. K. (2005). Evaluating a contextual model of responses to relational uncertainty increasing events: The role of intimacy, appraisals, and emotions. *Human Communication Research, 31,* 60–101.

Knobloch, L. K. (2006). Relational uncertainty and message production within courtship. *Human Communication Research, 32,* 244–273.

Knobloch, L. K. (in press). Perceptions of turmoil within courtship: Associations with intimacy, relational uncertainty, and interference from partners. *Journal of Social and Personal Relationships.*

Knobloch, L. K., & Carpenter-Theune, K. E. (2004). Topic avoidance in developing romantic relationships: Associations with intimacy and relational uncertainty. *Communication Research, 31,* 173–205.

Knobloch, L. K., & Donovan-Kicken, E. (2006). Perceived involvement of network members in courtships: A test of the relational turbulence model. *Personal Relationships, 13,* 281–302.

Knobloch, L. K., & Solomon, D. H. (1999). Measuring the sources and content of relational uncertainty. *Communication Studies, 50,* 261–278.

Knobloch, L. K., & Solomon, D. H. (2002a). Information seeking beyond initial interactions: Negotiating relational uncertainty within close relationships. *Human Communication Research, 28,* 243–257.

Knobloch, L. K., & Solomon, D. H. (2002b). Intimacy and the magnitude and experience of episodic uncertainty within romantic relationships. *Personal Relationships, 9,* 457–478.

Knobloch, L. K., & Solomon, D. H. (2003). Responses to changes in relational uncertainty within dating relationships: Emotions and communication strategies. *Communication Studies, 54,* 282–305.

Knobloch, L. K., & Solomon, D. H. (2004). Interference and facilitation from partners in the development of interdependence with romantic relationships. *Personal Relationships, 11,* 115–130.

Knobloch, L. K., & Solomon, D. H. (2005). Relational uncertainty and relational information processing. *Communication Research, 32,* 349–388.

Koehler, M. H. (2005). *Politics of privacy: The handling of privacy violations experienced by graduate teaching assistants.* Unpublished master's thesis, Arizona State University, Tempe.

Koeppel, L. B., Montagne-Miller, Y., O'Hair, D., & Cody, M. (1993). Friendly? Flirting? Wrong? In P. J. Kalbfleisch (Ed.), *Interpersonal communication: Evolving interpersonal relationships* (pp. 13–32). Hillsdale, NJ: Erlbaum.

Koerner, A. F., & Fitzpatrick, M. A. (2002). You never leave your family in a fight: The impact of family of origin on conflict behavior in romantic relationships. *Communication Studies, 53,* 234–251.

Koerner, A. F., & Fitzpatrick, M. A. (2006). Family conflict communication. In J. G. Oetzel & S. Ting-Toomey (Eds.), *The SAGE handbook of conflict communication* (pp. 159–183). Thousand Oaks, CA: Sage.

Kohn, M., Flood, H., Chase, J., & McMahon, P. M. (2000). Prevalence and health consequences of stalking—Louisiana, 1998–1999. *Morbidity and Mortality Weekly Report, 49*(29), 653–655.

Kollock, P., Blumstein, P., & Schwartz, P. (1985). Sex and power in interaction: Conversational privileges and duties. *American Sociological Review, 50,* 34–46.

Korda, M. (1975). *Power: How to get it, how to use it.* New York: Ballantine Books.

Krahl, J. R., & Wheeless, L. R. (1997). Retrospective analysis of previous relationship disengagement and current attachment style. *Communication Quarterly, 45,* 167–187.

Krokoff, L. J., Gottman, J. M., & Roy, A. K. (1988). Blue-collar and white-collar marital interaction and communication orientation. *Journal of Social and Personal Relationships, 5,* 201–221.

Krueger, R. F., & Caspi, A. (1993). Personality, arousal, and pleasure: A test of competing models of interpersonal attraction. *Personality and Individual Differences, 14,* 105–111.

Kruglanski, A. W. (1990). Motivations for judging and knowing: Implications for causal attribution. In E. T. Higgins & R. M. Sorrentino (Eds.), *Handbook of motivation and cognition: Foundation of social behavior* (Vol. 2, pp. 333–368). New York: Guilford Press.

Kruglanski, A. W., Webster, D. M., & Klem, A. (1993). Motivated resistance and openness to persuasion in the presence or absence of prior information. *Journal of Personality and Social Psychology, 65,* 861–876.

Kuczynski, L. (1984). Socialization goals and mother-child interaction: Strategies for long-term and short-term compliance. *Developmental Psychology, 20,* 1061–1073.

Kunce, L. J., & Shaver, P. R. (1994). An attachment-theoretical approach to caregiving in romantic relationships. In K. Bartholomew & D. Perlman (Eds.), *Advances in personal relationships: Vol. 5. Attachment processes in adulthood* (pp. 205–237). Bristol, PA: Kingsley.

Kurdek, L. A. (1989). Relationship quality in gay and lesbian cohabiting couples: A 1-year follow-up study. *Journal of Social and Personal Relationships, 6,* 39–59.

Kurdek, L. A. (1991). The dissolution of gay and lesbian couples. *Journal of Social and Personal Relationships, 8,* 265–278.

Kurdek, L. A. (1993a). The allocation of household labor in gay, lesbian, and heterosexual married couples. *Journal of Social Issues, 49*(3), 127–139.

Kurdek, L. A. (1993b). Predicting marital dissolution: A 5-year prospective longitudinal study of newlywed couples. *Journal of Personality and Social Psychology, 64,* 221–242.

LaFrance, M., & Mayo, C. (1978). *Moving bodies: Nonverbal communication in social relationships.* Monterey, CA: Brooks/Cole.

Laner, M. R., & Ventrone, N. A. (2000). Dating scripts revisited. *Journal of Family Issues, 21,* 488–500.

Lang, F. R. (2000). Endings and continuity of social relationships: Maximizing intrinsic benefits within personal networks when feeling near to death. *Journal of Social and Personal Relationships, 17,* 155–182.

Langer, E. J. (1989). *Mindfulness.* Reading, MA: Addison-Wesley.

Langlois, J. H., Kalakanis, L., Rubenstein, A. J., Larson, A., Hallam, M., & Smoot, M. (2000). Maxims or myths of beauty? A meta-analytic and theoretical review. *Psychological Bulletin, 126,* 390–423.

Lannutti, P. J., & Cameron, K. A. (2002). Beyond the breakup: Heterosexual and homosexual post—dissolution relationships. *Communication Quarterly, 50,* 153–170.

Lannutti, P. J., & Monahan, J. L. (2004). "Not now, maybe later": The influence of relationship type, request persistence and alcohol consumption on women's refusal strategies. *Communication Studies, 55,* 362–378.

Larkin, M. (1998). Easing the way to safer sex. *Lancet, 351,* 964–967.

Laumann, E. O., Gagnon, J. H., Michael, R. T., & Michaels, S. (1994). *The social organization of sexuality: Sexual practices in the United States.* Chicago: University of Chicago Press.

Laumann, E. O., Paik, A., & Rosen, R. C. (1999). Sexual dysfunction in the United States: Prevalence and predictors. *Journal of the American Medical Association, 281,* 537–544.

Laursen, B. (1989). *Relationships and conflict during adolescence.* Unpublished doctoral dissertation, University of Minnesota, Minneapolis.

Laursen, B., & Collins, W. A. (1994). Interpersonal conflict during adolescence. *Psychological Bulletin, 115,* 197–209.

Lawrence, K., & Byers, E. S. (1995). Sexual satisfaction in long-term heterosexual relationships: The interpersonal exchange model of sexual satisfaction. *Personal Relationships, 2,* 267–285.

Lazarus, R. S. (1985). The trivialization of distress. In J. C. Rose & L. J. Solomon (Eds.), *Primary prevention of psychopathology: Vol. 8. Prevention in health psychology* (pp. 279–298). Hanover, NH: University Press of New England.

Le, B., & Agnew, C. R. (2003). Commitment and its theorized determinants: A meta-analysis of the investment model. *Personal Relationships, 10,* 37–57.

Le Poire, B. A., Hallett, J. S., & Giles, H. (1998). Codependence: The paradoxical nature of the functional-afflicted relationship. In B. H. Spitzberg & W. R. Cupach (Eds.), *The dark side of relationships* (pp. 153–176). Mahwah, NJ: Erlbaum.

Le Poire, B. A., Shepard, C., & Duggan, A. (1999). Nonverbal involvement, expressiveness, and pleasantness as predicted by parental and partner attachment style. *Communication Monographs, 66,* 293–311.

Lea, M., & Spears, R. (1995). Love at first byte: Building personal relationships over computer networks. In J. T. Wood & S. Duck (Eds.), *Understudied relationships: Off the beaten track* (pp. 197–233). Thousand Oaks, CA: Sage.

Lear, D. (1997). *Sex and sexuality: Risk and relationships in the age of AIDS.* Thousand Oaks, CA: Sage.

Leary, M. R. (1995). *Self-presentation: Impression management and interpersonal behavior.* Madison, WI: Brown & Benchmark.

Leary, M. R., & Kowalski, R. M. (1990). Impression management: A literature review and two-component model. *Psychological Bulletin, 107,* 34–47.

Leary, M. R., Springer, C., Negel, L., Ansell, E., & Evans, K. (1998). The causes, phenomenology, and consequences of hurt feelings. *Journal of Personality and Social Psychology, 74,* 1225–1237.

Lee, J. A. (1973). *The colors of love: An exploration of the ways of loving.* Don Mills, Ontario, Canada: New Press.

Lee, J. A. (1977). A typology of styles of loving. *Personality and Social Psychology Bulletin, 3,* 173–182.

Lee, J. A. (1988). Love styles. In R. J. Sternberg & M. L. Barnes (Eds.), *The psychology of love* (pp. 38–67). New Haven, CT: Yale University Press.

Lee, J. W., & Guerrero, L. K. (2001). Types of touch in cross-sex relationships by coworkers: Perceptions of relational and emotional messages, inappropriateness and sexual harassment. *Journal of Applied Communication Research, 29,* 197–220.

Lepore, S. J., & Greenberg, M. A. (2002). Mending broken hearts: Effects of expressive writing on mood, cognitive processing, social adjustment, and health following a relationship breakup. *Psychology and Health, 17,* 547–560.

Levine, T. R., & Boster, F. J. (2001). The effects of power and message variables on compliance. *Communication Monographs, 68,* 28–48.

Levine, T. R., & McCornack, S. A. (1992). Linking love and lies: A formal test of the McCornack and Parks model of deception detection. *Journal of Social and Personal Relationships, 9,* 143–154.

Levinger, G., & Senn, D. J. (1967). Disclosure of feelings in marriage. *Merrill-Palmer Quarterly, 13,* 237–249.

Levitt, M. J. (1991). Attachment and close relationships: A life-span perspective. In J. L. Gerwitz & W. F. Kurtines (Eds.), *Intersections with attachment* (pp. 183–206). Mahwah, NJ: Erlbaum.

Levitt, M. J., Coffman, S., Guacci-Franco, N., & Loveless, S. C. (1994). Attachment relationships and life transitions: An expectancy model. In M. B. Sperling & W. H. Berman (Eds.), *Attachment in adults: Clinical and developmental perspectives* (pp. 232–255). New York: Guilford Press.

Lewis, M., & Rosenblum, L. A. (Eds.). (1974). *The effect of the infant on its caregiver.* New York: Wiley.

Lillard, L. L., Brien, M. J., & Waite, L. J. (1995). Premarital cohabitation and subsequent marital dissolution: A matter of self-selection? *Demography, 32,* 437–457.

Lippard, P. V. (1988). "Ask me no questions, I'll tell you no lies": Situational exigencies for interpersonal deception. *Western Journal of Speech Communication, 52,* 91–103.

Livingstone, K. R. (1980). Love as a process of reducing uncertainty. In K. S. Pope (Ed.), *On love and loving* (pp. 133–151). San Francisco: Jossey-Bass.

Lloyd, S. A., & Cate, R. M. (1985). The developmental course of conflict in dissolution of premarital relationships. *Journal of Social and Personal Relationships, 2,* 179–194.

Lloyd, S. A., Cate, R., & Henton, J. (1982). Equity and rewards as predictors of satisfaction in casual and intimate relationships. *Journal of Psychology, 110,* 43–48.

Lucchetti, A. N. (1999). Deception in disclosing one's sexual history: Safe-sex avoidance or ignorance? *Communication Quarterly, 47,* 300–314.

Lustig, M. W., & Koester, J. (2003). *Intercultural competence: Interpersonal communication across cultures* (4th ed.). Boston: Allyn & Bacon.

MacNeil, S., & Byers, E. S. (2005). Dyadic assessment of sexual self-disclosure and sexual satisfaction in heterosexual dating couples. *Journal of Social and Personal Relationships, 22,* 169–181.

Magai, C., & McFadden, S. H. (1995). *The role of emotion in social and personality development: History, theory, and research.* New York: Wiley.

Major, B., & Heslin, R. (1982). Perceptions of cross-sex and same-sex nonreciprocal touch: It is better to give than to receive. *Journal of Nonverbal Behavior, 6,* 148–162.

Marano, H. E. (1997, November/December). Gottman and Gray: The two Johns. *Psychology Today, 30*(6), 28.

Marks, M. A., & Nelson, E. S. (1993). Sexual harassment on campus: Effects of professor gender on perception of sexually harassing behaviors. *Sex Roles, 28,* 207–217.

Marshall, L. L. (1994). Physical and psychological abuse. In W. R. Cupach & B. H. Spitzberg (Eds.), *The dark side of interpersonal communication* (pp. 281–311). Hillsdale, NJ: Lawrence Erlbaum.

Marston, P. J., & Hecht, M. L. (1994). Love ways: An elaboration and application to relational maintenance. In D. J. Canary & L. Stafford (Eds.), *Communication and relational maintenance* (pp. 87–202). Orlando, FL: Academic Press.

Marston, P. J., Hecht, M. L., Manke, M., McDaniel, S., & Reeder, H. (1998). The subjective experience of intimacy, passion, and commitment in heterosexual loving relationships. *Personal Relationships, 5,* 15–30.

Marston, P. J., Hecht, M. L., & Robers, T. (1987). True love ways: The subjective experience and communication of romantic love. *Journal of Social and Personal Relationships, 4,* 387–407.

Martin, J. G., & Westie, F. R. (1959). The intolerant personality. *American Sociological Review, 24,* 521–528.

Masheter, C. (1997). Former spouses who are friends: Three case studies. *Journal of Social and Personal Relationships, 14,* 207–222.

Mast, M. S. (2002). Dominance as expressed and inferred through speaking time: A meta-analysis. *Human Communication Research, 28,* 420–450.

Mast, M. S. (2005). The world according to men: It is hierarchical and stereotypical. *Sex Roles, 53,* 919–924.

Masters, W. H., & Johnson, V. E. (1979). *Homosexuality in perspective.* Boston: Little, Brown.

Matthews, S. (1986). *Friendships through the life course: Oral biographies in old age.* Beverly Hills, CA: Sage.

May, J. L., & Hamilton, P. A. (1980). Effects of musically evoked affect on women's interpersonal attraction toward and perceptual judgments of physical attractiveness of men. *Journal of Social and Clinical Psychology, 6,* 180–190.

Mayback, K. L., & Gold, S. R. (1994). Hyperfemininity and attraction to macho and non-macho men. *Journal of Sex Research, 31,* 91–98.

Mazur, M. A., & Hubbard, A. S. E. (2004). "Is there something I should know?" Topic avoidant responses in parent-adolescent communication. *Communication Reports, 17,* 27–37.

McAdams, D. P. (1985). Motivation and friendship. In S. Duck & D. Perlman (Eds.), *Understanding personal relationships: An interdisciplinary approach* (pp. 85–105). London: Sage.

McAdams, D. P. (1988). Personal needs and personal relationships. In S. Duck (Ed.), *Handbook of personal relationships: Theory, research, and intervention* (pp. 7–22). New York: Wiley.

McCabe, M. P. (1999). The interrelationship between intimacy, relationship functioning, and sexuality among men and women in committed relationships. *Canadian Journal of Human Sexuality, 8,* 31–39.

McCornack, S. A. (1992). Information manipulation theory. *Communication Monographs, 59,* 1–16.

McCornack, S. A., & Levine, T. R. (1990). When lies are uncovered: Emotional and relational outcomes of discovered deception. *Communication Monographs, 57,* 119–138.

McCornack, S. A., & Parks, M. R. (1986). Deception detection and relationship development: The other side of trust. In M. L. McLaughlin (Ed.), *Communication yearbook 9* (pp. 377–389). Beverly Hills, CA: Sage.

McCroskey, J. C., & McCain, T. A. (1974). The measurement of interpersonal attraction. *Speech Monographs, 41,* 261–266.

McCroskey, J. C., Larson, C. E., & Knapp, M. L. (1971). *An introduction to interpersonal communication.* Englewood Cliffs, NJ: Prentice Hall.

McCullough, M. E., Rachal, K. C., Sandage, S. J., Worthington, E. L., Brown, S. W., & Hight, T. L. (1998). Interpersonal forgiving in close relationships: II. Theoretical elaboration and measurement. *Journal of Personality and Social Psychology, 75,* 1586–1603.

McCullough, M. E., Worthington, E. L., & Rachal, K. C. (1997). Interpersonal forgiving in close relationships. *Journal of Personality and Social Psychology, 73,* 321–336.

McDonald, G. W. (1981). Structural exchange and marital interaction. *Journal of Marriage and the Family, 43,* 825–839.

McGoldrick, M., & Carter, E. (1982). The family life cycle. In F. Walsh (Ed.), *Normal family processes* (pp. 167–195). New York: Guilford Press.

McGonagle, K. A., Kessler, R. C., & Schilling, E. A. (1992). The frequency and determinants of marital disagreements in a community sample. *Journal of Social and Personal Relationships, 9,* 507–524.

McKinnell, J. (2006, May 15). Who not to marry. *Maclean's,* pp. 41–42.

Mead, D. E., Vatcher, G. M., Wyne, B. A., & Roberts, S. L. (1990). The comprehensive areas of change questionnaire: Assessing marital couples' presenting complaints. *American Journal of Family Therapy, 18,* 65–79.

Mearns, J. (1991). Copying with a breakup: Negative mood regulation expectancies and depression following the end of a romantic relationship. *Journal of Personality and Social Psychology, 60,* 327–334.

Mehrabian, A. (1971). *Silent messages.* Belmont, CA: Wadsworth.

Mehrabian, A. (1981). *Silent messages: Implicit communication of emotions and attitudes* (2nd ed.). Belmont, CA: Wadsworth.

Mehrabian, A., & Ksionzky, S. (1974). *A theory of affiliation.* Lexington, MA: Lexington Books.

Meloy, J. R., & Gothard, S. (1995). Demographic and clinical comparisons of obsessional followers and offenders with mental disorders. *American Journal of Psychiatry, 152,* 258–263.

Menzies-Toman, D. A., & Lydon, J. E. (2005). Commitment-motivated benign appraisals of partner transgressions: Do they facilitate accommodation? *Journal of Social and Personal Relationships, 22,* 111–128.

Merolla, A. J., Weber, K. D., Myers, S. A., & Booth-Butterfield, M. (2004). The impact of past dating relationship solidarity on commitment, satisfaction, and investment in current relationships. *Communication Quarterly, 52,* 251–264.

Merton, R. K. (1948). The self-fulfilling prophecy. *Antioch Review, 8,* 193–210.

Messman, S. J., Canary, D. J., & Hause, K. S. (2000). Motives to remain platonic, equity, and the use of maintenance strategies in opposite-sex friendships. *Journal of Social and Personal Relationships, 17,* 67–94.

Metts, S. (1989). An exploratory investigation of deception in close relationships. *Journal of Social and Personal Relationships, 6,* 159–179.

Metts, S. (1991, February). *The wicked things you say, the wicked things you do: A pilot study of relational transgressions.* Paper presented at the annual meeting of the Western States Communication Association, Phoenix, AZ.

Metts, S. (1992). The language of disengagement: A face-management perspective. In T. L. Orbuch (Ed.), *Close relationships loss: Theoretical approaches* (pp. 111–127). New York: Springer-Verlag.

Metts, S. (1994). Relational transgressions. In W. R. Cupach & B. H. Spitzberg (Eds.), *The dark side of interpersonal communication* (pp. 217–240). Hillsdale, NJ: Erlbaum.

Metts, S. (1997). Face and facework: Implications for the study of personal relationships. In S. Duck (Ed.), *Handbook of personal relationships: Theory,* research and interventions (pp. 373–390). Chichester, UK: Wiley.

Metts, S. (2004). First sexual involvement in romantic relationships: An empirical investigation of communicative framing, romantic beliefs, and attachment orientation in the passion turning point. In J. H. Harvey, A. Wenzel, & S. Sprecher (Eds.), *The handbook of sexuality in close relationships* (pp. 135–158). Mahwah, NJ: Lawrence Erlbaum.

Metts, S., & Bowers, J. W. (1994). Emotion in interpersonal communication. In M. L. Knapp & G. R. Miller (Eds.), *Handbook of interpersonal communication* (2nd ed., pp. 508–541). Thousand Oaks, CA: Sage.

Metts, S., & Chronis, H. (1986, May). *An exploratory investigation of relational deception.* Paper presented at the annual meeting of the International Communication Association, Chicago.

Metts, S., & Cupach, W. R. (1986, February). *Disengagement themes in same-sex and opposite-sex friendships.* Paper presented at the annual meeting of the Western Speech Communication Association, Tucson, AZ.

Metts, S., Cupach, W. R., & Bejlovich, R. A. (1989). "I love you too much to ever start liking you": Redefining romantic relationships. *Journal of Social and Personal Relationships, 6,* 259–274.

Metts, S., Cupach, W. R., & Imahori, T. T. (1992). Perceptions of compliance-resisting messages in three types of cross-sex relationships. *Western Journal of Communication, 56,* 1–17.

Metts, S., & Grohskopf, E. (2003). Impression management: Goals, strategies, and skills. In J. O. Greene & B. R. Burleson (Eds.), *Handbook of communication and social interaction skills* (pp. 357–402). Mahwah, NJ: Lawrence Erlbaum.

Metts, S., Sprecher, S., & Regan, P. C. (1998). Communication and sexual desire. In P. A. Andersen & L. K. Guerrero (Eds.), *Handbook of communication and emotion: Research, theory, applications, and contexts* (pp. 353–377). San Diego, CA: Academic Press.

Meurling, C. N., Ray, G. E., & LoBello, S. G. (1999). Children's evaluations of classroom friend and classroom best friend relationships. *Child Study Journal, 29,* 79–83.

Mikulincer, M., & Nachshon, O. (1991). Attachment styles and patterns of self-disclosure. *Journal of Personality and Social Psychology, 61,* 321–331.

Miller, A. L., Notaro, P. C., & Zimmerman, M. A. (2002). Stability and change in internal working models of friendship: Associations with multiple domains of urban adolescent functioning. *Journal of Social and Personal Relationships, 19,* 233–259.

Miller, G. R. (1976). *Explorations in interpersonal communication.* Beverly Hills, CA: Sage.

Miller, G. R., & Boster, F. (1988). Persuasion in personal relationships. In S. Duck (Ed.), *Handbook of personal relationships: Theory, research and interventions* (pp. 275–287). Chichester, UK: Wiley.

Miller, G. R., Boster, F., Roloff, M., & Siebold, D. (1977). Compliance-gaining message strategies: A typology and some findings concerning the effects of situational differences. *Communication Monographs, 44,* 37–51.

Miller, G. R., & Steinberg, M. (1975). *Between people: A new analysis of interpersonal communication.* Chicago: Science Research Associates.

Miller, L. C., Cody, M. J., & McLaughlin, M. L. (1994). Situations and goals as fundamental constructs in interpersonal communication research. In M. L. Knapp & G. R. Miller (Eds.), *Handbook of interpersonal communication* (pp. 162–198). Thousand Oaks, CA: Sage.

Miller, R. S. (1996). *Embarrassment: Poise and peril in everyday life.* New York: Guilford Press.

Miller, S. (2004, November). 6 secret ways to turn her on. *Men's Health,* pp. 138, 140.

Miller, S. M. (1987). Monitoring and blunting: Validation of a questionnaire to assess styles of information-seeking under threat. *Journal of Personality and Social Psychology, 52,* 345–353.

Miller, S. M., Brody, D. S., & Summerton, J. (1988). Styles of coping with threat: Implications for health. *Journal of Personality and Social Psychology, 54,* 142–148.

Mills, R. S. L., Nazar, J., & Farrell, H. M. (2002). Child and parent perceptions of hurtful messages. *Journal of Social and Personal Relationships, 19,* 731–754.

Mischel, M. H. (1981). The measurement of uncertainty in illness. *Nursing Research, 30,* 258–263.

Mischel, M. H. (1988). Uncertainty in illness. *Image: Journal of Nursing Scholarship, 20,* 225–232.

Mischel, M. H. (1990). Reconceptualization of the uncertainty in illness theory. *Image: Journal of Nursing Scholarship, 22,* 256–262.

Modigliani, A. (1968). Embarrassment, facework, and eye contact: Testing a theory of embarrassment. *Sociometry, 31,* 313–326.

Moller, N. P., Fouladi, R. T., McCarthy, C. J., & Hatch, K. D. (2003). Relationship of attachment and social support to college students' adjustment following relationship breakup. *Journal of Counseling and Development, 81,* 354–369.

Mongeau, P. A., & Carey, C. M. (1996). Who's wooing whom II? An experimental investigation of date-initiation and expectancy violation. *Western Journal of Communication, 60,* 195–213.

Mongeau, P. A., Hale, J. L., & Alles, M. (1994). An experimental investigation of accounts and attributions following sexual infidelity. *Communication Monographs, 61,* 326–344.

Mongeau, P. A., Hale, J. L., Johnson, K. L., & Hillis, J. D. (1993). Who's wooing whom?: An investigation of female-initiated dating. In P. J. Kalbfleisch (Ed.), *Interpersonal communication: Evolving interpersonal relationships* (pp. 51–68). Hillsdale, NJ: Lawrence Erlbaum.

Mongeau, P. A., & Johnson, K. L. (1995). Predicting cross-sex first-date sexual expectations and involvement: Contextual and individual difference factors. *Personal Relationships, 2,* 301–312.

Mongeau, P. A., Ramirez, A., & Vorrell, M. (2003, February). *Friends with benefits: Initial exploration of sexual, non-romantic relationships.* Paper presented at the annual meeting of the Western States Communication Association, Salt Lake City, UT.

Mongeau, P. A., & Schulz, B. E. (1997). What he doesn't know won't hurt him (or me): Verbal responses and attributions following sexual infidelity. *Communication Reports, 10,* 143–152.

Mongeau, P. A., Serewicz, M. C. M., Henningsen, M. L. M., & Davis, K. L. (2006). Sex differences in the transition to a heterosexual romantic relationship. In K. Dindia & D. J. Canary (Eds.), *Sex differences and similarities in communication* (2nd ed., pp. 337–358). Mahwah, NJ: Lawrence Erlbaum.

Mongeau, P. A., Serewicz, M. C. M., & Therrien. (2004). Goals for cross-sex first dates: The identification, measurement, and influence of contextual factors. *Communication Monographs, 71,* 121–147.

Monroe, S. M., Rohde, P., Seeley, J. R., & Lewinsohn, P. M. (1999). Life events and depression in adolescence: Relationship loss as a prospective risk factor for first onset of major depressive disorder. *Journal of Abnormal Psychology, 108,* 606–614.

Monsour, M. (1992). Meanings of intimacy in cross- and same-sex friendships. *Journal of Social and Personal Relationships, 9,* 277–295.

Montagu, A. (1971/1978). *Touching: The human significance of the skin.* New York: Harper & Row.

Montgomery, B. M. (1988). Quality communication in personal relationships. In S. Duck (Ed.), *Handbook of personal relationships* (pp. 343–362). New York: Wiley.

Moore, M. M. (1985). Nonverbal courtship patterns in women: Context and consequences. *Ethology and Sociobiology, 6,* 237–247.

Morman, M. T., & Floyd, K. (1999). Affectionate communication between fathers and young adult sons: Individual- and relational-level correlates. *Communication Studies, 50,* 294–309.

Morr, M. C., & Mongeau, P. A. (2004). First-date expectations: The impact of sex of initiator, alcohol consumption, and relationship type. *Communication Research, 31,* 3–35.

Morris, D. (1977). *Manwatching: A field guide to human behavior.* New York: Harry N. Abrams.

Morrison, R. L., Van Hasselt, V. B., & Bellack, A. S. (1987). Assessment of assertion and problem-solving skills in wife abusers and their spouses. *Journal of Family Violence, 2,* 227–256.

Morry, M. M. (2005). Relationship satisfaction as a predictor of similarity ratings: A test of the attraction-similarity hypothesis. *Journal of Social and Personal Relationships, 22,* 561–584.

Motley, M. T., & Reeder, H. M. (1995). Unwanted escalation of sexual intimacy: Male and female perceptions of connotations and relational consequences of resistance messages. *Communication Monographs, 62,* 355–382.

Muehlenhard, C. L., & Cook, S. W. (1988). Men's self-reports of unwanted sexual activity. *Journal of Sex Research, 24,* 58–72.

Muehlenhard, C. L., Koralewski, M. A., Andrews, S. L., & Burdick, C. A. (1986). Verbal and nonverbal cues that convey interest in dating: Two studies. *Behavior Therapy, 17,* 404–419.

Muehlenhard, C. L., & Scardino, T. J. (1985). What will he think? Men's impressions of women to initiate dates and achieve academically. *Journal of Counseling Psychology, 32,* 560–569.

Mullen, P. E., & Pathe, M. (1994). Stalking and pathologies of love. *Australian and New Zealand Journal of Psychiatry, 28,* 469–477.

Murnan, S. K., Perot, A., & Byrne, D. (1989). Coping with unwanted sexual activity: Normative responses, situational determinants, and individual differences. *Journal of Sex Research, 26,* 85–106.

Murray, S. L., Holmes, J. G., & Griffin, D. W. (1996). The benefits of positive illusions: Idealization and the construction of satisfaction in close relationships. *Journal of Personality and Social Psychology, 70,* 79–98.

Najib, A., Lorberbaum, J. P., Kose, S., Bohning, D. E., & George, M. S. (2004). Regional brain activity in women grieving a romantic relationship breakup. *American Journal of Psychiatry, 161,* 2245–2256.

Nanus, S. E. (2005, November). How to deal with his ex. *Seventeen,* p. 104.

Neff, K. D., & Harter, S. (2002). The role of power and authenticity in relationship styles emphasizing autonomy, connectedness, or mutuality among adult couples. *Journal of Social and Personal Relationships, 19,* 835–857.

Nell, K., & Ashton, N. (1996). Gender, self-esteem, and perception of own attractiveness. *Perceptual and Motor Skills, 83,* 1105–1106.

Newcomb, T. M. (1961). *The acquaintance process.* New York: Holt, Rinehart & Winston.

Niehuis, S., & Bartell, D. (2006). The marital disillusionment scale: Development and psychometric properties. *North American Journal of Psychology, 8,* 69–83.

Niehuis, S., & Huston, T. L. (2002, July). *The premarital roots of disillusionment in early marriage.* Paper presented at the International Conference on Personal Relationships, Halifax, Nova Scotia, Canada.

Noar, S. M., Zimmerman, R. S., & Atwood, K. A. (2004). Safer sex and sexually transmitted infections from a relationships perspective. In J. H. Harvey, A. Wenzel, & S. Sprecher (Eds.), *The handbook of sexuality in close relationships* (pp. 519–544). Mahwah, NJ: Erlbaum.

Nock, S. L. (1995). A comparison of marriages and cohabiting relationships. *Journal of Family Issues, 16,* 53–76.

O'Connell-Corcoran, K., & Mallinckrodt, B. (2000). Adult attachment, self-efficacy, perspective taking, and conflict resolution. *Journal of Counseling and Development, 78,* 473–483.

O'Hair, D. H., & Cody, M. J. (1994). Deception. In W. R. Cupach & B. H. Spitzberg (Eds.), *The dark side of interpersonal communication* (pp. 181–213). Hillsdale, NJ: Erlbaum.

O'Meara, J. D. (1989). Cross-sex friendships: Four basic challenges of an ignored relationship. *Sex Roles, 21,* 525–543.

O'Sullivan, L. F., & Allgeier, E. R. (1994). Disassembling a stereotype: Gender differences in the use of token resistance. *Journal of Applied Social Psychology, 24,* 1035–1055.

O'Sullivan, L. F., & Allgeier, E. R. (1998). Feigning sexual desire: Consenting to unwanted sexual activity in heterosexual dating relationships. *Journal of Sex Research, 35,* 234–243.

O'Sullivan, L. F., & Byers, E. S. (1993). Eroding stereotypes: College women's attempts to influence reluctant male partners. *Journal of Sex Research, 30,* 270–282.

O'Sullivan, L. F., & Gaines, M. E. (1998). Decision-making in college students' heterosexual dating relationship: Ambivalence about engaging in sexual activity. *Journal of Social and Personal Relationships, 15,* 347–363.

Oakes, P. (1987). The salience of social categories. In J. C. Turner (Ed.), *Rediscovering the social group* (pp. 117–141). New York: Basil Blackwell.

Owen, W. F. (1987). The verbal expression of love by women and men as a critical communication event in personal relationships. *Women's Studies in Communication, 10,* 15–24.

Owen, W. F. (1993). Metaphors in accounts of romantic relationship terminations. In P. J. Kalbfleisch (Ed.), *Interpersonal communication: Evolving interpersonal relationships* (pp. 271–272). Hillsdale, NJ: Erlbaum.

Paikoff, R. L., & Brooks-Gunn, J. (1991). Do parent-child relationships change during puberty? *Psychological Bulletin, 110,* 47–66.

Papa, M. J., & Canary, D. J. (1995). Communication in organizations: A competence-based approach. In A. M. Nicotera (Ed.), *Conflict and organizations: Communicative processes* (pp. 153–179). Albany: State University of New York Press.

Papini, D. R., Sebby, R. A., & Clark, S. (1989). Affective quality of family relations and adolescent identity exploration. *Adolescence, 24,* 457–466.

Parker, B. L., & Drummond-Reeves, S. J. (1993). The death of a dyad: Relational autopsy, analysis and aftermath. *Journal of Divorce and Remarriage, 21,* 95–119.

Parks, M. R. (1982). Ideology of interpersonal communication: Off the couch and into the world. In M. Burgoon (Ed.), *Communication yearbook 5* (pp. 79–108). New Brunswick, NJ: Transaction Books.

Parks, M. R., & Adelman, M. B. (1983). Communication networks and the development of romantic relationships: An expansion of uncertainty reduction theory. *Human Communication Research, 10,* 55–79.

Parks, M. R., & Floyd, K. (1996). Meanings for closeness and intimacy in friendship. *Journal of Social and Personal Relationships, 13,* 85–107.

Patterson, M. L. (1983). *Nonverbal behavior: A functional perspective.* New York: Springer-Verlag.

Pearson, J., & Thoennes, N. (1990). Custody after divorce: Demographic and attitudinal patterns. *American Journal of Orthopsychiatry, 60,* 233–249.

Pendell, S. D. (2002). Affection in interpersonal relationships: Not just a fond or tender feeling. In W. B. Gudykunst (Ed.), *Communication yearbook 26* (pp. 70–115). Mahwah, NJ: Erlbaum.

Pennebaker, J. W. (1989). Confession, inhibition, and disease. In L. Berkowitz (Ed.), *Advances in experimental social psychology* (Vol. 22, pp. 211–244). San Diego, CA: Academic Press.

Pennebaker, J. W. (1990). *Opening up: The healing power of confiding in others.* New York: Morrow.

Pennebaker, J. W., Colder, M., & Sharp, L. K. (1990). Accelerating the coping process. *Journal of Personality and Social Psychology, 58,* 528–537.

Pennebaker, J. W., Dyer, M. A., Caulkins, R. S., Litowitz, D. L., Ackerman, P. L., Anderson, D. B., et al. (1979). Don't the girls get prettier at closing time: A country and western application to psychology. *Personality and Social Psychology Bulletin, 5,* 122–125.

Peplau, L. A., & Campbell, S. M. (1989). The balance of power in dating and marriage. In J. Freeman (Ed.) *Women: A feminist perspective* (4th ed., pp. 121–137). Mountain View, CA: Mayfield.

Peplau, L. A., Fingerhut, A., & Beals, K. P. (2004). In J. H. Harvey, A. Wenzel, & S. Sprecher (Eds.), *The handbook of sexuality in close relationships* (pp. 349–369). Mahwah, NJ: Erlbaum.

Peplau, L. A., & Spalding, L. R. (2000). The close relationships of lesbians, gay men, and bisexuals. In C. Hendrick & S. S. Hendrick (Eds.), *Close relationships: A sourcebook* (pp. 111–123). Thousand Oaks, CA: Sage.

Perras, M. T., & Lustig, M. W. (1982, February). *The effects of intimacy level and intent to disengage on the selection of relational disengagement strategies.* Paper presented at the annual meeting of the Western Speech Communication Association, Denver, CO.

Peterson, C. C. (1990). Husbands' and wives' perceptions of marital fairness across the family life cycle. *International Journal of Aging and Human Development, 31,* 179–188.

Petras, R., & Petras, K. (1993). *The 775 stupidest things ever said.* New York: Doubleday.

Petronio, S. (1991). Communication boundary management: A theoretical model of managing disclosure of private information between marital couples. *Communication Theory, 1,* 311–335.

Petronio, S. (2000). The boundaries of privacy: Praxis of everyday life. In S. Petronio (Ed.), *Balancing secrets of private disclosure* (pp. 37–49). Mahwah, NJ: Erlbaum.

Petronio, S. (2002). *Boundaries of privacy: Dialectics of disclosure.* Albany: State University of New York Press.

Petronio, S., & Harriman, S. (1990, October). *Parental privacy invasion: Tactics and reactions to encroachment.* Paper presented at the annual meeting of the Speech Communication Association, Chicago.

Petronio, S., Sargent, J., Andea, L., Reganis, P., & Cichocki, D. (2004). Family and friends as healthcare advocates: Dilemmas of confidentiality and privacy. *Journal of Social and Personal Relationships, 21,* 33–52.

Pfouts, J. H. (1978). Violent families: Coping responses of abused wives. *Child Welfare, 57,* 101–111.

Philliber, S. (1980). Socialization for childbearing. *Journal of Social Issues, 36,* 20–44.

Phillips, G. M., & Metzger, N. J. (1976). *Intimate communication.* Boston: Allyn & Bacon.

Phillips, R. (1988). *Putting asunder: A history of divorce in Western society.* Cambridge, UK: Cambridge University Press.

Pierce, C. A. (1996). Body height and romantic attraction: A meta-analytic test of the male-taller norm. *Social Behavior and Personality, 24,* 143–149.

Pierce, T., & Lydon, J. E. (2001). Global and specific relational models in the experience of social interactions. *Journal of Personality and Social Psychology, 80,* 613–631.

Pines, A. (1992). *Romantic jealousy: Understanding and conquering the shadow of love.* New York: St. Martin's Press.

Pines, A. (1998). A prospective study of personality and gender differences in romantic attraction. *Personality and Individual Differences, 25,* 147–157.

Pistole, M. C. (1989). Attachment in adult romantic relationships: Style of conflict resolution and relationship satisfaction. *Journal of Social and Personal Relationships, 6,* 505–510.

Planalp, S., & Honeycutt, J. M. (1985). Events that increase uncertainty in personal relationships. *Human Communication Research, 11,* 593–604.

Prager, K. J. (1995). *The psychology of intimacy.* New York: Guilford Press.

Prager, K. J. (2000). Intimacy in personal relationships. In C. Hendrick & S. S. Hendrick (Eds.), *Close relationships: A sourcebook* (pp. 229–242). Thousand Oaks, CA: Sage.

Prager, K. J., & Buhrmester, D. (1998). Intimacy and need fulfillment in couple relationships. *Journal of Social and Personal Relationships, 15,* 435–469.

Prager, K. J., & Roberts, L. J. (2004). Deep intimate connection: Self and intimacy in couple relationships. In D. J. Mashek & A. P. Aron (Eds.), *Handbook of closeness and intimacy* (pp. 43–60). Mahwah, NJ: Lawrence Erlbaum.

Pruitt, D. G., & Carnevale, P. J. (1993). *Negotiation in social conflict.* Pacific Grove, CA: Brooks/Cole.

Putnam, L. L., & Wilson, C. E. (1982). Communicative strategies in organizational conflicts: Reliability and validity of a measurement scale. In M. Burgoon (Ed.), *Communication yearbook 6* (pp. 629–652). Beverly Hills, CA: Sage.

Rabby, M. K., & Walther, J. B. (2003). Computer mediated communication effects on relationship formation and maintenance. In D. J. Canary & M. Dainton (Eds.), *Maintaining relationships through communication: Relational, contextual, and cultural variations* (pp. 141–162). Mahwah, NJ: Lawrence Erlbaum.

Rahim, M. A. (1986). *Managing conflicts in organizations.* New York: Praeger.

Rahim, M. A., & Bonoma, T. V. (1979). Managing organizational conflict: A model for diagnosis and intervention. *Psychological Reports, 44,* 36–48.

Rathus, S. A., Nevid, J. S., & Fichner-Rathus, L. (1993). *Human sexuality in a world of diversity.* Boston: Allyn & Bacon.

Rawlins, W. K. (1983a). Negotiating close friendships: The dialectic of conjunctive freedoms. *Human Communication Research, 9,* 255–266.

Rawlins, W. K. (1983b). Openness as problematic in ongoing friendships: Two conversational dilemmas. *Communication Monographs, 50,* 1–13.

Rawlins, W. K. (1989). A dialectical analysis of the tensions, functions, and strategic challenges of communication in young adult friendships. In J. A. Anderson (Ed.), *Communication yearbook 12* (pp. 157–189). Newbury Park, CA: Sage.

Rawlins, W. K. (1992). *Friendship matters: Communication, dialectics, and the life course.* Hawthorne, NY: Aldine de Gruyter.

Rawlins, W. K. (1994). Being there and growing apart: Sustaining friendships during adulthood. In D. J. Canary & L. Stafford (Eds.), *Communication and relational maintenance* (pp. 275–294). San Diego, CA: Academic Press.

Ray, G. B., & Floyd, K. (2006). Nonverbal expressions of liking and disliking in initial interaction: Encoding and decoding perspectives. *Southern Communication Journal, 71,* 45–64.

Redmond, M. V., & Virchota, D. A. (1994, November). *The effects of varying lengths of initial interaction on attraction and uncertainty reduction.* Paper presented at the annual meeting of the Speech Communication Association, New Orleans, LA.

Reece, M. M., & Whitman, R. N. (1962). Expressive movements, warmth, and verbal reinforcement. *Journal of Abnormal and Social Psychology, 64,* 234–236.

Reel, B. W., & Thompson, T. L. (1994). A test of the effectiveness of strategies for talking about the effectiveness of condom use. *Journal of Applied Communication Research, 22,* 127–140.

Reese-Weber, S., & Bartle-Haring, S. (1998). Conflict resolution styles in family subsystems and adolescent romantic relationships. *Journal of Youth and Adolescence, 27,* 735–752.

Regan, P. C. (1998a). Of lust and love: Beliefs about the role of sexual desire in romantic relationships. *Personal Relationships, 5,* 139–157.

Regan, P. C. (1998b). What if you can't get what you want? Willingness to compromise ideal mate selection standards as a function of sex, mate value, and relationship context. *Personality and Social Psychology Bulletin, 24,* 1294–1303.

Regan, P. C. (2004). Sex and the attraction process: Lessons learned from science (and Shakespeare) on lust, love, chastity, and fidelity. In J. H. Harvey, A. Wenzel, & S. Sprecher (Eds.), *The handbook of sexuality in close relationships* (pp. 115–133). Mahwah, NJ: Erlbaum.

Regan, P. C., & Berscheid, E. (1995). Gender differences in beliefs about the causes of male and female sexual desire. *Personal Relationships, 2,* 345–358.

Regan, P. C., & Berscheid, E. (1999). *Lust: What we know about sexual desire.* Thousand Oaks, CA: Sage.

Regan, P. C., & Dreyer, C. S. (1999). Lust? Love? Status? Young adults' motives for engaging in casual sex. *Journal of Psychology and Human Sexuality, 11,* 1–24.

Reilly, M. E., & Lynch, J. M. (1990). Power-sharing in lesbian partnerships. *Journal of Homosexuality, 19*(1), 1–30.

Reined, C., Byers, E. S., & Pan, S. (1997). Sexual and relational satisfaction in mainland China. *Journal of Sex Research, 34,* 399–410.

Reinisch, J. M., & Beasley, R. (1990). *The Kinsey Institute report on sex: What you must know to be sexually literate.* New York: St. Martin's Press.

Reis, H. T., & Shaver, P. (1988). Intimacy as an interpersonal process. In S. Duck (Ed.), *Handbook of personal relationships* (pp. 367–389). New York: Wiley.

Reissman, C., Aron, A., & Bergen, M. R. (1993). Shared activities and marital satisfaction: Causal direction and self-expansion versus boredom. *Journal of Social and Personal Relationships, 10,* 249–254.

Remland, M. S. (1981). Developing leadership skills in nonverbal communication: A situational perspective. *Journal of Business Communication, 18,* 17–29.

Remland, M. S. (1982, November). *Leadership impressions and nonverbal communication in a superior subordinate situation.* Paper presented at the annual meeting of the Speech Communication Association, Louisville, KY.

Reyes, M., Afifi, W., Krawchuk, A., Imperato, N., Shelley, D., & Lee, J. (June, 1999). *Just (don't) talk: Comparing the impact of interaction style on sexual desire and social attraction.* Paper presented at the joint conference of the International Network on Personal Relationships and the International Society for the Study of Personal Relationships, Louisville, KY.

Riordan, C. A., & Tedeschi, J. T. (1983). Attraction in aversive environments: Some evidence for classical conditioning and negative reinforcement. *Journal of Personality and Social Psychology, 44,* 683–692.

Roberson, B. F., & Wright, R. A. (1994). Difficulty as a determinant of interpersonal appeal: A social-motivational application of energization theory. *Basic and Applied Social Psychology, 15,* 373–388.

Roberto, K. A., & Scott, J. P. (1986). Friendships of older men and women: Exchange patterns and satisfaction. *Psychology and Aging, 1,* 103–109.

Robinson, T., & Smith-Lovin, L. (1992). Selective interaction as a strategy for identity maintenance: An affect control model. *Social Psychology Quarterly, 55,* 12–28.

Rodman, H. (1972). Marital power and the theory of resources in cultural context. *Journal of Comparative Family Studies, 3,* 50–69.

Rogers, E. M. (1995). *Diffusion of innovations* (4th ed.). New York: Free Press.

Rogers, L. A., & Farace, R. V. (1975). Analysis of relational communication in dyads: New measurement procedures. *Human Communication Research, 1,* 222–239.

Rogers, L. A., & Millar, F. E. (1988). Relational communication. In S. Duck (Ed.), *Handbook of personal relationships* (pp. 289–305). New York: Wiley.

Rohlfing, M. E. (1995). "Doesn't anybody stay in one place anymore?" An exploration of the understudied phenomenon of long-distance relationships. In J. T. Wood & S. Duck (Eds.), *Understudied relationships: Off the beaten track* (pp. 173–196). Thousand Oaks, CA: Sage.

Roiger, J. F. (1993). Power in friendship and use of influence strategies. In P. J. Kalbfleisch (Ed.), *Interpersonal communication: Evolving interpersonal relationships* (pp. 133–145). Hillsdale, NJ: Erlbaum.

Roloff, M. E., & Cloven, D. H. (1990). The chilling effect in interpersonal relationships: The reluctance to speak one's mind. In D. D. Cahn (Ed.), *Intimates in conflict: A communication perspective* (pp. 49–76). Hillsdale, NJ: Erlbaum.

Roloff, M. E., & Ifert, D. E. (2000). Conflict management through avoidance: Withholding complaints, suppressing arguments, and declaring topics taboo. In S. Petronio (Ed.), *Balancing the secrets of private disclosures* (pp. 151–163). Mahwah, NJ: Lawrence Erlbaum.

Roloff, M. E., & Miller, C. W. (2006). Social cognition approaches to understanding conflict and communication. In J. G. Oetzel & S. Ting-Toomey (Eds.), *The SAGE handbook of conflict communication* (pp. 97–128). Thousand Oaks, CA: Sage.

Roloff, M. E., Soule, K. P., & Carey, C. M. (2001). Reasons for remaining in a relationship and responses to relational transgressions. *Journal of Social and Personal Relationships, 18,* 362–385.

Roscoe, B., Cavanaugh, L. E., & Kennedy, D. R. (1988). Dating infidelity: Behaviors, reasons, and consequences. *Adolescence, 89,* 36–43.

Rose, S. M. (1985). Same- and cross-sex friendships and the psychology of homosociology. *Sex Roles, 12,* 63–74.

Rosen, K. H., & Stith, S. M. (1995). Women terminating abusive relationships: A qualitative study. *Journal of Social and Personal Relationships, 12,* 155–160.

Rosenbluth, P. C., Steil, J. M., & Whitcomb, J. H. (1998). Marital equality: What does it mean? *Journal of Family Issues, 19,* 227–244.

Rosenfeld, L. B. (1979). Self-disclosure avoidance: Why I am afraid to tell you who I am. *Communication Monographs, 46,* 63–74.

Rosenfeld, L. B. (2000). Overview of the ways privacy, secrecy, disclosure are balanced in today's society. In S. Petronio (Ed.), *Balancing secrets of private disclosure* (pp. 3–17). Mahwah, NJ: Erlbaum.

Rosenfeld, L. B., & Kendrick, W. L. (1984). Choosing to be open: An empirical investigation of subjective reasons for self-disclosing. *Western Journal of Speech Communication, 48,* 326–343.

Rosenfeld, L. B., & Welsh, S. M. (1985). Differences in self-disclosure in dual-career and single-career marriages. *Communication Monographs, 52,* 253–261.

Rosenthal, D., Gifford, S., & Moore, S. (1998). Safe sex or safe love: Competing discourses. *AIDS Care, 10,* 35–47.

Rosenthal, R., & Jacobson, L. (1968). *Pygmalion in the classroom: Teacher expectation and pupils' intellectual development.* New York: Holt, Rinehart & Winston.

Rosenzweig, J. M., & Lebow, W. C. (1992). Femme on the streets, butch in the sheets? Lesbian sex roles, dyadic adjustment, and sexual satisfaction. *Journal of Homosexuality, 23,* 1–20.

Ross, M., & Sicoly, F. (1979). Egocentric biases in availability and attribution. *Journal of Personality and Social Psychology, 37,* 273–285.

Rowatt, W. C., Cunningham, M. R., & Druen, P. B. (1998). Deception to get a date. *Personality and Social Psychology Bulletin, 24,* 1228–1242.

Rowatt, W. C., Cunningham, M. R., & Druen, P. B. (1999). Lying to get a date: The effects of facial physical attractiveness on the willingness to deceive prospective dating partners. *Journal of Social and Personal Relationships, 16,* 209–233.

Rozema, H. J. (1986). Defensive communications climate as a barrier to sex education in the home. *Family Relations, 35,* 531–537.

Rubin, Z. (1970). Measurement of romantic love. *Journal of Personality and Social Psychology, 16,* 265–273.

Rubin, Z. (1973). *Loving and liking: An invitation to social psychology.* New York: Holt, Rinehart & Winston.

Rubin, Z. (1974). Lovers and other strangers. The development of intimacy in encounters and relationships. *American Scientist, 62,* 182–190.

Rubovits, P. C., & Maher, M. L. (1973). Pygmalion black and white. *Journal of Personality and Social Psychology, 25,* 210–218.

Ruesch, J. (1951). Communication and human relations: An interdisciplinary approach. In J. Ruesch & G. Bateson (Eds.), *Communication: The social matrix of psychiatry* (pp. 21–49). New York: Norton.

Rusbult, C. E. (1980). Commitment and satisfaction in romantic associations: A test of the investment model. *Journal of Experimental Social Psychology, 16,* 172–186.

Rusbult, C. E. (1983). A longitudinal test of the investment model: The development (and deterioration) of satisfaction and commitment in heterosexual involvements. *Journal of Personality and Social Psychology, 45,* 101–117.

Rusbult, C. E. (1987). Responses to dissatisfaction in close relationships: The exit-voice-loyalty-neglect model. In D. Perlman & S. Duck (Eds.), *Intimacy relationships: Development, dynamics and deterioration* (pp. 209–237). Newbury Park, CA: Sage.

Rusbult, C. E., Arriaga, X. B., & Agnew, C. R. (2001). Interdependence in close relationships. In G. J. O. Fletcher & M. S. Clark (Eds.), *Blackwell handbook of social psychology: Interpersonal processes* (pp. 359–387). Oxford: Blackwell.

Rusbult, C. E., Bissonnette, V. L., Arriaga, X. B., & Cox, C. L. (1998). Accommodation processes during the early years of marriage. In T. N. Bradbury (Ed.), *The developmental course of marital dysfunction* (pp. 74–113). New York: Cambridge University Press.

Rusbult, C. E., & Buunk, B. P. (1993). Commitment processes in close relationships: An interdependence analysis. *Journal of Social and Personal Relationships, 10,* 175–204.

Rusbult, C. E., Drigotas, S. M., & Verette, J. (1994). The investment model: An interdependence analysis of commitment processes and relationship maintenance phenomena. In D. J. Canary & L. Stafford (Eds.), *Communication and relational maintenance* (pp. 115–139). San Diego, CA: Academic Press.

Rusbult, C. E., & Farrell, D. (1983). A longitudinal test of the investment model: The impact on job satisfaction, job commitment, and turnover of variations in rewards, costs, alternatives, and investments. *Journal of Applied Psychology, 68,* 429–438.

Rusbult, C. E., Johnson, D. J., & Morrow, G. D. (1986). Impact of couple patterns of problems solving on distress and nondistress in dating relationships. *Journal of Personality and Social Psychology, 50,* 744–753.

Rusbult, C. E., & Martz, J. (1995). Remaining in an abusive relationship: An investment model analysis of nonvoluntary dependence. *Personality and Social Psychology Bulletin, 21,* 558–571.

Rusbult, C. E., Olsen, N., Davis, J. L., & Hannon, P. A. (2001). Commitment and relationship maintenance mechanisms. In J. H. Harvey & A. Wenzel (Eds.), *Close romantic relationships: Maintenance and enhancement* (pp. 87–113). Mahwah, NJ: Lawrence Erlbaum.

Rusbult, C. E., Van Lange, P. A. M., Wildschut, T., Yovetich, N. A., & Verette, J. (2000). Perceived superiority in close relationships: Why it exists and persists. *Journal of Personality and Social Psychology, 79,* 521–545.

Rusbult, C. E., Verette, J., Whitney, G. A., Slovik, L. F., & Lipkus, I. (1991). Accommodation processes in close relationships: Theory and preliminary empirical evidence. *Journal of Personality and Social Psychology, 60,* 53–78.

Rusbult, C. E., & Zembrodt, I. M. (1983). Responses to dissatisfaction in romantic involvements: A multidimensional scaling analysis. *Journal of Experimental Social Psychology, 19,* 274–293.

Rusbult, C. E., Zembrodt, I. M., & Gunn, L. K. (1982). Exit, voice, loyalty and neglect: Responses to dissatisfaction in romantic involvements. *Journal of Personality and Social Psychology, 43,* 1230–1242.

Russell, B. (1938). *Power: A new social analysis.* London: Allen & Unwin.

Sabatelli, R. M. (1984). The marital comparison level index: A measure for assessing outcomes related to expectations. *Journal of Marriage and the Family, 46,* 651–662.

Sabatelli, R. M., & Mazor, A. (1985). Differentiation, individuation, and identity formation: The integration of family system and individual development perspectives. *Adolescence, 20,* 619–633.

Sadalla, E. K., Kenrick, D. T., & Vershure, B. (1987). Dominance and heterosexual attraction. *Journal of Personality and Social Psychology, 52,* 730–738.

Safilios-Rothschild, C. (1970). The study of family power structure: A review 1960–1969. *Journal of Marriage and the Family, 32,* 539–552.

Safron, C. (1979). Troubles that pull couples apart: A Redbook report. *Redbook, 83,* 138–141.

Sagrestano, L. M. (1992). Power strategies in interpersonal relationships. *Psychology of Women Quarterly, 16,* 481–495.

Sagrestano, L. M., Heavey, C. L., & Christensen, A. (1998). Theoretical approaches to understanding sex differences and similarities in conflict behavior. In D. J. Canary & K. Dindia (Eds.), *Sex differences and similarities in communication* (pp. 287–302). Mahwah, NJ: Lawrence Erlbaum.

Sagrestano, L. M., Heavey, C. L., & Christensen, A. (2006). Individual differences versus social structural approaches to explaining demand-withdraw and social influence behaviors. In K. Dindia & D. J. Canary (Eds.), *Sex differences and similarities in communication* (2nd ed., pp. 379–395). Mahwah, NJ: Lawrence Erlbaum.

Salovey, P., & Rodin, J. (1985, September). The heart of jealousy. *Psychology Today, 19,* 22–25, 28–29.

Salovey, P., & Rodin, J. (1986). Differentiation of social-comparison jealousy and romantic jealousy. *Journal of Personality and Social Psychology, 50,* 1100–1112.

Salovey, P., & Rodin, J. (1989). Envy and jealousy in close relationships. In C. Hendrick (Ed.), *Close relationships* (pp. 221–246). Newbury Park, CA: Sage.

Samp, J. A., & Solomon, D. H. (2001). Coping with problematic events in dating relationships: The influence of dependence power on severity appraisals and decisions to communicate. *Western Journal of Communication, 65,* 138–160.

Sanderson, C. A., Rahm, K. B., Beigbeder, S. A, & Metts, S. (2005). The link between the pursuit of intimacy goals and satisfaction in close same-sex friendships: An examination of the underlying processes. *Journal of Social and Personal Relationships, 22,* 75–98.

Scheflen, A. E. (1965). Quasi-courtship behavior in psychotherapy. *Psychiatry, 27,* 245–257.

Scheflen, A. E. (1972). *Body language and the social order: Communication as behavior control.* Englewood Cliffs, NJ: Prentice Hall.

Scheflen, A. E. (1974). *How behavior means.* Garden City, NY: Anchor/Doubleday.

Scherer, K. R. (1972). Judging personality from voice: A cross-cultural approach to an old issue in interpersonal perception. *Journal of Personality, 40,* 191–210.

Scherer, K. R. (1979). Acoustic concomitants of emotional dimensions: Judging affect from synthesized tone sequences. In S. Weitz (Ed.), *Nonverbal communication: Readings with commentary* (pp. 249–253). New York: Oxford University Press.

Schlenker, B. R. (1980). Impression management: The self-concept, social identity, and interpersonal relations. Monterey, CA: Brooks/Cole.

Schlenker, B. R. (1984). Identities, identifications, and relationships. In V. Derlega (Ed.), *Communication, intimacy, and close relationships* (pp. 71–104). San Diego, CA: Academic Press.

Schlenker, B. R. (Ed.). (1985). *The self and social life.* New York: McGraw-Hill.

Schlenker, B. R., Britt, T. W., & Pennington, J. (1996). Impression regulation and management: Highlights of a theory of self-identification. In R. M. Sorrentino & E. T. Higgins (Eds.), *Handbook of motivation and cognition: The interpersonal context* (Vol. 3, pp. 118–142). New York: Guilford Press.

Schlenker, B. R., Britt, T. W., Pennington, J., Murphy, R., & Doherty, K. J. (1994). The triangle model of responsibility. *Psychological Review, 101,* 632–652.

Schlenker, B. R., & Darby, B. W. (1981). The use of apologies in social predicaments. *Social Psychology Quarterly, 44,* 271–278.

Schlenker, B. R., & Weigold, M. F. (1990). Self-consciousness and self-presentation: Being autonomous versus appearing autonomous. *Journal of Personality and Social Psychology, 59,* 820–828.

Schlenker, B. R., & Weigold, M. F. (1992). Interpersonal processes involving impression regulation and management. *Annual Review of Psychology, 43,* 133–168.

Schneider, K. T., Swan, S., & Fitzgerald, L. F. (1997). Job-related and psychological effects of sexual harassment in the workplace: Empirical evidence from two organizations. *Journal of Applied Psychology, 82,* 401–415.

Schoen, R., & Owens, D. (1992). A further look at first marriages and first unions. In S. J. South & S. E. Tolnay (Eds.), *The changing American family: Sociological and demographic perspectives* (pp. 109–117). Boulder, CO: Westview.

Schutz, W. C. (1958). *The interpersonal underworld.* Palo Alto, CA: Science and Behavior Books.

Schwartz, J. C., & Shaver, P. (1987). Emotions and emotion knowledge in interpersonal relations. In W. H. Jones & D. Perlman (Eds.), *Advances in personal relationships* (pp. 197–241). Greenwich, CT: JAI Press.

Schwartz, P. (1994). *Peer marriage: How love between equals really works.* New York: Macmillan.

Schweinle, W. E., Ickes, W., & Bernstein, I. H. (2002). Empathic inaccuracy in husband to wife aggression: The overattribution bias. *Personal Relationships, 9,* 141–158.

Scobie, E. D., & Scobie, G. E. (1998). Damaging events: The perceived need for forgiveness. *Journal for the Theory of Social Behavior, 28,* 373–401.

Scott, M. D., & Powers, W. G. (1978). *Interpersonal communication: A question of needs.* Boston: Houghton Mifflin.

Segrin, C. (1998). Interpersonal communication problems associated with depression and loneliness. In P. A. Andersen & L. K. Guerrero (Eds.), *Handbook of communication and emotion: Research, theory, applications, and contexts* (pp. 215–242). San Diego, CA: Academic Press.

Segrin, C., Taylor, M. E., & Altman, J. (2005). Social cognitive mediators and relational outcomes associated with parental divorce. *Journal of Social and Personal Relationships, 22,* 361–377.

Seltzer, J. A. (1991). Relationships between fathers and children who live apart: The father's role after separation. *Journal of Marriage and the Family, 53,* 79–101.

Shackelford, T. K., & Buss, D. M. (1997). Cues to infidelity. *Personality and Social Psychology Bulletin, 23,* 1034–1045.

Shackelford, T. K., Buss, D. M., & Bennett, K. (2002). Forgiveness or breakups: Sex differences in responses to a partner's responses to a partner's infidelity. *Cognition and Emotion, 16,* 299–307.

Shantz, C. U. (1993). Children's conflicts: Representations and lessons learned. In R. R. Cocking & D. A. Renninger (Eds.), *The development and meaning of psychological distance* (pp. 185–202). Hillsdale, NJ: Erlbaum.

Sharabany, R., Gershoni, R., & Hoffman, J. E. (1981). Girlfriend, boyfriend: Age and sex differences in intimate friendship. *Developmental Psychology, 17,* 800–808.

Sharma, V., & Kaur, I. (1996). Interpersonal attraction in relation to the loss-gain hypothesis. *Journal of Social Psychology, 136,* 635–638.

Sharpsteen, D. J. (1991). The organization of jealousy knowledge: Romantic jealousy as a blended emotion. In P. Salovey (Ed.), *The psychology of jealousy and envy* (pp. 31–51). New York: Guilford Press.

Sharpsteen, D. J., & Kirkpatrick, L. A. (1997). Romantic jealousy and adult romantic attachment. *Journal of Personality and Social Psychology, 72,* 627–640.

Shaver, P. R., Collins, N., & Clark, C. L. (1996). Attachment styles and internal working models of self and relationship partners. In G. J. O. Fletcher & J. Fitness (Eds.), *Knowledge structures in close relationships: A social psychological approach* (pp. 25–61). Mahwah, NJ: Lawrence Erlbaum.

Shaver, P. R., Furman, W., & Buhrmester, D. (1995). Aspects of a life transition: Network changes, social skills and loneliness. In S. W. Duck & D. Perlman (Eds.), *Understanding personal relationships research: An interdisciplinary approach* (pp. 193–219). London: Sage.

Shaver, P. R., Morgan, H. J., & Wu, S. (1996). Is love a "basic" emotion? *Personal Relationships, 3,* 81–96.

Shaver, P. R., Schwartz, J., Kirson, D., & O'Connor, C. (1987). Emotion knowledge: Further explorations of a prototype approach. *Journal of Personality and Social Psychology, 52,* 1061–1086.

Shea, B. C., & Pearson, J. (1986). The effects of relationship type, partner intent, and gender on the selection of relationship maintenance strategies. *Communication Monographs, 53,* 352–364.

Shelov, S. P. (Ed.). (1998). *Caring for your baby and young child.* New York: Bantam Books.

Shelton, B. A., & Johnson, D. (1996). The division of household labor. *Annual Review of Sociology, 22,* 299–322.

Shen, L., & Dillard, J. P. (2005). Psychometric properties of the Hong psychological reactance scale. *Journal of Personality Assessment, 85,* 74–81.

Sheppard, B. M., Hartwick, J., & Warshaw, P. R. (1988). The theory of reasoned action: A meta-analysis of past research with recommendations for modification and future research. *Journal of Consumer Research, 15,* 325–343.

Sheppard, V. J., Nelson, E. S., & Andreoli-Mathie, V. (1995). Dating relationships and infidelity: Attitudes and behaviors. *Journal of Sex and Marital Therapy, 21,* 202–212.

Sherrod, D. (1989). The influence of gender on same-sex friendships. In C. Hendrick & S. S. Hendrick (Ed.), *Close relationships: A sourcebook* (pp. 164–186). Newbury Park, CA: Sage.

Shotland, R. L., & Craig, J. M. (1988). Can men and women differentiate between friendly and sexually interested behavior? *Social Psychology Quarterly, 51,* 66–73.

Sias, P. M., & Cahill, D. J. (1998). From coworkers to friends: The development of peer friendships in the workplace. *Western Journal of Communication, 62,* 273–299.

Sias, P. M., Smith, G., & Avdeyera, T. (1999, November). *Developmental influences and communication in peer workplace friendships.* Paper presented at the annual meeting of the National Communication Association, Chicago.

Siegert, J. R., & Stamp, G. H. (1994). "Our first big fight" as a milestone in the development of close relationships. *Communication Monographs, 61,* 345–360.

Sigall, H., & Landy, D. (1973). Radiating beauty: The effects of having a physically attractive partner on perception. *Journal of Personality and Social Psychology, 28,* 218–224.

Sillars, A. L. (1980). Attributions and communication in roommate conflicts. *Communication Monographs, 47,* 180–200.

Sillars, A. L., Canary, D. J., & Tafoya, M. (2004). Communication, conflict, and the quality of family relationships. In A. L. Vangelisti (Ed.), *Handbook of family interaction* (pp. 413–446). Mahwah, NJ: Lawrence Erlbaum.

Sillars, A. L., Coletti, S. F., Parry, D., & Rogers, M. A. (1982). Coding verbal conflicts: Nonverbal and perceptual correlates of the "avoidance-distributive-integrative" distinction. *Human Communication Research, 9,* 83–95.

Sillars, A., Roberts, L. J., Leonard, K. E., & Dun, T. (2000). Cognition during marital conflict: The relationship of thought and talk. *Journal of Social and Personal Relationships, 17,* 479–502.

Silver, R. L., Boone, C., & Stones, M. H. (1983). Searching for meaning in misfortune: Making sense of incest. *Journal of Social Issues, 39,* 81–102.

Simon, E. P., & Baxter, L. A. (1993). Attachment-style differences in relationship maintenance strategies. *Western Journal of Communication, 57,* 416–430.

Simpson, J. A. (1987). The dissolution of romantic relationships: Factors involved in relational stability and emotional distress. *Journal of Personality and Social Psychology, 53,* 683–692.

Simpson, J. A., & Gangestad, S. W. (1991). Individual differences in sociosexuality: Evidence for convergent and discriminant validity. *Journal of Personality and Social Psychology, 60,* 870–883.

Simpson, J. A., Gangestad, S. W., & Lerma, M. (1990). Perception of physical attractiveness: Mechanisms involved in the maintenance of romantic relationships. *Journal of Personality and Social Psychology, 59,* 1192–1201.

Simpson, J. A., & Harris, B. A. (1994). Interpersonal attraction. In A. L. Weber & J. H. Harvey (Eds.), *Perspectives on close relationships* (pp. 45–66). Boston: Allyn & Bacon.

Simpson, J. A., Ickes, W., & Grich, J. (1999). When accuracy hurts: Reactions of anxiously-attached dating partners to a relationship-threatening situation. *Journal of Personality and Social Psychology, 76,* 754–769.

Simpson, J. A., & Rholes, W. S. (1994). Stress and secure base relationships in adulthood. In K. Bartholomew & D. Perlman (Eds.), *Attachment processes in adulthood: Advances in personal relationships* (Vol. 5, pp. 181–204). Bristol, PA: Kingsley.

Simpson, J. A., Wilson, C. L., & Winterheld, H. A. (2004). Sociosexuality and romantic relationships. In J. H. Harvey, A. Wenzel, & S. Sprecher (Eds.), *The handbook of sexuality in close relationships* (pp. 87–112). Mahwah, NJ: Erlbaum.

Singh, D. (1993). Adaptive significance of female attractiveness: Role of the waist-to-hip ratio. *Journal of Personality and Social Psychology, 65,* 293–307.

Singh, D. (1995). Female judgment of male attractiveness and desirability for relationships: Role of the waist-to-hip ratio and financial status. *Journal of Personality and Social Psychology, 69,* 1089–1101.

Smith, D. A., Vivian, D., & O'Leary, K. D. (1990). Longitudinal prediction of marital discord from premarital expressions of affect. *Journal of Consulting and Clinical Psychology, 59,* 790–798.

Snow, D. A., & Anderson, L. (1987). Identity work among the homeless: The verbal construction and avowal of personal identities. *American Journal of Sociology, 93,* 1336–1371.

Snyder, M., Berscheid, E., & Glick, P. (1985). Focusing on the exterior and interior. Two investigations of the initiation of personal relationships. *Journal of Personality and Social Psychology, 48,* 1427–1439.

Snyder, M., & Gangestad, S. (1986). On the nature of self-monitoring: Matters of assessment, matters of validity. *Journal of Personality and Social Psychology, 51,* 125–139.

Snyder, M., & Simpson, J. A. (1987). Orientations toward romantic relationships. In D. Perlman & S. Duck (Eds.), *Intimate relationships: Development, dynamics, and deterioration* (pp. 45–62). Newbury Park, CA: Sage.

Snyder, M., Tanke, E. D., & Berscheid, E. (1977). Social perception and interpersonal behavior: On the self-fulfilling nature of social stereotypes. *Journal of Personality and Social Psychology, 35,* 656–666.

Solomon, D. H., & Knobloch, L. K. (2001). Relationship uncertainty, partner interference, and intimacy within dating relationships. *Journal of Social and Personal Relationships, 18,* 804–820.

Solomon, D. H., & Knobloch, L. K. (2004). A model of relational turbulence: The role of intimacy, relational uncertainty, and interference from partners in appraisal of irritations. *Journal of Social and Personal Relationships, 21,* 795–816.

Solomon, D. H., Knobloch, L. K., & Fitzpatrick, M. A. (2004). Relational power, marital schema, and decisions to withhold complaints: An investigation of the chilling effect of confrontation in marriage. *Communication Studies, 55,* 146–167.

Solomon, D. H., & Samp, J. A. (1998). Power and problem appraisal: Perceptual foundations of the chilling effect in dating relationship. *Journal of Social and Personal Relationships, 15,* 191–209.

Sorensen, R. C. (1973). *Adolescent sexuality in contemporary America.* New York: World.

Sorrentino, R. M., Holmes, J. G., Hanna, S. E., & Sharp, A. (1995). Uncertainty orientation and trust in close relationships: Individual differences in cognitive styles. *Journal of Personality and Social Psychology, 68,* 314–327.

Sorrentino, R. M., & Short, J. C. (1986). Uncertainty orientation, motivation, and cognition. In R. M. Sorrentino & E. T. Higgins (Eds.), *Handbook of motivation and* cognition: Foundations of social behavior (Vol. 1, pp. 379–403). New York: Guilford Press.

Sorrentino, R. M., Short, J. C., & Raynor, J. O. (1984). Uncertainty orientation: Implications for affective and cognitive views of achievement behavior. *Journal of Personality and Social Psychology, 46,* 189–206.

Sperling, M. B., & Borgaro, S. (1995). Attachment anxiety and reciprocity as moderators of interpersonal attraction. *Psychological Reports, 76,* 323–335.

Spiegel, D. (1992). Effects of psychosocial support on patients with metastatic breast cancer. *Journal of Psychosocial Oncology, 10,* 113–120.

Spitzberg, B. H., & Cupach, W. R. (1988). *Handbook of interpersonal communication competence.* New York: Springer-Verlag.

Spitzberg, B. H., & Cupach, W. R. (Eds.). (1998). *The dark side of close relationships.* Mahwah, NJ: Erlbaum.

Sprecher, S. (1986). The relation between emotion and equity in close relationships. *Social Psychological Bulletin, 49,* 309–321.

Sprecher, S. (1987). The effects of self-disclosure given and received on affect for an intimate partner and the stability of the relationship. *Journal of Personal and Social Relationships, 4,* 115–128.

Sprecher, S. (1989). The importance to males and females of physical attractiveness, earning potential, and expressiveness in initial attraction. *Sex Roles, 12,* 449–462.

Sprecher, S. (1998a). Insiders' perspectives on reasons for attraction to a close other. *Social Psychology Quarterly, 61,* 287–300.

Sprecher, S. (1998b). Social exchange theories and sexuality. *Journal of Sex Research, 35,* 32–43.

Sprecher, S. (2001). A comparison of emotional consequences of and changes in equity over time using global and domain-specific measures of equity. *Journal of Social and Personal Relationships, 18,* 477–501.

Sprecher, S., & Cate, R. M. (2004). Sexual satisfaction and sexual expression as predictors of relationship satisfaction and stability. In J. H. Harvey, A. Wenzel, & S. Sprecher (Eds.). *The handbook of sexuality in close relationships* (pp. 235–256). Mahwah, NJ: Erlbaum.

Sprecher, S., & Fehr, B. (2005). Compassionate love for close others and humanity. *Journal of Social and Personal Relationships, 22,* 629–651.

Sprecher, S., & Felmlee, D. (1992). The influence of parents and friends on the quality and stability of romantic relationships: A three-wave longitudinal study. *Journal of Marriage and the Family, 54,* 888–900.

Sprecher, S., & Felmlee, D. (1997). The balance of power in romantic heterosexual couples over time from "his" and "her" perspectives. *Sex Roles, 37,* 361–378.

Sprecher, S., Felmlee, D., Metts, S., Fehr, B., & Vanni, D. (1998). Factors associated with distress following the breakup of a close relationship. *Journal of Social and Personal Relationships, 15,* 791–809.

Sprecher, S., & McKinney, K. (1993). *Sexuality.* Newbury Park, CA: Sage.

Sprecher, S., McKinney, K., Walsh, R., & Anderson, C. (1988). A revision of the Reiss premarital sexual permissiveness scale. *Journal of Marriage and the Family, 50,* 821–828.

Sprecher, S., & Regan, P. C. (1996). College virgins: How men and women perceive their sexual status. *Journal of Sex Research, 33,* 3–15.

Sprecher, S., & Regan, P. C. (2000). Sexuality in a relational context. In C. Hendrick & S. S. Hendrick (Eds.), *Close relationships: A sourcebook* (pp. 217–227). Thousand Oaks, CA: Sage.

Stafford, L. (2003). Maintaining romantic relationships: Summary and analysis of one research program. In D. J. Canary & M. Dainton (Eds.), *Maintaining relationships through communication: Relational, contextual, and cultural variations* (pp. 51–77). Mahwah, NJ: Lawrence Erlbaum.

Stafford, L., & Canary, D. J. (1991). Maintenance strategies and romantic relationship type, gender and relational characteristics. *Journal of Social and Personal Relationships, 8,* 217–242.

Stafford, L., Daly, J., & Reske, J. (1987, November). The effects of romantic reltionships on friendship networks. Paper presented at the annual conference of the Speech Communication Association, Boston.

Stafford, L., Kline, S. L., & Rankin, C. T. (2004). Married individuals, cohabiters, and cohabiters who marry: A longitudinal study of relational and individual well-being. *Journal of Social and Personal Relationships, 21,* 231–248.

Stafford, L., & Reske, J. R. (1990). Idealization and communication in long-distance premarital relationships. *Family Relations, 39,* 274–279.

Staines, G., & Libby, P. (1986). Men and women in role relationships. In R. Ashmore & F. Del Bocca (Eds.), *The social psychology of female-male relationships: A critical analysis of central concepts* (pp. 211–257). New York: Academic Press.

Stangor, C., & Ruble, D. H. (1989). Strength of expectancies and memory for social information: What we remember depends on how much we know. *Journal of Experimental Social Psychology, 25,* 18–35.

Stark, P. B. (1994). *It's negotiable: The how-to handbook of win/win tactics.* San Diego, CA: Pfeiffer.

Steil, J. M. (2000). Contemporary marriage: Still an unequal partnership. In C. Hendrick & S. S. Hendrick (Eds.), *Close relationships: A sourcebook* (pp. 125–136). Thousand Oaks, CA: Sage.

Steil, L. K., Barker, L. L., & Watson, K. W. (1983). *Effective listening: Keys to success.* Reading, MA: Addison-Wesley.

Steinberg, L. D. (1981). Transformations in family relations at puberty. *Developmental Psychology, 17,* 833–840.

Steinberg, L. D. (1987). Impact of puberty on family relations: Effects of pubertal status and pubertal timing. *Developmental Psychology, 23,* 451–460.

Steinberg, L. D., & Silverberg, S. B. (1986). The vicissitudes of autonomy in early adolescence. *Child Development, 57,* 841–851.

Steinbugler, A. C. (2005). Visibility as privilege and danger: Heterosexual and same-sex interracial intimacy in the 21st century. *Sexualities, 8,* 425–443.

Steinmetz, S. K. (1979). Disciplinary techniques and their relationship to aggressiveness, dependency, and conscience. In W. Burr, R. Hill, R. I. Nye, & I. L. Reiss (Eds.), *Contemporary theories about the family* (Vol. 1, pp. 405–438). New York: Free Press.

Stephan, C. W., & Bachman, G. F. (1999). What's sex got to do with it? Attachment, love schemas, and sexuality. *Personal Relationships, 6,* 111–123.

Sternberg, R. J. (1986). A triangular theory of love. *Psychological Review, 93,* 119–135.

Sternberg, R. J. (1987). *The triangle of love: Intimacy, passion, commitment.* New York: Basic Books.

Sternberg, R. J. (1988). Triangulating love. In R. J. Sternberg & M. L. Barnes (Eds.), *The psychology of love* (pp. 119–138). New Haven, CT: Yale University Press.

Stier, D. S., & Hall, J. A. (1984). Gender differences in touch: An empirical and theoretical review. *Journal of Personality and Social Psychology, 47,* 440–459.

Stiff, J. B., Dillard, J. P., Somera, L., Kim, H., & Sleight, C. (1988). Empathy, communication, and prosocial behavior. *Communication Monographs, 55,* 198–213.

Stiff, J. B., Kim, H. J., & Ramesh, C. N. (1992). Truth biases and aroused suspicion in relational deception. *Communication Research, 19,* 326–345.

Stiles, W. B. (1987). "I have to talk to somebody": A fever model of disclosure. In V. J. Derlega & J. H. Berg (Eds.), *Self-disclosure: Theory, research, and therapy* (pp. 257–282). New York: Plenum Press.

Stiles, W. B., Shuster, P. L., & Harrigan, J. A. (1992). Disclosure and anxiety: A test of the fever model. *Journal of Personality and Social Psychology, 63,* 980–988.

Stillwell, R., & Dunn, J. (1985). Continuities in sibling relationships: Patterns of aggression and friendliness. *Journal of Child Psychology and Psychiatry, 26,* 627–637.

Stranger, J. D. (1997). *Television in the home: The 1997 survey of parents and children.* Philadelphia: Annenberg Public Policy Center, University of Pennsylvania. Retrieved January 1, 2007, from www.annenbergpublicpolicycenter.org/05_media_developing_child/mediasurvey/SURVEY2.PDF

Straus, M. A., & Gelles, R. J. (1990). How violent are American families? Estimates from the National Family Violence Resurvey and other studies. In M. A. Straus & R. J. Gelles (Eds.), *Physical violence in American families: Risk factors and adaptations to violence in 8,145 families* (pp. 95–112). New Brunswick, NJ: Transaction Publishers.

Street, R. L., Jr., & Giles, H. (1982). Speech accommodation theory: A social cognitive approach to language and speech behavior. In M. Roloff & C. Berger (Eds.), *Social cognition and communication* (pp. 193–226). Beverly Hills, CA: Sage.

Strong, B., DeVault, C., & Sayad, B. W. (1999). *Human sexuality: Diversity in contemporary America.* Mountain View, CA: Mayfield.

Strong, S. R., Hills, H. J., Kilmartin, C. T., DeVries, H., Lanier, K., Nelson, B. N., et al. (1988). The dynamic relations among interpersonal behaviors: A test of complementarity and anti-complementarity. *Journal of Personality and Social Psychology, 54,* 798–810.

Struckman-Johnson, C. (1988). Forced sex on dates: It happens to men too. *Journal of Sex Research, 24,* 234–241.

Struckman-Johnson, C., & Struckman-Johnson, D. (1991). Men's and women's acceptance of sexually coercive strategies varied by initiator gender and couple intimacy. *Sex Roles, 25,* 661–676.

Struckman-Johnson, C., & Struckman-Johnson, D. (1994). Men pressured and forced into sexual experience. *Archives of Sexual Behavior, 23,* 93–114.

Student Health Services. (1998). *HIV/AIDS facts.* San Diego, CA: San Diego State University.

Sunnafrank, M. (1986). Predicted outcome value during initial interactions: A reformulation of uncertainty reduction theory. *Human Communication Research, 13,* 3–33.

Sunnafrank, M. (1990). Predicted outcome value and uncertainty reduction theories: A test of competing perspectives. *Human Communication Research, 17,* 76–103.

Sunnafrank, M. (1991). Interpersonal attraction and attitude similarity: A communication-based assessment. In J. A. Anderson (Ed.), *Communication yearbook 14* (pp. 451–483). Newbury Park, CA: Sage.

Sunnafrank, M. (1992). On debunking the attitude similarity myth. *Communication Monographs, 59,* 164–179.

Sunnafrank, M., & Ramirez, A., Jr. (2004). At first sight: Persistent relational effects of get-acquainted conversations. *Journal of Social and Personal Relationships, 21,* 361–379.

Swan, S. C. (1997). Explaining the job-related and psychological consequences of sexual harassment in the workplace: A contextual model. *Dissertation Abstracts International, 58*(6-B), 3371.

Swann, W. B. (1983). Self-verification: Bringing social reality into harmony with the self. In J. Suls & G. Greenwald (Eds.), *Psychology perspectives on the self* (Vol. 2, pp. 33–66). Hillsdale, NJ: Erlbaum.

Swann, W. B., De La Ronde, C., & Hixon, G. (1994). Authenticity and positive strivings in marriage and courtship. *Journal of Personality and Social Psychology, 6,* 857–869.

Swann, W. B., Griffin, J. J., Predmore, S., & Gaines, B. (1987). The cognitive-affective crossfire: When self-consistency confronts self-enhancement. *Journal of Personality and Social Psychology, 52,* 881–889.

Swann, W. B., & Read, S. J. (1981). Self-verification processes. How we sustain our self-conceptions. *Journal of Experimental Social Psychology, 54,* 268–273.

Swann, W. B., Silvera, D. H., & Proske, C. U. (1995). On "knowing your partner": Dangerous illusions in the age of AIDS? *Personal Relationships, 2,* 173–186.

Tannen, D. (1990). *You just don't understand: Women and men in conversation.* New York: Morrow.

Taraban, C. B., Hendrick, S. S., & Hendrick, C. (1998). Loving and liking. In P. A. Andersen & L. K., Guerrero (Eds.), *Handbook of communication and emotion: Research, theory, applications, and contexts* (pp. 331–351). San Diego, CA: Academic Press.

Tardy, C. H. (Ed.). (1988). *A handbook for the study of human communication: Methods for observing, measuring, and assessing communication processes.* Norwood, NJ: Ablex.

Tashiro, T., & Frazier, P. (2003). I'll never be in a relationship like that again: Personal growth following romantic relationship breakups. *Personal Relationships, 10,* 113–138.

Teachman, J. D. (2000). Diversity of family structure: Economic and social influences. In D. H. Demo, K. A. Allen, & M. A. Fine (Eds.), *Handbook of family diversity* (pp. 32–58). New York: Oxford University Press.

Tedeschi, J. T. (1986). Private and public experiences of the self. In R. Baumeister (Ed.), *Public self and private self* (pp. 1–20). New York: Springer-Verlag.

Tesser, A., & Achee, J. (1994). Aggression, love, conformity and other social psychological catastrophes. In R. R. Vallacher & A. Nowak (Eds.), *Dynamical systems in social psychology* (pp. 95–109). San Diego, CA: Academic Press.

Thagaard, T. (1997). Gender, power, and love. *Acta Sociologica, 38,* 357–376.

Theiss, J. A., & Solomon, D. H. (2006). A relational turbulence model of communication about irritations in romantic relationships. *Communication Research, 33,* 391–418.

Thibaut, J. W., & Kelley, J. J. (1959). *The psychology of groups.* New York: Wiley.

Thieme, A., & Rouse, C. (1991, November). *Terminating intimate relationships: An examination of the interactions among disengagement strategies, acceptance, and causal attributions.* Paper presented at the annual meeting of the Speech Communication Association, Atlanta, GA.

Thompson, A. P. (1984). Emotional and sexual components of extramarital relations. *Journal of Marriage and the Family, 46,* 35–42.

Thompson, L., & Walker, A. J. (1989). Gender in families: Women and men in marriage, work, and parenthood. *Journal of Marriage and the Family, 51,* 845–871.

Thorne, B., & Luria, Z. (1986). Sexuality and gender in children's daily worlds. *Social Problems, 33,* 176–190.

Thorton, A., Axinn, W. G., & Teachman, J. D. (1995). The influence of school enrollment and accumulation of cohabitation and marriage in early adulthood. *American Sociological Review, 60,* 207–220.

Tice, D. M., Butler, J. L., Muraven, M. B., & Stillwell, A. M. (1995). When modesty prevails: Differential favorability of self-presentation to friends and strangers. *Journal of Personality and Social Psychology, 69,* 1120–1138.

Timmerman, L. M. (2002). Comparing the production of power in language on the basis of sex. In M. Allen, R. W. Preiss, B. M. Gayke, & N. Burell (Eds.), *Interpersonal* communication research: Advances through meta-analysis (pp. 73–88). Mahwah, NJ: Erlbaum.

Tolhuizen, J. H. (1989). Communication strategies for intensifying dating relationships: Identification, use, and structure. *Journal of Social and Personal Relationships, 6,* 413–434.

Tolstedt, B. E., & Stokes, J. P. (1984). Self-disclosure, intimacy and the depenetration process. *Journal of Personality and Social Psychology, 46,* 84–90.

Tooke, W., & Camire, L. (1991). Patterns of deception in intersexual and intrasexual mating strategies. *Ethology and Sociobiology, 12,* 345–364.

Tornblom, K. Y., & Fredholm, E. M. (1984). Attribution of friendship: The influence of the nature and comparability of resources given and received. *Social Psychology Quarterly, 47,* 50–61.

Tracy, K. (1990). The many faces of facework. In H. Giles & W. P. Robinson (Eds.), *Handbook of language and social psychology* (pp. 209–226). Chichester, UK: Wiley.

Traupmann, J., Hatfield, E., & Wexler, P. (1983). Equity and sexual satisfaction in dating couples. *British Journal of Social Psychology, 22,* 33–40.

Trivers, R. (1985). *Social evolution.* Menlo Park, CA: Benjamin/Cummings.

Trost, M. R., & Alberts, J. K. (2006). How men and women communicate attraction: An evolutionary view. In D. J. Canary & K. Dindia (Eds.), *Sex differences and similarities in communication* (2nd ed., pp. 317–336). Mahwah, NJ: Erlbaum.

Troy, B. A., Lewis-Smith, J., & Laurenceau, J. (2006). Interracial and intraracial romantic relationships: The search for differences in satisfaction, conflict, and attachment style. *Journal of Social and Personal Relationships, 23,* 65–80.

Tucker, J. S., & Anders, S. L. (1998). Adult attachment style and nonverbal closeness in dating couples. *Journal of Nonverbal Behavior, 22,* 109–124.

Turner, L. H. (1990). The relationship between communication and marital uncertainty: Is "her" marriage different from "his" marriage? *Women's Studies in Communication, 13,* 57–83.

Turner, R. E., Edgley, C., & Olmstead, G. (1975). Information control in conversations: Honesty is not always the best policy. *Kansas Journal of Speech, 11,* 69–89.

Tusing, K. J., & Dillard, J. P. (2000). The sounds of dominance: Vocal precursors of perceived dominance during interpersonal influence. *Human Communication Research, 16,* 148–171.

Tutzauer, F., & Roloff, M. E. (1988). Communication processes leading to integrative agreements: Three paths to joint benefits. *Communication Research, 15,* 360–380.

Twenge, J. M., Campbell, W. K., & Foster, C. A. (2003). Parenthood and marital satisfaction: A meta-analytic review. *Journal of Marriage and Family, 65,* 574–583.

Ugbah, S., & DeWine, S. (1986, November). *Conflict and relational development: Are the communication strategies the same?* Paper presented at the annual meeting of the Speech Communication Association, Chicago.

Van Horn, K. R., Arnone, A., Nesbitt, K., Desilets, L., Sears, T., Giffin, M., et al. (1997). Physical distance and interpersonal characteristics in college students' romantic relationships. *Personal Relationships, 4,* 15–24.

Van Lange, P. A. M., Rusbult, C. E., Drigotas, S. M., Arriaga, X. B., Witcher, B. S., & Cox, C. L. (1997). Willingness to sacrifice in close relationships. *Journal of Personality and Social Psychology, 72,* 1373–1395.

Van Willigen, M., & Drentea, P. (2001). Benefits of equitable relationships: The impact of sense of fairness, household division of labor, and decision making power on perceived social support. *Sex Roles, 44,* 571–597.

Vangelisti, A. L. (1994a). Family secrets: Forms, functions, and correlates. *Journal of Social and Personal Relationships, 11,* 113–135.

Vangelisti, A. L. (1994b). Messages that hurt. In W. R. Cupach & B. H. Spitzberg (Eds.), *The dark side of interpersonal communication* (pp. 53–82). Hillsdale, NJ: Lawrence Erlbaum.

Vangelisti, A. L. (2001). Making sense of hurtful interactions in close relationships: When hurt feelings create distance. In V. Manusov & J. H. Harvey (Eds.), *Attribution, communication behavior, and close relationships: Advances in personal relations* (pp. 38–58). New York: Cambridge University Press.

Vangelisti, A. L. (2002). Interpersonal processes in romantic relationships. In M. L. Knapp & J. A. Daly (Eds.), *Handbook of interpersonal communication* (3rd ed., pp. 643–679). Thousand Oaks, CA: Sage.

Vangelisti, A. L., & Caughlin, J. P. (1997). Revealing family secrets: The influence of topic, function, and relationships. *Journal of Social and Personal Relationships, 14,* 679–706.

Vangelisti, A. L., & Crumley, L. P. (1998). Reactions to messages that hurt: The influence of relational contexts. *Communication Monographs, 65,* 173–196.

Vangelisti, A. L., & Huston, T. L. (1994). Maintaining marital satisfaction and love. In D. J. Canary & L. Stafford (Eds.), *Communication and relational maintenance* (pp. 165–186). San Diego, CA: Academic Press.

Vangelisti, A. L., Knapp, M. L., & Daly, J. A. (1990). Conversational narcissism. *Communication Monographs, 57,* 251–274.

Vangelisti, A. L., & Sprague, R. J. (1998). Guilt and hurt: Similarities, distinctions, and conversational strategies. In P. A. Andersen & L. K. Guerrero (Eds.), *Handbook of communication and emotion: Research, theory, applications, and contexts* (pp. 123–153). San Diego, CA: Academic Press.

Vangelisti, A. L., & Young, S. L. (2000). When words hurt: The effects of perceived intentionality on interpersonal relationships. *Journal of Social and Personal Relationships, 17,* 393–424.

VanLear, C. A., Jr. (1987). The formation of social relationships: A longitudinal study of social penetration. *Human Communication Research, 13,* 299–322.

Vaughn, D. (1986). *Uncoupling: Turning points in intimate relationships.* New York: Oxford.

Verhoff, J., Young, A. M., & Coon, H. M. (1997). The early years of marriage. In S. Duck (Ed.), *Handbook of personal relationships* (pp. 431–450). New York: Wiley.

Vohs, K. D., Catanese, K. R., & Baumeister, R. E. (2004). Sex in "his" versus "her" relationship. In J. H. Harvey, A. Wenzel, & S. Sprecher (Eds.), *The handbook of sexuality in close relationships* (pp. 455–474). Mahwah, NJ: Erlbaum.

Waldron, V. R., & Kelley, D. L. (2005). Forgiving communication as a response to relational transgressions. *Journal of Social and Personal Relationships, 22,* 723–742.

Wallace, H., & Silverman, J. (1996). Stalking and post traumatic stress syndrome. *Police Journal, 69,* 203–206.

Waller, W. W., & Hill, R. (1951). *The family: A dynamic interpretation.* New York: Dryden Press.

Walster, E., Berscheid, E., & Walster, G. W. (1973). Equity and extramarital sexuality. *Archives of Sexual Behavior, 7,* 127–141.

Walster, E., & Walster, G. W. (1978). *A new look at love.* Reading, MA: Addison-Wesley.

Walster, E., Walster, G. W., & Berscheid, E. (1978). *Equity: Theory and research.* Boston: Allyn & Bacon.

Walster, E., Walster, G. W., Piliavin, J., & Schmidt, L. (1973). "Playing hard-to-get": Understanding an elusive phenomenon. *Journal of Personality and Social Psychology, 26,* 113–121.

Walster, E., Walster, G. W., & Traupmann, J. (1978). Equity and premarital sex. *Journal of Personality, 36,* 82–92.

Ward, L. M. (1995). Talking about sex: Common themes about sexuality in prime-time television programs children and adolescents view most. *Journal of Youth and Adolescence, 5,* 595–615.

Warren, C. (1995). Parent-child communication about sex. In T. Socha & G. H. Stamp (Eds.), *Parents, children, and communication: Frontiers of theory and research* (pp. 173–201). Mahwah, NJ: Erlbaum.

Watzlawick, P., Beavin, J. H., & Jackson, D. D. (1967). *Pragmatics of human communication.* New York: Norton.

Webb, L., Delaney, J. J., & Young, L. R. (1989). Age, interpersonal attraction, and social interaction: A review and assessment. *Research on Aging, 11,* 107–123.

Weber, A. L. (1998). Losing, leaving, and letting go: Coping with nonmarital breakups. In B. H. Spitzberg & W. R. Cupach (Eds.), *The dark side of close relationships* (pp. 267–306). Mahwah, NJ: Erlbaum.

Weger, H., & Polcar, L. E. (2002). Attachment style and person-centered comforting. *Western Journal of Communication, 66,* 64–103.

Wegner, D. M. (1989). *White bears and other unwanted thoughts.* New York: Viking Press.

Wegner, D. M. (1992). You can't always think what you want: Problems in the suppression of unwanted thoughts. In M. Zanna (Ed.), *Advances in experimental social psychology* (Vol. 25, pp. 193–225). San Diego, CA: Academic Press.

Wegner, D. M., & Erber, R. (1992). The hyperaccessibility of suppressed thoughts. *Journal of Personality and Social Psychology, 63,* 903–912.

Wegner, D. M., Lane, J. D., & Dimitri, S. (1994). The allure of secret relationships. *Journal of Personality and Social Psychology, 66,* 287–300.

Wegner, D. M., Schneider, D. J., Carter, S. R., III, & White, T. L. (1987). Paradoxical effects of thought suppression. *Journal of Personality and Social Psychology, 53,* 5–13.

Weigel, D. J., & Ballard-Reisch, D. S. (1999). The influence of marital duration on the use of relationship maintenance behaviors. *Communication Reports, 12,* 59–70.

Weigel, D. J., & Ballard-Reisch, D. S. (2001). The impact of relational maintenance behaviors on marital satisfaction: A longitudinal analysis. *Journal of Family Communication, 1,* 265–279.

Weinbach, R. (1989). Sudden death and the secret survivors: Helping those who grieve alone. *Social Work, 34,* 57–60.

Weiner, B., Graham, S., Peter, O., & Zmuidinas, M. (1991). Public confession and forgiveness. *Journal of Personality, 59,* 281–312.

Weiner, M., & Mehrabian, A. (1968). *Language within language: Immediacy, a channel in verbal communication.* New York: Appleton-Century-Crofts.

Weis, D. L., & Slosnerick, M. (1981). Attitudes toward sexual and nonsexual extramarital involvement among a sample of college students. *Journal of Marriage and the Family, 43,* 349–358.

Wells, B. E., & Twenge, J. M. (2005). Changes in young people's sexual behavior and attitudes, 1943–1999. A cross-temporal analysis. *Review of General Psychology, 9,* 249–261.

Werking, K. (1997). *We're just good friends: Women and men in nonromantic relationships.* New York: Guilford Press.

Werner, C. M., Altman, I., Brown, B. B., & Ganat, J. (1993). Celebrations in personal relationships: A transactional/dialectical perspective. In S. Duck (Ed.), *Social context and relationships* (pp. 109–138). Newbury Park, CA: Sage.

Westenhoefer, S., & Mapa, A. (2006, August 15). Five sex tips. . . What can lesbians and gay men teach each other about great sex? *Advocate,* p. 41.

Westhoff, L. A. (1985). *Corporate romance.* New York: Times Books.

Wheeless, L. R., Wheeless, V. E., & Baus, R. (1984). Sexual communication, communication satisfaction, and solidarity in the development stages of intimate relationships. *Western Journal of Speech Communication, 48,* 217–230.

White, G. L. (1981). Jealousy and partner's perceived motives for attraction to a rival. *Social Psychology Quarterly, 44,* 24–30.

White, G. L., Fishbein, S., & Rutstein, J. (1981). Passionate love: The misattribution of arousal. *Journal of Personality and Social Psychology, 41,* 56–62.

White, G. L., & Mullen, P. E. (1989). *Jealousy: Theory, research, and clinical strategies.* New York: Guilford Press.

Wiederman, M. W., & Allgeier, E. R. (1993). Gender differences in sexual jealousy: Adaptationist or social learning explanation? *Ethology and Sociobiology, 14,* 115–140.

Wiederman, M. W., & Hurd, C. (1999). Extradyadic involvement during dating. *Journal of Social and Personal Relationships, 16,* 265–274.

Wiener, M., & Mehrabian, A. (1968). *Language within language: Immediacy, a channel in verbal communication.* New York: Appleton-Century-Crofts.

Wieselquist, J., Rusbult, C. E., Foster, C. A., & Agnew, C. R. (1999). Commitment, pro-relationship behavior, and trust in close relationships. *Journal of Personality and Social Psychology, 77,* 942–966.

Wiggins, J. D., & Lederer, D. A. (1984). Differential antecedents of infidelity in marriage. *American Mental Health Counseling Association Journal, 6,* 152–161.

Willetts, M. C., Sprecher, S., & Beck, F. D. (2004). Overview of sexual practices and attitudes within relational contexts. In J. H. Harvey, A. Wenzel, & S. Sprecher (Eds.), *The handbook of sexuality in close relationships* (pp. 57–85). Mahwah, NJ: Erlbaum.

Williams, S., & Andersen, P. A. (1998). Toward an expanded view of interracial romantic relationships. In V. Duncan (Ed.), *Toward achieving maat.* Dubuque, IA: Kendall-Hunt.

Wilmot, W. W. (1994). Relationship rejuvenation. In D. J. Canary & L. Stafford (Eds.), *Communication and relational maintenance* (pp. 255–273). San Diego, CA: Academic Press.

Wilmot, W. W. (1995). *Relational communication.* New York: McGraw-Hill.

Wilmot, W. W., Carbaugh, D. A., & Baxter, L. A. (1985). Communicative strategies used to terminate romantic relationships. *Western Journal of Speech Communication, 49,* 204–216.

Wiseman, J. P. (1986). Friendship: Bonds and binds in a voluntary relationship. *Journal of Social and Personal Relationships, 3,* 191–211.

Wiseman, R. L., & Schenck-Hamlin, W. (1981). A multidimensional scaling validation of an inductively-derived set of compliance gaining strategies. *Communication Monographs, 48,* 251–270.

Witteman, H., & Fitzpatrick, M. A. (1986). Compliance-gaining in marital interaction: Power bases, processes and outcomes. *Communication Monographs, 53,* 130–143.

Wolfinger, N. H. (1999). Trends in the intergenerational transmission of divorce. *Demography, 36,* 415–420.

Wood, J. T. (1994). *Gendered lives: Communications, gender, and culture.* Belmont, CA: Wadsworth.

Wood, J. T. (Ed.). (1996). *Gendered relationships.* Mountain View, CA: Mayfield.

Wood, J. T., & Dindia, K. (1998). What's the difference? A dialogue about the differences and similarities between women and men. In D. J. Canary & K. Dindia (Eds.), *Sex differences and similarities in communication* (pp. 19–39). Mahwah, NJ: Erlbaum.

Wood, J. T., & Duck, S. (1995). Off the beaten track: New shores for relationships research. In J. T. Wood & S. Duck (Eds.), *Understudied relationships: Off the beaten track* (pp. 1–21). Thousand Oaks, CA: Sage.

Worthington, E. L., & Wade, N. G. (1999). The psychology of forgiveness and unforgiveness and implications for clinical practice. *Journal of Social and Clinical Psychology, 18,* 385–418.

Wright, K. B. (2004). On-line relational maintenance strategies and perceptions of partners within exclusively Internet-based and primarily Internet-based relationships. *Communication Studies, 55,* 239–253.

Wright, P. H. (1982). Men's friendship, women's friendships, and the alleged inferiority of the latter. *Sex Roles, 8,* 1–20.

Wright, R. A., & Contrada, R. J. (1986). Dating selectivity and interpersonal attractiveness: Toward a better understanding of the "elusive phenomenon." *Journal of Social and Personal Relationships, 3,* 131–148.

Wright, R. A., Toi, M., & Brehm, J. W. (1984). Difficulty and interpersonal attraction. *Motivation and Emotion, 8,* 327–341.

Yelsma, P. (1986). Marriage vs. cohabitation: Couples' communication practices and satisfaction. *Journal of Communication, 36,* 94–107.

Yingling, J. (1995). The first relationship: Infant-parent communication. In T. J. Socha & G. H. Stamp (Eds.), *Parents, children, and communication: Frontiers of theory and research* (pp. 23–41). Hillsdale, NJ: Erlbaum.

Young, S. L. (2004). Factors that influence recipients' appraisals of hurtful communication. *Journal of Social and Personal Relationships, 21,* 291–303.

Young, S. L., & Bippus, A. M. (2001). Does it make a difference if they hurt you in a funny way? *Communication Quarterly, 49,* 35–52.

Zeeman, E. C. (1977). Catastrophe theory. *Scientific American, 234,* 65–83.

Zillman, D. (1978). Attribution and misattribution of excitatory reactions. In J. H. Harvey, W. Ickes, & R. F. Kidd (Eds.), *New directions in attribution research* (Vol. 2, pp. 335–368). Hillsdale, NJ: Erlbaum.

Zillman, D. (1990). The interplay of cognition and excitation in aggravated conflict. In D. D. Cahn (Ed.), *Intimates in conflict: A communication perspective* (pp. 187–208). Hillsdale, NJ: Erlbaum.

Zimmerman, S., & Applegate, J. L. (1994). Communicating social support in organizations. In B. R. Burleson, T. L. Albrecht, & I. G. Sasason (Eds.), *Communication of social support: Messages, interactions, relationships, and community* (pp. 50–70). Thousand Oaks, CA: Sage.

Zuckerman, M., DePaulo, B. M., & Rosenthal, R. (1981). Verbal and nonverbal communication of deception. In L. Berkowitz (Ed.), *Advances in experimental social psychology* (Vol. 14, pp. 1–59). New York: Academic Press.

Name Index

Subject Index

ABOUT THE AUTHORS

Laura K. Guerrero (PhD, University of Arizona, 1994) is a professor in the Hugh Downs School of Human Communication at Arizona State University, Tempe, where she teaches courses in relational communication, nonverbal communication, emotional communication, research methods, and data analysis. Most of her research focuses on communication within close relationships, such as those between romantic partners, friends, and family members. Her research has examined both the "bright side" of personal relationships, including nonverbal intimacy, relational maintenance, communication skill, and forgiveness; and the "dark side" of personal relationships, including jealousy, hurtful events, conflict, and anger. She has published more than 70 journal articles and book chapters related to these topics. In addition to *Close Encounters*, her book credits include *Nonverbal Communication in Close Relationships* (coauthored with Kory Floyd), *The Handbook of Communication and Emotion* (coedited with Peter Andersen), and *The Nonverbal Reader: Classic and Contemporary Readings* (coedited with Joseph DeVito and Michael Hecht). She has received several research awards, including the Early Career Achievement Award from the International Association for Relationship Research in 2001, the Dickens Research Award from the Western States Communication Association in 1995 and 2001, and the Outstanding Doctoral Dissertation Award from the Interpersonal Communication Division of The International Communication Association in 1995.

She lives in Phoenix (during the school year) and San Diego (during the summer) with her husband Vico and her young daughters Gabrielle and Kristiana. She enjoys reading, dancing, biking, and taking long walks in the mountains or on the beach.

Peter A. Andersen (PhD, Florida State University, 1975) teaches in the School of Communication at San Diego State University. He has authored more than 100 book chapters and journal articles as well as more than 100 research papers. Before earning his PhD, he earned a bachelor's degree in political science from the University of Illinois, Chicago, and a master's degree in communication from Illinois State University. He has received recognition as one of the 100 most published scholars in the history of the field of communication. He has taught relational communication, nonverbal communication, political communication, persuasion, and quantitative research methods at San Diego State University for the past 25 years. He has served as the President of the Western Communication Association, Director of Research for the Japan-U.S. Telecommunications Research Institute, and Editor of the *Western Journal of Communication*. In addition to *Close Encounters*, he is the author of *The Handbook of Communication and Emotion* (1998, edited with L. Guerrero), *Nonverbal Communication: Forms and Functions* (1999), and *The Complete Idiot's Guide to Understanding Body Language* (2004). He has served as a coinvestigator or consultant on tobacco prevention grants from the National

Cancer Institute, sun-safety grants from the National Cancer Institute, and risk communication grants from the U.S. office of Homeland Security and the County of San Diego. He cherishes the relationships he has with Janis, his wife of 34 years; his daughter Kirsten, who lives in Los Angeles; and his mother, who lives in Chicago. He is an avid skier, marathon runner, swimmer, and a really mediocre tennis player.

Walid A. Afifi (PhD, University of Arizona, 1996) joined the faculty at the University of Delaware for 3 years after earning his PhD. He then worked at The Pennsylvania State University for 8 years before moving to the University of California, Santa Barbara in 2006. His primary research program revolves around people's experience of uncertainty and their decisions to seek or avoid information in relational contexts. He has applied these interests across several domains, including family discussions about organ donation, college students' search for information about their partners' sexual health, people's negotiation of cross-sex friendships, and family members' management of privacy boundaries around sensitive topics. He has also examined people's decisions to avoid disclosure and/or keep secrets. His most recent research projects approach the construct from a more sociological lens, examining people's experience of "ambient" uncertainty following traumatic societal episodes (e.g., natural disasters, terrorism, war) and assessing its impact on relational processes. He has published more than 35 articles and chapters, serves as a member on several editorial boards, has occupied the role of Associate Editor for *Personal Relationships*, and recently completed his tenure as Chair of the Interpersonal Division of the National Communication Association. He teaches several courses, including interpersonal communication, relational communication, and nonverbal communication. He grew up in Beirut, Lebanon, where his sister and her family still reside. He lives in Goleta (right outside Santa Barbara), California, with his wife Tammy (who studies family communication and is a faculty member in the same department), two daughters (Leila and Rania), and two dogs (Meshi and Maddie). He is an avid sports fan and loves outdoor activities of all kinds.